Taking Sides: Clashing
Views on Legal Issues, 18/e

M. Ethan Katsh

http://create.mheducation.com

ISBN-10: 125988368X   ISBN-13: 9781259883682

Contents

Detailed Table of Contents

Unit 4: Law and the Community

<u>**Issue: Is There a Constitutional Right to Possess a Firearm for Private Use?**</u>
Yes: Antonin Scalia, from "Majority Opinion, *District of Columbia, et al., v. Heller*," *United States Supreme Court* (2008)
No: John Paul Stevens, from "Dissenting Opinion, *District of Columbia, et al., v. Heller*," *United States Supreme Court* (2008)

Supreme Court Justice Antonin Scalia argues that the Second Amendment protects the right of a private citizen to own a handgun for self-defense. Supreme Court Justice John Paul Stevens argues that a previous case, *United States v. Miller*, held that the Second Amendment did not protect the right of a private citizen to own a handgun for self-defense.

<u>**Issue: Are Blanket Prohibitions on Cross Burnings Unconstitutional?**</u>
Yes: Sandra Day O'Connor, from "Plurality Opinion, *Virginia v. Black*," *United States Supreme Court* (2003)
No: Clarence Thomas, from "Dissenting Opinion, *Virginia v. Black*," *United States Supreme Court* (2003)

Supreme Court Justice Sandra Day O'Connor argues that part of a Virginia statute proscribing cross burning with the intent to intimidate is constitutional because it is content discrimination based on the very reasons that make it constitutional; however, part of the statute is unconstitutional insofar as it requires an inference of intent to intimidate solely based on the action of cross burning itself, which is symbolic speech. Supreme Court Justice Clarence Thomas disagrees with part of the statute being held unconstitutional, arguing that the history and nature of cross burning in the United States inextricably links the act to threatening and menacing violence and that the intent to intimidate can therefore be inferred solely from the act of cross burning itself.

<u>**Issue: Does the Fourth Amendment Prohibit the Police from Collecting a DNA Sample from a Person Arrested, But Not Yet Convicted on Felony Charges?**</u>
Yes: Anthony Kennedy, from "Majority Opinion, *Maryland v. King*," *United States Supreme Court* (2013)
No: Antonin Scalia, from "Dissenting Opinion, *Maryland v. King*," *United States Supreme Court* (2013)

Justice Anthony Kennedy rules that using a cheek swab to collect a person's DNA during postarrest processing is a reasonable search under the Fourth Amendment because it is predominantly used to confirm the identity of the arrestee. Justice Antonin Scalia argues that DNA collection at the time of arrest is an unreasonable search because the arrestee's DNA profile is predominantly used to investigate unrelated crimes.

<u>**Issue: Is Same-sex Marriage Protected by the Fourteenth Amendment to the U.S. Constitution?**</u>
Yes: Anthony Kennedy, from "Majority Opinion, *Obergefell v. Hodges*," *United States Supreme Court* (2015)
No: John Roberts, from "Dissenting Opinion, *Obergefell v. Hodges*," *United States Supreme Court* (2015)

Supreme Court Justice Anthony Kennedy holds that marriage is a fundamental right, and bans on same-sex marriage are unconstitutional under the Due Process and Equal Protection Clauses of the Fourteenth Amendment. Supreme Court Chief Justice John Roberts argues that it is no place for the Court, as unelected lawyers, to make the determination of what defines "marriage," as that is the job of the legislature and not the judiciary.

<u>**Issue: Are Race-conscious Public University Admissions Policies Permitted Under the Fourteenth Amendment?**</u>
Yes: Anthony Kennedy, from "Majority Opinion, *Fisher v. University of Texas at Austin II*," *United States Supreme Court* (2016)
No: Samuel Anthony Alito, Jr., from "Dissenting Opinion, *Fisher v. University of Texas at Austin II*," *United States Supreme Court* (2016)

Justice Anthony Kennedy holds that the race-conscious admissions program in use at the University of Texas does not violate the Equal Protection Clause of the Fourteenth Amendment. Justice Samuel Anthony Alito argues that the university failed to effectively demonstrate that its admission policy needs a racial element and that the one it employs does, in fact, foster diversity.

<u>**Issue: Is It Unconstitutional for States to Imprison Undocumented Immigrants?**</u>
Yes: Anthony Kennedy, from "Majority Opinion, *Arizona v. United States*," *United States Supreme Court* (2012)
No: Antonin Scalia, from "Dissenting Opinion, *Arizona v. United States*," *United States Supreme Court* (2012)

Justice Anthony Kennedy argues that a recent state law making it a crime to be an undocumented immigrant in Arizona impinges on the U.S. federal government's authority to regulate immigration. Justice Antonin Scalia argues that it is not unconstitutional for a state to supplement U.S. federal immigration law with its own, harsher penalties for illegal immigration.

Introduction

The Role of Law

More than 200 years ago, Edmund Burke, the influential British statesman and orator, commented that "in no other country, perhaps, in the world, is the law so general a study as it is in the United States." Today, in America, general knowledge about law is at a disappointing level. In one study, 69 percent of those surveyed mistakenly believed that when it was first written, the U.S. Constitution outlawed slavery. In a 2010 survey, nearly two-thirds of the people questioned could not name even one member of the U.S. Supreme Court and only 1 percent knew all nine justices.

One purpose of this volume is to provide information about some specific and important legal issues. In your local newspaper today, there is probably at least one story concerning an issue in this book. The quality of your life will be directly affected by how many of these issues are resolved. But affirmative action, abortion, copyrighted material on the Internet, and other issues in this book are often the subject of superficial, misleading, or inaccurate statements. *Taking Sides* is designed to encourage you to become involved in the public debate on these issues and to raise the level of the discussion on them.

The issues that are debated in this book represent some of the most important challenges our society faces, and the issues raise questions about what kind of society we will have in the future. Although it is important to look at and study the issues separately, it is equally necessary to think about their relationship to each other and about the fact that there is a tool called "law," which is being called upon to solve a series of difficult conflicts.

The study of discrete legal issues should enable you to gain insight into some broad theoretical questions about law. This introduction, therefore, will focus on several basic characteristics of law and the legal process that you should keep in mind as you read this book.

The Nature of Law

The eminent legal anthropologist E. Adamson Hoebel once noted that the search for a definition of law is as difficult as the search for the Holy Grail. Law is certainly complicated, and trying to define it precisely can be frustrating. What follows, therefore, is not a definition of law but a framework or perspective for looking at and understanding law.

Law as a Body of Rules

One of the common incorrect assumptions about law is that it is merely a body of rules invoked by those who need them and then applied by a judge. Under this view, the judge is essentially a machine whose task is simply to find and apply the right rule to the dispute in question. This perspective makes the mistake of equating law with the rules of law. It is sometimes even assumed that there exists somewhere in the libraries or computers of lawyers and judges one book or file with all the rules or laws in it, which can be consulted to answer legal questions. As may already be apparent, such a resource could not exist. Rules alone do not supply the solutions to many legal problems. The late Supreme Court Justice William O. Douglas once wrote, "The law is not a series of calculating machines where definitions and answers come tumbling out when the right levers are pushed." As you read the debates about the issues in this book, you will see that much more goes into a legal argument than the recitation of rules.

Law as a Process

A more meaningful way of thinking about law is to look at it as a process or system, keeping in mind that legal rules are one of the elements in the process. This approach requires a considerably broader vision of law: to think not only of the written rules but also of the judges, the lawyers, the police, and all the other people in the system. It requires an even further consideration of all the things that influence these people, such as their values and economic status.

"Law," one legal commentator has stated, "is very much like an iceberg; only one-tenth of its substance appears above the social surface in the explicit form of documents, institutions, and professions, while the nine-tenths of its substance that supports its visible fragment leads a subaquatic existence, living in the habits, attitudes, emotions and aspirations of men."[1] In reading the discussions of controversial issues in this book, try to identify what forces are influencing the content of the rules and the position of the writers. Three of the most important influences on the nature of law are economics, moral values, and public opinion.

Law and Economics

Laws that talk about equality, such as the Fourteenth Amendment, which guarantees that no state shall "deny to any person . . . equal protection of the laws," suggest that economic status is irrelevant in the making and application of the law. As Anatole France, the nineteenth-century French satirist, once wrote, however, "The law, in its majestic equality, forbids the rich as well as the poor to sleep under bridges, to beg in streets, and to steal bread." Sometimes the purpose and effect of the law cannot be determined merely from the words of the law.

Critics of law in capitalistic societies assert that poverty results from the manipulation of the law by the wealthy and powerful. It is possible to look at several issues in this book and make some tentative judgments about the influence of economic power on law. For example, what role does economics play in the debate over the sharing of music files through the Internet? Is the controversy over providing incentives for creators and musicians or maximizing profits for record companies?

Law and Values

The relationship between law and values has been a frequent theme of legal writers and a source of debate. Clearly, there is, in most societies, some relationship between law and morality. One writer has summarized the relationship as follows:

1. *There is a moral order in society.* Out of the many different and often conflicting values of the individuals and institutions that make up society may emerge a dominant moral position, a core of the moral order. The position of this core is dynamic, and as it changes, the moral order of society moves in the direction of that change.
2. *There is a moral content to the law.* The moral content of law also changes over time, and as it changes, the law moves in the direction of that change.
3. *The moral content of the law and moral order in society are seldom identical.*
4. *A natural and necessary affinity exists between the two "bodies" of law and moral order.*
5. *When there is a gap between the moral order of society and the law, some movement to close the gap is likely.* The law will move closer to the moral order of society, or the moral order will move closer to the law, or each will move toward the other. The likelihood of the movement to close the gap between law and moral order depends upon the size of the gap between the two bodies and the perceived significance of the subject matter concerning which the gap exists.[2]

Law and morality will not be identical in a pluralistic society, but there will also be attempts by dominant groups to insert their views of what is right into the legal code. The First Amendment prohibition against establishment of religion and the guarantee of freedom of religion are designed to protect those whose beliefs are different. Yet there have also been many historical examples of legal restrictions or limitations being imposed on minorities or of laws being ineffective because of the resistance of powerful groups. Prayers in the public schools, for example, which have been forbidden since the early 1960s, are still said in a few local communities.

Of the topics in this book, the insertion of morality into legal discussions has occurred most frequently in the abortion debate. It is probably fair to say that this issue remains high on the agenda of public debate because it involves strongly held values and beliefs. The nature of the debate is also colored by strong feelings that are held by the parties. Although empirical evidence about public health and abortion does exist, the debate is generally more emotional than objective.

Public Opinion and the Law

It is often claimed that the judicial process is insulated from public pressures. Judges are elected or appointed for long terms or for life, and the theory is that they will, therefore, be less subject to the force of public opinion. As a result, the law should be uniformly applied in different places, regardless of the nature of the community. It is fair to say that the judicial process is less responsive to public sentiment than is the political process, but that is not really saying much. What is important is that the legal process is not totally immune from public pressure. The force of public opinion is not applied directly through lobbying, but it would be naive to think that the force of what large numbers of people believe and desire never gets reflected in what happens in court. The most obvious examples are trials in which individuals are tried as much for their dissident beliefs as for their actions. Less obvious is the fact that the outcomes of cases may be determined in some measure by popular will. Judicial complicity in slavery and the internment of Japanese Americans during World War II are blatant examples of this. A more recent example would be changes in public attitudes about same-sex marriages and the impact of that on judicial decisions involving this issue.

Many of the issues selected for this volume are controversial because a large group is opposed to some practice sanctioned by the courts. Does this mean that the judges have taken a courageous stand and ignored public opinion? Not necessarily. Only in a few of the issues have courts adopted an uncompromising position. In most of the other issues, the trend of court decisions reflects a middle-of-the-road approach that could be interpreted as trying to satisfy everyone but those at the extremes. For example, in affirmative action, the *Bakke* decision, while generally approving of affirmative action, was actually won by Bakke and led to the abolition of all such programs that contained rigid quotas.

Assessing Influences on the Law

This summary of what can influence legal decisions is not meant to suggest that judges consciously ask what the public desires when interpretations of law are made. There are subtle forces at work on judges that may not be obvious in any particular opinion but that can be discerned in a line of cases over a period of time. This may be explicitly denied by judges, such as in this statement by Justice Harry A. Blackmun in his majority opinion for the landmark *Roe v. Wade* abortion case: "Our task, of course, is to resolve the issue by constitutional measurement, free of emotion and predilection." However, a reading of that opinion raises the question of whether or not Blackmun succeeds in being totally objective in his interpretation of law and history.

Do these external and internal influences corrupt the system, create injustice, inject bias and discrimination, and pervert the law? Or do these influences enable judges to be flexible, to treat individual circumstances, and to fulfill the spirit of the law? Both of these ends are possible and do occur. What is important to realize is that there are so many points in the legal system where discretion is employed that it is hopeless to think that we could be governed by rules alone. "A government of laws, not men," aside from the sexism of the language, is not a realistic possibility, and it is not an alternative that many would find satisfying either.

On the other hand, it is also fair to say that the law, in striving to get the public to trust in it, must persuade citizens that it is more than the whim of those who are in power. Although it cannot be denied that the law may be used in self-serving ways, there are also mechanisms at work that are designed to limit abuses of discretionary power. One quality of law that is relevant to this problem is that the legal process is fundamentally a conservative institution, which is, by nature, resistant to radical change. Lawyers are trained to give primary consideration in legal arguments to precedent—previous cases involving similar facts. As attention is focused on how the present case is similar to or different from past cases, some pressure is exerted on new decisions to be consistent with old ones and on the law to be stable. Thus, the way in which a legal argument is constructed tends to reduce the influence of currently popular psychological, sociological, philosophical, or anthropological theories. Prior decisions will reflect ideologies, economic considerations, and ethical values that were influential when these decisions were made, and, if no great change has occurred in the interim, the law will tend to preserve the status quo, both perpetuating old injustices and protecting traditional freedoms.

Legal Procedure

The law's great concern with the procedure of decision making is one of its more basic and important characteristics. Any discussion of the law that did not note the importance of procedure would be inadequate. Legal standards are often phrased not in terms of results but in terms of procedure. For example, it is not unlawful to convict the innocent if the right procedures are used (and it *is* unlawful to convict the guilty if the wrong procedures are followed). The law feels that it cannot guarantee that the right result will always be reached and that only the guilty will be caught, so it minimizes the risk of reaching the wrong result or convicting the innocent by specifying procedural steps to be followed. Lawyers, more than most people, are satisfied if the right procedures are followed even if there is something disturbing about the outcome. Law, therefore, has virtually eliminated the word *justice* from its vocabulary and has substituted the phrase *due process*, meaning that the proper procedures, such as right to counsel, right to a public trial, and right to cross-examine witnesses, have been followed. This concern with method is one of the pillars upon which law is based. It is one of the characteristics of law that distinguishes it from nonlegal methods of dispute resolution, where the atmosphere will be more informal and there may be no set procedures.

Conclusion

Law is a challenging area of study because many questions may not be amenable to simple solutions. The legal approach to problem solving is usually methodical and often slow. We frequently become frustrated with this process, and, in fact, it may be an inappropriate way to deal with some problems. For the issues in this book, however, an approach that pays careful attention to the many different aspects of these topics will be the most rewarding. Many of the readings provide historical, economic, and sociological data as well as information about law. The issues examined in *Taking Sides* involve basic cultural institutions such as religion, schools, and the family as well as basic cultural values such as privacy, individualism, and equality. While the law takes a narrow approach to problems, reading these issues should broaden your outlook on the problems discussed and, perhaps, encourage you to do further reading on those topics that are of particular interest to you.

Notes

1. Iredell Jenkins, *Social Order and the Limits of Law* (Princeton University Press, 1980), p. xi.
2. Lynn Wardle, "The Gap Between Law and Moral Order: An Examination of the Legitimacy of the Supreme Court Abortion Decisions," 1980(4) BYU L. Rev. 811–835 (1980).

Preface

The study of law should be introduced as part of a liberal education, to train and enrich the mind. . . . I am convinced that, like history, economics, and metaphysics—and perhaps even to a greater degree than these—the law could be advantageously studied with a view to the general development of the mind.

—*Justice Louis D. Brandeis*

The general study of law in colleges, universities, and even high schools has grown rapidly during the last 30 years. Accompanying this development has been the publication of new curriculum materials that go beyond the analyses of legal cases and doctrines that make up much of professional law study in law schools. This book is part of the effort to view and study law as an institution that continuously interacts with other social institutions. Law should be examined from an interdisciplinary perspective and be accessible to all students.

This book focuses on a series of controversial issues involving law and the legal system. It is, we believe, an appropriate starting point for law study because controversy and conflict are inherent in law. Law is based on an adversary approach to conflict resolution, in which two advocates representing opposing sides are pitted against each other. Judicial decisions often contain both majority and dissenting opinions, which reveal some of the arguments that went on in the judges' chambers. Perhaps most relevant to a discussion of the place of controversy in the legal system is the First Amendment guarantee of freedom of speech and of the press, which presumes that we all benefit by a vigorous debate of important issues.

Since many of the issues in *Taking Sides* are often in the news, you probably already have opinions on them. What you should remember, however, is that there is usually more to learn about any given issue, and the topics discussed here are best approached with an open mind. You should not be surprised if your views change as you read the selections.

Organization of the book   This book contains selections presented in a pro-and-con format that debate legal issues. Following each selection, contributor information is provided on the legal scholars, commentators, and judges whose views are debated in each issue. Each *issue introduction* has been expanded to include more information and appreciation for the context of the debate. Each *issue introduction* also includes a section on key *Learning Outcomes*, which lists the specific information that students should take out of each issue. The *Exploring the Issue* section that follows the pro–con articles presents *Critical Thinking and Reflection* questions to guide student reflection. This section also includes an *Is There Common Ground?* commentary that explores whether contrasting viewpoints can be reconciled. Finally, the *Additional Resources* and *Internet References* sections provide sources for further information on the topic and points for further research.

A word to the instructor   A general guidebook, *Using Taking Sides in the Classroom*, which discusses methods and techniques for integrating the pro–con approach into any classroom setting, is available through the publisher for the instructor using *Taking Sides* in the classroom. An online version of *Using Taking Sides in the Classroom* and a correspondence service for *Taking Sides* adopters can be found at www.createcentral.com.

Taking Sides: Clashing Views on Legal Issues is only one title in the *Taking Sides* collection. If you are interested in seeing the table of contents for any of the other titles, please visit The *Taking Sides* Collection at www.mcgrawhillcreate.com.

Acknowledgments   This edition has benefited greatly from the research conducted by Justin Rostoff of the New England School of Law.

M. Ethan Katsh
University of Massachusetts—Amherst
To Ari

Editor of This Volume

M. ETHAN KATSH is professor emeritus of legal studies and director of the National Center for Information Technology and Dispute Resolution at the University of Massachusetts at Amherst (www.odr.info/ethan-katsh). A graduate of the Yale Law School, he has authored books on law and technology: *Law in a Digital World* (Oxford University Press, 1995), *The Electronic Media and the Transformation of Law* (Oxford University Press, 1989), and, with Professor Janet Rifkin, *Online Dispute Resolution: Resolving Conflicts in Cyberspace* (2001). Professor Katsh is one of the founders of the field of online dispute resolution (www.odr.info). He may be reached at Katsh@legal.umass.edu.

Academic Advisory Board Members

Members of the Academic Advisory Board are instrumental in the final selection of articles for *Takings Sides* books. Their review of the articles for content, level, and appropriateness provides critical direction to the editor(s) and staff. We think that you will find their careful consideration reflected in this book.

Scott Kelly
Penn State Altoona

Charles Thomas Kelly, Jr.
Louisiana State University

Steven Kempisty
Bryant & Stratton College

Nancy Keppenhan
Liberty University

John Kuzenski
North Carolina Central University

Anthony La Manna
Ramapo College of New Jersey

Barbara Limbach
Chadron State College

Adam Lippe
Stevenson University

Robert Lockwood
Portland State University

Terry Lyons
University of Mississippi

Joel Maatman
Lansing Community College

Sheryl A. MacDougall
Community College of Rhode Island

Victoria Mantzopoulos
University of Detroit Mercy

Joan Mars
University of Michigan - Flint

Jeff McAlpin
Northwestern Oklahoma State University

Brian McCully
Fresno City College

Deshannon McDonald
Alabama State University

Larry Menter
Clayton State University

Craig Miller
Penn College

Deborah Mitchell Robinson
Valdosta State University

Samuel Monk
Jacksonville State University

Odell Moon
Victor Valley College

Cliff Olson
Southern Adventist University

Angela L. Ondrus
Owens State Community College

Scott Paulsen
Illinois Central College

Shelly Peffer
Blackburn College

Liana Pennington
University of Alabama

Michael Polakowski
University of Arizona

Rick Poland
Flagler College

Mike Pouraryan
Mohave Community College

Steven Pyser
Rutgers University

Jonah Raskin
Sonoma State University

Virginia Rich
Caldwell College

Raymond Rushboldt
SUNY Fredonia

Foster Russell
Guilford Technical Community College

Kurt Saunders
California State University

Carl Schwarz
University of California Irvine

Calvin Shaw
Gaston College

Unit 1

UNIT

Law and Terrorism

*T**he events of September 11, 2001, and the subsequent war on terror have had a significant impact on the law. We are continuously being confronted with choices about what we want law to do and how we want law to do it. These choices touch many deeply held values, affect our identity as individuals and as a country, and pose questions that we are likely to visit and revisit for some time.*

Should U.S. Citizens Who Are Declared to Be "Enemy Combatants" Be Able to Contest Their Detention before a Judge? by Katsh

15

Selected, Edited, and with Issue Framing Material by:
M. Ethan Katsh, *University of Massachusetts, Amherst*

ISSUE

Should U.S. Citizens Who Are Declared to Be "Enemy Combatants" Be Able to Contest Their Detention before a Judge?

YES: **Sandra Day O'Connor**, from "Majority Opinion, *Hamdi v. Rumsfeld,*" *United States Supreme Court* (2004)

NO: **Clarence Thomas**, from "Minority Opinion, *Hamdi v. Rumsfeld,*" *United States Supreme Court* (2004)

Learning Outcomes
After reading this issue, you will be able to: • Describe the writ of *habeas corpus*. • Describe who generally qualifies as an "enemy combatant." • Discuss the differing views of the Supreme Court justices with regards to reviewing presidential wartime decisions. • Identify other historical Supreme Court cases involving *habeas corpus*.

ISSUE SUMMARY

YES: Supreme Court Justice Sandra Day O'Connor finds that the Authorization for Use of Military Force passed by Congress does not authorize the indefinite detainment of a person found to be an "enemy combatant."

NO: Justice Clarence Thomas believes that the detention of an "enemy combatant" is permitted under the federal government's war powers.

The factual background to this issue is well known. On September 11, 2001, the al Qaeda terrorist network launched a coordinated attack on the United States, striking the twin towers of the World Trade Center in New York City and the Pentagon. They failed to strike a third target in Washington, D.C., presumably the White House or the U.S. Capitol. Approximately 3,000 people were killed with thousands more injured. The attacks' immediate economic damages were calculated in the hundreds of millions of dollars. Their long-term effects, human, legal, and economic, are still accumulating. It was the deadliest foreign attack on U.S. soil in this nation's history.

President George W. Bush took swift retaliatory action in response to the al Qaeda attacks. With the Authorization for Use of Military Force (AUMF), Pub. L. No. 107–40, secs. 1–2, 115 Stat. 224, Congress provided overwhelming bipartisan support for the president's use of "all necessary and appropriate force against those nations, organizations, or persons he determines planned, authorized, committed, or aided the terrorist attacks or harbored such organizations or persons." In addition to the power to commit military forces to battle, President Bush also claimed the authority to detain, indefinitely, those persons he designated as "enemy combatants"; a term whose definition has fluctuated over the last decade, but which the court in *Hamdi* defines as an individual who was "'part of or supporting forces hostile to the United States or coalition partners' in Afghanistan and who 'engaged in an armed conflict against the United States there'.'" In 2009, the Obama administration issued a statement saying that they were no longer using the phrase. However, the phrase has become part of the American political lexicon, and there have been calls, predominantly by conservatives, that even alleged domestic terrorists should be considered "enemy combatants."

Yaser Esam Hamdi, a United States citizen, was captured by Northern Alliance forces on the battlefields of Afghanistan in late 2001 and was eventually turned over to the American military. Hamdi was designated an "enemy combatant" by the President and therefore subject to detention away from the battlefield for the duration of "hostilities."

Although he claimed to have been a noncombatant, Hamdi was held by the Department of Defense, without access to legal counsel for more than a year. Ultimately, Hamdi's father, acting as his "next friend," petitioned a federal district court for a writ of *habeas corpus*, alleging that his son had been wrongfully seized and was being unlawfully held by the U.S. government.

The writ of *habeas corpus* has a long and storied history, originating in English law, but a look back in U.S. history is also instructive. On April 27, 1861, President Abraham Lincoln first suspended the writ of *habeas corpus*, nearly two weeks after Fort Sumpter fell to Confederate forces. He would do so again two more times before the end of the Civil War, in response to the profound nature of the threat posed to the nation's security by the war. Lambdin Milligan, Indiana lawyer and sympathizer of the Southern cause, was one of several thousand civilians arrested during this period. Sentenced to death for insurrectionary activities by a military commission, Milligan ultimately challenged his conviction before the U.S. Supreme Court. Rendering its decision after the war had come to an end, the Court overturned Milligan's conviction, holding that he had been denied his constitutional rights to a jury trial in a court of law (not the military tribunal that convicted him). Writing for the Court, Justice Davis observed: "During the late wicked Rebellion, the temper of the times did not allow that calmness in deliberation and discussion so necessary to a correct conclusion of a purely judicial question. Then, considerations of safety were mingled with the exercise of power; and feelings and interests prevailed which are happily terminated. Now that the public safety is assured, this question, as well as all others, can be discussed and decided without passion or the admixture of any element not required to form a legal judgment." (Ex parte Milligan, 24 Wall. [71 U.S.] 2, 1866)

Although Justice Davis would concede that constitutional protections of individual rights are "elastic,"

narrowing in a time of crisis and expanding in a time of calm, he would go on to insist on the absolute necessity for judicial review of executive action, even in time of war. The scope of such judicial review, however, would remain in question. In one of the next great crises to confront this nation, World War II, a majority of the Supreme Court would uphold the constitutionality of the forced internment of innocent American citizens of Japanese descent (*Korematsu v. United States*, 323 U.S. 214, 1944). In doing so, the Court articulated the need on the part of the judiciary, in the name of security, to defer to the military and the executive branch in times of national emergency. *Korematsu v. United States* was not a unanimous decision, however, and three justices wrote stinging dissents accusing the majority of sanctioning racism, overlooking a clear violation of citizens' constitutional rights, and shirking the Court's time-honored responsibility to protect U.S. citizens from unjust executive detention. Although never reversed, the *Korematsu* decision was in later years repudiated.

In 1980, Congress established a Commission on Wartime Relocation and Internment of Civilians to study the Japanese internment during World War II. In its report, *Personal Justice Denied*, the Commission found that the internment program "was done out of fear," rather than the claimed military necessity, and "inflicted tremendous human cost" without any benefit. In 1993, President Clinton issued a formal apology to Japanese Americans interned during the war, stating that "[i]n retrospect, we understand that the nation's actions were rooted deeply in racial prejudice, wartime hysteria, and a lack of political leadership." Clinton later awarded Fred Korematsu the Presidential Medal of Freedom. As you will read, *ex Parte Milligan* and *Korematsu* offer interesting analogies to Hamdi.

The legal challenge to Hamdi's detention moved back and forth between federal district court and the U.S. Court of Appeals. The U.S. government was ordered to grant a federal public defender's request to gain access to Hamdi in order to facilitate a due process challenge to his continued detention. Federal District Court Judge Robert Doumar characterized the government's factual declarations regarding Hamdi's original seizure as little more than their "say-so." He went on to insist that if the Court were to accept the government's factual claims alone as sufficient justification for Hamdi's continued detention, "it would in effect be abdicating any semblance of the most minimal level of judicial review. In effect, this Court would be acting as little more than a rubber-stamp" (*Hamdi v. Rumsfeld*, 243 F. Supp. 2d 527, 535 (E.D., Va. 2002)).

On appeal, however, the Fourth Circuit Court of Appeals rejected the lower court's analysis, urging instead the need for limited judicial review during times of war. Fourth Circuit Judge J. Harvey Wilkinson, citing separation of powers concerns and the need to defer to the war-making powers of the executive and legislative branches, observed that "[t]he safeguards that all Americans have come to expect in criminal prosecutions do not translate neatly to the arena of armed conflict. In fact, if deference to the executive branch is not exercised with respect to military judgments in the field, it is difficult to see where deference would ever obtain" (*Hamdi v. Rumsfeld*, 316 F. 3d 450 (4th Cir. 2003)). With this decision, the Fourth Circuit Court denied further inquiry into the facts alleged by the U.S. government that justified Hamdi's status as an "enemy combatant."

The *Hamdi* case asks the question of whether one can challenge their classification as an "enemy combatant."

Interestingly, what is not discussed in detail, but taken as fact from a government brief, is the definition of the term itself. While the court acknowledges in *Hamdi* that there "is some debate as to the proper scope of this term," and leaves it at that, the issue would resurface in Supreme Court jurisprudence. Shortly after the Court's decision in *Hamdi*, the Bush administration created Combatant Status Review Tribunals (CSRTs), which were charged with making "enemy combatant" status determinations of those in custody and to avoid future *habeas corpus* challenges in federal court by providing alternative due process procedures. However, in *Boumediene v. Bush*, the Supreme Court ruled that CSRTs and its implementing legislation, the Detainee Treatment Act, were inadequate substitutions for the writ of *habeas corpus*, and that detainees could still avail themselves of federal courts to make *habeas* petitions.

YES ⤶

Sandra Day O'Connor

Majority Opinion, *Hamdi v. Rumsfeld*

JUSTICE O'CONNOR announced the judgment of the Court and delivered an opinion, in which the CHIEF JUSTICE, JUSTICE KENNEDY, and JUSTICE BREYER join.

At this difficult time in our Nation's history, we are called upon to consider the legality of the Government's detention of a United States citizen on United States soil as an "enemy combatant" and to address the process that is constitutionally owed to one who seeks to challenge his classification as such. The United States Court of Appeals for the Fourth Circuit held that petitioner's detention was legally authorized and that he was entitled to no further opportunity to challenge his enemy-combatant label. We now vacate and remand. We hold that although Congress authorized the detention of combatants in the narrow circumstances alleged here, due process demands that a citizen held in the United States as an enemy combatant be given a meaningful opportunity to contest the factual basis for that detention before a neutral decisionmaker.

I

. . . This case arises out of the detention of a man whom the Government alleges took up arms with the Taliban during this conflict. . . . The Government contends that Hamdi is an "enemy combatant," and that this status justifies holding him in the United States indefinitely—without formal charges or proceedings—unless and until it makes the determination that access to counsel or further process is warranted. . . .

The petition contends that Hamdi's detention was not legally authorized. *Id.*, at 105. It argues that, "[a]s an American citizen, . . . Hamdi enjoys the full protections of the Constitution," and that Hamdi's detention in the United States without charges, access to an impartial tribunal, or assistance of counsel "violated and continue[s] to violate the Fifth and Fourteenth Amendments to the United States Constitution. . . .

[The] District Court had failed to extend appropriate deference to the Government's security and intelligence interests. 296 F. 3d 278, 279, 283 (2002). It directed the

District Court to consider "the most cautious procedures first," *id.*, at 284, and to conduct a deferential inquiry into Hamdi's status. . . .

The Fourth Circuit emphasized that the "vital purposes" of the detention of uncharged enemy combatants—preventing those combatants from rejoining the enemy while relieving the military of the burden of litigating the circumstances of wartime captures halfway around the globe—were interests "directly derived from the war powers of Articles I and II." *Id.*, at 465–466. In that court's view, because "Article III contains nothing analogous to the specific powers of war so carefully enumerated in Articles I and II," *id.*, at 463, separation of powers principles prohibited a federal court from "delv[ing] further into Hamdi's status and capture," *id.*, at 473. Accordingly, the District Court's more vigorous inquiry "went far beyond the acceptable scope of review.". . .

II

The threshold question before us is whether the Executive has the authority to detain citizens who qualify as "enemy combatants." There is some debate as to the proper scope of this term, and the Government has never provided any court with the full criteria that it uses in classifying individuals as such. It has made clear, however, that, for purposes of this case, the "enemy combatant" that it is seeking to detain is an individual who, it alleges, was "'part of or supporting forces hostile to the United States or coalition partners'" in Afghanistan and who "'engaged in an armed conflict against the United States'" there. Brief for Respondents 3. We therefore answer only the narrow question before us: whether the detention of citizens falling within that definition is authorized.

The Government maintains that no explicit congressional authorization is required, because the Executive possesses plenary authority to detain pursuant to Article II of the Constitution. We do not reach the question whether Article II provides such authority, however, because we agree with the Government's alternative

From Supreme Court of the United States, June 28, 2004.

position, that Congress has in fact authorized Hamdi's detention, through the AUMF. . . .

The AUMF authorizes the President to use "all necessary and appropriate force" against "nations, organizations, or persons" associated with the September 11, 2001, terrorist attacks. 115 Stat. 224. There can be no doubt that individuals who fought against the United States in Afghanistan as part of the Taliban, an organization known to have supported the al Qaeda terrorist network responsible for those attacks, are individuals Congress sought to target in passing the AUMF. We conclude that detention of individuals falling into the limited category we are considering, for the duration of the particular conflict in which they were captured, is so fundamental and accepted an incident to war as to be an exercise of the "necessary and appropriate force" Congress has authorized the President to use.

The capture and detention of lawful combatants and the capture, detention, and trial of unlawful combatants, by "universal agreement and practice," are "important incident[s] of war.". . .

There is no bar to this Nation's holding one of its own citizens as an enemy combatant. . . .

Hamdi objects, nevertheless, that Congress has not authorized the *indefinite* detention to which he is now subject. . . . We take Hamdi's objection to be not to the lack of certainty regarding the date on which the conflict will end, but to the substantial prospect of perpetual detention. We recognize that the national security underpinnings of the "war on terror," although crucially important, are broad and malleable. As the Government concedes, "given its unconventional nature, the current conflict is unlikely to end with a formal cease-fire agreement." *Ibid*. The prospect Hamdi raises is therefore not far-fetched. If the Government does not consider this unconventional war won for two generations, and if it maintains during that time that Hamdi might, if released, rejoin forces fighting against the United States, then the position it has taken throughout the litigation of this case suggests that Hamdi's detention could last for the rest of his life. . . .

III

Even in cases in which the detention of enemy combatants is legally authorized, there remains the question of what process is constitutionally due to a citizen who disputes his enemy-combatant status. Hamdi argues that he is owed a meaningful and timely hearing and that "extra-judicial detention [that] begins and ends with the submission of an affidavit based on third-hand hearsay" does not comport with the Fifth and Fourteenth Amendments. . . .

A

. . . All agree that, absent suspension, the writ of habeas corpus remains available to every individual detained within the United States. U. S. Const., Art. I, §9, cl. 2. . . . Only in the rarest of circumstances has Congress seen fit to suspend the writ. . . . At all other times, it has remained a critical check on the Executive, ensuring that it does not detain individuals except in accordance with law. . . . All agree suspension of the writ has not occurred here. Thus, it is undisputed that Hamdi was properly before an Article III court to challenge his detention under 28 U. S. C. §2241. . . .

C

The Government's second argument requires closer consideration. This is the argument that further factual exploration is unwarranted and inappropriate in light of the extraordinary constitutional interests at stake. Under the Government's most extreme rendition of this argument, "[r]espect for separation of powers and the limited institutional capabilities of courts in matters of military decision-making in connection with an ongoing conflict" ought to eliminate entirely any individual process, restricting the courts to investigating only whether legal authorization exists for the broader detention scheme. At most, the Government argues, courts should review its determination that a citizen is an enemy combatant under a very deferential "some evidence" standard. *Id.*, at 34 ("Under the some evidence standard, the focus is exclusively on the factual basis supplied by the Executive to support its own determination."). . .

In response, Hamdi emphasizes that this Court consistently has recognized that an individual challenging his detention may not be held at the will of the Executive without recourse to some proceeding before a neutral tribunal to determine whether the Executive's asserted justifications for that detention have basis in fact and warrant in law. . . . He argues that the Fourth Circuit inappropriately "ceded power to the Executive during wartime to define the conduct for which a citizen may be detained, judge whether that citizen has engaged in the proscribed conduct, and imprison that citizen indefinitely," . . . and that due process demands that he receive a hearing in which he may challenge the Mobbs Declaration and adduce his own counter evidence. . . .

Both of these positions highlight legitimate concerns. And both emphasize the tension that often exists between the autonomy that the Government asserts is necessary in order to pursue effectively a particular goal and the process that a citizen contends he is due before he is deprived of a constitutional right. The ordinary mechanism that we use for balancing such serious competing interests, and for determining the procedures that are necessary to ensure that a citizen is not deprived of life, liberty, or property, . . .

1

It is beyond question that substantial interests lie on both sides of the scale in this case. Hamdi's "private interest . . . affected by the official action," *ibid.*, is the most elemental of liberty interests—the interest in being free from physical detention by one's own government. . . . "In our society liberty is the norm," and detention without trial "is the carefully limited exception.". . .

Nor is the weight on this side of the *Mathews* scale offset by the circumstances of war or the accusation of treasonous behavior, for "[i]t is clear that commitment for *any* purpose constitutes a significant deprivation of liberty that requires due process protection," . . . Indeed, as *amicus* briefs from media and relief organizations emphasize, the risk of erroneous deprivation of a citizen's liberty in the absence of sufficient process here is very real. . . . Moreover, as critical as the Government's interest may be in detaining those who actually pose an immediate threat to the national security of the United States during ongoing international conflict, history and common sense teach us that an unchecked system of detention carries the potential to become a means for oppression and abuse of others who do not present that sort of threat. . . . We reaffirm today the fundamental nature of a citizen's right to be free from involuntary confinement by his own government without due process of law, and we weigh the opposing governmental interests against the curtailment of liberty that such confinement entails.

2

On the other side of the scale are the weighty and sensitive governmental interests in ensuring that those who have in fact fought with the enemy during a war do not return to battle against the United States. . . . Without doubt, our Constitution recognizes that core strategic matters of warmaking belong in the hands of those who are best positioned and most politically accountable for making them. . . .

3

Striking the proper constitutional balance here is of great importance to the Nation during this period of ongoing combat. But it is equally vital that our calculus not give short shrift to the values that this country holds dear or to the privilege that is American citizenship. It is during our most challenging and uncertain moments that our Nation's commitment to due process is most severely tested; and it is in those times that we must preserve our commitment at home to the principles for which we fight abroad. . . .

With due recognition of these competing concerns, we believe that neither the process proposed by the Government nor the process apparently envisioned by the District Court below strikes the proper constitutional balance when a United States citizen is detained in the United States as an enemy combatant. That is, "the risk of erroneous deprivation" of a detainee's liberty interest is unacceptably high under the Government's proposed rule, while some of the "additional or substitute procedural safeguards" suggested by the District Court are unwarranted in light of their limited "probable value" and the burdens they may impose on the military in such cases. *Mathews*, 424 U. S., at 335.

We therefore hold that a citizen-detainee seeking to challenge his classification as an enemy combatant must receive notice of the factual basis for his classification, and a fair opportunity to rebut the Government's factual assertions before a neutral decisionmaker. . . . "For more than a century the central meaning of procedural due process has been clear: 'Parties whose rights are to be affected are entitled to be heard; and in order that they may enjoy that right they must first be notified.' It is equally fundamental that the right to notice and an opportunity to be heard 'must be granted at a meaningful time and in a meaningful manner.'" . . . These essential constitutional promises may not be eroded.

At the same time, the exigencies of the circumstances may demand that, aside from these core elements, enemy combatant proceedings may be tailored to alleviate their uncommon potential to burden the Executive at a time of ongoing military conflict. . . .

We think it unlikely that this basic process will have the dire impact on the central functions of warmaking that the Government forecasts. . . .

In sum, while the full protections that accompany challenges to detentions in other settings may prove unworkable and inappropriate in the enemy-combatant setting, the threats to military operations posed by a basic system of independent review are not so weighty as to trump a citizen's core rights to challenge meaningfully the Government's case and to be heard by an impartial adjudicator.

D

In so holding, we necessarily reject the Government's assertion that separation of powers principles mandate a

Should U.S. Citizens Who Are Declared to Be "Enemy Combatants" Be Able to Contest Their Detention before a Judge? by Katsh

21

heavily circumscribed role for the courts in such circumstances. . . . We have long since made clear that a state of war is not a blank check for the President when it comes to the rights of the Nation's citizens. . . . Whatever power the United States Constitution envisions for the Executive in its exchanges with other nations or with enemy organizations in times of conflict, it most assuredly envisions a role for all three branches when individual liberties are at stake. . . . Likewise, we have made clear that, unless Congress acts to suspend it, the Great Writ of habeas corpus allows the Judicial Branch to play a necessary role in maintaining this delicate balance of governance, serving as an important judicial check on the Executive's discretion in the realm of detentions. . . .

SANDRA DAY O'CONNOR was an associate justice of the U.S. Supreme Court. She worked in various legal capacities both in the United States and in Germany until she was appointed to the Arizona State Senate in 1969. She served as a state senator for four years and served in the Arizona judiciary for six years before she was nominated to the Supreme Court by President Ronald Reagan in 1981.

Clarence Thomas  **NO**

Minority Opinion, *Hamdi v. Rumsfeld*

JUSTICE THOMAS, dissenting.

The Executive Branch, acting pursuant to the powers vested in the President by the Constitution and with explicit congressional approval, has determined that Yaser Hamdi is an enemy combatant and should be detained. This detention falls squarely within the Federal Government's war powers, and we lack the expertise and capacity to second-guess that decision. As such, petitioners' habeas challenge should fail, and there is no reason to remand the case. The plurality reaches a contrary conclusion by failing adequately to consider basic principles of the constitutional structure as it relates to national security and foreign affairs and by using the balancing scheme of *Mathews v. Eldridge,* 424 U. S. 319 (1976). I do not think that the Federal Government's war powers can be balanced away by this Court. Arguably, Congress could provide for additional procedural protections, but until it does, we have no right to insist upon them. But even if I were to agree with the general approach the plurality takes, I could not accept the particulars. The plurality utterly fails to account for the Government's compelling interests and for our own institutional inability to weigh competing concerns correctly. I respectfully dissent.

I

"It is 'obvious and unarguable' that no governmental interest is more compelling than the security of the Nation." *Haig v. Agee,* 453 U. S. 280, 307 (1981). . . . The national security, after all, is the primary responsibility and purpose of the Federal Government. . . . But because the Founders understood that they could not foresee the myriad potential threats to national security that might later arise, they chose to create a Federal Government that necessarily possesses sufficient power to handle any threat to the security of the Nation. The power to protect the Nation

> "ought to exist without limitation . . . *[b]ecause it is impossible to foresee or define the extent and variety of national exigencies, or the correspondent extent &*

variety of the means which may be necessary to satisfy them. The circumstances that endanger the safety of nations are infinite; and for this reason no constitutional shackles can wisely be imposed on the power to which the care of it is committed." *Id.,* at 147.

. . . The Founders intended that the President have primary responsibility—along with the necessary power—to protect the national security and to conduct the Nation's foreign relations. They did so principally because the structural advantages of a unitary Executive are essential in these domains. "Energy in the executive is a leading character in the definition of good government. It is essential to the protection of the community against foreign attacks." The Federalist No. 70. The principle "ingredien[t]" for "energy in the executive" is "unity.". . . This is because "[d]ecision, activity, secrecy, and dispatch will generally characterise the proceedings of one man, in a much more eminent degree, than the proceedings of any greater number."

These structural advantages are most important in the national-security and foreign-affairs contexts. "Of all the cares or concerns of government, the direction of war most peculiarly demands those qualities which distinguish the exercise of power by a single hand.". . . Also for these reasons, John Marshall explained that "[t]he President is the sole organ of the nation in its external relations, and its sole representative with foreign nations.". . . To this end, the Constitution vests in the President "[t]he executive Power," Art. II, §1, provides that he "shall be Commander in Chief of the" armed forces, §2, and places in him the power to recognize foreign governments, §3.

This Court has long recognized these features and has accordingly held that the President has *constitutional* authority to protect the national security and that this authority carries with it broad discretion. . . .

The Court has acknowledged that the President has the authority to "employ [the Nation's Armed Forces] in the manner he may deem most effectual to harass and conquer and subdue the enemy.". . . With respect to foreign affairs as well, the Court has recognized the President's independent authority and need to be free from interference. . . .

From Supreme Court of the United States, June 28, 2004.

Congress, to be sure, has a substantial and essential role in both foreign affairs and national security. But it is crucial to recognize that *judicial* interference in these domains destroys the purpose of vesting primary responsibility in a unitary Executive. I cannot improve on Justice Jackson's words, speaking for the Court:

> "The President, both as Commander-in-Chief and as the Nation's organ for foreign affairs, has available intelligence services whose reports are not and ought not to be published to the world. It would be intolerable that courts, without the relevant information, should review and perhaps nullify actions of the Executive taken on information properly held secret. Nor can courts sit *in camera* in order to be taken into executive confidences. But even if courts could require full disclosure, the very nature of executive decisions as to foreign policy is political, not judicial. Such decisions are wholly confided by our Constitution to the political departments of the government, Executive and Legislative. They are delicate, complex, and involve large elements of prophecy. They are and should be undertaken only by those directly responsible to the people whose welfare they advance or imperil. They are decisions of a kind for which the Judiciary has neither aptitude, facilities nor responsibility and which has long been held to belong in the domain of political power not subject to judicial intrusion or inquiry." *Ibid.*

Several points . . . are worth emphasizing. First, with respect to certain decisions relating to national security and foreign affairs, the courts simply lack the relevant information and expertise to second-guess determinations made by the President based on information properly withheld. Second, even if the courts could compel the Executive to produce the necessary information, such decisions are simply not amenable to judicial determination because "[t]hey are delicate, complex, and involve large elements of prophecy." Third, the Court . . . has correctly recognized the primacy of the political branches in the foreign-affairs and national-security contexts.

For these institutional reasons and because "Congress cannot anticipate and legislate with regard to every possible action the President may find it necessary to take or every possible situation in which he might act," it should come as no surprise that "[s]uch failure of Congress . . . does not, 'especially . . . in the areas of foreign policy and national security,' imply 'congressional disapproval' of action taken by the Executive.". . . Rather, in these domains, the fact that Congress has provided the President with broad authorities does not imply—and the Judicial Branch should not infer—that Congress intended to deprive him of particular powers not specifically enumerated. See *Dames & Moore*, 453 U. S., at 678. As far as the courts are concerned, "the enactment of legislation closely related to the question of the President's authority in a particular case which evinces legislative intent to accord the President broad discretion may be considered to 'invite' 'measures on independent presidential responsibility.'" *Ibid.* (quoting *Youngstown*, 343 U. S., at 637 (Jackson, J., concurring)). . . .

I acknowledge that the question whether Hamdi's executive detention is lawful is a question properly resolved by the Judicial Branch, though the question comes to the Court with the strongest presumptions in favor of the Government. The plurality agrees that Hamdi's detention is lawful if he is an enemy combatant. But the question whether Hamdi is actually an enemy combatant is "of a kind for which the Judiciary has neither aptitude, facilities nor responsibility and which has long been held to belong in the domain of political power not subject to judicial intrusion or inquiry.". . . That is, although it is appropriate for the Court to determine the judicial question whether the President has the asserted authority . . . we lack the information and expertise to question whether Hamdi is actually an enemy combatant, a question the resolution of which is committed to other branches.[1] . . .

II

"The war power of the national government is 'the power to wage war successfully.'". . . The Authorization for Use of Military Force (AUMF), 115 Stat. 224, authorizes the President to "use all necessary and appropriate force against those nations, organizations, or persons he determines planned, authorized, committed, or aided the terrorist attacks" of September 11, 2001. Indeed, the Court has previously concluded that language materially identical to . . .

The plurality, however, qualifies its recognition of the President's authority to detain enemy combatants in the war on terrorism in ways that are at odds with our precedent. . . . [We] are bound by the political branches' determination that the United States is at war. . . . [The] power to detain does not end with the cessation of formal hostilities. . . .

Accordingly, the President's action here is "supported by the strongest of presumptions and the widest latitude of judicial interpretation.". . . The question becomes whether the Federal Government (rather than the President acting alone) has power to detain Hamdi as an enemy combatant. More precisely, we must determine whether the Government may detain Hamdi given the procedures that were used.

III

I agree with the plurality that the Federal Government has power to detain those that the Executive Branch determines to be enemy combatants. See *ante*, at 10. But I do not think that the plurality has adequately explained the breadth of the President's authority to detain enemy combatants, an authority that includes making virtually conclusive factual findings. In my view, the structural considerations discussed above, as recognized in our precedent, demonstrate that we lack the capacity and responsibility to second-guess this determination. . . .

The Court has held that an executive, acting pursuant to statutory and constitutional authority may, consistent with the Due Process Clause, unilaterally decide to detain an individual if the executive deems this necessary for the public safety *even if he is mistaken.*

. . . In *Luther v. Borden,* 7 How. 1 (1849), . . . the Court also addressed the natural concern that placing "this power in the President is dangerous to liberty, and may be abused." The Court noted that "[a]ll power may be abused if placed in unworthy hands," and explained that "it would be difficult . . . to point out any other hands in which this power would be more safe, and at the same time equally effectual." Putting that aside, the Court emphasized that this power "is conferred upon him by the Constitution and laws of the United States, and must therefore be respected and enforced in its judicial tribunals." Finally, the Court explained that if the President abused this power "it would be in the power of Congress to apply the proper remedy. But the courts must administer the law as they find it." *Id.,* at 45. . . .

The Government's asserted authority to detain an individual that the President has determined to be an enemy combatant, at least while hostilities continue, comports with the Due Process Clause. As these cases also show, the Executive's decision that a detention is necessary to protect the public need not and should not be subjected to judicial second-guessing. Indeed, at least in the context of enemy-combatant determinations, this would defeat the unity, secrecy, and dispatch that the Founders believed to be so important to the warmaking function. . . .

Accordingly, I conclude that the Government's detention of Hamdi as an enemy combatant does not violate the Constitution. By detaining Hamdi, the President, in the prosecution of a war and authorized by Congress, has acted well within his authority. Hamdi thereby received all the process to which he was due under the circumstances. I therefore believe that this is no occasion to balance the competing interests, as the plurality unconvincingly attempts to do.

IV

Although I do not agree with the plurality that the balancing approach of *Mathews v. Eldridge,* 424 U. S. 319 (1976), is the appropriate analytical tool with which to analyze this case,[2] I cannot help but explain that the plurality misapplies its chosen framework, one that if applied correctly would probably lead to the result I have reached. . . .

Undeniably, Hamdi has been deprived of a serious interest, one actually protected by the Due Process Clause. Against this, however, is the Government's overriding interest in protecting the Nation. If a deprivation of liberty can be justified by the need to protect a town, the protection of the Nation, *a fortiori,* justifies it.

I acknowledge that under the plurality's approach, it might, at times, be appropriate to give detainees access to counsel and notice of the factual basis for the Government's determination. See *ante,* at 25–27. But properly accounting for the Government's interests also requires concluding that access to counsel and to the factual basis would not always be warranted. . . .

Notes

1. Although I have emphasized national-security concerns, the President's foreign-affairs responsibilities are also squarely implicated by this case. The Government avers that Northern Alliance forces captured Hamdi, and the District Court demanded that the Government turn over information relating to statements made by members of the Northern Alliance. See 316 F. 3d 450, 462 (CA4 2003).

2. Evidently, neither do the parties, who do not cite *Mathews* even once.

CLARENCE THOMAS is an associate justice of the U.S. Supreme Court. A former judge on the U.S. Court of Appeals for the District of Columbia, he was nominated by President George H. W. Bush to the Supreme Court in 1991. He received his J.D. from the Yale University School of Law in 1974.

EXPLORING THE ISSUE

Should U.S. Citizens Who Are Declared to Be "Enemy Combatants" Be Able to Contest Their Detention before a Judge?

Critical Thinking and Reflection

1. In a time of war, how do democracies negotiate the difficult balance between the security of the many and protection of individual liberties?
2. If the war against al Qaeda is an ongoing fight without a clear end, should enemy combatants be held indefinitely?
3. How much deference do you believe the President should have in making detention determinations?
4. Should only U.S. citizens be entitled to *habeas corpus,* or should everyone being detained by the United States?

Is There Common Ground?

Although the events of September 11 were unique in American history, many of the legal questions they entail are not. As discussed, separation of powers issues assumed center stage in *Hamdi*. While the court differed on the amount of deference that should be given to the President on decisions of detention during wartime, it is clear that all of the justices were in agreement that the President, as the Commander-in-Chief, is clearly charged with this responsibility. Given the strategy requirements of war, and his access to the most confidential of wartime information, as well as the fact that he is also politically accountable to the American people, the President is uniquely positioned to make such determinations.

Both the Majority and Dissenting opinions also agree that it is for the Judicial Branch to determine whether Hamdi's detention by the Executive is lawful. However, they disagree on the method for analyzing the issue. In its decision, the Court relies on the procedural due process balancing test established by a 1970s Supreme Court case (*Mathews v. Eldridge,* 424 U.S. 319 (1976)). The test consists of three factors: (1) the private interest at stake that will be affected by the government's action; (2) the risk of erroneous deprivation given the procedures implemented, and the value of additional or substitute procedural safeguards; and (3) the government's interest, including the government's function involved, and the burdens of additional

or substitute procedures. The Matthews test is used to protect the procedural due process rights provided by the Fifth Amendment, which states that no person shall "be deprived of life, liberty, or property, without due process." While Justice Thomas writes in his dissent that he does not believe "that the Federal Government's war powers can be balanced away by this Court," a clear attack on using *Matthews*, he nonetheless frames part of his arguments within the balancing test. Interestingly, as Justice Thomas also notes, neither Hamdi nor the government relied on *Matthews* in making its arguments. Why? Perhaps because the interest at stake in *Matthews* was not liberty, but property—the denial of social security disability payments.

Additional Resources

Allison M. Danner, "Defining Unlawful Enemy Combatants: A Centripetal Story," 43 *Tex. Int'l L. J.* 1 (2007–2008).

Louis Fisher, *Military Tribunals and Presidential Power* (University Press of Kansas, 2005); *Presidential War Power* (University Press of Kansas, 2004).

Michael Ignatieff, *The Lesser Evil: Political Ethics in an Age of Terror* (Princeton University Press, 2004).

Chief Justice William Rehnquist, *All the Laws but One: Civil Liberties in Wartime* (Vintage, 2000).

Internet References . . .

New York City Bar Association's Committee on Federal Courts

The Committee analyzes the *Hamdi* decision and its implications for U.S. detention policy in its report *The Indefinite Detention of "Enemy Combatants": Balancing Due Process and National Security in the Context of the War on Terror,* March 2004 (updated edition).

www.911familiesforamerica.org/pdf/1C_WL06!.pdf

New York Times

U.S. Won't Label Terror Suspects as 'Combatants'

www.nytimes.com/2009/03/14/us /politics/14gitmo.html?_r=0

G.O.P. Lawmakers Push to Have Boston Suspect Questioned as Enemy Combatant

www.nytimes.com/2013/04/22/us/gop-lawmakers -push-to-hold-boston-suspect-as-enemy-combatant .html?pagewanted=all

Legal Information Institute at Cornell University Law School

Full decision of ex parte *Milligan*

www.law.cornell.edu/supct/html/historics /USSC_CR_0071_0002_ZS.html

Full decision of *Korematsu*

www.law.cornell.edu/supct/html/historics /USSC_CR_0323_0214_ZS.html

Full decision of *Matthews*

www.law.cornell.edu/supct/html/historics /USSC_CR_0424_0319_ZO.html

Full decision of *Boumediene*

www.law.cornell.edu/supct/html/06-1195 .ZS.html

Selected, Edited, and with Issue Framing Material by:
M. Ethan Katsh, *University of Massachusetts, Amherst*

ISSUE

Does the President Possess Constitutional Authority to Order Wiretaps on U.S. Citizens?

YES: U.S. Department of Justice, from "Legal Authorities Supporting the Activities of the National Security Agency Described by the President," *United States Department of Justice* (2006)

NO: Letter to Congress, from "14 Law Professors and Former Government Attorneys to Congressional Leaders" (2006)

Learning Outcomes

After reading this issue, you will be able to:

- Discuss how presidential and congressional authority intertwine in the context of war powers.
- Identify and discuss legislation related to the surveillance of electronic communications.
- Discuss how the Fourth Amendment to the Constitution is used by advocates both for and against the President's right to wiretap U.S. citizens without a warrant.
- Discuss how the Foreign Intelligence Surveillance Act (FISA) regulates the President's ability to wiretap U.S. citizens.
- Discuss how courts have avoided deciding the substantive issue of the legality of warrantless wiretaps.

ISSUE SUMMARY

YES: The Department of Justice argues that the Constitution gives the President the right to engage in electronic surveillance, with or without congressional approval or judicial oversight. It further claims that the National Security Agency (NSA) wiretapping program ordered by President Bush does not violate federal law, specifically the Foreign Intelligence Surveillance Act (FISA), because such surveillance falls under the auspices of the military response to the 9/11 attacks, which was authorized by Congress.

NO: Several lawyers with expertise in constitutional law or experience in the federal government argue that the NSA wiretapping program violates FISA and the Fourth Amendment of the U.S. Constitution. They further argue that the President does not have any inherent authority either to engage in warrantless wiretapping or to violate federal law that limits such surveillance.

After discovering that President Nixon had used the FBI and other law enforcement mechanisms to spy on political opponents, the Senate voted in 1975 to establish a committee, chaired by Senator Frank Church, to investigate the government's recent intelligence gathering and whether it had involved any "illegal, improper, or unethical activities . . . by any agency of the Federal Government" (S. Res. 21, 1975). The Church Committee found, as many had speculated, that the FBI and CIA had engaged in massive spying on American citizens with little or no judicial oversight.

In issuing its numerous recommendations to Congress for how it should address the abuses that intelligence-gathering agencies had perpetrated, the Church Committee stated that it "believe[d] that there should be no electronic surveillance within the United States which is not subject to a judicial warrant procedure." The Supreme Court largely agreed: By the time of the Church Committee report, it had already ruled that most electronic surveillance, such as wiretapping phone calls, required a warrant issued by a judge. In *United States v. United States District Court* (1972), the majority declared that "Fourth Amendment freedoms cannot properly be guaranteed if domestic security surveillances may be conducted solely within the discretion of the Executive Branch . . . the Government's concerns do not justify departure in this case from the customary Fourth Amendment requirement of judicial approval prior to initiation of a search or surveillance."

However, in its decision in *United States v. U.S. District Court*, the Court was careful to state that it was not passing judgment "on the scope of the President's surveillance power with respect to the activities of foreign powers, within or without this country" [emphasis added]. Congress similarly had avoided the subject of "foreign intelligence surveillance" in federal legislation on electronic surveillance. Thus, while there were constitutional and statutory restrictions on how law enforcement could conduct surveillance on criminal suspects and "domestic" national security threats, there were no guidelines on measures that the government undertook in the name of foreign intelligence surveillance.

To address this issue, Congress in 1978 passed the Foreign Intelligence Surveillance Act (FISA). FISA established a special court, the Foreign Intelligence Surveillance Court (FISC), that meets in secret to issue warrants for wiretapping and searches that relate to threats from "a foreign power or an agent of a foreign power," including potential acts of "sabotage and international terrorism" (FISA, codified as 50 USC 1801(e)(1)). FISA also established civil and criminal penalties for any government official who "engages in electronic surveillance under color of law except as authorized by statute" (50 USC 1809(a)(1)). Congress believed that in passing FISA and in establishing a method whereby intelligence agencies could obtain warrants secretly and without any public record, it had balanced the Church Committee and the Supreme Court's concerns about civil liberties with the need of those agencies to collect information vital to national security.

In a 2002 presidential order, President Bush authorized the National Security Agency (NSA) to engage in warrantless wiretapping as part of its antiterrorism surveillance. The domestic wiretapping program put in place by President Bush's order was not known until December 2005, when the *New York Times* broke the story, reporting that the NSA had monitored "the international telephone calls and international e-mail messages of hundreds, perhaps thousands, of people inside the United States." The day after the *New York Times's* story went to press, President Bush acknowledged the program, arguing that it was within his constitutional powers to authorize such measures and sharply criticized the *New York Times* for endangering the safety of the United States by reporting the story.

Over the following months, the President and his administration made a concerted effort to explain and justify the "terrorist surveillance program," as it was characterized. Among these efforts was a memorandum released by the Department of Justice (DOJ), which is excerpted here, outlining the legal justification for the program. The DOJ relies on both constitutional and statutory authority for the President's power to authorize warrantless wiretapping of individuals within the United States, including U.S. citizens. Implicating the powers granted to the Executive under Article II of the Constitution to conduct matters involving foreign affairs and as Commander in Chief of the Armed Forces, the DOJ argues that it is the President who is tasked with protection of the Nation, and as such may do as he/she deems necessary to fulfill this constitutional obligation.

The DOJ also relies heavily on the Authorization for Use of Military Force (AUMF) granted to the President by Congress and its sweeping language allowing the President "to use all necessary and appropriate force" against those involved in 9/11. The DOJ further reasons that wiretapping and intelligence gathering, essential elements of any armed conflict, are therefore fully authorized by the AUMF and not subject to the procedural requirements imposed by FISA.

Not surprisingly, critics of the wiretapping program, including the former government attorneys and legal scholars who authored the second excerpted reading here, read FISA to continue to restrict the President's authority to direct wiretaps without a warrant, regardless of the AUMF. They argue that FISA was enacted specifically for the purpose of preventing the precise measures that the President was implementing. These scholars further point to the fact that the President is inferring his wiretapping powers from the AUMF, whereas FISA provides the "exclusive means" by which wiretapping in the United States may be conducted. In addition, it was argued, FISA provides for the realities and necessities of intelligence gathering, allowing warrantless wiretaps if immediately necessary, but subsequently requiring a warrant to be obtained after 72 hours.

At the heart of the criticism of the wiretapping program is the Fourth Amendment to the Constitution, which provides that "[t]he right of the people to be secure in their persons, houses, papers, and effects, against unreasonable searches and seizures shall not be violated, and no Warrants shall issue, but upon probable cause . . . ." Relying on principles of legal interpretation, as well as the Court's history in protecting the privacy of ordinary Americans, these critics argue that legislation should not be read to violate constitutional rights, but rather to protect them.

In 2007, the Bush administration claimed to have stopped the NSA wiretapping program, and with the inauguration of President Obama, many believed that the program and debates of its legality would be put to rest. However, this was not the case. Hundreds of lawsuits related to the wiretapping program have been filed to challenge its legality, but success has proved illusive.

Given the difficulties of finding actual proof of a rights violation under a highly secretive program, plaintiffs have had to rely on showing a high probability of their rights being violated in the future under the program, as was the case in *Clapper v. Amnesty International USA*. While Clapper had some success in lower courts, the Supreme Court, in February 2013, failed to address the substantive issue of the legality of the program by ruling that the plaintiffs could not bring their case because they were relying on a chain of contingencies that would have to fall into place to show that their communications were at risk of wiretapping. The case was dismissed.

In *al-Haramain Islamic Foundation v. Obama*, actual proof of warrantless wiretapping was available because the government accidentally sent the plaintiff copies of phone conversations he had with his attorneys. Even so, plaintiffs were again unsuccessful. In August 2012, the Ninth Circuit Court of Appeals ruled that under the FISA statute, the only remedy for the plaintiffs were monetary damages against the United States, but sovereign immunity prevented any such remedy and the case was dismissed.

Recognizing the difficulties of prevailing in a legal battle with the United States, critics of the wiretapping program set their sights on telecommunication companies, which had allegedly been assisting the Bush administration according to several whistleblowers. However, in 2008, Congress passed the FISA Amendments Act of 2008, which protected telecommunication companies from lawsuits for past or future cooperation with federal agencies under the wiretapping program. The FISA Amendments

Act also gave law enforcement greater leniency in conducting wiretaps by providing them with 7 days, rather than 48 hours, to obtain a warrant, and by allowing them to engage in some forms of indirect warrantless wiretapping of Americans within the United States if the government does not *intentionally* target domestic conversations. If the government intends to wiretap conversations involving someone within the United States, or has good reason to believe one of the speakers is within the United States, it is still required to obtain a warrant from the Foreign Intelligence Surveillance Court (FISC).

With FISA no longer providing strict limits on the government's ability to wiretap without warrants and absolving the telecommunication companies of wrongdoing, only one notable legal challenge remains, as of the writing of this book. Relying on whistleblower evidence provided by former AT&T and NSA employees, the case *Jewell v. NSA* is attempting to hold not only the government agencies tasked with carrying out the wiretapping responsible, but those who initially authorized the programs, including President Bush and former Vice-President Dick Cheney. The government's latest defense, based on sovereign immunity and that litigation would result in the United States disclosing state secrets, is being considered before a federal district court in San Francisco.

So-called "whistleblowers" have increasingly become a key element to bringing transparency to otherwise highly secretive surveillance programs being carried out by the U.S. government. In early June 2013, Edward Snowden, a former NSA Infrastructure Analyst, and Booz Allen, an employee of the government security contractor, disclosed to several newspapers highly confidential information on several comprehensive U.S. surveillance programs. These programs included the gathering of metadata related to virtually all telephone calls on the Verizon network; unfettered access to e-mail, Internet searches and other online communications in conjunction with Internet service providers under a program known as PRISM; and programs aimed at obtaining the private communications of foreign embassies, trade delegations, and diplomats, including those of U.S. allies. As of the writing of this book, Snowden is wanted on various charges, including espionage, and is seeking asylum in several jurisdictions that do not have extradition treaties with the United States.

YES ⤶

U.S. Department of Justice

Legal Authorities Supporting the Activities of the National Security Agency Described by the President

As the President has explained, since shortly after the attacks of September 11, 2001, he has authorized the National Security Agency ("NSA") to intercept international communications into and out of the United States of persons linked to al Qaeda or related terrorist organizations. The purpose of these intercepts is to establish an early warning system to detect and prevent another catastrophic terrorist attack on the United States. This paper addresses, in an unclassified form, the legal basis for the NSA activities described by the President ("NSA activities"). . . .

In its first legislative response to the terrorist attacks of September 11th, Congress authorized the President to "use all necessary and appropriate force against those nations, organizations, or persons he determines planned, authorized, committed, or aided the terrorist attacks" of September 11th in order to prevent "any future acts of international terrorism against the United States." Authorization for Use of Military Force, Pub. L. No. 107–40, § 2(a), 115 Stat. 224, 224 (Sept. 18, 2001) (reported as a note to 50 U.S.C.A. § 1541) ("AUMF"). History conclusively demonstrates that warrantless communications intelligence targeted at the enemy in time of armed conflict is a traditional and fundamental incident of the use of military force authorized by the AUMF. The Supreme Court's interpretation of the AUMF in *Hamdi v. Rumsfeld*, 542 U.S. 507 (2004), confirms that Congress in the AUMF gave its express approval to the military conflict against al Qaeda and its allies and thereby to the President's use of all traditional and accepted incidents of force in this current military conflict—including warrantless electronic surveillance to intercept enemy communications both at home and abroad. This understanding of the AUMF demonstrates Congress's support for the President's authority to protect the Nation and, at the same time, adheres to Justice O'Connor's admonition that "a state of war is not a blank check for the President," *Hamdi*, 542 U.S. at 536 (plurality opinion), particularly in view of the narrow scope of the NSA activities. . . .

Background

A. The Attacks of September 11, 2001

On September 14, 2001, the President declared a national emergency "by reason of the terrorist attacks at the World Trade Center, New York, New York, and the Pentagon, and the continuing and immediate threat of further attacks on the United States." Proclamation No. 7463, 66 Fed. Reg. 48,199 (Sept. 14, 2001). The same day, Congress passed a joint resolution authorizing the President "to use all necessary and appropriate force against those nations, organizations, or persons he determines planned, authorized, committed, or aided the terrorist attacks" of September 11th, which the President signed on September 18th. AUMF § 2(a). Congress also expressly acknowledged that the attacks rendered it "necessary and appropriate" for the United States to exercise its right "to protect United States citizens both at home and abroad," and in particular recognized that "the President has authority under the Constitution to take action to deter and prevent acts of international terrorism against the United States." *Id.* pmbl. Congress emphasized that the attacks "continue to pose an unusual and extraordinary threat to the national security and foreign policy of the United States." *Id.* The United States also launched a large-scale military response, both at home and abroad. In the United States, combat air patrols were immediately established over major metropolitan areas and were maintained 24 hours a day until April 2002. The United States also immediately began plans for a military response directed at al Qaeda's base of operations in Afghanistan. Acting under his constitutional authority as Commander in Chief, and with the support of Congress, the President dispatched forces to Afghanistan and, with the assistance of the Northern Alliance, toppled the Taliban regime.

As the President made explicit in his Military Order of November 13, 2001, authorizing the use of military commissions to try terrorists, the attacks of September 11th

Memorandum released by the U.S. Department of Justice, January 19, 2006.

"created a state of armed conflict." Military Order § l(a), 66 Fed. Reg. 57,833 (Nov. 13, 2001). Indeed, shortly after the attacks, NATO—for the first time in its 46-year history—invoked article 5 of the North Atlantic Treaty, which provides that an "armed attack against one or more of [the parties] shall be considered an attack against them all." . . . The President also determined in his Military Order that al Qaeda and related terrorists organizations "possess both the capability and the intention to undertake further terrorist attacks against the United States that, if not detected and prevented, will cause mass deaths, mass injuries, and massive destruction of property, and may place at risk the continuity of the operations of the United States Government," and concluded that "an extraordinary emergency exists for national defense purposes." Military Order, § l(c), (g), 66 Fed. Reg. at 57,833–34.

B. The NSA Activities

Against this unfolding background of events in the fall of 2001, there was substantial concern that al Qaeda and its allies were preparing to carry out another attack within the United States. Al Qaeda had demonstrated its ability to introduce agents into the United States undetected and to perpetrate devastating attacks, and it was suspected that additional agents were likely already in position within the Nation's borders. As the President has explained, unlike a conventional enemy, al Qaeda has infiltrated "our cities and communities and communicated from here in America to plot and plan with bin Laden's lieutenants in Afghanistan, Pakistan and elsewhere." Press Conference of President Bush (Dec. 19, 2005). . . . To this day, finding al Qaeda sleeper agents in the United States remains one of the paramount concerns in the War on Terror. As the President has explained, "[t]he terrorists want to strike America again, and they hope to inflict even more damage than they did on September the 11th." *Id.*

The President has acknowledged that, to counter this threat, he has authorized the NSA to intercept international communications into and out of the United States of persons linked to al Qaeda or related terrorist organizations. The same day, the Attorney General elaborated and explained that in order to intercept a communication, there must be "a reasonable basis to conclude that one party to the communication is a member of al Qaeda, affiliated with al Qaeda, or a member of an organization affiliated with al Qaeda." Press Briefing by Attorney General Alberto Gonzales and General Michael Hayden, Principal Deputy Director for National Intelligence . . . (Dec. 19, 2005) (statement of Attorney General Gonzales). The purpose of these intercepts is to establish an early warning

system to detect and prevent another catastrophic terrorist attack on the United States. The President has stated that the NSA activities "ha[ve] been effective in disrupting the enemy, while safeguarding our civil liberties." President's Press Conference. . . .

Analysis

I. The President Has Inherent Constitutional Authority to Order Warrantless Foreign Intelligence Surveillance

As Congress expressly recognized in the AUMF, "the President has authority under the Constitution to take action to deter and prevent acts of international terrorism against the United States," AUMF pmbl., especially in the context of the current conflict. Article II of the Constitution vests in the President all executive power of the United States, including the power to act as Commander in Chief of the Armed Forces, *see* U.S. Const. art. II, § 2, and authority over the conduct of the Nation's foreign affairs. . . .

To carry out these responsibilities, the President must have authority to gather information necessary for the execution of his office. The Founders, after all, intended the federal Government to be clothed with all authority necessary to protect the Nation. . . . Because of the structural advantages of the Executive Branch, the Founders also intended that the President would have the primary responsibility and necessary authority as Commander in Chief and Chief Executive to protect the Nation and to conduct the Nation's foreign affairs. . . . Thus, it has been long recognized that the President has the authority to use secretive means to collect intelligence necessary for the conduct of foreign affairs and military campaigns. . . .

In reliance on these principles, a consistent understanding has developed that the President has inherent constitutional authority to conduct warrantless searches and surveillance within the United States for foreign intelligence purposes. Wiretaps for such purposes thus have been authorized by Presidents at least since the administration of Franklin Roosevelt in 1940. *See, e.g., United States v. United States District Court,* 444 F.2d 651, 669–71 (6th Cir. 1971) (reproducing as an appendix memoranda from Presidents Roosevelt, Truman, and Johnson). In a Memorandum to Attorney General Jackson, President Roosevelt wrote on May 21, 1940:

> You are, therefore, authorized and directed in such cases as you may approve, after investigation of the need in each case, to authorize the necessary

investigation agents that they are at liberty to secure information by listening devices directed to the conversation or other communications of persons suspected of subversive activities against the Government of the United States, including suspected spies. You are requested furthermore to limit these investigations so conducted to a minimum and limit them insofar as possible to aliens.

. . . In *United States v. United States District Court*, 407 U.S. 297 (1972) (the *"Keith"* case), the Supreme Court concluded that the Fourth Amendment's warrant requirement applies to investigations of wholly *domestic* threats to security—such as domestic political violence and other crimes. But the Court in the *Keith* case made clear that it was not addressing the President's authority to conduct *foreign* intelligence surveillance without a warrant and that it was expressly reserving that question: "[T]he instant case requires no judgment on the scope of the President's surveillance power with respect to the activities of foreign powers, within or without this country." *Id.* at 308; *see also id.* at 321–22 & n. 20 ("We have not addressed, and express no opinion as to, the issues which may be involved with respect to activities of foreign powers or their agents."). That *Keith* does not apply in the context of protecting against a foreign attack has been confirmed by the lower courts. After *Keith,* each of the three courts of appeals that have squarely considered the question have concluded—expressly taking the Supreme Court's decision into account—that the President has inherent authority to conduct warrantless surveillance in the foreign intelligence context. *See, e.g., Truong Dinh Hung,* 629 F.2d at 913–14; *Butenko,* 494 F.2d at 603; *Brown,* 484 F.2d 425–26.

From a constitutional standpoint, foreign intelligence surveillance such as the NSA activities differs fundamentally from the domestic security surveillance at issue in *Keith*. As the Fourth Circuit observed, the President has uniquely strong constitutional powers in matters pertaining to foreign affairs and national security. "Perhaps most crucially, the executive branch not only has superior expertise in the area of foreign intelligence, it is also constitutionally designated as the pre-eminent authority in foreign affairs." *Truong,* 629 F.2d at 914. . . .

The present circumstances that support recognition of the President's inherent constitutional authority to conduct the NSA activities are considerably stronger than were the circumstances at issue in the earlier courts of appeals cases that recognized this power. All of the cases described above addressed inherent executive authority under the foreign affairs power to conduct surveillance in a peacetime context. The courts in these cases therefore had no

occasion even to consider the fundamental authority of the President, as Commander in Chief, to gather intelligence in the context of an ongoing armed conflict in which the United States already had suffered massive civilian casualties and in which the intelligence gathering efforts at issue were specifically designed to thwart further armed attacks. Indeed, intelligence gathering is particularly important in the current conflict, in which the enemy attacks largely through clandestine activities and which, as Congress recognized, "pose[s] an unusual and extraordinary threat," AUMF pmbl. . . .

II. The AUMF Confirms and Supplements the President's Inherent Power to Use Warrantless Surveillance Against the Enemy in the Current Armed Conflict

In the Authorization for Use of Military Force enacted in the wake of September 11th, Congress confirms and supplements the President's constitutional authority to protect the Nation, including through electronic surveillance, in the context of the current post–September 11th armed conflict with al Qaeda and its allies. The broad language of the AUMF affords the President, at a minimum, discretion to employ the traditional incidents of the use of military force. The history of the President's use of warrantless surveillance during armed conflicts demonstrates that the NSA surveillance described by the President is a fundamental incident of the use of military force that is necessarily included in the AUMF. . . .

The AUMF passed by Congress on September 14, 2001, does not lend itself to a narrow reading. Its expansive language authorizes the President "to use *all necessary and appropriate force* against those nations, organizations, or persons *he determines* planned, authorized, committed, or aided the terrorist attacks that occurred on September 11, 2001." AUMF § 2(a) (emphases added). In the field of foreign affairs, and particularly that of war powers and national security, congressional enactments are to be broadly construed where they indicate support for authority long asserted and exercised by the Executive Branch. . . . Although Congress's war powers under Article I, Section 8 of the Constitution empower Congress to legislate regarding the raising, regulation, and material support of the Armed Forces and related matters, rather than the prosecution of military campaigns, the AUMF indicates Congress's endorsement of the President's use of his constitutional war powers. This authorization transforms the struggle against al Qaeda and related terrorist organizations from what Justice Jackson called "a zone of twilight," in which the President and the Congress may have concurrent powers whose "distribution is uncertain," *Youngstown Sheet & Tube Co. v. Sawyer,* 343 U.S. 579, 637 (1952) (Jackson, J., concurring), into a situation in which the President's authority is at is maximum because "it includes all that he possesses in his own right plus all that Congress can delegate," *id.* at 635. With regard to these fundamental tools of warfare—and, as demonstrated below, warrantless electronic surveillance against the declared enemy is one such tool—the AUMF places the President's authority at its zenith under *Youngstown.* . . .

Warrantless Electronic Surveillance Aimed at Intercepting Enemy Communications Has Long Been Recognized as a Fundamental Incident of the Use of Military Force

The history of warfare—including the consistent practice of Presidents since the earliest days of the Republic—demonstrates that warrantless intelligence surveillance against the enemy is a fundamental incident of the use of military force, and this history confirms the statutory authority provided by the AUMF. Electronic surveillance is a fundamental tool of war that must be included in any natural reading of the AUMF's authorization to use "all necessary and appropriate force."

As one author has explained:

> It is *essential* in warfare for a belligerent to be as fully informed as possible about the enemy—his strength, his weaknesses, measures taken by him and measures contemplated by him. This applies not only to military matters, but . . . anything which bears on and is material to his ability to wage the war in which he is engaged. *The laws of war recognize and sanction this aspect of warfare.*

Morris Greenspan, *The Modern Law of Land Warfare* 325 (1959) (emphases added). . . .

In accordance with these well-established principles, the Supreme Court has consistently recognized the President's authority to conduct intelligence activities. *See, e.g., Totten v. United States,* 92 U.S. 105, 106 (1876) (recognizing President's authority to hire spies); *Tenet v. Doe,* 544 U.S. 1 (2005) (reaffirming *Totten* and counseling against judicial interference with such matters); *see also Chicago & S. Air Lines v. Waterman S.S. Corp.,* 333 U.S. 103, 111 (1948) ("The President, both as Commander-in-Chief and as the Nation's organ for foreign affairs, has available intelligence services whose reports neither are not and ought not to be published to the world."); *United States v. Curtiss-Wright*

Export Corp., 299 U.S. 304, 320 (1936) (The President "has his confidential sources of information. He has his agents in the form of diplomatic, consular, and other officials."). Chief Justice John Marshall even described the gathering of intelligence as a military duty. *See Tatum v. Laird,* 444 F.2d 947, 952–53 (D.C. Cir. 1971) ("As Chief Justice John Marshall said of Washington, 'A general must be governed by his intelligence and must regulate his measures by his information. It is his duty to obtain correct information. . . .'") (quoting Foreword, U.S. Army Basic Field Manual, Vol. X, circa 1938), *rev'd on other grounds,* 408 U.S. 1 (1972). . . .

The interception of communications, in particular, has long been accepted as a fundamental method for conducting wartime surveillance. *See, e.g.,* Greenspan, *supra,* at 326 (accepted and customary means for gathering intelligence "include air reconnaissance and photography; ground reconnaissance; observation of enemy positions; *interception of enemy messages, wireless and other;* examination of captured documents; . . . and interrogation of prisoners and civilian inhabitants") (emphasis added). Indeed, since its independence, the United States has intercepted communications for wartime intelligence purposes and, if necessary, has done so within its own borders. During the Revolutionary War, for example, George Washington received and used to his advantage reports from American intelligence agents on British military strength, British strategic intentions, and British estimates of American strength.

More specifically, warrantless electronic surveillance of wartime communications has been conducted in the United States since electronic communications have existed, *i.e.,* since at least the Civil War, when "[t]elegraph wiretapping was common, and an important intelligence source for both sides." G.J.A. O'Toole, *The Encyclopedia of American Intelligence and Espionage* 498 (1988). Confederate General J.E.B. Stuart even "had his own personal wiretapper travel along with him in the field" to intercept military telegraphic communications. . . .

In light of the long history of prior wartime practice, the NSA activities fit squarely within the sweeping terms of the AUMF. The use of signals intelligence to identify and pinpoint the enemy is a traditional component of wartime military operations—or, to use the terminology of *Hamdi,* a "fundamental and accepted . . . incident to war," 542 U.S. at 518 (plurality opinion)—employed to defeat the enemy and to prevent enemy attacks in the United States. Here, as in other conflicts, the enemy may use public communications networks, and some of the enemy may already be in the United States. Although those factors may be present in this conflict to a greater degree than in the past, neither is novel. Certainly, both factors were well known at the time Congress enacted the AUMF. Wartime interception of international communications made by the enemy thus should be understood, no less than the wartime detention at issue in *Hamdi,* as one of the basic methods of engaging and defeating the enemy that Congress authorized in approving "*all* necessary and appropriate force" that the President would need to defend the Nation. AUMF § 2(a) (emphasis added).

⋖⟐⋗

III. The NSA Activities Are Consistent with the Foreign Intelligence Surveillance Act

The President's exercise of his constitutional authority to conduct warrantless wartime electronic surveillance of the enemy, as confirmed and supplemented by statute in the AUMF, is fully consistent with the requirements of the Foreign Intelligence Surveillance Act ("FISA").[1] FISA is a critically important tool in the War on Terror. The United States makes full use of the authorities available under FISA to gather foreign intelligence information, including authorities to intercept communications, conduct physical searches, and install and use pen registers and trap and trace devices. While FISA establishes certain procedures that must be followed for these authorities to be used (procedures that usually involve applying for and obtaining an order from a special court), FISA also expressly contemplates that a later legislative enactment could authorize electronic surveillance outside the procedures set forth in FISA itself. The AUMF constitutes precisely such an enactment. To the extent there is any ambiguity on this point, the canon of constitutional avoidance requires that such ambiguity be resolved in favor of the President's authority to conduct the communications intelligence activities he has described. Finally, if FISA could not be read to allow the President to authorize the NSA activities during the current congressionally authorized armed conflict with al Qaeda, FISA would be unconstitutional as applied in this narrow context.

A. The Requirements of FISA

FISA was enacted in 1978 to regulate "electronic surveillance," particularly when conducted to obtain "foreign intelligence information," as those terms are defined in section 101 of FISA, 50 U.S.C. § 1801. As a general matter, the statute requires that the Attorney General approve an application for an order from a special court composed of Article III judges and created by FISA—the Foreign Intelligence Surveillance Court ("FISC"). *See* 50 U.S.C. §§ 1803–1804. The application must demonstrate, among other things, that there is probable cause to believe that the target is a foreign power or an agent of a foreign power. *See id.* § 1805(a)(3)(A). It must also contain a certification from the Assistant to the President for National Security Affairs or an officer of the United States appointed by the President with the advice and consent of the Senate and having responsibilities in the area of national security or defense that the information sought is foreign intelligence information and cannot reasonably be obtained by normal investigative means. *See id.* § 1804(a)(7). FISA further requires the Government to state the means that it proposes to use to obtain the information and the basis for its belief that the facilities at which the surveillance will be directed are being used or are about to be used by a foreign power or an agent of a foreign power. *See id.* § 1804(a)(4), (a)(8).

FISA was the first congressional measure that sought to impose restrictions on the Executive Branch's authority to engage in electronic surveillance for foreign intelligence purposes, an authority that, as noted above, had been repeatedly recognized by the federal courts. . . .

In addition, Congress addressed, to some degree, the manner in which FISA might apply after a formal declaration of war by expressly allowing warrantless surveillance for a period of fifteen days following such a declaration. Section 111 of FISA allows the President to "authorize electronic surveillance without a court order under this subchapter to acquire foreign intelligence information for a period not to exceed fifteen calendar days following a declaration of war by the Congress." 50 U.S.C. § 1811.

The legislative history of FISA shows that Congress understood it was legislating on fragile constitutional ground and was pressing or even exceeding constitutional limits in regulating the President's authority in the field of foreign intelligence. The final House Conference Report, for example, recognized that the statute's restrictions might well impermissibly infringe on the President's constitutional powers. That report includes the extraordinary acknowledgment that "[t]he conferees agree that the establishment by this act of exclusive means by which the President may conduct electronic surveillance does not foreclose a different decision by the Supreme Court." H.R. Conf. Rep. No. 95-1720, at 35, *reprinted in* 1978 U.S.C.C.A.N. 4048, 4064. But, invoking Justice Jackson's concurrence in the *Steel Seizure* case, the Conference Report explained that Congress intended in FISA to exert whatever power Congress constitutionally had over the subject matter to restrict foreign intelligence surveillance and to leave the President solely with whatever inherent constitutional authority he might be able to invoke against Congress's express wishes. . . .

B. FISA Contemplates and Allows Surveillance Authorized "by Statute"

Congress did not attempt through FISA to prohibit the Executive Branch from using electronic surveillance. Instead, Congress acted to bring the exercise of that power under more stringent congressional control. *See, e.g.,* H. Conf. Rep. No. 95-1720, at 32, *reprinted in* 1978 U.S.C.C.A.N. 4048, 4064. Congress therefore enacted a regime intended to supplant the President's reliance on his own constitutional authority. Consistent with this overriding purpose of bringing the use of electronic surveillance under *congressional* control and with the commonsense notion that the Congress that enacted FISA could not bind future Congresses, FISA expressly contemplates that the Executive Branch may conduct electronic surveillance outside FISA's express procedures if and when a subsequent statute authorizes such surveillance.

Thus, section 109 of FISA prohibits any person from intentionally "engag[ing] . . . in electronic surveillance under color of law *except as authorized by statute.*" 50 U.S.C. § 1809(a)(1) (emphasis added). Because FISA's prohibitory provision broadly exempts surveillance "authorized by statute," the provision demonstrates that Congress did not attempt to regulate through FISA electronic surveillance authorized by Congress through a subsequent enactment. The use of the term "statute" here is significant because it strongly suggests that *any* subsequent authorizing statute, not merely one that amends FISA itself, could legitimately authorize surveillance outside FISA's standard procedural requirements. . . . In enacting FISA, therefore, Congress contemplated the possibility that the President might be permitted to conduct electronic surveillance pursuant to a later-enacted statute that did not incorporate all of the procedural requirements set forth in FISA or that did not expressly amend FISA itself. . . .

C. The AUMF Is a "Statute" Authorizing Surveillance Outside the Confines of FISA

The AUMF qualifies as a "statute" authorizing electronic surveillance within the meaning of section 109 of FISA.

First, because the term "statute" historically has been given broad meaning, the phrase "authorized by statute" in section 109 of FISA must be read to include joint resolutions such as the AUMF. . . .

Second, the longstanding history of communications intelligence as a fundamental incident of the use of force

and the Supreme Court's decision in *Hamdi v. Rumsfeld* strongly suggest that the AUMF satisfies the requirement of section 109 of FISA for statutory authorization of electronic surveillance. As explained above, it is not necessary to demarcate the outer limits of the AUMF to conclude that it encompasses electronic surveillance targeted at the enemy. Just as a majority of the Court concluded in *Hamdi* that the AUMF authorizes detention of U.S. citizens who are enemy combatants without expressly mentioning the President's long-recognized power to detain, so too does it authorize the use of electronic surveillance without specifically mentioning the President's equally long-recognized power to engage in communications intelligence targeted at the enemy. . . .

D. The Canon of Constitutional Avoidance Requires Resolving in Favor of the President's Authority any Ambiguity About Whether FISA Forbids the NSA Activities

As explained above, the AUMF fully authorizes the NSA activities. Because FISA contemplates the possibility that subsequent statutes could authorize electronic surveillance without requiring FISA's standard procedures, the NSA activities are also consistent with FISA and related provisions in title 18. Nevertheless, some might argue that sections 109 and 111 of FISA, along with section 2511(2)(f)'s "exclusivity" provision and section 2511(2)(e)'s liability exception for officers engaged in FISA-authorized surveillance, are best read to suggest that FISA requires that subsequent authorizing legislation specifically amend FISA in order to free the Executive from FISA's enumerated procedures. As detailed above, this is not the better reading of FISA. But even if these provisions were ambiguous, any doubt as to whether the AUMF and FISA should be understood to allow the President to make tactical military decisions to authorize surveillance outside the parameters of FISA must be resolved to avoid the serious constitutional questions that a contrary interpretation would raise.

It is well established that the first task of any interpreter faced with a statute that may present an unconstitutional infringement on the powers of the President is to determine whether the statute may be construed to avoid the constitutional difficulty. "[I]f an otherwise acceptable construction of a statute would raise serious constitutional problems, and where an alternative interpretation of the statute is 'fairly possible,' we are obligated to construe the statute to avoid such problems." *INS v. St. Cyr*, 533 U.S. 289, 299–300 (2001) (citations omitted); *Ashwander v. TVA*, 297 U.S. 288, 345–48 (1936) (Brandeis, J., concurring). Moreover, the canon of constitutional avoidance has particular importance in the realm of national security, where the

President's constitutional authority is at its highest. . . . Thus, courts and the Executive Branch typically construe a general statute, even one that is written in unqualified terms, to be implicitly limited so as not to infringe on the President's Commander in Chief powers.

Reading FISA to prohibit the NSA activities would raise two serious constitutional questions, both of which must be avoided if possible: (1) whether the signals intelligence collection the President determined was necessary to undertake is such a core exercise of Commander in Chief control over the Armed Forces during armed conflict that Congress cannot interfere with it at all and (2) whether the particular restrictions imposed by FISA are such that their application would impermissibly impede the President's exercise of his constitutionally assigned duties as Commander in Chief. Constitutional avoidance principles require interpreting FISA, at least in the context of the military conflict authorized by the AUMF, to avoid these questions, if "fairly possible." Even if Congress intended FISA to use the full extent of its constitutional authority to "occupy the field" of "electronic surveillance," as FISA used that term, during peacetime, the legislative history indicates that Congress had not reached a definitive conclusion about its regulation during wartime. *See* H.R. Conf. Rep. No. 95-1720, at 34, *reprinted in* 1978 U.S.C.C.A.N. at 4063 (noting that the purpose of the fifteen-day period following a declaration of war in section 111 of FISA was to "allow time for consideration of any amendment to this act that may be appropriate during a wartime emergency"). Therefore, it is not clear that Congress, in fact, intended to test the limits of its constitutional authority in the context of wartime electronic surveillance.

Whether Congress may interfere with the President's constitutional authority to collect foreign intelligence information through interception of communications reasonably believed to be linked to the enemy poses a difficult constitutional question. As explained in Part I, it had long been accepted at the time of FISA's enactment that the President has inherent constitutional authority to conduct warrantless electronic surveillance for foreign intelligence purposes. Congress recognized at the time that the enactment of a statute purporting to eliminate the President's ability, even during peacetime, to conduct warrantless electronic surveillance to collect foreign intelligence was near or perhaps beyond the limit of Congress's Article I powers. The NSA activities, however, involve signals intelligence performed in the midst of a congressionally authorized armed conflict undertaken to prevent further hostile attacks on the United States. The NSA activities lie at the very core of the Commander in Chief power, especially in light of the AUMF's explicit authorization for the President

to take *all* necessary and appropriate military action to stop al Qaeda from striking again. The constitutional principles at stake here thus involve not merely the President's well-established inherent authority to conduct warrantless surveillance for foreign intelligence purposes during peacetime, but also the powers and duties expressly conferred on him as Commander in Chief by Article II. . . .

IV. The NSA Activities Are Consistent with the Fourth Amendment

The Fourth Amendment prohibits "unreasonable searches and seizures" and directs that "no Warrants shall issue, but upon probable cause, supported by Oath or affirmation, and particularly describing the place to be searched, and the persons or things to be seized." U.S. Const. amend. IV. The touchstone for review of government action under the Fourth Amendment is whether the search is "reasonable." *See, e.g., Vernonia Sch. Dist. v. Acton,* 515 U.S. 646, 653 (1995).

As noted above, . . . all of the federal courts of appeals to have addressed the issue have affirmed the President's inherent constitutional authority to collect foreign intelligence without a warrant. *See In re Sealed Case,* 310 F.3d at 742. Properly understood, foreign intelligence collection in general, and the NSA activities in particular, fit within the "special needs" exception to the warrant requirement of the Fourth Amendment. Accordingly, the mere fact that no warrant is secured prior to the surveillance at issue in the NSA activities does not suffice to render the activities unreasonable. Instead, reasonableness in this context must be assessed under a general balancing approach, "'by assessing, on the one hand, the degree to which it intrudes upon an individual's privacy and, on the other, the degree to which it is needed for the promotion of legitimate governmental interests.'" *United States v. Knights,* 534 U.S. 112, 118–19 (2001) (quoting *Wyoming v. Houghton,* 526 U.S. 295, 300 (1999)). The NSA activities are reasonable because the Government's interest, defending the Nation from another foreign attack in time of armed conflict, outweighs the individual privacy interests at stake, and because they seek to intercept only international communications where one party is linked to al Qaeda or an affiliated terrorist organization.

A. The Warrant Requirement of the Fourth Amendment Does Not Apply to the NSA Activities

In "the criminal context," the Fourth Amendment reasonableness requirement "usually requires a showing of probable cause" and a warrant. *Board of Educ. v. Earls,* 536 U.S. 822, 828 (2002). The requirement of a warrant supported by probable cause, however, is not universal. Rather, the Fourth Amendment's "central requirement is one of reasonableness," and the rules the Court has developed to implement that requirement "[s]ometimes . . . require warrants." *Illinois v. McArthur,* 531 U.S. 326, 330 (2001). . . .

In particular, the Supreme Court repeatedly has made clear that in situations involving "special needs" that go beyond a routine interest in law enforcement, the warrant requirement is inapplicable. . . . It is difficult to encapsulate in a nutshell all of the different circumstances the Court has found to qualify as "special needs" justifying warrantless searches. But one application in which the Court has found the warrant requirement inapplicable is in circumstances in which the Government faces an increased need to be able to react swiftly and flexibly, or when there are at stake interests in public safety beyond the interests in ordinary law enforcement. One important factor in establishing "special needs" is whether the Government is responding to an emergency that goes beyond the need for general crime control. . . .

Thus, the Court has permitted warrantless searches of property of students in public schools, *see New Jersey v. T.L.O.,* 469 U.S. 325, 340 (1985) (noting that warrant requirement would "unduly interfere with the maintenance of the swift and informal disciplinary procedures needed in the schools"), to screen athletes and students involved in extracurricular activities at public schools for drug use, *see Vernonia,* 515 U.S. at 654–55; *Earls,* 536 U.S. at 829–38, to conduct drug testing of railroad personnel involved in train accidents, *see Skinner v. Railway Labor Executives' Ass'n,* 489 U.S. 602, 634 (1989), and to search probationers' homes, *see Griffin,* 483 U.S. 868. Many special needs doctrine and related cases have upheld *suspicionless* searches or seizures. *See, e.g., Illinois v. Lidster,* 540 U.S. 419, 427 (2004) (implicitly relying on special needs doctrine to uphold use of automobile checkpoint to obtain information about recent hit-and-run accident); *Earls,* 536 U.S. at 829–38 (suspicionless drug testing of public school students involved in extracurricular activities); *Michigan Dep't of State Police v. Sitz,* 496 U.S. 444, 449–55 (1990) (road block to check all motorists for signs of drunken driving); *United States v. Martinez-Fuerte,* 428 U.S. 543 (1976) (road block near the border to check vehicles for illegal immigrants); *cf. In re Sealed Case,* 310 F.3d at 745–46 (noting that suspicionless searches and seizures in one sense are a greater encroachment on privacy than electronic surveillance under FISA because they are not based on any particular suspicion, but "[o]n the other hand, wiretapping is a good deal more intrusive than an automobile stop accompanied by questioning"). To fall within the "special needs" exception to the warrant requirement, the purpose

of the search must be distinguishable from ordinary general crime control. *See, e.g., Ferguson v. Charleston,* 532 U.S. 67 (2001); *City of Indianapolis v. Edmond,* 531 U.S. 32, 41 (2000).

Foreign intelligence collection, especially in the midst of an armed conflict in which the adversary has already launched catastrophic attacks within the United States, fits squarely within the area of "special needs, beyond the normal need for law enforcement" where the Fourth Amendment's touchstone of reasonableness can be satisfied without resort to a warrant. *Vernonia,* 515 U.S. at 653. The Executive Branch has long maintained that collecting foreign intelligence is far removed from the ordinary criminal law enforcement action to which the warrant requirement is particularly suited. . . .

In particular, the NSA activities are undertaken to prevent further devastating attacks on our Nation, and they serve the highest government purpose through means other than traditional law enforcement. The NSA activities are designed to enable the Government to act quickly and flexibly (and with secrecy) to find agents of al Qaeda and its affiliates—an international terrorist group which has already demonstrated a capability to infiltrate American communities without being detected—in time to disrupt future terrorist attacks against the United States. As explained by the Foreign Intelligence Surveillance Court of Review, the nature of the "emergency" posed by al Qaeda "takes the matter out of the realm of ordinary crime control." *In re Sealed Case,* 310 F.3d at 746. Thus, under the "special needs" doctrine, no warrant is required by the Fourth Amendment for the NSA activities.

B. The NSA Activities Are Reasonable

As the Supreme Court has emphasized repeatedly, "[t]he touchstone of the Fourth Amendment is reasonableness, and the reasonableness of a search is determined by assessing, on the one hand, the degree to which it intrudes upon an individual's privacy and, on the other, the degree to which it is needed for the promotion of legitimate governmental interests." . . . Under the standard balancing of interests analysis used for gauging reasonableness, the NSA activities are consistent with the Fourth Amendment.

With respect to the individual privacy interests at stake, there can be no doubt that, as a general matter, interception of telephone communications implicates a significant privacy interest of the individual whose conversation is intercepted. The Supreme Court has made clear at least since *Katz v. United States,* 389 U.S. 347 (1967), that individuals have a substantial and constitutionally protected reasonable expectation of privacy that their telephone conversations will not be subject to governmental eavesdropping. Although the individual privacy interests at stake may be substantial, it is well recognized that a variety of governmental interests—including routine law enforcement and foreign-intelligence gathering—can overcome those interests.

On the other side of the scale here, the Government's interest in engaging in the NSA activities is the most compelling interest possible—securing the Nation from foreign attack in the midst of an armed conflict. One attack already has taken thousands of lives and placed the Nation in state of armed conflict. Defending the Nation from attack is perhaps the most important function of the federal Government—and one of the few express obligations of the federal Government enshrined in the Constitution. *See* U.S. Const. art. IV, § 4 ("The United States shall guarantee to every State in this Union a Republican Form of Government, *and shall protect each of them against Invasion* . . . .") (emphasis added); *The Prize Cases,* 67 U.S. (2 Black) 635, 668 (1863) ("If war be made by invasion of a foreign nation, the President is not only authorized but bound to resist force by force."). As the Supreme Court has declared, "[i]t is 'obvious and unarguable' that no governmental interest is more compelling than the security of the Nation." *Haig v. Agee,* 453 U.S. 280, 307 (1981).

The Government's overwhelming interest in detecting and thwarting further al Qaeda attacks is easily sufficient to make reasonable the intrusion into privacy involved in intercepting one-end foreign communications where there is "a reasonable basis to conclude that one party to the communication is a member of al Qaeda,

affiliated with al Qaeda, or a member of an organization affiliated with al Qaeda." . . .

Conclusion

For the foregoing reasons, the President—in light of the broad authority to use military force in response to the attacks of September 11th and to prevent further catastrophic attack expressly conferred on the President by the Constitution and confirmed and supplemented by Congress in the AUMF—has legal authority to authorize the NSA to conduct the signals intelligence activities he has described. Those activities are authorized by the Constitution and by statute, and they violate neither FISA nor the Fourth Amendment.

Note

1. To avoid revealing details about the operation of the program, it is assumed for purposes of this paper that the activities described by the President constitute "electronic surveillance," as defined by FISA, 50 U.S.C. § 1801(f).

THE UNITED STATES DEPARTMENT OF JUSTICE has a mission to enforce the law and defend the interests of the United States according to the law to ensure public safety against threats foreign and domestic, to provide federal leadership in preventing and controlling crime, to seek just punishment for those guilty of unlawful behavior, and to ensure fair and impartial administration of justice for all Americans.

Letter to Congress

 **NO**

Letter to Congress from 14 Law Professors and Former Government Attorneys to Congressional Leaders

Dear Members of Congress:

We are scholars of constitutional law and former government officials. We write in our individual capacities as citizens concerned by the Bush Administration's National Security Agency domestic spying program, as reported in the New York Times, and in particular to respond to the Justice Department's December 22, 2005, letter to the majority and minority leaders of the House and Senate Intelligence Committees setting forth the administration's defense of the program. Although the program's secrecy prevents us from being privy to all of its details, the Justice Department's defense of what it concedes was secret and warrantless electronic surveillance of persons within the United States fails to identify any plausible legal authority for such surveillance. Accordingly the program appears on its face to violate existing law.

The basic legal question here is not new. In 1978, after an extensive investigation of the privacy violations associated with foreign intelligence surveillance programs, Congress and the President enacted the Foreign Intelligence Surveillance Act (FISA). Pub. L. 95–511, 92 Stat. 1783. FISA comprehensively regulates electronic surveillance within the United States, striking a careful balance between protecting civil liberties and preserving the "vitally important government purpose" of obtaining valuable intelligence in order to safeguard national security. S. Rep. No. 95-604, pt. 1, at 9 (1977).

With minor exceptions, FISA authorizes electronic surveillance only upon certain specified showings, and only if approved by a court. The statute specifically allows for warrantless *wartime* domestic electronic surveillance— but only for the first fifteen days of a war. 50 U.S.C. § 1811. It makes criminal any electronic surveillance not authorized by statute, *id.* § 1809; and it expressly establishes FISA and specified provisions of the federal criminal code (which govern wiretaps for criminal investigation) as the

"*exclusive* means by which electronic surveillance . . . may be conducted," 18 U.S.C. § 2511(2)(f) (emphasis added).[1]

The Department of Justice (DOJ) concedes that the NSA program was not authorized by any of the above provisions. It maintains, however, that the program did not violate existing law because Congress implicitly authorized the NSA program when it enacted the Authorization for Use of Military Force (AUMF) against al Qaeda, Pub. L. No. 107–40, 115 Stat. 224 (2001). But the AUMF cannot reasonably be construed to implicitly authorize warrantless electronic surveillance in the United States during wartime, where Congress has expressly and specifically addressed that precise question in FISA and limited any such warrantless surveillance to the first fifteen days of war.

The DOJ also invokes the President's inherent constitutional authority as Commander in Chief to collect "signals intelligence" targeted at the enemy, and maintains that construing FISA to prohibit the President's actions would raise constitutional questions. But even conceding that the President in his role as Commander in Chief may generally collect signals intelligence on the enemy abroad, Congress indisputably has authority to regulate electronic surveillance within the United States, as it has done in FISA. Where Congress has so regulated, the President can act in contravention of statute only if his authority is *exclusive,* and not subject to the check of statutory regulation. The DOJ letter pointedly does not make that extraordinary claim.

Moreover, to construe the AUMF as the DOJ suggests would itself raise serious constitutional questions under the Fourth Amendment. The Supreme Court has never upheld warrantless wiretapping within the United States. Accordingly, the principle that statutes should be construed to avoid serious constitutional questions provides an additional reason for concluding that the AUMF does not authorize the President's actions here.

I. Congress Did Not Implicitly Authorize the NSA Domestic Spying Program in the AUMF, and in Fact Expressly Prohibited It in FISA

The DOJ concedes . . . that the NSA program involves "electronic surveillance," which is defined in FISA to mean the interception of the *contents* of telephone, wire, or email communications that occur, at least in part, in the United States. 50 U.S.C. §§ 1801(f)(1)–(2), 1801(n). NSA engages in such surveillance without judicial approval, and apparently without the substantive showings that FISA requires—e.g., that the subject is an "agent of a foreign power." *Id.* § 1805(a). The DOJ does not argue that FISA itself authorizes such electronic surveillance; and, as the DOJ letter acknowledges, 18 U.S.C. § 1809 makes criminal any electronic surveillance not authorized by statute.

The DOJ nevertheless contends that the surveillance is authorized by the AUMF, signed on September 18, 2001, which empowers the President to use "all necessary and appropriate force against" al Qaeda. According to the DOJ, collecting "signals intelligence" on the enemy, even if it involves tapping U.S. phones without court approval or probable cause, is a "fundamental incident of war" authorized by the AUMF. This argument fails for four reasons.

First, and most importantly, the DOJ's argument rests on an unstated general "implication" from the AUMF that directly contradicts *express* and *specific* language in FISA. Specific and "carefully drawn" statutes prevail over general statutes where there is a conflict. *Morales v. TWA, Inc.,* 504 U.S. 374, 384–85 (1992) (quoting *International Paper Co. v. Ouelette,* 479 U.S. 481, 494 (1987)). In FISA, Congress has directly and specifically spoken on the question of domestic warrantless wiretapping, including during wartime, and it could not have spoken more clearly.

As noted above, Congress has comprehensively regulated all electronic surveillance in the United States, and authorizes such surveillance only pursuant to specific statutes designated as the "*exclusive* means by which electronic surveillance . . . and the interception of domestic wire, oral, and electronic communications may be conducted." 18 U.S.C. § 2511(2)(f) (emphasis added). Moreover, FISA *specifically* addresses the question of domestic wiretapping during wartime. In a provision entitled "Authorization during time of war," FISA dictates that "[n]otwithstanding any other law, the President, through the Attorney General, may authorize electronic surveillance without a court order under this subchapter to acquire foreign intelligence information *for a period not to exceed fifteen calendar days following a declaration of war by the Congress.*" 50 U.S.C. §

1811 (emphasis added). Thus, even where Congress has declared war—a more formal step than an authorization such as the AUMF—the law limits warrantless wiretapping to the first fifteen days of the conflict. Congress explained that if the President needed further warrantless surveillance during wartime, the fifteen days would be sufficient for Congress to consider and enact further authorization.[2] Rather than follow this course, the President acted unilaterally and secretly in contravention of FISA's terms. The DOJ letter remarkably does not even *mention* FISA's fifteen-day war provision, which directly refutes the President's asserted "implied" authority. . . .

Second, the DOJ's argument would require the conclusion that Congress implicitly and *sub silentio* repealed 18 U.S.C. § 2511(2)(f), the provision that identifies FISA and specific criminal code provisions as "the *exclusive* means by which electronic surveillance . . . may be conducted." Repeals by implication are strongly disfavored; they can be established only by "overwhelming evidence," *J.E.M. Ag. Supply, Inc. v. Pioneer Hi-Bred Int'l, Inc.,* 534 U.S. 124, 137 (2001), and "'the only permissible justification for a repeal by implication is when the earlier and later statutes are irreconcilable,'" *id.* at 141–142 (quoting *Morton v. Mancari,* 417 U.S. 535, 550 (1974)). The AUMF and § 2511(2)(f) are not irreconcilable, and there is *no* evidence, let alone overwhelming evidence, that Congress intended to repeal § 2511(2)(f).

Third, Attorney General Alberto Gonzales has admitted that the administration did not seek to amend FISA to authorize the NSA spying program because it was advised that Congress would reject such an amendment.[3] The administration cannot argue on the one hand that Congress authorized the NSA program in the AUMF, and at the same time that it did not ask Congress for such authorization because it feared Congress would say no.[4]

Finally, the DOJ's reliance upon *Hamdi v. Rumsfeld,* 542 U.S. 507 (2004), to support its reading of the AUMF, . . . is misplaced. A plurality of the Court in *Hamdi* held that the AUMF authorized military detention of enemy combatants captured on the battlefield abroad as a "fundamental incident of waging war." *Id.* at 519. The plurality expressly limited this holding to individuals who were "part of or supporting forces hostile to the United States or coalition partners *in Afghanistan and who engaged in an armed conflict against the United States there.*" *Id.* at 516 (emphasis added). It is one thing, however, to say that foreign battlefield capture of enemy combatants is an incident of waging war that Congress intended to authorize. It is another matter entirely to treat unchecked warrantless *domestic* spying as included in that authorization, especially where an existing statute specifies that other laws are the "exclusive means" by which electronic surveillance may be conducted and provides that even a declaration of war authorizes such spying only for a fifteen-day emergency period.

II. Construing FISA to Prohibit Warrantless Domestic Wiretapping Does Not Raise Any Serious Constitutional Question, Whereas Construing the AUMF to Authorize Such Wiretapping Would Raise Serious Questions Under the Fourth Amendment

The DOJ argues that FISA and the AUMF should be construed to permit the NSA program's domestic surveillance because otherwise there might be a "conflict between FISA and the President's Article II authority as Commander-in-Chief." DOJ Letter at 4. The statutory scheme described above is not ambiguous, and therefore the constitutional avoidance doctrine is not even implicated. *See United States v. Oakland Cannabis Buyers' Coop.*, 532 U.S. 483, 494 (2001) (the "canon of constitutional avoidance has no application in the absence of statutory ambiguity"). But were it implicated, it would work against the President, not in his favor. Construing FISA and the AUMF according to their plain meanings raises no serious constitutional questions regarding the President's duties under Article II. Construing the AUMF to *permit* unchecked warrantless wiretapping without probable cause, however, would raise serious questions under the Fourth Amendment.

A. FISA's Limitations Are Consistent with the President's Article II Role

We do not dispute that, absent congressional action, the President might have inherent constitutional authority to collect "signals intelligence" about the enemy abroad. Nor do we dispute that, had Congress taken no action in this area, the President might well be constitutionally empowered to conduct domestic surveillance directly tied and narrowly confined to that goal—subject, of course, to Fourth Amendment limits. Indeed, in the years before FISA was enacted, the federal law involving wiretapping specifically provided that "[n]othing contained in this chapter or in section 605 of the Communications Act of 1934 shall limit the constitutional power of the President . . . to obtain foreign intelligence information deemed essential to the security of the United States." 18 U.S.C. § 2511(3) (1976).

But FISA specifically *repealed* that provision. FISA § 201(c), 92 Stat. 1797, and replaced it with language dictating that FISA and the criminal code are the "exclusive means" of conducting electronic surveillance. In doing so, Congress did not deny that the President has constitutional power to conduct electronic surveillance for national security purposes; rather, Congress properly concluded that "even if the President has the inherent authority *in the absence of legislation* to authorize warrantless electronic surveillance for foreign intelligence purposes, Congress has the power to regulate the conduct of such surveillance by legislating a reasonable procedure, which then becomes the exclusive means by which such surveillance may be conducted." H.R. Rep. No. 95-1283, pt. 1, at 24 (1978) (emphasis added). This analysis, Congress noted, was "supported by two successive Attorneys General." *Id.*

To say that the President has inherent authority does not mean that his authority is exclusive, or that his conduct is not subject to statutory regulations enacted (as FISA was) pursuant to Congress's Article I powers. As Justice Jackson famously explained in his influential opinion in *Youngstown Sheet & Tube Co. v. Sawyer*, 343 U.S. at 635 (Jackson, J., concurring), the Constitution "enjoins upon its branches separateness but interdependence, autonomy but reciprocity. Presidential powers are not fixed but fluctuate, depending upon their disjunction or conjunction with those of Congress." For example, the President in his role as Commander in Chief directs military operations. But the Framers gave Congress the power to prescribe rules for the regulation of the armed and naval forces, Art. I, § 8, cl. 14, and if a duly enacted statute prohibits the military from engaging in torture or cruel, inhuman, and degrading treatment, the President must follow that dictate. As Justice Jackson wrote, when the President acts in defiance of "the expressed or implied will of Congress," his power is "at its lowest ebb." 343 U.S. at 637. In this setting, Jackson wrote, "Presidential power [is] most vulnerable to attack and in the least favorable of possible constitutional postures." *Id.* at 640.

Congress plainly has authority to regulate domestic wiretapping by federal agencies under its Article I powers, and the DOJ does not suggest otherwise. Indeed, when FISA was enacted, the Justice Department agreed that Congress had power to regulate such conduct, and could require judicial approval of foreign intelligence surveillance. FISA does not prohibit foreign intelligence surveillance, but merely imposes reasonable regulation to protect legitimate privacy rights. (For example, although FISA generally requires judicial approval for electronic surveillance of persons within the United States, it permits the executive branch to install a wiretap immediately so long as it obtains judicial approval within 72 hours. 50 U.S.C. § 1805(f).)

Just as the President is bound by the statutory prohibition on torture, he is bound by the statutory dictates of FISA. The DOJ once infamously argued that the President as Commander in Chief could ignore even the criminal prohibition on torture,[5] and, more broadly still, that statutes may not "place *any* limits on the President's determinations as to any terrorist threat, the amount of military force to be used in response, or the method, timing, and nature of the response."[6] But the administration withdrew the August 2002 torture memo after it was disclosed, and for good reason the DOJ does not advance these extreme arguments here. Absent a serious question about FISA's constitutionality, there is no reason even to consider construing the AUMF to have implicitly overturned the carefully designed regulatory regime that FISA establishes. *See, e.g., Reno v. Flores*, 507 U.S. 292, 314 n.9 (1993) (constitutional avoidance canon applicable only if the constitutional question to be avoided is a serious one, "not to eliminate all possible contentions that the statute *might* be unconstitutional") (emphasis in original; citation omitted).[7]

B. Construing the AUMF to Authorize Warrantless Domestic Wiretapping Would Raise Serious Constitutional Questions

The principle that ambiguous statutes should be construed to avoid serious constitutional questions works against the administration, not in its favor. Interpreting the AUMF and FISA to permit unchecked domestic wiretapping for the duration of the conflict with al Qaeda would certainly raise serious constitutional questions. The Supreme Court has never upheld such a sweeping power to invade the privacy of Americans at home without individualized suspicion or judicial oversight.

The NSA surveillance program permits wiretapping within the United States without *either* of the safeguards presumptively required by the Fourth Amendment for electronic surveillance—individualized probable cause and a warrant or other order issued by a judge or magistrate. The Court has long held that wiretaps generally require a warrant and probable cause. *Katz v. United States*, 389 U.S. 347 (1967). And the only time the Court considered the question of national security wiretaps, it held that the Fourth Amendment prohibits domestic security wiretaps without those safeguards. *United States v. United States Dist. Court*, 407 U.S. 297 (1972). Although the Court in that case left open the question of the Fourth Amendment validity of warrantless wiretaps for foreign intelligence

purposes, its precedents raise serious constitutional questions about the kind of open-ended authority the President has asserted with respect to the NSA program. *See id.* at 316–18 (explaining difficulty of guaranteeing Fourth Amendment freedoms if domestic surveillance can be conducted solely in the discretion of the executive branch).

Indeed, serious Fourth Amendment questions about the validity of warrantless wiretapping led Congress to enact FISA, in order to "provide the secure framework by which the executive branch may conduct legitimate electronic surveillance for foreign intelligence purposes within the context of this nation's commitment to privacy and individual rights." S. Rep. No. 95-604, pt. 1, at 15 (1977) (citing, *inter alia, Zweibon v. Mitchell*, 516 F.2d 594 (D.C. Cir. 1975), in which "the court of appeals held that a warrant must be obtained before a wiretap is installed on a domestic organization that is neither the agent of, nor acting in collaboration with, a foreign power").

Relying on *In re Sealed Case No. 02-001*, the DOJ argues that the NSA program falls within an exception to the warrant and probable cause requirement for reasonable searches that serve "special needs" above and beyond ordinary law enforcement. But the existence of "special needs" has never been found to permit warrantless wiretapping. "Special needs" generally excuse the warrant and individualized suspicion requirements only where those requirements are impracticable and the intrusion on privacy is minimal. . . . Wiretapping is not a minimal intrusion on privacy, and the experience of FISA shows that foreign intelligence surveillance can be carried out through warrants based on individualized suspicion.

The court in *Sealed Case* upheld FISA itself, which requires warrants issued by Article III federal judges upon an individualized showing of probable cause that the subject is an "agent of a foreign power." The NSA domestic spying program, by contrast, includes none of these safeguards. It does not require individualized judicial approval, and it does not require a showing that the target is an "agent of a foreign power." According to Attorney General Gonzales, the NSA may wiretap any person in the United States who so much as receives a communication from anyone abroad, if the administration deems either of the parties to be affiliated with al Qaeda, a member of an organization affiliated with al Qaeda, "working in support of al Qaeda," or "part of" an organization or group "that is supportive of al Qaeda." Under this reasoning, a U.S. citizen living here who received a phone call from another U.S. citizen who attends a mosque that the administration believes is "supportive" of al Qaeda could be wiretapped without a warrant. The absence of meaningful safeguards on the NSA program at a minimum raises serious questions about the validity of the program under the Fourth Amendment, and therefore supports an interpretation of the AUMF that does not undercut FISA's regulation of such conduct.

◆

In conclusion, the DOJ letter fails to offer a plausible legal defense of the NSA domestic spying program. If the Administration felt that FISA was insufficient, the proper course was to seek legislative amendment, as it did with other aspects of FISA in the Patriot Act, and as Congress expressly contemplated when it enacted the wartime wiretap provision in FISA. One of the crucial features of a constitutional democracy is that it is always open to the President—or anyone else—to seek to change the law. But it is also beyond dispute that, in such a democracy, the President cannot simply violate criminal laws behind closed doors because he deems them obsolete or impracticable.[8]

We hope you find these views helpful to your consideration of the legality of the NSA domestic spying program.

Notes

1. More detail about the operation of FISA can be found in Congressional Research Service, "Presidential Authority to Conduct Warrantless Electronic Surveillance to Gather Foreign Intelligence Information" (Jan. 5, 2006). This letter was drafted prior to release of the CRS Report, which corroborates the conclusions drawn here.

2. "The Conferees intend that this [15-day] period will allow time for consideration of any amendment to this act that may be appropriate during a wartime emergency. . . . The conferees expect that such amendment would be reported with recommendations within 7 days and that each House would vote on the amendment within 7 days thereafter." H.R. Conf. Rep. No. 95-1720, at 34 (1978).

3. Attorney General Gonzales stated, "We have had discussions with Congress in the past—certain members of Congress—as to whether or not FISA could be amended to allow us to adequately deal with this kind of threat, and we were advised that that would be difficult, if not impossible." Press Briefing by Attorney General Alberto Gonzales and General Michael Hayden, Principal Deputy Director for National Intelligence (Dec. 19, 2005). . . .

4. The administration had a convenient vehicle for seeking any such amendment in the USA PATRIOT Act of 2001, Pub. L. No. 107–56, 115 Stat. 272, enacted in October 2001. The Patriot Act amended FISA in several respects, including in sections 218 (allowing FISA wiretaps in criminal investigations) and 215 (popularly known as the "libraries provision"). Yet the administration did not ask Congress to amend FISA to authorize the warrantless electronic surveillance at issue here.

5. *See* Memorandum from Jay S. Bybee, Assistant Attorney General, Department of Justice Office of Legal Counsel, to Alberto R. Gonzales, Counsel to the President, Re: *Standards of Conduct for Interrogation under 18 U.S.C. §§ 2340-2340A* (Aug. 1, 2002), at 31.

6. Memorandum from John C. Yoo, Deputy Assistant Attorney General, Office of Legal Counsel, to the Deputy Counsel to the President, Re: *The President's Constitutional Authority to Conduct Military Operations against Terrorists and Nations Supporting Them* (Sept. 25, 2001) . . . (emphasis added).

7. Three years ago, the FISA Court of Review suggested in dictum that Congress cannot "encroach on the President's constitutional power" to conduct foreign intelligence surveillance. *In re Sealed Case No. 02-001,* 310 F.3d 717, 742 (FIS Ct. Rev. 2002) (per curiam). The FISA Court of Review, however, did not hold that FISA was unconstitutional, nor has any other court suggested that FISA's modest regulations constitute an impermissible encroachment on presidential authority. The FISA Court of Review relied upon *United States v. Truong Dihn Hung,* 629 F.2d 908 (4th Cir. 1980)—but that court did not suggest that the President's powers were beyond congressional control. To the contrary, the *Truong* court indicated that FISA's restrictions *were* constitutional. *See* 629 F.2d at 915 n.4 (noting that "the imposition of a warrant requirement, beyond the constitutional minimum described in this opinion, *should be left to the intricate balancing performed in the course of the legislative process by Congress and the President*") (emphasis added).

8. During consideration of FISA, the House of Representatives noted that "the decision as to the standards governing when and how foreign intelligence electronic surveillance should be conducted is and should be a political decision, in the best sense of the term, because it involves the weighing of important public policy concerns—civil liberties and national security. Such a political decision is one properly made by the political branches of Government together, not adopted by one branch on its own and with no regard for the other. Under our Constitution legislation is

the embodiment of just such political decisions." H. Rep. 95-1283, pt. I, at 21–22. Attorney General Griffin Bell supported FISA in part because "no matter how well intentioned or ingenious the persons in the Executive branch who formulate these measures, the crucible of the legislative process will ensure that the procedures will be affirmed by that branch of government which is more directly responsible to the electorate." Foreign Intelligence Surveillance Act of 1978: Hearings Before the Subcomm. on Intelligence and the Rights of Americans of the Senate Select Comm. on Intelligence, 95th Cong., 2d Sess. 12 (1977).

EXPLORING THE ISSUE

Does the President Possess Constitutional Authority to Order Wiretaps on U.S. Citizens?

Critical Thinking and Reflection

1. How does history play a part in each side's argument?
2. What are the key statutory and constitutional interpretation differences between the arguments?
3. When we travel into and out of the United States, we undergo customs and immigration procedures; why should our international communications not also be subject to inspection at the "digital" border?
4. Is sacrificing privacy the necessary price for our physical safety?

Is There Common Ground?

Both defenders and critics of the warrantless wiretapping program recognize the imperative nature of intelligence gathering in protecting the national security of the United States. The difficulty, as illustrated by the readings, is in determining with which body of government the decisions rest on how best to carry out matters of national security. Intimately connected to the debate regarding wiretapping is the debate over constitutional "war powers." The framers of the Constitution specifically sought to divide these powers between Congress and the President as a safeguard to one body making a hasty decision. The powers of Congress, which are more clearly defined by the Constitution, include the power to declare war, the power to raise armies, and the power to tax to support such armies. The President's power comes from his position as the Commander in Chief of the Armed Forces, and his authority over foreign affairs. Where the authority of one body of government ends and the other's begins has long been debated, not only since the Founding Fathers, but by the Founding Fathers themselves.

The *Youngstown* case, which both sides rely upon in their arguments, has historically been instrumental in assisting courts in determining whether the President has exceeded his constitutional powers. Justice Jackson, in a famous concurring opinion, articulated three different scenarios. In the first scenario, the President is acting with the express authorization of Congress, and thus his actions should be regarded with the highest deference toward being constitutional. Supporters of the President's power to wiretap argue that the AUMF has done just this, and thus his actions are clearly constitutional. In the

second scenario, Congress is silent as to its opinion on the President's actions. Here, the decision of constitutionality is often difficult to discern, or a "zone of twilight," because Congress and the President may share concurrent powers, as is the case with war. In the final scenario, the President acts in direct contravention to the stated imperatives of Congress. Here, the President is acting with the least amount of authority. As you have read, critics of the wiretapping program argue that FISA expressly contradicts the President's program, thus his actions should be regarded as having little to no constitutional validity.

The FISA Amendments Act, which was enacted after both of the readings were written, reiterated that it was the exclusive means by which electronic surveillance could be conducted. No doubt, critics of the wiretapping program would point to this as decisive evidence of their interpretation. Equally without a doubt, supporters of the wiretapping program would point to the fact that this was not a change from the original FISA and gave additional protections to those carrying out surveillance. While each side will advocate for its strongest position in terms of Youngstown analysis, both sides may be willing to admit that ultimately this is a "zone of twilight" with no simple answers. As Justice Jackson wrote, "In this area, any actual test of power is likely to depend on the imperatives of events and contemporary imponderables, rather than on abstract theories of law."

Additional Resources

Fletcher N. Baldwin, Jr., and Robert B. Shaw, "Down to the Wire: Assessing the Constitutionality of the National Security Agency's Warrantless

Wiretapping Program: Exit the Rule of Law," 17 *J. Law & Pub. Pol'y* 429 (2006).

Stephanie Cooper Blum, "What Really Is at Stake with the FISA Amendments Act of 2008 and Ideas for Future Surveillance Reform," *Boston University Public Interest Law Journal*, Spring 2009. Available at SSRN: http://ssrn.com/abstract=1398831

David D. Cole and Ruth Wedgwood, Symposium: 'Torture and the War on Terror': "NSA Wiretapping Controversy: A Debate Between Professor David D. Cole and Professor Ruth Wedgwood," 37 *Case W. Res. J. Int'l L.* 509 (2006).

Edward Keynes, *Undeclared War: Twilight Zone of Constitutional Power* (University Park, PA: The Pennsylvania State University Press, 1982).

Peter P. Swire, "The System of Foreign Intelligence Surveillance Law," *George Washington Law Review*, vol. 72 (2004) http://ssrn.com/abstract=586616.

Internet References . . .

U.S. Code

U.S. Code—Chapter 36: Foreign Intelligence Surveillance

http://codes.lp.findlaw.com/uscode/50/36

New York Times

This is the original article that brought to light the government's warrantless wiretapping program.

www.nytimes.com/2005/12/16/politics/16program .html?pagewanted=all&_r=0

Attorney General Gonzales' Letter

This is the letter sent by Attorney General Gonzales to members of Congress stating that the Bush administration had ceased its warrantless surveillance program and was abiding by all of the procedural requirements of FISA.

http://graphics8.nytimes.com/packages/pdf /politics/20060117gonzales_Letter.pdf

Article on al-Haramain

www.washingtonpost.com/wp-dyn/content /article/2006/03/01/AR2006030102585.html

Electronic Frontier Foundation

The Electronic Frontier Foundation filed the first case against a telecommunication company for its part in the warrantless wiretapping programs in *Hepting v. AT&T* and is also representing victims in *Jewel v. NSA*. More information on their efforts is available at the below website link.

www.eff.org/nsa-spying

Guardian and *Washington Post*

The following links are the original stories from the *Guardian* and *Washington Post* newspapers based on the classified NSA information leaked by Edward Snowden.

www.guardian.co.uk/world/interactive/2013 /jun/06/verizon-telephone-data-court-order

www.washingtonpost.com/investigations /us-intelligence-mining-data-from-nine -us-internet-companies-in-broad-secret -program/2013/06/06/3a0c0da8-cebf-11e2-8845 -d970ccb04497_story.html

www.guardian.co.uk/world/2013/jun/06/us-tech -giants-nsa-data

www.guardian.co.uk/world/2013/jun/09 /nsa-secret-surveillance-lawmakers-live#block -51b4f1cee4b0bfa7376c4902

www.guardian.co.uk/uk/2013/jun/16/gchq-intercepted -communications-g20-summits

Unit 2

UNIT

Law and the Individual

*T*he American legal and political systems are oriented around protection of the individual. The law does not provide absolute protection for the individual, however, because legitimate state interests are often recognized as being controlling. This unit examines issues that affect individual choice and the dignity of the individual.

Selected, Edited, and with Issue Framing Material by:
M. Ethan Katsh, *University of Massachusetts, Amherst*

ISSUE

Is It Unconstitutional for a State to Require Physicians Who Perform Abortions to Have Admitting Privileges at a Nearby Hospital and for Abortion Clinics to Have Facilities Comparable to an Ambulatory Surgical Center?

YES: Stephen Breyer, from "Majority Opinion, *Whole Woman's Health v. Hellerstedt*," *U.S. Supreme Court* (2016)

NO: Clarence Thomas, from "Dissenting Opinion, *Whole Woman's Health v. Hellerstedt*," *U.S. Supreme Court* (2016)

Learning Outcomes
After reading this issue, you will be able to: • Identify the central holding in *Roe v. Wade*.   • Discuss how Supreme Court decisions following *Roe v. Wade* have shaped abortion jurisprudence.   • Identify principles by which courts evaluate the constitutionality of a law regulating abortion.   • Describe the legal concept *of stare decisis*.

ISSUE SUMMARY

YES: Justice Breyer argues that two provisions in a Texas law—requiring physicians who perform abortions to have admitting privileges at a nearby hospital and requiring abortion clinics in the state to have facilities comparable to an ambulatory surgical center—place a substantial obstacle in the path of women seeking an abortion, constitute an "undue burden" on abortion access, and therefore violate the Constitution.

NO: Justice Thomas finds that there is no "undue burden."

Abortion is an issue that has never left the spotlight, even though it has been more than four decades since the Supreme Court ruled, in *Roe v. Wade* (410 U.S. 113, 1973), that laws banning the procedure violated the Constitution. The Supreme Court has repeatedly upheld and reaffirmed its decision in *Roe* that the Due Process Clause of the Fourteenth Amendment provides a right to privacy that encompasses a woman's right to choose whether to terminate a pregnancy. However, the Court did not say in *Roe* that this right was absolute.

The recognition in *Roe* and, two decades later, in *Planned Parenthood v. Casey* (505 U.S. 833, 1992) that the government has a "legitimate interest" in "protecting the potentiality of human life" has led to considerable litigation surrounding the extent to which both state and federal legislatures can pass laws regulating abortion. The difficulty of deciding which types of laws cross the ill-defined line that separates legitimate governmental action from unconstitutional interference in a private decision is evident in the Supreme Court's mixed holdings in post-*Roe* abortion cases. For instance, can states mandate that doctors perform all second-trimester abortions in hospitals? No, according to the Court's decision in *Planned Parenthood of Kansas City, MO, v. Ashcroft*, 462 U.S. 476 (1983). Can states mandate that a second doctor be present at all late term abortions? Yes, according to the same ruling.

Adding to this confusion was the Court's decision in *Planned Parenthood v. Casey* to reaffirm *Roe*'s "central holding" while modifying some of its methodology for determining which laws violate a woman's right to choose. In *Casey*, the Court stated that in many of its rulings since *Roe*, it had gone "too far" and "[struck] down . . . some abortion regulations which in no real sense deprived women of the ultimate decision." Part of the problem, according to the Court, was its use of *Roe*'s "trimester approach," under which "almost no regulation at all [wa]s permitted during the first trimester of pregnancy; regulations designed to protect the woman's health, but not to further the State's interest in potential life, [were] permitted during the second trimester; and during the third trimester, when the fetus is viable, prohibitions [were] permitted provided the life or health of the mother [wa]s not at stake." The Court announced in *Casey* that it would adopt a new standard to determine the constitutionality of abortion regulations— whether they posed an "undue burden" to a woman's exercise of her right to choose—and it overruled some of its previous abortion decisions, for example, its holding in two cases that states could not require doctors to provide certain information to all women seeking abortions.

In 2000, the Court faced one of its most significant post-*Casey* abortion cases, *Stenberg v. Carhart*. *Stenberg* required the Court to weigh in, using its "undue burden" standard, on the constitutionality of a Nebraska state law banning certain types of late-term abortions that critics have dubbed "partial-birth" abortions. Nevertheless, the Court, in a 5–4 opinion, held the Nebraska law unconstitutional for two reasons. First, it lacked an exception, required by *Roe* and *Casey*, to allow for the banned procedure when necessary to safeguard the mother's health. Second, the language was so broad that it could be read to outlaw the most common types of second-trimester abortions, "thereby unduly burdening the right to choose abortion itself."

In 2007, the Court once again addressed the constitutionality of a law prohibiting partial-birth abortions in *Gonzales v. Carhart*. This time, however, the Court—again in a 5–4 decision—upheld the ban. According to Justice Anthony Kennedy's decision for the five-justice majority,

the law at issue—the federal Partial-Birth Abortion Ban Act of 2003—was sufficiently different from the Nebraska statute in *Stenberg* that the Court could not conclude that it posed an "undue burden." However, in her dissent, Justice Ruth Bader Ginsburg argued that the law clearly contravenes the Court's holding, in both *Roe* and *Casey*, that any regulation limiting a woman's access to abortion, even postviability, must include a health exception.

In claiming that the Court's decision in *Gonzales v. Carhart* is "in undisguised conflict with *Stenberg*" and "surely would not survive under the close scrutiny that previously attended state-decreed limitations on a woman's reproductive choices," Justice Ginsburg hints at one factor that could explain the Court's divergent opinions in these two cases: the change in the composition of the Supreme Court between 2000 and 2007. In 2005, Justice Sandra Day O'Connor, who was generally pro-choice and even coauthored the Court's decision in *Casey*, announced she was planning to retire. She was soon replaced by Justice Samuel Alito, who sided with the Court's majority in *Gonzales v. Carhart*.

Former Justice Potter Stewart once lamented that a "basic change in the law upon a ground no firmer than a change in our membership invites the popular misconception that this institution is little different from the two political branches of the Government. No misconception could do more lasting injury to this Court and to the system of law which it is our abiding mission to serve" (Dissenting Opinion, *Michell v. W. T. Grant Co.*, 416 U.S. 600, 1974). The need to maintain a consistent approach to legal issues and downplay the effect of justices' own value systems on its decision-making process is part of the reason the Supreme Court has adopted the principle of *stare decisis* as one of its central tenets.

Stare decisis, Latin for "to stand by decisions," is the concept that the Court will restrain itself when possible from overruling previous decisions that have set important legal precedents. As former Justice Byron White once described it, "The rule of ci is essential if case-by-case judicial decision-making is to be reconciled with the principle of the rule of law, for when governing legal standards are open to revision in every case, deciding cases becomes a mere exercise of judicial will, with arbitrary and unpredictable results" (Dissenting Opinion, *Akron v. Akron Reproductive Health*, 462 U.S. 416, 1983). According to Justice O'Connor in her *Casey* decision, stare decisis was a key reason why the Court should hesitate to overrule *Roe*:

> The obligation to follow precedent begins with necessity, and a contrary necessity marks its outer limit . . . no judicial system could do society's

work if it eyed each issue afresh in every case that raised it. . . . Indeed, the very concept of the rule of law underlying our own Constitution requires such continuity over time that a respect for precedent is, by definition, indispensable.

Nevertheless, there are, of course, times when the Court has found it both prudent and necessary to overrule precedent, especially in constitutional cases. Whereas Congress can overcome the Court's judgments on statutory issues by passing new laws, the difficulty of amending the Constitution has made the Supreme Court more willing to review its constitutional holdings when previous decisions have proven difficult in practice or no longer seem defensible on principle. For instance, the Court has shown willingness to revisit periodically its decisions on what constitutes "cruel and unusual punishment" under the Eighth Amendment, citing as its justification former Chief Justice Warren's assertion that "the words of the Amendment are not precise . . . their scope is not static. The Amendment must draw its meaning from the evolving standards of decency that mark the progress of a maturing society" (*Trop v. Dulles,* 356 U.S. 86, 1958). Of course, one could make a similar pronouncement about many of the amendments to the Constitution, making the Supreme Court's determination of which of its decisions are worthy of adherence, and which should be overruled, an important part of its constitutional jurisprudence.

The following case again requires determining whether a state statute imposes an "undue burden." It was decided by a 5-3 vote, Justice Scalia having passed away earlier in the year. He undoubtedly would have voted with the minority, so his replacement on the court is not likely to change the alignment of the justices in any future case. If, during the Trump administration, more justices retire and are replaced, there would likely be a significant change in the majority and minority in abortion-related cases.

YES ↵

Stephen Breyer

Majority Opinion, *Whole Woman's Health v. Hellerstedt*

Justice Breyer delivered the opinion of the Court.

In *Planned Parenthood of Southeastern Pa.* v. *Casey*, 505 U.S. 833, 878 (1992), a plurality of the Court concluded that there "exists" an "undue burden" on a woman's right to decide to have an abortion, and consequently, a provision of law is constitutionally invalid, if the "*purpose or effect*" of the provision "*is to place a substantial obstacle* in the path of a woman seeking an abortion before the fetus attains viability" (emphasis added.) The plurality added that "[u]nnecessary health regulations that have the purpose or effect of presenting a substantial obstacle to a woman seeking an abortion impose an undue burden on the right" *Ibid.*

We must here decide whether two provisions of Texas' House Bill 2 violate the Federal Constitution as interpreted in *Casey*. The first provision, which we shall call the "*admitting-privileges requirement*," says that

> [a] physician performing or inducing an abortion . . . must, on the date the abortion is performed or induced, have active admitting privileges at a hospital that . . . is located not further than 30 miles from the location at which the abortion is performed or induced. (Tex. Health & Safety Code Ann. §171.0031(a); West Cum. Supp. 2015).

This provision amended Texas law that had previously required an abortion facility to maintain a written protocol "for managing medical emergencies and the transfer of patients requiring further emergency care to a hospital" (38 Tex. Reg. 6546, 2013).

The second provision, which we shall call the "*surgical-center requirement*," says that

> the minimum standards for an abortion facility must be equivalent to the minimum standards adopted under the Texas Health and Safety Code section] for ambulatory surgical centers. (Tex. Health & Safety Code Ann. §245.010(a)).

We conclude that neither of these provisions offers medical benefits sufficient to justify the burdens upon access that each imposes. Each places a substantial obstacle in the path of women seeking a previability abortion, each constitutes an undue burden on abortion access, and each violates the Federal Constitution.

In July 2013, the Texas Legislature enacted House Bill 2 (HB2 or Act). In September (before the new law took effect), a group of Texas abortion providers filed an action in Federal District Court, seeking facial invalidation of the law's admitting-privileges provision. In late October, the District Court granted the injunction. *Planned Parenthood of Greater Tex. Surgical Health Servs.* v. *Abbott*, 951 F. Supp. 2d 891, 901 (WD Tex. 2013). But three days later, the Fifth Circuit vacated the injunction, thereby permitting the provision to take effect (*Planned Parenthood of Greater Tex. Surgical Health Servs*. V. *Abbott*, 734 F. 3d 406, 419, 2013).

The Fifth Circuit subsequently upheld the provision and set forth its reasons in an opinion released late the following March.

. . .

Undue Burden—Legal Standard

We begin with the standard, as described in *Casey*. We recognize that the "State has a legitimate interest in seeing to it that abortion, like any other medical procedure, is performed under circumstances that insure maximum safety for the patient" (*Roe* v. *Wade*, 410 U.S. 113, 150, 1973). But, we added, "a statute which, while furthering [a] valid state interest, has the effect of placing a substantial obstacle in the path of a woman's choice cannot be considered a permissible means of serving its legitimate ends" (*Casey*, 505 U.S., at 877, plurality opinion). Moreover, "[u]nnecessary health regulations that have the purpose or effect of presenting a substantial obstacle to a woman seeking an abortion impose an undue burden on the right" (Id., at 878).

Majority Opinion, Whole Woman's Health v. Hellerstedt, U.S. Supreme Court, 136 S.Ct. 2992, June 27, 2016.

Is It Unconstitutional to Require Physicians Who Perform Abortions to Have Admitting Privileges at a Nearby Hospital? by Katsh

53

The court of appeals wrote that a state law is . . .

The Court of Appeals' articulation of the relevant standard is incorrect. The first part of the Court of Appeals' test may be read to imply that a district court should not consider the existence or nonexistence of medical benefits when considering whether a regulation of abortion constitutes an undue burden. The rule announced in *Casey*, however, requires that courts consider the burdens a law imposes on abortion access together with the benefits those laws confer. See 505 U.S., at 887–898 (opinion of the Court) (performing this balancing with respect to a spousal notification provision); id., at 899–901 (joint opinion of O'Connor, KENNEDY, and Souter, JJ.) (same balancing with respect to a parental notification provision). . . .

The Court of Appeals' approach simply does not match the standard that this Court laid out in *Casey*, which asks courts to consider whether any burden imposed on abortion access is "undue."

The statement that legislatures, and not courts, must resolve questions of medical uncertainty is also inconsistent with this Court's case law. Instead, the Court, when determining the constitutionality of laws regulating abortion procedures, has placed considerable weight upon evidence and argument presented in judicial proceedings. In *Casey*, for example, we relied heavily on the District Court's factual findings and the research-based submissions of *amici* in declaring a portion of the law at issue unconstitutional (505 U.S., at 888–894, opinion of the Court; discussing evidence related to the prevalence of spousal abuse in determining that a spousal notification provision erected an undue burden to abortion access). And, in *Gonzales* the Court, while pointing out that we must review legislative "factfinding under a deferential standard," added that we must not "place dispositive weight" on those "findings" (550 U.S., at 165). *Gonzales* went on to point out that the "*Court retains an independent constitutional duty to review factual findings where constitutional rights are at stake*" (Ibid; emphasis added). Although there we upheld a statute regulating abortion, we did not do so solely on the basis of legislative findings explicitly set forth in the statute, noting that "evidence presented in the District Courts contradicts" some of the legislative findings (Id., at 166). In these circumstances, we said, "[u]ncritical deference to Congress' factual findings . . . is inappropriate" *Ibid*.

. . .

Undue Burden—Admitting-privileges Requirement

Turning to the lower courts' evaluation of the evidence, we first consider the admitting-privileges requirement. Before the enactment of HB2, doctors who provided abortions were required to "have admitting privileges *or* have a working arrangement with a physician(s) who has admitting privileges at a local hospital in order to ensure the necessary back up for medical complications" (Tex. Admin. Code, tit. 25, §139.56, 2009; emphasis added). The new law changed this requirement by requiring that a "physician performing or inducing an abortion . . . must, on the date the abortion is performed or induced, have active admitting privileges at a hospital that . . . is located not further than 30 miles from the location at which the abortion is performed or induced" (Tex. Health & Safety Code Ann. §171.0031(a)). The District Court held that the legislative change imposed an "undue burden" on a woman's right to have an abortion. We conclude that there is adequate legal and factual support for the District Court's conclusion.

The purpose of the admitting-privileges requirement is to help ensure that women have easy access to a hospital should complications arise during an abortion procedure. But the District Court found that it brought about no such health-related benefit. The court found that "[t]he great weight of evidence demonstrates that, before the act's passage, abortion in Texas was extremely safe with particularly low rate of serious complications and virtually no deaths occurring on account of the procedure" (46 F. Supp. 3d, at 684). Thus, there was no significant health-related problem that the new law helped to cure.

The evidence upon which the court based this conclusion included, among other things:

- A collection of at least five peer-reviewed studies on abortion complications in the first trimester, showing that the highest rate of major complications—including those complications requiring hospital admission—was less than one-quarter of 1 percent.
- Figures in three peer-reviewed studies showing that the highest complication rate found for the much rarer second trimester abortion was less than one-half of 1 percent (0.45 percent or about 1 of about 200).
- Expert testimony to the effect that complications rarely require hospital admission, much less immediate transfer to a hospital from an outpatient clinic (citing a study of complications occurring within six weeks after 54,911 abortions that

had been paid for by the fee-for-service California Medicaid Program finding that the incidence of complications was 2.1 percent, the incidence of complications requiring hospital admission was 0.23 percent, and that of the 54,911 abortion patients included in the study, only 15 required immediate transfer to the hospital on the day of the abortion).

- Expert testimony stating that "it is extremely unlikely that a patient will experience a serious complication at the clinic that requires emergent hospitalization" and "in the rare case in which [one does], the quality of care that the patient receives is not affected by whether the abortion provider has admitting privileges at the hospital."
- Expert testimony stating that in respect to surgical abortion patients who do suffer complications requiring hospitalization, most of these complications occur in the days after the abortion, not on the spot.
- Expert testimony stating that a delay before the onset of complications is also expected for medical abortions, as "abortifacient drugs take time to exert their effects, and thus, the abortion itself almost always occurs after the patient has left the abortion facility."
- Some experts added that, if a patient needs a hospital in the day or week following her abortion, she will likely seek medical attention at the hospital nearest her home.

We have found nothing in Texas' record evidence that shows that, compared to prior law (which required a "working arrangement" with a doctor with admitting privileges), the new law advanced Texas' legitimate interest in protecting women's health.

We add that, when directly asked at oral argument whether Texas knew of a single instance in which the new requirement would have helped even one woman obtain better treatment, Texas admitted that there was no evidence in the record of such a case.

This answer is consistent with the findings of the other Federal District Courts that have considered the health benefits of other States' similar admitting-privileges laws (see *Planned Parenthood of Wis., Inc.* v. *Van Hollen*, 94). . . .

At the same time, the record evidence indicates that the admitting-privileges requirement places a "substantial obstacle in the path of a woman's choice" (*Casey*, 505 U.S., at 877, plurality opinion). The District Court found, as of the time the admitting-privileges requirement began to be enforced, the number of facilities providing abortions

dropped in half, from about 40 to about 20. Eight abortion clinics closed in the months leading up to the requirement's effective date. See App. 229–230; cf. Brief for Planned Parenthood Federation of America et al. as *Amici Curiae* 14 (noting that abortion facilities in Waco, San Angelo, and Midland no longer operate because Planned Parenthood is "unable to find local physicians in those communities with privileges who are willing to provide abortions due to the size of those communities and the hostility that abortion providers face"). Eleven more closed on the day the admitting privileges requirement took effect.

Other evidence helps to explain why the new requirement led to the closure of clinics. We read that other evidence in light of a brief filed in this Court by the Society of Hospital Medicine. That brief describes the undisputed general fact that "hospitals often condition admitting privileges on reaching a certain number of admissions per year." Returning to the District Court record, we note that, in direct testimony, the president of Nova Health Systems, implicitly relying on this general fact, pointed out that it would be difficult for doctors regularly performing abortions at the El Paso clinic to obtain admitting privileges at nearby hospitals because "[d]uring the past 10 years, over 17,000 abortion procedures were performed at the El Paso clinic [and n]ot a single one of those patients had to be transferred to a hospital for emergency treatment, much less admitted to the hospital." App. 730. In a word, doctors would be unable to maintain admitting privileges or obtain those privileges for the future, because the fact that abortions are so safe meant that providers were unlikely to have any patients to admit.

. . .

In our view, the record contains sufficient evidence that the admitting-privileges requirement led to the closure of half of Texas' clinics or thereabouts. Those closures meant fewer doctors, longer waiting times, and increased crowding. Record evidence also supports the finding that after the admitting-privileges provision went into effect, the "number of women of reproductive age living in a county . . . more than 150 miles from a provider increased from approximately 86,000 to 400,000 . . . and the number of women living in a county more than 200 miles from a provider from approximately 10,000 to 290,000."

. . .

Undue Burden—Surgical-center Requirement

The second challenged provision of Texas' new law sets forth the surgical-center requirement. Prior to enactment of the new requirement, Texas law required abortion facilities to meet a host of health and safety requirements. Under those preexisting laws, facilities were subject to annual reporting and recordkeeping requirements, a quality assurance program, personnel policies and staffing requirements, physical and environmental requirements, infection control standards, disclosure requirements, patient-rights standards, and medical and clinical-services standards, including anesthesia standards. These requirements are policed by random and announced inspections, at least annually, as well as administrative penalties, injunctions, civil penalties, and criminal penalties for certain violations (Admin. Code, tit. 25, §139.33; Tex. Health & Safety Code).

HB2 added the requirement that an "abortion facility" meets the "minimum standards . . . for ambulatory surgical centers" under Texas law. The surgical-center regulations include, among other things, detailed specifications relating to the size of the nursing staff, building dimensions, and other building requirements. The nursing staff must comprise at least "an adequate number of [registered nurses] on duty to meet the following minimum staff requirements: director and staff personnel for each service area to assure the immediate availability of [a registered nurse] for emergency care or for any patient when needed" as well as "a second individual on duty on the premises who is trained and currently certified in basic cardiac life support until all patients have been discharged from the facility" for facilities that provide moderate sedation, such as most abortion facilities. Facilities must include a full surgical suite with an operating room that has "a clear floor area of at least 240 square feet" in which "[t]he minimum clear dimension between built-in cabinets, counters, and shelves shall be 14 feet." There must be a preoperative patient holding room and a postoperative recovery suite. The former "shall be provided and arranged in a one-way traffic pattern so that patients entering from outside the surgical suite can change, gown, and move directly into the restricted corridor of the surgical suite," and the latter "shall be arranged to provide a one-way traffic pattern from the restricted surgical corridor to the postoperative recovery suite, and then to the extended observation rooms or discharge." Surgical centers must meet numerous other spatial requirements, including specific corridor widths. Surgical

centers must also have an advanced heating, ventilation, and air conditioning system and must satisfy particular piping system and plumbing requirements. Dozens of other sections list additional requirements that apply to surgical centers.

There is considerable evidence in the record supporting the District Court's findings indicating that the statutory provision requiring all abortion facilities to meet all surgical-center standards does not benefit patients and is not necessary. The District Court found that "risks are not appreciably lowered for patients who undergo abortions at ambulatory surgical centers as compared to nonsurgical-center facilities." The court added that women "will not obtain better care or experience more frequent positive outcomes at an ambulatory surgical center as compared to a previously licensed facility." And these findings are well supported.

The record makes clear that the surgical-center requirement provides no benefit when complications arise in the context of an abortion produced through medication. That is because, in such a case, complications would almost always arise only after the patient has left the facility. The record also contains evidence indicating that abortions taking place in an abortion facility are safe—indeed, safer than numerous procedures that take place outside hospitals and to which Texas does not apply its surgical-center requirements. The total number of deaths in Texas from abortions was five in the period from 2001 to 2012, or about one every two years (that is to say, one of about 120,000 to 144,000 abortions; Id., at 272). Nationwide, childbirth is 14 times more likely than abortion to result in death, but Texas law allows a midwife to oversee childbirth in the patient's own home. Colonoscopy, a procedure that typically takes place outside a hospital (or surgical center) setting, has a mortality rate 10 times higher than an abortion.. . . These facts indicate that the surgical-center provision imposes "a requirement that simply is not based on differences" between abortion and other surgical procedures "that are reasonably related to" preserving women's health, the asserted "purpos[e] of the Act in which it is found," *Doe*, 410 U.S., at 194 (quoting *Morey* v. *Doud*, 354 U.S. 457, 465 (1957); internal quotation marks omitted).

· · ·

More fundamentally, in the face of no threat to women's health, Texas seeks to force women to travel long distances to get abortions in crammed-to-capacity superfacilities. Patients seeking these services are less likely to get the kind of individualized attention, serious conversation, and emotional support that doctors at less taxed facilities may have offered. Health-care facilities and medical professionals are not fungible commodities. Surgical centers attempting to accommodate sudden, vastly increased demand, may find that quality of care declines. Another commonsense inference that the District Court made is that these effects would be harmful to, not supportive of, women's health.

Finally, the District Court found that the costs that a currently licensed abortion facility would have to incur to meet the surgical-center requirements were considerable, ranging from US$1 million per facility (for facilities with adequate space) to US$3 million per facility (where additional land must be purchased). This evidence supports the conclusion that more surgical centers will not soon fill the gap when licensed facilities are forced to close.

We agree with the District Court that the surgical-center requirement, like the admitting-privileges requirement, provides few, if any, health benefits for women, poses a substantial obstacle to women seeking abortions, and constitutes an "undue burden" on their constitutional right to do so.

. . .

For these reasons, the judgment of the Court of Appeals is reversed, and the case is remanded for further proceedings consistent with this opinion.

It is so ordered.

Stephen Breyer is an associate justice of the U.S. Supreme Court. He received an AB from Stanford University, a BA from Magdalen College, Oxford, and an LLB from Harvard Law School. He served as a law clerk to Justice Arthur Goldberg of the Supreme Court of the United States during the 1964 term. Prior to being appointed as a judge of the United States Court of Appeals for the First Circuit, he was a professor at Harvard Law School. From 1990 to 1994, he served as a Chief Judge for the First Circuit Court of Appeals. President Clinton nominated him as an associate justice of the Supreme Court in 1994.

Clarence Thomas

 **NO**

Dissenting Opinion, *Whole Woman's Health v. Hellerstedt*

Today, the Court strikes down two state statutory provisions in all of their applications, at the behest of abortion clinics and doctors. That decision exemplifies the Court's troubling tendency "to bend the rules when any effort to limit abortion, or even to speak in opposition to abortion, is at issue" (*Stenberg* v. *Carhart*, 530 U.S. 914, 954, 2000; Scalia, J., dissenting).

. . .

To begin, the very existence of this suit is a jurisprudential oddity. Ordinarily, plaintiffs cannot file suits to vindicate the constitutional rights of others. But the Court employs a different approach to rights that it favors. So in this case and many others, the Court has erroneously allowed doctors and clinics to vicariously vindicate the putative constitutional right of women seeking abortions.

This case also underscores the Court's increasingly common practice of invoking a given level of scrutiny—here, the abortion-specific undue burden standard—while applying a different standard of review entirely. Whatever scrutiny the majority applies to Texas' law, it bears little resemblance to the undue-burden test the Court articulated in *Planned Parenthood of Southeastern Pa.* v. *Casey*, 505 U.S. 833 (1992), and its successors. Instead, the majority eviscerates important features of that test to return to a regime like the one that Casey repudiated.

Ultimately, this case shows why the Court never should have bent the rules for favored rights in the first place. Our law is now so riddled with special exceptions for special rights that our decisions deliver neither predictability nor the promise of a judiciary bound by the rule of law.

I

This suit is possible only because the Court has allowed abortion clinics and physicians to invoke a putative constitutional right that does not belong to them—a woman's right to abortion. The Court's third-party standing jurisprudence is no model of clarity (see *Kowalski* v. *Tesmer*, 543 U.S. 125, 135, 2004; THOMAS, J., concurring). Driving this doctrinal confusion, the Court has shown a particular willingness to undercut restrictions on third-party standing when the right to abortion is at stake. And this case reveals a deeper flaw in straying from our normal rules: when the wrong party litigates a case, we end up resolving disputes that make for bad law.

For most of our Nation's history, plaintiffs could not challenge a statute by asserting someone else's constitutional rights. This Court would "not listen to an objection made to the constitutionality of an act by a party whose rights it does not affect and who has therefore no interest in defeating it" (*Clark* v. *Kansas City*, 176 U.S. 114, 118, 1900; internal quotation marks omitted). And for good reason: "[C]ourts are not roving commissions assigned to pass judgment on the validity of the Nation's laws" (*Broadrick* v. *Oklahoma*, 413 U.S. 601, 610–611, 1973).

In the 20th century, the Court began relaxing that rule. But even as the Court started to recognize exceptions for certain types of challenges, it stressed the strict limits of those exceptions. A plaintiff could assert a third party's rights, the Court said, but only if the plaintiff had a "close relation to the third party" and the third party faced a formidable "hindrance" to asserting his own rights (*Powers* v. *Ohio*, 499 U.S. 400, 411 1991); accord, *Kowalski, supra,* at 130–133, similar).

. . .

Those limits broke down, however, because the Court has been "quite forgiving" in applying these standards to certain claims.

Above all, the Court has been especially forgiving of third-party standing criteria for one particular category of cases: those involving the purported substantive due process right of a woman to abort her unborn child. In *Singleton*

Dissenting Opinion, Whole Woman's Health v. Hellerstedt, U.S. Supreme Court, 136 S.Ct. 2992, June 27, 2016.

v. *Wulff*, 428 U.S. 106 (1976), a plurality of this Court fashioned a blanket rule allowing third-party standing in abortion cases. "[I]t generally is appropriate," said the Court, "to allow a physician to assert the rights of women patients as against governmental interference with the abortion decision." Yet the plurality conceded that the traditional criteria for an exception to the third-party standing rule were not met. There are no "insurmountable" obstacles stopping women seeking abortions from asserting their own rights, the plurality admitted. Nor are there jurisdictional barriers. *Roe* v. *Wade*, 410 U.S. 113 (1973), held that women seeking abortions fell into the mootness exception for cases "'capable of repetition, yet seeking review,'" enabling them to sue after they terminated their pregnancies without showing that they intended to become pregnant and seek an abortion again. Yet, since *Singleton*, the Court has unquestioningly accepted doctors' and clinics' vicarious assertion of the constitutional rights of hypothetical patients, even as women seeking abortions have successfully and repeatedly asserted their own rights before this Court.

Here too, the Court does not question whether doctors and clinics should be allowed to sue on behalf of Texas women seeking abortions as a matter of course. They should not. The central question under the Court's abortion precedents is whether there is an undue burden on a woman's access to abortion (see *Casey*, 505 U.S., at 877, plurality opinion). But the Court's permissive approach to third-party standing encourages litigation that deprives us of the information needed to resolve that issue. Our precedents encourage abortion providers to sue—and our cases then relieve them of any obligation to prove what burdens women actually face.

I find it astonishing that the majority can discover an "undue burden" on women's access to abortion for "those [women] for whom [Texas' law] is an actual rather than an irrelevant restriction," without identifying how many women fit this description; their proximity to open clinics; or their preferences as to where they obtain abortions, and from whom. "[C]ommonsense inference[s]" that such a burden exists are no substitute for actual evidence. There should be no surer sign that our jurisprudence has gone off the rails than this: after creating a constitutional right to abortion because it "involve[s] the most intimate and personal choices a person may make in a lifetime, choices central to personal dignity and autonomy," the Court has created special rules that cede its enforcement to others.

II

Nearly 25 years ago, in *Planned Parenthood of Southeastern Pa. v. Casey*, 505 U.S. 833, a plurality of this Court invented the "undue burden" standard as a special test for gauging the permissibility of abortion restrictions. *Casey* held that a law is unconstitutional if it imposes an "undue burden" on a woman's ability to choose to have an abortion, meaning that it "has the purpose or effect of placing a substantial obstacle in the path of a woman seeking an abortion of a nonviable fetus." *Casey* thus instructed courts to look to whether a law substantially impedes women's access to abortion, and whether it is reasonably related to legitimate state interests. As the Court explained, "[w]here it has a rational basis to act, and it does not impose an undue burden, the State may use its regulatory power" to regulate aspects of abortion procedures, "all in furtherance of its legitimate interests in regulating the medical profession in order to promote respect for life, including life of the unborn" (*Gonzales* v. *Carhart*, 550 U.S. 124, 158, 2007).

I remain fundamentally opposed to the Court's abortion jurisprudence. Even taking *Casey* as the baseline, however, the majority radically rewrites the undue-burden test in three ways. First, today's decision requires courts to "consider the burdens a law imposes on abortion access together with the benefits those laws confer." Second, today's opinion tells the courts that, when the law's justifications are medically uncertain, they need not defer to the legislature and must instead assess medical justifications for abortion restrictions by scrutinizing the record themselves. Finally, even if a law imposes no "substantial obstacle" to women's access to abortions, the law now must have more than a "reasonabl[e] relat[ion] to . . . a legitimate state interest." These precepts are nowhere to be found in *Casey* or its successors and transform the undue-burden test to something much more akin to strict scrutiny.

First, the majority's free-form balancing test is contrary to *Casey*. When assessing Pennsylvania's recordkeeping requirements for abortion providers, for instance, *Casey* did not weigh its benefits and burdens. Rather, *Casey* held that the law had a legitimate purpose because data collection advances medical research, "so it cannot be said that the requirements serve no purpose other than to make abortions more difficult" (505 U.S., at 901, joint opinion of O'Connor, KENNEDY, and Souter, JJ.). The opinion then asked whether the recordkeeping requirements imposed a "substantial obstacle" and found none. Contrary to the majority's statements, Casey did not balance the benefits and burdens of Pennsylvania's spousal and parental notification provisions, either. Pennsylvania's spousal notification requirement, the plurality said, imposed an undue burden because findings established that the requirement would "likely . . . prevent a significant number of women from obtaining an abortion"—not because these burdens outweighed its benefits (505 U.S., at 893, majority opinion; see id., at 887–894). And *Casey* summarily upheld parental notification provisions because even pre-*Casey* decisions had done so.

Decisions in *Casey*'s wake further refute the majority's benefits-and-burdens balancing test. The Court in *Mazurek* v. *Armstrong*, 520 U.S. 968 (1997) (*per curiam*), had no difficulty upholding a Montana law authorizing only physicians to perform abortions—even though no legislative findings supported the law, and the challengers claimed that "all health evidence contradict[ed] the claim that there is any health basis for the law." *Mazurek* also deemed objections to the law's lack of benefits "squarely foreclosed by *Casey* itself." Instead, the Court explained, "'the Constitution gives the States broad latitude to decide that particular functions may be performed only by licensed professionals, *even if an objective assessment might suggest that those same tasks could be performed by others.*'"

Second, by rejecting the notion that "legislatures, and not courts, must resolve questions of medical uncertainty," the majority discards another core element of the *Casey* framework. Before today, this Court had "given state and federal legislatures wide discretion to pass legislation in areas where there is medical and scientific uncertainty" (Gonzales, 550 U.S., at 163). This Court emphasized that this "traditional rule" of deference "is consistent with *Casey*." This Court underscored that legislatures should not be hamstrung "if some part of the medical community were disinclined to follow the proscription." And this Court concluded that "[c]onsiderations of marginal safety, including the balance of risks, are within the legislative competence when the regulation is rational and in pursuit of legitimate ends" ("the right of the legislature to resolve matters on which physicians disagreed" is "establish[ed] beyond doubt"). This Court could not have been clearer: whenever medical justifications for an abortion restriction are debatable, that "provides a sufficient basis to conclude in [a] facial attack that the [law] does not impose an undue burden" (*Gonzales*, 550 U.S., at 164). Otherwise, legislatures would face "to exacting" a standard.

Today, however, the majority refuses to leave disputed medical science to the legislature because past cases "placed considerable weight upon the evidence and argument presented in judicial proceedings." But while *Casey* relied on record evidence to uphold Pennsylvania's spousal-notification requirement, that requirement had nothing to do with debated medical science. And while

Gonzales observed that courts need not blindly accept all legislative findings, that does not help the majority. *Gonzales* refused to accept Congress' finding of "a medical consensus that the prohibited procedure is never medically necessary" because the procedure's necessity was debated within the medical community. Having identified medical uncertainty, *Gonzales* explained how courts should resolve conflicting positions: by respecting the legislature's judgment.

Finally, the majority overrules another central aspect of *Casey* by requiring laws to have more than a rational basis even if they do not substantially impede access to abortion. "Where [the State] *has a rational basis to act* and it does not impose an undue burden," this Court previously held, "the State may use its regulatory power" to impose regulations "in furtherance of its legitimate interests in regulating the medical profession in order to promote respect for life, including life of the unborn." No longer. Though the majority declines to say how substantial a State's interest must be, one thing is clear: the State's burden has been ratcheted to a level that has not applied for a quarter century.

Today's opinion does resemble *Casey* in one respect: after disregarding significant aspects of the Court's prior jurisprudence, the majority applies the undue-burden standard in a way that will surely mystify lower courts for years to come. As in *Casey*, today's opinion "simply . . . highlight[s] certain facts in the record that apparently strike the . . . Justices as particularly significant in establishing (or refuting) the existence of an undue burden." As in *Casey*, "the opinion then simply announces that the provision either does or does not impose a 'substantial obstacle' or an 'undue burden.'"

And still "[w]e do not know whether the same conclusions could have been reached on a different record, or in what respects the record would have had to differ before an opposite conclusion would have been appropriate" (505 U.S., at 991). All we know is that an undue burden now has little to do with whether the law, in a "real sense, deprive[s] women of the ultimate decision" (*Casey, supra*, at 875), and more to do with the loss of "individualized attention, serious conversation, and emotional support."

The majority's undue-burden test looks far less like our post-*Casey* precedents and far more like the strict-scrutiny standard that *Casey* rejected, under which only the most compelling rationales justified restrictions on abortion. One searches the majority opinion in vain for any acknowledgment of the "premise central" to Casey's rejection of strict scrutiny: "that the government has a legitimate and substantial interest in preserving and promoting fetal life" from conception, not just in regulating medical procedures. Meanwhile, the majority's undue burden balancing approach risks ruling out even minor, previously valid infringements on access to abortion. Moreover, by second-guessing medical evidence and making its own assessments of "quality of care" issues, the majority reappoints this Court as "the country's *ex officio* medical board with powers to disapprove medical and operative practices and standards throughout the United States." And the majority seriously burdens States, which must guess at how much more compelling their interests must be to pass muster and what "commonsense inferences" of an undue burden this Court will identify next.

. . .

Today's decision will prompt some to claim victory, just as it will stiffen opponents' will to object.

But the entire Nation has lost something essential. The majority's embrace of a jurisprudence of rights-specific exceptions and balancing tests is "a regrettable concession of defeat—an acknowledgment that we have passed the point where 'law,' properly speaking, has any further application" (Scalia, The Rule of Law as a Law of Rules, 56 U. Chi. L. Rev. 1175, 1182, 1989). I respectfully dissent.

CLARENCE THOMAS is an associate justice of the U.S. Supreme Court. A former judge on the U.S. Court of Appeals for the District of Columbia, he was nominated by President George H. W. Bush to the Supreme Court in 1991. He received his J.D. from the Yale University School of Law in 1974.

EXPLORING THE ISSUE

Is It Unconstitutional for a State to Require Physicians Who Perform Abortions to Have Admitting Privileges at a Nearby Hospital and for Abortion Clinics to Have Facilities Comparable to an Ambulatory Surgical Center?

Critical Thinking and Reflection

1. Is this a legal debate or a political debate?
2. Do you think it is possible for judges to fairly rule based on the law regarding such a highly charged emotional and moral issue?
3. How should the Courts handle situations where there is a strong divergence of medical opinion as to a key issue in a case?
4. The viability of a fetus outside its mother is a key issue in evaluating an abortion regulation, but viability has improved greatly over the last 40 years. Should improvements to technology be able to directly affect legal standards?

Is There Common Ground?

It is difficult to find common ground on a subject as divisive and impassioned as abortion. In this case, both the Majority and Dissenting opinions invoke strong language for the preservation of life and the rights of women, and both opinions are reticent to find any validity with the other's arguments. However, even the dissent and the Majority both recognize the main tenets of past abortion jurisprudence: the right of a woman to have an abortion and the right of the State to regulate to protect the health of an unborn child. While the extent to which these rights may be exercised or restricted vary greatly between the differing opinions, it is clear from both opinions that the tenets of *stare decisis* have not been wholly discarded.

Additional Resources

Hull, N. E. H., and Hoffer Peter Charles, *Roe v. Wade: The Abortion Rights Controversy in American History* (University Press of Kansas, 2001).

Hull, N.E.H., Hoffer, William James, and Hoffer, Peter, eds., *The Abortion Rights Controversy in America: A Legal Reader* (University of North Carolina Press, 2004).

Balkin, Jack, ed., *What* Roe v. Wade *Should Have Said: The Nation's Top Legal Experts Rewrite America's Most Controversial Decision* (New York University Press, 2005).

Solinger, Rickie, *Reproductive Politics: What Everyone Needs to Know* (Oxford University Press, 2013).

Wilson, Joshua C., *The New States of Abortion Politics* (Stanford University Press, 2016).

Internet References . . .

Abstract and Recording of Oral Arguments of *Gonzales v. Carhart*

http://www.oyez.org/cases/2000-2009/2006/2006_05_380

Abstract and Recording of Oral Arguments of *Planned Parenthood v. Casey*

http://www.oyez.org/cases/1990-1999/1991/1991_91_744

Abstract and Recording of Oral Arguments of *Roe v. Wade*

http://www.oyez.org/cases/1970-1979/1971/1971_70_18

Full text of *Whole Woman's Health v Hellerstedt and* recording of *Oral* Argument

https://www.oyez.org/cases/2015/15-274

Guttmacher Institute U.S. Abortion Rate Continues to Decline, Hits Historic Low January 17, 2017

https://www.guttmacher.org/news-release/2017/us-abortion-rate-continues-decline-hits-historic-low

Melissa Deckman January 20, 2017

https://www.washingtonpost.com/news/monkey-cage/wp/2017/01/20/can-pro-choice-and-pro-life-women-find-common-ground-its-complicated/?utm_term=.0837b7ba361a

Selected, Edited, and with Issue Framing Material by:
M. Ethan Katsh, *University of Massachusetts, Amherst*

ISSUE

Are Violent Video Games Protected by the First Amendment?

YES: Antonin Scalia, from "Majority Opinion, *Brown v. Entertainment Merchants Association*," *United States Supreme Court* (2011)

NO: Stephen Breyer, from "Dissenting Opinion, *Brown v. Entertainment Merchants Association*," *United States Supreme Court* (2011)

Learning Outcomes

After reading this issue, you will be able to:

- Explain what the exceptions are to protected speech in the First Amendment.
- Discuss why Justice Scalia rejected the claim that video games are a new category of unprotected speech because they are interactive.
- Compare the arguments on each side about whether the State of California has a compelling interest in protecting its children and how this law would or would not help.
- Assess the psychological evidence that supports the State's claim that playing violent video games promotes violent behavior in children.
- Understand how this case can be seen by one side as unnecessary censorship and by the other as protecting children.

ISSUE SUMMARY

YES: Supreme Court Justice Antonin Scalia argues that legislation creating a whole new category of speech that is banned only for children violates the First Amendment.

NO: Justice Stephen Breyer believes that the California law restricting the purchase of video games by minors is clear and constitutional.

Cyberspace is, increasingly, the "place" where people shop, socialize, learn, and so on. It has been equated with such physical places as a library, a shopping mall, a school, a conference center, an arcade, and a casino, because we can read, buy, learn, converse, play games, and gamble online. Looked at most simply, cyberspace allows information to be distributed and exchanged extremely quickly over great distances and at much lower costs than existed before. As a result, its continuing growth in our lives should not be surprising.

What cyberspace is not is a harmonious place or a problem-free environment. This, too, should not be surprising; since there is an enormous amount of activity in cyberspace, there is a great deal of money being spent there, and there are numerous relationships being formed there. When so much is happening so fast, you have conditions in which there will be problems and a demand for law.

Many activities that rely on technology or occur in cyberspace may seem familiar. Buying something online, for example, may seem like purchasing something from a catalog or on the phone. Looking at an electronic health record or a school transcript may seem not all that different from looking through a paper record. Or, ebooks may seem like regular books. For law, the question is whether we need new rules, new frameworks for thinking about traditional rules, and new processes for dealing with disputes that arise online or are affected by the use of technology.

These are difficult challenges because it is not yet clear whether we need revisions of old rules or to create completely new legal categories and areas of regulation. What we do know is that we can do more things at a distance than ever before, that we can do many things that were too complex for any of us to do before, that we can do many activities faster than ever before, and that it is often, as a result, harder for the state and other previously powerful entities to exercise control over some online activities. How difficult it is to control something is significant to law because it affects how effective the law will be and whether new norms and regulations will be enforced. Even if a law seems desirable as a matter of substance, it is not desirable to have a law if it is not enforceable.

Supreme Court justice Oliver Wendell Holmes once wrote that "the life of the law is not logic; it is experience." What Holmes meant is that outside forces shape the law at the same time that the law is shaping those forces. The emergence of powerful information technologies certainly qualifies as an "experience," for all of us as well as for the law. It is, in all likelihood, one of the most powerful experiences the law has encountered in a long time and this presents us with a broad range of interesting, significant and challenging issues to explore. It also means that there will be many attempts at legal regulation over a period of time, some successful and some requiring addressing a problem more than once.

The readings that follow involve a challenge to a law enacted by the California legislature in 2005. It imposed a fine of up to $1,000 upon any person who distributed a violent video game in California without labeling it "18," or who sold or rented a labeled violent video game to a person under the age of 18. The law defined a violent video game as one in which

1. a player "kill[s], maim[s], dismember[s], or sexually assault[s] an image of a human being";
2. "[a] reasonable person, considering the game as a whole, would find [the game] appeals to a deviant or morbid interest of minors";
3. "[the game] is patently offensive to prevailing standards in the community as to what is suitable for minors"; and
4. "the game, as a whole, . . . lack[s] serious literary, artistic, political, or scientific value for minors."

This language was chosen with care and is very similar to the language that the Supreme Court had used in carving out an exception to the First Amendment for obscenity. In *Miller v. United States*, the Court had ruled that obscene works could be banned and that the test for determining whether a work was obscene was

1. whether the average person, applying contemporary community standards, would find that the work, taken as a whole, appealed to the prurient interest;
2. whether the work depicted or described, in a patently offensive way, sexual conduct or excretory functions specifically defined by applicable state law; and
3. whether the work, taken as a whole, lacked serious literary, artistic, political, or scientific value.

In *Miller*, the Court was dealing with obscenity, a category difficult to define but one that everyone agrees is not protected by the First Amendment. It was trying to distinguish obscenity from pornography, which, for adults, is protected by the First Amendment and cannot be banned.

The difficulty here is that while obscenity can be banned for everyone, pornography can only be banned for children. While the distribution of pornography to adults is a protected activity, child pornography is not and is illegal under all circumstances. The challenge here is that video games are not obscene and the court is being asked to recognize a new exception to the First Amendment for video games. It is being asked to do this when children are involved and reach a result that parallels pornography in allowing an activity for adults while regulating that same activity for children.

Computer games are rated by an organization called the Entertainment Software Rating Board (ESRB). Each game contains a symbol suggesting age appropriateness and a description of content that influenced the rating. Looking up Mortal Kombat, for example, one of the longest running games sold in the United States, reveals a rating of M (Mature), meaning that it should not be played by anyone under 17. It is accompanied by the following content descriptor: "Blood and Gore, Intense Violence, Partial Nudity, Strong Language" and the following paragraph explaining the rating.

Players use swords, guns, chains, spikes, and supernatural attacks (e.g., fire, ice, lightning) to defeat a cast of human-like characters. After an opponent is defeated at the end of a match, players have the option to perform finishing moves called 'Fatalities.' Many of these finishing moves depict over-the-top instances of violence: impalement, bone-crushing body snaps, execution-style gunshots to the head; large blood-splatter effects occur during these sequences, staining characters' bodies and the ground. Several of these exaggerated finishing moves depict characters getting dismembered, ripped or sliced in half, stabbed, set on fire, or set to explode. (www.esrb.org/ratings/synopsis.jsp?Certificate=30816&searchkeyword=mortal%20kombat)

Justice Scalia wrote in his majority opinion:

California claims that video games present special problems because they are "interactive," in that the player participates in the violent action on screen and determines its outcome. The latter feature is nothing new: Since at least the publication of The Adventures of You: Sugarcane Island in 1969, young readers of choose-your-own-adventure stories have been able to make decisions that determine the plot by following instructions about which page to turn to . . . . As for the argument that video games enable participation in the violent action, that seems to us more a matter of degree than of kind. As Judge Posner has observed, all literature is interactive. "[T]he better it is, the more interactive. Literature when it is successful draws the reader into the story, makes him identify with the characters, invites him to judge them and quarrel with them, to experience their joys and sufferings as the reader's own."

Is the interactive quality of violent video games "nothing new" and to be reasonably equated with the kind of interaction between reader and character that occurs when one is immersed in a novel? Or would Justice Scalia have been better off writing only that without much stronger evidence of harm, removing First Amendment protection is unwarranted.

YES ⤸

Antonin Scalia

Majority Opinion, *Brown v. Entertainment Merchants Association*

JUSTICE SCALIA delivered the opinion of the Court.

We consider whether a California law imposing restrictions on violent video games comports with the First Amendment.

. . .

II

California correctly acknowledges that video games qualify for First Amendment protection. The Free Speech Clause exists principally to protect discourse on public matters, but we have long recognized that it is difficult to distinguish politics from entertainment, and dangerous to try. "Everyone is familiar with instances of propaganda through fiction. What is one man's amusement, teaches another's doctrine." *Winters v. New York*, 333 U.S. 507, 510 (1948). Like the protected books, plays, and movies that preceded them, video games communicate ideas—and even social messages—through many familiar literary devices (such as characters, dialogue, plot, and music) and through features distinctive to the medium (such as the player's interaction with the virtual world). That suffices to confer First Amendment protection. Under our Constitution, "esthetic and moral judgments about art and literature . . . are for the individual to make, not for the Government to decree, even with the mandate or approval of a majority." *United States v. Playboy Entertainment Group, Inc.*, 529 U.S. 803, 818 (2000). And whatever the challenges of applying the Constitution to ever-advancing technology, "the basic principles of freedom of speech and the press, like the First Amendment's command, do not vary" when a new and different medium for communication appears. *Joseph Burstyn, Inc. v. Wilson*, 343 U.S. 495, 503 (1952).

The most basic of those principles is this: "[A]s a general matter, . . . government has no power to restrict expression because of its message, its ideas, its subject matter, or its content." *Ashcroft v. American Civil Liberties Union*, 535 U.S. 564, 573 (2002). There are of course exceptions. "'From 1791 to the present,' . . . the First Amendment has 'permitted restrictions upon the content of speech in a few limited areas,' and has never 'include[d] a freedom to disregard these traditional limitations.'" *United States v. Stevens*, 559 U.S. ___, ___ (2010) (slip op., at 5) (quoting *R. A. V. v. St. Paul*, 505 U.S. 377, 382–383 (1992)). These limited areas—such as obscenity, *Roth v. United States*, 354 U.S. 476, 483 (1957), incitement, *Brandenburg v. Ohio*, 395 U.S. 444, 447–449 (1969) (*per curiam*), and fighting words, *Chaplinsky v. New Hampshire*, 315 U.S. 568, 572 (1942)—represent "well-defined and narrowly limited classes of speech, the prevention and punishment of which have never been thought to raise any Constitutional problem," *id.*, at 571–572.

Last Term, in *Stevens*, we held that new categories of unprotected speech may not be added to the list by a legislature that concludes certain speech is too harmful to be tolerated. *Stevens* concerned a federal statute purporting to criminalize the creation, sale, or possession of certain depictions of animal cruelty. See 18 U.S. C. §48 (amended 2010). The statute covered depictions "in which a living animal is intentionally maimed, mutilated, tortured, wounded, or killed" if that harm to the animal was illegal where the "the creation, sale, or possession t[ook] place," §48(c)(1). A saving clause largely borrowed from our obscenity jurisprudence, see *Miller v. California*, 413 U.S. 15, 24 (1973), exempted depictions with "serious religious, political, scientific, educational, journalistic, historical, or artistic value," §48(b). We held that statute to be an impermissible content-based restriction on speech. There was no American tradition of forbidding the *depiction of* animal cruelty—though States have long had laws against *committing* it.

The Government argued in *Stevens* that lack of a historical warrant did not matter; that it could create new categories of unprotected speech by applying a "simple balancing test" that weighs the value of a particular category of speech against its social costs and then punishes that category of speech if it fails the test. . . . We emphatically rejected that "startling and dangerous" proposition. . . . "Maybe there are some categories of speech that have been historically unprotected, but have not yet been specifically identified or discussed as such in our case law." . . . But without persuasive evidence that a novel restriction on content is part of a long (if heretofore unrecognized) tradition of proscription, a legislature may not revise the "judgment [of] the American people," embodied in the First Amendment, "that the benefits of its restrictions on the Government outweigh the costs." . . .

That holding controls this case. As in *Stevens*, California has tried to make violent-speech regulation look like obscenity regulation by appending a saving clause required for the latter. That does not suffice. Our cases have been clear that the obscenity exception to the First Amendment does not cover whatever a legislature finds shocking, but only depictions of "sexual conduct," *Miller, supra*, at 24. See also *Cohen v. California*, 403 U.S. 15, 20 (1971); *Roth, supra*, at 487, and n. 20.

Stevens was not the first time we have encountered and rejected a State's attempt to shoehorn speech about violence into obscenity. In *Winters*, we considered a New York criminal statute "forbid[ding] the massing of stories of bloodshed and lust in such a way as to incite to crime against the person," 333 U.S., at 514. The New York Court of Appeals upheld the provision as a law against obscenity. "[T]here can be no more precise test of written indecency or obscenity," it said, "than the continuing and changeable experience of the community as to what types of books are likely to bring about the corruption of public morals or other analogous injury to the public order." *Id.*, at 514. That is of course the same expansive view of governmental power to abridge the freedom of speech based on interest-balancing that we rejected in *Stevens*. Our opinion in *Winters*, which concluded that the New York statute failed a heightened vagueness standard applicable to restrictions upon speech entitled to First Amendment protection, 333 U.S., at 517–519, made clear that violence is not part of the obscenity that the Constitution permits to be regulated. The speech reached by the statute contained "no indecency or obscenity in any sense heretofore known to the law." *Id.*, at 519.

Because speech about violence is not obscene, it is of no consequence that California's statute mimics the New York statute regulating obscenity-for-minors that we upheld in *Ginsberg v. New York*, 390 U.S. 629 (1968). That case approved a prohibition on the sale to minors of *sexual* material that would be obscene from the perspective of a child.[1] We held that the legislature could "adjus[t] the definition of obscenity 'to social realities by permitting the appeal of this type of material to be assessed in terms of the sexual interests . . .' of . . . minors." *Id.*, at 638 (quoting *Mishkin v. New York*, 383 U.S. 502, 509 (1966)). And because "obscenity is not protected expression," the New York statute could be sustained so long as the legislature's judgment that the proscribed materials were harmful to children "was not irrational." 390 U.S., at 641.

The California Act is something else entirely. It does not adjust the boundaries of an existing category of unprotected speech to ensure that a definition designed for adults is not uncritically applied to children. California does not argue that it is empowered to prohibit selling offensively violent works *to adults*—and it is wise not to, since that is but a hair's breadth from the argument rejected in *Stevens*. Instead, it wishes to create a wholly new category of content-based regulation that is permissible only for speech directed at children.

That is unprecedented and mistaken. "[M]inors are entitled to a significant measure of First Amendment protection, and only in relatively narrow and well-defined circumstances may government bar public dissemination of protected materials to them." *Erznoznik v. Jacksonville*, 422 U.S. 205, 212–213 (1975) (citation omitted). No doubt a State possesses legitimate power to protect children from harm, *Ginsberg, supra*, at 640–641; *Prince v. Massachusetts*, 321 U.S. 158, 165 (1944), but that does not include a free-floating power to restrict the ideas to which children may be exposed. "Speech that is neither obscene as to youths nor subject to some other legitimate proscription cannot be suppressed solely to protect the young from ideas or images that a legislative body thinks unsuitable for them." *Erznoznik, supra*, at 213–214.[2]

California's argument would fare better if there were a longstanding tradition in this country of specially restricting children's access to depictions of violence, but there is none. Certainly the *books* we give children to read—or read to them when they are younger—contain no shortage of gore. Grimm's Fairy Tales, for example, are grim indeed. As her just deserts for trying to poison Snow White, the wicked queen is made to dance in red hot slippers "till she fell dead on the floor, a sad example of envy and jealousy." The Complete Brothers Grimm Fairy Tales 198 (2006 ed.). Cinderella's evil stepsisters have their eyes pecked out by doves. *Id.*, at 95. And Hansel and Gretel (children!) kill their captor by baking her in an oven. *Id.*, at 54.

High-school reading lists are full of similar fare. Homer's Odysseus blinds Polyphemus the Cyclops by grinding out his eye with a heated stake. The Odyssey of Homer, Book IX, p. 125 (S. Butcher & A. Lang transls. 1909) ("Even so did we seize the fiery-pointed brand and whirled it round in his eye, and the blood flowed about the heated bar. And the breath of the flame singed his eyelids and brows all about, as the ball of the eye burnt away, and the roots thereof crackled in the flame"). In the Inferno, Dante and Virgil watch corrupt politicians struggle to stay submerged beneath a lake of boiling pitch, lest they be skewered by devils above the surface. Canto XXI, pp. 187–189 (A. Mandelbaum transl. Bantam Classic ed. 1982). And Golding's Lord of the Flies recounts how a schoolboy called Piggy is savagely murdered *by other children* while marooned on an island. W. Golding, Lord of the Flies 208–209 (1997 ed.).[3]

This is not to say that minors' consumption of violent entertainment has never encountered resistance. In the 1800's, dime novels depicting crime and "penny dreadfuls" (named for their price and content) were blamed in some quarters for juvenile delinquency. See Brief for Cato Institute as *Amicus Curiae* 6–7. When motion pictures came along, they became the villains instead. "The days when the police looked upon dime novels as the most dangerous of textbooks in the school for crime are drawing to a close. . . . They say that the moving picture machine . . . tends even more than did the dime novel to turn the thoughts of the easily influenced to paths which sometimes lead to prison." Moving Pictures as Helps to Crime, N. Y. Times, Feb. 21, 1909, quoted in Brief for Cato Institute, at 8. For a time, our Court did permit broad censorship of movies because of their capacity to be "used for evil," see *Mutual Film Corp. v. Industrial Comm'n of Ohio,* 236 U.S. 230, 242 (1915), but we eventually reversed course, *Joseph Burstyn, Inc.,* 343 U.S., at 502; see also *Erznoznik, supra,* at 212–214 (invalidating a drive-in movies restriction designed to protect children). Radio dramas were next, and then came comic books. Brief for Cato Institute, at 10–11. Many in the late 1940's and early 1950's blamed comic books for fostering a "preoccupation with violence and horror" among the young, leading to a rising juvenile crime rate. See Note, Regulation of Comic Books, 68 Harv. L. Rev. 489, 490 (1955). But efforts to convince Congress to restrict comic books failed. Brief for Comic Book Legal Defense Fund as *Amicus Curiae* 11–15.[4] And, of course, after comic books came television and music lyrics.

California claims that video games present special problems because they are "interactive," in that the player participates in the violent action on screen and determines its outcome. The latter feature is nothing new: Since at least the publication of The Adventures of You: Sugarcane Island in 1969, young readers of choose-your-own adventure stories have been able to make decisions that determine the plot by following instructions about which page to turn to. Cf. *Interactive Digital Software Assn. v. St. Louis County,* 329 F. 3d 954, 957–958 (CA8 2003). As for the argument that video games enable participation in the violent action, that seems to us more a matter of degree than of kind. As Judge Posner has observed, all literature is interactive. "[T]he better it is, the more interactive. Literature when it is successful draws the reader into the story, makes him identify with the characters, invites him to judge them and quarrel with them, to experience their joys and sufferings as the reader's own." *American Amusement Machine Assn. v. Kendrick,* 244 F. 3d 572, 577 (CA7 2001) (striking down a similar restriction on violent video games).

JUSTICE ALITO has done considerable independent research to identify . . . video games in which "the violence is astounding," "Victims are dismembered, decapitated, disemboweled, set on fire, and chopped into little pieces. . . . Blood gushes, splatters, and pools.". . . JUSTICE ALITO recounts all these disgusting video games in order to disgust us—but disgust is not a valid basis for restricting expression. And the same is true of JUSTICE ALITO's description, . . . of those video games he has discovered that have a racial or ethnic motive for their violence—" 'ethnic cleansing' [of] . . . African Americans, Latinos, or Jews." To what end does he relate this? Does it somehow increase the "aggressiveness" that California wishes to suppress? Who knows? But it does arouse the reader's ire, and the reader's desire to put an end to this horrible message. Thus, ironically, JUSTICE ALITO's argument highlights the precise danger posed by the California Act: that the *ideas* expressed by speech—whether it be violence, or gore, or racism—and not its objective effects, may be the real reason for governmental proscription.

III

Because the Act imposes a restriction on the content of protected speech, it is invalid unless California can demonstrate that it passes strict scrutiny—that is, unless it is justified by a compelling government interest and is narrowly drawn to serve that interest. *R. A. V.,* 505 U.S., at 395. The State must specifically identify an "actual problem" in need of solving, *Playboy,* 529 U.S., at 822–823, and the curtailment of free speech must be actually necessary to the solution, see *R. A. V., supra,* at 395. That is a demanding standard. "It is rare that a regulation restricting speech because of its content will ever be permissible." *Playboy, supra,* at 818.

California cannot meet that standard. At the outset, it acknowledges that it cannot show a direct causal link between violent video games and harm to minors. Rather, relying upon our decision in *Turner Broadcasting System, Inc. v. FCC,* 512 U.S. 622 (1994), the State claims that it need not produce such proof because the legislature can make a predictive judgment that such a link exists, based on competing psychological studies. But reliance on *Turner Broadcasting* is misplaced. That decision applied *intermediate scrutiny* to a content-neutral regulation. . . . California's burden is much higher, and because it bears the risk of uncertainty, . . . ambiguous proof will not suffice.

The State's evidence is not compelling. California relies primarily on the research of Dr. Craig Anderson and a few other research psychologists whose studies purport to show a connection between exposure to violent video games and harmful effects on children. These studies have been rejected by every court to consider them, and with good reason: They do not prove that violent video games *cause* minors to *act* aggressively (which would at least be a beginning). Instead, "[n]early all of the research is based on correlation, not evidence of causation, and most of the studies suffer from significant, admitted flaws in methodology." *Video Software Dealers Assn.* 556 F. 3d, at 964. They show at best some correlation between exposure to violent entertainment and minuscule real-world effects, such as children's feeling more aggressive or making louder noises in the few minutes after playing a violent game than after playing a nonviolent game.[5]

Even taking for granted Dr. Anderson's conclusions that violent video games produce some effect on children's feelings of aggression, those effects are both small and indistinguishable from effects produced by other media. In his testimony in a similar lawsuit, Dr. Anderson admitted that the "effect sizes" of children's exposure to violent video games are "about the same" as that produced by their exposure to violence on television. . . . And he admits that the *same* effects have been found when children watch cartoons starring Bugs Bunny or the Road Runner, *id.*, at 1304, or when they play video games like Sonic the Hedgehog that are rated "E" (appropriate for all ages), . . . or even when they "vie[w] a picture of a gun.". . .[6]

Of course, California has (wisely) declined to restrict Saturday morning cartoons, the sale of games rated for young children, or the distribution of pictures of guns. The consequence is that its regulation is wildly underinclusive when judged against its asserted justification, which in our view is alone enough to defeat it. Underinclusiveness raises serious doubts about whether the government is in fact pursuing the interest it invokes, rather than disfavoring a particular speaker or viewpoint. . . . Here, California has singled out the purveyors of video games for disfavored treatment—at least when compared to booksellers, cartoonists, and movie producers—and has given no persuasive reason why.

The Act is also seriously underinclusive in another respect—and a respect that renders irrelevant the contentions of the concurrence and the dissents that video games are qualitatively different from other portrayals of violence. The California Legislature is perfectly willing to leave this dangerous, mind-altering material in the hands of children so long as one parent (or even an aunt or uncle) says it's OK. And there are not even any requirements as to how this parental or avuncular relationship is to be verified; apparently the child's or putative parent's, aunt's, or uncle's say-so suffices. That is not how one addresses a serious social problem.

California claims that the Act is justified in aid of parental authority: By requiring that the purchase of violent video games can be made only by adults, the Act ensures that parents can decide what games are appropriate. At the outset, we note our doubts that punishing third parties for conveying protected speech to children *just in case* their parents disapprove of that speech is a proper governmental means of aiding parental authority. Accepting that position would largely vitiate the rule that "only in relatively narrow and well-defined circumstances may government bar public dissemination of protected materials to [minors]." *Erznoznik,* 422 U.S., at 212–213.

But leaving that aside, California cannot show that the Act's restrictions meet a substantial need of parents who wish to restrict their children's access to violent video games but cannot do so. The video-game industry has in place a voluntary rating system designed to inform consumers about the content of games. The system, implemented by the Entertainment Software Rating Board (ESRB), assigns age-specific ratings to each video game submitted: EC (Early Childhood); E (Everyone); E10+ (Everyone 10 and older); T (Teens); M (17 and older); and AO (Adults Only—18 and older). . . . The Video Software Dealers Association encourages retailers to prominently display information about the ESRB system in their stores; to refrain from renting or selling adults-only games to minors; and to rent or sell "M" rated games to minors only with parental consent. . . . In 2009, the Federal Trade Commission (FTC) found that, as a result of this system, "the video game industry outpaces the movie and music industries" in "(1) restricting target-marketing of mature-rated products to children; (2) clearly and prominently disclosing rating information; and (3) restricting children's access to mature-rated products at retail." FTC, Report to Congress, Marketing Violent Entertainment to Children 30 (Dec. 2009). . . . This system does much to ensure that minors cannot purchase seriously violent games on their own, and that parents who care about the matter can readily evaluate the games their children bring home. Filling the remaining modest gap in concerned-parents' control can hardly be a compelling state interest.[7]

And finally, the Act's purported aid to parental authority is vastly overinclusive. Not all of the children who are forbidden to purchase violent video games on their own have parents who *care* whether they purchase violent video games. While some of the legislation's effect may indeed be in support of what some parents of the restricted children actually want, its entire effect is only in support of what the State thinks parents *ought* to want. This is not the narrow tailoring to "assisting parents" that restriction of First Amendment rights requires.

＊

California's effort to regulate violent video games is the latest episode in a long series of failed attempts to censor violent entertainment for minors. While we have pointed out above that some of the evidence brought forward to support the harmfulness of video games is unpersuasive, we do not mean to demean or disparage the concerns that underlie the attempt to regulate them—concerns that may and doubtless do prompt a good deal of parental oversight. We have no business passing judgment on the view of the California Legislature that violent video games (or, for that matter, any other forms of speech) corrupt the young or harm their moral development. Our task is only to say whether or not such works constitute a "well-defined and narrowly limited clas[s] of speech, the prevention and punishment of which have never been thought to raise any Constitutional problem," *Chaplinsky*, 315 U.S., at 571–572 (the answer plainly is no); and if not, whether the regulation of such works is justified by that high degree of necessity we have described as a compelling state interest (it is not). Even where the protection of children is the object, the constitutional limits on governmental action apply.

California's legislation straddles the fence between (1) addressing a serious social problem and (2) helping concerned parents control their children. Both ends are legitimate, but when they affect First Amendment rights they must be pursued by means that are neither seriously underinclusive nor seriously overinclusive. . . . As a means of protecting children from portrayals of violence, the legislation is seriously underinclusive, not only because it excludes portrayals other than video games, but also because it permits a parental or avuncular veto. And as a means of assisting concerned parents it is seriously overinclusive because it abridges the First Amendment rights of young people whose parents (and aunts and uncles) think violent video games are a harmless pastime. And the overbreadth in achieving one goal is not cured by the underbreadth in achieving the other. Legislation such as this, which is neither fish nor fowl, cannot survive strict scrutiny.

We affirm the judgment below.

It is so ordered.

Notes

1. The statute in *Ginsberg* restricted the sale of certain depictions of "nudity, sexual conduct, sexual excitement, or sado-masochistic abuse," that were "'[h]armful to minors.'" A depiction was harmful to minors if it:

"(i) predominantly appeals to the prurient, shameful or morbid interests of minors, and

"(ii) is patently offensive to prevailing standards in the adult community as a whole with respect to what is suitable material for minors, and

"(iii) is utterly without redeeming social importance for minors." 390 U.S., at 646 (Appendix A to opinion of the Court) (quoting N. Y. Penal Law §484–h(1)(f)).

2. JUSTICE THOMAS ignores the holding of *Erznoznik*, and denies that persons under 18 have any constitutional right to speak or be spoken to without their parents' consent. He cites no case, state or federal, supporting this view, and to our knowledge there is none. Most of his dissent is devoted to the proposition that parents have traditionally had the power to control what their children hear and say. This is true enough. And it perhaps follows from this that the state has the power to *enforce* parental prohibitions—to require, for example, that the promoters of a rock concert exclude those minors whose parents have advised the promoters that their children are forbidden to attend. But it does not follow that the state has the power to prevent children from hearing or saying anything *without their parents' prior consent.* The latter would mean, for example, that it could be made criminal to admit persons under 18 to a political rally without their parents' prior written consent—even a political rally in support of laws against corporal punishment of children, or laws in favor of greater rights for minors. And what is good for First Amendment rights of speech must be good for First Amendment rights of religion as well: It could be made criminal to admit a person under 18 to church, or to give a person under 18 a religious tract, without his parents' prior consent. Our point is not, as JUSTICE THOMAS believes, *post*, at 16, n. 2, merely that such laws are "undesirable." They are obviously an infringement upon the religious freedom of young people and those who wish to proselytize young people. Such laws do not enforce *parental* authority over children's speech and religion; they impose *governmental* authority, subject only to a parental veto. In the absence of any precedent for state control, uninvited by the parents, over a child's speech and religion (JUSTICE THOMAS cites none), and in the absence of any justification for such control that would satisfy strict scrutiny, those laws must be unconstitutional.

This argument is not, as JUSTICE THOMAS asserts, "circular," . . . It is the absence of any historical warrant or compelling justification for such restrictions, not our *ipse dixit,* that renders them invalid.

3. JUSTICE ALITO accuses us of pronouncing that playing violent video games "is not different in 'kind' " from reading violent literature. *Post,* at 2. Well of course it is different in kind, but not in a way that causes the provision and viewing of violent video games, unlike the provision and reading of books, not to be expressive activity and hence not to enjoy First Amendment protection. Reading Dante is unquestionably more cultured and intellectually edifying than playing Mortal Kombat. But these cultural and intellectual differences are not *constitutional* ones. Crudely violent video games, tawdry TV shows, and cheap novels and magazines are no less forms of speech than The Divine Comedy, and restrictions upon them must survive strict scrutiny—a question to which we devote our attention in Part III, *infra.* Even if we can see in them "nothing of any possible value to society . . . , they are as much entitled to the protection of free speech as the best of literature." *Winters v. New York,* 333 U.S. 507, 510 (1948).

4. The crusade against comic books was led by a psychiatrist, Frederic Wertham, who told the Senate Judiciary Committee that "as long as the crime comic books industry exists in its present forms there are no secure homes." Juvenile Delinquency (Comic Books): Hearings before the Subcommittee to Investigate Juvenile Delinquency, 83d Cong., 2d Sess., 84 (1954). Wertham's objections extended even to Superman comics, which he described as "particularly injurious to the ethical development of children." *Id.,* at 86. Wertham's crusade did convince the New York Legislature to pass a ban on the sale of certain comic books to minors, but it was vetoed by Governor Thomas Dewey on the ground that it was unconstitutional given our opinion in *Winters, supra.* See *People v. Bookcase, Inc.,* 14 N. Y. 2d 409, 412–413, 201 N. E. 2d 14, 15–16 (1964).

5. One study, for example, found that children who had just finished playing violent video games were more likely to fill in the blank letter in "explo_e" with a "d" (so that it reads "explode") than with an "r" ("explore"). App. 496, 506 (internal quotation marks omitted). The prevention of this phenomenon, which might have been anticipated with common sense, is not a compelling state interest.

6. JUSTICE ALITO is mistaken in thinking that we fail to take account of "new and rapidly evolving technology." . . . The studies in question pertain to that new and rapidly evolving technology, and fail to show, with the degree of certitude that strict scrutiny

requires, that this subject-matter restriction on speech is justified. Nor is JUSTICE ALITO correct in attributing to us the view that "violent video games really present no serious problem." . . . Perhaps they do present a problem, and perhaps none of us would allow our own children to play them. But there are all sorts of "problems"—some of them surely more serious than this one—that cannot be addressed by governmental restriction of free expression: for example, the problem of encouraging anti-Semitism (*National Socialist Party of America v. Skokie,* 432 U.S. 43 (1977) (*per curiam*)), the problem of spreading a political philosophy hostile to the Constitution (*Noto v. United States,* 367 U.S. 290 (1961)), or the problem of encouraging disrespect for the Nation's flag (*Texas v. Johnson,* 491 U.S. 397 (1989)).

JUSTICE BREYER would hold that California has satisfied strict scrutiny based upon his own research into the issue of the harmfulness of violent video games. . . . (Appendixes to dissenting opinion) (listing competing academic articles discussing the harmfulness *vel non* of violent video games). The vast preponderance of this research is outside the record—and in any event we do not see how it could lead to JUSTICE BREYER's conclusion, since he admits he cannot say whether the studies on his side are right or wrong. . . . Similarly, JUSTICE ALITO says he is not "sure" whether there are any constitutionally dispositive differences between video games and other media. . . . If that is so, then strict scrutiny plainly has not been satisfied.

7. JUSTICE BREYER concludes that the remaining gap is compelling because, according to the FTC's report, some "20% of those under 17 are still able to buy M-rated games." *Post,* at 18 (citing FTC Report 28). But some gap in compliance is unavoidable. The sale of alcohol to minors, for example, has long been illegal, but a 2005 study suggests that about 18% of retailers still sell alcohol to those under the drinking age. . . . Even if the sale of violent video games to minors could be deterred further by increasing regulation, the government does not have a compelling interest in each marginal percentage point by which its goals are advanced.

ANTONIN SCALIA is an associate justice of the U.S. Supreme Court. He taught law at the University of Virginia, the American Enterprise Institute, Georgetown University, and the University of Chicago before being nominated to the U.S. Court of Appeals by President Ronald Reagan in 1982. He served in that capacity until he was nominated by Reagan to the Supreme Court in 1986.

Stephen Breyer

 **NO**

Dissenting Opinion, *Brown v. Entertainment Merchants Association*

JUSTICE BREYER, dissenting.

California imposes a civil fine of up to $1,000 upon any person who distributes a violent video game in California without labeling it "18," or who sells or rents a labeled violent video game to a person under the age of 18. Representatives of the video game and software industries, claiming that the statute violates the First Amendment on its face, seek an injunction against its enforcement. Applying traditional First Amendment analysis, I would uphold the statute as constitutional on its face and would consequently reject the industries' facial challenge.

I

A

California's statute defines a violent video game as: A game in which a player "kill[s], maim[s], dismember[s], or sexually assault[s] an image of a human being," *and*

> "[a] reasonable person, considering the game as a whole, would find [the game] appeals to a deviant or morbid interest of minors,"

and

> "[the game] is patently offensive to prevailing standards in the community as to what is suitable for minors,"

and

> "the game, as a whole, . . . lack[s] serious literary, artistic, political, or scientific value for minors." Cal. Civ. Code Ann. §1746(d)(1).

The statute in effect forbids the sale of such a game to minors unless they are accompanied by a parent; it requires the makers of the game to affix a label identifying it as a game suitable only for those aged 18 and over; it exempts retailers from liability unless such a label is properly affixed to the game; and it imposes a civil fine of up to $1,000 upon a violator. . . .

B

A facial challenge to this statute based on the First Amendment can succeed only if "a substantial number of its applications are unconstitutional, judged in relation to the statute's plainly legitimate sweep." *United States v. Stevens*, 559 U.S. __, __ (2010). . . . Moreover, it is more difficult to mount a facial First Amendment attack on a statute that seeks to regulate activity that involves action as well as speech. See *Broadrick v. Oklahoma*, 413 U.S. 601, 614–615 (1973). Hence, I shall focus here upon an area within which I believe the State can legitimately apply its statute, namely sales to minors under the age of 17 (the age cutoff used by the industry's own ratings system), of highly realistic violent video games, which a reasonable game maker would know meet the Act's criteria. That area lies at the heart of the statute. I shall assume that the number of instances in which the State will enforce the statute within that area is comparatively large, and that the number outside that area (for example, sales to 17-year-olds) is comparatively small. And the activity the statute regulates combines speech with action (a virtual form of target practice).

C

In determining whether the statute is unconstitutional, I would apply both this Court's "vagueness" precedents and a strict form of First Amendment scrutiny. In doing so, the special First Amendment category I find relevant is not (as the Court claims) the category of "depictions of violence," . . . but rather the category of "protection of children." This Court has held that the "power of the state to control the conduct of children reaches beyond the scope of its authority over adults." *Prince v. Massachusetts,*

From Supreme Court of the United States, June 27, 2011.

321 U.S. 158, 170 (1944). And the "'regulatio[n] of communication addressed to [children] need not conform to the requirements of the [F]irst [A]mendment in the same way as those applicable to adults.'" *Ginsberg v. New York*, 390 U.S. 629, 638, n. 6 (1968) (quoting Emerson, Toward a General Theory of the First Amendment, 72 Yale L. J. 877, 939 (1963)).

The majority's claim that the California statute, if upheld, would create a "new categor[y] of unprotected speech," . . . is overstated. No one here argues that depictions of violence, even extreme violence, *automatically* fall outside the First Amendment's protective scope as, for example, do obscenity and depictions of child pornography. We properly speak of *categories* of expression that lack protection when, like "child pornography," the category is broad, when it applies automatically, and when the State can prohibit everyone, including adults, from obtaining access to the material within it. But where, as here, careful analysis must precede a narrower judicial conclusion (say, denying protection to a shout of "fire" in a crowded theater, or to an effort to teach a terrorist group how to peacefully petition the United Nations), we do not normally describe the result as creating a "new category of unprotected speech." See *Schenck v. United States*, 249 U.S. 47, 52 (1919); *Holder v. Humanitarian Law Project*, 561 U.S. __ (2010).

Thus, in *Stevens*, after rejecting the claim that *all* depictions of animal cruelty (a category) fall outside the First Amendment's protective scope, we went on to decide whether the particular statute at issue violates the First Amendment under traditional standards; and we held that, because the statute was overly broad, it was invalid. Similarly, here the issue is whether, applying traditional First Amendment standards, this statute does, or does not, pass muster.

II

In my view, California's statute provides "fair notice of what is prohibited," and consequently it is not impermissibly vague. *United States v. Williams*, 553 U.S. 285, 304 (2008). *Ginsberg* explains why that is so. The Court there considered a New York law that forbade the sale to minors of a

> "picture, photograph, drawing, sculpture, motion picture film, or similar visual representation or image of a person or portion of the human body which depicts nudity . . . ,"

that

> "predominately appeals to the prurient, shameful or morbid interest of minors,"

and

> "is patently offensive to prevailing standards in the adult community as a whole with respect to what is suitable material for minors,"

and

> "is utterly without redeeming social importance for minors." 390 U.S., at 646–647.

This Court upheld the New York statute in *Ginsberg* (which is sometimes unfortunately confused with a very different, earlier case, *Ginzburg v. United States*, 383 U.S. 463 (1966)). The five-Justice majority, in an opinion written by Justice Brennan, wrote that the statute was sufficiently clear. 390 U.S., at 643–645. No Member of the Court voiced any vagueness objection. See *id.*, at 648–650 (Stewart, J., concurring in result); *id.*, at 650–671 (Douglas, J., joined by Black, J., dissenting); *id.*, at 671–675 (Fortas, J., dissenting).

Comparing the language of California's statute . . . with the language of New York's statute (set forth immediately above), it is difficult to find any vagueness-related difference. Why are the words "kill," "maim," and "dismember" any more difficult to understand than the word "nudity?" JUSTICE ALITO objects that these words do "not perform the narrowing function" that this Court has required in adult obscenity cases, where statutes can only cover "'hard core'" depictions. . . . But the relevant comparison is not to adult obscenity cases but to *Ginsberg*, which dealt with "nudity," a category no more "narrow" than killing and maiming. And in any event, *narrowness* and *vagueness* do not necessarily have anything to do with one another. All that is required for vagueness purposes is that the terms "kill," "maim," and "dismember" give fair notice as to what they cover, which they do.

The remainder of California's definition copies, almost word for word, the language this Court used in *Miller v. California*, 413 U.S. 15 (1973), in permitting a *total* ban on material that satisfied its definition (one enforced with *criminal* penalties). The California law's reliance on "community standards" adheres to *Miller*, and in *Fort Wayne Books, Inc. v. Indiana*, 489 U.S. 46, 57–58 (1989), this Court specifically upheld the use of *Miller*'s language against charges of vagueness. California only departed from the *Miller* formulation in two significant respects: It substituted the word "deviant" for the words "prurient" and "shameful," and it three times added the words "for minors." The word "deviant" differs from "prurient" and "shameful," but it would seem no less suited to defining and narrowing the reach of the statute. And the addition of "for minors" to a version of the *Miller* standard was approved in *Ginsberg*, 390 U.S., at 643, even though the New York law "dr[ew] no distinction between young children and adolescents who are nearing the age of majority," *ante*, at 8 (opinion of ALITO, J.).

Both the *Miller* standard and the law upheld in *Ginsberg* lack perfect clarity. But that fact reflects the difficulty of the Court's long search for words capable of protecting expression without depriving the State of a legitimate constitutional power to regulate. As is well known, at one point Justice Stewart thought he could do no better in defining obscenity than, "I know it when I see it." *Jacobellis v. Ohio*, 378 U.S. 184, 197 (1964) (concurring opinion). And Justice Douglas dissented from *Miller*'s standard, which he thought was still too vague. 413 U.S., at 39–40. Ultimately, however, this Court accepted the "community standards" tests used in *Miller* and *Ginsberg*. They reflect the fact that sometimes, even when a precise standard proves elusive, it is easy enough to identify instances that fall within a legitimate regulation. And they seek to draw a line, which, while favoring free expression, will nonetheless permit a legislature to find the words necessary to accomplish a legitimate constitutional objective . . . (the Constitution does not always require " 'perfect clarity and precise guidance,' " even when " 'expressive activity' " is involved).

What, then, is the difference between *Ginsberg* and *Miller* on the one hand and the California law on the other? It will often be easy to pick out cases at which California's statute directly aims, involving, say, a character who shoots out a police officer's knee, douses him with gasoline, lights him on fire, urinates on his burning body, and finally kills him with a gunshot to the head. (Footage of one such game sequence has been submitted in the record.) . . . As in *Miller* and *Ginsberg*, the California law clearly *protects* even the most violent games that possess serious literary, artistic, political, or scientific value. §1746(d)(1)(A)(iii). And it is easier here than in *Miller* or *Ginsberg* to separate the sheep from the goats at the statute's border. That is because here the industry itself has promulgated standards and created a review process, in which adults who "typically have experience with children" assess what games are inappropriate for minors. . . .

There is, of course, one obvious difference: The *Ginsberg* statute concerned depictions of "nudity," while California's statute concerns extremely violent video games. But for purposes of vagueness, why should that matter? JUSTICE ALITO argues that the *Miller* standard sufficed because there are "certain generally accepted norms concerning expression related to sex," whereas there are no similarly "accepted standards regarding the suitability of

violent entertainment." . . . But there is no evidence that is so. The Court relied on "community standards" in *Miller* precisely because of the difficulty of articulating "accepted norms" about depictions of sex. I can find no difference—historical or otherwise—that is *relevant* to the vagueness question. Indeed, the majority's examples of literary descriptions of violence, on which JUSTICE ALITO relies, do not show anything relevant at all.

After all, one can find in literature as many (if not more) descriptions of physical love as descriptions of violence. Indeed, sex "has been a theme in art and literature throughout the ages." *Ashcroft v. Free Speech Coalition*, 535 U.S. 234, 246 (2002). For every Homer, there is a Titian. For every Dante, there is an Ovid. And for all the teenagers who have read the original versions of Grimm's Fairy Tales, I suspect there are those who know the story of Lady Godiva.

Thus, I can find no meaningful vagueness-related differences between California's law and the New York law upheld in *Ginsberg*. And if there remain any vagueness problems, the state courts can cure them through interpretation. See *Erznoznik v. Jacksonville*, 422 U.S. 205, 216 (1975) ("[S]tate statute should not be deemed facially invalid unless it is not readily subject to a narrowing construction by the state courts"). Cf. *Ginsberg, supra,* at 644 (relying on the fact that New York Court of Appeals would read a knowledge requirement into the statute); *Berry v. Santa Barbara*, 40 Cal. App. 4th 1075, 1088– 1089, 47 Cal. Rptr. 2d 661, 669 (1995) (reading a knowledge requirement into a statute). Consequently, for purposes of this facial challenge, I would not find the statute unconstitutionally vague.

III

Video games combine physical action with expression. Were physical activity to predominate in a game, government could appropriately intervene, say by requiring parents to accompany children when playing a game involving actual target practice, or restricting the sale of toys presenting physical dangers to children. See generally Consumer Product Safety Improvement Act of 2008, 122 Stat. 3016 ("Title I—Children's Product Safety"). But because video games also embody important expressive and artistic elements, I agree with the Court that the First Amendment significantly limits the State's power to regulate. And I would determine whether the State has exceeded those limits by applying a strict standard of review.

Like the majority, I believe that the California law must be "narrowly tailored" to further a "compelling interest," without there being a "less restrictive" alternative that would be "at least as effective." *Reno v. American Civil Liberties Union,* 521 U.S. 844, 874, 875, 879 (1997). I would not apply this strict standard "mechanically." *United States v. Playboy Entertainment Group, Inc.,* 529 U.S. 803, 841 (2000) (Breyer, J., joined by Rehnquist, C. J., and O'Connor and Scalia, JJ., dissenting). Rather, in applying it, I would evaluate the degree to which the statute injures speech-related interests, the nature of the potentially-justifying "compelling interests," the degree to which the statute furthers that interest, the nature and effectiveness of possible alternatives, and, in light of this evaluation, whether, overall, "the statute works speech-related harm . . . out of proportion to the benefits that the statute seeks to provide." . . .

First Amendment standards applied in this way are difficult but not impossible to satisfy. Applying "strict scrutiny" the Court has upheld restrictions on speech that, for example, ban the teaching of peaceful dispute resolution to a group on the State Department's list of terrorist organizations, *Holder,* 561 U.S., at ___ (slip op., at 22–34); but cf. *id.,* at ___ (slip op., at 1) (Breyer, J., dissenting), and limit speech near polling places, *Burson, supra,* at 210–211 (plurality opinion). And applying less clearly defined but still rigorous standards, the Court has allowed States to require disclosure of petition signers, *Doe v. Reed,* 561 U.S. ___ (2010), and to impose campaign contribution limits that were "'closely drawn' to match a 'sufficiently important interest,'" *Nixon v. Shrink Missouri Government PAC,* 528 U.S. 377, 387–388 (2000).

Moreover, although the Court did not specify the "level of scrutiny" it applied in *Ginsberg,* we have subsequently described that case as finding a "compelling interest" in protecting children from harm sufficient to justify limitations on speech. See *Sable Communications of Cal., Inc. v. FCC,* 492 U.S. 115, 126 (1989). Since the Court in *Ginsberg* specified that the statute's prohibition applied to material that was *not* obscene, 390 U.S., at 634, I cannot dismiss *Ginsberg* on the ground that it concerned obscenity. . . . Nor need I depend upon the fact that the Court in *Ginsberg* insisted only that the legislature have a "rational" basis for finding the depictions there at issue harmful to children. . . . For in this case, California has substantiated its claim of harm with considerably stronger evidence.

A

California's law imposes no more than a modest restriction on expression. The statute prevents no one from playing a video game, it prevents no adult from buying a video game, and it prevents no child or adolescent from obtaining a game provided a parent is willing to help. §1746.1(c). All it prevents is a child or adolescent from buying, without a parent's assistance, a gruesomely violent video game of a kind that the industry *itself* tells us it wants to keep out of the hands of those under the age of 17. . . .

Nor is the statute, if upheld, likely to create a precedent that would adversely affect other media, say films, or videos, or books. A typical video game involves a significant amount of physical activity. See *ante,* at 13–14 (Alito, J., concurring in judgment). . . . And pushing buttons that achieve an interactive, virtual form of target practice (using images of human beings as targets), while containing an expressive component, is not just like watching a typical movie.

B

The interest that California advances in support of the statute is compelling. As this Court has previously described that interest, it consists of both (1) the "basic" parental claim "to authority in their own household to direct the rearing of their children," which makes it proper to enact "laws designed to aid discharge of [parental] responsibility," and (2) the State's "independent interest in the well-being of its youth." *Ginsberg,* 390 U.S., at 639–640. . . . ("'[O]ne can well distinguish laws which do not impose a morality on children, but which support the right of parents to deal with the morals of their children as they see fit'" (quoting Henkin, Morals and the Constitution: The Sin of Obscenity, 63 Colum. L. Rev. 391, 413, n. 68 (1963))). And where these interests work in tandem, it is not fatally "underinclusive" for a State to advance its interests in protecting children against the special harms present in an interactive video game medium through a default rule that still allows parents to provide their children with what their parents wish.

Both interests are present here. As to the need to help parents guide their children, the Court noted in 1968 that "'parental control or guidance cannot always be provided.'" 390 U.S., at 640. Today, 5.3 million grade-school-age children of working parents are routinely home alone. See Dept. of Commerce, Census Bureau, Who's Minding the Kids? Child Care Arrangements: Spring 2005/Summer 2006, p. 12 (2010). . . . Thus, it has, if anything, become more important to supplement parents' authority to guide their children's development.

As to the State's independent interest, we have pointed out that juveniles are more likely to show a "'lack of maturity'" and are "more vulnerable or susceptible to negative influences and outside pressures," and that their "character . . . is not as well formed as that of an adult." *Roper v. Simmons,* 543 U.S. 551, 569–570 (2005). And we have therefore recognized "a compelling interest in protecting the physical and psychological well-being of minors." *Sable Communications, supra,* at 126.

At the same time, there is considerable evidence that California's statute significantly furthers this compelling interest. That is, in part, because video games are excellent teaching tools. Learning a practical task often means developing habits, becoming accustomed to performing the task, and receiving positive reinforcement when performing that task well. Video games can help develop habits, accustom the player to performance of the task, and reward the player for performing that task well. Why else would the Armed Forces incorporate video games into its training? See CNN, War Games: Military Training Goes High-Tech (Nov. 22, 2001). . . .

When the military uses video games to help soldiers train for missions, it is using this medium for a beneficial purpose. But California argues that when the teaching features of video games are put to less desirable ends, harm can ensue. In particular, extremely violent games can harm children by rewarding them for being violently aggressive in play, and thereby often teaching them to be violently aggressive in life. And video games can cause more harm in this respect than can typically passive media, such as books or films or television programs.

There are many scientific studies that support California's views. Social scientists, for example, have found *causal* evidence that playing these games results in harm. Longitudinal studies, which measure changes over time, have found that increased exposure to violent video games causes an increase in aggression over the same period. . . .

Experimental studies in laboratories have found that subjects randomly assigned to play a violent video game subsequently displayed more characteristics of aggression than those who played nonviolent games. See, *e.g.,* Anderson et al., Violent Video Games: Specific Effects of Violent Content on Aggressive Thoughts and Behavior, 36 Advances in Experimental Soc. Psychology 199 (2004).

Surveys of 8th and 9th grade students have found a correlation between playing violent video games and aggression. See, *e.g.,* Gentile, Lynch, Linder, & Walsh, The Effects of Violent Video Game Habits On Adolescent Hostility, Aggressive Behaviors, and School Performance, 27 J. Adolescence 5 (2004).

Cutting-edge neuroscience has shown that "virtual violence in video game playing results in those neural patterns that are considered characteristic for aggressive cognition and behavior." Weber, Ritterfeld, & Mathiak, Does Playing Violent Video Games Induce Aggression? Empirical Evidence of a Functional Magnetic Resonance Imaging Study, 8 Media Psychology 39, 51 (2006).

And "meta-analyses," *i.e.,* studies of all the studies, have concluded that exposure to violent video games "was positively associated with aggressive behavior, aggressive cognition, and aggressive affect," and that "playing violent video games is a *causal* risk factor for long-term harmful outcomes." Anderson et al., Violent Video Game Effects on Aggression, Empathy, and Prosocial Behavior in Eastern and Western Countries: A Meta-Analytic Review, 136 Psychological Bulletin 151, 167, 169 (2010) (emphasis added).

Some of these studies take care to explain in a common-sense way why video games are potentially more harmful than, say, films or books or television. In essence, they say that the closer a child's behavior comes, not to watching, but to *acting* out horrific violence, the greater the potential psychological harm. See Bushman & Huesmann, Aggression, in 2 Handbook of Social Pscyhology 833, 851 (S. Fiske, D. Gilbert, & G. Lindzey eds., 5th ed. 2010) (video games stimulate more aggression because "[p]eople learn better when they are actively involved," players are "more likely to identify with violent characters," and "violent games directly reward violent behavior"); Polman, de Castro, & van Aken, Experimental Study of the Differential Effects of Playing Versus Watching Violent Video Games on Children's Aggressive Behavior, 34 Aggressive Behavior 256 (2008) (finding greater aggression resulting from playing, as opposed to watching, a violent game); C. Anderson, D. Gentile, & K. Buckley, Violent Video Game Effects on Children and Adolescents 136–137 (2007) (three studies finding greater effects from games as opposed to television). See also *infra,* at 15–16 (statements of expert public health associations agreeing that interactive games can be more harmful than "passive" media like television); *ante,* at 12–17 (ALITO, J., concurring in judgment).

Experts debate the conclusions of all these studies. Like many, perhaps most, studies of human behavior, each study has its critics, and some of those critics have produced studies of their own in which they reach different conclusions. (I list both sets of research in the appendixes.) I, like most judges, lack the social science expertise to say definitively who is right. But associations of public health professionals who do possess that expertise have reviewed many of these studies and found a significant risk that violent video games, when compared with more passive media, are particularly likely to cause children harm.

Eleven years ago, for example, the American Academy of Pediatrics, the American Academy of Child & Adolescent Psychiatry, the American Psychological Association, the American Medical Association, the American Academy of Family Physicians, and the American Psychiatric Association released a joint statement, which said:

"[O]ver 1000 studies . . . point overwhelmingly to a causal connection between media violence and aggressive behavior in some children . . . [and, though less research had been done at that time, preliminary studies indicated that] the impact of violent interactive entertainment (video games and other interactive media) on young people . . . may be *significantly more severe* than that wrought by television, movies, or music." Joint Statement on the Impact of Entertainment Violence on Children (2000) (emphasis added). . . .

Five years later, after more research had been done, the American Psychological Association adopted a resolution that said:

"[C]omprehensive analysis of violent interactive video game research suggests such exposure . . . increases aggressive behavior, . . . increases aggressive thoughts, . . . increases angry feelings, . . . decreases helpful behavior, and . . . increases physiological arousal." Resolution on Violence in Video Games and Interactive Media (2005). . . .

The Association added:

"[T]he practice, repetition, and rewards for acts of violence may be *more conducive* to increasing aggressive behavior among children and youth than passively watching violence on TV and in films." *Ibid.* (emphasis added).

Four years after that, in 2009, the American Academy of Pediatrics issued a statement in significant part about interactive media. It said:

"Studies of these rapidly growing and ever-more-sophisticated types of media have indicated that the effects of child-initiated virtual violence may be *even more profound than those of passive media* such as television. In many games the child or teenager is 'embedded' in the game and uses a 'joystick' (handheld controller) that enhances both the experience and the aggressive feelings." Policy Statement—Media Violence, 124 Pediatrics 1495, 1498 (2009) (emphasis added).

It added:

"Correlational and experimental studies have revealed that violent video games lead to increases in aggressive behavior and aggressive thinking and decreases in prosocial behavior. Recent longitudinal studies . . . have revealed that in as little as 3 months, high exposure to violent video games increased physical aggression. Other recent

longitudinal studies . . . have revealed similar effects across 2 years." *Ibid.* (footnotes omitted).

Unlike the majority, I would find sufficient grounds in these studies and expert opinions for this Court to defer to an elected legislature's conclusion that the video games in question are particularly likely to harm children. This Court has always thought it owed an elected legislature some degree of deference in respect to legislative facts of this kind, particularly when they involve technical matters that are beyond our competence, and even in First Amendment cases. . . . The majority, in reaching its own, opposite conclusion about the validity of the relevant studies, grants the legislature no deference at all. . . .

C

I can find no "less restrictive" alternative to California's law that would be "at least as effective." . . . The majority points to a voluntary alternative: The industry tries to prevent those under 17 from buying extremely violent games by labeling those games with an "M" (Mature) and encouraging retailers to restrict their sales to those 17 and older. . . . But this voluntary system has serious enforcement gaps. When California enacted its law, a Federal Trade Commission (FTC) study had found that nearly 70% of unaccompanied 13- to 16-year-olds were able to buy M-rated video games. FTC, Marketing Violent Entertainment to Children 27 (2004). . . . Subsequently the voluntary program has become more effective. But as of the FTC's most recent update to Congress, 20% of those under 17 are still able to buy M-rated video games, and, breaking down sales by store, one finds that this number rises to nearly 50% in the case of one large national chain. FTC, Marketing Violent Entertainment to Children 28 (2009). . . . And the industry could easily revert back to the substantial noncompliance that existed in 2004, particularly after today's broad ruling reduces the industry's incentive to police itself.

The industry also argues for an alternative technological solution, namely "filtering at the console level." Brief for Respondents 53. But it takes only a quick search of the Internet to find guides explaining how to circumvent any such technological controls. YouTube viewers, for example, have watched one of those guides (called "How to bypass parental controls on the Xbox 360") more than 47,000 times. . . .

IV

The upshot is that California's statute, as applied to its heartland of applications (*i.e.,* buyers under 17; extremely violent, realistic video games), imposes a restriction on speech that is modest at most. That restriction is justified by a compelling interest (supplementing parents' efforts to prevent their children from purchasing potentially harmful violent, interactive material). And there is no equally effective, less restrictive alternative. California's statute is consequently constitutional on its face—though litigants remain free to challenge the statute as applied in particular instances, including any effort by the State to apply it to minors aged 17.

I add that the majority's different conclusion creates a serious anomaly in First Amendment law. *Ginsberg* makes clear that a State can prohibit the sale to minors of depictions of nudity; today the Court makes clear that a State cannot prohibit the sale to minors of the most violent interactive video games. But what sense does it make to forbid selling to a 13-year-old boy a magazine with an image of a nude woman, while protecting a sale to that 13-year-old of an interactive video game in which he actively, but virtually, binds and gags the woman, then tortures and kills her? What kind of First Amendment would permit the government to protect children by restricting sales of that extremely violent video game *only* when the woman—bound, gagged, tortured, and killed—is also topless?

This anomaly is not compelled by the First Amendment. It disappears once one recognizes that extreme violence, where interactive, and *without literary, artistic, or similar justification,* can prove at least as, if not more, harmful to children as photographs of nudity. And the record here is more than adequate to support such a view. That is why I believe that *Ginsberg* controls the outcome here *a fortiori*. And it is why I believe California's law is constitutional on its face.

This case is ultimately less about censorship than it is about education. Our Constitution cannot succeed in securing the liberties it seeks to protect unless we can raise future generations committed cooperatively to making our system of government work. Education, however, is about choices. Sometimes, children need to learn by making choices for themselves. Other times, choices are made for children—by their parents, by their teachers, and by the people acting democratically through their governments. In my view, the First Amendment does not disable government from helping parents make such a choice here—a choice not to have their children buy extremely violent, interactive video games, which they more than reasonably fear pose only the risk of harm to those children.

For these reasons, I respectfully dissent.

STEPHEN BREYER is an associate justice of the U.S. Supreme Court. He received an AB from Stanford University, a BA from Magdalen College, Oxford, and an LLB from Harvard Law School. He served as a law clerk to Justice Arthur Goldberg of the Supreme Court of the United States during the 1964 term. Prior to being appointed as a judge of the United States Court of Appeals for the First Circuit, he was a professor at Harvard Law School. From 1990 to 1994, he served as Chief Judge for the First Circuit Court of Appeals. President Clinton nominated him as an associate justice of the Supreme Court in 1994.

EXPLORING THE ISSUE

Are Violent Video Games Protected by the First Amendment?

Critical Thinking and Reflection

1. Explain the free speech guarantee in the First Amendment. What kinds of expressions are exceptions and what does that mean?
2. Describe how Justice Scalia saw the Court's findings in the *Stevens* case concerning not adding new categories of unprotected speech related to this case.
3. Define the term "compelling interest" and explain how this concept is used in the arguments for and against restricting the availability of violent video games for minors.
4. How does Justice Breyer explain his view that the CA law "imposes no more than a modest restriction" on free expression? Explain how the law does or does not prevent people from playing violent video games.
5. Contrast the opposing views of each justice about the scientific research related to the effects on children of playing violent video games. What is a causal relationship, and how does that figure in the argument?

Is There Common Ground?

In a concurring opinion, Justice Alito wrote

> In considering the application of unchanging constitutional principles to new and rapidly evolving technology, this Court should proceed with caution. We should make every effort to understand the new technology. We should take into account the possibility that developing technology may have important societal implications that will become apparent only with time. We should not jump to the conclusion that new technology is fundamentally the same as some older thing with which we are familiar. And we should not hastily dismiss the judgment of legislators, who may be in a better position than we are to assess the implications of new technology. The opinion of the Court exhibits none of this caution.

A recent *New York Times* story began by recounting, "The young men who opened fire at Columbine High School, at the movie theater in Aurora, Colo., and in other massacres had this in common: they were video gamers who seemed to be acting out some dark digital fantasy. It was as if all that exposure to computerized violence gave them the idea to go on a rampage—or at least fueled their urges." At the same time, gun violence is relatively low in countries such as South Korea and the Netherlands where the per capita spending on video games is high. One leading researcher, Dr. Craig A. Anderson of Iowa State University,

concluded that "none of these extreme acts, like a school shooting, occurs because of only one risk factor; there are many factors, including feeling socially isolated, being bullied, and so on. But if you look at the literature, I think it's clear that violent media is one factor; it's not the largest factor, but it's also not the smallest." Anderson concludes that "at the very least, parents should be aware of what's in the games their kids are playing, and think of it from a socialization point of view: what kind of values, behavioral skills, and social scripts is the child learning?"

Additional Resources

Craig A. Anderson, Douglas A. Gentile, and Katherine E. Buckley. *Violent Video Game Effects on Children and Adolescents: Theory, Research, and Public Policy* (Oxford University Press, 2007).

Amitai Etzioni, "Do Children Have the Same First Amendment Rights as Adults?" 79 *Chicago-Kent Law Review* 3 (2004).

Lawrence Kutner and Cheryl Olson. *Grand Theft Childhood: The Surprising Truth About Violent Video Games and What Parents Can Do* (Simon & Schuster, 2008).

Rodney A. Smolla, "The Paladin Case and the Limits of Protection for Violent Speech." Available at: www.freedomforum.org/publications/first/violenceandmedia/violenceandthemedia.pdf

Internet References . . .

Huffington Post's "10 Most Violent Video Games (and 10+ Alternatives)"

www.huffingtonpost.com/common-sense-media/10
-most-violent-video-games_b_3480497.html

Erik Kain, "The Truth About Video Games and Gun Violence: Do Brutal Games Lead to Mass Shootings? What Do Three Decades of Research Really Tell Us?"

www.motherjones.com/politics/2013/06/video-games
-violence-guns-explainer

Benedict Carey, "Shooting in the Dark," *New York Times* (February 11, 2013)

www.nytimes.com/2013/02/12/science/studying-the
-effects-of-playing-violent-video-games.html?_r=0

Selected, Edited, and with Issue Framing Material by:
M. Ethan Katsh, *University of Massachusetts, Amherst*

ISSUE

Can States Ban Physician Aid-in-Dying for Terminally Ill Patients?

YES: William H. Rehnquist, from "Majority Opinion, *Washington v. Glucksberg*," United States Supreme Court (1997)

NO: Stephen Reinhardt, from "Majority Opinion, *Compassion in Dying v. State of Washington*," United States Supreme Court (1996)

Learning Outcomes

After reading this issue, you will be able to:

- Appreciate the intensely private and emotionally complex nature of end-of-life decision making by patients, their families, and physicians, and analyze the relationship of such decisions to individual liberties protected by the Constitution.
- Discuss and evaluate several legitimate state interests that might be advanced by legislation that seeks to structure end-of-life decision making, including physician aid-in-dying, and discuss the difficulties inherent in using law to regulate such decision making.
- Consider medical, ethical, and legal implications of various ways in which physicians might assist patients who refuse life-sustaining medical care or who choose palliative care that reduces suffering or that may hasten an imminent death.
- Distinguish between the end-of-life decisions made by a terminally ill patient who is legally capable of making treatment decisions, and decisions made by healthcare proxies or surrogates for a terminally ill patient who is not competent to make such decisions.
- Discuss with friends and family your own views about end-of-life care, and participate in public policy discussions about whether and how state legislation should seek to structure, support, or ban various options for end-of-life care.

ISSUE SUMMARY

YES: Former Supreme Court Chief Justice William H. Rehnquist, writing one of six opinions of a unanimous Court in *Washington v. Glucksberg*, rules that although patients have the right to refuse life-sustaining medical treatment, "physician-assisted suicide" is not constitutionally protected, and states may ban that practice.

NO: Judge Stephen Reinhardt, writing the majority opinion for the Ninth Circuit case that became *Washington v. Glucksberg* when it reached the U.S. Supreme Court, argues that criminalizing physician assistance in hastening the death of competent, terminally ill patients who request life-ending prescriptions violates the Due Process Clause of the Constitution.

Extraordinary increases in the quality of medical care and advances in medical technology have increased life expectancy and quality of life for millions of people. But sometimes medical science seems to advance at a far greater pace than our moral, ethical, and policy concepts about how to respond to the new challenges presented by the medical care that is available to us. The problem of end-of-life care decision making is among the most difficult of these medical/moral challenges. Terminally ill individuals, for whom a host of life-extending treatment options may compete with palliative or comfort care options, or even with the desire to end intractable pain, suffering, and indignity by hastening an approaching death, may regard these decisions as intensely personal expressions of individual liberty. They reflect an individual's beliefs about the human condition, the meaning of life and of personhood in a complex society, about family and spirituality, and about the mystery of death.

For a society already uncertain and divided on ethical, spiritual, and policy issues of many kinds, however, these same end-of-life care decisions may seem to be not intensely personal expressions of individual freedom, but basic moral questions upon which law should pronounce civilized standards applicable to all. In this mix of individual liberties and moral imperatives in healthcare, physician aid-in-dying is perhaps the most difficult and most important challenge to resolve. Consider the personal tragedy that struck the Cruzan family in 1983, and that became a political battle, a media circus, and a *cause celebre* in the culture wars before a 1990 decision in the U.S. Supreme Court sought to put to rest a young woman who seemed to have died seven years earlier.

In the 1990 case, the Supreme Court issued a 5–4 landmark ruling concerning the right to refuse or withdraw medical treatment in *Cruzan v. Director, Missouri Department of Health,* 497 U.S. 261 (1990). Seven years earlier, 26-year-old Nancy Beth Cruzan had sustained severe and irreversible injuries in a one-car automobile accident, and her brain had been deprived of oxygen for 12–14 minutes before emergency medical personnel arrived and were able to restore her pulse and respiration. After several weeks of being in a coma, and after numerous tests and attempts by physicians to improve her condition—during which time an artificial feeding and hydration tube had been surgically inserted in her stomach with the consent of her father—her condition was not improved. After many more months, Nancy Cruzan was diagnosed as being in a "persistent vegetative state." She had, in other words, no discernible cognitive or higher brain functioning, no awareness, and did not react to any stimuli; her injuries and anorexia had been so severe that she was incapable of regaining any of these functions. But though completely unresponsive, she seemed to be "awake" and could breathe on her own; her heart was strong. Her doctors believed that although she would never regain consciousness or be able to take care of her own bodily needs, or have any cognitive functioning, she could be kept "alive" for 20–30 years through skilled nursing care and the use of the artificial hydration and feeding equipment.

In 1987, four years after the accident, Nancy's parents requested that the feeding and hydration tube be removed and that Nancy be allowed to die. Nancy Cruzan had left no living will and had appointed no health care proxy prior to her accident. The Missouri public hospital in which Nancy was located—and which supplied all her medical care at public expense—refused to honor the family's request without a court order. The Cruzan's then began proceedings in a Missouri state trial court so that they could provide evidence that, although she had left no explicit directions about end-of-life care, Nancy was the kind of person who would not have wanted to live in a persistent vegetative state and had indicated such intentions in a general conversation with a friend a year or so before the accident.

The Missouri trial court ruled that there was sufficient evidence to justify removing the feeding tube as the parents had requested. However, the State of Missouri intervened, claiming an "unqualified governmental interest in preserving the sanctity of human life." In an appeal to the Missouri Supreme Court, the State argued that in the absence of a living will, "clear and convincing evidence" of the wishes of a patient who could not decide for or express herself was required to authorize the removal of life-sustaining devices. (Ironically, Missouri's living will statute did not allow a person to use a living will to require the withdrawal of feeding and hydration equipment.) Agreeing with the Missouri Attorney General that this higher standard of proof was appropriate, the Missouri Supreme Court reversed the trial court order. The family then appealed the Missouri Supreme Court's ruling to the U.S. Supreme Court. Did Nancy Cruzan have a right to refuse life-sustaining medical treatment, and if so, did her family have a sufficient basis for exercising that right on her behalf once she was no longer able to articulate that decision for herself? Did the State of Missouri have a legitimate interest in preventing the removal of the artificial feeding and hydration tube, and if so, what was the nature of state's interest in resisting the family's request?

In its decision in *Cruzan,* the U.S. Supreme Court assumed that there exists a constitutionally protected liberty interest in refusing unwanted medical treatment, even if that meant hastening one's death. But the question remained as to how much evidence of the patient's intentions prior to becoming unconscious was required to justify honoring this liberty interest in the face of the state's claim to be upholding the sanctity of human life. The five Justices of the majority ruled that Missouri's legitimate state interest in preserving life justified its more stringent evidentiary requirement. Requiring clear and convincing evidence of an unconscious patient's previous desire to refuse life-sustaining treatment did not, in other words, violate what the majority characterized as an individual's constitutionally protected "right to die."

Although Nancy Cruzan was not terminally ill in the ordinary sense of the term, by examining the parameters of a constitutional right to refuse even life-saving medical treatment, the *Cruzan* case sets the stage for the later cases like *Glucksberg* that consider what kind of assistance, if any, a physician may provide to a terminally ill patient who wants to hasten an end to the intractable pain and suffering of an approaching death. In *Cruzan*, Justice Rehnquist's majority opinion concedes that the Court's prior decisions grant a competent person a "constitutionally protected liberty interest" in refusing unwanted medical treatment, including lifesaving nutrition and hydration. But the nature and importance of this right of personal autonomy were not fully explored until Justice Brennan took up the issue in his dissent. In rejecting the majority's decision that Missouri could restrict the right to refuse medical treatment more than it would have been allowed to restrict other constitutional liberties, Brennan classified the right to refuse medical treatment as "fundamental" and "deeply rooted in this Nation's traditions." Brennan went still further in acknowledging the importance of being free to use one's own values to evaluate the benefits and consequences of medical treatment, writing that "Dying is personal. And it is profound," and that for some people "the burden of maintaining the corporeal existence degrades the very humanity it was meant to serve."

Clearly it is not only one's concept of the personal freedom at stake that influences judgments about the "right to die," but one's concept of dying and of death itself. Justice Stevens made this explicit in his dissenting opinion in *Cruzan*, and in doing so raised yet another constitutional dimension—that of religious freedom—imbedded in the question of how far states may restrict the liberty of individuals in end-of-life decision making. Stevens wrote, "Not much may be said with confidence about death unless it is said from faith, and that alone is reason enough to protect the freedom to conform choices about death to individual conscience." It may be that religious concepts of death and of individual autonomy also lie at the core of the issues raised in challenges to state bans of physician aid-in-dying.

The State of Missouri had formidable interests it sought to protect by intervening in the intensely personal and constitutionally important decisions with which the Cruzan family was confronted as a result of Nancy Cruzan's tragic accident. The process followed by the Court, as in most cases pitting individual liberty against state interests, required balancing the importance of the asserted right

against the state interests claimed by Missouri. Those state interests were distilled by the Court as including "the preservation of life, the protection of the interests of innocent third parties, the prevention of suicide, and the maintenance of the ethical integrity of the medical profession." Of these, the Court leaned most heavily on the state's profound interest in the preservation of human life, making the *Cruzan* case similar in some ways to abortion cases in which states may try to define life as a means of advancing the state interest in protecting it. Indeed it might be argued that Missouri's intervention in the *Cruzan* case was as much about advancing the constitutional status of the right-to-life principle as it was in whether Nancy Cruzan was allowed to refuse the medical treatment that was keeping her artificially alive.

The majority's reasoning in *Cruzan* also relied on the claim that the higher standard of evidence that Missouri sought to require would assure that a decision to remove the feeding tube and allow Nancy to die accurately reflected her wishes. Thus, the State not only declined to make judgments about the quality of Nancy's—or anyone's—life, it also sought to impose a greater burden on the Cruzan family as it sought to articulate the decision they believed their daughter would have made if she had been able to do so. The majority thus argued that the consequences of an erroneous decision that Nancy would have wanted the feeding tube removed would be her irreversible death, and therefore a more severe mistake than if an erroneous decision to continue artificial feeding and hydration were made.

The problem of assessing the nature and importance of individual autonomy at the end of life can be put in bold relief by asking the following question: What would have been lost by simply keeping Nancy Cruzan "alive" for the 20–30 years that her doctors thought she might live with the artificial feeding and hydration being provided? By all accounts Nancy could feel no pain and was aware of no suffering. Missouri was paying $100,000 per year toward her care cost in a public hospital. And perhaps there would be a medical advance or a miracle that would restore her awareness and cognitive functioning to some degree. The answer lies in part in one's assessment of the importance of individual autonomy and freedom of decision in matters that touch so deeply the nature of being human, the mysteries of life and death, and the value of liberty under the Constitution. As Justice Brennan put it in his dissenting opinion, a person might choose to forgo further medical treatment rather than "visiting a prolonged and anguished vigil on one's parents, spouse, and children. A long, drawn-out death can have a debilitating effect on family members. . . . For some, the idea of being remembered in their persistent vegetative states rather than as they were before their illness or accident may be very disturbing." These and similar questions about the constitutional importance of individual autonomy are raised by considering the limits that states may place upon a terminally ill individual's relationship to his or her physicians, upon the types of care that such physicians may legally provide, and upon the constitutionally protected liberty and dignity of dying individuals.

The State of Missouri also relied upon its claimed interest in preventing suicide. Nowhere was this concept more clearly stated in *Cruzan* than in Justice Scalia's concurring opinion. He argued that ". . . American law has always accorded the State the power to prevent, by force if necessary, suicide—including suicide by refusing to take appropriate measures necessary to preserve one's life. . . ." By describing the right to refuse life-sustaining medical treatment as a claim to a " right to suicide," Justice Scalia not only sought to transform the debate in *Cruzan*, but to cast all consideration of the "right to die" in terms that many terminally ill patients and their families and physicians might consider not only disrespectful and inaccurate, but incendiary. In reading the cases concerning state bans on the kinds of care that physicians may provide to their terminally ill patients, it is important to evaluate carefully the differences as well as the similarities between "physician aid-in-dying" and "physician-assisted suicide."

Shortly after the Supreme Court's 5–4 decision in *Cruzan*, the family returned to the trial court for a rehearing on their request to have the feeding tube removed from Nancy's abdomen. The judge in the case heard some new evidence but also much of the same evidence as had been presented in the initial hearing. Applying the "clear and convincing evidence" standard that the Missouri Court had ordered and the U.S. Supreme Court affirmed, the trial court again ordered that the feeding tube be removed. About 10 days later in accordance with what the court found to be her wishes, Nancy Cruzan died. It had been almost eight years—and four major court hearings—since

her automobile accident had left her in a persistent vegetative state.

Other than the removal of the feeding and hydration tube, Nancy Cruzan had not required any physician's aid or medical treatment beyond a hospital room and nursing attention to her medical condition in case of unforeseen developments. But many people who refuse life-preserving medical treatment, or choose to have it withdrawn, do require and receive palliative care—medical assistance in dying. Physicians may provide something as simple as sedatives to reduce agitation; or it may be necessary to institute complex regimes of pain management and other treatments designed to alleviate the suffering that often comes with dying. Some of these treatments, for example, active management of intractable pain, may themselves hasten death as a secondary effect of pain reduction. Few if any legal questions are raised about the provision of these forms of physician aid-in-dying.

The issues raised in the *Cruzan* case illustrate that the law has generally recognized the right of competent adults to refuse medical treatment and has viewed the act of forcing treatment on an unconsenting person as violating his or her liberty rights as guaranteed by the Constitution. The assistance of physicians in withdrawing unwanted medical treatment and in helping dying patients to finish the dying process with as little suffering as possible has been found to violate no law. In fact, palliative care is a growing field of medicine because it responds to the needs of so many terminally ill people. Patients have a legal right to reject life-saving treatment, knowing that the decision will hasten death, but that their doctors may be able to help reduce the suffering that accompanies that death. Shouldn't competent, terminally ill individuals also have a right to a doctor's aid in ameliorating their suffering by hastening an imminent death through the use of self-administered prescription drugs? Cruzan introduces many of the legal and policy issues that underlie this controversial moral and legal issue, and a U.S. Court of Appeals and the Supreme Court of the United States consider the issue in greater depth.

YES ↵   **William H. Rehnquist**

Majority Opinion, *Washington v. Glucksberg*

CHIEF JUSTICE REHNQUIST delivered the opinion of the Court.

The question presented in this case is whether Washington's prohibition against "causing" or "aiding" a suicide offends the Fourteenth Amendment to the United States Constitution. We hold that it does not.

It has always been a crime to assist a suicide in the State of Washington. In 1854, Washington's first Territorial Legislature outlawed "assisting another in the commission of self-murder." Today, Washington law provides: "A person is guilty of promoting a suicide attempt when he knowingly causes or aids another person to attempt suicide." Wash. Rev. Code 9A.36.060(1)(1994). "Promoting a suicide attempt" is a felony, punishable by up to five years' imprisonment and up to a $10,000 fine. §§ 9A.36.060(2) and 9A.20.021(1)(c). At the same time, Washington's Natural Death Act, enacted in 1979, states that the "withholding or withdrawal of life-sustaining treatment" at a patient's direction "shall not, for any purpose, constitute a suicide." Wash. Rev. Code § 70.122.070(1).[1]

Petitioners in this case are the State of Washington and its Attorney General. Respondents Harold Glucksberg, M.D., Abigail Halperin, M.D., Thomas A. Preston, M.D., and Peter Shalit, M.D., are physicians who practice in Washington. These doctors occasionally treat terminally ill, suffering patients, and declare that they would assist these patients in ending their lives if not for Washington's assisted-suicide ban. In January 1994, respondents, along with three gravely ill, pseudonymous plaintiffs who have since died and Compassion in Dying, a nonprofit organization that counsels people considering physician-assisted suicide, sued in the United States District Court, seeking a declaration that Wash. Rev. Code 9A.36.060(1) (1994) is, on its face, unconstitutional. *Compassion in Dying v. Washington, 850 F. Supp. 1454, 1459 (WD Wash. 1994).*

The plaintiffs asserted "the existence of a liberty interest protected by the Fourteenth Amendment which extends to a personal choice by a mentally competent, terminally ill adult to commit physician-assisted suicide." Relying primarily on *Planned Parenthood v. Casey, 505 U.S. 833 (1992),* and *Cruzan v. Director, Missouri Dept. of Health, 497 U.S. 261 (1990),* the District Court agreed, *850 F. Supp., at 1459–1462,* and concluded that Washington's assisted-suicide ban is unconstitutional because it "places an undue burden on the exercise of [that] constitutionally protected liberty interest." The District Court also decided that the Washington statute violated the Equal Protection Clause's requirement that "'all persons similarly situated . . . be treated alike.'"

A panel of the Court of Appeals for the Ninth Circuit reversed, emphasizing that "in the two hundred and five years of our existence no constitutional right to aid in killing oneself has ever been asserted and upheld by a court of final jurisdiction." *Compassion in Dying v. Washington, 49 F.3d 586, 591 (1995).* The Ninth Circuit reheard the case en banc, reversed the panel's decision, and affirmed the District Court. *Compassion in Dying v. Washington, 79 F.3d 790, 798 (1996).* Like the District Court, the en banc Court of Appeals emphasized our *Casey* and *Cruzan* decisions. The court also discussed what it described as "historical" and "current societal attitudes" toward suicide and assisted suicide, and concluded that "the Constitution encompasses a due process liberty interest in controlling the time and manner of one's death—that there is, in short, a constitutionally-recognized 'right to die.'" After "weighing and then balancing" this interest against Washington's various interests, the court held that the State's assisted-suicide ban was unconstitutional "as applied to terminally ill competent adults who wish to hasten their deaths with medication prescribed by their physicians." The court did not reach the District Court's equal-protection holding. We granted certiorari, and now reverse.

I

We begin, as we do in all due-process cases, by examining our Nation's history, legal traditions, and practices. In almost every State—indeed, in almost every western democracy—it is a crime to assist a suicide. The States' assisted-suicide bans are not innovations. Rather, they are longstanding expressions of the States' commitment to the protection and preservation of all human life.

More specifically, for over 700 years, the Anglo-American common-law tradition has punished or otherwise disapproved of both suicide and assisting suicide. In the 13th century, Henry de Bracton, one of the first legal-treatise writers, observed that "just as a man may commit felony by slaying another so may he do so by slaying himself." Bracton on Laws and Customs of England 423 (f. 150) (G. Woodbine ed., S. Thorne transl., 1968). The real and personal property of one who killed himself to avoid conviction and punishment for a crime were forfeit to the king; however, thought Bracton, "if a man slays himself in weariness of life or because he is unwilling to endure further bodily pain . . . [only] his movable goods [were] confiscated." Thus, "the principle that suicide of a sane person, for whatever reason, was a punishable felony was . . . introduced into English common law."

For the most part, the early American colonies adopted the common-law approach. For example, the legislators of the Providence Plantations, which would later become Rhode Island, declared, in 1647, that "self-murder is by all agreed to be the most unnatural, and it is by this present Assembly declared, to be that, wherein he that doth it, kills himself out of a premeditated hatred against his own life or other humor: . . . his goods and chattels are the king's custom, but not his debts nor lands; but in case he be an infant, a lunatic, mad or distracted man, he forfeits nothing." The Earliest Acts and Laws of the Colony of Rhode Island and Providence Plantations 1647–1719, p. 19 (J. Cushing ed. 1977). Virginia also required ignominious burial for suicides, and their estates were forfeit to the crown. A. Scott, Criminal Law in Colonial Virginia 108, and n. 93, 198, and n. 15 (1930).

Over time, however, the American colonies abolished these harsh common-law penalties. William Penn abandoned the criminal-forfeiture sanction in Pennsylvania in 1701, and the other colonies (and later, the other States) eventually followed this example. *Cruzan, 497 U.S. at 294* (SCALIA, J., concurring). . . .

[T]he movement away from the common law's harsh sanctions did not represent an acceptance of suicide; rather, as Chief Justice Swift observed, this change reflected the growing consensus that it was unfair to punish the suicide's family for his wrongdoing. Nonetheless, although States moved away from Blackstone's treatment of suicide, courts continued to condemn it as a grave public wrong.

That suicide remained a grievous, though nonfelonious, wrong is confirmed by the fact that colonial and early state legislatures and courts did not retreat from prohibiting assisting suicide. Swift, in his early 19th century treatise on the laws of Connecticut, stated that "if one counsels another to commit suicide, and the other by reason of the advice kills himself, the advisor is guilty of murder as principal." Z. Swift, *A Digest of the Laws of the State of Connecticut* 270 (1823). This was the well established common-law view.

And the prohibitions against assisting suicide never contained exceptions for those who were near death. Rather, "the life of those to whom life had become a burden—of those who [were] hopelessly diseased or fatally wounded—nay, even the lives of criminals condemned to death, [were] under the protection of law, equally as the lives of those who [were] in the full tide of life's enjoyment, and anxious to continue to live." *Blackburn v. State, 23 Ohio St. 146, 163 (1872).*

The earliest American statute explicitly to outlaw assisting suicide was enacted in New York in 1828, and many of the new States and Territories followed New York's example. Between 1857 and 1865, a New York commission led by Dudley Field drafted a criminal code that prohibited "aiding" a suicide and, specifically, "furnishing another person with any deadly weapon or poisonous drug, knowing that such person intends to use such weapon or drug in taking his own life." By the time the Fourteenth Amendment was ratified, it was a crime in most States to assist a suicide. The Field Penal Code was adopted in the Dakota Territory in 1877, in New York in 1881, and its language served as a model for several other western States' statutes in the late 19th and early 20th centuries. California, for example, codified its assisted-suicide prohibition in 1874, using language similar to the Field Code's. In this century, the Model Penal Code also prohibited "aiding" suicide, prompting many States to enact or revise their assisted-suicide bans. . . .

Though deeply rooted, the States' assisted-suicide bans have in recent years been reexamined and, generally, reaffirmed. Because of advances in medicine and technology, Americans today are increasingly likely to die in institutions, from chronic illnesses. Public concern and democratic action are therefore sharply focused on how best to protect dignity and independence at the end of life, with the result that there have been many significant changes in state laws and in the attitudes these laws reflect. Many States, for example, now permit "living wills," surrogate health-care decisionmaking, and the withdrawal or refusal of life-sustaining medical treatment. At the same time, however, voters and legislators continue for the most part to reaffirm their States' prohibitions on assisting suicide.

The Washington statute at issue in this case, Wash. Rev. Code § 9A.36.060 (1994), was enacted in 1975 as part of a revision of that State's criminal code. Four years later, Washington passed its Natural Death Act, which specifically stated that the "withholding or withdrawal of life-sustaining treatment . . . shall not, for any purpose, constitute a suicide" and that "nothing in this chapter shall be construed to condone, authorize, or approve mercy killing. . . ." In 1991, Washington voters rejected a ballot initiative which, had it passed, would have permitted a form of physician-assisted suicide. Washington then added a provision to the Natural Death Act expressly excluding physician-assisted suicide.

California voters rejected an assisted-suicide initiative similar to Washington's in 1993. On the other hand, in 1994, voters in Oregon enacted, also through ballot initiative, that State's "Death With Dignity Act," which legalized physician-assisted suicide for competent, terminally ill adults. Since the Oregon vote, many proposals to legalize assisted suicide have been and continue to be introduced in the States' legislatures, but none has been enacted. And just last year, Iowa and Rhode Island joined the overwhelming majority of States explicitly prohibiting assisted suicide. See Iowa Code Ann. §§ 707A.2, 707A.3 (Supp. 1997); R. I. Gen. Laws §§ 11-60-1, 11-60-3 (Supp. 1996). Also, on April 30, 1997, President Clinton signed the Federal Assisted Suicide Funding Restriction Act of 1997, which prohibits the use of federal funds in support of physician-assisted suicide. . . .

Attitudes toward suicide itself have changed since Bracton, but our laws have consistently condemned, and continue to prohibit, assisting suicide. Despite changes in medical technology and notwithstanding an increased emphasis on the importance of end-of-life decisionmaking, we have not retreated from this prohibition. Against this backdrop of history, tradition, and practice, we now turn to respondents' constitutional claim.

II

. . . In a long line of cases, we have held that, in addition to the specific freedoms protected by the Bill of Rights, the "liberty" specially protected by the Due Process Clause includes the rights to marry, *Loving v. Virginia, 388 U.S. 1 (1967)*; to have children, *Skinner v. Oklahoma ex rel. Williamson, 316 U.S. 535 (1942)*; to direct the education and upbringing of one's children, *Meyer v. Nebraska, 262 U.S. 390 (1923); Pierce v. Society of Sisters, 268 U.S. 510 (1925)*; to marital privacy, *Griswold v. Connecticut, 381 U.S. 479 (1965)*; to use contraception, ibid; *Eisenstadt v. Baird, 405 U.S. 438 (1972)*; to bodily integrity, *Rochin v. California, 342 U.S. 165 (1952)*, and to abortion, Casey, supra. We have also assumed, and strongly suggested, that the Due Process Clause protects the traditional right to refuse unwanted lifesaving medical treatment. *Cruzan, 497 U.S. at 278–279.*

But we "have always been reluctant to expand the concept of substantive due process because guideposts for responsible decisionmaking in this unchartered area are scarce and open-ended." *Collins, 503 U.S. at 125.* By extending constitutional protection to an asserted right or liberty interest, we, to a great extent, place the matter outside the arena of public debate and legislative action. We must therefore "exercise the utmost care whenever we are asked to break new ground in this field," ibid, lest the liberty protected by the Due Process Clause be subtly transformed into the policy preferences of the members of this Court, *Moore, 431 U.S. at 502* (plurality opinion).

Our established method of substantive-due-process analysis has two primary features: First, we have regularly observed that the Due Process Clause specially protects those fundamental rights and liberties which are, objectively, "deeply rooted in this Nation's history and tradition," *id.,* at 503 (plurality opinion); *Snyder v. Massachusetts, 291 U.S. 97, 105 (1934)* ("so rooted in the traditions and conscience of our people as to be ranked as fundamental"), and "implicit in the concept of ordered liberty," such that "neither liberty nor justice would exist if they were sacrificed," *Palko v. Connecticut, 302 U.S. 319, 325, 326 (1937).* Second, we have required in substantive-due-process cases a "careful description" of the asserted fundamental liberty interest. Our Nation's history, legal traditions, and practices thus provide the crucial "guideposts for responsible decisionmaking," that direct and restrain our exposition of the Due Process Clause. As we stated recently in Flores, the Fourteenth Amendment "forbids the government to infringe . . . 'fundamental' liberty interests at all, no matter what process is provided, unless the infringement is narrowly tailored to serve a compelling state interest." *507 U.S. at 302.*

JUSTICE SOUTER, relying on Justice Harlan's dissenting opinion in Poe v. Ullman, would largely abandon this restrained methodology, and instead ask "whether [Washington's] statute sets up one of those 'arbitrary impositions' or 'purposeless restraints' at odds with the Due Process Clause of the Fourteenth Amendment," post, at 1 (quoting *Poe, 367 U.S. 497, 543 (1961)* (Harlan, J., dissenting)). In our view, however, the development of this Court's substantive-due-process jurisprudence, described briefly above, has been a process whereby the outlines of the "liberty" specially protected by the Fourteenth Amendment— never fully clarified, to be sure, and perhaps not capable of being fully clarified— have at least been carefully refined by concrete examples involving fundamental rights found to be deeply rooted in our legal tradition. This approach tends to rein in the subjective elements that are necessarily present in due-process judicial review. In addition, by establishing a threshold requirement—that a challenged state action implicate a fundamental right—before requiring more than a reasonable relation to a legitimate state interest to justify the action, it avoids the need for complex balancing of competing interests in every case.

Turning to the claim at issue here, the Court of Appeals stated that "properly analyzed, the first issue to be resolved is whether there is a liberty interest in determining the time and manner of one's death," or, in other words, "is there a right to die?" Similarly, respondents assert a "liberty to choose how to die" and a right to "control of one's final days," and describe the asserted liberty as "the right to choose a humane, dignified death," and "the liberty to shape death." As noted above, we have a tradition of carefully formulating the interest at stake in substantive-due-process cases. For example, although *Cruzan* is often described as a "right to die" case, see *79 F.3d, at 799;* post, at 9 (STEVENS, J., concurring in judgment) (*Cruzan* recognized "the more specific interest in making decisions about how to confront an imminent death"), we were, in fact, more precise: we assumed that the Constitution granted competent persons a "constitutionally protected right to refuse lifesaving hydration and nutrition." *Cruzan, 497 U.S. at 279; id., at 287* (O'CONNOR, J., concurring) ("[A] liberty interest in refusing unwanted medical treatment may be inferred from our prior decisions"). The Washington statute at issue in this case prohibits "aiding another person to attempt suicide," Wash. Rev. Code § 9A.36.060(1) (1994), and, thus, the question before us is whether the "liberty" specially protected by the Due Process Clause includes a right to commit suicide which itself includes a right to assistance in doing so.

We now inquire whether this asserted right has any place in our Nation's traditions. Here, as discussed above, we are confronted with a consistent and almost universal tradition that has long rejected the asserted right, and continues explicitly to reject it today, even for terminally ill, mentally competent adults. To hold for respondents, we would have to reverse centuries of legal doctrine and practice, and strike down the considered policy choice of almost every State.

Respondents contend, however, that the liberty interest they assert is consistent with this Court's substantive-due-process line of cases, if not with this Nation's history and practice. Pointing to *Casey* and *Cruzan,* respondents read our jurisprudence in this area as reflecting a general tradition of "self-sovereignty," and as teaching that the "liberty" protected by the Due Process Clause includes "basic and intimate exercises of personal autonomy" ("It is a promise of the Constitution that there is a realm of personal liberty which the government may not enter").

According to respondents, our liberty jurisprudence, and the broad, individualistic principles it reflects, protects the "liberty of competent, terminally ill adults to make end-of-life decisions free of undue government interference." Brief for Respondents 10. The question presented in this case, however, is whether the protections of the Due Process Clause include a right to commit suicide with another's assistance. With this "careful description" of respondents' claim in mind, we turn to *Casey* and *Cruzan.*

In *Cruzan,* we considered whether Nancy Beth Cruzan, who had been severely injured in an automobile accident and was in a persistive vegetative state, "had a right under the United States Constitution which would require the hospital to withdraw life-sustaining treatment" at her parents' request. We began with the observation that "at common law, even the touching of one person by another without consent and without legal justification was a battery." We then discussed the related rule that "informed consent is generally required for medical treatment." After reviewing a long line of relevant state cases, we concluded that "the common-law doctrine of informed consent is viewed as generally encompassing the right of a competent individual to refuse medical treatment." Next, we reviewed our own cases on the subject, and stated that "the principle that a competent person has a constitutionally protected liberty interest in refusing unwanted medical treatment may be inferred from our prior decisions." Therefore, "for purposes of [that] case, we assumed that the United States Constitution would grant a competent person a constitutionally protected right to refuse lifesaving hydration and nutrition." We concluded that, notwithstanding this right, the Constitution permitted Missouri to require clear and convincing evidence of an incompetent patient's wishes concerning the withdrawal of life-sustaining treatment.

Respondents contend that in *Cruzan* we "acknowledged that competent, dying persons have the right to direct the removal of life-sustaining medical treatment and thus hasten death," Brief for Respondents 23, and that "the constitutional principle behind recognizing the patient's liberty to direct the withdrawal of artificial life support applies at least as strongly to the choice to hasten impending death by consuming lethal medication." Similarly, the Court of Appeals concluded that "*Cruzan,* by recognizing a liberty interest that includes the refusal of artificial provision of life-sustaining food and water, necessarily recognized a liberty interest in hastening one's own death." *79 F.3d, at 816.*

The right assumed in *Cruzan,* however, was not simply deduced from abstract concepts of personal autonomy. Given the common-law rule that forced medication was a battery, and the long legal tradition protecting the decision to refuse unwanted medical treatment, our assumption was entirely consistent with this Nation's history and constitutional traditions. The decision to commit suicide with the assistance of another may be just as personal and profound as the decision to refuse unwanted medical treatment, but it has never enjoyed similar legal protection. Indeed, the two acts are widely and reasonably regarded as quite distinct. In *Cruzan* itself, we recognized that most States outlawed assisted suicide—and even more do today—and we certainly gave no intimation that the right to refuse unwanted medical treatment could be somehow transmuted into a right to assistance in committing suicide.

Respondents also rely on *Casey*. There, the Court's opinion concluded that "the essential holding of Roe v. Wade should be retained and once again reaffirmed." *Casey, 505 U.S. at 846.* We held, first, that a woman has a right, before her fetus is viable, to an abortion "without undue interference from the State"; second, that States may restrict post-viability abortions, so long as exceptions are made to protect a woman's life and health; and third, that the State has legitimate interests throughout a pregnancy in protecting the health of the woman and the life of the unborn child. Ibid. In reaching this conclusion, the opinion discussed in some detail this Court's substantive-due-process tradition of interpreting the Due Process Clause to protect certain fundamental rights and "personal decisions relating to marriage, procreation, contraception, family relationships, child rearing, and education," and noted that many of those rights and liberties "involve the most intimate and personal choices a person may make in a lifetime."

The Court of Appeals, like the District Court, found *Casey* "'highly instructive'" and "'almost prescriptive'" for determining "'what liberty interest may inhere in a terminally ill person's choice to commit suicide'":

> "Like the decision of whether or not to have an abortion, the decision how and when to die is one of 'the most intimate and personal choices a person may make in a lifetime,' a choice 'central to personal dignity and autonomy.'" *79 F.3d, at 813–814.*

Similarly, respondents emphasize the statement in *Casey* that:

> "At the heart of liberty is the right to define one's own concept of existence, of meaning, of the universe, and of the mystery of human life. Beliefs about these matters could not define the attributes of personhood were they formed under compulsion of the State." *Casey, 505 U.S. at 851.*

. . . By choosing this language, the Court's opinion in *Casey* described, in a general way and in light of our prior cases, those personal activities and decisions that this Court has identified as so deeply rooted in our history and traditions, or so fundamental to our concept of constitutionally ordered liberty, that they are protected by the Fourteenth Amendment. The opinion moved from the recognition that liberty necessarily includes freedom of conscience and belief about ultimate considerations to the observation that "though the abortion decision may originate within the zone of conscience and belief, it is more than a philosophic exercise." *Casey, 505 U.S. at 852. . . .* That many of the rights and liberties protected by the Due Process Clause sound in personal autonomy does not warrant the sweeping conclusion that any and all important, intimate, and personal decisions are so protected, *San Antonio Independent School Dist. v. Rodriguez, 411 U.S. 1, 33–35 (1973),* and *Casey* did not suggest otherwise.

The history of the law's treatment of assisted suicide in this country has been and continues to be one of the rejection of nearly all efforts to permit it. That being the case, our decisions lead us to conclude that the asserted "right" to assistance in committing suicide is not a fundamental liberty interest protected by the Due Process Clause. The Constitution also requires, however, that Washington's assisted-suicide ban be rationally related to legitimate government interests. See *Heller v. Doe, 509 U.S. 312, 319–320 (1993); Flores, 507 U.S. at 305.* This requirement is unquestionably met here. As the court below recognized, Washington's assisted-suicide ban implicates a number of state interests.

First, Washington has an "unqualified interest in the preservation of human life." *Cruzan, 497 U.S. at 282.* The State's prohibition on assisted suicide, like all homicide laws, both reflects and advances its commitment to this interest. ("The interests in the sanctity of life that are represented by the criminal homicide laws are threatened by one who expresses a willingness to participate in taking the life of another"). This interest is symbolic and aspirational as well as practical:

> "While suicide is no longer prohibited or penalized, the ban against assisted suicide and euthanasia shores up the notion of limits in human relationships. It reflects the gravity with which we view the decision to take one's own life or the life of another, and our reluctance to encourage or promote these decisions." New York Task Force 131–132.

Respondents admit that "the State has a real interest in preserving the lives of those who can still contribute to society and enjoy life." Brief for Respondents 35, n.23. The Court of Appeals also recognized Washington's interest in protecting life, but held that the "weight" of this interest depends on the "medical condition and the wishes of the person whose life is at stake." *79 F.3d, at 817.* Washington, however, has rejected this sliding-scale approach and, through its assisted-suicide ban, insists that all persons' lives, from beginning to end, regardless of physical or mental condition, are under the full protection of the law. See *United States v. Rutherford, 442, U.S. 544, 558 (1979)* (". . . Congress could reasonably have determined to protect the terminally ill, no less than other patients, from the vast range of self-styled panaceas that inventive minds can devise"). As we have previously affirmed, the States "may properly decline to make judgments about the 'quality' of life that a particular individual may enjoy," *Cruzan, 497 U.S. at 282.* This remains true, as *Cruzan* makes clear, even for those who are near death.

Relatedly, all admit that suicide is a serious public-health problem, especially among persons in otherwise vulnerable groups.

Those who attempt suicide—terminally ill or not—often suffer from depression or other mental disorders. Research indicates, however, that many people who request physician-assisted suicide withdraw that request if their depression and pain are treated. The New York Task Force, however, expressed its concern that, because depression is difficult to diagnose, physicians and medical professionals often fail to respond adequately to seriously ill patients' needs. Thus, legal physician-assisted suicide could make it more difficult for the State to protect depressed or mentally ill persons, or those who are suffering from untreated pain, from suicidal impulses.

The State also has an interest in protecting the integrity and ethics of the medical profession. In contrast to the Court of Appeals' conclusion that "the integrity of the medical profession would [not] be threatened in any way [by physician-assisted suicide]," *79 F.3d, at 827,* the American Medical Association, like many other medical and physicians' groups, has concluded that "physician-assisted suicide is fundamentally incompatible with the physician's role as healer." American Medical Association, Code of Ethics § 2.211 (1994); see Council on Ethical and Judicial Affairs, Decisions Near the End of Life, *267 JAMA 2229, 2233 (1992)* ("The societal risks of involving physicians in medical interventions to cause patients' deaths is too great"); New York Task Force 103–109 (discussing physicians' views). And physician-assisted suicide could, it is argued, undermine the trust that is essential to the doctor-patient relationship by blurring the time-honored line between healing and harming.

Next, the State has an interest in protecting vulnerable groups—including the poor, the elderly, and disabled persons—from abuse, neglect, and mistakes. The Court of Appeals dismissed the State's concern that disadvantaged persons might be pressured into physician-assisted suicide as "ludicrous on its face." *79 F.3d, at 825.* We have recognized, however, the real risk of subtle coercion and undue influence in end-of-life situations. *Cruzan, 497 U.S. at 281.* Similarly, the New York Task Force warned that "legalizing physician-assisted suicide would pose profound risks to many individuals who are ill and vulnerable. . . . The risk of harm is greatest for the many individuals in our society whose autonomy and well-being are already compromised by poverty, lack of access to good medical care, advanced age, or membership in a stigmatized social group." If physician-assisted suicide were permitted, many might resort to it to spare their families the substantial financial burden of end-of-life health-care costs.

The State's interest here goes beyond protecting the vulnerable from coercion; it extends to protecting disabled and terminally ill people from prejudice, negative and inaccurate stereotypes, and "societal indifference." *49 F.3d, at 592.* The state's assisted-suicide ban reflects and reinforces its policy that the lives of terminally ill, disabled, and elderly people must be no less valued than the lives of the young and healthy, and that a seriously disabled person's suicidal impulses should be interpreted and treated the same way as anyone else's.

Finally, the State may fear that permitting assisted suicide will start it down the path to voluntary and perhaps even involuntary euthanasia. The Court of Appeals struck down Washington's assisted-suicide ban only "as applied to competent, terminally ill adults who wish to hasten their deaths by obtaining medication prescribed by their doctors." *79 F.3d, at 838.* Washington insists, however, that the impact of the court's decision will not and cannot be so limited. If suicide is protected as a matter of constitutional right, it is argued, "every man and woman in the United States must enjoy it."

The Court of Appeals' decision, and its expansive reasoning, provide ample support for the State's concerns. The court noted, for example, that the "decision of a duly appointed surrogate decision maker is for all legal purposes the decision of the patient himself," *79 F.3d, at 832, n.120;* that "in some instances, the patient may be unable to self-administer the drugs and . . . administration by the physician . . . may be the only way the patient may be able to receive them," *id., at 831;* and that not only physicians, but also family members and loved ones, will inevitably participate in assisting suicide. *Id., at 838, n.140.* Thus, it turns out that what is couched as a limited right to "physician-assisted suicide" is likely, in effect, a much broader license, which could prove extremely difficult to police and contain. Washington's ban on assisting suicide prevents such erosion.

This concern is further supported by evidence about the practice of euthanasia in the Netherlands. The Dutch government's own study revealed that in 1990, there were 2,300 cases of voluntary euthanasia (defined as "the deliberate termination of another's life at his request"), 400 cases of assisted suicide, and more than 1,000 cases of euthanasia without an explicit request. In addition to these latter 1,000 cases, the study found an additional 4,941 cases where physicians administered lethal morphine overdoses without the patients' explicit consent. Physician-Assisted Suicide and Euthanasia in the Netherlands: A Report of Chairman Charles T. Canady, at 12–13 (citing Dutch study). This study suggests that, despite the existence of various reporting procedures, euthanasia in the Netherlands has not been limited to competent, terminally ill adults who are enduring physical suffering, and that regulation of the practice may not have prevented abuses in cases involving vulnerable persons, including severely disabled neonates and elderly persons suffering from dementia. The New York Task Force, citing the Dutch experience, observed that "assisted suicide and euthanasia are closely linked," New York Task Force 145, and concluded that the "risk of . . . abuse is neither speculative nor distant." Washington, like most other States, reasonably ensures against this risk by banning, rather than regulating, assisting suicide.

We need not weigh exactly the relative strengths of these various interests. They are unquestionably important and legitimate, and Washington's ban on assisted suicide is at least reasonably related to their promotion and protection. We therefore hold that Wash. Rev. Code § 9A.36.060(1) (1994) does not violate the Fourteenth Amendment, either on its face or "as applied to competent, terminally ill adults who wish to hasten their deaths by obtaining medication prescribed by their doctors." *79 F.3d, at 838.*

Throughout the Nation, Americans are engaged in an earnest and profound debate about the morality, legality, and practicality of physician-assisted suicide. Our holding permits this debate to continue, as it should in a democratic society. The decision of the en banc Court of Appeals is reversed, and the case is remanded for further proceedings consistent with this opinion.

Note

1. Under Washington's Natural Death Act, "adult persons have the fundamental right to control the decisions relating to the rendering of their own health care, including the decision to have life-sustaining treatment withheld or withdrawn in instances of a terminal condition or permanent unconscious condition." Wash. Rev. Code § 70.122.010 (1994). In Washington, "any adult person may execute a directive directing the withholding or withdrawal of life-sustaining treatment in a terminal condition or permanent unconscious condition," § 70.122.030, and a physician who, in accordance with such a directive, participates in the withholding or withdrawal of life-sustaining treatment is immune from civil, criminal, or professional liability. § 70.122.051.

WILLIAM H. REHNQUIST (1924–2005) became the 16th chief justice of the U.S. Supreme Court in 1986. He engaged in a general practice of law with primary emphasis on civil litigation for 16 years before being appointed assistant attorney general, Office of Legal Counsel, by President Richard Nixon in 1969. He was nominated by Nixon to the Supreme Court in 1972.

Stephen Reinhardt

 **NO**

Majority Opinion, *Compassion in Dying v. State of Washington*

I.

This case raises an extraordinarily important and difficult issue. It compels us to address questions to which there are no easy or simple answers, at law or otherwise. It requires us to confront the most basic of human concerns—the mortality of self and loved ones—and to balance the interest in preserving human life against the desire to die peacefully and with dignity. People of good will can and do passionately disagree about the proper result, perhaps even more intensely than they part ways over the constitutionality of restricting a woman's right to have an abortion. Heated though the debate may be, we must determine whether and how the United States Constitution applies to the controversy before us, a controversy that may touch more people more profoundly than any other issue the courts will face in the foreseeable future.

Today, we are required to decide whether a person who is terminally ill has a constitutionally-protected liberty interest in hastening what might otherwise be a protracted, undignified, and extremely painful death. If such an interest exists, we must next decide whether or not the state of Washington may constitutionally restrict its exercise by banning a form of medical assistance that is frequently requested by terminally ill people who wish to die. We first conclude that there is a constitutionally-protected liberty interest in determining the time and manner of one's own death, an interest that must be weighed against the state's legitimate and countervailing interests, especially those that relate to the preservation of human life. After balancing the competing interests, we conclude by answering the narrow question before us: We hold that insofar as the Washington statute prohibits physicians from prescribing life-ending medication for use by terminally ill, competent adults who wish to hasten their own deaths, it violates the Due Process Clause of the Fourteenth Amendment.

II. Preliminary Matters and History of the Case

. . . The plaintiffs do not challenge Washington statute RCW 9A.36.060 in its entirety. Specifically they do not object to the portion of the Washington statute that makes it unlawful for a person knowingly to cause another to commit suicide. Rather, they only challenge the statute's "or aids" provision. They challenge that provision both on its face and as applied to terminally ill, mentally competent adults who wish to hasten their own deaths with the help of medication prescribed by their doctors. The plaintiffs contend that the provision impermissibly prevents the exercise by terminally ill patients of a constitutionally-protected liberty interest in violation of the Due Process Clause of the Fourteenth Amendment, and also that it impermissibly distinguishes between similarly situated terminally ill patients in violation of the Equal Protection Clause. . . .

III. Overview of Legal Analysis: Is There a Due Process Violation?

In order to answer the question whether the Washington statute violates the Due Process Clause insofar as it prohibits the provision of certain medical assistance to terminally ill, competent adults who wish to hasten their own deaths, we first determine whether there is a liberty interest in choosing the time and manner of one's death—a question sometimes phrased in common parlance as: Is there a right to die? Because we hold that there is, we must then determine whether prohibiting physicians from prescribing life-ending medication for use by terminally ill patients who wish to die violates the patients' due process rights.

The mere recognition of a liberty interest does not mean that a state may not prohibit the exercise of that

From Supreme Court of the United States, 1996.

interest in particular circumstances, nor does it mean that a state may not adopt appropriate regulations governing its exercise. Rather, in cases like the one before us, the courts must apply a balancing test under which we weigh the individual's liberty interests against the relevant state interests in order to determine whether the state's actions are constitutionally permissible. . . .

Defining the Liberty Interest and Other Relevant Terms

. . . While some people refer to the liberty interest implicated in right-to-die cases as a liberty interest in committing suicide, we do not describe it that way. We use the broader and more accurate terms, "the right to die," "determining the time and manner of one's death," and "hastening one's death" for an important reason. The liberty interest we examine encompasses a whole range of acts that are generally not considered to constitute "suicide." Included within the liberty interest we examine, is for example, the act of refusing or terminating unwanted medical treatment . . . a competent adult has a liberty interest in refusing to be connected to a respirator or in being disconnected from one, even if he is terminally ill and cannot live without mechanical assistance. The law does not classify the death of a patient that results from the granting of his wish to decline or discontinue treatment as "suicide." Nor does the law label the acts of those who help the patient carry out that wish, whether by physically disconnecting the respirator or by removing an intravenous tube, as assistance in suicide. Accordingly, we believe that the broader terms—"the right to die," "controlling the time and manner of one's death," and "hastening one's death"—more accurately describe the liberty interest at issue here. . . .

Like the Court in *Roe [v. Wade]*, we begin with ancient attitudes. In Greek and Roman times, far from being universally prohibited, suicide was often considered commendable in literature, mythology, and practice. . . .

While Socrates counseled his disciples against committing suicide, he willingly drank the hemlock as he was condemned to do, and his example inspired others to end their lives. Plato, Socrates' most distinguished student, believed suicide was often justifiable.

He suggested that if life itself became immoderate, then suicide became a rational, justifiable act. Painful disease, or intolerable constraint were sufficient reasons to depart. And this when religious superstitions faded was philosophic justification enough.

Many contemporaries of Plato were even more inclined to find suicide a legitimate and acceptable act.

In *Roe*, while surveying the attitudes of the Greeks toward abortion, the Court stated that "only the Pythagorean school of philosophers frowned on the related act of suicide," 410 U.S. at 131; it then noted that the Pythagorean school represented a distinctly minority view. *Id.*

The Stoics glorified suicide as an act of pure rational will. Cato, who killed himself to avoid dishonor when Ceasar crushed his military aspirations, was the most celebrated of the many suicides among the Stoics. Montaigne wrote of Cato: "This was a man chosen by nature to show the heights which can be attained by human steadfastness and constancy. . . . Such courage is above philosophy."

Like the Greeks, the Romans often considered suicide to be acceptable or even laudable.

To live nobly also meant to die nobly and at the right time. Everything depended on a dominant will and a rational choice. . . .

Suicide was a crime under the English common law, at least in limited circumstances, probably as early as the thirteenth century. Bracton, incorporating Roman Law as set forth in Justinian's Digest, declared that if someone commits suicide to avoid conviction of a felony, his property escheats to his lords. Bracton said "[i]t ought to be otherwise if he kills himself through madness or unwillingness to endure suffering." Despite his general fidelity to Roman law, Bracton did introduce a key innovation: "[I]f a man slays himself in weariness of life or because he is unwilling to endure further bodily pain . . . he may have a successor, but his movable goods [personal property] are confiscated. He does not lose his inheritance [real property], only his movable goods." Bracton's innovation was incorporated into English common law, which has thus treated suicides resulting from the inability to "endure further bodily pain" with compassion and understanding ever since a common law scheme was firmly established. . . .

English attitudes toward suicide, including the tradition of ignominious burial, carried over to America where they subsequently underwent a transformation. By 1798, six of the 13 original colonies had abolished all penalties for suicide either by statute or state constitution. There is no evidence that any court ever imposed a punishment for suicide or attempted suicide under common law in post-revolutionary America. By the time the Fourteenth Amendment was adopted in 1868, suicide was generally not punishable, and in only nine of the 37 states is it clear that there were statutes prohibiting assisting suicide.

The majority of states have not criminalized suicide or attempted suicide since the turn of the century. The New Jersey Supreme Court declared in 1901 that since suicide was not punishable it should not be considered a crime. "[A]ll will admit that in some cases it is ethically defensible," the court said, as when a woman kills herself to escape being raped or "when a man curtails weeks or months of agony of an incurable disease." *Campbell v. Supreme Conclave Improved Order Heptasophs,* 66 N.J.L. 274, 49 A. 550, 553 (1901). Today, no state has a statute prohibiting suicide or attempted suicide; nor has any state had such a statute for at least 10 years. A majority of states do, however, still have laws on the books against assisting suicide.

Current Societal Attitudes

Clearly the absence of a criminal sanction alone does not show societal approbation of a practice. Nor is there any evidence that Americans approve of suicide in general. In recent years, however, there has been increasingly widespread support for allowing the terminally ill to hasten their deaths and avoid painful, undignified, and inhumane endings to their lives. Most Americans simply do not appear to view such acts as constituting suicide, and there is much support in reason for that conclusion.

Polls have repeatedly shown that a large majority of Americans—sometimes nearing 90%—fully endorse recent legal changes granting terminally ill patients, and sometimes their families, the prerogative to accelerate their death by refusing or terminating treatment. Other polls indicate that a majority of Americans favor doctor-assisted suicide for the terminally ill. In April, 1990, the Roper Report found that 64% of Americans believed that the terminally ill should have the right to request and receive physician aid-in-dying. Another national poll, conducted in October 1991, shows that "nearly two out of three Americans favor doctor-assisted suicide and euthanasia for terminally ill patients who request it." A 1994 Harris poll found 73% of Americans favor legalizing physician-assisted suicide. Three states have held referenda on proposals to allow physicians to help terminally ill, competent adults commit suicide with somewhat mixed results. In Oregon, voters approved the carefully-crafted referendum by a margin of 51 to 49 percent in November of 1994. In Washington and California where the measures contained far fewer practical safeguards, they narrowly failed to pass. . . . Accounts of doctors who have helped their patients end their lives have appeared both in professional journals and in the daily press. . . .

Liberty Interest Under Casey

In *[Planned Parenthood v.] Casey,* the Court surveyed its prior decisions affording "constitutional protection to personal decisions relating to marriage, procreation, contraception, family relationships, child rearing, and education," *id.* at 2807 and then said:

These matters, involving the most intimate and personal choices a person may make in a lifetime, choices central to personal dignity and autonomy, are central to the liberty protected by the Fourteenth Amendment. At the heart of liberty is the right to define one's own concept of existence, of meaning, of the universe, and of the mystery of human life. Beliefs about these matters could not define the attributes of personhood were they formed under compulsion of the State. The district judge in this case found the Court's reasoning in *Casey* "highly instructive" and "almost prescriptive" for determining "what liberty interest may inhere in a terminally ill person's choice to commit suicide." Compassion In Dying, 850 F. Supp. at 1459. We agree.

Like the decision of whether or not to have an abortion, the decision how and when to die is one of "the most intimate and personal choices a person may make in a lifetime," a choice "central to personal dignity and autonomy." A competent terminally ill adult, having lived nearly the full measure of his life, has a strong liberty interest in choosing a dignified and humane death rather than being reduced at the end of his existence to a childlike state of helplessness, diapered, sedated, incontinent. How a person dies not only determines the nature of the final period of his existence, but in many cases, the enduring memories held by those who love him.

Prohibiting a terminally ill patient from hastening his death may have an even more profound impact on that person's life than forcing a woman to carry a pregnancy to term. The case of an AIDS patient treated by Dr. Peter Shalit, one of the physician-plaintiffs in this case, provides a compelling illustration. In his declaration, Dr. Shalit described his patient's death this way:

One patient of mine, whom I will call Smith, a fictitious name, lingered in the hospital for weeks, his lower body so swollen from oozing Kaposi's lesions that he could not walk, his genitals so swollen that he required a catheter to drain his bladder, his fingers gangrenous from clotted arteries. Patient Smith's friends stopped visiting him because it gave them nightmares. Patient Smith's agonies could not be relieved by medication or by the excellent nursing care he received. Patient Smith begged for assistance in hastening his death. As his treating doctor, it was my professional opinion that patient Smith was mentally competent to make a choice with respect to shortening his period of suffering before inevitable death. I felt that I should accommodate his request. However, because of the statute, I was unable to assist him and he died after having been tortured for weeks by the end-phase of his disease.

For such patients, wracked by pain and deprived of all pleasure, a state-enforced prohibition on hastening their deaths condemns them to unrelieved misery or torture. Surely, a person's decision whether to endure or avoid such an existence constitutes one of the most, if not the most, "intimate and personal choices a person may make in a life-time," a choice that is "central to personal dignity and autonomy." *Casey,* 112 S.Ct. at 2807. . . .

Cruzan stands for the proposition that there is a due process liberty interest in rejecting unwanted medical treatment, including the provision of food and water by artificial means. Moreover, the Court majority clearly recognized that granting the request to remove the tubes through which Cruzan received artificial nutrition and hydration would lead inexorably to her death. *Cruzan,* 497 U.S. at 267–68, 283. Accordingly, we conclude that *Cruzan,* by recognizing a liberty interest that includes the refusal of artificial provision of life-sustaining food and water, necessarily recognizes a liberty interest in hastening one's own death.

Summary

Casey and *Cruzan* provide persuasive evidence that the Constitution encompasses a due process liberty interest in controlling the time and manner of one's death—that there is, in short, a constitutionally recognized "right to die." Our conclusion is strongly influenced by, but not limited to, the plight of mentally competent, terminally ill adults. We are influenced as well by the plight of others, such as those whose existence is reduced to a vegetative state or a permanent and irreversible state of unconsciousness.

Our conclusion that there is a liberty interest in determining the time and manner of one's death does not mean that there is a concomitant right to exercise that interest in all circumstances or to do so free from state regulation. To the contrary, we explicitly recognize that some prohibitory and regulatory state action is fully consistent with constitutional principles.

In short, finding a liberty interest constitutes a critical first step toward answering the question before us. The determination that must now be made is whether the state's attempt to curtail the exercise of that interest is constitutionally justified.

V. Relevant Factors and Interests

To determine whether a state action that impairs a liberty interest violates an individual's substantive due process rights we must identify the factors relevant to the case at hand, assess the state's interests and the individual's liberty interest in light of those factors, and then weigh and balance the competing interests. The relevant factors generally include: 1) the importance of the various state interests, both in general and in the factual context of the case; 2) the manner in which those interests are furthered by the state law or regulation; 3) the importance of the liberty interest, both in itself and in the context in which it is being exercised; 4) the extent to which that interest is burdened by the challenged state action; and, 5) the consequences of upholding or overturning the statute or regulation. . . .

B. The Means by Which the State Furthers Its Interests

In applying the balancing test, we must take into account not only the strength of the state's interests but also the means by which the state has chosen to further those interests.

1. Prohibition—A Total Ban for the Terminally Ill

Washington's statute prohibiting assisted suicide has a drastic impact on the terminally ill. By prohibiting physician assistance, it bars what for many terminally ill patients is the only palatable, and only practical, way to end their lives. Physically frail, confined to wheelchairs or beds, many terminally ill patients do not have the means or ability to kill themselves in the multitude of ways that healthy individuals can. Often, for example, they cannot even secure the medication or devices they would need to carry out their wishes.

Some terminally ill patients stockpile prescription medicine, which they can use to end their lives when they decide the time is right. The successful use of the stockpile technique generally depends, however, on the assistance of a physician, whether tacit or unknowing (although it is possible to end one's life with over-the-counter medication). Even if the terminally ill patients are able to accumulate sufficient drugs, given the pain killers and other medication they are taking, most of them would lack the knowledge to determine what dose of any given drug or drugs they must take, or in what combination. Miscalculation can be tragic. It can lead to an even more painful and lingering death. Alternatively, if the medication reduces respiration enough to restrict the flow of oxygen to the brain but not enough to cause death, it can result in the patient's falling into a comatose or vegetative state.

Thus for many terminally ill patients, the Washington statute is effectively a prohibition. While technically it only prohibits one means of exercising a liberty interest, practically it prohibits the exercise of that interest as effectively as prohibiting doctors from performing abortions prevented women from having abortions in the days before *Roe.*

*2. Regulation—A Permissible Means
of Promoting State Interests*

State laws or regulations governing physician-assisted suicide are both necessary and desirable to ensure against errors and abuse, and to protect legitimate state interests. Any of several model statutes might serve as an example of how these legitimate and important concerns can be addressed effectively.

By adopting appropriate, reasonable, and properly drawn safeguards Washington could ensure that people who choose to have their doctors prescribe lethal doses of medication are truly competent and meet all of the requisite standards. Without endorsing the constitutionality of any particular procedural safeguards, we note that the state might, for example, require: witnesses to ensure voluntariness; reasonable, though short, waiting periods to prevent rash decisions; second medical opinions to confirm a patient's terminal status and also to confirm that the patient has been receiving proper treatment, including adequate comfort care; psychological examinations to ensure that the patient is not suffering from momentary or treatable depression; reporting procedures that will aid in the avoidance of abuse. Alternatively, such safeguards could be adopted by interested medical associations and other organizations involved in the provision of health care, so long as they meet the state's needs and concerns. . . .

E. The Consequences of Upholding or Overturning the Statutory Provision

In various earlier sections of this opinion, we have discussed most of the consequences of upholding or overturning the Washington statutory provision at issue, because in this case those consequences are best considered as part of the discussion of the specific factors or interests. The one remaining consequence of significance is easy to identify: Whatever the outcome here, a host of painful and agonizing issues involving the right to die will continue to confront the courts. More important, these problems will continue to plague growing numbers of Americans of advanced age as well as their families, dependents, and loved ones. The issue is truly one which deserves the most thorough, careful, and objective attention from all segments of society.

VI. Application of the Balancing Test and Holding

Weighing and then balancing a constitutionally-protected interest against the state's countervailing interests, while bearing in mind the various consequences of the decision, is quintessentially a judicial role. Despite all of the efforts of generations of courts to categorize and objectify, to create multi-part tests and identify weights to be attached to the various factors, in the end balancing entails the exercise of judicial judgment rather than the application of scientific or mathematical formulae. No legislative body can perform the task for us. Nor can any computer. In the end, mindful of our constitutional obligations, including the limitations imposed on us by that document, we must rely on our judgment, guided by the facts and the law as we perceive them.

As we have explained, in this case neither the liberty interest in choosing the time and manner of death nor the state's countervailing interests are static. The magnitude of each depends on objective circumstances and generally varies inversely with the other. The liberty interest in hastening death is at its strongest when the state's interest in protecting life and preventing suicide is at its weakest, and vice-versa.

The liberty interest at issue here is an important one and, in the case of the terminally ill, is at its peak. Conversely, the state interests, while equally important in the abstract, are for the most part at a low point here. We recognize that in the case of life and death decisions the state has a particularly strong interest in avoiding undue influence and other forms of abuse. Here, that concern is ameliorated in large measure because of the mandatory involvement in the decision-making process of physicians, who have a strong bias in favor of preserving life, and because the process itself can be carefully regulated and rigorous safeguards adopted. Under these circumstances, we believe that the possibility of abuse, even when considered along with the other state interests, does not outweigh the liberty interest at issue.

The state has chosen to pursue its interests by means of what for terminally ill patients is effectively a total prohibition, even though its most important interests could be adequately served by a far less burdensome measure. The consequences of rejecting the as-applied challenge would be disastrous for the terminally ill, while the adverse consequences for the state would be of a far lesser order. This, too, weighs in favor of upholding the liberty interest.

We consider the state's interests in preventing assisted suicide as being different only in degree and not in kind from its interests in prohibiting a number of other medical practices that lead directly to a terminally ill patient's death. Moreover, we do not consider those interests to be significantly greater in the case of assisted suicide than they are in the case of those other medical practices, if indeed they are greater at all. However, even if the difference were one of kind and not degree, our result would be no different. For no matter how much weight we could legitimately afford the state's interest in preventing suicide, that weight, when combined with the weight we give all the other state's interests, is insufficient to outweigh the terminally ill individual's interest in deciding whether to end his agony and suffering by hastening the time of his death with medication prescribed by his physician. The individual's interest in making that vital decision is compelling indeed, for no decision is more painful, delicate, personal, important, or final than the decision how and when one's life shall end. If broad general state policies can be used to deprive a terminally ill individual of the right to make that choice, it is hard to envision where the exercise of arbitrary and intrusive power by the state can be halted. In this case, the state has wide power to regulate, but it may not ban the exercise of the liberty interest, and that is the practical effect of the program before us. Accordingly, after examining one final legal authority, we hold that the "or aids" provision of Washington statute RCW 9A.36.06 is unconstitutional as applied to terminally ill competent adults who wish to hasten their deaths with medication prescribed by their physicians. . . .

VII. Conclusion

We hold that a liberty interest exists in the choice of how and when one dies, and that the provision of the Washington statute banning assisted suicide, as applied to competent, terminally ill adults who wish to hasten their deaths by obtaining medication prescribed by their doctors, violates the Due Process Clause. We recognize that this decision is a most difficult and controversial one, and that it leaves unresolved a large number of equally troublesome issues that will require resolution in the years ahead. We also recognize that other able and dedicated jurists, construing the Constitution as they believe it must be construed, may disagree not only with the result we reach but with our method of constitutional analysis. Given the nature of the judicial process and the complexity of the

task of determining the rights and interests comprehended by the Constitution, good faith disagreements within the judiciary should not surprise or disturb anyone who follows the development of the law. For these reasons, we express our hope that whatever debate may accompany the future exploration of the issues we have touched on today will be conducted in an objective, rational, and constructive manner that will increase, not diminish, respect for the Constitution.

There is one final point we must emphasize. Some argue strongly that decisions regarding matters affecting life or death should not be made by the courts. Essentially, we agree with that proposition. In this case, by permitting the individual to exercise the right to choose we are following the constitutional mandate to take such decisions out of the hands of the government, both state and federal, and to put them where they rightly belong, in the hands of the people. We are allowing individuals to make the decisions that so profoundly affect their very existence—and precluding the state from intruding excessively into that critical realm. The Constitution and the courts stand as a bulwark between individual freedom and arbitrary and intrusive governmental power. Under our constitutional system, neither the state nor the majority of the people in a state can impose its will upon the individual in a matter so highly "central to personal dignity and autonomy," *Casey*, 112 S.Ct. at 2807. Those who believe strongly that death must come without physician assistance are free to follow that creed, be they doctors or patients. They are not free, however, to force their views, their religious convictions, or their philosophies on all the other members of a democratic society, and to compel those whose values differ with theirs to die painful, protracted, and agonizing deaths.

Affirmed.

STEPHEN REINHARDT is a judge on the U.S. Court of Appeals for the Ninth Circuit in Seattle, Washington.

EXPLORING THE ISSUE

Can States Ban Physician Aid-in-Dying for Terminally Ill Patients?

Critical Thinking and Reflection

1. Should a terminally ill patient's right to a doctor's assistance in dying be judicially established by being equated with the individual liberty rights guaranteed by the Constitution, such as freedom of religion and belief, privacy, and the right to refuse medical treatment?
2. What are the strongest policy arguments *for and against* a state's establishing a regulated right to "Death with Dignity" such as has been done in Oregon (referenda, 1994 and 1997), Washington State (referendum, 2008), and Montana (state court decriminalizing decision, 2010), and Vermont (legislation, 2013)?
3. What would the judicial establishment of a "right to palliative care," rather than a "right to a physician's aid-in-dying," have to include in order to be an effective compromise between the sides and a useful policy for dying patients, their families, and physicians?
4. Does it appear to be ethically justifiable and humane to legally permit a doctor to hasten a terminally ill patient's death by removing life support at the patient's request, but not to permit a doctor to hasten a terminally ill patient's death by prescribing a life-ending prescription requested by the patient?
5. Do the regulations and years of experience under Oregon's Death with Dignity Act allay the concerns of the opponents of such laws that the value of life will be diminished, that vulnerable patients will be abused or pressured, or that the ethics of the doctor–patient relationship will be eroded?

Is There Common Ground?

The litigants and their backers in cases like *Glucksberg* appear to be polarized and disinclined to compromise. But there may be some common ground between those who advocate a carefully regulated right to "death with dignity," such as that provided by the statute established in Oregon, and those who want to criminalize this form of physician aid-in-dying. In Professor Burt's analysis of the six *Glucksberg* opinions (see "Additional Resources" below), for example, he suggests that while the Court was unwilling to find a constitutional right to "assisted suicide," it might be willing to establish a "constitutional right to palliative care." In exploring the putative right to palliative care, Burt comes close to approving not only a doctor's provision of pain relief that might hasten death, but comfort care that might be responsive to a patient's desire to die in a particular time and way. Some of Burt's analysis is based on the concurring opinion of Justice Breyer, in which the Justice wrote that the right claimed might better be described as a "right to die with dignity." Such a right, Breyer continued, would have at its core ". . . personal control over the manner of death, professional medical assistance, and the avoidance of unnecessary and severe physical suffering—combined." Burt's analysis also discusses the discomfort of

several Justices with the possibility—not presented by the facts in *Glucksberg*—that there might be state laws that in an effort to prevent drug abuse might prevent doctors from providing the kind of aggressive pain relief that some terminally ill patients need. What the content of a common-ground right to palliative care might be, and how much freedom for decision making such a right would leave in the doctor–patient relationship are questions that remain to be answered.

A second reason for believing that there may be common ground among most of the interest groups involved in litigation like *Glucksberg* concerns the medical practices that already exist for alleviating the suffering of dying patients. One such practice is the administration of pain relievers that may also hasten death as a secondary effect. Morphine is one such medicine, because there are circumstances in which increasing the morphine administered to a level that is effective for a terminally ill patient may also slow respiration and thereby hasten the approaching death. This practice is widely accepted among physicians because of what is known as the "rule of double effect," in which patients and their families are informed that it is the primary intent of the doctor to reduce extreme pain, even though it is foreseeable that a secondary result—hastening death—is possible. Another generally accepted practice for relief of intractable pain and other suffering is "palliative sedation," in which the patient voluntarily agrees to be sedated to unconsciousness as the only means of having suffering relieved. This sedation may be maintained until the patient dies from the underlying disease, or that death may be hastened by not providing artificial feeding and hydration during the period of sedation. These and similar practices for relieving the extreme suffering of some terminally ill patients may be more readily available to wealthier persons with long-term relationships to their doctors than they are to others equally in need. And it might be that the administration of these practices could benefit from some oversight to ensure that they are not the product of undue pressures applied to vulnerable patients. Both expanding the availability and restricting the abuse of these practices might be the common ground that could advance a regulated and legalized regime of physician aid-in-dying.

Finally, Chief Justice Rehnquist's opinion for the Court in *Glucksberg* ends with the following expression of federalism: "Throughout the Nation, Americans are engaged in an earnest and profound debate about the morality, legality, and practicality of physician-assisted suicide. Our holding permits this debate to continue, as it should in a democratic society." The forms of common ground suggested above may be contributing to the thoughtfulness of this state-by-state discourse, and the recent renaming of its subject as "physician aid-in-dying" rather than "assisted suicide" may have helped as well. In any case, common ground has been found for advancing the availability of a regulated regime of medically assisting terminally ill patients who are suffering extreme pain or existential angst. One can see this common ground in the fact that three states have followed Oregon's example since 1997, Washington State, Vermont, and Montana. One can also see some unexpected positive results from the statistics of Oregon's experience with its Death with Dignity Act. In the past 12 years only about two-thirds of those who have received prescriptions for life-ending medications have actually used them, indicating that it is control—having the mere possibility of being able to escape unendurable pain or suffering—that eases dying and makes it more dignified. And in that same time period, there has been a significant increase in the availability and quality of palliative care for all of Oregon's citizens—an indication that common ground may be enhanced by the creation of benefits even for those who oppose the adoption of a Death with Dignity Act.

Additional Resources

Stephen Arons, "Palliative Care in the U.S. Healthcare System: Constitutional Right or Criminal Act?" 29(2) *W. New Eng. L. Rev.* 309–356 (2007).

Robert A. Burt, "The Supreme Court Speaks. Not Assisted Suicide but a Constitutional Right to Palliative Care." 337 *New Eng. J. Med.* 1234 (1997).

Lewis M. Cohen, *No Good Deed: A Story of Medicine, Murder Accusations, and the Debate over How We Die* (HarperCollins, 2010).

William H. Colby, *Long Goodbye: The Deaths of Nancy Cruzan* ((Hay House, 2002).

Ronald Dworkin, *Life's Dominion: An Argument about Abortion, Euthanasia, and Individual Freedom* (Vintage, 1994).

Internet References . . .

The Experience of Oregon's Death with Dignity Act

This is the official site of the Oregon Health Authority, and contains links to the text of the statute, forms required, and yearly statistics compiled since the law's its first year of operation in 1998.

http://public.health.oregon.gov/ProviderPartner Resources/Evaluationresearch/deathwithdignityact /Pages/index.aspx

Principled and Articulate Opposition to Physician Aid-in-Dying

This lengthy 2012 article by a renowned legal scholar in the *Journal of Law, Medicine and Ethics*, by Yale Kamisar, is available through most online library search engines: "Are the Decisions Drawn in the Debate about End-of-Life Decision Making 'Principled'? If Not, How Much Does It Matter?"

http://onlinelibrary.wiley.com/doi/10.1111 /j.1748-720X.2012.00647.x/abstract

The Euthanasia and Law in Europe

This lengthy, thorough, and readable book explores the experiences and policies about euthanasia in Europe. The above-titled book by Griffiths, Weyers, and Adams evaluates the "slippery slope" argument often made against physician aid-in-dying in the United States—that there will be no principled way to prevent a slide into involuntary euthanasia once a death with dignity act is adopted by a U.S. jurisdiction or approved by the courts.

www.amazon.com/Euthanasia-Law-Europe-John -Griffiths/dp/1841137006

The Prosecution of Doctors Who Provide Palliative Care

In a television presentation entitled, "American Justice: A Questionable Doctor," the History Channel presents the case of Dr L. Stanley Naramore who provided two terminally ill patients with palliative care but was tried and convicted of murder and attempted murder by a Kansas jury in spite of the expert medical testimony that he was providing standard medical care. Naramore was eventually acquitted on appeal, but not before his career, finances, and family were ruined by the experience. The trial exemplifies the ambiguity and conflict that so often accompanies the death of a loved one and the medical options available to the terminally ill.

http://shop.history.com/american-justice-a -questionable-doctor-dvd/detail.php?p=67451

Selected, Edited, and with Issue Framing Material by:
M. Ethan Katsh, *University of Massachusetts, Amherst*

ISSUE

Does the Sharing of Music Files Through the Internet Violate Copyright Laws?

YES: Ruth Bader Ginsburg, from "Concurring Opinion, *Metro-Goldwyn-Mayer Studios Inc., et al., v. Grokster, Ltd., et al.," United States Supreme Court* (2005)

NO: Stephen Breyer, from "Concurring Opinion, *Metro-Goldwyn-Mayer Studios Inc., et al.,* Petitioners *v. Grokster, Ltd., et al.," United States Supreme Court* (2005)

Learning Outcomes

After reading this issue, you will be able to:

- Identify what facts a court will look to in determining whether a new technology violates copyright law.
- Discuss the legal conundrums faced by peer-to-peer sharing networks.
- Discuss how courts attempt to balance protecting the rights of copyright holders and not deterring technological innovation.
- Distinguish between the results in *Sony v. Universal City Studios* and *Grokster v. MGM*.

ISSUE SUMMARY

YES: Justice Ruth Bader Ginsburg believes that copyright laws are violated by a company when its software is used primarily for illegal file sharing, and lawful uses in the future are unlikely.

NO: Justice Stephen Breyer does not want copyright laws to hinder technological innovation and is more willing to take into account the potential use of the software for lawful file sharing.

When the first edition of *Taking Sides: Legal Issues* was published 30 years ago, it would have been impossible to think of a copyright issue that was controversial and newsworthy enough to include in the book. Today, however, with our avid use of computers and the Internet, issues of copyright now touch our daily lives, even if we are not always aware of it. Several decades ago, it would have been difficult for ordinary citizens to commit a copyright violation that would provoke a response from the copyright owner. Today, every person who downloads music from a free file-sharing site, uses a friend's copy of a software package, or streams a television show from an unauthorized website exposes himself or herself to some measure of risk.

The decision in *MGM Studios v. Grokster* was unanimous and held that Grokster could be held liable for violating copyright laws by providing peer-to-peer file sharing software to the public, although Grokster itself did not directly infringe on others' intellectual property. The justices were willing to hold Grokster liable since Grokster, in addition to making its software available, encouraged users to copy copyrighted files. The Court did not, however, go so far as to state that all file-sharing programs would violate copyright laws. But what if a developer simply made software available online that could be used for file sharing but did not actively encourage file sharing of copyrighted works? What if a developer made available software that in fact was used by many to exchange copyrighted works but was also used to exchange nonprotected works?

While *Grokster* was the first file-sharing case for the U.S. Supreme Court, it was not the first case involving a technology that made possible the copying of copyrighted works. The landmark case in this area is *Sony v. Universal City Studios,* 464 U.S. 417 (1984), a case questioning whether the VCR manufactured by Sony violated copyright law. This new technology represented an enormous threat in the eyes of Hollywood. In 1983, Jack Valenti, the president of the Motion Picture Association of America (MPAA), appeared before a House of Representatives Committee and testified that "the VCR is to the motion picture industry and the American public what the Boston strangler is to the woman alone." He felt that if the *Sony* case were decided in favor of Sony, as it was, copying would be rampant, and the movie industry would suffer terribly. As it turned out, however, the VCR may have saved the movie industry by providing new outlets and new sources of revenue.

The *Sony* decision was very close, 5–4, and held that machines that were being used to violate copyright law and that also were being used in ways that didn't violate copyright law could not be banned. The majority reasoned that the "time-shifting" VCR technology was not infringing, even though it was marketed as a means to record copyrighted programming, because a significant amount of the recordings would be authorized. That authorized number, although not precise, was estimated to be around 10 percent of the copying done with the VCR and that was sufficient to keep the technology from being banned. The *Sony* Court further held that a technology that could be used for both lawful and unlawful copying does not violate copyright laws if it is "capable of substantial non-infringing use." What the *Sony* court did not expound upon was what "substantial" meant. Even though capable of broad lawful use, Grokster's technology represented copyright infringement on many orders of magnitude larger than that reasonably capable with the VCR.

It is the different reading and application of the Court's *Sony* holding to Grokster that lead us to the selections here. On this issue, the Court was not unanimous. The two concurring opinions differ greatly on what the standard should be for a company that produces software that is used unlawfully, an issue that the Court will have to decide in some future case as neither side held a majority. In the YES selection, Justice Ruth Bader Ginsburg writes that with little or no evidence of noninfringing uses, a company that distributes a product used to violate copyright law should be held responsible. Justice Stephen

Breyer, on the other hand, emphasizes the need to encourage the development of new technologies, something that will not happen if creators are worried that their creations will be held to violate copyright law. Thus, Justice Breyer believes that it is sufficient in a case like this merely to show a capability of future noninfringing use in order to escape liability under copyright laws.

Similar to Jack Valenti's warnings in 1983, dire predictions are continually made today about the music and film industries, but it is less clear whether piracy or changing technology is to blame. Music industry revenues are less than half of their peak over a decade ago, and film industry revenue is well off its highs as well. But in terms of legal consumption by units, the numbers have never been greater. More people are legally buying music and watching movies than ever before. The diminished revenues, however, reflect a change in the many different ways in which we are now capable of consuming content. Today, the music and film industries are seeing enormous growth in the very mediums they once most feared—digital consumption. While this growth is often at the expense of older, more profitable distribution methods (e.g., CD and DVD sales), wholly new methods of entertainment consumption are taking hold, such as video on demand, IMAX, 3-D movies, and music streaming services like Spotify and Pandora.

While the *Grokster* opinion no doubt piqued the fear of other peer-to-peer sharing networks, it did not have the effect of deterring them altogether, and in fact some continued to thrive. Even in the wake of Grokster, other file-sharing services, such as LimeWire, Megaupload, and Pirate Bay, grew to enormous size and provided consumers with the continued ability to download vast amounts of copyrighted materials. However, copyright holders have been unrelenting, and each has since met their demise: LimeWire settled its lawsuit with the major record labels for $105 million, only to later be sued by the major film studios—it is presently defunct; Megaupload's founder, Kim Dotcom, is currently being criminally prosecuted for copyright infringement and money laundering; and Pirate Bay's founders were convicted of copyright infringement and sentenced to pay $6.5 million in damages and serve jail time.

While copyright holders and their respective trade groups have had numerous successes in prosecuting peer-to-peer network providers as well as thousands of individual infringers, their recent efforts to stem the tide of piracy have been met with sharp criticism. In early 2012, legislation was introduced in Congress that created new penalties and regulations for copyright infringement and those that aided infringers, including advertising services, payment providers, and Internet search engines. Known as the Stop Online Piracy Act (SOPA), and strongly supported by the MPAA and the Recording Industry Association of America (RIAA), the Act found worthy adversaries in the likes of some of the largest names in technology, including Google and Wikipedia. With the help of a massive online campaign, an online blackout protest by thousands of major websites, and a general outcry by consumers, SOPA never reached a vote. *Grokster* by no means settles the issue of how far courts are willing to curtail new technologies to protect intellectual property rights, but it does foretell how future cases will no doubt be argued.

YES ↵

Ruth Bader Ginsburg

Concurring Opinion, *Metro-Goldwyn-Mayer Studios Inc., et al., v. Grokster, Ltd., et al.*

JUSTICE GINSBURG, with whom THE CHIEF JUSTICE AND JUSTICE KENNEDY join, concurring.

I concur in the Court's decision, which vacates in full the judgment of the Court of Appeals for the Ninth Circuit, and write separately to clarify why I conclude that the Court of Appeals misperceived, and hence misapplied, our holding in *Sony Corp. of America v. Universal City Studios, Inc.,* 464 U.S. 417 (1984). There is here at least a "genuine issue as to [a] material fact," Fed. Rule Civ. Proc. 56(c), on the liability of Grokster or StreamCast, not only for actively inducing copyright infringement, but also or alternatively, based on the distribution of their software products, for contributory copyright infringement. On neither score was summary judgment for Grokster and StreamCast warranted.

At bottom, however labeled, the question in this case is whether Grokster and StreamCast are liable for the direct infringing acts of others. Liability under our jurisprudence may be predicated on actively encouraging (or inducing) infringement through specific acts (as the Court's opinion develops) or on distributing a product distributees use to infringe copyrights, if the product is not capable of "substantial" or "commercially significant" noninfringing uses. *Sony,* 464 U.S., at 442. While the two categories overlap, they capture different culpable behavior. Long coexisting, both are now codified in patent law. Compare 35 U. S. C. §271(b) (active inducement liability), with §271(c) (contributory liability for distribution of a product not "suitable for substantial noninfringing use").

In *Sony,* 464 U.S. 417, the Court considered Sony's liability for selling the Betamax video cassette recorder. It did so enlightened by a full trial record. Drawing an analogy to the staple article of commerce doctrine from patent law, the *Sony* Court observed that the "sale of an article . . . adapted to [a patent] infringing use" does not suffice "to make the seller a contributory infringer" if the article "is also adapted to other and lawful uses." *Id.,* at 441 (quoting *Henry v. A. B. Dick Co.,* 224 U.S. 1, 48 (1912),

overruled on other grounds, *Motion Picture Patents Co. v. Universal Film Mfg. Co.,* 243 U.S. 502, 517 (1917)).

"The staple article of commerce doctrine" applied to copyright, the Court stated, "must strike a balance between a copyright holder's legitimate demand for effective—not merely symbolic—protection of the statutory monopoly, and the rights of others freely to engage in substantially unrelated areas of commerce." *Sony,* 464 U.S., at 442. "Accordingly," the Court held, "the sale of copying equipment, like the sale of other articles of commerce, does not constitute contributory infringement if the product is widely used for legitimate, unobjectionable purposes. Indeed, it need merely be capable of substantial noninfringing uses." Thus, to resolve the *Sony* case, the Court explained, it had to determine "whether the Betamax is capable of commercially significant noninfringing uses."

To answer that question, the Court considered whether "a significant number of [potential uses of the Betamax were] noninfringing." The Court homed in on one potential use—private, noncommercial time-shifting of television programs in the home (*i.e.,* recording a broadcast TV program for later personal viewing). Time-shifting was noninfringing, the Court concluded, because in some cases trial testimony showed it was authorized by the copyright holder, and in others it qualified as legitimate fair use. Most purchasers used the Betamax principally to engage in time-shifting, a use that "plainly satisfie[d]" the Court's standard. Thus, there was no need in *Sony* to "give precise content to the question of how much [actual or potential] use is commercially significant." *Ibid.*[1] Further development was left for later days and cases.

The Ninth Circuit went astray, I will endeavor to explain, when that court granted summary judgment to Grokster and StreamCast on the charge of contributory liability based on distribution of their software products. Relying on its earlier opinion in *A&M Records, Inc. v. Napster, Inc.,* 239 F. 3d 1004 (CA9 2001), the Court of Appeals held that "if substantial noninfringing use was shown, the copyright owner would be required to show that the defendant had reasonable knowledge of specific infringing files." 380 F. 3d 1154, 1161 (CA9 2004). "A careful examination of the record," the court concluded, "indicates that there is no genuine issue of material fact as to noninfringing use." The appeals court pointed to the band Wilco, which made one of its albums available for free downloading, to other recording artists who may have authorized free distribution of their music through the Internet, and to public domain literary works and films available through Grokster's and StreamCast's software. Although it acknowledged MGM's assertion that "the vast majority of the software use is for copyright infringement," the court concluded that Grokster's and StreamCast's proffered evidence met *Sony*'s requirement that "a product need only be *capable* of substantial noninfringing uses." 380 F. 3d, at 1162.[2]

This case differs markedly from *Sony*. Cf. Peters, Brace Memorial Lecture: Copyright Enters the Public Domain, 51 J. Copyright Soc. 701, 724 (2004) ("The *Grokster* panel's reading of *Sony* is the broadest that any court has given it. . . ."). Here, there has been no finding of any fair use and little beyond anecdotal evidence of noninfringing uses. In finding the Grokster and StreamCast software products capable of substantial noninfringing uses, the District Court and the Court of Appeals appear to have relied largely on declarations submitted by the defendants. These declarations include assertions (some of them hearsay) that a number of copyright owners authorize distribution of their works on the Internet and that some public domain material is available through peer-to-peer networks including those accessed through Grokster's and StreamCast's software. 380 F. 3d, at 1161; 259 F. Supp. 2d 1029, 1035–1036 (CD Cal. 2003); App. 125–171.

The District Court declared it "undisputed that there are substantial noninfringing uses for Defendants' software," thus obviating the need for further proceedings. 259 F. Supp. 2d, at 1035. This conclusion appears to rest almost entirely on the collection of declarations submitted by Grokster and StreamCast. Review of these declarations reveals mostly anecdotal evidence, sometimes obtained second-hand, of authorized copyrighted works or public domain works available online and shared through peer-to-peer networks, and general statements about the benefits of peer-to-peer technology. See, *e.g.*, Decl. of Janis Ian ¶13, App. 128 ("P2P technologies offer musicians an alternative channel for promotion and distribution."); Decl. of Gregory Newby ¶12, *id.*, at 136 ("Numerous authorized and public domain Project Gutenberg eBooks are made available on Morpheus, Kazaa,

Gnutella, Grokster, and similar software products."); Decl. of Aram Sinnreich ¶6, *id.*, at 151 ("file sharing seems to have a net positive impact on music sales"); Decl. of John Busher ¶8, *id.*, at 166 ("I estimate that Acoustica generates sales of between $1,000 and $10,000 per month as a result of the distribution of its trialware software through the Gnutella and FastTrack Networks."); Decl. of Patricia D. Hoekman ¶¶3–4, *id.*, at 169–170 (search on Morpheus for "President Bush speeches" found several video recordings, searches for "Declaration of Independence" and "Bible" found various documents and declarant was able to download a copy of the Declaration); Decl. of Sean L. Mayers ¶11, *id.*, at 67 ("Existing open, decentralized peer-to-peer file-sharing networks . . . offer content owners distinct business advantages over alternate online distribution technologies."). Compare Decl. of Brewster Kahle ¶20, *id.*, at 142 ("Those who download the Prelinger films . . . are entitled to redistribute those files, and the Archive welcomes their redistribution by the Morpheus-Grokster-KaZaa community of users."), with Deposition of Brewster Kahle, *id.*, at 396–403 (Sept. 18, 2002) (testifying that he has no knowledge of any person downloading a Prelinger film using Morpheus, Grokster, or Kazaa). Compare also Decl. of Richard Prelinger ¶17, *id.*, at 147 ("[W]e welcome further redistribution of the Prelinger films . . . by individuals using peer-to-peer software products like Morpheus, Kazaa and Grokster."), with Deposition of Richard Prelinger, *id.*, at 410–411 (Oct. 1, 2002) ("Q. What is your understanding of Grokster? A. I have no understanding of Grokster. . . . Q. Do you know whether any user of the Grokster software has made available to share any Prelinger film? A. No."). See also Deposition of Aram Sinnreich, *id.*, at 390 (Sept. 25, 2002) (testimony about the band Wilco based on "[t]he press and industry news groups and scuttlebutt."). These declarations do not support summary judgment in the face of evidence, proffered by MGM, of overwhelming use of Grokster's and StreamCast's software for infringement.[3]

Even if the absolute number of noninfringing files copied using the Grokster and StreamCast software is large, it does not follow that the products are therefore put to substantial noninfringing uses and are thus immune from liability. The number of noninfringing copies may be reflective of, and dwarfed by, the huge total volume of files shared. Further, the District Court and the Court of Appeals did not sharply distinguish between uses of Grokster's and StreamCast's software products (which this case is about) and uses of peer-to-peer technology generally (which this case is not about).

In sum, when the record in this case was developed, there was evidence that Grokster's and StreamCast's products were, and had been for some time, overwhelmingly used to infringe, and that this infringement was the overwhelming source of revenue from the products. Fairly appraised, the evidence was insufficient to demonstrate, beyond genuine debate, a reasonable prospect that substantial or commercially significant noninfringing uses were likely to develop over time. On this record, the District Court should not have ruled dispositively on the contributory infringement charge by granting summary judgment to Grokster and StreamCast.[4]

If, on remand, the case is not resolved on summary judgment in favor of MGM based on Grokster and StreamCast actively inducing infringement, the Court of Appeals, I would emphasize, should reconsider, on a fuller record, its interpretation of *Sony*'s product distribution holding.

Notes

1. JUSTICE BREYER finds in *Sony Corp. of America v. Universal City Studios, Inc.,* 464 U.S. 417 (1984), a "clear" rule permitting contributory liability for copyright infringement based on distribution of a product only when the product "will be used *almost exclusively* to infringe copyrights." *Post*, at 9–10. But cf. *Sony*, 464 U.S., at 442 (recognizing "copyright holder's legitimate demand for effective—not merely symbolic—protection"). *Sony*, as I read it, contains no clear, near-exclusivity test. Nor have Courts of Appeals unanimously recognized JUSTICE BREYER'S clear rule. Compare *A&M Records, Inc. v. Napster, Inc.,* 239 F. 3d 1004, 1021 (CA9 2001) ("[E]vidence of actual knowledge of specific acts of infringement is required to hold a computer system operator liable for contributory copyright infringement."), with *In re Aimster Copyright Litigation*, 334 F. 3d 643, 649–650 (CA7 2003) ("[W]hen a supplier is offering a product or service that has noninfringing as well as infringing uses, some estimate of the respective magnitudes of these uses is necessary for a finding of contributory infringement. . . . But the balancing of costs and benefits is necessary only in a case in which substantial non-infringing uses, present or prospective, are demonstrated."). See also *Matthew Bender & Co., Inc. v. West Pub. Co.*, 158 F. 3d 693, 707 (CA2 1998) ("The Supreme Court applied [the *Sony*] test to prevent copyright holders from leveraging the copyrights in their original work to control distribution of . . . products that might be used incidentally for infringement, but that

had substantial noninfringing uses. . . . The same rationale applies here [to products] that have substantial, predominant and noninfringing uses as tools for research and citation."). All Members of the Court agree, moreover, that "the Court of Appeals misapplied *Sony*," at least to the extent it read that decision to limit "secondary liability" to a hardly-ever category, "quite beyond the circumstances to which the case applied." *Ante*, at 16.

2. Grokster and StreamCast, in the Court of Appeals' view, would be entitled to summary judgment unless MGM could show that that the software companies had knowledge of specific acts of infringement and failed to act on that knowledge—a standard the court held MGM could not meet. 380 F. 3d, at 1162–1163.

3. JUSTICE BREYER finds support for summary judgment in this motley collection of declarations and in a survey conducted by an expert retained by MGM. *Post*, at 4–8. That survey identified 75% of the files available through Grokster as copyrighted works owned or controlled by the plaintiffs, and 15% of the files as works likely copyrighted. App. 439. As to the remaining 10% of the files, "there was not enough information to form reasonable conclusions either as to what those files even consisted of, and/or whether they were infringing or non-infringing." App. 479. Even assuming, as JUSTICE BREYER does, that the *Sony* Court would have absolved Sony of contributory liability solely on the basis of the use of the Betamax for authorized time-shifting, *post*, at 3–4, summary judgment is not inevitably appropriate here. *Sony* stressed that the plaintiffs there owned "well below 10%" of copyrighted television programming, 464 U.S., at 443, and found, based on trial testimony from representatives of the four major sports leagues and other individuals authorized to consent to home-recording of their copyrighted broadcasts, that a similar percentage of program copying was authorized, *id.*, at 424. Here, the plaintiffs allegedly control copyrights for 70% or 75% of the material exchanged through the Grokster and StreamCast software, 380 F. 3d, at 1158; App. 439, and the District Court does not appear to have relied on comparable testimony about authorized copying from copyright holders.

4. The District Court's conclusion that "[p]laintiffs do not dispute that Defendants' software is being used, and could be used, for substantial noninfringing purposes," 259 F. Supp. 2d 1029,

1036 (CD Cal. 2003); accord 380 F. 3d, at 1161, is, to say the least, dubious. In the courts below and in this Court, MGM has continuously disputed any such conclusion. Brief for Motion Picture Studio and Recording Company Petitioners 30–38; Brief for MGM Plaintiffs-Appellants in No. 03-55894, etc. (CA9), p. 41; App. 356–357, 361–365.

RUTH BADER GINSBURG is an associate justice of the U.S. Supreme Court. She graduated at the top of her law school class at Columbia University and taught at Rutgers and Columbia Law Schools. She has served as director of the ACLU Women's Rights Project, and between 1972 and 1978, she argued six cases involving sex-role stereotyping before the Court and won five. She was appointed to the Supreme Court by President Bill Clinton in 1993.

Stephen Breyer

 **NO**

Concurring Opinion, *Metro-Goldwyn-Mayer Studios Inc., et al., Petitioners v. Grokster, Ltd., et al.*

JUSTICE BREYER, with whom JUSTICE STEVENS and JUSTICE O'CONNOR join, concurring.

I agree with the Court that the distributor of a dual-use technology may be liable for the infringing activities of third parties where he or she actively seeks to advance the infringement. I further agree that, in light of our holding today, we need not now "revisit" *Sony Corp. of America v. Universal City Studios, Inc.,* 464 U.S. 417 (1984). Other Members of the Court, however, take up the *Sony* question: whether Grokster's product is "capable of 'substantial' or 'commercially significant' noninfringing uses." (GINSBURG, J., concurring) (quoting *Sony, supra,* at 442). And they answer that question by stating that the Court of Appeals was wrong when it granted summary judgment on the issue in Grokster's favor. I write to explain why I disagree with them on this matter.

I

The Court's opinion in *Sony* and the record evidence (as described and analyzed in the many briefs before us) together convince me that the Court of Appeals' conclusion has adequate legal support.

A

I begin with *Sony*'s standard. In *Sony,* the Court considered the potential copyright liability of a company that did not itself illegally copy protected material, but rather sold a machine—a Video Cassette Recorder (VCR)—that could be used to do so. A buyer could use that machine for *non*infringing purposes, such as recording for later viewing (sometimes called "'time-shifting,'" *Sony,* 464 U.S., at 421) uncopyrighted television programs or copyrighted programs with a copyright holder's permission. The buyer could use the machine for infringing purposes as well, such as building libraries of taped copyrighted programs. Or, the

buyer might use the machine to record copyrighted programs under circumstances in which the legal status of the act of recording was uncertain (*i.e.,* where the copying may, or may not, have constituted a "fair use." Sony knew many customers would use its VCRs to engage in unauthorized copying and "'library-building.'" *Id.,* at 458–459 (Blackmun, J., dissenting). But that fact, said the Court, was insufficient to make Sony itself an infringer. And the Court ultimately held that Sony was not liable for its customers' acts of infringement.

In reaching this conclusion, the Court recognized the need for the law, in fixing *secondary* copyright liability, to "strike a balance between a copyright holder's legitimate demand for effective—not merely symbolic—protection of the statutory monopoly, and the rights of others freely to engage in substantially unrelated areas of commerce." *Id.,* at 442. It pointed to patent law's "staple article of commerce" doctrine, under which a distributor of a product is not liable for patent infringement by its customers unless that product is "unsuited for any commercial noninfringing use." *Dawson Chemical Co. v. Rohm & Haas Co.,* 448 U.S. 176, 198 (1980). The Court wrote that the sale of copying equipment, "like the sale of other articles of commerce, does not constitute contributory infringement if the product is widely used for legitimate, unobjectionable purposes. Indeed, it need merely be capable of substantial noninfringing uses." *Sony,* 464 U.S., at 442 (emphasis added). The Court ultimately characterized the legal "question" in the particular case as "whether [Sony's VCR] is *capable of commercially significant noninfringing uses*" (while declining to give "precise content" to these terms). *Ibid.* (emphasis added).

It then applied this standard. The Court had before it a survey (commissioned by the District Court and then prepared by the respondents) showing that roughly 9% of all VCR recordings were of the type—namely, religious, educational, and sports programming—owned by producers and distributors testifying on Sony's behalf who did not object to time-shifting. See Brief for Respondent Universal Studios et al. O. T. 1983, No. 81-1687, pp. 52–53; see also *Sony, supra,* at 424 (7.3% of all Sony VCR use is to record sports programs; representatives of the sports leagues do not object). A much higher percentage of VCR *users* had at one point taped an authorized program, in addition to taping unauthorized programs. And the plaintiffs—not a large class of content providers as in this case—owned only a small percentage of the total available *un*authorized programming. See *ante,* at 6–7, and n. 3 (GINSBURG, J., concurring). But of all the taping actually done by Sony's customers, only around 9% was of the sort the Court referred to as authorized.

The Court found that the magnitude of authorized programming was "significant," and it also noted the "significant potential for future authorized copying." 464 U.S., at 444. The Court supported this conclusion by referencing the trial testimony of professional sports league officials and a religious broadcasting representative. It also discussed (1) a Los Angeles educational station affiliated with the Public Broadcasting Service that made many of its programs available for home taping, and (2) Mr. Rogers' Neighborhood, a widely watched children's program. On the basis of this testimony and other similar evidence, the Court determined that producers of this kind had authorized duplication of their copyrighted programs "in significant enough numbers to create a *substantial* market for a noninfringing use of the" VCR. *Id.,* at 447, n. 28 (emphasis added).

The Court, in using the key word "substantial," indicated that these circumstances alone constituted a sufficient basis for rejecting the imposition of secondary liability. See *id.,* at 456 ("Sony demonstrated a significant likelihood that *substantial* numbers of copyright holders" would not object to time-shifting (emphasis added)). Nonetheless, the Court buttressed its conclusion by finding separately that, in any event, *un*authorized time-shifting often constituted not infringement, but "fair use."

B

When measured against *Sony*'s underlying evidence and analysis, the evidence now before us shows that Grokster passes *Sony*'s test—that is, whether the company's product is capable of substantial or commercially significant noninfringing uses. For one thing, petitioners' (hereinafter MGM) own expert declared that 75% of current files available on Grokster are infringing and 15% are "likely infringing." See App. 436–439, ¶¶6–17 (Decl. of Dr. Ingram Olkin); cf. *ante,* at 4 (opinion of the Court). That leaves some number of

files near 10% that apparently are noninfringing, a figure very similar to the 9% or so of authorized time-shifting uses of the VCR that the Court faced in *Sony.*

As in *Sony,* witnesses here explained the nature of the noninfringing files on Grokster's network without detailed quantification. Those files include:

- Authorized copies of music by artists such as Wilco, Janis Ian, Pearl Jam, Dave Matthews, John Mayer, and others. See App. at 152–153, ¶¶9–13 (Decl. of Aram Sinnreich) (Wilco's "lesson has already been adopted by artists still signed to their major labels"); *id.,* at 170, ¶¶5–7 (Decl. of Patricia D. Hoekman) (locating "numerous audio recordings" that were authorized for swapping); *id.,* at 74, ¶10 (Decl. of Daniel B. Rung) (describing Grokster's partnership with a company that hosts music from thousands of independent artists)
- Free electronic books and other works from various online publishers, including Project Gutenberg. See *id.,* at 136, ¶12 (Decl. of Gregory B. Newby) ("Numerous authorized and public domain Project Gutenberg eBooks are made available" on Grokster. Project Gutenberg "welcomes this widespread sharing . . . using these software products[,] since they assist us in meeting our objectives"); *id.,* at 159–160, ¶32 (Decl. of Sinnreich)
- Public domain and authorized software, such as WinZip 8.1. *Id.,* at 170, ¶8 (Decl. of Hoekman); id., at 165, ¶¶4–7 (Decl. of John Busher)
- Licensed music videos and television and movie segments distributed via digital video packaging with the permission of the copyright holder. Id., at 70, ¶24 (Decl. of Sean L. Mayers)

The nature of these and other lawfully swapped files is such that it is reasonable to infer quantities of current lawful use roughly approximate to those at issue in *Sony.* At least, MGM has offered no evidence sufficient to survive summary judgment that could plausibly demonstrate a significant quantitative difference. See *ante,* at 4 (opinion of the Court); see also Brief for Motion Picture Studio and Recording Company Petitioners i (referring to "at least 90% of the total use of the services"); but see *ante,* at 6–7, n. 3 (GINSBURG, J., concurring). To be sure, in quantitative terms these uses account for only a small percentage of the total number of uses of Grokster's product. But the same was true in *Sony,* which characterized the relatively limited authorized copying market as "substantial." (The Court made clear as well in *Sony* that the amount of material then presently available for lawful copying—if not actually copied—was significant, see 464 U.S., at 444, and the same is certainly true in this case.)

Importantly, *Sony* also used the word "capable," asking whether the product is *"capable of"* substantial noninfringing uses. Its language and analysis suggest that a figure like 10%, if fixed for all time, might well prove insufficient, but that such a figure serves as an adequate foundation where there is a reasonable prospect of expanded legitimate uses over time. See *ibid.* (noting a "significant potential for future authorized copying"). And its language also indicates the appropriateness of looking to potential future uses of the product to determine its "capability."

Here the record reveals a significant future market for noninfringing uses of Grokster-type peer-to-peer software. Such software permits the exchange of *any* sort of digital file—whether that file does, or does not, contain copyrighted material. As more and more uncopyrighted information is stored in swappable form, it seems a likely inference that lawful peer-to-peer sharing will become increasingly prevalent. See, *e.g.*, App. 142, ¶20 (Decl. of Brewster Kahle) ("The [Internet Archive] welcomes [the] redistribution [of authorized films] by the Morpheus-Grokster-KaZaa community of users"); *id.*, at 166, ¶8 (Decl. of Busher) (sales figures of $1,000 to $10,000 per month through peer-to-peer networks "will increase in the future as Acoustica's trialware is more widely distributed through these networks"); *id.*, at 156–164, ¶¶21–40 (Decl. of Sinnreich).

And that is just what is happening. Such legitimate noninfringing uses are coming to include the swapping of: *research information* (the initial purpose of many peer-to-peer networks); *public domain films* (*e.g.*, those owned by the Prelinger Archive); *historical recordings and digital educational materials* (*e.g.*, those stored on the Internet Archive); *digital photos* (OurPictures, for example, is starting a P2P photo-swapping service); *"shareware" and "freeware"* (*e.g.*, Linux and certain Windows software); *secure licensed music and movie files* (Intent MediaWorks, for example, protects licensed content sent across P2P networks); *news broadcasts past and present* (the BBC Creative Archive lets users "rip, mix and share the BBC"); *user-created audio and video files* (including "podcasts" that may be distributed through P2P software); *and all manner of free "open content" works collected by Creative Commons* (one can search for Creative Commons material on StreamCast). See Brief for Distributed Computing Industry Association as *Amicus Curiae* 15–26; Merges, A New Dynamism in the Public Domain, 71 U. Chi. L. Rev. 183 (2004). I can find nothing in the record that suggests that this course of events will *not* continue to flow naturally as a consequence of the character of the software taken together with the foreseeable development of the Internet and of information technology. Cf. *ante*, at 1–2 (opinion of the Court) (discussing the significant benefits of peer-to-peer technology).

There may be other now-unforeseen noninfringing uses that develop for peer-to-peer software, just as the home-video rental industry (unmentioned in *Sony*) developed for the VCR. But the foreseeable development of such uses, when taken together with an estimated 10% noninfringing material, is sufficient to meet *Sony*'s standard. And while *Sony* considered the record following a trial, there are no facts asserted by MGM in its summary judgment filings that lead me to believe the outcome after a trial here could be any different. The lower courts reached the same conclusion.

Of course, Grokster itself may not want to develop these other noninfringing uses. But *Sony*'s standard seeks to protect not the Groksters of this world (which in any event may well be liable under today's holding), but the development of technology more generally. And Grokster's desires in this respect are beside the point.

II

The real question here, I believe, is not whether the record evidence satisfies *Sony*. As I have interpreted the standard set forth in that case, it does. And of the Courts of Appeals that have considered the matter, only one has proposed interpreting *Sony* more strictly than I would do—in a case where the product might have failed under *any* standard. *In re Aimster Copyright Litigation*, 334 F. 3d 643, 653 (CA7 2003) (defendant "failed to show that its service is *ever* used for any purpose other than to infringe" copyrights (emphasis added)); see *Matthew Bender & Co., Inc. v. West Pub. Co.*, 158 F. 3d 693, 706–707 (CA2 1998) (court did not *require* that noninfringing uses be "predominant," it merely found that they *were* predominant, and therefore provided no analysis of *Sony*'s boundaries; but see *ante*, at 3 n. 1 (GINSBURG, J., concurring); see also *A&M Records v. Napster, Inc.*, 239 F. 3d 1004, 1020 (CA9 2001) (discussing *Sony*); *Cable/Home Communication Corp. v. Network Productions, Inc.*, 902 F. 2d 829, 842–847 (CA11 1990) (same); *Vault Corp. v. Quaid Software, Ltd.*, 847 F. 2d 255, 262 (CA5 1988) (same); cf. *Dynacore Holdings Corp. v. U.S. Philips Corp.*, 363 F. 3d 1263, 1275 (CA Fed. 2004) (same); see also *Doe v. GTE Corp.*, 347 F. 3d 655, 661 (CA7 2003) ("A person may be liable as a contributory infringer if the product or service it sells has no (or only slight) legal use").

Instead, the real question is whether we should modify the *Sony* standard, as MGM requests, or interpret *Sony* more strictly, as I believe JUSTICE GINSBURG's approach would do in practice. Compare *ante*, at 4–8 (concurring) (insufficient evidence in this case of both present lawful uses and of a reasonable prospect that substantial noninfringing uses would develop over time), with *Sony*, 464 U.S., at 442–447 (basing conclusion as to the likely existence of a substantial market for authorized copying upon general declarations, some survey data, and common sense).

As I have said, *Sony* itself sought to "strike a balance between a copyright holder's legitimate demand for effective—not merely symbolic—protection of the statutory monopoly, and the rights of others freely to engage in substantially unrelated areas of commerce." *Id.*, at 442. Thus, to determine whether modification, or a strict interpretation, of *Sony* is needed, I would ask whether MGM has shown that *Sony* incorrectly balanced copyright and new-technology interests. In particular: (1) Has *Sony* (as I interpret it) worked to protect new technology? (2) If so, would modification or strict interpretation significantly weaken that protection? (3) If so, would new or necessary copyright-related benefits outweigh any such weakening?

A

The first question is the easiest to answer. *Sony*'s rule, as I interpret it, has provided entrepreneurs with needed assurance that they will be shielded from copyright liability as they bring valuable new technologies to market.

Sony's rule is clear.   That clarity allows those who develop new products that are capable of substantial noninfringing uses to know, *ex ante*, that distribution of their product will not yield massive monetary liability. At the same time, it helps deter them from distributing products that have no other real function than—or that are specifically intended for—copyright infringement, deterrence that the Court's holding today reinforces (by adding a weapon to the copyright holder's legal arsenal).

Sony's rule is strongly technology protecting.   The rule deliberately makes it difficult for courts to find secondary liability where new technology is at issue. It establishes that the law will not impose copyright liability upon the distributors of dual-use technologies (who do not themselves engage in unauthorized copying) unless the product in question will be used *almost exclusively* to infringe copyrights (or unless they actively induce infringements as we today describe). *Sony* thereby recognizes that the copyright laws are not intended to discourage or to control the emergence of new technologies, including (perhaps especially) those that help disseminate information and ideas more broadly or more efficiently. Thus *Sony*'s rule shelters VCRs, typewriters, tape recorders, photocopiers, computers, cassette players, compact disc burners, digital video recorders, MP3 players, Internet search engines, and peer-to-peer software. But *Sony*'s rule does not shelter descramblers, even if one could *theoretically* use a descrambler in a noninfringing way. 464 U.S., at 441–442; compare *Cable/Home Communication Corp.*, *supra*, at 837–850 (developer liable for advertising television signal descrambler), with *Vault Corp.*, *supra*, at 262 (primary use infringing but a substantial noninfringing use).

Sony's rule is forward looking.   It does not confine its scope to a static snapshot of a product's current uses (thereby threatening technologies that have undeveloped future markets). Rather, as the VCR example makes clear, a product's market can evolve dramatically over time. And *Sony*—by referring to a *capacity* for substantial noninfringing uses—recognizes that fact. *Sony*'s word "capable" refers to a plausible, not simply a theoretical, likelihood that such uses will come to pass, and that fact anchors *Sony* in practical reality.

Sony's rule is mindful of the limitations facing judges where matters of technology are concerned. Judges have no specialized technical ability to answer questions about present or future technological feasibility or commercial viability where technology professionals, engineers, and venture capitalists themselves may radically disagree and where answers may differ depending upon whether one focuses upon the time of product development or the time of distribution. Consider, for example, the question whether devices can be added to Grokster's software that will filter out infringing files. MGM tells us this is easy enough to do, as do several *amici* that produce and sell the filtering technology. See, *e.g.*, Brief for Motion Picture Studio Petitioners 11; Brief for Audible Magic Corp. et al. as *Amicus Curiae* 3–10. Grokster says it is not at all easy to do, and not an efficient solution in any event, and several apparently disinterested computer science professors agree. See Brief for Respondents 31; Brief for Computer Science Professors as *Amicus Curiae* 6–10, 14–18. Which account should a judge credit? *Sony* says that the judge will not necessarily have to decide.

Given the nature of the *Sony* rule, it is not surprising that in the last 20 years, there have been relatively few contributory infringement suits—based on a product distribution theory—brought against technology providers (a small handful of federal appellate court cases and perhaps fewer than two dozen District Court cases in the last 20 years). I have found nothing in the briefs or the record that shows that *Sony* has failed to achieve its innovation-protecting objective.

B

The second, more difficult, question is whether a modified *Sony* rule (or a strict interpretation) would significantly weaken the law's ability to protect new technology. Justice Ginsburg's approach would require defendants to produce considerably more concrete evidence—more than was presented here—to earn *Sony*'s shelter. That heavier evidentiary demand, and especially the more dramatic (case-by-case balancing) modifications that MGM and the Government seek, would, I believe, undercut the protection that *Sony* now offers.

To require defendants to provide, for example, detailed evidence—say business plans, profitability estimates, projected technological modifications, and so forth—would doubtless make life easier for copyright holder plaintiffs. But it would simultaneously increase the legal uncertainty that surrounds the creation or development of a new technology capable of being put to infringing uses. Inventors and entrepreneurs (in the garage, the dorm room, the corporate lab, or the boardroom) would have to fear (and in many cases endure) costly and extensive trials when they create, produce, or distribute the sort of information technology that can be used for copyright infringement. They would often be left guessing as to how a court, upon later review of the product and its uses, would decide when necessarily rough estimates amounted to sufficient evidence. They would have no way to predict how courts would weigh the respective values of infringing and noninfringing uses; determine the efficiency and advisability of technological changes; or assess a product's potential future markets. The price of a wrong guess—even if it involves a good-faith effort to assess technical and commercial viability—could be large statutory damages (not less than $750 and up to $30,000 *per infringed work*). 17 U. S. C. §504(c)(1). The additional risk and uncertainty would mean a consequent additional chill of technological development.

C

The third question—whether a positive copyright impact would outweigh any technology-related loss—I find the most difficult of the three. I do not doubt that a more intrusive *Sony* test would generally provide greater revenue security for copyright holders. But it is harder to conclude that the gains on the copyright swings would exceed the losses on the technology roundabouts.

For one thing, the law disfavors equating the two different kinds of gain and loss; rather, it leans in favor of protecting technology. As *Sony* itself makes clear, the producer of a technology which *permits* unlawful copying does not himself *engage* in unlawful copying—a fact that makes the attachment of copyright liability to the creation, production, or distribution of the technology an exceptional thing. See 464 U.S., at 431 (courts "must be circumspect" in construing the copyright laws to preclude distribution of new technologies). Moreover, *Sony* has been the law for some time. And that fact imposes a serious burden upon copyright holders like MGM to show a need for change in the current rules of the game, including a more strict interpretation of the test. See, *e.g.*, Brief for Motion Picture Studio Petitioners 31 (*Sony* should not protect products when the "primary or principal" use is infringing).

In any event, the evidence now available does not, in my view, make out a sufficiently strong case for change. To say this is not to doubt the basic need to protect copyrighted material from infringement. The Constitution itself stresses the vital role that copyright plays in advancing the "useful Arts." Art. I, §8, cl. 8. No one disputes that "reward to the author or artist serves to induce release to the public of the products of his creative genius." *United States v. Paramount Pictures, Inc.*, 334 U.S. 131, 158 (1948). And deliberate unlawful copying is no less an unlawful taking of property than garden-variety theft. See, *e.g.*, 18 U. S. C. §2319 (criminal copyright infringement); §1961(1) (B) (copyright infringement can be a predicate act under the Racketeer Influenced and Corrupt Organizations Act); §1956(c)(7)(D) (money laundering includes the receipt of proceeds from copyright infringement). But these highly general principles cannot by themselves tell us how to balance the interests at issue in *Sony* or whether *Sony*'s standard needs modification. And at certain key points, information is lacking.

Will an unmodified *Sony* lead to a significant diminution in the amount or quality of creative work produced? Since copyright's basic objective is creation and its revenue objectives but a means to that end, this is the underlying copyright question. See *Twentieth Century Music Corp. v. Aiken*, 422 U.S. 151, 156 (1975) ("Creative work is to be encouraged and rewarded, but private motivation must ultimately serve the cause of promoting broad public availability of literature, music, and the other arts"). And its answer is far from clear.

Unauthorized copying likely diminishes industry revenue, though it is not clear by how much. Compare S. Liebowitz, Will MP3 Downloads Annihilate the Record Industry? The Evidence So Far, p. 2 (June 2003) . . . (all Internet materials as visited June 24, 2005, and available in Clerk of Court's case file) (file sharing has caused a decline in music sales), and Press Release, Informa Media Group Report (citing Music on the Internet (5th ed. 2004)) (estimating total lost sales to the music industry in the range of

$2 billion annually) . . . with F. Oberholzer & K. Strumpf, The Effect of File Sharing on Record Sales: An Empirical Analysis, p. 24 (Mar. 2004) . . . (academic study concluding that "file sharing has no statistically significant effect on purchases of the average album"), and McGuire, Study: File-Sharing No Threat to Music Sales (Mar. 29, 2004) . . . (discussing mixed evidence).

The extent to which related production has actually and resultingly declined remains uncertain, though there is good reason to believe that the decline, if any, is not substantial. See, *e.g.*, M. Madden, Pew Internet & American Life Project, Artists, Musicians, and the Internet, p. 21 . . . (nearly 70% of musicians believe that file sharing is a minor threat or no threat at all to creative industries); Benkler, Sharing Nicely: On Shareable Goods and the Emergence of Sharing as a Modality of Economic Production, 114 Yale L. J. 273, 351–352 (2004) ("Much of the actual flow of revenue to artists—from performances and other sources—is stable even assuming a complete displacement of the CD market by peer-to-peer distribution. . . . [I]t would be silly to think that music, a cultural form without which no human society has existed, will cease to be in our world [because of illegal file swapping]").

More importantly, copyright holders at least potentially have other tools available to reduce piracy and to abate whatever threat it poses to creative production. As today's opinion makes clear, a copyright holder may proceed against a technology provider where a provable specific intent to infringe (of the kind the Court describes) is present. *Ante*, at 24 (opinion of the Court). Services like Grokster may well be liable under an inducement theory.

In addition, a copyright holder has always had the legal authority to bring a traditional infringement suit against one who wrongfully copies. Indeed, since September 2003, the Recording Industry Association of America (RIAA) has filed "thousands of suits against people for sharing copyrighted material." Walker, New Movement Hits Universities: Get Legal Music, *Washington Post*, Mar. 17, 2005, p. E1. These suits have provided copyright holders with damages; have served as a teaching tool, making clear that much file sharing, if done without permission, is unlawful; and apparently have had a real and significant deterrent effect. See, *e.g.*, L. Rainie, M. Madden, D. Hess, & G. Mudd, Pew Internet Project and comScore Media Metrix Data Memo: The state of music downloading and file-sharing online, pp. 2, 4, 6, 10 (Apr. 2004) . . . (number of people downloading files fell from a peak of roughly 35 million to roughly 23 million in the year following the first suits; 38% of current downloaders report downloading fewer files because of the suits); M. Madden & L. Rainie, Pew Internet Project Data Memo: Music

and video downloading moves beyond P2P, p. 7 (March 2005) . . . (number of downloaders has "inched up" but "continues to rest well below the peak level"); Groennings, Note, Costs and Benefits of the Recording Industry's Litigation Against Individuals, 20 Berkeley Technology L. J. 571 (2005); but see Evangelista, Downloading Music and Movie Files Is as Popular as Ever, San Francisco Chronicle, Mar. 28, 2005, p. E1 (referring to the continuing "tide of rampant copyright infringement," while noting that the RIAA says it believes the "campaign of lawsuits and public education has at least contained the problem").

Further, copyright holders may develop new technological devices that will help curb unlawful infringement. Some new technology, called "digital 'watermarking'" and "digital fingerprint[ing]," can encode within the file information about the author and the copyright scope and date, which "fingerprints" can help to expose infringers. RIAA Reveals Method to Madness, Wired News, Aug. 28, 2003; . . . Besek, Anti-Circumvention Laws and Copyright: A Report from the Kernochan Center for Law, Media and the Arts, 27 Colum. J. L. & Arts 385, 391, 451 (2004). Other technology can, through encryption, potentially restrict users' ability to make a digital copy. See J. Borland, Tripping the Rippers, C/net News.com (Sept. 28, 2001); . . . but see Brief for Bridgemar Services Ltd. as *Amicus Curiae* 5–8 (arguing that peer-to-peer service providers can more easily block unlawful swapping).

At the same time, advances in technology have discouraged unlawful copying by making *lawful* copying (*e.g.*, downloading music with the copyright holder's permission) cheaper and easier to achieve. Several services now sell music for less than $1 per song. (Walmart.com, for example, charges $0.88 each). Consequently, many consumers initially attracted to the convenience and flexibility of services like Grokster are now migrating to lawful paid services (services with copying permission) where they can enjoy at little cost even greater convenience and flexibility without engaging in unlawful swapping. See Wu, When Code Isn't Law, 89 Va. L. Rev. 679, 731–735 (2003) (noting the prevalence of technological problems on unpaid swapping sites); K. Dean, P2P Tilts Toward Legitimacy, Wired.com, Wired News (Nov. 24, 2004); . . . M. Madden & L. Rainie, March 2005 Data Memo, *supra*, at 6–7 (percentage of current downloaders who have used paid services rose from 24% to 43% in a year; number using free services fell from 58% to 41%).

Thus, lawful music downloading services—those that charge the customer for downloading music and pay royalties to the copyright holder—have continued to grow and to produce substantial revenue. See Brief for Internet Law Faculty as *Amici Curiae* 5–20; Bruno,

Digital Entertainment: Piracy Fight Shows Encouraging Signs (Mar. 5, 2005), available at LEXIS, News Library, Billboard File (in 2004, consumers worldwide purchased more than 10 times the number of digital tracks purchased in 2003; global digital music market of $330 million in 2004 expected to double in 2005); Press Release, Informa Media Report, *supra* (global digital revenues will likely exceed $3 billion in 2010); Ashton [International Federation of the Phonographic Industry] Predicts Downloads Will Hit the Mainstream, Music Week, Jan. 29, 2005, p. 6 (legal music sites and portable MP3 players "are helping transform the digital music market" into "an everyday consumer experience"). And more advanced types of *non*-music-oriented P2P networks have also started to develop, drawing in part on the lessons of Grokster.

Finally, as *Sony* recognized, the legislative option remains available. Courts are less well suited than Congress to the task of "accommodat[ing] fully the varied permutations of competing interests that are inevitably implicated by such new technology." *Sony*, 464 U.S., at 431; see, *e.g.*, Audio Home Recording Act of 1992, 106 Stat. 4237 (adding 17 U. S. C., ch. 10); Protecting Innovation and Art While Preventing Piracy: Hearing Before the Senate Comm. on the Judiciary, 108th Cong., 2d Sess. (July 22, 2004).

I do not know whether these developments and similar alternatives will prove sufficient, but I am reasonably certain that, given their existence, a strong demonstrated need for modifying *Sony* (or for interpreting *Sony*'s standard more strictly) has not yet been shown. That fact, along with the added risks that modification (or strict interpretation) would impose upon technological innovation, leads me to the conclusion that we should maintain *Sony*, reading its standard as I have read it. As so read, it requires affirmance of the Ninth Circuit's determination of the relevant aspects of the *Sony* question.

For these reasons, I disagree with JUSTICE GINSBURG, but I agree with the Court and join its opinion.

Stephen Breyer is an associate justice of the U.S. Supreme Court. He received an AB from Stanford University, a BA from Magdalen College, Oxford, and an LLB from Harvard Law School. He served as a law clerk to Justice Arthur Goldberg of the Supreme Court of the United States during the 1964 term. Prior to being appointed as a judge of the United States Court of Appeals for the First Circuit, he was a professor at Harvard Law School. From 1990 to 1994, he served as chief judge for the First Circuit Court of Appeals. President Clinton nominated him as an associate justice of the Supreme Court in 1994.

EXPLORING THE ISSUE

Does the Sharing of Music Files Through the Internet Violate Copyright Laws?

Critical Thinking and Reflection

1. Is the decision to illegally download movies and music only an economic one or are other factors at play as well?
2. Will more aggressive enforcement of copyright laws encourage the investment of time and money and lead to more creative activity, or will it interfere with the process of creation and inhibit those trying to express themselves in new ways?
3. In an increasingly interconnected world, is it reasonable to think that a U.S. court decision will prevent new infringing technologies from developing? Rather than lawsuits, what other methods of protecting their craft might content creators embrace?
4. Has the decade of technological innovation since *Grokster* reinforced or further justified either the Majority's or the Dissent's opinions?

Is There Common Ground?

Both concurring opinions recognize the importance copyrights have in our society, as did our Founding Fathers. Article I, Section 8, of the U.S. Constitution states that the purpose of copyright is "To promote the progress of science and useful arts, by securing for limited times to authors and inventors the exclusive right to their respective writings and discoveries." Copyright, therefore, is for the benefit of society, and rewarding authors and creators is the means to do this; on this point, there is little debate. However, there is little consensus on the degree to which the courts should inhibit new technologies that are readily used for copyright infringement, but that might otherwise possess other lawful purposes. Interestingly, both Justice Ginsburg and Justice Breyer's decisions are similarly motivated—to establish frameworks that incentivize, rather than inhibit, innovation and creation. In Justice Ginsburg's opinion, society benefits to a greater degree by protecting its copyright creators, where a new technology directly allows for infringement and the vast majority of its use is for that purpose. To not adequately protect those copyright holders whose works are being infringed upon results in a direct loss of income, which may ultimately interfere with future copyrights coming to the market. In Justice Breyer's opinion, the greater benefit is in innovative new technologies that allow for some noninfringing sharing of works and can possibly be used for noninfringing uses in the future. Here, the value of the new technology is not as immediately quantifiable, but in the future may ultimately prove to be immensely beneficial.

Less clear from the opinions, but no less important to the discussion, are the practicalities of enforcing the court's ruling issues, which most likely were at least considered by the Justices. The discussion of incentivizing and protecting innovation is equally a discussion of economic value, as this is in most instances the method of incentivizing. As the U.S. economy shifts from being principally based on manufacturing to services and technology, the importance of information and communication technologies and intellectual property become even more paramount. We can speculate that both opinions in coming to their conclusions are also, at least in part, weighing in on the Internet revolution that is before them. Perhaps knowing that absolute protection is impossible, Justice Ginsburg may be more willing to give an allowance to copyright holders to protect themselves, even if it may mean that certain noninfringing practices are being stymied. Justice Breyer, on the other hand, may recognize that technological innovation cannot be stopped, and thus the best method is for all parties to accept and adapt to new technologies rather than dragging one's feet to protect the old ways. Indeed, these are the criticisms that have been levied at the film and music industries. Many believe that had they been more willing to adopt new technologies, rather than fight them, they would not be in the positions they are in today.

Additional Resources

Geller, Paul Edward, "Copyright's History and the Future: What's Culture Got To Do with It?" 47 *J. Copyright Soc'y U.S.A.* 209, 264 (2000).

Lessig, Lawrence, *The Future of Ideas* (Vintage, 2002).

Lessig, Lawrence, *Free Culture* (Penguin Books, 2004).

Litman, Jessica, *Digital Copyright: Protecting Intellectual Property on the Internet* (Prometheus Books, 2001).

Merges, Robert P., Menell, Peter S., and Lemley, Mark A., *Intellectual Property in the New Technological Age*, 2nd ed. (Aspen Law and Business Publishers, 2000).

Internet References . . .

Abstract and Recording of Oral Arguments of *Sony Corp. v. Universal City Studios*

www.oyez.org/cases/1980-1989/1982/1982_81_1687/

Abstract and Recording of Oral Arguments of *MGM Studios v. Grokster*

www.oyez.org/cases/2000-2009/2004/2004_04_480

Eldred v. Ashcroft (2003)

An interesting case about how "limited" the term of a copyright should be is *Eldred v. Ashcroft* (2003).

http://supct.law.cornell.edu/supct/html/01-618.ZS.html

2012 Box Office Report

This *Entertainment Weekly* article, "Box Office Report 2012: Film Industry Climbs to Record Breaking 10.8 billion," discusses how 2012 was the best year ever for the film Industry at the box office.

http://insidemovies.ew.com/2012/12/31/box-office-report-2012/

New York Times

This article, "Music Industry Sales Rise, and Digital Revenue Gets the Credit," discusses how the digital revolution is now being embraced by the music industry.

www.nytimes.com/2013/02/27/technology/music-industry-records-first-revenue-increase-since-1999.html

Wall Street Journal

"Home Movie Sales Log Rare Increase" article discusses how even the home entertainment business is rebounding thanks to digital distribution.

http://online.wsj.com/article/SB10001424127887323706704578229911000744452.html

The Nielsen Company & Billboard's 2012 Music Industry Report

www.businesswire.com/news/home/20130104005149/en/Nielsen-Company-Billboard's-2012-Music-Industry-Repor

Selected, Edited, and with Issue Framing Material by:
M. Ethan Katsh, *University of Massachusetts, Amherst*

ISSUE

Is the Eighth Amendment Protection Violated If Prisoners Are Deprived of Basic Sustenance?

YES: Anthony Kennedy, from "Majority Opinion, *Brown v. Plata*," *United States Supreme Court* (2011)

NO: Antonin Scalia, from "Dissenting Opinion, *Brown v. Plata*," *United States Supreme Court* (2011)

Learning Outcomes

After reading this issue, you will be able to:

- Discuss the State of California's prison system and how it came to be.
- Discuss the Prison Litigation Reform Act and its implications.
- Discuss how different Supreme Court justices view the role of the Judiciary and how they review Constitutional issues.
- Discuss the historical significance of the Eighth Amendment.

ISSUE SUMMARY

YES: Supreme Court Justice Anthony Kennedy rules that if a prison deprives prisoners of basic sustenance, including adequate medical care, the courts have a responsibility to remedy the resulting violation of the Eighth Amendment.

NO: Justice Antonin Scalia believes that a ruling that may result in the release of 40,000 prisoners is unwarranted and unprecedented.

The Eighth Amendment to the U.S. Constitution states: "Excessive bail shall not be required, nor excessive fines imposed, nor cruel and unusual punishments inflicted." While each of these three restrictions provided for in the Eighth Amendment has gone before the Supreme Court, none has posed as great a challenge as the interpretation of "cruel and unusual punishment." When reviewing a case involving the cruel and unusual punishment clause, the Court most often is reviewing a challenge to a form of punishment, such as the death penalty or a lengthy prison term for a nonviolent crime. However, as you will read in the majority and dissenting opinions of the 2011 Supreme Court case, *Brown v. Plata*, which forms the arguments for

and against the question at hand, the scope of the Court's "cruel and unusual" inquiry does not end with the punishment determination of a jury, judge, or even a legislature.

The history of the Eighth Amendment confirms that the prohibition of specific forms of punishment is generally what was intended by the Framers in including the Amendment in the Bill of Rights. As an "originalist," or one who believes that the Constitution should be interpreted based on norms at the time it was drafted, Justice Scalia argues in the dissent that the courts should not look beyond this meaning. Given the history in Europe of torturous methods of punishment, such as drawing and quartering criminals or burning them at the stake, the Framers sought to ensure that such forms of punishment would not reappear in the American criminal justice system. As one critic of the pre–Bill of Rights Constitution argued, "[Congress is] nowhere restrained from inventing the most cruel and unheard-of punishments, and annexing them to crimes; and there is no constitutional check on [it], but that racks and gibbets may be amongst the most mild instruments of [its] discipline."

Few would argue that, all else being equal, imprisonment is a form of cruel and unusual punishment. It is a far cry from physical torture to merely segregate someone from the general population, and insofar as it is the default method of punishment in the modern world, it hardly qualifies as "unusual." However, even if imprisonment is generally considered humane, the conditions under which someone is imprisoned could be so gruesome as to bring into question whether the prisoner is being subjected to cruel and unusual punishment. In the 1970s, the Supreme Court made clear that the Eighth Amendment outlawed both inhumane punishments and the inhumane treatment of prisoners while incarcerated:

> The Eighth Amendment's ban on inflicting cruel and unusual punishments, made applicable to the States by the Fourteenth Amendment, proscribe[s] more than physically barbarous punishments. It prohibits penalties that . . . transgress today's broad and idealistic concepts of dignity, civilized standards, humanity, and decency. Confinement in a prison or in an isolation cell is a form of punishment subject to scrutiny under Eighth Amendment standards.

> *Hutto v. Finney,* 437 U.S. 678, 685 (1978)

While the majority opinion in *Brown,* authored by Justice Kennedy, no doubt holds this precedential interpretation of the Eighth Amendment as the foundation for its arguments, Justice Scalia is reluctant to agree. He, along with the other three dissenting justices, sees the application of the Eighth Amendment to prison conditions as unwarranted and the intervention of the judiciary into prison management as impractical. Furthermore, they argue that Congress has agreed with their latter sentiment by adopting the Prison Litigation Reform Act (PLRA), which they claim restricts the majority from doing precisely what it is doing with its opinion—legislating from the bench.

With respect to the origins of the PLRA, Justice Scalia is correct. Concerned with the number of lawsuits challenging prison conditions and the costly results of those suits, Congress, in 1995, enacted the PLRA. The PLRA limits the ability of federal courts to impose or sanction expansive remedial measures (as had been done prior to 1995 in a number of

settlement agreements between prisons and inmates). The PLRA requires all relief to be "narrowly drawn" to address the specific violations at issue before the court. The PLRA also imposed an exhaustion requirement to all federal lawsuits, forcing prisoners to first utilize all available administrative remedies prior to being able to file in court. However, even with the hurdles enacted by the PLRA, *Brown v. Plata* found its way to the highest court in the land.

At issue in *Brown* is the validity of an order issued by a specially convened three-judge district court that ordered the release of thousands of prisoners due to the inability of the prison system to provide adequate care to the inmates, a violation of the Eighth Amendment's cruel and unusual punishment clause. This relief was necessary, according to the Court, because California, fraught with budget problems, could not enact the most obvious solution—and one that would avoid the potential dangers associated with releasing prisoners—building new prison facilities and increasing the medical services available to prisoners. As background to the Court's decision, California's elected officials are limited in their ability to raise taxes because of a 1978 ballot initiative, Proposition 13, which amended the state constitution to limit property tax increases and require supermajorities to increase other tax rates. Meanwhile, California's prison population has exploded over the past two decades, in part because of harsher sentencing laws and a "three strikes" policy that mandates a 25-year prison sentence for any defendant convicted of a third felony offense.

Brown v. Plata highlights some of the often-overlooked complexities involved in administering a criminal justice system. The California "three strikes" law was passed as a popular ballot initiative, Proposition 184 in 1994, by an overwhelming margin, but another popular measure—Proposition 13—has impeded California from raising the billions of dollars necessary to accommodate the increased prison population that resulted from Proposition 184.

Few would want to return to the times of corporal punishment, public executions, or banishment of citizens to penal colonies, but the alternative—a prison system—requires the expenditure of public funds, and taxpayers often loathe to have their hard-earned tax dollars go to support food and medical care for those who violate the law. If these competing interests cannot be resolved, prison conditions may deteriorate, as they did here, to the point where judicial intervention is the only option. However, even the courts would admit that the solutions at their disposal, such as ordering the release of convicted criminals, are hardly ideal.

YES ⤺

Anthony Kennedy

Majority Opinion, *Brown v. Plata*

JUSTICE KENNEDY delivered the opinion of the Court.

This case arises from serious constitutional violations in California's prison system. The violations have persisted for years. They remain uncorrected. The appeal comes to this Court from a three-judge District Court order directing California to remedy two ongoing violations of the Cruel and Unusual Punishments Clause, a guarantee binding on the States by the Due Process Clause of the Fourteenth Amendment. The violations are the subject of two class actions in two Federal District Courts. The first involves the class of prisoners with serious mental disorders. That case is *Coleman v. Brown*. The second involves prisoners with serious medical conditions. That case is *Plata v. Brown*. The order of the three-judge District Court is applicable to both cases.

After years of litigation, it became apparent that a remedy for the constitutional violations would not be effective absent a reduction in the prison system population. The authority to order release of prisoners as a remedy to cure a systemic violation of the Eighth Amendment is a power reserved to a three-judge district court, not a single-judge district court. . . . In accordance with that rule, the *Coleman* and *Plata* District Judges independently requested that a three-judge court be convened. The Chief Judge of the Court of Appeals for the Ninth Circuit convened a three-judge court composed of the *Coleman* and *Plata* District Judges and a third, Ninth Circuit Judge. Because the two cases are interrelated, their limited consolidation for this purpose has a certain utility in avoiding conflicting decrees and aiding judicial consideration and enforcement. . . . The State . . . objects to the substance of the three-judge court order, which requires the State to reduce overcrowding in its prisons.

The appeal presents the question whether the remedial order issued by the three-judge court is consistent with requirements and procedures set forth in a congressional statute, the Prison Litigation Reform Act of 1995 (PLRA) . . . The order leaves the choice of means to reduce overcrowding to the discretion of state officials. But absent compliance through new construction, out-of-state transfers, or other means—or modification of the order upon a further showing by the State—the State will be required to release some number of prisoners before their full sentences have been served. High recidivism rates must serve as a warning that mistaken or premature release of even one prisoner can cause injury and harm. The release of prisoners in large numbers—assuming the State finds no other way to comply with the order—is a matter of undoubted, grave concern.

At the time of trial, California's correctional facilities held some 156,000 persons. This is nearly double the number that California's prisons were designed to hold, and California has been ordered to reduce its prison population to 137.5% of design capacity. By the three-judge court's own estimate, the required population reduction could be as high as 46,000 persons. Although the State has reduced the population by at least 9,000 persons during the pendency of this appeal, this means a further reduction of 37,000 persons could be required. As will be noted, the reduction need not be accomplished in an indiscriminate manner or in these substantial numbers if satisfactory, alternate remedies or means for compliance are devised. The State may employ measures, including good-time credits and diversion of low-risk offenders and technical parole violators to community-based programs, that will mitigate the order's impact. The population reduction potentially required is nevertheless of unprecedented sweep and extent.

Yet so too is the continuing injury and harm resulting from these serious constitutional violations. For years the medical and mental health care provided by California's prisons has fallen short of minimum constitutional requirements and has failed to meet prisoners' basic health needs. Needless suffering and death have been the well documented result. Over the whole course of years during which this litigation has been pending, no other remedies have been found to be sufficient. Efforts to remedy the violation have been frustrated by severe overcrowding in California's prison system. Short term gains in the provision of care have been eroded by the long-term effects of severe and pervasive overcrowding.

Supreme Court of the United States, May 23, 2011.

Overcrowding has overtaken the limited resources of prison staff; imposed demands well beyond the capacity of medical and mental health facilities; and created unsanitary and unsafe conditions that make progress in the provision of care difficult or impossible to achieve. The overcrowding is the "primary cause of the violation of a Federal right," 18 U. S. C. §3626(a)(3)(E)(i), specifically the severe and unlawful mistreatment of prisoners through grossly inadequate provision of medical and mental health care.

This Court now holds that the PLRA does authorize the relief afforded in this case and that the court-mandated population limit is necessary to remedy the violation of prisoners' constitutional rights. The order of the three judge court, subject to the right of the State to seek its modification in appropriate circumstances, must be affirmed.

I

A

The degree of overcrowding in California's prisons is exceptional. California's prisons are designed to house a population just under 80,000, but at the time of the three-judge court's decision the population was almost double that. The State's prisons had operated at around 200% of design capacity for at least 11 years. Prisoners are crammed into spaces neither designed nor intended to house inmates. As many as 200 prisoners may live in a gymnasium, monitored by as few as two or three correctional officers. . . . As many as 54 prisoners may share a single toilet. . . .

The Corrections Independent Review Panel, a body appointed by the Governor and composed of correctional consultants and representatives from state agencies, concluded that California's prisons are "'severely overcrowded, imperiling the safety of both correctional employees and inmates. . . .'"

In 2006, then-Governor Schwarzenegger declared a state of emergency in the prisons, as "'immediate action is necessary to prevent death and harm caused by California's severe prison overcrowding.'". . . The consequences of overcrowding identified by the Governor include "'increased, substantial risk for transmission of infectious illness'" and a suicide rate "'approaching an average of one per week.'". . .

Prisoners in California with serious mental illness do not receive minimal, adequate care. Because of a shortage of treatment beds, suicidal inmates may be held for prolonged periods in telephone-booth sized cages without toilets. . . . A psychiatric expert reported observing an inmate who had been held in such a cage for nearly 24 hours, standing in a pool of his own urine, unresponsive and nearly catatonic. Prison officials explained they had "'no place to put him.'". . . Other inmates awaiting care may be held for months in administrative segregation, where they endure harsh and isolated conditions and receive only limited mental health services. Wait times for mental health care range as high as 12 months. . . . In 2006, the suicide rate in California's prisons was nearly 80% higher than the national average for prison populations; and a court-appointed Special Master found that 72.1% of suicides involved "some measure of inadequate assessment, treatment, or intervention, and were therefore most probably foreseeable and/or preventable.". . .

Prisoners suffering from physical illness also receive severely deficient care. California's prisons were designed to meet the medical needs of a population at 100% of design capacity and so have only half the clinical space needed to treat the current population. . . . A correctional officer testified that, in one prison, up to 50 sick inmates may be held together in a 12- by 20-foot cage for up to five hours awaiting treatment. . . . The number of staff is inadequate, and prisoners face significant delays in access to care. . . .

D

The *Coleman* and *Plata* plaintiffs, believing that a remedy for unconstitutional medical and mental health care could not be achieved without reducing overcrowding, moved their respective District Courts to convene a three- judge court empowered under the PLRA to order reductions in the prison population. . . .

The three-judge court heard 14 days of testimony and issued a 184-page opinion, making extensive findings of fact. The court ordered California to reduce its prison population to 137.5% of the prisons' design capacity within two years. Assuming the State does not increase capacity through new construction, the order requires a population reduction of 38,000 to 46,000 persons. Because it appears all but certain that the State cannot complete sufficient construction to comply fully with the order, the prison population will have to be reduced to at least some extent. The court did not order the State to achieve this reduction in any particular manner. Instead, the court ordered the State to formulate a plan for compliance and submit its plan for approval by the court.

The State appealed to this Court. . . .

II

As a consequence of their own actions, prisoners may be deprived of rights that are fundamental to liberty. Yet the law and the Constitution demand recognition of certain other rights. Prisoners retain the essence of human dignity inherent in all persons. Respect for that dignity animates the Eighth Amendment prohibition against cruel and unusual punishment. "'The basic concept underlying the Eighth Amendment is nothing less than the dignity of man.'" *Atkins v. Virginia,* 536 U.S. 304, 311 (2002) (quoting *Trop v. Dulles,* 356 U.S. 86, 100 (1958) (plurality opinion)).

To incarcerate, society takes from prisoners the means to provide for their own needs. Prisoners are dependent on the State for food, clothing, and necessary medical care. A prison's failure to provide sustenance for inmates "may actually produce physical 'torture or a lingering death.'" *Estelle v. Gamble,* 429 U.S. 97, 103 (1976) (quoting *In re Kemmler,* 136 U.S. 436, 447 (1890)); . . . Just as a prisoner may starve if not fed, he or she may suffer or die if not provided adequate medical care. A prison that deprives prisoners of basic sustenance, including adequate medical care, is incompatible with the concept of human dignity and has no place in civilized society.

If government fails to fulfill this obligation, the courts have a responsibility to remedy the resulting Eighth Amendment violation. . . . Courts must be sensitive to the State's interest in punishment, deterrence, and rehabilitation, as well as the need for deference to experienced and expert prison administrators faced with the difficult and dangerous task of housing large numbers of convicted criminals. . . . Courts nevertheless must not shrink from their obligation to "enforce the constitutional rights of all 'persons,' including prisoners." *Cruz v. Beto,* 405 U.S. 319, 321 (1972) *(per curiam).* Courts may not allow constitutional violations to continue simply because a remedy would involve intrusion into the realm of prison administration. . . .

B

[Under the PLRA,] Once a three-judge court has been convened, the court must find additional requirements satisfied before it may impose a population limit. The first of these requirements is that "crowding is the primary cause of the violation of a Federal right." 18 U. S. C. §3626(a)(3)(E)(i).

1

The three-judge court found the primary cause requirement satisfied by the evidence at trial. The court found that overcrowding strains inadequate medical and mental health facilities; overburdens limited clinical and custodial staff; and creates violent, unsanitary, and chaotic conditions that contribute to the constitutional violations and frustrate efforts to fashion a remedy. The three-judge court also found that "until the problem of overcrowding is overcome it will be impossible to provide constitutionally compliant care to California's prison population." . . .

The record documents the severe impact of burgeoning demand on the provision of care. At the time of trial, vacancy rates for medical and mental health staff ranged as high as 20% for surgeons, 25% for physicians, 39% for nurse practitioners, and 54.1% for psychiatrists. . . . These percentages are based on the number of positions budgeted by the State. Dr. Ronald Shansky, former medical director of the Illinois prison system, concluded that these numbers understate the severity of the crisis because the State has not budgeted sufficient staff to meet demand. According to Dr. Shansky, "even if the prisons were able to fill all of their vacant health care positions, which they have not been able to do to date, . . . the prisons would still be unable to handle the level of need given the current overcrowding." . . . Dr. Craig Haney, a professor of psychology, reported that mental health staff are "managing far larger caseloads than is appropriate or effective." . . . A prison psychiatrist told Dr. Haney that "'we are doing about 50% of what we should be doing.'" . . . In the context of physical care Dr. Shansky agreed that "demand for care, particularly for the high priority cases, continues to overwhelm the resources. . . .

Crowding also creates unsafe and unsanitary living conditions that hamper effective delivery of medical and mental health care. A medical expert described living quarters in converted gymnasiums or dayrooms, where large numbers of prisoners may share just a few toilets and showers, as "'breeding grounds for disease.'" . . . Cramped conditions promote unrest and violence, making it difficult for prison officials to monitor and control the prison population. On any given day, prisoners in the general prison population may become ill, thus entering the plaintiff class; and overcrowding may prevent immediate medical attention necessary to avoid suffering, death, or spread of disease. After one prisoner was assaulted in a crowded gymnasium, prison staff did not even learn of the injury until the prisoner had been dead for several hours. . . . Living in crowded, unsafe, and unsanitary conditions can cause prisoners with latent mental illnesses to worsen and develop overt symptoms. Crowding may also impede efforts to improve delivery of care. Two prisoners committed suicide by hanging after being placed in cells that had been identified as requiring a simple fix to remove attachment points that could support a noose. The repair was not made because doing so would involve removing prisoners from the cells, and there was no place to put them. . . . More generally, Jeanne Woodford, the former acting secretary of California's prisons, testified that there "'are simply too many issues that arise from such a large number of prisoners,'" and that, as a result, "'management spends virtually all of its time fighting fires instead of engaging in thoughtful decision-making and planning'" of the sort needed to fashion an effective remedy for these constitutional violations. . . .

Increased violence also requires increased reliance on lockdowns to keep order, and lockdowns further impede the effective delivery of care. In 2006, prison officials instituted 449 lockdowns. . . . The average lockdown lasted 12 days, and 20 lockdowns lasted 60 days or longer. . . . During lockdowns, staff must either escort prisoners to medical facilities or bring medical staff to the prisoners. Either procedure puts additional strain on already overburdened medical and custodial staff. Some programming for the mentally ill even may be canceled altogether during lockdowns, and staff may be unable to supervise the delivery of psychotropic medications. . . .

Numerous experts testified that crowding is the primary cause of the constitutional violations. The former warden of San Quentin and former acting secretary of the California prisons concluded that crowding "makes it 'virtually impossible for the organization to develop, much less implement, a plan to provide prisoners with adequate care.'". . .

3

The three-judge court acknowledged that the violations were caused by factors in addition to overcrowding and that reducing crowding in the prisons would not entirely cure the violations. This is consistent with the reports of the *Coleman* Special Master and *Plata* Receiver, both of whom concluded that even a significant reduction in the prison population would not remedy the violations absent continued efforts to train staff, improve facilities, and reform procedures. . . . The three-judge court nevertheless found that overcrowding was the primary cause in the sense of being the foremost cause of the violation. . . .

As this case illustrates, constitutional violations in conditions of confinement are rarely susceptible of simple or straightforward solutions. In addition to overcrowding the failure of California's prisons to provide adequate medical and mental health care may be ascribed to chronic and worsening budget shortfalls, a lack of political will in favor of reform, inadequate facilities, and systemic administrative failures. The *Plata* District Judge,

in his order appointing the Receiver, compared the problem to "'a spider web, in which the tension of the various strands is determined by the relationship among all the parts of the web, so that if one pulls on a single strand, the tension of the entire web is redistributed in a new and complex pattern.'". . . Only a multifaceted approach aimed at many causes, including overcrowding, will yield a solution.

The PLRA should not be interpreted to place undue restrictions on the authority of federal courts to fashion practical remedies when confronted with complex and intractable constitutional violations. Congress limited the availability of limits on prison populations, but it did not forbid these measures altogether. . . . The House Report accompanying the PLRA explained:

> "While prison caps must be the remedy of last resort, a court still retains the power to order this remedy despite its intrusive nature and harmful consequences to the public if, but only if, it is truly necessary to prevent an actual violation of a prisoner's federal rights." H. R. Rep. No. 104–21, p. 25 (1995).

Courts should presume that Congress was sensitive to the real-world problems faced by those who would remedy constitutional violations in the prisons and that Congress did not leave prisoners without a remedy for violations of their constitutional rights. . . .

C

The three-judge court was also required to find by clear and convincing evidence that "no other relief will remedy the violation of the Federal right.". . .

The State argues that the violation could have been remedied through a combination of new construction, transfers of prisoners out of State, hiring of medical personnel, and continued efforts by the *Plata* Receiver and *Coleman* Special Master. The order in fact permits the State to comply with the population limit by transferring prisoners to county facilities or facilities in other States, or by constructing new facilities to raise the prisons' design capacity. And the three-judge court's order does not bar the State from undertaking any other remedial efforts. If the State does find an adequate remedy other than a population limit, it may seek modification or termination of the three-judge court's order on that basis. The evidence at trial, however, supports the three-judge court's conclusion that an order limited to other remedies would not provide effective relief. . . .

The common thread connecting the State's proposed remedial efforts [in order to avoid releasing prisoners] is that they would require the State to expend large amounts of money absent a reduction in overcrowding. The Court cannot ignore the political and fiscal reality behind this case. California's Legislature has not been willing or able to allocate the resources necessary to meet this crisis absent a reduction in overcrowding. There is no reason to believe it will begin to do so now, when the State of California is facing an unprecedented budgetary shortfall. As noted above, the legislature recently failed to allocate funds for planned new construction. *Supra,* at 30–31. Without a reduction in overcrowding, there will be no efficacious remedy for the unconstitutional care of the sick and mentally ill in California's prisons. . . .

In reaching its decision, the three-judge court gave "substantial weight" to any potential adverse impact on public safety from its order. The court devoted nearly 10 days of trial to the issue of public safety, and it gave the question extensive attention in its opinion. Ultimately, the court concluded that it would be possible to reduce the prison population "in a manner that preserves public safety and the operation of the criminal justice system.". . .

The PLRA's requirement that a court give "substantial weight" to public safety does not require the court to certify that its order has no possible adverse impact on the public. A contrary reading would depart from the statute's text by replacing the word "substantial" with "conclusive." Whenever a court issues an order requiring the State to adjust its incarceration and criminal justice policy, there is a risk that the order will have some adverse impact on public safety in some sectors. This is particularly true when the order requires release of prisoners before their sentence has been served. Persons incarcerated for even one offense may have committed many other crimes prior to arrest and conviction, and some number can be expected to commit further crimes upon release. Yet the PLRA contemplates that courts will retain authority to issue orders necessary to remedy constitutional violations, including authority to issue population limits when necessary. . . . A court is required to consider the public safety consequences of its order and to structure, and monitor, its ruling in a way that mitigates those consequences while still achieving an effective remedy of the constitutional violation.

This inquiry necessarily involves difficult predictive judgments regarding the likely effects of court orders. Although these judgments are normally made by state officials, they necessarily must be made by courts when those courts fashion injunctive relief to remedy serious constitutional violations in the prisons. These questions are difficult and sensitive, but they are factual questions and should be treated as such. Courts can, and should, rely on relevant and informed expert testimony when making factual findings. It was proper for the three-judge court to rely on the testimony of prison officials from California and other States. Those experts testified on the basis of empirical evidence and extensive experience in the field of prison administration.

The three-judge court credited substantial evidence that prison populations can be reduced in a manner that does not increase crime to a significant degree. Some evidence indicated that reducing overcrowding in California's prisons could even improve public safety. Then-Governor Schwarzenegger, in his emergency proclamation on overcrowding, acknowledged that "'overcrowding causes harm to people and property, leads to inmate unrest and misconduct, . . . and increases recidivism as shown within this state and in others.'" . . . The former warden of San Quentin and acting secretary of the California prison system testified that she "'absolutely believe[s] that we make people worse, and that we are not meeting public safety by the way we treat people.'". . . And the head of Pennsylvania's correctional system testified that measures to reduce prison population may "actually improve on public safety because they address the problems that brought people to jail." . . .

Expert witnesses produced statistical evidence that prison populations had been lowered without adversely affecting public safety in a number of jurisdictions, including certain counties in California, as well as Wisconsin, Illinois, Texas, Colorado, Montana, Michigan, Florida, and Canada. . . . Washington's former secretary of corrections testified that his State had implemented population reduction methods, including parole reform and expansion of good time credits, without any "deleterious effect on crime." . . . In light of this evidence, the three-judge court concluded that any negative impact on public safety would be "substantially offset, and perhaps entirely eliminated, by the public safety benefits" of a reduction in overcrowding. Juris. App. 248a.

The court found that various available methods of reducing overcrowding would have little or no impact on public safety. Expansion of good-time credits would allow the State to give early release to only those prisoners who pose the least risk of reoffending. Diverting low-risk offenders to community programs such as drug treatment, day reporting centers, and electronic monitoring would likewise lower the prison population without releasing violent convicts. The State now sends large numbers of persons to prison for violating a technical term or condition of their parole, and it could reduce the prison population by punishing technical parole violations through community-based programs. This last measure would be particularly beneficial as it would reduce crowding in the reception centers, which are especially hard hit by overcrowding. . . . The court's order took account of public safety concerns by giving the State substantial flexibility to select among these and other means of reducing overcrowding. . . .

III

Establishing the population at which the State could begin to provide constitutionally adequate medical and mental health care, and the appropriate time frame within which to achieve the necessary reduction, requires a degree of judgment. The inquiry involves uncertain predictions regarding the effects of population reductions, as well as difficult determinations regarding the capacity of prison officials to provide adequate care at various population levels. Courts have substantial flexibility when making these judgments. . . .

A

The three-judge court concluded that the population of California's prisons should be capped at 137.5% of design capacity. This conclusion is supported by the record. . . . The medical and mental health care provided by California's prisons falls below the standard of decency that inheres in the Eighth Amendment. This extensive and ongoing constitutional violation requires a remedy, and a remedy will not be achieved without a reduction in overcrowding. The relief ordered by the three-judge court is required by the Constitution and was authorized by Congress in the PLRA. The State shall implement the order without further delay.

The judgment of the three-judge court is affirmed.

It is so ordered.

ANTHONY KENNEDY is an associate justice of the U.S. Supreme Court. He received his LLB from Harvard Law School in 1961 and worked for law firms in San Francisco and Sacramento, California, until he was nominated by President Gerald Ford to the U.S. Court of Appeals for the Ninth Circuit in 1975. He was nominated by President Ronald Reagan to the Supreme Court in 1988.

Antonin Scalia

 **NO**

Dissenting Opinion, *Brown v. Plata*

Justice Scalia, with whom Justice Thomas joins, dissenting.

Today the Court affirms what is perhaps the most radical injunction issued by a court in our Nation's history: an order requiring California to release the staggering number of 46,000 convicted criminals.

There comes before us, now and then, a case whose proper outcome is so clearly indicated by tradition and common sense, that its decision ought to shape the law, rather than vice versa. One would think that, before allowing the decree of a federal district court to release 46,000 convicted felons, this Court would bend every effort to read the law in such a way as to avoid that outrageous result. Today, quite to the contrary, the Court disregards stringently drawn provisions of the governing statute, and traditional constitutional limitations upon the power of a federal judge, in order to uphold the absurd.

The proceedings that led to this result were a judicial travesty. I dissent because the institutional reform the District Court has undertaken violates the terms of the governing statute, ignores bedrock limitations on the power of Article III judges, and takes federal courts wildly beyond their institutional capacity.

I

A

The Prison Litigation Reform Act (PLRA) states that "[p]rospective relief in any civil action with respect to prison conditions shall extend no further than necessary to correct the violation of the Federal right of a particular plaintiff or plaintiffs"; that such relief must be "narrowly drawn, [and] exten[d] no further than necessary to correct the violation of the Federal right"; and that it must be "the least intrusive means necessary to correct the violation of the Federal right."... In deciding whether these multiple limitations have been complied with, it is necessary to identify with precision what is the "violation of the Federal right of a particular plaintiff or plaintiffs" that has been alleged. What has been alleged here, and what

the injunction issued by the Court is tailored (narrowly or not) to remedy is the running of a prison system with inadequate medical facilities. That may result in the denial of needed medical treatment to "a particular [prisoner] or [prisoners]," thereby violating (according to our cases) his or their Eighth Amendment rights. But the mere existence of the inadequate system does not subject to cruel and unusual punishment the entire prison population in need of medical care, including those who receive it.

The Court acknowledges that the plaintiffs "do not base their case on deficiencies in care provided on any one occasion"; rather, "[p]laintiffs rely on systemwide deficiencies in the provision of medical and mental health care that, taken as a whole, subject sick and mentally ill prisoners in California to 'substantial risk of serious harm' and cause the delivery of care in the prisons to fall below the evolving standards of decency that mark the progress of a maturing society."... But our judge-empowering "evolving standards of decency" jurisprudence.... does not prescribe (or at least has not until today prescribed) rules for the "decent" running of schools, prisons, and other government institutions. It forbids "indecent" treatment of individuals—in the context of this case, the *denial of medical care* to those who need it. And the persons who have a constitutional claim for denial of medical care are those who are denied medical care—not all who face a "substantial risk" (whatever that is) of being denied medical care.

The *Coleman* litigation involves "the class of seriously mentally ill persons in California prisons,"... and the *Plata* litigation involves "the class of state prisoners with serious medical conditions"... The plaintiffs do not appear to claim—and it would absurd to suggest—that every single one of those prisoners has personally experienced "torture or a lingering death,"... as a consequence of that bad medical system. Indeed, it is inconceivable that anything more than a small proportion of prisoners in the plaintiff classes have personally received sufficiently atrocious treatment that their Eighth Amendment right was violated—which, as the Court recognizes, is why the plaintiffs do not premise their claim on "deficiencies in care provided on any one occasion."... Rather, the plaintiffs' claim is that they are all part of a medical system so defective that some number of prisoners will inevitably be injured by incompetent medical care, and that this number is sufficiently high so as to render the system, as a whole, unconstitutional.

But what procedural principle justifies certifying a class of plaintiffs so they may assert a claim of systemic unconstitutionality? I can think of two possibilities, both of which are untenable. The first is that although some or most plaintiffs in the class do not *individually* have viable Eighth Amendment claims, the class as a whole has collectively suffered an Eighth Amendment violation. That theory is contrary to the bedrock rule that the sole purpose of classwide adjudication is to aggregate claims that are individually viable. "A class action, no less than traditional joinder (of which it is a species), merely enables a federal court to adjudicate claims of multiple parties at once, instead of in separate suits. And like traditional joinder, it leaves the parties' legal rights and duties intact and the rules of decision unchanged." . . .

The second possibility is that every member of the plaintiff class *has* suffered an Eighth Amendment violation merely by virtue of being a patient in a poorly-run prison system, and the purpose of the class is merely to aggregate all those individually viable claims. This theory has the virtue of being consistent with procedural principles, but at the cost of a gross substantive departure from our case law. Under this theory, each and every prisoner who happens to be a patient in a system that has systemic weaknesses—such as "hir[ing] any doctor who had a license, a pulse and a pair of shoes," . . . —has suffered cruel or unusual punishment, even if that person cannot make an individualized showing of mistreatment. Such a theory of the Eighth Amendment is preposterous. And we have said as much in the past: "If . . . a healthy inmate who had suffered no deprivation of needed medical treatment were able to claim violation of his constitutional right to medical care . . . simply on the ground that the prison medical facilities were inadequate, the essential distinction between judge and executive would have disappeared: it would have become the function of the courts to assure adequate medical care in prisons." . . .

Whether procedurally wrong or substantively wrong, the notion that the plaintiff class can allege an Eighth Amendment violation based on "systemwide deficiencies" is assuredly wrong. It follows that the remedy decreed here is also contrary to law, since the theory of systemic unconstitutionality is central to the plaintiffs' case. The PLRA requires plaintiffs to establish that the systemwide injunction entered by the District Court was "narrowly drawn" and "extends no further than necessary" to correct "the

violation of the Federal right of a particular plaintiff or plaintiffs." If (as is the case) the only viable constitutional claims consist of individual instances of mistreatment, then a remedy reforming the system as a whole goes far beyond what the statute allows.

It is also worth noting the peculiarity that the vast majority of inmates most generously rewarded by the release order—the 46,000 whose incarceration will be ended—do not form part of any aggrieved class even under the Court's expansive notion of constitutional violation. Most of them will not be prisoners with medical conditions or severe mental illness; and many will undoubtedly be fine physical specimens who have developed intimidating muscles pumping iron in the prison gym.

B

Even if I accepted the implausible premise that the plaintiffs have established a systemwide violation of the Eighth Amendment, I would dissent from the Court's endorsement of a decrowding order. That order is an example of what has become known as a "structural injunction." As I have previously explained, structural injunctions are radically different from the injunctions traditionally issued by courts of equity, and presumably part of "the judicial Power" conferred on federal courts by Article III:

> "The mandatory injunctions issued upon termination of litigation usually required 'a single simple act.' . . . Indeed, there was a 'historical prejudice of the court of chancery against rendering decrees which called for more than a single affirmative act.' . . . And where specific performance of contracts was sought, it was the categorical rule that no decree would issue that required ongoing supervision. . . . Compliance with these 'single act' mandates could, in addition to being simple, be quick; and once it was achieved the contemnor's relationship with the court came to an end, at least insofar as the subject of the order was concerned. Once the document was turned over or the land conveyed, the litigant's obligation to the court, and the court's coercive power over the litigant, ceased. . . . The court did not engage in any ongoing supervision of the litigant's conduct, nor did its order continue to regulate its behavior." *Mine Workers v. Bagwell*, 512 U.S. 821, 841–842 (1994) (SCALIA, J., concurring).

Structural injunctions depart from that historical practice, turning judges into long-term administrators of complex social institutions such as schools, prisons, and police departments. Indeed, they require judges to play a role essentially indistinguishable from the role ordinarily played by executive officials. Today's decision not only affirms the structural injunction but vastly expands its use, by holding that an entire system is unconstitutional because it *may produce* constitutional violations.

The drawbacks of structural injunctions have been described at great length elsewhere. . . . This case illustrates one of their most pernicious aspects: that they force judges to engage in a form of factfinding-as-policymaking that is outside the traditional judicial role. The factfinding judges traditionally engage in involves the determination of past or present facts based (except for a limited set of materials of which courts may take "judicial notice") exclusively upon a closed trial record. That is one reason why a district judge's factual findings are entitled to clear-error review: because having viewed the trial first hand he is in a better position to evaluate the evidence than a judge reviewing a cold record. In a very limited category of cases, judges have also traditionally been called upon to make some predictive judgments: which custody will best serve the interests of the child, for example, or whether a particular one-shot injunction will remedy the plaintiff's grievance. When a judge manages a structural injunction, however, he will inevitably be required to make very broad empirical predictions necessarily based in large part upon policy views—the sort of predictions regularly made by legislators and executive officials, but inappropriate for the Third Branch.

This feature of structural injunctions is superbly illustrated by the District Court's proceeding concerning the decrowding order's effect on public safety. The PLRA requires that, before granting "[p]rospective relief in [a] civil action with respect to prison conditions," a court must "give substantial weight to any adverse impact on public safety or the operation of a criminal justice system caused by the relief." . . . Here, the District Court discharged that requirement by making the "factual finding" that "the state has available methods by which it could readily reduce the prison population to 137.5% design capacity or less without an adverse impact on public safety or the operation of the criminal justice system." . . . It found the evidence "clear" that prison overcrowding would "perpetuate a criminogenic prison system that itself threatens public safety," . . . and volunteered its opinion that "[t]he population could be reduced even further with the reform of California's antiquated sentencing policies and other related changes to the laws." . . . It "reject[ed] the testimony that inmates released early from prison would commit additional new crimes," finding that "shortening the length of stay through earned credits

would give inmates incentives to participate in programming designed to lower recidivism," . . . and that "slowing the flow of technical parole violators to prison, thereby substantially reducing the churning of parolees, would by itself improve both the prison and parole systems, and public safety." . . . It found that "the diversion of offenders to community correctional programs has significant beneficial effects on public safety," . . . and that "additional rehabilitative programming would result in a significant population reduction while improving public safety" . . .

The District Court cast these predictions (and the Court today accepts them) as "factual findings," made in reliance on the procession of expert witnesses that testified at trial. Because these "findings" have support in the record, it is difficult to reverse them under a plain-error standard of review. . . . And given that the District Court devoted nearly 10 days of trial and 70 pages of its opinion to this issue, it is difficult to dispute that the District Court has discharged its statutory obligation to give "substantial weight to any adverse impact on public safety."

But the idea that the three District Judges in this case relied solely on the credibility of the testifying expert witnesses is fanciful. *Of course* they were relying largely on their own beliefs about penology and recidivism. And *of course* different district judges, of different policy views, would have "found" that rehabilitation would not work and that releasing prisoners would increase the crime rate. I am not saying that the District Judges rendered their factual findings in bad faith. I am saying that it is impossible for judges to make "factual findings" without inserting their own policy judgments, when the factual findings *are* policy judgments. What occurred here is no more judicial factfinding in the ordinary sense than would be the factual findings that deficit spending will not lower the unemployment rate, or that the continued occupation of Iraq will decrease the risk of terrorism. Yet, because they have been branded "factual findings" entitled to deferential review, the policy preferences of three District Judges now govern the operation of California's penal system.

It is important to recognize that the dressing-up of policy judgments as factual findings is not an error peculiar to this case. It is an unavoidable concomitant of institutional-reform litigation. When a district court issues an injunction, it must make a factual assessment of the anticipated consequences of the injunction. And when the injunction undertakes to restructure a social institution, assessing the factual consequences of the injunction is necessarily the sort of predictive judgment that our system of government allocates to other government officials.

But structural injunctions do not simply invite judges to indulge policy preferences. They invite judges to indulge *incompetent* policy preferences. Three years of law school and familiarity with pertinent Supreme Court precedents give no insight whatsoever into the management of social institutions. Thus, in the proceeding below the District Court determined that constitutionally adequate medical services could be provided if the prison population was 137.5% of design capacity. This was an empirical finding it was utterly unqualified to make. Admittedly, the court did not generate that number entirely on its own; it heard the numbers 130% and 145% bandied about by various witnesses and decided to split the difference. But the ability of judges to spit back or even average-out numbers spoon-fed to them by expert witnesses does not render them competent decisionmakers in areas in which they are otherwise unqualified. . . .

C

My general concerns associated with judges' running social institutions are magnified when they run prison systems, and doubly magnified when they force prison officials to release convicted criminals. As we have previously recognized:

> "[C]ourts are ill equipped to deal with the increasingly urgent problems of prison administration and reform. . . . [T]he problems of prisons in America are complex and intractable, and, more to the point, they are not readily susceptible of resolution by decree. . . . Running a prison is an inordinately difficult undertaking that requires expertise, planning, and the commitment of resources, all of which are peculiarly within the province of the legislative and executive branches of government. Prison is, moreover, a task that has been committed to the responsibility of those branches, and separation of powers concerns counsel a policy of judicial restraint. Where a state penal system is involved, federal courts have . . . additional reason to accord deference to the appropriate prison authorities." *Turner v. Safley,* 482 U.S. 78, 84–85 (1987) (internal quotation marks omitted).

These principles apply doubly to a prisoner-release order. As the author of today's opinion explained earlier this Term, granting a writ of habeas corpus "'disturbs the State's significant interest in repose for concluded litigation, denies society the right to punish some admitted offenders, and intrudes on state sovereignty to a degree matched by few exercises of federal judicial authority.'" *Harrington v. Richter,* 562 U.S. ___, ___ (2011) (slip op., at 13) (quoting *Harris v. Reed,* 489 U.S. 255, 282 (1989) (Kennedy, J., dissenting)). Recognizing that habeas relief

must be granted sparingly, we have reversed the Ninth Circuit's erroneous grant of habeas relief to individual California prisoners four times this Term alone. . . . And yet here, the Court affirms an order granting the functional equivalent of 46,000 writs of habeas corpus, based on its paean to courts' "substantial flexibility when making these judgments." . . . It seems that the Court's respect for state sovereignty has vanished in the case where it most matters. . . .

III

In view of the incoherence of the Eighth Amendment claim at the core of this case, the nonjudicial features of institutional reform litigation that this case exemplifies, and the unique concerns associated with mass prisoner releases, I do not believe this Court can affirm this injunction. I will state my approach briefly: In my view, a court may not order a prisoner's release unless it determines that the prisoner is suffering from a violation of his constitutional rights, and that his release, and no other relief, will remedy that violation. Thus, if the court determines that a particular prisoner is being denied constitutionally required medical treatment, and the release of that prisoner (and no other remedy) would enable him to obtain medical treatment, then the court can order his release; but a court may not order the release of prisoners who have suffered no violations of their constitutional rights, merely to make it less likely that that will happen to them in the future.

This view follows from the PLRA's text that I discussed at the outset, . . . "[N]arrowly drawn" means that the relief applies only to the "particular [prisoner] or [prisoners]" whose constitutional rights are violated; "extends no further than necessary" means that prisoners whose rights are not violated will not obtain relief; and "least intrusive means necessary to correct the violation of the Federal right" means that no other relief is available.

I acknowledge that this reading of the PLRA would severely limit the circumstances under which a court could issue structural injunctions to remedy allegedly unconstitutional prison conditions, although it would not eliminate them entirely. If, for instance, a class representing all prisoners in a particular institution alleged that the temperature in their cells was so cold as to violate the Eighth Amendment, or that they were deprived of all exercise time, a court could enter a prisonwide injunction ordering that the temperature be raised or exercise time be provided. Still, my approach may invite the objection that the PLRA appears to contemplate structural injunctions in general and mass prisoner-release orders in particular.

The statute requires courts to "give substantial weight to any adverse impact on public safety or the operation of a criminal justice system caused by the relief" and authorizes them to appoint Special Masters . . . provisions that seem to presuppose the possibility of a structural remedy. It also sets forth criteria under which courts may issue orders that have "the purpose or effect of reducing or limiting the prisoner population" . . .

I do not believe that objection carries the day. In addition to imposing numerous limitations on the ability of district courts to order injunctive relief with respect to prison conditions, the PLRA states that "[n]othing in this section shall be construed to . . . repeal or detract from otherwise applicable limitations on the remedial powers of the courts." . . . The PLRA is therefore best understood as an attempt to constrain the discretion of courts issuing structural injunctions—not as a mandate for their use. For the reasons I have outlined, structural injunctions, especially prisoner-release orders, raise grave separation-of-powers concerns and veer significantly from the historical role and institutional capability of courts. It is appropriate to construe the PLRA so as to constrain courts from entering injunctive relief that would exceed that role and capability.

* * *

The District Court's order that California release 46,000 prisoners extends "further than necessary to correct the violation of the Federal right of a particular plaintiff or plaintiffs" who have been denied needed medical care. . . . It is accordingly forbidden by the PLRA—besides defying all sound conception of the proper role of judges.

ANTONIN SCALIA is an associate justice of the U.S. Supreme Court. He taught law at the University of Virginia, the American Enterprise Institute, Georgetown University, and the University of Chicago before being nominated to the U.S. Court of Appeals by President Ronald Reagan in 1982. He served in that capacity until he was nominated by Reagan to the Supreme Court in 1986.

EXPLORING THE ISSUE

Is the Eighth Amendment Protection Violated If Prisoners Are Deprived of Basic Sustenance?

Critical Thinking and Reflection

1. Were the courts right to intervene in this case, or is Justice Scalia correct that these are issues of public policy, not constitutionalism?
2. Is there any legislation that could be passed by Congress that would have restricted the Court's decision here?
3. Has the court created a "right" to health care?
4. Should the fact that millions of Americans not behind bars live without adequate medical care affect the court's decision?

Is There Common Ground?

It is clear from Justice Kennedy's opinion that the majority's decision releasing thousands of prisoners from California's jails was not an easy one. Indeed, he called the release "a matter of undoubted, grave concern." This sentiment was strongly echoed by the dissent, which made a point to emphasize the sheer number of individuals that had been found guilty by our justice system but that would be released as a result of this decision. What was not shared by both decisions was the level of concern over the gravity of prisoner access to health resources. Nor was there agreement that reducing the prison population was the method to remedy the problem.

While the main issue before the Court was whether the PLRA was violated by upholding the order, several other fundamental issues of jurisprudence were also at front in *Brown*: the appropriate checks and balances between the legislative, judicial, and executive branches of government; the extent of the power of courts to dictate what actions a State must take to remedy constitutional violations; and differing means of interpreting the Constitution. These issues are by no means unique to *Brown*, but their strong overlapping in this case does make for interesting contrasts.

The majority is far more willing to intrude into matters typically left to local government administration. The dissent, recognizing a far more restrictive role for the Courts, as well as a belief that Congress has already spoken directly to this point, believes that dictating a particular course of action far exceeds their authority. Although the majority and dissenting opinions differ on the breadth of their responsibility, all of the justices recognize that there are limits to the authority of the Judiciary to right wrongs. The majority of lawsuits in the United States are resolved not by requiring that specific actions be taken (injunctive relief), but by awarding compensation (monetary damages). However, when, as in this case, money is part of the fundamental problem, there will be no easy solutions.

Additional Resources

Dolovich, Sharon, "Cruelty, Prison Conditions, and the Eighth Amendment" 84 *NYU Law Rev.* 4 (2009).

Feeley, Malcolm M. and Rubin, Edward L., *Judicial Policy Making and the Modern State: How the Courts Reformed American Prisons* (Cambridge University Press, 1999).

Granucci, Anthony, "Nor Cruel and Unusual Punishment Inflicted:' The Original Meaning," 57 *California Law Rev.* 4 (1969).

Kuzinski, Eugene J., "The End of the Prison Law Firm?: Frivolous Inmate Litigation, Judicial Oversight, and the Prison Litigation Reform Act of 1995," 29 *Rutgers Law J.* 361 (1997–1998).

van Zyl Smit, Dirk and Dunkel, Frieder (eds.), *Imprisonment Today and Tomorrow: International Perspectives on Prisoners' Rights and Prison Conditions*, 2nd ed. (Kluwer Law International, 2001).

Internet References . . .

Text of the Prison Litigation Reform Act

www.law.cornell.edu/uscode/text/18/3626

Center for the Study of Constitutional Originalism

A center at the University of San Diego School of Law that explores all aspects of originalism.

www.sandiego.edu/law/centers/csco/events.php

Recording of Oral Arguments of *Brown v. Plata*

www.oyez.org/cases/2010-2019/2010/2010_09_1233

Human Rights Watch

Human Rights Watch criticizes the PLRA for blocking legitimate lawsuits about abusive prison conditions in its 2009 report *No Equal Justice: The Prison Litigation Reform Act in the United States.*

www.hrw.org/en/reports/2009/06/15/no-equal-justice

Unit 3

UNIT

Law and the State

*T*he use of state power can be seen in various ways, including the promotion of patriotic and moral values, in efforts to deal with crime, in responses to public opinion, and in choices of policies to be implemented. The majority is not always allowed to rule, and determining when state interests are compelling and legitimate is often difficult. The issues in this unit confront some of these challenges.

Selected, Edited, and with Issue Framing Material by:
M. Ethan Katsh, *University of Massachusetts, Amherst*

ISSUE

Does the Constitution's Commerce Clause Allow Congress to Require Uninsured Individuals to Buy Health Insurance?

YES: Ruth Bader Ginsburg, from "Majority Opinion, *National Federation of Independent Businesses v. Sebelius*," *United States Supreme Court* (2012)

NO: John G. Roberts, Jr., from "Dissenting Opinion, *National Federation of Independent Businesses v. Sebelius*," *United States Supreme Court* (2012)

Learning Outcomes

After reading this issue, you will be able to:

- Explain what the Commerce Clause is, what it allows Congress to do, and its relevance to the Affordable Care Act.
- Explain why Justice Ginsburg sees the market for medical care as different from all other commerce.
- Explain what is meant by the two principles of "rational basis" and "reasonable connection" regulation of commerce and why Justice Ginsburg thinks that the Affordable Care Act meets these requirements.
- Explain why Justice Roberts thinks that Congress does not have the authority to force every citizen to buy health insurance. Contrast this with Justice Ginsburg's view of this requirement of the law.

ISSUE SUMMARY

YES: Justice Ruth Bader Ginsburg argues that, under existing Supreme Court interpretations of the Constitution's Commerce Clause, Congress has the constitutional authority to require uninsured Americans to buy health insurance or pay a penalty.

NO: Chief Justice John G. Roberts, Jr., argues that a federal mandate to buy a service or product exceeds Congress's power under the Commerce Clause.

As we were finishing this book in May 2017, Congress voted to repeal Obamacare. This does not mean that Obamacare is no longer the law. Quite the contrary. Until the Senate votes on a bill, the House and Senate agree on a bill and the President signs it, all of the provisions of Obamacare, officially the Affordable Care Act (ACA), remain the law of the land.

The most eagerly awaited Supreme Court decision of the 2011–2012 term involved the constitutionality of ACA. The main goal of the ACA was to provide a means for the approximately 50 million uninsured to obtain health insurance. The bill that was passed was lengthy and complex. One of its key elements was the so-called "individual mandate," a requirement that individuals purchase insurance or pay a penalty. The theory was that with a larger number of insured persons, particularly your healthy people, insurance would be more affordable. In addition, the legislation prohibited insurance companies from refusing to insure persons with existing conditions.

The "individual mandate" was the most controversial aspect of health-care reform, with proponents arguing that it was the only way that coverage could be extended to all under a market-based insurance system, and opponents claiming that it was unconstitutional for the U.S. federal government to force people to buy a product or service they did not want. Supporters of the bill primarily focused on the Commerce Clause as the constitutional justification, noting that the Supreme Court has historically given Congress wide latitude in how it regulates interstate economic issues such as health care. Its detractors, however, maintained that the clause allows Congress only to regulate existing commerce, whereas forcing Americans to buy insurance would be creating commerce.

Progressives often favor an expansive reading of the Commerce Clause, one that allows the U.S. federal government to play a more active role in setting social policy, even policy that might not seem related to interstate commerce. For instance, when Congress passed the 1964 Civil Rights Act—which, among other things, outlawed race-based discrimination in public accommodations, such as restaurants and hotels—it justified its ability to force private businesses to take on certain customers by claiming that those business owners were engaged in interstate commerce. In *Heart of Atlanta Motel v. United States* (1964), the Supreme Court sustained that reading of the Commerce Clause. A motel in Atlanta, GA, that refused to rent rooms to African Americans claimed that Congress could not regulate it because it was locally owned and operated and thus couldn't be considered "interstate commerce." The Court disagreed: "the power of Congress to promote interstate commerce also includes the power to regulate the local incidents thereof, including local activities in both the States of origin and destination, which might have a substantial and harmful effect upon that commerce" (379 U.S. 241, 258, 1964).

From the time of the New Deal in the 1930s until the 1990s, the Supreme Court sided with Congress on almost every challenge to its Commerce Clause power. That changed under the Rehnquist Court, when more-conservative justices gained a majority. In 1995, in a 5–4 ruling (*United States v. Lopez*), the Supreme Court held for the first time in decades that a U.S. federal law exceeded Congress's authority under the Commerce Clause. The law in question, which made it a federal crime to have a firearm near a school, "neither regulates a commercial activity nor contains a requirement that the possession be connected in any way to interstate commerce" (514 U.S. 549, 551, 1995) according to Chief Justice Rehnquist's majority opinion. Five years later, the Court used a similar rationale to strike down part of the Violence Against Women Act (*United States v. Morrison*).

The individual mandate was upheld by the Court 5–4 but the five in the majority did not all have the same rationale for finding the law constitutional. Four of the justices agreed with Justice Ginsburg that the individual mandate was justified under the Commerce Clause. Chief Justice Roberts provided the fifth vote for upholding the law but his reasoning was different from Ginsburg's and the other justices in the majority.

Although Chief Justice Roberts declared the individual mandate unconstitutional under the Commerce Clause, he did not strike down the whole ACA. Instead, he crafted an unusual argument for its constitutionality. Noting that under the Supreme Court's precedent, the Court is supposed to uphold a federal statute if any convincing argument can be made for its constitutionality, Roberts said that the individual mandate could be viewed as a tax, since noncompliance only results in a small fine. The mandate could therefore be seen as constitutional under the Taxing Clause, which gives Congress the "power to lay and collect taxes, duties, imposts and excises, to pay the debts and provide for the common defense and general welfare of the United States" (Article I, §8, cl. 1). This was a surprising view, given that the statute itself repeatedly refers to a "penalty" but never portrayed that as a tax. Moreover, most lower court judges who considered the argument rejected it, as did the other four conservative Supreme Court justices, who wanted the entire law struck down as unconstitutional. The more-liberal justices on the Court joined with Ginsburg in viewing the individual mandate as constitutional under the Commerce Clause; however, in order to ensure a majority in favor of the mandate, they joined with Roberts's holding—though not his reasoning—that the law could be upheld under the Taxing Clause. Therefore, although no other justice agreed with Roberts's argument, his opinion effectively controlled the outcome of the case.

Why did Roberts not simply uphold the mandate under the Commerce Clause or join with the four dissenters who wanted the law struck down as unconstitutional? Because the Supreme Court deliberates in secret, the public can only speculate about what happens behind the scenes. Nonetheless, many legal commentators have noted that Roberts's opinion accomplished two conflicting goals: it provided a narrow interpretation of the Commerce Clause, one favored by most conservative jurists, but allowed the Court nevertheless to uphold the ACA. The ACA was President Obama's largest domestic achievement during his first term, and as Ginsburg notes, there is much precedent to support the idea that Congress has the authority to enact the mandate. Even many conservative lower court judges concluded that, under existing precedent, Congress has wide latitude to legislate on interstate commerce, as long as the subject of the legislation is directly related to commerce. As one prominent conservative judge on an appeals court put it, the individual mandate "certainly is an encroachment on individual liberty, but it is no more so than a command that restaurants or hotels are obliged to serve all customers regardless of race, that gravely ill individuals cannot use a substance their doctors described as the only effective palliative for excruciating pain, or that a farmer cannot grow enough wheat to support his own family" (Judge Laurence Silberman, *Seven-Sky v. Holder*, 661 F.3d 1, 20, 2011).

If the Court had used novel interpretations of the Commerce Clause to issue a 5–4 ruling striking down the law, with all five justices in the majority being Republican appointees, the decision might be seen as partisan and politically motivated. Instead, Roberts managed to establish precedent for future limits on the Commerce Clause while at the same time portraying the Court as an impartial, and apolitical, enforcer of the law. That is not to say that all, or even most, Americans are satisfied with the Court's ruling; it simply means that future debates about the individual mandate will happen in the political, rather than the judicial, realm.

YES ⤶

Ruth Bader Ginsburg

Majority Opinion, *National Federation of Independent Businesses v. Sebelius*

. . . Justice Ginsburg concurring in part, concurring in the judgment in part, and dissenting in part.

. . . The provision of health care is today a concern of national dimension, just as the provision of old-age and survivors' benefits was in the 1930s. In the Social Security Act, Congress installed a federal system to provide monthly benefits to retired wage earners and, eventually, to their survivors. Beyond question, Congress could have adopted a similar scheme for health care. Congress chose, instead, to preserve a central role for private insurers and state governments. According to The Chief Justice, the Commerce Clause does not permit that preservation. This rigid reading of the Clause makes scant sense and is stunningly retrogressive.

Since 1937, our precedent has recognized Congress' large authority to set the Nation's course in the economic and social welfare realm. . . . The Chief Justice's crabbed reading of the Commerce Clause harks back to the era in which the Court routinely thwarted Congress' efforts to regulate the national economy in the interest of those who labor to sustain it. . . . It is a reading that should not have staying power.

I

In enacting the Patient Protection and Affordable Care Act (ACA), Congress comprehensively reformed the national market for health-care products and services. By any measure, that market is immense. Collectively, Americans spent $2.5 trillion on health care in 2009, accounting for 17.6% of our Nation's economy. Within the next decade, it is anticipated, spending on health care will nearly double.

The health-care market's size is not its only distinctive feature. Unlike the market for almost any other product or service, the market for medical care is one in which all individuals inevitably participate. Virtually every person residing in the United States, sooner or later, will visit a doctor or other health-care professional. Most people will do so repeatedly.

When individuals make those visits, they face another reality of the current market for medical care: its high cost. In 2010, on average, an individual in the United States incurred over $7,000 in health-care expenses. Over a lifetime, costs mount to hundreds of thousands of [dollars]. When a person requires nonroutine care, the cost will generally exceed what he or she can afford to pay. A single hospital stay, for instance, typically costs upwards of $10,000. Treatments for many serious, though not uncommon, conditions similarly cost a substantial sum.

Although every U. S. domiciliary will incur significant medical expenses during his or her lifetime, the time when care will be needed is often unpredictable. An accident, a heart attack, or a cancer diagnosis commonly occurs without warning. Inescapably, we are all at peril of needing medical care without a moment's [notice].

To manage the risks associated with medical care—its high cost, its unpredictability, and its inevitability—most people in the United States obtain health insurance. Many (approximately 170 million in 2009) are insured by private insurance companies. Others, including those over 65 and certain poor and disabled persons, rely on government-funded insurance programs, notably Medicare and Medicaid. Combined, private health insurers and State and Federal Governments finance almost 85% of the medical care administered to U. S. residents.

Not all U. S. residents, however, have health insurance. In 2009, approximately 50 million people were uninsured, either by choice or, more likely, because they could not afford private insurance and did not qualify for government aid. As a group, uninsured individuals annually consume more than $100 billion in health-care services, nearly 5% of the Nation's total. Over 60% of those without insurance visit a doctor's office or emergency room in a given year. The large number of individuals without health insurance, Congress found, heavily burdens the national health-care market. As just noted, the cost of emergency care or treatment for a serious illness generally exceeds what an individual can afford to pay on her own. Unlike markets for most products, however, the inability to pay for care does not mean that an uninsured individual will

From Supreme Court of the United States, 2012.

receive no care. Federal and state law, as well as professional obligations and embedded social norms, require hospitals and physicians to provide care when it is most needed, regardless of the patient's ability to pay.

As a consequence, medical-care providers deliver significant amounts of care to the uninsured for which the providers receive no payment. In 2008, for example, hospitals, physicians, and other health-care professionals received no compensation for $43 billion worth of the $116 billion in care they administered to those without insurance.

Health-care providers do not absorb these bad debts. Instead, they raise their prices, passing along the cost of uncompensated care to those who do pay reliably: the government and private insurance companies. In response, private insurers increase their premiums, shifting the cost of the elevated bills from providers onto those who carry insurance. The net result: Those with health insurance subsidize the medical care of those without it. As economists would describe what happens, the uninsured "free ride" on those who pay for health insurance.

The size of this subsidy is considerable. Congress found that the cost-shifting just described "increases family [insurance] premiums by on average over $1,000 a year." Higher premiums, in turn, render health insurance less affordable, forcing more people to go without insurance and leading to further cost-shifting. . . .

States cannot resolve the problem of the uninsured on their own. Like Social Security benefits, a universal health-care system, if adopted by an individual State, would be "bait to the needy and dependent elsewhere, encouraging them to migrate and seek a haven of repose." An influx of unhealthy individuals into a State with universal health care would result in increased spending on medical services. To cover the increased costs, a State would have to raise taxes, and private health-insurance companies would have to increase premiums. Higher taxes and increased insurance costs would, in turn, encourage businesses and healthy individuals to leave the State.

States that undertake health-care reforms on their own thus risk "placing themselves in a position of economic disadvantage as compared with neighbors or competitors." Facing that risk, individual States are unlikely to take the initiative in addressing the problem of the uninsured, even though solving that problem is in all States' best interests. Congress' intervention was needed to overcome this collective-action impasse.

Aware that a national solution was required, Congress could have taken over the health-insurance market by establishing a tax-and-spend federal program like Social Security. Such a program, commonly referred to as a single-payer system (where the sole payer is the Federal Government), would have left little, if any, room for private enterprise or the States. Instead of going this route, Congress enacted the ACA, a solution that retains a robust role for private insurers and state governments. To make its chosen approach work, however, Congress had to use some new tools, including a requirement that most individuals obtain private health insurance coverage. As explained below, by employing these tools, Congress was able to achieve a practical, altogether reasonable, solution.

A central aim of the ACA is to reduce the number of uninsured U. S. residents. The minimum coverage provision advances this objective by giving potential recipients of health care a financial incentive to acquire insurance. Per the minimum coverage provision, an individual must either obtain insurance or pay a toll constructed as a tax penalty.

The minimum coverage provision serves a further purpose vital to Congress' plan to reduce the number of uninsured. Congress knew that encouraging individuals to purchase insurance would not suffice to solve the problem, because most of the uninsured are not uninsured by choice. Of particular concern to Congress were people who, though desperately in need of insurance, often cannot acquire it: persons who suffer from preexisting medical conditions.

Before the ACA's enactment, private insurance companies took an applicant's medical history into account when setting insurance rates or deciding whether to insure an individual. Because individuals with preexisting medical conditions cost insurance companies significantly more than those without such conditions, insurers routinely refused to insure these individuals, charged them substantially higher premiums, or offered only limited coverage that did not include the preexisting illness.

To ensure that individuals with medical histories have access to affordable insurance, Congress devised a three-part solution. First, Congress imposed a "guaranteed issue" requirement, which bars insurers from denying coverage to any person on account of that person's medical condition or history. Second, Congress required insurers to use "community rating" to price their insurance policies. Community rating, in effect, bars insurance companies from charging higher premiums to those with preexisting conditions.

But these two provisions, Congress comprehended, could not work effectively unless individuals were given a powerful incentive to obtain insurance.

In the 1990s, several States—including New York, New Jersey, Washington, Kentucky, Maine, New Hampshire, and Vermont—enacted guaranteed-issue and community-rating laws without requiring universal acquisition of insurance coverage. The results were disastrous. "All seven states suffered from skyrocketing insurance premium costs, reductions in individuals with coverage, and reductions in insurance products and providers."

Congress comprehended that guaranteed-issue and community-rating laws alone will not work. When insurance companies are required to insure the sick at affordable prices, individuals can wait until they become ill to buy insurance. Pretty soon, those in need of immediate medical care—*i.e.*, those who cost insurers the most—become the insurance companies' main customers. This "adverse selection" problem leaves insurers with two choices: They can either raise premiums dramatically to cover their ever-increasing costs or they can exit the market. In the seven States that tried guaranteed-issue and community-rating requirements without a minimum coverage provision, that is precisely what insurance companies did.

Massachusetts, Congress was told, cracked the adverse selection problem. By requiring most residents to obtain insurance, the Commonwealth ensured that insurers would not be left with only the sick as customers. As a result, federal lawmakers observed, Massachusetts succeeded where other States had failed. In coupling the minimum coverage provision with guaranteed-issue and community-rating prescriptions, Congress followed Massachusetts' lead.

* * *

In sum, Congress passed the minimum coverage provision as a key component of the ACA to address an economic and social problem that has plagued the Nation for decades: the large number of U. S. residents who are unable or unwilling to obtain health insurance. Whatever one thinks of the policy decision Congress made, it was Congress' prerogative to make it. Reviewed with appropriate deference, the minimum coverage provision, allied to the guaranteed-issue and community-rating prescriptions, should survive measurement under the Commerce and Necessary and Proper Clauses.

II

A

The Commerce Clause, it is widely acknowledged, "was the Framers' response to the central problem that gave rise to the Constitution itself." Under the Articles of Confederation, the Constitution's precursor, the regulation of commerce was left to the States. This scheme proved unworkable, because the individual States, understandably focused on their own economic interests, often failed to take actions critical to the success of the Nation as a whole.

What was needed was a "national Government . . . armed with a positive & compleat authority in all cases

where uniform measures are necessary." The Framers' solution was the Commerce Clause, which, as they perceived it, granted Congress the authority to enact economic legislation "in all Cases for the general Interests of the Union, and also in those Cases to which the States are separately incompetent."

The Framers understood that the "general Interests of the Union" would change over time, in ways they could not anticipate. Accordingly, they recognized that the Constitution was of necessity a "great outlin[e]," not a detailed blueprint, and that its provisions included broad concepts, to be "explained by the context or by the facts of the case.". . .

Consistent with the Framers' intent, we have repeatedly emphasized that Congress' authority under the Commerce Clause is dependent upon "practical" considerations, including "actual experience." We afford Congress the leeway "to undertake to solve national problems directly and realistically."

Until today, this Court's pragmatic approach to judging whether Congress validly exercised its commerce power was guided by two familiar principles. First, Congress has the power to regulate economic activities "that substantially affect interstate commerce." This capacious power extends even to local activities that, viewed in the aggregate, have a substantial impact on interstate commerce.

Second, we owe a large measure of respect to Congress when it frames and enacts economic and social legislation. When appraising such legislation, we ask only (1) whether Congress had a "rational basis" for concluding that the regulated activity substantially affects interstate commerce, and (2) whether there is a "reasonable connection between the regulatory means selected and the asserted ends." In answering these questions, we presume the statute under review is constitutional and may strike it down only on a "plain showing" that Congress acted irrationally.

Straightforward application of these principles would require the Court to hold that the minimum coverage provision is proper Commerce Clause legislation. Beyond dispute, Congress had a rational basis for concluding that the uninsured, as a class, substantially affect interstate commerce. Those without insurance consume billions of dollars of health-care products and services each year. Those goods are produced, sold, and delivered largely by national and regional companies who routinely transact business across state lines. The uninsured also cross state lines to receive care. Some have medical emergencies while away from home. Others, when sick, go to a neighboring State that provides better care for those who have not prepaid for care.

Not only do those without insurance consume a large amount of health care each year; critically, as earlier explained, their inability to pay for a significant portion of that consumption drives up market prices, foists costs on other consumers, and reduces market efficiency and stability. Given these far-reaching effects on interstate commerce, the decision to forgo insurance is hardly inconsequential or equivalent to "doing nothing" it is, instead, an economic decision Congress has the authority to address under the Commerce Clause.

The minimum coverage provision, furthermore, bears a "reasonable connection" to Congress' goal of protecting the health-care market from the disruption caused by individuals who fail to obtain insurance. By requiring those who do not carry insurance to pay a toll, the minimum coverage provision gives individuals a strong incentive to insure. This incentive, Congress had good reason to believe, would reduce the number of uninsured and, correspondingly, mitigate the adverse impact the uninsured have on the national health-care market.

Congress also acted reasonably in requiring uninsured individuals, whether sick or healthy, either to obtain insurance or to pay the specified penalty. As earlier observed, because every person is at risk of needing care at any moment, all those who lack insurance, regardless of their current health status, adversely affect the price of health care and health insurance. Moreover, an insurance-purchase requirement limited to those in need of immediate care simply could not work. Insurance companies would either charge these individuals prohibitively expensive premiums, or, if community-rating regulations were in place, close up [shop].

"[W]here we find that the legislators . . . have a rational basis for finding a chosen regulatory scheme necessary to the protection of commerce, our investigation is at an end." Congress' enactment of the minimum coverage provision, which addresses a specific interstate problem in a practical, experience-informed manner, easily meets this criterion.

Rather than evaluating the constitution of the minimum coverage provision in the manner established by our precedents, The Chief Justice relies on a newly minted constitutional doctrine. The commerce power does not, The Chief Justice announces, permit Congress to "compe[l] individuals to become active in commerce by purchasing a product."

The Chief Justice's novel constraint on Congress' commerce power gains no force from our precedent and for that reason alone warrants disapprobation. But even assuming, for the moment, that Congress lacks authority under the Commerce Clause to "compel individuals not engaged in commerce to purchase an unwanted product," such a limitation would be inapplicable here. Everyone will, at some point, consume health-care products and services. Thus,

if The Chief Justice is correct that an insurance-purchase requirement can be applied only to those who "actively" consume health care, the minimum coverage provision fits the bill.

The Chief Justice does not dispute that all U. S. residents participate in the market for health services over the course of their lives. But, The Chief Justice insists, the uninsured cannot be considered active in the market for health care, because "[t]he proximity and degree of connection between the [uninsured today] and [their] subsequent commercial activity is too lacking."

This argument has multiple flaws. First, more than 60% of those without insurance visit a hospital or doctor's office each year. Nearly 90% will within five years. An uninsured's consumption of health care is thus quite proximate: It is virtually certain to occur in the next five years and more likely than not to occur this year.

Equally evident, Congress has no way of separating those uninsured individuals who will need emergency medical care today (surely their consumption of medical care is sufficiently imminent) from those who will not need medical services for years to come. No one knows when an emergency will occur, yet emergencies involving the uninsured arise daily. To capture individuals who unexpectedly will obtain medical care in the very near future, then, Congress needed to include individuals who will not go to a doctor anytime soon. Congress, our decisions instruct, has authority to cast its net that wide.

Second, it is Congress' role, not the Court's, to delineate the boundaries of the market the Legislature seeks to regulate. The Chief Justice defines the health-care market as including only those transactions that will occur either in the next instant or within some (unspecified) proximity to the next instant. But Congress could reasonably have viewed the market from a long-term perspective, encompassing all transactions virtually certain to occur over the next decade, not just those occurring here and now.

Third, contrary to The Chief Justice's contention, our precedent does indeed support "[t]he proposition that Congress may dictate the conduct of an individual today because of prophesied future activity." In *Wickard*, the Court upheld a penalty the Federal Government imposed on a farmer who grew more wheat than he was permitted to grow under the Agricultural Adjustment Act of 1938 (AAA). He could not be penalized, the farmer argued, as he was growing the wheat for home consumption, not for sale on the open market. The Court rejected this argument. Wheat intended for home consumption, the Court noted, "overhangs the market, and if induced by rising prices, tends to flow into the market and check price increases [intended by the AAA]." . . .

Maintaining that the uninsured are not active in the health-care market, THE CHIEF JUSTICE draws an analogy to the car market. An individual "is not 'active in the car market,'" THE CHIEF JUSTICE observes, simply because he or she may someday buy a car. The analogy is inapt. The inevitable yet unpredictable need for medical care and the guarantee that emergency care will be provided when required are conditions nonexistent in other markets. That is so of the market for cars, and of the market for broccoli as well. Although an individual *might* buy a car or a crown of broccoli one day, there is no certainty she will ever do so. And if she eventually wants a car or has a craving for broccoli, she will be obliged to pay at the counter before receiving the vehicle or nourishment. She will get no free ride or food, at the expense of another consumer forced to pay an inflated price. Upholding the minimum coverage provision on the ground that all are participants or will be participants in the health-care market would therefore carry no implication that Congress may justify under the Commerce Clause a mandate to buy other products and services. . . .

THE CHIEF JUSTICE also calls the minimum coverage provision an illegitimate effort to make young, healthy individuals subsidize insurance premiums paid by the less hale and hardy. This complaint, too, is spurious. Under the current health-care system, healthy persons who lack insurance receive a benefit for which they do not pay: They are assured that, if they need it, emergency medical care will be available, although they cannot afford it. Those who have insurance bear the cost of this guarantee. By requiring the healthy uninsured to obtain insurance or pay a penalty structured as a tax, the minimum coverage provision ends the free ride these individuals currently enjoy.

In the fullness of time, moreover, today's young and healthy will become society's old and infirm. Viewed over a lifespan, the costs and benefits even out: The young who pay more than their fair share currently will pay less than their fair share when they become senior citizens. And even if, as undoubtedly will be the case, some individuals, over their lifespans, will pay more for health insurance than they receive in health services, they have little to complain about, for that is how insurance works. Every insured person receives protection against a catastrophic loss, even though only a subset of the covered class will ultimately need that protection.

a

In any event, THE CHIEF JUSTICE's limitation of the commerce power to the regulation of those actively engaged in commerce finds no home in the text of the Constitution or our decisions. Article I, §8, of the Constitution grants Congress the power "[t]o regulate Commerce . . . among the several States." Nothing in this language implies that Congress' commerce power is limited to regulating those actively engaged in commercial transactions. . . .

In separating the power to regulate from the power to bring the subject of the regulation into existence, THE CHIEF JUSTICE asserts, "[t]he language of the Constitution reflects the natural understanding that the power to regulate assumes there is already something to be regulated."

This argument is difficult to fathom. Requiring individuals to obtain insurance unquestionably regulates the interstate health-insurance and health-care markets, both of them in existence well before the enactment of the ACA. Thus, the "something to be regulated" was surely there when Congress created the minimum coverage provision.

Nor does our case law toe the activity versus inactivity line. In *Wickard*, for example, we upheld the penalty imposed on a farmer who grew too much wheat, even though the regulation had the effect of compelling farmers to purchase wheat in the open market. "[F]orcing some farmers into the market to buy what they could provide for themselves" was, the Court held, a valid means of regulating commerce. In another context, this Court similarly upheld Congress' authority under the commerce power to compel an "inactive" landholder to submit to an unwanted sale. . . .

It is not hard to show the difficulty courts (and Congress) would encounter in distinguishing statutes that regulate "activity" from those that regulate "inactivity." As Judge Easterbrook noted, "it is possible to restate most actions as corresponding inactions with the same effect." Take this case as an example. An individual who opts not to purchase insurance from a private insurer can be seen as actively selecting another form of insurance: self-insurance. The minimum coverage provision could therefore be described as regulating activists in the self-insurance market. *Wickard* is another example. Did the statute there at issue target activity (the growing of too much wheat) or inactivity (the farmer's failure to purchase wheat in the marketplace)? If anything, the Court's analysis suggested the latter. . . .

1 Underlying THE CHIEF JUSTICE's view that the Commerce Clause must be confined to the regulation of active participants in a commercial market is a fear that the commerce power would otherwise know no limits. . . .

When contemplated in its extreme, almost any power looks dangerous. The commerce power, hypothetically, would enable Congress to prohibit the purchase and home production of all meat, fish, and dairy goods, effectively compelling Americans to eat only vegetables. Yet no one would offer the "hypothetical and unreal possibilit[y]" of a vegetarian state as a credible reason to deny Congress the authority ever to ban the possession and sale of goods. THE CHIEF JUSTICE accepts just such specious logic when he cites the broccoli horrible as a reason to deny Congress the power to pass the individual mandate.

2   To bolster his argument that the minimum coverage provision is not valid Commerce Clause legislation, THE CHIEF JUSTICE emphasizes the provision's novelty. . . . For decades, the Court has declined to override legislation because of its novelty, and for good reason. As

our national economy grows and changes, we have recognized, Congress must adapt to the changing "economic and financial realities." Hindering Congress' ability to do so is shortsighted; if history is any guide, today's constriction of the Commerce Clause will not endure. . . .

RUTH BADER GINSBURG is an associate justice of the U.S. Supreme Court. She graduated at the top of her law school class at Columbia University and taught at Rutgers and Columbia Law Schools. She served as director of the ACLU Women's Rights Project, and between 1972 and 1978 she argued six cases involving sex-role stereotyping before the Court and won five. She was appointed to the Supreme Court by President Bill Clinton in 1993.

John G. Roberts, Jr.  **NO**

Dissenting Opinion, *National Federation of Independent Businesses v. Sebelius*

CHIEF JUSTICE ROBERTS announced the judgment of the Court. . . .

Today we resolve constitutional challenges to two provisions of the Patient Protection and Affordable Care Act of 2010: the individual mandate, which requires individuals to purchase a health insurance policy providing a minimum level of coverage; and the Medicaid expansion, which gives funds to the States on the condition that they provide specified health care to all citizens whose income falls below a certain threshold. We do not consider whether the Act embodies sound policies. That judgment is entrusted to the Nation's elected leaders. We ask only whether Congress has the power under the Constitution to enact the challenged provisions.

In our federal system, the National Government possesses only limited powers; the States and the people retain the remainder. Nearly two centuries ago, Chief Justice Marshall observed that "the question respecting the extent of the powers actually granted" to the Federal Government "is perpetually arising, and will probably continue to arise, as long as our system shall exist." In this case we must again determine whether the Constitution grants Congress powers it now asserts, but which many States and individuals believe it does not possess. Resolving this controversy requires us to examine both the limits of the Government's power, and our own limited role in policing those boundaries.

The Federal Government "is acknowledged by all to be one of enumerated powers." That is, rather than granting general authority to perform all the conceivable functions of government, the Constitution lists, or enumerates, the Federal Government's powers. Congress may, for example, "coin Money," "establish Post Offices," and "raise and support Armies." The enumeration of powers is also a limitation of powers, because "[t]he enumeration presupposes something not enumerated." The Constitution's express conferral of some powers makes clear that it does not grant others. And the Federal Government "can exercise only the powers granted to it."

Today, the restrictions on government power foremost in many Americans' minds are likely to be affirmative prohibitions, such as contained in the Bill of Rights. These affirmative prohibitions come into play, however, only where the Government possesses authority to act in the first place. If no enumerated power authorizes Congress to pass a certain law, that law may not be enacted, even if it would not violate any of the express prohibitions in the Bill of Rights or elsewhere in the Constitution.

Indeed, the Constitution did not initially include a Bill of Rights at least partly because the Framers felt the enumeration of powers sufficed to restrain the Government. . . . And when the Bill of Rights was ratified, it made express what the enumeration of powers necessarily implied: "The powers not delegated to the United States by the Constitution . . . are reserved to the States respectively, or to the people." The Federal Government has expanded dramatically over the past two centuries, but it still must show that a constitutional grant of power authorizes each of its actions.

The same does not apply to the States, because the Constitution is not the source of their power. The Constitution may restrict state governments—as it does, for example, by forbidding them to deny any person the equal protection of the laws. But where such prohibitions do not apply, state governments do not need constitutional authorization to act. The States thus can and do perform many of the vital functions of modern government—punishing street crime, running public schools, and zoning property for development, to name but a few—even though the Constitution's text does not authorize any government to do so. Our cases refer to this general power of governing, possessed by the States but not by the Federal Government, as the "police power."

"State sovereignty is not just an end in itself: Rather, federalism secures to citizens the liberties that derive from the diffusion of sovereign power." Because the police power is controlled by 50 different States instead of one national sovereign, the facets of governing that touch on citizens' daily lives are normally administered by smaller governments closer to the governed. The Framers thus

From Supreme Court of the United States, 2012.

ensured that powers which "in the ordinary course of affairs, concern the lives, liberties, and properties of the people" were held by governments more local and more accountable than a distant federal bureaucracy. The independent power of the States also serves as a check on the power of the Federal Government: "By denying any one government complete jurisdiction over all the concerns of public life, federalism protects the liberty of the individual from arbitrary power."

This case concerns two powers that the Constitution does grant the Federal Government, but which must be read carefully to avoid creating a general federal authority akin to the police power. The Constitution authorizes Congress to "regulate Commerce with foreign Nations, and among the several States, and with the Indian Tribes." Our precedents read that to mean that Congress may regulate "the channels of interstate commerce," "persons or things in interstate commerce," and "those activities that substantially affect interstate commerce." The power over activities that substantially affect interstate commerce can be expansive. That power has been held to authorize federal regulation of such seemingly local matters as a farmer's decision to grow wheat for himself and his livestock, and a loan shark's extortionate collections from a neighborhood butcher shop. . . .

The reach of the Federal Government's enumerated powers is broader still because the Constitution authorizes Congress to "make all Laws which shall be necessary and proper for carrying into Execution the foregoing Powers." We have long read this provision to give Congress great latitude in exercising its powers: "Let the end be legitimate, let it be within the scope of the constitution, and all means which are appropriate, which are plainly adapted to that end, which are not prohibited, but consist with the letter and spirit of the constitution, are constitutional."

Our permissive reading of these powers is explained in part by a general reticence to invalidate the acts of the Nation's elected leaders. "Proper respect for a co-ordinate branch of the government" requires that we strike down an Act of Congress only if "the lack of constitutional authority to pass [the] act in question is clearly demonstrated." Members of this Court are vested with the authority to interpret the law; we possess neither the expertise nor the prerogative to make policy judgments. Those decisions are entrusted to our Nation's elected leaders, who can be thrown out of office if the people disagree with them. It is not our job to protect the people from the consequences of their political choices.

Our deference in matters of policy cannot, however, become abdication in matters of law. "The powers of the legislature are defined and limited; and that those limits may not be mistaken, or forgotten, the constitution is written." Our respect for Congress's policy judgments thus can never extend so far as to disavow restraints on federal power that the Constitution carefully constructed. "The peculiar circumstances of the moment may render a measure more or less wise, but cannot render it more or less constitutional." And there can be no question that it is the responsibility of this Court to enforce the limits on federal power by striking down acts of Congress that transgress those limits.

The questions before us must be considered against the background of these basic principles.

I

In 2010, Congress enacted the Patient Protection and Affordable Care Act. The Act aims to increase the number of Americans covered by health insurance and decrease the cost of health care. . . .

The individual mandate requires most Americans to maintain "minimum essential" health insurance coverage. The mandate does not apply to some individuals, such as prisoners and undocumented aliens. Many individuals will receive the required coverage through their employer, or from a government program such as Medicaid or Medicare. But for individuals who are not exempt and do not receive health insurance through a third party, the means of satisfying the requirement is to purchase insurance from a private company.

Beginning in 2014, those who do not comply with the mandate must make a "[s]hared responsibility payment" to the Federal Government. That payment, which the Act describes as a "penalty," is calculated as a percentage of household income, subject to a floor based on a specified dollar amount and a ceiling based on the average annual premium the individual would have to pay for qualifying private health insurance. In 2016, for example, the penalty will be 2.5 percent of an individual's household income, but no less than $695 and no more than the average yearly premium for insurance that covers 60 percent of the cost of 10 specified services (e.g., prescription drugs and hospitalization). The Act provides that the penalty will be paid to the Internal Revenue Service with an individual's taxes, and "shall be assessed and collected in the same manner" as tax penalties, such as the penalty for claiming too large an income tax refund. The Act, however, bars the IRS from using several of its normal enforcement tools, such as criminal prosecutions and levies. And some individuals who are subject to the mandate are nonetheless exempt from the penalty—for example, those with income below a certain threshold and members of Indian tribes.

On the day the President signed the Act into law, Florida and 12 other States filed a complaint in the Federal District Court for the Northern District of Florida. Those plaintiffs—who are both respondents and petitioners here, depending on the issue—were subsequently joined by 13 more States, several individuals, and the National Federation of Independent Business. The plaintiffs alleged, among other things, that the individual mandate provisions of the Act exceeded Congress's powers under Article I of the Constitution. The District Court agreed, holding that Congress lacked constitutional power to enact the individual mandate. The District Court determined that the individual mandate could not be severed from the remainder of the Act, and therefore struck down the Act in its entirety.

The Court of Appeals for the Eleventh Circuit affirmed in part and reversed in part. The court affirmed the District Court's holding that the individual mandate exceeds Congress's power. The panel unanimously agreed that the individual mandate did not impose a tax, and thus could not be authorized by Congress's power to "lay and collect Taxes." U. S. Const., A majority also held that the individual mandate was not supported by Congress's power to "regulate Commerce . . . among the several States." According to the majority, the Commerce Clause does not empower the Federal Government to order individuals to engage in commerce, and the Government's efforts to cast the individual mandate in a different light were unpersuasive. Judge Marcus dissented, reasoning that the individual mandate regulates economic activity that has a clear effect on interstate commerce.

Having held the individual mandate to be unconstitutional, the majority examined whether that provision could be severed from the remainder of the Act. The majority determined that, contrary to the District Court's view, it could. The court thus struck down only the individual mandate, leaving the Act's other provisions intact.

Other Courts of Appeals have also heard challenges to the individual mandate. The Sixth Circuit and the D. C. Circuit upheld the mandate as a valid exercise of Congress's commerce power. . . .

II

The Government advances two theories for the proposition that Congress had constitutional authority to enact the individual mandate. First, the Government argues that Congress had the power to enact the mandate under the Commerce Clause. Under that theory, Congress may order individuals to buy health insurance because the failure to do so affects interstate commerce, and could undercut the Affordable Care Act's other reforms. Second, the Government argues that if the commerce power does not support the mandate, we should nonetheless uphold it as an exercise of Congress's power to tax. According to the Government, even if Congress lacks the power to direct individuals to buy insurance, the only effect of the individual mandate is to raise taxes on those who do not do so, and thus the law may be upheld as a tax.

A

The Government's first argument is that the individual mandate is a valid exercise of Congress's power under the Commerce Clause and the Necessary and Proper Clause. According to the Government, the health care market is characterized by a significant cost-shifting problem. Everyone will eventually need health care at a time and to an extent they cannot predict, but if they do not have insurance, they often will not be able to pay for it. Because state and federal laws nonetheless require hospitals to provide a certain degree of care to individuals without regard to their ability to pay, hospitals end up receiving compensation for only a portion of the services they provide. To recoup the losses, hospitals pass on the cost to insurers through higher rates, and insurers, in turn, pass on the cost to policy holders in the form of higher premiums. Congress estimated that the cost of uncompensated care raises family health insurance premiums, on average, by over $1,000 per year.

In the Affordable Care Act, Congress addressed the problem of those who cannot obtain insurance coverage because of preexisting conditions or other health issues. It did so through the Act's "guaranteed-issue" and "community-rating" provisions. These provisions together prohibit insurance companies from denying coverage to those with such conditions or charging unhealthy individuals higher premiums than healthy individuals.

The guaranteed-issue and community-rating reforms do not, however, address the issue of healthy individuals who choose not to purchase insurance to cover potential health care needs. In fact, the reforms sharply exacerbate that problem, by providing an incentive for individuals to delay purchasing health insurance until they become sick, relying on the promise of guaranteed and affordable coverage.

The reforms also threaten to impose massive new costs on insurers, who are required to accept unhealthy individuals but prohibited from charging them rates necessary to pay for their coverage. This will lead insurers to significantly increase premiums on everyone.

The individual mandate was Congress's solution to these problems. By requiring that individuals purchase health insurance, the mandate prevents cost-shifting by those who would otherwise go without it. In addition, the mandate forces into the insurance risk pool more healthy individuals, whose premiums on average will be higher than their health care expenses. This allows insurers to subsidize the costs of covering the unhealthy individuals the reforms require them to accept. The Government claims that Congress has power under the Commerce and Necessary and Proper Clauses to enact this solution.

1

The Government contends that the individual mandate is within Congress's power because the failure to purchase insurance "has a substantial and deleterious effect on interstate commerce" by creating the cost-shifting problem. The path of our Commerce Clause decisions has not always run smooth, but it is now well established that Congress has broad authority under the Clause. We have recognized, for example, that "[t]he power of Congress over interstate commerce is not confined to the regulation of commerce among the states," but extends to activities that "have a substantial effect on interstate commerce." Congress's power, moreover, is not limited to regulation of an activity that by itself substantially affects interstate commerce, but also extends to activities that do so only when aggregated with similar activities of others.

Given its expansive scope, it is no surprise that Congress has employed the commerce power in a wide variety of ways to address the pressing needs of the time. But Congress has never attempted to rely on that power to compel individuals not engaged in commerce to purchase an unwanted product.[1] Legislative novelty is not necessarily fatal; there is a first time for everything. But sometimes "the most telling indication of [a] severe constitutional problem . . . is the lack of historical precedent" for Congress's action. At the very least, we should "pause to consider the implications of the Government's arguments" when confronted with such new conceptions of federal power.

The Constitution grants Congress the power to "*regulate* Commerce." The power to *regulate* commerce presupposes the existence of commercial activity to be regulated. If the power to "regulate" something included the power to create it, many of the provisions in the Constitution would be superfluous. For example, the Constitution gives Congress the power to "coin Money," in addition to the power to "regulate the Value thereof." And it gives Congress the power to "raise and support Armies" and to "provide and maintain a Navy," in addition to the power

to "make Rules for the Government and Regulation of the land and naval Forces." If the power to regulate the armed forces or the value of money included the power to bring the subject of the regulation into existence, the specific grant of such powers would have been unnecessary. The language of the Constitution reflects the natural understanding that the power to regulate assumes there is already something to be regulated.

Our precedent also reflects this understanding. As expansive as our cases construing the scope of the commerce power have been, they all have one thing in common: They uniformly describe the power as reaching "activity." It is nearly impossible to avoid the word when quoting them.

The individual mandate, however, does not regulate existing commercial activity. It instead compels individuals to *become* active in commerce by purchasing a product, on the ground that their failure to do so affects interstate commerce. Construing the Commerce Clause to permit Congress to regulate individuals precisely *because* they are doing nothing would open a new and potentially vast domain to congressional authority. Every day individuals do not do an infinite number of things. In some cases they decide not to do something; in others they simply fail to do it. Allowing Congress to justify federal regulation by pointing to the effect of inaction on commerce would bring countless decisions an individual could *potentially* make within the scope of federal regulation, and—under the Government's theory—empower Congress to make those decisions for him.

Applying the Government's logic to the familiar case of *Wickard v. Filburn* shows how far that logic would carry us from the notion of a government of limited powers. In *Wickard*, the Court famously upheld a federal penalty imposed on a farmer for growing wheat for consumption on his own farm. That amount of wheat caused the farmer to exceed his quota under a program designed to support the price of wheat by limiting supply. The Court rejected the farmer's argument that growing wheat for home consumption was beyond the reach of the commerce power. It did so on the ground that the farmer's decision to grow wheat for his own use allowed him to avoid purchasing wheat in the market. That decision, when considered in the aggregate along with similar decisions of others, would have had a substantial effect on the interstate market for wheat.

Wickard has long been regarded as "perhaps the most far reaching example of Commerce Clause authority over intrastate activity," but the Government's theory in this case would go much further. Under *Wickard* it is within Congress's power to regulate the market for wheat by supporting its price. But price can be supported by increasing demand as well as by decreasing supply. The aggregated decisions of some consumers not to purchase wheat have a substantial effect on the price of wheat, just as decisions not to purchase health insurance have on the price of insurance. Congress can therefore command that those not buying wheat do so, just as it argues here that it may command that those not buying health insurance do so. The farmer in *Wickard* was at least actively engaged in the production of wheat, and the Government could regulate that activity because of its effect on commerce. The Government's theory here would effectively override that limitation, by establishing that individuals may be regulated under the Commerce Clause whenever enough of them are not doing something the Government would have them do.

Indeed, the Government's logic would justify a mandatory purchase to solve almost any problem. To consider a different example in the health care market, many Americans do not eat a balanced diet. That group makes up a larger percentage of the total population than those without health insurance. The failure of that group to have a healthy diet increases health care costs, to a greater extent than the failure of the uninsured to purchase insurance. Those increased costs are borne in part by other Americans who must pay more, just as the uninsured shift costs to the insured. Congress addressed the insurance problem by ordering everyone to buy insurance. Under the Government's theory, Congress could address the diet problem by ordering everyone to buy vegetables.

People, for reasons of their own, often fail to do things that would be good for them or good for society. Those failures—joined with the similar failures of others—can readily have a substantial effect on interstate commerce. Under the Government's logic, that authorizes Congress to use its commerce power to compel citizens to act as the Government would have them act.

That is not the country the Framers of our Constitution envisioned. James Madison explained that the Commerce Clause was "an addition which few oppose and from which no apprehensions are entertained." While Congress's authority under the Commerce Clause has of course expanded with the growth of the national economy, our cases have "always recognized that the power to regulate commerce, though broad indeed, has limits." The Government's theory would erode those limits, permitting Congress to reach beyond the natural extent of its authority, "everywhere extending the sphere of its activity and drawing all power into its impetuous vortex." Congress already enjoys vast power to regulate much of what

we do. Accepting the Government's theory would give Congress the same license to regulate what we do not do, fundamentally changing the relation between the citizen and the Federal Government.[2]

To an economist, perhaps, there is no difference between activity and inactivity; both have measurable economic effects on commerce. But the distinction between doing something and doing nothing would not have been lost on the Framers, who were "practical statesmen," not metaphysical philosophers. The Framers gave Congress the power to *regulate* commerce, not to *compel* it, and for over 200 years both our decisions and Congress's actions have reflected this understanding. There is no reason to depart from that understanding now.

The Government sees things differently. It argues that because sickness and injury are unpredictable but unavoidable, "the uninsured as a class are active in the market for health care, which they regularly seek and obtain." The individual mandate "merely regulates how individuals finance and pay for that active participation—requiring that they do so through insurance, rather than through attempted self-insurance with the back-stop of shifting costs to others."

The Government repeats the phrase "active in the market for health care" throughout its brief, but that concept has no constitutional significance. An individual who bought a car two years ago and may buy another in the future is not "active in the car market" in any pertinent sense. The phrase "active in the market" cannot obscure the fact that most of those regulated by the individual mandate are not currently engaged in any commercial activity involving health care, and that fact is fatal to the Government's effort to "regulate the uninsured as a class." Our precedents recognize Congress's power to regulate "class[es] of *activities*," not classes of *individuals*, apart from any activity in which they are engaged.

The individual mandate's regulation of the uninsured as a class is, in fact, particularly divorced from any link to existing commercial activity. The mandate primarily affects healthy, often young adults who are less likely to need significant health care and have other priorities for spending their money. It is precisely because these individuals, as an actuarial class, incur relatively low health care costs that the mandate helps counter the effect of forcing insurance companies to cover others who impose greater costs than their premiums are allowed to reflect. If the individual mandate is targeted at a class, it is a class whose commercial inactivity rather than activity is its defining feature.

The Government, however, claims that this does not matter. The Government regards it as sufficient to trigger Congress's authority that almost all those who are uninsured will, at some unknown point in the future, engage in a health care transaction. Asserting that "[t]here is no temporal limitation in the Commerce Clause," the Government argues that because "[e]veryone subject to this regulation is in or will be in the health care market," they can be "regulated in advance."

The proposition that Congress may dictate the conduct of an individual today because of prophesied future activity finds no support in our precedent. We have said that Congress can anticipate the *effects* on commerce of an economic activity. But we have never permitted Congress to anticipate that activity itself in order to regulate individuals not currently engaged in commerce. . . .

Everyone will likely participate in the markets for food, clothing, transportation, shelter, or energy; that does not authorize Congress to direct them to purchase particular products in those or other markets today. The Commerce Clause is not a general license to regulate an individual from cradle to grave, simply because he will predictably engage in particular transactions. Any police power to regulate individuals as such, as opposed to their activities, remains vested in the States.

The Government argues that the individual mandate can be sustained as a sort of exception to this rule, because health insurance is a unique product. According to the Government, upholding the individual mandate would not justify mandatory purchases of items such as cars or broccoli because, as the Government puts it, "[h]ealth insurance is not purchased for its own sake like a car or broccoli; it is a means of financing health-care consumption and covering universal risks." But cars and broccoli are no more purchased for their "own sake" than health insurance. They are purchased to cover the need for transportation and food.

The Government says that health insurance and health care financing are "inherently integrated." But that does not mean the compelled purchase of the first is properly regarded as a regulation of the second. No matter how "inherently integrated" health insurance and health care consumption may be, they are not the same thing: They involve different transactions, entered into

at different times, with different providers. And for most of those targeted by the mandate, significant health care needs will be years, or even decades, away. The proximity and degree of connection between the mandate and the subsequent commercial activity is too lacking to justify an exception of the sort urged by the Government. The individual mandate forces individuals into commerce precisely because they elected to refrain from commercial activity. Such a law cannot be sustained under a clause authorizing Congress to "regulate Commerce." . . .

Notes

1. The examples of other congressional mandates cited by JUSTICE GINSBURG are not to the contrary. Each of those mandates—to report for jury duty, to register for the draft, to purchase firearms in anticipation of militia service, to exchange gold currency for paper currency, and to file a tax return—[is] based on constitutional provisions other than the Commerce Clause.

2. In an attempt to recast the individual mandate as a regulation of commercial activity, JUSTICE GINSBURG suggests that "[a]n individual who opts not to purchase insurance from a private insurer can be seen as actively selecting another form of insurance: self-insurance." But "self-insurance" is, in this context, nothing more than a description of the failure to purchase insurance. Individuals are no more "activ[e] in the self-insurance market" when they fail to purchase insurance, than they are active in the "rest" market when doing nothing.

JOHN G. ROBERTS, JR., is the current Chief Justice of the U.S. Supreme Court. He received an AB from Harvard College in 1976 and a JD from Harvard Law School in 1979. He served as a law clerk for former U.S. Supreme Court Chief Justice William Rehnquist during the 1980 term and in various other legal capacities until his appointment to the U.S. Court of Appeals for the District of Columbia Circuit in 2003. President George W. Bush nominated him as Chief Justice in 2005.

EXPLORING THE ISSUE

Does the Constitution's Commerce Clause Allow Congress to Require Uninsured Individuals to Buy Health Insurance?

Critical Thinking and Reflection

1. Explain the provisions of the Commerce Clause and its relevance to interstate commerce. How do the uninsured, as a class, affect interstate commerce?
2. What were the differences of opinion between Justices Ginsburg and Roberts on the issue of the Affordable Care Act requiring everyone to buy health insurance?
3. What does Justice Roberts mean when he says that the Framers of the Constitution gave Congress the power to regulate but not to compel commerce?
4. Why does Justice Ginsburg reject Justice Roberts's view that the Affordable Care Act is an illegal effort to force young and healthy people to subsidize other and sicker people?

Is There Common Ground?

What has come to be called Obamacare is an extraordinarily complex piece of legislation. The "individual mandate" is one of many requirements and although the Affordable Care Act (ACA) was passed in 2010, it is being put into practice gradually. For example, beginning in January 2014, individuals will be required to obtain health insurance or face a fine.

The enactment of the ACA followed another piece of health-care legislation that was passed in 2008. That Act, the Health Information Technology for Economic and Clinical Health (HITECH) Act, provides subsidies to physicians and hospitals that adopt the use of electronic health records for patients. HITECH and Obamacare share two goals. The first is to improve the health of individuals by encouraging better and more efficient medical treatment for the ill. The second, often not noted, is to improve public health by obtaining better statistics and understanding of patterns of illnesses and medical conditions in the United States. The goal is as much prevention as it is treatment, and the hope is that improved public health will also lead to reduced expenditures on health care.

As was well advertised during the 2012 presidential campaign, much of the ACA was modeled after the health insurance legislation passed by Massachusetts in 2006 when Mitt Romney was governor of the state. In general, the individual mandate in Massachusetts has been a success. In 2012, 98.1 percent of its residents and 99.8 percent of its children were insured. The number of employers offering insurance coverage has increased from 70 percent to 77 percent since 2006, and 88 percent of Massachusetts physicians believe reform either improved, or did not affect, care or quality of care. On the other hand, per capita health care spending in Massachusetts is projected to nearly double by 2020.

Additional Resources

Blue Cross Blue Shield of Massachusetts Foundation, "Health Reform in Massachusetts Expanding Access to Health Insurance Coverage," May, 2012, https://www.mahealthconnector.org/portal/binary/com.epicentric.contentmanagement.servlet.ContentDeliveryServlet/Health%2520Care%2520Reform/Overview/HealthReformAssessingtheResults.pdf

Avik Roy, "The Tortuous History of Conservatives and the Individual Mandate," Forbes, February 7, 2012, http://www.forbes.com/sites/aroy/2012/02/07/the-tortuous-conservative-history-of-the-individual-mandate/

Ilya Somin, "A Mandate for Mandates: Is the Individual Health Insurance Case a Slippery Slope?" 75 Law & Contemporary Problems, 75 (2012).

Wendy K. Mariner, "The Affordable Care Act Individual Coverage Requirement: Ways to Frame the Commerce Clause Issue," 21 Annals of Health Law, 45 (2012).

Internet References . . .

How Does the Affordable Care Act Help People Like Me (from healthcare.gov)?

www.healthcare.gov/how-does-the-affordable-care-act-affect-me

Meaningful Use Standards for Increasing Usage of Electronic Health Records

www.healthit.gov/policy-researchers-implementers/meaningful-use

Timeline for Health care Reform

www.whitehouse.gov/healthreform

Selected, Edited, and with Issue Framing Material by:
M. Ethan Katsh, *University of Massachusetts, Amherst*

ISSUE

Is It Constitutional to Open a Town Meeting with a Prayer?

YES: Anthony Kennedy, from "Majority Opinion, *Town of Greece, New York v. Susan Galloway,*" *United States Supreme Court* (2014)

NO: Elena Kagan et al., from "Dissenting Opinion, *Town of Greece, New York v. Susan Galloway,*" *United States Supreme Court* (2014)

Learning Outcomes

After reading this issue, you will be able to:

- Discuss how this case departs from the Court's usual analysis of Establishment Clause cases.
- Describe how local government legislative bodies differ from State and Federal legislatures.
- Provide examples of how religion could be unlawfully incorporated into legislative functions.
- Discuss the historical significance of prayer and our system of government.

ISSUE SUMMARY

YES: Supreme Court Justice Anthony Kennedy, writing for the Majority, affirms the right of local government bodies to hold a prayer prior to conducting official business maintaining that the history of the United States is consistent with such a practice, and thus the Establishment Clause is not implicated.

NO: Supreme Court Justice Elena Kagan, dissenting from the Court's opinion, argues that prayer prior to local town meetings is a violation of the Establishment Clause of the Constitution and is materially different from prayer held in other governmental forums, which had been previously upheld by the Court.

Is the United States a Christian nation? Are we a religious nation? A monotheistic nation? If that is too bold, is it fair to say that we are a nation based on Judeo-Christian-Islamic values? Should any of this matter in terms of how our government functions? To truly understand the role of religion in politics, must we look to the role religion plays in the lives of every day Americans? The "separation of church and state" is one of the main tenets of our system of government taught in civics classes across the country, but does anyone believe it is that simple?

Other than in the Free Exercise and Establishment Clauses of the First Amendment, the word "God" does not appear in the U.S. Constitution, and Article VI, Section 3 specifically forbids the use of a religious test to qualify an individual for political office. However, the U.S. Constitution does refer to "Blessings," and the date is provided in terms of "the Year of our Lord." While one could debate whether these references are truly religious or mere illustrations of contemporary parlance, there is little debating the religiosity of State governments. Every State Constitution makes reference to a higher power, with almost all making specific reference to "God," and all but a handful making that reference as early as the Constitution's Preamble. Some State Constitutions even go so far as to deny nonbelievers the right to hold State office or testify as a witness at trial, which one could reasonably assume violates the U.S. Constitution.

Many of our nation's earliest European immigrants came to the shores of Massachusetts, Connecticut, and across the eastern seaboard seeking refuge from religious persecution. Along with their families and all their worldly possessions, they also brought strong, devout beliefs. These beliefs in turn made religion an integral part of all aspects of their lives, including government. In fact, the land itself became a destiny of divine providence, or the opportunity to create a "City Upon a Hill," a phrase taken from Jesus' Sermon on the Mount by the Puritan leader, John Winthrop, as a call to create a community that exemplified moral and religious purity. This phrase still continues in the lexicon of American politicians seeking to empower their constituencies.

These early religious settler communities and their leaders, whom historian Frank Lambert refers to as the "Planting Fathers," no doubt had an effect on the evolution of our modern day government. But as time progressed and as more European immigrants arrived, a broader swath of distinct cultural and religious identities took root in the United States, and the desire for religious freedom became a great uniting factor, and as made clear by the Founding Fathers in the First Amendment. As the case remains today, opportunity for a better life in general, not necessarily religious freedom was the driving force for many to embark upon the arduous journey to the New World.

The journey from the ideologies of the Planting Fathers to the Founding Fathers was not without its share of hardship. Courts in the Massachusetts Bay Colony were known to render punishments on strictly religious grounds, including fining individuals for not properly observing the Sabbath. The Puritan leader, Roger Williams, was banished from Massachusetts in the dead of winter for his outspoken criticism of religion's role in their government. He would go on to found Rhode Island, in part, based on the principle of religious freedom. Among his more colorful quotations was that "forced worship stinks in God's nostrils."

From this short discussion alone, it is clear the United States has a convoluted history related to religion and political governance. In the Supreme Court case that follows, *Town of Greece v. Galloway*, history and religion are once again at the forefront of the debate between the Court's conservative and liberal Justices. As you will read, history plays a particularly decisive role in the Majority's conclusion, as is often the case with the originalist members of the Court who seek to determine and base their decisions on the intent of our Founding Fathers. However, here, their inspection of history goes beyond the Founding Fathers and looks to the sustained practices of our legislative branch, noting that Chaplains have always been a paid position within Congress and that their position was

appointed days after the First Amendment was approved. Their reliance on history is further sanctioned by the Court's previous decision in *Marsh v. Chambers,* 463 U.S. 783 (1983).

In *Marsh*, the practice of Nebraska's legislature to pay a Chaplain and preside over a prayer said prior to legislative meetings for the legislators was upheld by the Supreme Court. The *Marsh* opinion was unique in that it departed from the usual analysis of Establishment Clause cases by not applying the "Lemon Test," which was first formed in the Supreme Court case *Lemon v. Kurtzman* (1971). The Lemon Test requires courts to analyze three issues: whether a statute (1) has a "secular legislative purpose"; (2) advances or inhibits religion; and (3) creates an excessive entanglement between government and religion. In *Lemon*, the Court found, after applying its newly determined test, that the practice of certain States to provide funding to nonpublic religious schools, even if related to secular subjects, was a violation of the Establishment Clause. In *Marsh*, and similarly in *Town of Greece*, the Court renders its opinion by applying no test, but by relying principally on the historical significance of the practice of prayer in a legislative body of the United States.

The Dissent also relies heavily on *Marsh* in reaching their conclusion, so much so that one wonders if they are, in fact, reading the same case. However, the Dissent uses *Marsh* as an opportunity to differentiate *Town of Greece* by emphasizing that it involves local government not State government, prayer not being bestowed upon legislators but upon the public in attendance, implied requests by the prayer giver for participation, and, in their opinion, religious invocations so dominated by Christian dogma that even one sharing in similar Judeo-Christian values would find the prayers to be intrusive. These differences, particularly given the intimate forum of local government, which generally involves more personal decisions related to the everyday lives of individuals, and decisions being made between neighbors, are too great for the Dissent to reconcile with *Marsh*.

One can infer from the Dissent's opinion that they would be more willing to tolerate individual prayers that invoke deeply religious symbolism reflective of one particular religion if the local government more widely accepted the participation of different faiths. This would be in line with what some scholars believe that the Founding Fathers sought to achieve. By both allowing for freedom of religion and rejecting the establishment of any one religion, the Founding Fathers may have been striving to create a kind of religious economy, whereby a "marketplace of religion" would be allowed to prosper and where religions, based on their particular values, would vie for the following of individuals, rather than the other way around of imposing religion and withholding choice. However, the difficulty, as the Majority points out in describing the town's attempts to seek out other religions, is that there may not be a sufficient number of options to even create a marketplace.

The following case, which was decided 5 to 4, reflects the fact that religion continues to be a hot-button issue in both political and legal discourse.

YES ⮌

Anthony Kennedy

Majority Opinion, *Town of Greece, New York v. Susan Galloway*

Justice Kennedy delivered the opinion of the Court, except as to Part Il–B.

The Court must decide whether the town of Greece, New York, imposes an impermissible establishment of religion by opening its monthly board meetings with a prayer. It must be concluded, consistent with the Court's opinion in *Marsh v. Chambers*, 463 U.S. 783 (1983), that no violation of the Constitution has been shown.

I

Greece, a town with a population of 94,000, is in upstate New York. For some years, it began its monthly town board meetings with a moment of silence. In 1999, the newly elected town supervisor, John Auberger, decided to replicate the prayer practice he had found meaningful while serving in the county legislature. Following the roll call and recitation of the Pledge of Allegiance, Auberger would invite a local clergyman to the front of the room to deliver an invocation. . . .

The town followed an informal method for selecting prayer givers, all of whom were unpaid volunteers. A town employee would call the congregations listed in a local directory until she found a minister available for that month's meeting. The town eventually compiled a list of willing "board chaplains" who had accepted invitations and agreed to return in the future. The town at no point excluded or denied an opportunity to a would-be prayer giver. Its leaders maintained that a minister or layperson of any persuasion, including an atheist, could give the invocation. But nearly all of the congregations in town were Christian; and from 1999 to 2007, all of the participating ministers were too.

Greece neither reviewed the prayers in advance of the meetings nor provided guidance as to their tone or content, in the belief that exercising any degree of control over the prayers would infringe both the free exercise and speech rights of the ministers. The town instead left the guest clergy free to compose their own devotions. The resulting prayers often sounded both civic and religious themes. Typical were invocations that asked the divinity to abide at the meeting and bestow blessings on the community:

> "Lord we ask you to send your spirit of servanthood upon all of us gathered here this evening to do your work for the benefit of all in our community. We ask you to bless our elected and appointed officials so they may deliberate with wisdom and act with courage. Bless the members of our community who come here to speak before the board so they may state their cause with honesty and humility. . . . Lord we ask you to bless us all, that everything we do here tonight will move you to welcome us one day into your kingdom as good and faithful servants. We ask this in the name of our brother Jesus. Amen."

Some of the ministers spoke in a distinctly Christian idiom; and a minority invoked religious holidays, scripture, or doctrine, as in the following prayer:

> "Lord, God of all creation, we give you thanks and praise for your presence and action in the world. We look with anticipation to the celebration of Holy Week and Easter. It is in the solemn events of next week that we find the very heart and center of our Christian faith. We acknowledge the saving sacrifice of Jesus Christ on the cross. We draw strength, vitality, and confidence from his resurrection at Easter. . . . We pray for peace in the world, an end to terrorism, violence, conflict, and war. We pray for stability, democracy, and good government in those countries in which our armed forces are now serving, especially in Iraq and Afghanistan. . . . Praise and glory be yours, O Lord, now and forever more. Amen."

Respondents Susan Galloway and Linda Stephens attended town board meetings to speak about issues of local concern, and they objected that the prayers violated their religious or philosophical views. At one meeting, Galloway admonished board members that she found the prayers "offensive," "intolerable," and an affront to a "diverse community." After respondents complained that Christian themes pervaded the prayers, to the exclusion of citizens who did not share those beliefs, the town invited a Jewish layman and the chairman of the local Baha'i temple to deliver prayers. A Wiccan priestess who had read press reports about the prayer controversy requested, and was granted, an opportunity to give the invocation.

Galloway and Stephens brought suit in the United States District Court for the Western District of New York. They alleged that the town violated the First Amendment's Establishment Clause by preferring Christians over other prayer givers and by sponsoring sectarian prayers, such as those given "in Jesus' name." They did not seek an end to the prayer practice, but rather requested an injunction that would limit the town to "inclusive and ecumenical" prayers that referred only to a "generic God" and would not associate the government with any one faith or belief.

The District Court on summary judgment upheld the prayer practice as consistent with the First Amendment. It found no impermissible preference for Christianity, noting that the town had opened the prayer program to all creeds and excluded none. Although most of the prayer givers were Christian, this fact reflected only the predominantly Christian identity of the town's congregations, rather than an official policy or practice of discriminating against minority faiths. . . .

The Court of Appeals for the Second Circuit reversed. 681 F. 3d 20, 34 (2012). It held that some aspects of the prayer program, viewed in their totality by a reasonable observer, conveyed the message that Greece was endorsing Christianity. The town's failure to promote the prayer opportunity to the public, or to invite ministers from congregations outside the town limits, all but "ensured a Christian viewpoint." Although the court found no inherent problem in the sectarian content of the prayers, it concluded that the "steady drumbeat" of Christian prayer, unbroken by invocations from other faith traditions, tended to affiliate the town with Christianity. Finally, the court found it relevant that guest clergy sometimes spoke on behalf of all present at the meeting, as by saying "let us pray," or by asking audience members to stand and bow their heads. . . That board members bowed their heads or made the sign of the cross further conveyed the message that the town endorsed Christianity. The Court of Appeals emphasized that it was the "interaction of the facts present in this case," rather than any single element, that rendered the prayer unconstitutional.

Having granted certiorari to decide whether the town's prayer practice violates the Establishment Clause, 569 U.S._ _ _ (2013), the Court now reverses the judgment of the Court of Appeals.

II

In *Marsh v. Chambers*, 463 U.S. 783, the Court found no First Amendment violation in the Nebraska Legislature's practice of opening its sessions with a prayer delivered by a chaplain paid from state funds. The decision concluded that legislative prayer, while religious in nature, has long been understood as compatible with the Establishment Clause. As practiced by Congress since the framing of the Constitution, legislative prayer lends gravity to public business, reminds lawmakers to transcend petty differences in pursuit of a higher purpose, and expresses a common aspiration to a just and peaceful society. The Court has considered this symbolic expression to be a "tolerable acknowledgement of beliefs widely held," Marsh, 463 U.S., at 792, rather than a first, treacherous step towards establishment of a state church.

Marsh is sometimes described as "carving out an exception" to the Court's Establishment Clause jurisprudence because it sustained legislative prayer without subjecting the practice to "any of the formal 'tests' that have traditionally structured" this inquiry. (Brennan, J., dissenting). The Court in Marsh found those tests unnecessary because history supported the conclusion that legislative invocations are compatible with the Establishment Clause. The First Congress made it an early item of business to appoint and pay official chaplains, and both the House and Senate have maintained the office virtually uninterrupted since that time. But see Marsh, (noting dissenting views among the Framers). When Marsh was decided, in 1983, legislative prayer had persisted in the Nebraska Legislature for more than a century, and the majority of the other States also had the same, consistent practice. . . .

Yet Marsh must not be understood as permitting a practice that would amount to a constitutional violation if not for its historical foundation. The case teaches instead that the Establishment Clause must be interpreted "by reference to historical practices and understandings." County of Allegheny, 492 U.S., at 670. That the First Congress provided for the appointment of chaplains only days after approving language for the First Amendment demonstrates that the Framers considered legislative prayer a benign acknowledgment of religion's role in society.

. . . Marsh stands for the proposition that it is not necessary to define the precise boundary of the Establishment Clause where history shows that the specific practice is permitted. Any test the Court adopts must acknowledge a practice that was accepted by the Framers and has withstood the critical scrutiny of time and political change. County of Allegheny. . . . A test that would sweep away what has so long been settled would create new controversy and begin anew the very divisions along religious lines that the Establishment Clause seeks to prevent. See *Van Orden v. Perry*, 545 U.S. 677–704 (2005).

The Court's inquiry, then, must be to determine whether the prayer practice in the town of Greece fits within the tradition long followed in Congress and the state legislatures. Respondents assert that the town's prayer exercise falls outside that tradition and transgresses the Establishment Clause for two independent but mutually reinforcing reasons. First, they argue that Marsh did not approve prayers containing sectarian language or themes, such as the prayers offered in Greece that referred to the "death, resurrection, and ascension of the Savior Jesus Christ," and the "saving sacrifice of Jesus Christ on the crosst." Second, they argue that the setting and conduct of the town board meetings create social pressures that force nonadherents to remain in the room or even feign participation in order to avoid offending the representatives who sponsor the prayer and will vote on matters citizens bring before the board. The sectarian content of the prayers compounds the subtle coercive pressures, they argue, because the nonbeliever who might tolerate ecumenical prayer is forced to do the same for prayer that might be inimical to his or her beliefs.

A

Respondents maintain that prayer must be nonsectarian, or not identifiable with any one religion; and they fault the town for permitting guest chaplains to deliver prayers that "use overtly Christian terms" or "invoke specifics of Christian theology." A prayer is fitting for the public sphere, in their view, only if it contains the "most general, nonsectarian reference to God," (quoting M. Meyerson, Endowed by Our Creator: The Birth of Religious Freedom in America 11–12 (2012)), and eschews mention of doctrines associated with any one faith, Brief. They argue that prayer which contemplates "the workings of the Holy Spirit, the events of Pentecost, and the belief that God 'has raised up the Lord Jesus' and 'will raise us, in our turn, and put us by His side'" would be impermissible, as would any prayer that reflects dogma particular to a single faith tradition.

An insistence on nonsectarian or ecumenical prayer as a single, fixed standard is not consistent with the tradition of legislative prayer outlined in the Court's cases. The Court found the prayers in Marsh consistent with the First Amendment not because they espoused only a generic theism but because our history and tradition have shown that prayer in this limited context could "coexis[t] with the principles of disestablishment and religious freedom." The Congress that drafted the First Amendment would have been accustomed to invocations containing explicitly religious themes of the sort respondents find objectionable. One of the Senate's first chaplains, the Rev. William White, gave prayers in a series that included the Lord's Prayer, the Collect for Ash Wednesday, prayers for peace and grace, a general thanksgiving, St. Chrysostom's Prayer, and a prayer seeking "the grace of our Lord Jesus Christ." The decidedly Christian nature of these prayers must not be dismissed as the relic of a time when our Nation was less pluralistic than it is today. Congress continues to permit its appointed and visiting chaplains to express themselves in a religious idiom. It acknowledges our growing diversity not by proscribing sectarian content but by welcoming ministers of many creeds.

The contention that legislative prayer must be generic or nonsectarian derives from dictum in County of Allegheny, that was disputed when written and has been repudiated by later cases. There the Court held that a crèche placed on the steps of a county courthouse to celebrate the Christmas season violated the Establishment Clause because it had "the effect of endorsing a patently Christian message." Four dissenting Justices disputed that endorsement could be the proper test, as it likely would condemn a host of traditional practices that recognize the role religion plays in our society, among them legislative prayer and the "forthrightly religious" Thanksgiving proclamations issued by nearly every President since Washington. The Court sought to counter this criticism by recasting Marsh to permit only prayer that contained no overtly Christian references:

> "However history may affect the constitutionality of nonsectarian references to religion by the government, history cannot legitimate practices that demonstrate the government's allegiance to a particular sect or creed. . . . The legislative prayers involved in Marsh did not violate this principle because the particular chaplain had 'removed all references to Christ.'" (quoting Marsh).

This proposition is irreconcilable with the facts of Marsh and with its holding and reasoning. Marsh nowhere suggested that the constitutionality of legislative prayer turns on the neutrality of its content. The opinion noted that Nebraska's chaplain, the Rev. Robert E. Palmer, modulated the "explicitly Christian" nature of his prayer and "removed all references to Christ" after a Jewish lawmaker complained. 463 U.S., at 793, n. 14. With this footnote, the Court did no more than observe the practical demands placed on a minister who holds a permanent, appointed position in a legislature and chooses to write his or her prayers to appeal to more members, or at least to give less offense to those who object. Marsh did not suggest that Nebraska's prayer practice would have failed had the chaplain not acceded to the legislator's request. Nor did the Court imply the rule that prayer violates the Establishment Clause any time it is given in the name of a figure deified by only one faith or creed. To the contrary, the Court instructed that the "content of the prayer is not of concern to judges," provided "there is no indication that the prayer opportunity has been exploited to proselytize or advance any one, or to disparage any other, faith or belief."

To hold that invocations must be nonsectarian would force the legislatures that sponsor prayers and the courts that are asked to decide these cases to act as supervisors and censors of religious speech, a rule that would involve government in religious matters to a far greater degree than is the case under the town's current practice of neither editing or approving prayers in advance nor criticizing their content after the fact. Our Government is prohibited from prescribing prayers to be recited in our public institutions in order to promote a preferred system of belief or code of moral behavior. *Engel v. Vitale*, 370 U.S. 421, 430 (1962). It would be but a few steps removed from that prohibition for legislatures to require chaplains to redact the religious content from their message in order to make it acceptable for the public sphere. Government may not mandate a civic religion that stifles any but the most generic reference to the sacred any more than it may prescribe a religious orthodoxy. See *Lee v. Weisman*, 505 U.S. 577, 590 (1992).

Respondents argue, in effect, that legislative prayer may be addressed only to a generic God. The law and the Court could not draw this line for each specific prayer or seek to require ministers to set aside their nuanced and deeply personal beliefs for vague and artificial ones. There is doubt, in any event, that consensus might be reached as to what qualifies as generic or nonsectarian. Honorifics like "Lord of Lords" or "King of Kings" might strike a Christian audience as ecumenical, yet these titles may have no place in the vocabulary of other faith traditions. . . . [E]ven seemingly general references to God or the Father might alienate nonbelievers or polytheists. *McCreary County v. American Civil Liberties Union of Ky.*, 545 U.S. 844, 893 (2005) (Scalia, J., dissenting). Because it is unlikely that prayer will be inclusive beyond dispute, it would be unwise to adopt what respondents think is the next-best option: permitting those religious words, and only those words, that are acceptable to the majority, even if they will exclude some. *Torcaso v. Watkins*, 367 U.S. 488, 495 (1961). The First Amendment is not a majority rule, and government may not seek to define permissible categories of religious speech. Once it invites prayer into the public sphere, government must permit a prayer giver to address his or her own God or gods as conscience dictates, unfettered by what an administrator or judge considers to be nonsectarian.

In rejecting the suggestion that legislative prayer must be nonsectarian, the Court does not imply that no constraints remain on its content. The relevant constraint derives from its place at the opening of legislative sessions, where it is meant to lend gravity to the occasion and reflect values long part of the Nation's heritage. Prayer that is solemn and respectful in tone, that invites lawmakers to reflect upon shared ideals and common ends before they embark on the fractious business of governing, serves that legitimate function. If the course and practice over time shows that the invocations denigrate nonbelievers or religious minorities, threaten damnation, or preach conversion, many present may consider the prayer to fall short of the desire to elevate the purpose of the occasion and to unite lawmakers in their common effort. That circumstance would present a different case than the one presently before the Court.

The tradition reflected in Marsh permits chaplains to ask their own God for blessings of peace, justice, and freedom that find appreciation among people of all faiths. That a prayer is given in the name of Jesus, Allah, or Jehovah, or that it makes passing reference to religious doctrines, does not remove it from that tradition. These religious themes provide particular means to universal ends. Prayer that reflects beliefs specific to only some creeds can still serve to solemnize the occasion, so long as the practice over time is not "exploited to proselytize or advance any one, or to disparage any other, faith or belief." Marsh, 463 U.S., at 794–795.

It is thus possible to discern in the prayers offered to Congress a commonality of theme and tone. While these prayers vary in their degree of religiosity, they often seek peace for the Nation, wisdom for its lawmakers, and justice for its people, values that count as universal and that are embodied not only in religious traditions, but in our founding documents and laws. . . .

From the earliest days of the Nation, these invocations have been addressed to assemblies comprising many different creeds. These ceremonial prayers strive for the idea that people of many faiths may be united in a community of tolerance and devotion. Even those who disagree as to religious doctrine may find common ground in the desire to show respect for the divine in all aspects of their lives and being. Our tradition assumes that adult citizens, firm in their own beliefs, can tolerate and perhaps appreciate a ceremonial prayer delivered by a person of a different faith.

. . . A number of the prayers did invoke the name of Jesus, the Heavenly Father, or the Holy Spirit, but they also invoked universal themes, as by celebrating the changing of the seasons or calling for a "spirit of cooperation" among town leaders. App. 31 a, 38a. . . .

Respondents point to other invocations that disparaged those who did not accept the town's prayer practice. One guest minister characterized objectors as a "minority" who are "ignorant of the history of our country," id., at 108a, while another lamented that other towns did not have "God-fearing" leaders, id., at 79a. Although these two remarks strayed from the rationale set out in Marsh, they do not despoil a practice that on the whole reflects and embraces our tradition. Absent a pattern of prayers that over time denigrate, proselytize, or betray an impermissible government purpose, a challenge based solely on the content of a prayer will not likely establish a constitutional violation. Marsh, indeed, requires an inquiry into the prayer opportunity as a whole, rather than into the contents of a single prayer. 463 U.S., at 794–795.

Finally, the Court disagrees with the view taken by the Court of Appeals that the town of Greece contravened the Establishment Clause by inviting a predominantly Christian set of ministers to lead the prayer. The town made reasonable efforts to identify all of the congregations located within its borders and represented that it would welcome a prayer by any minister or layman who wished to give one. That nearly all of the congregations in town turned out to be Christian does not reflect an aversion or bias on the part of town leaders against minority faiths. So long as the town maintains a policy of nondiscrimination, the Constitution does not require it to search beyond its borders for non-Christian prayer givers in an effort to achieve religious balancing. The quest to promote "a 'diversity' of religious views" would require the town "to make wholly inappropriate judgments about the number of religions [it] should sponsor and the relative frequency with which it should sponsor each," Lee, 505 U.S., at 617 (Souter, J., concurring), a form of government entanglement with religion that is far more troublesome than the current approach.

B

Respondents further seek to distinguish the town's prayer practice from the tradition upheld in Marsh on the ground that it coerces participation by nonadherents. They and some amici contend that prayer conducted in the intimate setting of a town board meeting differs in fundamental ways from the invocations delivered in Congress and state legislatures, where the public remains segregated from legislative activity and may not address the body except by occasional invitation. Citizens attend town meetings, on the other hand, to accept awards; speak on matters of local importance; and petition the board for action that may affect their economic interests, such as the granting of permits, business licenses, and zoning variances. Respondents argue that the public may feel subtle pressure to participate in prayers that violate their beliefs in order to please the board members from whom they are about to seek a favorable ruling. In their view the fact that board members in small towns know many of their constituents by name only increases the pressure to conform.

It is an elemental First Amendment principle that government may not coerce its citizens "to support or participate in any religion or its exercise." County of Allegheny, 492 U.S., at 659 (Kennedy, J., concurring in judgment in part and dissenting in part). On the record in this case the Court is not persuaded that the town of Greece, through the act of offering a brief, solemn, and respectful prayer to open its monthly meetings, compelled its citizens to engage in a religious observance. The inquiry remains a fact-sensitive one that considers both the setting in which the prayer arises and the audience to whom it is directed.

The prayer opportunity in this case must be evaluated against the backdrop of historical practice. As a practice that has long endured, legislative prayer has become part of our heritage and tradition, part of our expressive idiom, similar to the Pledge of Allegiance, inaugural prayer, or the recitation of "God save the United States and this honorable Court" at the opening of this Court's sessions. See Lynch, 465 U.S., at 693 (O'Connor, J., concurring). It is presumed that the reasonable observer is acquainted with this tradition and understands that its purposes are to lend gravity to public proceedings and to acknowledge the place religion holds in the lives of many private citizens, not to afford government an opportunity to proselytize or force truant constituents into the pews. . . .

The principal audience for these invocations is not, indeed, the public but lawmakers themselves, who may find that a moment of prayer or quiet reflection sets the mind to a higher purpose and thereby eases the task of governing. The District Court in Marsh described the prayer exercise as "an internal act" directed at the Nebraska Legislature's "own members," *Chambers v. Marsh*, 504 F. Supp. 585, 588 (Neb. 1980), rather than an effort to promote religious observance among the public.

. . . To be sure, many members of the public find these prayers meaningful and wish to join them. But their purpose is largely to accommodate the spiritual needs of lawmakers and connect them to a tradition dating to the time of the Framers. For members of town boards and commissions, who often serve part-time and as volunteers, ceremonial prayer may also reflect the values they hold as private citizens. The prayer is an opportunity for them to show who and what they are without denying the right to dissent by those who disagree.

The analysis would be different if town board members directed the public to participate in the prayers, singled out dissidents for opprobrium, or indicated that their decisions might be influenced by a person's acquiescence in the prayer opportunity. No such thing occurred in the town of Greece. Although board members themselves stood, bowed their heads, or made the sign of the cross during the prayer, they at no point solicited similar gestures by the public. Respondents point to several occasions where audience members were asked to rise for the prayer. These requests, however, came not from town leaders but from the guest ministers, who presumably are accustomed to directing their congregations in this way and might have done so thinking the action was inclusive, not coercive. ("Would you bow your heads with me as we invite the Lord's presence here tonight?"). Respondents suggest that constituents might feel pressure to join the prayers to avoid irritating the officials who would be ruling on their petitions, but this argument has no evidentiary support. Nothing in the record indicates that town leaders allocated benefits and burdens based on participation in the prayer, or that citizens were received differently depending on whether they joined the invocation or quietly declined. . . . A practice that classified citizens based on their religious views would violate the Constitution, but that is not the case before this Court.

In their declarations in the trial court, respondents stated that the prayers gave them offense and made them feel excluded and disrespected. Offense, however, does not equate to coercion. Adults often encounter speech they find disagreeable, and an Establishment Clause violation is not made out any time a person experiences a sense of affront from the expression of contrary religious views in a legislative forum, especially where, as here, any member of the public is welcome in turn to offer an invocation reflecting his or her own convictions. If circumstances arise in which the pattern and practice of ceremonial, legislative prayer is alleged to be a means to coerce or intimidate others, the objection can be addressed in the regular course. But the showing has not been made here, where the prayers neither chastised dissenters nor attempted lengthy disquisition on religious dogma. Courts remain free to review the pattern of prayers over time to determine whether they comport with the tradition of solemn, respectful prayer approved in Marsh, or whether coercion is a real and substantial likelihood. But in the general course legislative bodies do not engage in impermissible coercion merely by exposing constituents to prayer they would rather not hear and in which they need not participate.

This case can be distinguished from the conclusions and holding of *Lee v. Weisman*, 505 U.S. 577. There the Court found that, in the context of a graduation where school authorities maintained close supervision over the conduct of the students and the substance of the ceremony, a religious invocation was coercive as to an objecting student. Id., at 592–594. Four Justices dissented in Lee, but the circumstances the Court confronted there are not present in this case and do not control its outcome. Nothing in the record suggests that members of the public are dissuaded from leaving the meeting room during the prayer, arriving late, or even, as happened here, making a later protest. In this case, as in Marsh, board members and constituents are "free to enter and leave with little comment and for any number of reasons." Lee, supra, at 597. Should nonbelievers choose to exit the room during a prayer they find distasteful, their absence will not stand out as disrespectful or even noteworthy. And should they remain, their quiet acquiescence will not, in light of our traditions, be interpreted as an agreement with the words or ideas expressed. Neither choice represents an unconstitutional imposition as to mature adults, who "presumably" are "not readily susceptible to religious indoctrination or peer pressure." Marsh, 463 U.S., at 792 (internal quotation marks and citations omitted). . . .

Ceremonial prayer is but a recognition that, since this Nation was founded and until the present day, many Americans deem that their own existence must be understood by precepts far beyond the authority of government to alter or define and that willing participation in civic affairs can be consistent with a brief acknowledgment of their belief in a higher power, always with due respect for those who adhere to other beliefs. The prayer in this case has a permissible ceremonial purpose. It is not an unconstitutional establishment of religion. . . .

The town of Greece does not violate the First Amendment by opening its meetings with prayer that comports with our tradition and does not coerce participation by nonadherents. The judgment of the U.S. Court of Appeals for the Second Circuit is reversed.

ANTHONY KENNEDY is an associate justice of the U.S. Supreme Court. He received his LLB from Harvard Law School in 1961 and worked for law firms in San Francisco and Sacramento, California, until he was nominated by President Gerald Ford to the U.S. Court of Appeals for the Ninth Circuit in 1975. He was nominated by President Ronald Reagan to the Supreme Court in 1988.

Elena Kagan et al.  **NO**

Dissenting Opinion, *Town of Greece, New York v. Susan Galloway*

Justice Kagan, with whom Justice Ginsburg, Justice Breyer, and Justice Sotomayor join, dissenting.

For centuries now, people have come to this country from every corner of the world to share in the blessing of religious freedom. Our Constitution promises that they may worship in their own way, without fear of penalty or danger, and that in itself is a momentous offering. Yet our Constitution makes a commitment still more remarkable— that however those individuals worship, they will count as full and equal American citizens. A Christian, a Jew, a Muslim (and so forth)—each stands in the same relationship with her country, with her state and local communities, and with every level and body of government. So that when each person performs the duties or seeks the benefits of citizenship, she does so not as an adherent to one or another religion, but simply as an American.

I respectfully dissent from the Court's opinion because I think the Town of Greece's prayer practices violate that norm of religious equality—the breathtakingly generous constitutional idea that our public institutions belong no less to the Buddhist or Hindu than to the Methodist or Episcopalian. I do not contend that principle translates here into a bright separationist line. To the contrary, I agree with the Court's decision in *Marsh v. Chambers*, 463 U.S. 783 (1983), upholding the Nebraska Legislature's tradition of beginning each session with a chaplain's prayer. And I believe that pluralism and inclusion in a town hall can satisfy the constitutional requirement of neutrality; such a forum need not become a religion-free zone. But still, the Town of Greece should lose this case. The practice at issue here differs from the one sustained in Marsh because Greece's town meetings involve participation by ordinary citizens, and the invocations given—directly to those citizens—were predominantly sectarian in content. Still more, Greece's Board did nothing to recognize religious diversity: In arranging for clergy members to open each meeting, the Town never sought (except briefly when this suit was filed) to involve, accommodate, or in any

way reach out to adherents of non-Christian religions. So month in and month out for over a decade, prayers steeped in only one faith, addressed toward members of the public, commenced meetings to discuss local affairs and distribute government benefits. In my view, that practice does not square with the First Amendment's promise that every citizen, irrespective of her religion, owns an equal share in her government.

I

To begin to see what has gone wrong in the Town of Greece, consider several hypothetical scenarios in which sectarian prayer—taken straight from this case's record— infuses governmental activities. None involves, as this case does, a proceeding that could be characterized as a legislative session, but they are useful to elaborate some general principles. In each instance, assume (as was true in Greece) that the invocation is given pursuant to government policy and is representative of the prayers generally offered in the designated setting.

You are a party in a case going to trial; let's say you have filed suit against the government for violating one of your legal rights. The judge bangs his gavel to call the court to order, asks a minister to come to the front of the room, and instructs the 10 or so individuals present to rise for an opening prayer. The clergyman faces those in attendance and says: "Lord, God of all creation, ... We acknowledge the saving sacrifice of Jesus Christ on the cross. We draw strength . . . from his resurrection at Easter. Jesus Christ, who took away the sins of the world, destroyed our death, through his dying and in his rising, he has restored our life. Blessed are you, who has raised up the Lord Jesus, you who will raise us, in our turn, and put us by His side. . . . Amen." App. 88a–89a. The judge then asks your lawyer to begin the trial.

It's election day, and you head over to your local polling place to vote. As you and others wait to give your names and receive your ballots, an election official asks everyone there to join him in prayer. He says: "We pray this [day] for the guidance of the Holy Spirit as [we vote] . . . . Let's just say the Our Father together. 'Our Father, who art in Heaven, hallowed be thy name; thy Kingdom come, thy will be done, on earth as it is in Heaven. . . .'" Id., at 56a. And after he concludes, he makes the sign of the cross, and appears to wait expectantly for you and the other prospective voters to do so too.

You are an immigrant attending a naturalization ceremony to finally become a citizen. The presiding official tells you and your fellow applicants that before administering the oath of allegiance, he would like a minister to pray for you and with you. The pastor steps to the front of the room, asks everyone to bow their heads, and recites: "[F]ather, son, and Holy Spirit—it is with a due sense of reverence and awe that we come before you [today] seeking your blessing . . . . You are . . . a wise God, oh Lord, . . . as evidenced even in the plan of redemption that is fulfilled in Jesus Christ. We ask that you would give freely and abundantly wisdom to one and to all. . . in the name of the Lord and Savior Jesus Christ, who lives with you and the Holy Spirit, one God for ever and ever. Amen." Id., at 99a–100a.

I would hold that the government officials responsible for the above practices—that is, for prayer repeatedly invoking a single religion's beliefs in these settings—crossed a constitutional line. I have every confidence the Court would agree. See ante, at 13 (Alito, J., concurring). And even Greece's attorney conceded that something like the first hypothetical (he was not asked about the others) would violate the First Amendment. See Tr. of Oral Arg. 3–4. Why?

The reason, of course, has nothing to do with Christianity as such. This opinion is full of Christian prayers, because those were the only invocations offered in the Town of Greece. But if my hypotheticals involved the prayer of some other religion, the outcome would be exactly the same. In any instance, the question would be why such government-sponsored prayer of a single religion goes beyond the constitutional pale.

One glaring problem is that the government in all these hypotheticals has aligned itself with, and placed its imprimatur on, a particular religious creed. "The clearest command of the Establishment Clause," this Court has held, "is that one religious denomination cannot be officially preferred over another." *Larson v. Valente*, 456 U.S. 228, 244 (1982). Justices have often differed about a further issue: whether and how the Clause applies to governmental policies favoring religion (of all kinds) over non-religion. Compare, e.g., *McCreary County v. American Civil Liberties Union of Ky.*, 545 U.S. 844, 860 (2005) ("[T]he First Amendment mandates governmental neutrality between . . . religion and nonreligion"), with, (Scalia, J., dissenting) ("[T]he Court's oft

repeated assertion that the government cannot favor religious practice [generally] is false"). But no one has disagreed with this much:

"[O]ur constitutional tradition, from the Declaration of Independence and the first inaugural address of Washington . . . down to the present day, has . . . ruled out of order government-sponsored endorsement of religion . . . where the endorsement is sectarian, in the sense of specifying details upon which men and women who believe in a benevolent, omnipotent Creator and Ruler of the world are known to differ (for example, the divinity of Christ)." *Lee v. Weisman*, 505 U.S. 577, 641 (1992) (Scalia, J., dissenting).

By authorizing and overseeing prayers associated with a single religion—to the exclusion of all others—the government officials in my hypothetical cases (whether federal, state, or local does not matter) have violated that foundational principle. They have embarked on a course of religious favoritism anathema to the First Amendment.

And making matters still worse: They have done so in a place where individuals come to interact with, and participate in, the institutions and processes of their government.

That is not the country we are, because that is not what our Constitution permits. Here, when a citizen stands before her government, whether to perform a service or request a benefit, her religious beliefs do not enter into the picture. The government she faces favors no particular religion, either by word or by deed. And that government, in its various processes and proceedings, imposes no religious tests on its citizens, sorts none of them by faith, and permits no exclusion based on belief. When a person goes to court, a polling place, or an immigration proceeding—I could go on: to a zoning agency, a parole board hearing, or the DMV—government officials do not engage in sectarian worship, nor do they ask her to do likewise. They all participate in the business of government not as Christians, Jews, Muslims (and more), but only as Americans—none of them different from any other for that civic purpose. Why not, then, at a town meeting?

II

In both Greece's and the majority's view, everything I have discussed is irrelevant here because this case involves "the tradition of legislative prayer outlined" in *Marsh v. Chambers*. And before I dispute the Town and Court, I want to give them their due: They are right that, under Marsh, legislative prayer has a distinctive constitutional warrant by virtue of tradition. As the Court today describes, a long history, stretching back to the first session of Congress (when chaplains began to give prayers in both Chambers), "ha[s] shown that prayer in this limited context could 'coexis[t] with the principles of disestablishment and religious freedom.'" (quoting Marsh). Relying on that "unbroken" national tradition, Marsh upheld (I think correctly) the Nebraska Legislature's practice of opening each day with a chaplain's prayer as "a tolerable acknowledgment of beliefs widely held among the people of this country." And so I agree with the majority that the issue here is "whether the prayer practice in the Town of Greece fits within the tradition long followed in Congress and the state legislatures."

Where I depart from the majority is in my reply to that question. The town hall here is a kind of hybrid. Greece's Board indeed has legislative functions, as Congress and state assemblies do—and that means some opening prayers are allowed there. But much as in my hypotheticals, the Board's meetings are also occasions for ordinary citizens to engage with and petition their government, often on highly individualized matters. That feature calls for Board members to exercise special care to ensure that the prayers offered are inclusive—that they respect each and every member of the community as an equal citizen. But the Board, and the clergy members it selected, made no such effort. Instead, the prayers given in Greece, addressed directly to the Town's citizenry, were more sectarian, and less inclusive, than anything this Court sustained in Marsh. For those reasons, the prayer in Greece departs from the legislative tradition that the majority takes as its benchmark.

A

Start by comparing two pictures, drawn precisely from reality. The first is of Nebraska's (unicameral) Legislature, as this Court and the state senators themselves described it. The second is of town council meetings in Greece, as revealed in this case's record.

It is morning in Nebraska, and senators are beginning to gather in the State's legislative chamber: It is the beginning of the official workday, although senators may not yet need to be on the floor. The chaplain rises to give the daily invocation. That prayer, as the senators emphasized when their case came to this Court, is "directed only at the legislative membership, not at the public at large." Any members of the public who happen to be in attendance—not very many at this early hour—watch only from the upstairs visitors' gallery.

The longtime chaplain says something like the following (the excerpt is from his own amicus brief supporting

Greece in this case): "O God, who has given all persons talents and varying capacities, Thou dost only require of us that we utilize Thy gifts to a maximum. In this Legislature to which Thou has entrusted special abilities and opportunities, may each recognize his stewardship for the people of the State." The chaplain is a Presbyterian minister, and "some of his earlier prayers" explicitly invoked Christian beliefs, but he "removed all references to Christ" after a single legislator complained. The chaplain also previously invited other clergy members to give the invocation, including local rabbis.

Now change the channel: It is evening in Greece, New York, and the Supervisor of the Town Board calls its monthly public meeting to order. Those meetings (so says the Board itself) are "the most important part of Town government." They serve assorted functions, almost all actively involving members of the public. The Board may swear in new Town employees and hand out awards for civic accomplishments; it always provides an opportunity (called a Public Forum) for citizens to address local issues and ask for improved services or new policies (for example, better accommodations for the disabled or actions to ameliorate traffic congestion); and it usually hears debate on individual applications from residents and local businesses to obtain special land-use permits, zoning variances, or other licenses.

The Town Supervisor, Town Clerk, Chief of Police, and four Board members sit at the front of the meeting room on a raised dais. But the setting is intimate: There are likely to be only 10 or so citizens in attendance. A few may be children or teenagers, present to receive an award or fulfill a high school civics requirement.

As the first order of business, the Town Supervisor introduces a local Christian clergy member—denominated the chaplain of the month—to lead the assembled persons in prayer. The pastor steps up to a lectern (emblazoned with the Town's seal) at the front of the dais, and with his back to the Town officials, he faces the citizens present. He asks them all to stand and to "pray as we begin this evening's town meeting." (He does not suggest that anyone should feel free not to participate.) And he says:

> "The beauties of spring . . . are an expressive symbol of the new life of the risen Christ. The Holy Spirit was sent to the apostles at Pentecost so that they would be courageous witnesses of the Good News to different regions of the Mediterranean world and beyond. The Holy Spirit continues to be the inspiration and the source of strength and virtue, which we all need in the world of today. And so . . . [w]e pray this evening for the guidance of the Holy Spirit as the Greece Town Board meets."

After the pastor concludes, Town officials behind him make the sign of the cross, as do some members of the audience, and everyone says "Amen." The Supervisor then announces the start of the Public Forum, and a citizen stands up to complain about the Town's contract with a cable company.

B

Let's count the ways in which these pictures diverge. First, the governmental proceedings at which the prayers occur differ significantly in nature and purpose. The Nebraska Legislature's floor sessions—like those of the U.S. Congress and other state assemblies—are of, by, and for elected lawmakers. Members of the public take no part in those proceedings; any few who attend are spectators only, watching from a high-up visitors' gallery. (In that respect, note that neither the Nebraska Legislature nor the Congress calls for prayer when citizens themselves participate in a hearing— say, by giving testimony relevant to a bill or nomination.) Greece's town meetings, by contrast, revolve around ordinary members of the community. Each and every aspect of those sessions provides opportunities for Town residents to interact with public officials. And the most important parts enable those citizens to petition their government. In the Public Forum, they urge (or oppose) changes in the Board's policies and priorities; and then, in what are essentially adjudicatory hearings, they request the Board to grant (or deny) applications for various permits, licenses, and zoning variances. So the meetings, both by design and in operation, allow citizens to actively participate in the Town's governance—sharing concerns, airing grievances, and both shaping the community's policies and seeking their benefits.

Second (and following from what I just said), the prayers in these two settings have different audiences. In the Nebraska Legislature, the chaplain spoke to, and only to, the elected representatives. Nebraska's senators were adamant on that point in briefing Marsh, and the facts fully supported them: As the senators stated, "[t]he activity is a matter of internal daily procedure directed only at the legislative membership, not at [members of] the public." The same is true in the U.S. Congress and, I suspect, in every other state legislature. As several Justices later noted (and the majority today agrees), Marsh involved "government officials invok[ing] spiritual inspiration entirely for their own benefit without directing any religious message at the citizens they lead."

The very opposite is true in Greece: Contrary to the majority's characterization, the prayers there are directed squarely at the citizens. Remember that the chaplain of

the month stands with his back to the Town Board; his real audience is the group he is facing—the 10 or so members of the public, perhaps including children. And he typically addresses those people, as even the majority observes, as though he is "directing [his] congregation." He almost always begins with some version of "Let us all pray together." Often, he calls on everyone to stand and bow their heads, and he may ask them to recite a common prayer with him. He refers, constantly, to a collective "we"—to "our" savior, for example, to the presence of the Holy Spirit in "our" lives, or to "our brother the Lord Jesus Christ." In essence, the chaplain leads, as the first part of a town meeting, a highly intimate (albeit relatively brief) prayer service, with the public serving as his congregation.

And third, the prayers themselves differ in their content and character. Marsh characterized the prayers in the Nebraska Legislature as "in the Judeo-Christian tradition," and stated, as a relevant (even if not dispositive) part of its analysis, that the chaplain had removed all explicitly Christian references at a senator's request. And as the majority acknowledges, Marsh hinged on the view that "that the prayer opportunity ha[d] [not] been exploited to proselytize or advance any one . . . faith or belief"; had it been otherwise, the Court would have reached a different decision.

But no one can fairly read the prayers from Greece's Town meetings as anything other than explicitly Christian—constantly and exclusively so. From the time Greece established its prayer practice in 1999 until litigation loomed nine years later, all of its monthly chaplains were Christian clergy. And after a brief spell surrounding the filing of this suit (when a Jewish layman, a Wiccan priestess, and a Baha'i minister appeared at meetings), the Town resumed its practice of inviting only clergy from neighboring Protestant and Catholic churches. About two-thirds of the prayers given over this decade or so invoked "Jesus," "Christ," "Your Son," or "the Holy Spirit"; in the 18 months before the record closed, 85% included those references. Many prayers contained elaborations of Christian doctrine or recitations of scripture. ("For unto us a child is born; unto us a son is given. And the government shall be upon his shoulder . . ."). And the prayers usually close with phrases like "in the name of Jesus Christ" or "in the name of Your son."

Still more, the prayers betray no understanding that the American community is today, as it long has been, a rich mosaic of religious faiths. See *Braunfeld v. Brown*, 366 U.S. 599, 606 (1961) (plurality opinion).

The monthly chaplains appear almost always to assume that everyone in the room is Christian (and of a kind who has no objection to government-sponsored worship). The Town itself has never urged its chaplains to reach out to members of other faiths, or even to recall that they might be present. And accordingly, few chaplains have made any effort to be inclusive; none has thought even to assure attending members of the public that they need not participate in the prayer session. Indeed, as the majority forthrightly recognizes, when the plaintiffs here began to voice concern over prayers that excluded some Town residents, one pastor pointedly thanked the Board "[o]n behalf of all God-fearing people" for holding fast, and another declared the objectors "in the minority and . . . ignorant of the history of our country."

C

Those three differences, taken together, remove this case from the protective ambit of Marsh and the history on which it relied. And so, contra the majority, Greece's prayers cannot simply ride on the constitutional coattails of the legislative tradition Marsh described. The Board's practice must, in its own particulars, meet constitutional requirements.

And the guideposts for addressing that inquiry include the principles of religious neutrality I discussed earlier. The government (whether federal, state, or local) may not favor, or align itself with, any particular creed. And that is nowhere more true than when officials and citizens come face to face in their shared institutions of governance. In performing civic functions and seeking civic benefits, each person of this nation must experience a government that belongs to one and all, irrespective of belief. And for its part, each government must ensure that its participatory processes will not classify those citizens by faith, or make relevant their religious differences.

None of this means that Greece's town hall must be religion- or prayer-free. "[W]e are a religious people," Marsh observed, and prayer draws some warrant from tradition in a town hall, as well as in Congress or a state legislature. What the circumstances here demand is the recognition that we are a pluralistic people too. When citizens of all faiths come to speak to each other and their elected representatives in a legislative session, the government must take especial care to ensure that the prayers they hear will seek to include, rather than serve to divide. No more is required—but that much is crucial—to treat every citizen, of whatever religion, as an equal participant in her government.

And contrary to the majority's (and Justice Alito's) view, that is not difficult to do. If the Town Board had let its chaplains know that they should speak in nonsectarian terms, common to diverse religious groups, then no one

would have valid grounds for complaint. (Such prayers show that "those of different creeds are in the end kindred spirits, united by a respect paid higher providence and by a belief in the importance of religious faith"). Priests and ministers, rabbis and imams give such invocations all the time; there is no great mystery to the project. (And providing that guidance would hardly have caused the Board to run afoul of the idea that "[t]he *First Amendment* is not a majority rule," as the Court (head spinningly) suggests; what does that is the Board's refusal to reach out to members of minority religious groups.) Or if the Board preferred, it might have invited clergy of many faiths to serve as chaplains, as the majority notes that Congress does. When one month a clergy member refers to Jesus, and the next to Allah or Jehovah—as the majority hopefully though counterfactually suggests happened here—the government does not identify itself with one religion or align itself with that faith's citizens, and the effect of even sectarian prayer is transformed. So Greece had multiple ways of incorporating prayer into its town meetings—reflecting all the ways that prayer (as most of us know from daily life) can forge common bonds, rather than divide.

But Greece could not do what it did: infuse a participatory government body with one (and only one) faith, so that month in and month out, the citizens appearing before it become partly defined by their creed—as those who share, and those who do not, the community's majority religious belief. In this country, when citizens go before the government, they go not as Christians or Muslims or Jews (or what have you), but just as Americans (or here, as Grecians). That is what it means to be an equal citizen, irrespective of religion. And that is what the Town of Greece precluded by so identifying itself with a single faith.

III

How, then, does the majority go so far astray, allowing the Town of Greece to turn its assemblies for citizens into a forum for Christian prayer? The answer does not lie in first principles: I have no doubt that every member of this Court believes as firmly as I that our institutions of government belong equally to all, regardless of faith. Rather, the error reflects two kinds of blindness. First, the majority misapprehends the facts of this case, as distinct from those characterizing traditional legislative prayer. And second, the majority misjudges the essential meaning of the religious worship in Greece's town hall, along with its capacity to exclude and divide.

The facts here matter to the constitutional issue; indeed, the majority itself acknowledges that the requisite inquiry—a "fact-sensitive" one—turns on "the setting in which the prayer arises and the audience to whom it is directed. But then the majority glides right over those considerations—at least as they relate to the Town of Greece. When the majority analyzes the "setting" and "audience" for prayer, it focuses almost exclusively on Congress and the Nebraska Legislature; it does not stop to analyze how far those factors differ in Greece's meetings. The majority thus gives short shrift to the gap—more like, the chasm— between a legislative floor session involving only elected officials and a town hall revolving around ordinary citizens. And similarly the majority neglects to consider how the prayers in Greece are mostly addressed to members of the public, rather than (as in the forums it discusses) to the lawmakers.

And of course—as the majority sidesteps as well—to pray in the name of Jesus Christ. In addressing the sectarian content of these prayers, the majority again changes the subject, preferring to explain what happens in other government bodies. The majority notes, for example, that Congress "welcom[es] ministers of many creeds," who commonly speak of "values that count as universal"; and in that context, the majority opines, the fact "[t]hat a prayer is given in the name of Jesus, Allah, or Jehovah . . . does not remove it from" Marsh's protection. But that case is not this one, as I have shown, because in Greece only Christian clergy members speak, and then mostly in the voice of their own religion; no Allah or Jehovah ever is mentioned. So all the majority can point to in the Town's practice is that the Board "maintains a policy of nondiscrimination," and "represent[s] that it would welcome a prayer by any minister or layman who wishe[s] to give one." But that representation has never been publicized; nor has the Board (except for a few months surrounding this suit's filing) offered the chaplain's role to any non-Christian clergy or layman, in either Greece or its environs; nor has the Board ever provided its chaplains with guidance about reaching out to members of other faiths, as most state legislatures and Congress do. The majority thus errs in assimilating the Board's prayer practice to that of Congress or the Nebraska Legislature. Unlike those models, the Board is determinedly—and relentlessly—noninclusive.

And the month in, month out sectarianism the Board chose for its meetings belies the majority's refrain that the prayers in Greece were "ceremonial" in nature. Ceremonial references to the divine surely abound: The majority is right that "the Pledge of Allegiance, inaugural prayer, or the recitation of 'God save the United States and this honorable Court'" each fits the bill. But prayers evoking "the saving sacrifice of Jesus Christ on the cross," "the plan of redemption that is fulfilled in Jesus Christ," the workings of the Holy Spirit, the events of Pentecost, and the belief that God "has raised up the Lord Jesus" and "will raise us, in our turn, and put us by His side"? No. These are statements of profound belief and deep meaning, subscribed to by many, denied by some. They "speak of the depths of [one's] life, of the source of [one's] being, of [one's] ultimate concern, of what [one] take[s] seriously without any reservation." P. "Tillich, *The Shaking of the Foundations* 57 (1948). If they (and the central tenets of other religions) ever become mere ceremony, this country will be a fundamentally different—and, I think, poorer—place to live.

But just for that reason, the not-so-implicit message of the majority's opinion—"What's the big deal, anyway?"—is mistaken. Contrary to the majority's apparent view, such sectarian prayers are not "part of our expressive idiom" or "part of our heritage and tradition," assuming the word "our" refers to all Americans. They express beliefs that are fundamental to some, foreign to others—and because that is so they carry the ever-present potential to both exclude and divide. The majority, I think, assesses too lightly the significance of these religious differences, and so fears too little the "religiously based divisiveness that the Establishment Clause seeks to avoid." *Van Orden v. Perry*, 545 U.S. 677, 704 (2005). I would treat more seriously the multiplicity of Americans' religious commitments, along with the challenge they can pose to the project—the distinctively American project—of creating one from the many, and governing all as united.

Elena Kagan is an associate justice of the Supreme Court of the United States. In 2009, President Obama appointed her Solicitor General of the United States and in 2010 the President nominated her to the Supreme Court to fill the vacancy from the impending retirement of Justice John Paul Stevens. Prior to these positions, she was a professor at Harvard Law School and was later named its first female dean.

EXPLORING THE ISSUE

Is It Constitutional to Open a Town Meeting with a Prayer?

Critical Thinking and Reflection

1. Have you ever been in a situation where you felt pressure to conform to another's religious beliefs or practices? How did you react?
2. Do you think local and state legislatures are sufficiently different to justify the Court's Majority opinion?
3. Is the United States a Christian nation? What evidence supports and contradicts your opinion?
4. How might changing demographics and religious beliefs influence religion's role in government in the future?
5. Recognizing the role of religion in the lives of most Americans, do you think an outspoken atheist will ever be elected President?

Is There Common Ground?

While the Justices take differing routes in their analyses, both the Majority and Dissenting opinions are willing to look to history and tradition for guidance in this case. Their recognition of the historical importance of religion in the United States, as well as its importance in the lives of everyday contemporary Americans, reflects their understanding that politics and religion, however hard our Founding Father's may have worked to separate the two, are inextricably intertwined. One might reasonably inquire that if the Justices are willing to look to history after the Founding Fathers' drafting of the Constitution for guidance on these issues, as was done in *Town of Greece*, should they also be equally willing to look to history before their time. In doing so, they might analyze the religious beliefs of the Planting Fathers and how they ultimately influenced the Founding Fathers. There can be little doubt that the Majority and Dissenting opinions would nonetheless still come to their prevailing opinions, with the Dissent finding it instructive how far the Founding Fathers departed from the governance ideals of the Planting Fathers in reaching their conclusions, and the Majority stressing the long-standing role religion has played in government from this nation's inception.

Additional Resources

Dow, George Francis, *Every Day Life in the Massachusetts Bay Colony* (New York, NY: Dover Publications, 1988).

Hudson, James H., *Religion and the Founding of the American Republic* (Washington, D.C.: Library of Congress, 1998).

Lambert, Frank, *The Founding Fathers and the Place of Religion in America* (Princeton, NJ: Princeton University Press, 2003).

The Library of Congress, *Religion and Founding of the American Republic, America as a Religious Refuge—The Seventeenth Century: Persecution in America.* http://www.loc.gov/exhibits/religion/rel01-2.html.

Meyerson, M., *Endowed by Our Creator: The Birth of Religious Freedom in America* (New Haven, CT: Yale University Press, 2012).

Internet References . . .

Abstract and Recording of Oral Arguments of *Marsh v. Chambers*

> http://www.oyez.org/cases/1980-1989/1982/1982_82_23

Abstract and Recording of Oral Arguments of *Lemon v. Kurtzman.*

> http://www.oyez.org/cases/1970-1979/1970/1970_89

Abstract and Recording of Oral Arguments of *Town of Greece v. Galloway*

> http://www.oyez.org/cases/2010-2019/2013/2013_12_696

The Town of Greece, NY, Town Board Meeting Schedule, Agenda, and Minutes

> http://greeceny.gov/planning/townboard

Address of President-Elect John F. Kennedy Delivered to a Joint Convention of the General Court of the Commonwealth of Massachusetts, The State House, Boston, January 9, 1961 (also known as the "City Upon a Hill" speech)

> http://www.jfklibrary.org/Asset-Viewer/OYhUZE2Qo0-ogdV7ok900A.aspx

Greene, Richard Allen, April 27, 2009; Americans Not Losing Their Religion, But Changing it Often

> http://www.cnn.com/2009/US/04/27/changing.religion.study/index.html?iref=24hours

Walenta, Craig, *God in the State Constitutions.* This is a non-exhausted list of the use of "God" and similar references in State Constitutions

> http://www.usconstitution.net/states_god.html

Selected, Edited, and with Issue Framing Material by:
M. Ethan Katsh, *University of Massachusetts, Amherst*

ISSUE

Is a Strip Search of Middle School Students That Is Aimed at Finding Drugs Prohibited Under the Fourth Amendment?

YES: David Souter, from "Majority Opinion, *Safford Unified School District, et al., v. April Redding*," *United States Supreme Court* (2009)

NO: Clarence Thomas, from "Dissenting Opinion, *Safford Unified School District, et al., v. April Redding*," *United States Supreme Court* (2009)

Learning Outcomes

After reading this issue, you will be able to:

- Identify exceptions to the Fourth Amendment's warrant requirement.
- Discuss how a Fourth Amendment search of a student differs from that of an ordinary citizen.
- Assess when the search of a student without a warrant might be appropriate and when it is likely barred.
- Discuss how Fourth Amendment jurisprudence has evolved with technology.

ISSUE SUMMARY

YES: Supreme Court Justice David Souter holds that a search in school requires a reasonable belief that evidence of wrongdoing will be found and that the search is not excessively intrusive in light of the age and sex of the student.

NO: Supreme Court Justice Clarence Thomas argues that the Fourth Amendment is not violated when there is reasonable suspicion that the student is in possession of drugs banned by school policy and the search is in an area where small pills could be concealed.

As a general rule, the Fourth Amendment to the Constitution requires authorities to obtain a search warrant before conducting a search. In order to do this, they must persuade a judge that probable cause exists that a crime has been committed and that the evidence sought will be found in the place to be searched. The warrant requirement is the key constitutional element restricting the power of the police to decide unilaterally to invade the privacy of someone's home.

There are exceptions to this requirement. For example, warrants are not required when a person is searched after an arrest or when the object seized is in plain view. Nor is a warrant needed if the invasion of privacy is less intrusive than a full-scale search. Patting down the outside of someone's clothing when the police believe the person might have a weapon only requires "reasonable suspicion." Such a search is commonly referred to as a "stop and frisk," or "Terry stop," after the case *Terry v. Ohio*, 392 U.S. 1 (1968). In such situations, the police do not need to meet the standard of probable cause but also may not extensively search the person.

Public schools are another context in which searches have been allowed even when probable cause was not present. In the seminal public school search case, *New Jersey v. T. L. O., A Juvenile,* 105 S. Ct. 733 (1985), the Court held that a search warrant was not required for school officials to search school lockers if there is reasonable suspicion that the search will reveal evidence of criminal behavior. The Court also added that the scope of the search must be reasonably related to the object being searched, and that the search could not be "excessively intrusive," taking into account the age and sex of the student and the reason for the search.

In this case, officials at a middle school in Arizona were told that a student, 13-year-old Savana Redding, had given a classmate four prescription-strength 400 mg ibuprofen (equivalent of two Advil) and a 200 mg over-the-counter naproxen. The assistant principal first searched her belongings, her clothing, and then her underwear. The officials did not find any contraband on Redding's person, and they did not contact Redding's parents at any point during the investigation. Redding's parents then sued the school district and the school officials for violating Ms. Redding's Fourth Amendment rights.

Pivotal to the Court's decision in the case here was not the question of whether reasonable suspicion existed, but whether the search itself was excessively intrusive. The Court looked to not only the method of search employed by the school officials, but also to the surrounding facts in order to come to its conclusion that the search was excessively intrusive. However, the Court, citing the uncertain status of student search jurisprudence as evidenced by court decisions from around the country, granted immunity to the school officials involved in the search. Interestingly, the Court's decision did not extend immunity to the school district and ultimately, the school district settled with Ms. Redding for $250,000.

The Supreme Court is not required to accept a case for review, and in recent decades, it has been deciding fewer and fewer cases. When it does decide to hear a case, it requires the parties to prepare and submit their legal arguments in writing and then to appear at an oral argument to answer questions that the justices might have. Often, observers at the oral argument make predictions about how the justices will vote based on the questions they ask and the comments they make at the oral argument.

The oral argument in the *Redding* case had many of the male members of the Court asking questions that appeared to be insensitive to the feelings of a 13-year-old girl subjected to a strip search. Justice Breyer, for example, asked, "Why is this a major thing to say strip down to your underclothes, which children do when they change for gym?" Justice Souter commented that if he were the principal in a school, he "would rather have the kid embarrassed by a strip search . . . than have some other kids dead because the stuff is distributed at lunchtime and things go awry." One correspondent at the Court wrote after the oral argument, "after today's argument, it's plain the court will overturn a Ninth Circuit Court of Appeals' opinion finding a school's decision to strip search a 13-year-old girl unconstitutional. That the school in question was looking for a prescription pill with the mind-altering force of a pair of Advil—and couldn't be bothered to call the child's mother first—hardly matters."

As it turned out, the case was decided 8 to 1 in favor of Ms. Redding, and the majority opinion was written by Justice Souter. For some, this was an example of the Justices, and the law, being influenced by public opinion. For others, who have seen many decisions that would not have been predicted given the questioning at the oral argument, the outcome in this case was much less of a surprise.

YES ↵

David Souter

Majority Opinion, *Safford Unified School District, et al., v. April Redding*

JUSTICE SOUTER delivered the opinion of the Court.

The issue here is whether a 13-year-old student's Fourth Amendment right was violated when she was subjected to a search of her bra and underpants by school officials acting on reasonable suspicion that she had brought forbidden prescription and over-the-counter drugs to school. Because there were no reasons to suspect the drugs presented a danger or were concealed in her underwear, we hold that the search did violate the Constitution, but because there is reason to question the clarity with which the right was established, the official who ordered the unconstitutional search is entitled to qualified immunity from liability.

I

The events immediately prior to the search in question began in 13-year-old Savana Redding's math class at Safford Middle School one October day in 2003. The assistant principal of the school, Kerry Wilson, came into the room and asked Savana to go to his office. There, he showed her a day planner, unzipped and open flat on his desk, in which there were several knives, lighters, a permanent marker, and a cigarette. Wilson asked Savana whether the planner was hers; she said it was, but that a few days before she had lent it to her friend, Marissa Glines. Savana stated that none of the items in the planner belonged to her.

Wilson then showed Savana four white prescription-strength ibuprofen 400-mg pills, and one over-the-counter blue naproxen 200-mg pill, all used for pain and inflammation but banned under school rules without advance permission. He asked Savana if she knew anything about the pills. Savana answered that she did not. Wilson then told Savana that he had received a report that she was giving these pills to fellow students; Savana denied it and agreed to let Wilson search her belongings. Helen Romero, an administrative assistant, came into the office, and

together with Wilson they searched Savana's backpack, finding nothing.

At that point, Wilson instructed Romero to take Savana to the school nurse's office to search her clothes for pills. Romero and the nurse, Peggy Schwallier, asked Savana to remove her jacket, socks, and shoes, leaving her in stretch pants and a T-shirt (both without pockets), which she was then asked to remove. Finally, Savana was told to pull her bra out and to the side and shake it, and to pull out the elastic on her underpants, thus exposing her breasts and pelvic area to some degree. No pills were found.

Savana's mother filed suit against Safford Unified School District #1, Wilson, Romero, and Schwallier for conducting a strip search in violation of Savana's Fourth Amendment rights. The individuals (hereinafter petitioners) moved for summary judgment, raising a defense of qualified immunity. The District Court for the District of Arizona granted the motion on the ground that there was no Fourth Amendment violation, and a panel of the Ninth Circuit affirmed. 504 F. 3d 828 (2007).

A closely divided Circuit sitting en banc, however, reversed. Following the two-step protocol for evaluating claims of qualified immunity, see *Saucier v. Katz,* 533 U.S. 194, 200 (2001), the Ninth Circuit held that the strip search was unjustified under the Fourth Amendment test for searches of children by school officials set out in *New Jersey v. T. L. O.,* 469 U.S. 325 (1985). 531 F. 3d 1071, 1081–1087 (2008). The Circuit then applied the test for qualified immunity, and found that Savana's right was clearly established at the time of the search: "'[t]hese notions of personal privacy are "clearly established" in that they inhere in all of us, particularly middle school teenagers, and are inherent in the privacy component of the Fourth Amendment's proscription against unreasonable searches.'" *Id.,* at 1088–1089 (quoting *Brannum v. Overton Cty. School Bd.,* 516 F. 3d 489, 499 (CA6 2008)). The upshot was reversal of summary judgment as to Wilson, while affirming the judgments in favor of Schwallier, the school nurse, and

From Supreme Court of the United States, June 25, 2009.

Romero, the administrative assistant, since they had not acted as independent decisionmakers. 531 F. 3d, at 1089.

We granted certiorari, 555 U.S. __ (2009), and now affirm in part, reverse in part, and remand.

II

The Fourth Amendment "right of the people to be secure in their persons . . . against unreasonable searches and seizures" generally requires a law enforcement officer to have probable cause for conducting a search. "Probable cause exists where 'the facts and circumstances within [an officer's] knowledge and of which [he] had reasonably trustworthy information [are] sufficient in themselves to warrant a man of reasonable caution in the belief that' an offense has been or is being committed," *Brinegar v. United States,* 338 U.S. 160, 175–176 (1949) (quoting *Carroll v. United States,* 267 U.S. 132, 162 (1925)), and that evidence bearing on that offense will be found in the place to be searched.

In *T. L. O.,* we recognized that the school setting "requires some modification of the level of suspicion of illicit activity needed to justify a search," 469 U.S., at 340, and held that for searches by school officials "a careful balancing of governmental and private interests suggests that the public interest is best served by a Fourth Amendment standard of reasonableness that stops short of probable cause". . . We have thus applied a standard of reasonable suspicion to determine the legality of a school administrator's search of a student, . . . and have held that a school search "will be permissible in its scope when the measures adopted are reasonably related to the objectives of the search and not excessively intrusive in light of the age and sex of the student and the nature of the infraction." . . .

A number of our cases on probable cause have an implicit bearing on the reliable knowledge element of reasonable suspicion, as we have attempted to flesh out the knowledge component by looking to the degree to which known facts imply prohibited conduct, see, *e.g., Adams v. Williams,* 407 U.S. 143, 148 (1972); *id.,* at 160, n. 9 (Marshall, J., dissenting), the specificity of the information received, see, *e.g., Spinelli v. United States,* 393 U.S. 410, 416–417 (1969), and the reliability of its source, see, *e.g., Aguilar v. Texas, 378* U.S. 108, 114 (1964). At the end of the day, however, we have realized that these factors cannot rigidly control, *Illinois v. Gates,* 462 U.S. 213, 230 (1983), and we have come back to saying that the standards are "fluid concepts that take their substantive content from the particular contexts" in which they are being assessed. *Ornelas v. United States,* 517 U.S. 690, 696 (1996).

Perhaps the best that can be said generally about the required knowledge component of probable cause for a law enforcement officer's evidence search is that it raise a "fair probability," *Gates,* 462 U.S., at 238, or a "substantial chance," *id.,* at 244, n. 13, of discovering evidence of criminal activity. The lesser standard for school searches could as readily be described as a moderate chance of finding evidence of wrongdoing.

III

A

In this case, the school's policies strictly prohibit the non-medical use, possession, or sale of any drug on school grounds, including "'[a]ny prescription or over-the-counter drug, except those for which permission to use in school has been granted pursuant to Board policy.'" . . .[1] A week before Savana was searched, another student, Jordan Romero (no relation of the school's administrative assistant), told the principal and Assistant Principal Wilson that "certain students were bringing drugs and weapons on campus," and that he had been sick after taking some pills that "he got from a classmate." . . . On the morning of October 8, the same boy handed Wilson a white pill that he said Marissa Glines had given him. He told Wilson that students were planning to take the pills at lunch.

Wilson learned from Peggy Schwallier, the school nurse, that the pill was Ibuprofen 400 mg, available only by prescription. Wilson then called Marissa out of class. Outside the classroom, Marissa's teacher handed Wilson the day planner, found within Marissa's reach, containing various contraband items. Wilson escorted Marissa back to his office.

In the presence of Helen Romero, Wilson requested Marissa to turn out her pockets and open her wallet. Marissa produced a blue pill, several white ones, and a razor blade. Wilson asked where the blue pill came from, and Marissa answered, "'I guess it slipped in when *she* gave me the IBU 400s.'" . . . When Wilson asked whom she meant, Marissa replied, "'Savana Redding.'" . . . Wilson then enquired about the day planner and its contents; Marissa denied knowing anything about them. Wilson did not ask Marissa any followup questions to determine whether there was any likelihood that Savana presently had pills: neither asking when Marissa received the pills from Savana nor where Savana might be hiding them.

Schwallier did not immediately recognize the blue pill, but information provided through a poison control hotline . . . indicated that the pill was a 200-mg dose of an anti-inflammatory drug, generically called naproxen, available over the counter. At Wilson's direction, Marissa was then subjected to a search of her bra and underpants by Romero and Schwallier, as Savana was later on. The search revealed no additional pills.

It was at this juncture that Wilson called Savana into his office and showed her the day planner. Their conversation established that Savana and Marissa were on friendly terms: while she denied knowledge of the contraband, Savana admitted that the day planner was hers and that she had lent it to Marissa. Wilson had other reports of their friendship from staff members, who had identified Savana and Marissa as part of an unusually rowdy group at the school's opening dance in August, during which alcohol and cigarettes were found in the girls' bathroom. Wilson had reason to connect the girls with this contra band, for Wilson knew that Jordan Romero had told the principal that before the dance, he had been at a party at Savana's house where alcohol was served. Marissa's statement that the pills came from Savana was thus sufficiently plausible to warrant suspicion that Savana was involved in pill distribution.

This suspicion of Wilson's was enough to justify a search of Savana's backpack and outer clothing.[2] If a student is reasonably suspected of giving out contraband pills, she is reasonably suspected of carrying them on her person and in the carryall that has become an item of student uniform in most places today. If Wilson's reasonable suspicion of pill distribution were not understood to support searches of outer clothes and backpack, it would not justify any search worth making. And the look into Savana's bag, in her presence and in the relative privacy of Wilson's office, was not excessively intrusive, any more than Romero's subsequent search of her outer clothing.

B

Here it is that the parties part company, with Savana's claim that extending the search at Wilson's behest to the point of making her pull out her underwear was constitutionally unreasonable. The exact label for this final step in the intrusion is not important, though strip search is a fair way to speak of it. Romero and Schwallier directed Savana to remove her clothes down to her underwear, and then "pull out" her bra and the elastic band on her underpants. . . . Although Romero and Schwallier stated that they did not see anything when Savana followed their instructions, . . . we would not define strip search and its Fourth Amendment consequences in a way that would guarantee litigation about who was looking and how much was seen. The very fact of Savana's pulling her underwear away from her body in the presence of the two officials who were able to see her necessarily exposed her breasts and pelvic area to some degree, and both subjective and reasonable societal expectations of personal privacy support the treatment of such a search as categorically distinct, requiring distinct elements of justification on the part of school authorities for going beyond a search of outer clothing and belongings.

Savana's subjective expectation of privacy against such a search is inherent in her account of it as embarrassing, frightening, and humiliating. The reasonableness of her expectation (required by the Fourth Amendment standard) is indicated by the consistent experiences of other young people similarly searched, whose adolescent vulnerability intensifies the patent intrusiveness of the exposure. See Brief for National Association of Social Workers et al. as *Amici Curiae* 6–14; Hyman & Perone, The Other Side of School Violence: Educator Policies and Practices that may Contribute to Student Misbehavior, 36 J. School Psychology 7, 13 (1998) (strip search can "result in serious emotional damage"). The common reaction of these adolescents simply registers the obviously different meaning of a search exposing the body from the experience of nakedness or near undress in other school circumstances. Changing for gym is getting ready for play; exposing for a search is responding to an accusation reserved for suspected wrongdoers and fairly understood as so degrading that a number of communities have decided that strip searches in schools are never reasonable and have banned them no matter what the facts may be, see, *e.g.*, New York City Dept. of Education, Reg. No. A-432, p. 2 (2005), . . . ("Under no circumstances shall a strip-search of a student be conducted").

The indignity of the search does not, of course, outlaw it, but it does implicate the rule of reasonableness as stated in *T. L. O.*, that "the search as actually conducted [be] reasonably related in scope to the circumstances which justified the interference in the first place." 469 U.S., at 341 (internal quotation marks omitted). The scope will be permissible, that is, when it is "not excessively intrusive in light of the age and sex of the student and the nature of the infraction." *Id.*, at 342.

Here, the content of the suspicion failed to match the degree of intrusion. Wilson knew beforehand that the pills were prescription-strength ibuprofen and over-the-counter naproxen, common pain relievers equivalent to two Advil, or one Aleve. . . . He must have been aware of the nature and limited threat of the specific drugs he was searching for, and while just about anything can be taken in quantities that will do real harm, Wilson had no reason to suspect that large amounts of the drugs were being passed around, or that individual students were receiving great numbers of pills.

Nor could Wilson have suspected that Savana was hiding common painkillers in her underwear. Petitioners suggest, as a truth universally acknowledged, that "students . . . hid[e] contraband in or under their clothing," Reply Brief for Petitioners 8, and cite a smattering of cases of students with contraband in their underwear, *id.*, at 8–9. But when the categorically extreme intrusiveness of a search down to the body of an adolescent requires some justification in suspected facts, general background possibilities fall short; a reasonable search that extensive calls for suspicion that it will pay off. But nondangerous school contraband does not raise the specter of stashes in intimate places, and there is no evidence in the record of any general practice among Safford Middle School students of hiding that sort of thing in underwear; neither Jordan nor Marissa suggested to Wilson that Savana was doing that, and the preceding search of Marissa that Wilson ordered yielded nothing. Wilson never even determined when Marissa had received the pills from Savana; if it had been a few days before, that would weigh heavily against any reasonable conclusion that Savana presently had the pills on her person, much less in her underwear.

In sum, what was missing from the suspected facts that pointed to Savana was any indication of danger to the students from the power of the drugs or their quantity, and any reason to suppose that Savana was carrying pills in her underwear. We think that the combination of these deficiencies was fatal to finding the search reasonable.

In so holding, we mean to cast no ill reflection on the assistant principal, for the record raises no doubt that his motive throughout was to eliminate drugs from his school and protect students from what Jordan Romero had gone through. Parents are known to overreact to protect their children from danger, and a school official with responsibility for safety may tend to do the same. The difference is that the Fourth Amendment places limits on the official, even with the high degree of deference that courts must pay to the educator's professional judgment.

We do mean, though, to make it clear that the *T. L. O.* concern to limit a school search to reasonable scope requires the support of reasonable suspicion of danger or of resort to underwear for hiding evidence of wrongdoing before a search can reasonably make the quantum leap from outer clothes and backpacks to exposure of intimate parts. The meaning of such a search, and the degradation its subject may reasonably feel, place a search that intrusive in a category of its own demanding its own specific suspicions.

IV

A school official searching a student is "entitled to qualified immunity where clearly established law does not show that the search violated the Fourth Amendment." *Pearson v. Callahan*, 555 U.S. __, __ (2009) (slip op., at 18). To be established clearly, however, there is no need that "the very action in question [have] previously been held unlawful." *Wilson v. Layne*, 526 U.S. 603, 615 (1999). The unconstitutionality of outrageous conduct obviously will be unconstitutional, this being the reason, as Judge Posner has said, that "[t]he easiest cases don't even arise." *K. H. v. Morgan*, 914 F. 2d 846, 851 (CA7 1990). But even as to action less than an outrage, "officials can still be on notice that their conduct violates established law . . . in novel factual circumstances." *Hope v. Pelzer*, 536 U.S. 730, 741 (2002).

T. L. O. directed school officials to limit the intrusiveness of a search, "in light of the age and sex of the student and the nature of the infraction," 469 U.S., at 342, and as we have just said at some length, the intrusiveness of the strip search here cannot be seen as justifiably related to the circumstances. But we realize that the lower courts have reached divergent conclusions regarding how the *T. L. O.* standard applies to such searches.

A number of judges have read *T. L. O.* as the en banc minority of the Ninth Circuit did here. The Sixth Circuit upheld a strip search of a high school student for a drug, without any suspicion that drugs were hidden next to her body. *Williams v. Ellington*, 936 F. 2d 881, 882–883, 887 (1991). And other courts considering qualified immunity for strip searches have read *T. L. O.* as "a series of abstractions, on the one hand, and a declaration of seeming deference to the judgments of school officials, on the other," *Jenkins v. Talladega City Bd. of Ed.*, 115 F. 3d 821, 828 (CA11 1997) (en banc), which made it impossible "to establish clearly the contours of a Fourth Amendment right . . . [in] the wide variety of possible school settings different from those involved in *T. L. O.*" itself. *Ibid.* See also *Thomas v. Roberts*, 323 F. 3d 950 (CA11 2003) (granting qualified immunity to a teacher and police officer who conducted a group strip search of a fifth grade class when looking for a missing $26).

We think these differences of opinion from our own are substantial enough to require immunity for the school officials in this case. We would not suggest that entitlement to qualified immunity is the guaranteed product of disuniform views of the law in the other federal, or state, courts, and the fact that a single judge, or even a group of judges, disagrees about the contours of a right does not automatically render the law unclear if we have been clear. That said, however, the cases viewing school strip searches differently from the way we see them are numerous enough, with well-reasoned majority and dissenting opinions, to counsel doubt that we were sufficiently clear in the prior statement of law. We conclude that qualified immunity is warranted.

V

The strip search of Savana Redding was unreasonable and a violation of the Fourth Amendment, but petitioners Wilson, Romero, and Schwallier are nevertheless protected from liability through qualified immunity. Our conclusions here do not resolve, however, the question of the liability of petitioner Safford Unified School District #1 under *Monell v. New York City Dept. of Social Servs.*, 436 U.S. 658, 694 (1978), a claim the Ninth Circuit did not address. The judgment of the Ninth Circuit is therefore affirmed in part and reversed in part, and this case is remanded for consideration of the *Monell* claim.

It is so ordered.

Notes

[1.] When the object of a school search is the enforcement of a school rule, a valid search assumes, of course, the rule's legitimacy. But the legitimacy of the rule usually goes without saying as it does here. The Court said plainly in *New Jersey v. T. L. O.*, 469 U.S. 325, 342, n. 9 (1985), that standards of conduct for schools are for school administrators to determine without second-guessing by courts lacking the experience to appreciate what may be needed. Except in patently arbitrary instances, Fourth Amendment analysis takes the rule as a given, as it obviously should do in this case. There is no need here either to explain the imperative of keeping drugs out of schools, or to explain the reasons for the school's rule banning all drugs, no matter how benign, without advance permission. Teachers are not pharmacologists trained to identify pills and powders, and an effective drug ban has to be enforceable fast. The plenary ban makes sense, and there is no basis to claim that the search was unreasonable owing to some defect or shortcoming of the rule it was aimed at enforcing.

[2.] 'There is no question here that justification for the school officials' search was required in accordance with the *T. L. O.* standard of reasonable suspicion, for it is common ground that Savana had a reasonable expectation of privacy covering the personal things she chose to carry in her backpack, cf. 469 U.S., at 339, and that Wilson's decision to look through it was a "search" within the meaning of the Fourth Amendment.

DAVID SOUTER retired as an associate justice of the U.S. Supreme Court in June 2009. Prior to his appointment to the Supreme Court, he was a former judge for the U.S. Court of Appeals for the First Circuit in Boston, Massachusetts. He was nominated by President George H. W. Bush to the Supreme Court in 1990.

Clarence Thomas

Dissenting Opinion, *Safford Unified School District, et al., v. April Redding*

J USTICE THOMAS, concurring in the judgment in part and dissenting in part.

I agree with the Court that the judgment against the school officials with respect to qualified immunity should be reversed. . . . Unlike the majority, however, I would hold that the search of Savana Redding did not violate the Fourth Amendment. The majority imposes a vague and amorphous standard on school administrators. It also grants judges sweeping authority to second-guess the measures that these officials take to maintain discipline in their schools and ensure the health and safety of the students in their charge. This deep intrusion into the administration of public schools exemplifies why the Court should return to the common-law doctrine of *in loco parentis* under which "the judiciary was reluctant to interfere in the routine business of school administration, allowing schools and teachers to set and enforce rules and to maintain order." *Morse v. Frederick,* 551 U.S. 393, 414 (2007) (THOMAS, J., concurring). But even under the prevailing Fourth Amendment test established by *New Jersey v. T. L. O.,* 469 U.S. 325 (1985), all petitioners, including the school district, are entitled to judgment as a matter of law in their favor.

I

"Although the underlying command of the Fourth Amendment is always that searches and seizures be reasonable, what is reasonable depends on the context within which a search takes place." *Id.,* at 337. Thus, although public school students retain Fourth Amendment rights under this Court's precedent, see *id.,* at 333–337, those rights "are different . . . than elsewhere; the 'reasonableness' inquiry cannot disregard the schools' custodial and tutelary responsibility for children," *Vernonia School Dist. 47J v. Acton,* 515 U.S. 646, 656 (1995); see also *T. L. O.,* 469 U.S., at 339 (identifying "the substantial interest of teachers and administrators in maintaining discipline in

the classroom and on school grounds"). For nearly 25 years this Court has understood that "[m]aintaining order in the classroom has never been easy, but in more recent years, school disorder has often taken particularly ugly forms: drug use and violent crime in the schools have become major social problems." . . . In schools, "[e]vents calling for discipline are frequent occurrences and sometimes require immediate, effective action." *Goss v. Lopez,* 419 U.S. 565, 580 (1975); see also *T. L. O.,* 469 U.S., at 340 (explaining that schools have a "legitimate need to maintain an environment in which learning can take place").

For this reason, school officials retain broad authority to protect students and preserve "order and a proper educational environment" under the Fourth Amendment. . . . This authority requires that school officials be able to engage in the "close supervision of schoolchildren, as well as . . . enforc[e] rules against conduct that would be perfectly permissible if undertaken by an adult." . . . Seeking to reconcile the Fourth Amendment with this unique public school setting, the Court in *T. L. O.* held that a school search is "reasonable" if it is "'justified at its inception'" and "'reasonably related in scope to the circumstances which justified the interference in the first place.'" . . . The search under review easily meets this standard.

A

A "search of a student by a teacher or other school official will be 'justified at its inception' when there are reasonable grounds for suspecting that the search will turn up evidence that the student has violated or is violating either the law or the rules of the school." *T. L. O., supra,* at 341–342 (footnote omitted). As the majority rightly concedes, this search was justified at its inception because there were reasonable grounds to suspect that Redding possessed medication that violated school rules. . . . A finding of reasonable suspicion "does not deal with hard certainties, but with probabilities." *United States v. Cortez,* 449 U.S. 411, 418 (1981); see also *T. L. O., supra,* at 346 ("[T]he requirement of reasonable suspicion is not a requirement of absolute certainty"). To satisfy this standard, more than a mere "hunch" of wrongdoing is required, but "considerably" less suspicion is needed than would be required to "satisf[y] a preponderance of the evidence standard." *United States v. Arvizu,* 534 U.S. 266, 274 (2002) (internal quotation marks omitted).

Furthermore, in evaluating whether there is a reasonable "particularized and objective" basis for conducting a search based on suspected wrongdoing, government officials must consider the "totality of the circumstances." . . . School officials have a specialized understanding of the school environment, the habits of the students, and the concerns of the community, which enables them to "'formulat[e] certain common-sense conclusions about human behavior.'" *United States v. Sokolow,* 490 U.S. 1, 8 (1989) (quoting *Cortez, supra,* at 418). And like police officers, school officials are "entitled to make an assessment of the situation in light of [this] specialized training and familiarity with the customs of the [school]." See *Arvizu, supra,* at 276.

Here, petitioners had reasonable grounds to suspect that Redding was in possession of prescription and non-prescription drugs in violation of the school's prohibition of the "non-medical use, possession, or sale of a drug" on school property or at school events. 531 F. 3d 1071, 1076 (CA9 2008) (en banc); see also *id.,* at 1107 (Hawkins, J., dissenting) (explaining that the school policy defined "drugs" to include "'[a]ny prescription or over-the-counter drug, except those for which permission to use in school has been granted'"). As an initial matter, school officials were aware that a few years earlier, a student had become "seriously ill" and "spent several days in intensive care" after ingesting prescription medication obtained from a classmate. . . . Fourth Amendment searches do not occur in a vacuum; rather, context must inform the judicial inquiry. . . . In this instance, the suspicion of drug possession arose at a middle school that had "a history of problems with students using and distributing prohibited and illegal substances on campus." . . .

The school's substance-abuse problems had not abated by the 2003–2004 school year, which is when the challenged search of Redding took place. School officials had found alcohol and cigarettes in the girls' bathroom during the first school dance of the year and noticed that a group of students including Redding and Marissa Glines smelled of alcohol. . . . Several weeks later, another student, Jordan Romero, reported that Redding had hosted a party before the dance where she served whiskey, vodka, and tequila. . . . Romero had provided this report to school officials as a result of a meeting his mother scheduled with the officials after Romero "bec[a]me violent" and "sick to his stomach" one night and admitted that "he had taken some pills that he had got[ten] from a classmate." . . . At that meeting, Romero admitted that "certain students were bringing drugs and weapons on campus." . . . One week later, Romero handed the assistant principal a white pill that he said he had received from Glines. . . . He reported "that a group of students [were] planning on taking the pills at lunch." . . .

School officials justifiably took quick action in light of the lunchtime deadline. The assistant principal took the pill to the school nurse who identified it as prescription-strength 400-mg Ibuprofen. . . . A subsequent search of Glines and her belongings produced a razor blade, a Naproxen 200-mg pill, and several Ibuprofen 400-mg pills. . . . When asked, Glines claimed that she had received the pills from Redding. . . . A search of Redding's planner, which Glines had borrowed, then uncovered "several knives, several lighters, a cigarette, and a permanent marker." . . . Thus, as the majority acknowledges, . . . the totality of relevant circumstances justified a search of Redding for pills.

B

The remaining question is whether the search was reasonable in scope. Under *T. L. O.,* "a search will be permissible in its scope when the measures adopted are reasonably related to the objectives of the search and not excessively intrusive in light of the age and sex of the student and the nature of the infraction." 469 U.S., at 342. The majority concludes that the school officials' search of Redding's underwear was not "'reasonably related in scope to the circumstances which justified the interference in the first place,'" . . . notwithstanding the officials' reasonable suspicion that Redding "was involved in pill distribution." . . . According to the majority, to be reasonable, this school search required a showing of "danger to the students from the power of the drugs or their quantity" or a "reason to suppose that [Redding] was carrying pills in her underwear." . . . Each of these additional requirements is an unjustifiable departure from bedrock Fourth Amendment law in the school setting, where this Court has heretofore read the Fourth Amendment to grant considerable leeway to school officials. Because the school officials searched in a location where the pills could have been hidden, the search was reasonable in scope under *T. L. O.*

1

The majority finds that "subjective and reasonable societal expectations of personal privacy support . . . treat[ing]" this type of search, which it labels a "strip search," as "categorically distinct, requiring distinct elements of justification on the part of school authorities for going beyond a search of clothing and belongings." . . . Thus, in the majority's view, although the school officials had reasonable suspicion to believe that Redding had the pills on her person, . . . they needed some greater level of particularized suspicion to conduct this "strip search." There is no support for this contortion of the Fourth Amendment.

The Court has generally held that the reasonableness of a search's scope depends only on whether it is limited to the area that is capable of concealing the object of the search. See, *e.g., Wyoming v. Houghton,* 526 U.S. 295, 307 (1999) (Police officers "may inspect passengers' belongings found in the car that are capable of concealing the object of the search"); *Florida v. Jimeno,* 500 U.S. 248, 251 (1991) ("The scope of a search is generally defined by its expressed object"); *United States v. Johns,* 469 U.S. 478, 487 (1985) (search reasonable because "there is no plausible argument that the object of the search could not have been concealed in the packages"); *United States v. Ross,* 456 U.S. 798, 820 (1982) ("A lawful search . . . generally extends to the entire area in which the object of the search may be found").[1]

In keeping with this longstanding rule, the "nature of the infraction" referenced in *T. L. O.* delineates the proper scope of a search of students in a way that is identical to that permitted for searches outside the school—*i.e.,* the search must be limited to the areas where the object of that infraction could be concealed. See *Horton v. California,* 496 U.S. 128, 141 (1990) ("Police with a warrant for a rifle may search only places where rifles might be" (internal quotation marks omitted)); *Ross, supra,* at 824 ("[P]robable cause to believe that undocumented aliens are being transported in a van will not justify a warrantless search of a suitcase"). A search of a student therefore is permissible in scope under *T. L. O.* so long as it is objectively reasonable to believe that the area searched could conceal the contraband. The dissenting opinion below correctly captured this Fourth Amendment standard, noting that "if a student brought a baseball bat on campus in violation of school policy, a search of that student's shirt pocket would be patently unjustified." 531 F. 3d, at 1104 (opinion of Hawkins, J.).

The analysis of whether the scope of the search here was permissible under that standard is straightforward. Indeed, the majority does not dispute that "general background possibilities" establish that students conceal "contraband in their underwear." . . . It acknowledges that school officials had reasonable suspicion to look in Redding's backpack and outer clothing because if

"Wilson's reasonable suspicion of pill distribution were not understood to support searches of outer clothes and backpack, it would not justify any search worth making." . . . The majority nevertheless concludes that proceeding any further with the search was unreasonable. See *ante,* at 8–10; see also *ante,* at 1 (Ginsburg, J., concurring in part and dissenting in part) ("Any reasonable search for the pills would have ended when inspection of Redding's backpack and jacket pockets yielded nothing"). But there is no support for this conclusion. The reasonable suspicion that Redding possessed the pills for distribution purposes did not dissipate simply because the search of her backpack turned up nothing. It was eminently reasonable to conclude that the backpack was empty because Redding was secreting the pills in a place she thought no one would look. See *Ross, supra,* at 820 ("Contraband goods rarely are strewn" about in plain view; "by their very nature such goods must be withheld from public view").

Redding would not have been the first person to conceal pills in her undergarments. See Hicks, Man Gets 17-Year Drug Sentence, [Corbin, KY] Times-Tribune, Oct. 7, 2008, p. 1 (Drug courier "told officials she had the [Oxycontin] pills concealed in her crotch"); Conley, Whitehaven: Traffic Stop Yields Hydrocodone Pills, [Memphis] Commercial Appeal, Aug. 3, 2007, p. B3 ("An additional 40 hydrocodone pills were found in her pants"); Caywood, Police Vehicle Chase Leads to Drug Arrests, [Worcester] Telegram & Gazette, June 7, 2008, p. A7 (25-year-old "allegedly had a cigar tube stuffed with pills tucked into the waistband of his pants"); Hubartt, 23-Year-Old Charged With Dealing Ecstasy, The [Fort Wayne] Journal Gazette, Aug. 8, 2007, p. C2 ("[W]hile he was being put into a squad car, his pants fell down and a plastic bag containing pink and orange pills fell on the ground"); Sebastian Residents Arrested in Drug Sting, Vero Beach Press Journal, Sept. 16, 2006, p. B2 (Arrestee "told them he had more pills 'down my pants'"). Nor will she be the last after today's decision, which announces the safest place to secrete contraband in school.

2

The majority compounds its error by reading the "nature of the infraction" aspect of the *T. L. O.* test as a license to limit searches based on a judge's assessment of a particular school policy. According to the majority, the scope of the search was impermissible because the school official "must have been aware of the nature and limited threat of the specific drugs he was searching for" and because he "had no reason to suspect that large amounts of the drugs were being passed around, or that individual students were receiving great numbers of pills." . . . Thus, in order to locate a rationale for finding a Fourth Amendment violation in this case, the majority retreats from its observation that the school's firm no-drug policy "makes sense, and there is no basis to claim that the search was unreasonable owing to some defect or shortcoming of the rule it was aimed at enforcing." . . .

Even accepting the majority's assurances that it is not attacking the rule's reasonableness, it certainly is attacking the rule's importance. This approach directly conflicts with *T. L. O.* in which the Court was "unwilling to adopt a standard under which the legality of a search is dependent upon a judge's evaluation of the relative importance of school rules." 469 U.S., at 342, n. 9. Indeed, the Court in *T. L. O.* expressly rejected the proposition that the majority seemingly endorses—that "some rules regarding student conduct are by nature too 'trivial' to justify a search based upon reasonable suspicion." . . .

The majority's decision in this regard also departs from another basic principle of the Fourth Amendment: that law enforcement officials can enforce with the same vigor all rules and regulations irrespective of the perceived importance of any of those rules. "In a long line of cases, we have said that when an officer has probable cause to believe a person committed even a minor crime in his presence, the balancing of private and public interests is not in doubt. The arrest is constitutionally reasonable." *Virginia v. Moore*, 553 U.S. __, __ (2008) (slip op., at 6). The Fourth Amendment rule for searches is the same: Police officers are entitled to search regardless of the perceived triviality of the underlying law. As we have explained, requiring police to make "sensitive, case-by-case determinations of government need," *Atwater v. Lago Vista*, 532 U.S. 318, 347 (2001), for a particular prohibition before conducting a search would "place police in an almost impossible spot," *id.*, at 350.

The majority has placed school officials in this "impossible spot" by questioning whether possession of Ibuprofen and Naproxen causes a severe enough threat to warrant investigation. Had the suspected infraction involved a street drug, the majority implies that it would have approved the scope of the search. . . . In effect, then, the majority has replaced a school rule that draws no distinction among drugs with a new one that does. As a result, a full search of a student's person for prohibited drugs will be permitted only if the Court agrees that the drug in question was sufficiently dangerous. Such a test is unworkable and unsound. School officials cannot be expected to halt searches based on the possibility that a court might later find that the particular infraction at issue is not severe enough to warrant an intrusive investigation.[2]

A rule promulgated by a school board represents the judgment of school officials that the rule is needed to maintain "school order" and "a proper educational environment." *T. L. O.*, 469 U.S., at 343, n. 9. Teachers, administrators, and the local school board are called upon both to "protect the . . . safety of students and school personnel" and "maintain an environment conducive to learning." *Id.*, at 353 (Blackmun, J., concurring in judgment). They are tasked with "watch[ing] over a large number of students" who "are inclined to test the outer boundaries of acceptable conduct and to imitate the misbehavior of a peer if that misbehavior is not dealt with quickly." *Id.*, at 352. In such an environment, something as simple as a "water pistol or peashooter can wreak [havoc] until it is taken away." *Ibid.* The danger posed by unchecked distribution and consumption of prescription pills by students certainly needs no elaboration.

Judges are not qualified to second-guess the best manner for maintaining quiet and order in the school environment. . . . It is a mistake for judges to assume the responsibility for deciding which school rules are important enough to allow for invasive searches and which rules are not.

3

Even if this Court were authorized to second-guess the importance of school rules, the Court's assessment of the importance of this district's policy is flawed. It is a crime to possess or use prescription-strength Ibuprofen without a prescription. See Ariz. Rev. Stat. Ann. §13–3406(A)(1) (West Supp. 2008) ("A person shall not knowingly . . . [p]ossess or use a prescription-only drug unless the person obtains the prescription-only drug pursuant to a valid prescription of a prescriber who is licensed pursuant to [state law]"). By prohibiting unauthorized prescription drugs on school grounds—and conducting a search to ensure students abide by that prohibition—the school rule here was consistent with a routine provision of the state criminal code. It hardly seems unreasonable for school officials to enforce a rule that, in effect, proscribes conduct that amounts to a crime. . . .

Admittedly, the Ibuprofen and Naproxen at issue in this case are not the prescription painkillers at the forefront of the prescription-drug-abuse problem. See Prescription for Danger 3 ("Pain relievers like Vicodin and OxyContin are the prescription drugs most commonly abused by teens"). But they are not without their own dangers. As nonsteroidal anti-inflammatory drugs (NSAIDs), they pose a risk of death from overdose. The Pill Book 821, 827 (H. Silverman, ed., 13th ed. 2008) (observing that

Is a Strip Search of Middle School Students That Is Aimed at Finding Drugs Prohibited Under the Fourth Amendment? by Katsh

181

Ibuprofen and Naproxen are NSAIDs and "[p]eople have died from NSAID overdoses"). Moreover, the side-effects caused by the use of NSAIDs can be magnified if they are taken in combination with other drugs. See, *e.g.,* Reactions Weekly, p. 18 (Issue no. 1235, Jan. 17, 2009) ("A 17-year-old girl developed allergic interstitial nephritis and renal failure while receiving escitalopram and ibuprofen"); *id.,* at 26 (Issue no. 1232, Dec. 13, 2008) ("A 16-month-old boy developed iron deficiency anaemia and hypoalbuminaemia during treatment with naproxen"); *id.,* at 15 (Issue no. 1220, Sept. 20, 2008) (18-year-old "was diagnosed with pill-induced oesophageal perforation" after taking ibuprofen "and was admitted to the [intensive care unit]"); *id.,* at 20 (Issue no. 1170, Sept. 22, 2007) ("A 12-year-old boy developed anaphylaxis following ingestion of ibuprofen").

If a student with a previously unknown intolerance to Ibuprofen or Naproxen were to take either drug and become ill, the public outrage would likely be directed toward the school for failing to take steps to prevent the unmonitored use of the drug. In light of the risks involved, a school's decision to establish and enforce a school prohibition on the possession of any unauthorized drug is thus a reasonable judgment.

In determining whether the search's scope was reasonable under the Fourth Amendment, it is therefore irrelevant whether officials suspected Redding of possessing prescription-strength Ibuprofen, nonprescription-strength Naproxen, or some harder street drug. Safford prohibited its possession on school property. Reasonable suspicion that Redding was in possession of drugs in violation of these policies, therefore, justified a search extending to any area where small pills could be concealed. The search did not violate the Fourth Amendment. . . .

Notes

[1.] The Court has adopted a different standard for searches involving an "intrusio[n] into the human body." *Schmerber v. California,* 384 U.S. 757, 770 (1966). The search here does not

implicate the Court's cases governing bodily intrusions, however, because it did not involve a "physical intrusion, penetrating beneath the skin," *Skinner v. Railway Labor Executives' Assn.,* 489 U.S. 602, 616 (1989).

[2.] JUSTICE GINSBURG suggests that requiring Redding to "sit on a chair outside [the assistant principal's] office for over two hours" and failing to call her parents before conducting the search constitutes an "[a]buse of authority" that "should not be shielded by official immunity." See *ante,* at 1–2. But the school was under no constitutional obligation to call Redding's parents before conducting the search: "[R]easonableness under the Fourth Amendment does not require employing the least intrusive means, because the logic of such elaborate less-restrictive-alternative arguments could raise insuperable barriers to the exercise of virtually all search-and-seizure powers." *Board of Ed. of Independent School Dist. No. 92 of Pottawatomie Cty. v. Earls,* 536 U.S. 822, 837 (2002) (internal quotation marks and brackets omitted). For the same reason, the Constitution did not require school officials to ask "followup questions" after they had already developed reasonable suspicion that Redding possessed drugs. See *ante,* at 6, 10 (majority opinion); *ante,* at 1 (opinion of GINSBURG, J.). In any event, the suggestion that requiring Redding to sit in a chair for two hours amounted to a deprivation of her constitutional rights, or that school officials are required to engage in detailed interrogations before conducting searches for drugs, only reinforces the conclusion that the Judiciary is ill-equipped to second-guess the daily decisions made by public administrators. Cf. *Beard v. Banks,* 548 U.S. 521, 536–537 (2006) (THOMAS, J., concurring in judgment).

CLARENCE THOMAS is an associate justice of the U.S. Supreme Court. A former judge on the U.S. Court of Appeals for the District of Columbia, he was nominated by President George H. W. Bush to the Supreme Court in 1991. He received his JD from the Yale University School of Law in 1974.

EXPLORING THE ISSUE

Is a Strip Search of Middle School Students That Is Aimed at Finding Drugs Prohibited Under the Fourth Amendment?

Critical Thinking and Reflection

1. Do you agree that students should be treated differently in terms of the constitutional protections they're afforded?
2. What circumstances might be sufficient to justify a student being strip searched in the Court's eye?
3. Should the Court have granted immunity to the school officials involved in the search?
4. With our willingness to share more information over the Internet and on social networks, is it fair to say that we have less of an expectation of privacy?

Is There Common Ground?

The decision in *Redding* was rendered by an 8 to 1 majority of the Supreme Court, meaning that there was considerable agreement among the Justices in regards to Ms. Redding's rights being violated. The lone dissenting opinion is that of Justice Thomas, who would have decided the case under the doctrine of *in loco parentis*, which in Latin means "in place of the parent." Applying the doctrine, Justice Thomas believes that the school acts in place of the parents when children are in their care, and that the Court should not pass judgment on how they, with their specialized knowledge of learning, set and enforce rules with regards to education.

Justice Thomas is not alone in his deference to the school and its educators. The majority opinion is also highly deferential, refusing to pass any judgment on the substantive rule itself that led to the search in *Redding*, the prohibition on use, possession, or sale of any drugs on school grounds, including prescription and over-the-counter drugs without the school's knowledge or consent. The Court also sided with the school in believing that sufficient suspicion existed to justify a search of Ms. Redding. However, Justice Thomas and the majority part ways as to the scope of the intrusion that is warranted by the justified suspicion. Once reasonable suspicion exists, Justice Thomas believes that the search should reflect the character of the sought-after contraband; since pills were being sought, the search should include any place where pills may be hidden.

Interestingly, the majority also relies on the character of the contraband as being instructive to the determination of the scope of the search, but reaches a different result. The majority relies on the fact that the sought-after pills were not believed to be of a significantly harmful nature, thereby reasoning that a less intrusive search was appropriate. Future student search cases are sure to carefully take into consideration the nature of the objects being searched for. However, we can fairly expect that the outcomes will not be as certain.

Additional Resources

Douglas E. Abrams, "Recognizing the Public Schools' Authority to Discipline Students' Off-Campus Cyberbullying of Classmates," 37 *N.E. J. Crim. & Civ. Con.* 181 (2011).

Sean Cooke, "Reasonable Suspicion, Unreasonable Search: Defining Fourth Amendment Protections Against Searches of Students' Personal Electronic Devices by Public School Officials," 40 *Cap. U.L. Rev.* 293.

Ryan J. Owens, and David A. Simon, "Explaining the Supreme Court's Shrinking Docket," 53 *Wm. & Mary L. Rev.* 1219 (2012).

A. James Spung, "From Backpacks to Blackberries: (Re)Examining *New Jersey v. T.L.O.* in the Age of the Cell Phone," 61 *Emory L.J.* 111 (2011).

Is a Strip Search of Middle School Students That Is Aimed at Finding Drugs Prohibited Under the Fourth Amendment? by Katsh

183

Internet References . . .

Abstract and Recording of Oral Arguments of Redding

www.oyez.org/cases/2000-2009/2008/2008_08_479

Drug Enforcement Administration of the United States

Background information on law enforcement and the drug problem can be found on the website of the Drug Enforcement Administration of the United States.

www.justice.gov/dea/

Slate Article

In this Slate article, "Search Me: The Supreme Court Is Neither Hot nor Bothered by Strip Searches," Dahlia Lithwick reports on the oral arguments in the *Redding* case.

www.slate.com/id/2216608

Student Press Law Center

Although school officials were given immunity for their actions in *Redding,* the court left open the possibility of the school district being held liable. This article discusses the settlement that resulted from *Redding* and the lengths that one journalist had to go through for that information to become public.

www.splc.org/news/newsflash.asp?id=2276

Selected, Edited, and with Issue Framing Material by:
M. Ethan Katsh, *University of Massachusetts, Amherst*

ISSUE

Is a Dog Sniffing for Drugs Outside a Home a Search Prohibited by the Fourth Amendment?

YES: **Antonin Scalia**, from "Majority Opinion, *Florida v. Jardines*," *United States Supreme Court* (2013)

NO: **Samuel Anthony Alito, Jr.**, from "Dissenting Opinion, *Florida v. Jardines*," *United States Supreme Court* (2013)

Learning Outcomes

After reading this issue, you will be able to:

- Explain what guarantees the Fourth Amendment provides to citizens.
- Explain why, according to Justice Scalia, the police engaged in a search and why the information gathered from their action was invalid.
- Explain how the law of trespass pertains to this case.
- Compare the views of the two justices on the use of the trained dog in deciding whether this action fulfills the requirement for a search, including the issue of "expectation of privacy."
- Explain why Justice Alito cited the case of *Kentucky v. King* in allowing the police to knock on the door.

ISSUE SUMMARY

YES: Supreme Court Justice Antonin Scalia finds that it is a search and a violation of the Fourth Amendment when police obtain evidence by allowing a trained dog to physically enter and occupy an area outside a home in which permission has not been obtained from the home owner.

NO: Supreme Court Justice Samuel Alito disagrees that there was a trespass here or that the dog sniff could be considered an invasion of any reasonable expectation of privacy given that one can expect that odors will float outside of a house.

In 1991 agent William Elliott of the U.S. Department of the Interior became suspicious that marijuana was being grown in the home of Danny Kyllo. Indoor marijuana growth typically requires high-intensity lamps, and at 3:20 a.m. on January 16, 1992, Elliott scanned Kyllo's home with a thermal imaging device. Such devices can detect infrared radiation, which virtually all objects emit but which is not visible to the naked eye. The imager converts radiation into images based on relative warmth—black is cool, white is hot, and shades of gray connote relative differences.

The scan of Kyllo's home took only a few minutes. It showed that the roof over the garage and a side wall of the home were relatively hot compared to the rest of the home and substantially warmer than neighboring homes. Elliott concluded that Kyllo was using special lamps to grow marijuana in his house. Based on tips from informants, utility bills, and the thermal imaging, a warrant was issued authorizing a search of Kyllo's home, where the agents found more than 100 plants being grown. Kyllo was indicted on one count of manufacturing marijuana. He unsuccessfully moved to suppress the evidence seized from his home and then entered a conditional guilty plea.

As a general rule, the Fourth Amendment to the Constitution requires authorities to obtain a search warrant before conducting a search. In order to do this, they must persuade a judge that probable cause exists that a crime has been committed and that the evidence sought will be found in the place to be searched. The warrant requirement is the key constitutional element restricting the power of the police to decide unilaterally to invade the privacy of someone's home. Thus, the task in Kyllo was to decide whether what thermal imaging revealed did constitute probable cause of a crime being committed.

The lower court ruled against Kyllo and found that the thermal imager "is a nonintrusive device which emits no rays or beams and shows a crude visual image of the heat being radiated from the outside of the house"; it "did not show any people or activity within the walls of the structure"; "the device used cannot penetrate walls or windows to reveal conversations or human activities"; and "no intimate details of the home were observed." Kyllo appealed to the Court of Appeals and then to the U.S. Supreme Court, which, in an opinion authored by Justice Scalia, ruled in his favor.

In this issue's reading, the issue is similar: namely can one get enough information while outside the home to justify obtaining a warrant to conduct a search inside the home? The technology at issue here, however, is not some kind of technological invention or device but a trained dog. Can one walk up to a home and allow the dog to sniff around and, in a sense, report his findings to a police handler? We have expectations of privacy when we are in our homes. We don't have such expectations for garbage we may put on the street outside our homes. What about the area right outside our front door, which is called the "curtilage"?

Even though Justice Scalia's majority opinion is a strong statement about the need for protecting privacy in a technological era, there will certainly be more cases in which challenging issues will be presented. Law enforcement's ability to invade privacy at a distance is increasing, and the Supreme Court has not, as it did in this case, always sided with the individual. Indeed, the Court has upheld various novel search techniques in other Fourth Amendment cases. Consider the following:

- *Dow Chemical Co. v. United States*, 476 U.S. 227 (1986)—The Court allowed aerial pictures taken by the Environmental Protection Agency (EPA) even though the company had refused to allow inspectors to enter.
- *Florida v. Riley,* 488 U.S. 445, 450 (1989)—The Court allowed a search in which a police officer in a helicopter looked into a greenhouse from a height of 400 feet and observed through openings in the roof what he thought was marijuana.
- *California v. Cariole*, 476 U.S. 207, 213–214 (1986)—The Court held that police officers were not "searching" when they flew over the defendant's property and observed marijuana growing.
- *Smith v. Maryland*, 442 U.S. 735, 742–744 (1979)—The Court allowed the authorities to look at "pen registers," or records of telephone numbers dialed, without a warrant.

This was also not the first case in which the Court had to rule on the propriety of a dog sniff. In 2005, in *Illinois v. Caballes* (543 U.S. 405 (2005)), the Court allowed a dog sniff during a legal traffic stop, and in 1986, in *United States v. Place* (462 U.S. 696 (1983)), the Court allowed federal agents to obtain a warrant based on a dog sniff of a suitcase for narcotics.

YES ↵

Antonin Scalia

Majority Opinion, *Florida v. Jardines*

JUSTICE SCALIA delivered the opinion of the Court.

We consider whether using a drug-sniffing dog on a homeowner's porch to investigate the contents of the home is a "search" within the meaning of the Fourth Amendment.

I

In 2006, Detective William Pedraja of the Miami-Dade Police Department received an unverified tip that marijuana was being grown in the home of respondent Joelis Jardines. One month later, the Department and the Drug Enforcement Administration sent a joint surveillance team to Jardines' home. Detective Pedraja was part of that team. He watched the home for fifteen minutes and saw no vehicles in the driveway or activity around the home, and could not see inside because the blinds were drawn. Detective Pedraja then approached Jardines' home accompanied by Detective Douglas Bartelt, a trained canine handler who had just arrived at the scene with his drug-sniffing dog. The dog was trained to detect the scent of marijuana, cocaine, heroin, and several other drugs, indicating the presence of any of these substances through particular behavioral changes recognizable by his handler.

Detective Bartelt had the dog on a six-foot leash, owing in part to the dog's "wild" nature and tendency to dart around erratically while searching. As the dog approached Jardines' front porch, he apparently sensed one of the odors he had been trained to detect, and began energetically exploring the area for the strongest point source of that odor. As Detective Bartelt explained, the dog "began tracking that airborne odor by . . . tracking back and forth," engaging in what is called "bracketing," "back and forth, back and forth." Detective Bartelt gave the dog "the full six feet of the leash plus whatever safe distance [he could] give him" to do this—he testified that he needed to give the dog "as much distance as I can." And Detective Pedraja stood back while this was occurring, so that he would not "get knocked over" when the dog was "spinning around trying to find" the source.

After sniffing the base of the front door, the dog sat, which is the trained behavior upon discovering the odor's strongest point. Detective Bartelt then pulled the dog away from the door and returned to his vehicle. He left the scene after informing Detective Pedraja that there had been a positive alert for narcotics.

On the basis of what he had learned at the home, Detective Pedraja applied for and received a warrant to search the residence. When the warrant was executed later that day, Jardines attempted to flee and was arrested; the search revealed marijuana plants, and he was charged with trafficking in cannabis.

At trial, Jardines moved to suppress the marijuana plants on the ground that the canine investigation was an unreasonable search. The trial court granted the motion, and the Florida Third District Court of Appeal reversed. On a petition for discretionary review, the Florida Supreme Court quashed the decision of the Third District Court of Appeal and approved the trial court's decision to suppress, holding (as relevant here) that the use of the trained narcotics dog to investigate Jardines' home was a Fourth Amendment search unsupported by probable cause, rendering invalid the warrant based upon information gathered in that search. 73 So. 3d 34 (2011).

We granted certiorari, limited to the question of whether the officers' behavior was a search within the meaning of the Fourth Amendment.

II

The Fourth Amendment provides in relevant part that the "right of the people to be secure in their persons, houses, papers, and effects, against unreasonable searches and seizures, shall not be violated." The Amendment establishes a simple baseline, one that for much of our history formed the exclusive basis for its protections: When "the Government obtains information by physically intruding" on persons, houses, papers, or effects, "a 'search' within the original meaning of the Fourth Amendment" has "undoubtedly occurred." *United States v. Jones,* 565 U. S. ___, ___, n. 3 (2012) (slip op., at 6, n. 3). By reason of our

From Supreme Court of the United States, March 26, 2013.

decision in *Katz v. United States,* 389 U. S. 347 (1967), property rights "are not the sole measure of Fourth Amendment violations," *Soldal v. Cook County,* 506 U. S. 56, 64 (1992)—but though *Katz* may add to the baseline, it does not subtract anything from the Amendment's protections "when the Government *does* engage in [a] physical intrusion of a constitutionally protected area," *United States v. Knotts,* 460 U. S. 276, 286 (1983) (Brennan, J., concurring in the judgment).

That principle renders this case a straightforward one. The officers were gathering information in an area belonging to Jardines and immediately surrounding his house—in the curtilage of the house, which we have held enjoys protection as part of the home itself. And they gathered that information by physically entering and occupying the area to engage in conduct not explicitly or implicitly permitted by the homeowner.

A

The Fourth Amendment "indicates with some precision the places and things encompassed by its protections": persons, houses, papers, and effects. The Fourth Amendment does not, therefore, prevent all investigations conducted on private property; for example, an officer may (subject to *Katz*) gather information in what we have called "open fields"—even if those fields are privately owned—because such fields are not enumerated in the Amendment's text. *Hester v. United States,* 265 U. S. 57 (1924).

But when it comes to the Fourth Amendment, the home is first among equals. At the Amendment's "very core" stands "the right of a man to retreat into his own home and there be free from unreasonable governmental intrusion." *Silverman v. United States,* 365 U. S. 505, 511 (1961). This right would be of little practical value if the State's agents could stand in a home's porch or side garden and trawl for evidence with impunity; the right to retreat would be significantly diminished if the police could enter a man's property to observe his repose from just outside the front window.

We therefore regard the area "immediately surrounding and associated with the home"—what our cases call the curtilage—as "part of the home itself for Fourth Amendment purposes." *Oliver, supra,* at 180. That principle has ancient and durable roots. Just as the distinction between the home and the open fields is "as old as the common law," *Hester, supra,* at 59, so too is the identity of home and what Blackstone called the "curtilage or homestall," for the "house protects and privileges all its branches and appurtenants." 4 W. Blackstone, Commentaries on the Laws of England 223, 225 (1769). This area around the home is "intimately linked to the home, both physically and psychologically," and is where "privacy expectations are most heightened." *California v. Ciraolo,* 476 U. S. 207, 213 (1986).

While the boundaries of the curtilage are generally "clearly marked," the "conception defining the curtilage" is at any rate familiar enough that it is "easily understood from our daily experience." *Oliver,* 466 U. S., at 182, n. 12. Here there is no doubt that the officers entered it: The front porch is the classic exemplar of an area adjacent to the home and "to which the activity of home life extends."

B

Since the officers' investigation took place in a constitutionally protected area, we turn to the question of whether it was accomplished through an unlicensed physical intrusion.[1] While law enforcement officers need not "shield their eyes" when passing by the home "on public thoroughfares," *Ciraolo,* 476 U. S., at 213, an officer's leave to gather information is sharply circumscribed when he steps off those thoroughfares and enters the Fourth Amendment's protected areas. In permitting, for example, visual observation of the home from "public navigable airspace," we were careful to note that it was done "in a physically nonintrusive manner." *Ibid. Entick v. Carrington,* 2 Wils. K. B. 275, 95 Eng. Rep. 807 (K. B. 1765), a case "undoubtedly familiar" to "every American statesman" at the time of the Founding, *Boyd v. United States,* 116 U. S. 616, 626 (1886), states the general rule clearly: "[O]ur law holds the property of every man so sacred, that no man can set his foot upon his neighbour's close without his leave." 2 Wils. K.B., at 291, 95 Eng. Rep., at 817. As it is undisputed that the detectives had all four of their feet and all four of their companion's firmly planted on the constitutionally protected extension of Jardines' home, the only question is whether he had given his leave (even implicitly) for them to do so. He had not.

"A license may be implied from the habits of the country," notwithstanding the "strict rule of the English common law as to entry upon a close." *McKee v. Gratz,* 260 U. S. 127, 136 (1922) (Holmes, J.). We have accordingly recognized that "the knocker on the front door is treated as an invitation or license to attempt an entry, justifying ingress to the home by solicitors, hawkers and peddlers of all kinds." *Breard v. Alexandria,* 341 U. S. 622, 626 (1951). This implicit license typically permits the visitor to approach the home by the front path, knock promptly, wait briefly to be received, and then (absent invitation to linger longer) leave. Complying with the terms of that traditional invitation does not require fine-grained legal knowledge; it is generally managed without incident by the Nation's Girl Scouts and trick-or-treaters. Thus, a police officer not armed with a warrant may approach a home and knock, precisely because that is "no more than any private citizen might do." *Kentucky v. King,* 563 U. S.___, ___ (2011) (slip op., at 16).

But introducing a trained police dog to explore the area around the home in hopes of discovering incriminating evidence is something else. There is no customary invitation to do *that.* An invitation to engage in canine forensic investigation assuredly does not inhere in the very act of hanging a knocker.[2] To find a visitor knocking on the door is routine (even if sometimes unwelcome); to spot that same visitor exploring the front path with a metal detector, or marching his bloodhound into the garden before saying hello and asking permission, would inspire most of us to—well, call the police. The scope of a license—express or implied—is limited not only to a particular area but also to a specific purpose. Consent at a traffic stop to an officer's checking out an anonymous tip that there is a body in the trunk does not permit the officer to rummage through the trunk for narcotics. Here, the background social norms that invite a visitor to the front door do not invite him there to conduct a search. . . .

III

The State argues that investigation by a forensic narcotics dog by definition cannot implicate any legitimate privacy interest. The State cites for authority our decisions in *United States v. Place,* 462 U. S. 696 (1983), *United States v. Jacobsen,* 466 U. S. 109 (1984), and *Illinois v. Caballes,* 543 U. S. 405 (2005), which held, respectively, that canine inspection of luggage in an airport, chemical testing of a substance that had fallen from a parcel in transit, and canine inspection of an automobile during a lawful traffic stop, do not violate the "reasonable expectation of privacy" described in *Katz.*

Just last Term, we considered an argument much like this. *Jones* held that tracking an automobile's whereabouts using a physically-mounted GPS receiver is a Fourth Amendment search. The Government argued that the *Katz* standard "show[ed] that no search occurred," as the defendant had "no 'reasonable expectation of privacy'" in his whereabouts on the public roads, *Jones,* 565 U. S., at ___ (slip op., at 5)—a proposition with at least as much support in our case law as the one the State marshals here. See, *e.g., United States v. Knotts,* 460 U. S. 276, 278 (1983). But because the GPS receiver had been physically

mounted on the defendant's automobile (thus intruding on his "effects"), we held that tracking the vehicle's movements was a search: a person's "Fourth Amendment rights do not rise or fall with the *Katz* formulation." The *Katz* reasonable expectations test "has been *added to,* not *substituted for,*" the traditional property-based understanding of the Fourth Amendment, and so is unnecessary to consider when the government gains evidence by physically intruding on constitutionally protected areas.

Thus, we need not decide whether the officers' investigation of Jardines' home violated his expectation of privacy under *Katz.* One virtue of the Fourth Amendment's property-rights baseline is that it keeps easy cases easy. That the officers learned what they learned only by physically intruding on Jardines' property to gather evidence is enough to establish that a search occurred.

For a related reason we find irrelevant the State's argument (echoed by the dissent) that forensic dogs have been commonly used by police for centuries. This argument is apparently directed to our holding in *Kyllo v. United States,* 533 U. S. 27 (2001), that surveillance of the home is a search where "the Government uses a device that is not in general public use" to "explore details of the home that would previously have been unknowable *without physical intrusion.*" *Id.,* at 40 (emphasis added). But the implication of that statement (*inclusio unius est exclusio alterius*) is that when the government uses a physical intrusion to explore details of the home (including itscurtilage), the antiquity of the tools that they bring along is irrelevant. . . .

The government's use of trained police dogs to investigate the home and its immediate surroundings is a "search" within the meaning of the Fourth Amendment. The judgment of the Supreme Court of Florida is therefore affirmed.

It is so ordered.

Notes

1. At oral argument, the State and its *amicus* the Solicitor General argued that Jardines conceded in the lower courts that the officers had a right to be where they were. This misstates the record. Jardines conceded nothing more than the unsurprising proposition that the officers could have lawfully approached his home to knock on the front door in hopes of speaking with him. Of course, that is not what they did.
2. The dissent insists that our argument must rest upon "the particular instrument that Detective Bartelt used to detect the odor of marijuana"— the dog. *Post,* at 8. It is not the dog that is the problem, but the behavior that here involved

use of the dog. We think a typical person would find it "'a cause for great alarm'" (the kind of reaction the dissent quite rightly relies upon to justify its no-night-visits rule) to find a stranger snooping about his front porch *with or without a dog*. The dissent would let the police do whatever they want by way of gathering evidence so long as they stay on the base-path, to use a baseball analogy—so long as they "stick to the path that is typically used to approach a front door, such as a paved walkway." From that vantage point they can presumably peer into the house through binoculars with impunity. That is not the law, as even the State concedes.

Antonin Scalia is an associate justice of the U.S. Supreme Court. He taught law at the University of Virginia, the American Enterprise Institute, Georgetown University, and the University of Chicago before being nominated to the U.S. Court of Appeals by President Ronald Reagan in 1982. He served in that capacity until he was nominated by Reagan to the Supreme Court in 1986.

Samuel Anthony Alito, Jr.

Dissenting Opinion, *Florida v. Jardines*

JUSTICE ALITO, with whom THE CHIEF JUSTICE, JUSTICE KENNEDY, and JUSTICE BREYER join, dissenting.

The Court's decision in this important Fourth Amendment case is based on a putative rule of trespass law that is nowhere to be found in the annals of Anglo-American jurisprudence.

The law of trespass generally gives members of the public a license to use a walkway to approach the front door of a house and to remain there for a brief time. This license is not limited to persons who intend to speak to an occupant or who actually do so. (Mail carriers and persons delivering packages and flyers are examples of individuals who may lawfully approach a front door without intending to converse.) Nor is the license restricted to categories of visitors whom an occupant of the dwelling is likely to welcome; as the Court acknowledges, this license applies even to "solicitors, hawkers and peddlers of all kinds." And the license even extends to police officers who wish to gather evidence against an occupant (by asking potentially incriminating questions).

According to the Court, however, the police officer in this case, Detective Bartelt, committed a trespass because he was accompanied during his otherwise lawful visit to the front door of respondent's house by his dog, Franky. Where is the authority evidencing such a rule? Dogs have been domesticated for about 12,000 years;[1] they were ubiquitous in both this country and Britain at the time of the adoption of the Fourth Amendment;[2] and their acute sense of smell has been used in law enforcement for centuries.[3] Yet the Court has been unable to find a single case—from the United States or any other common-law nation—that supports the rule on which its decision is based. Thus, trespass law provides no support for the Court's holding today.

The Court's decision is also inconsistent with the reasonable-expectations-of-privacy test that the Court adopted in *Katz v. United States*, 389 U. S. 347 (1967). A reasonable person understands that odors emanating from a house may be detected from locations that are open to the public, and a reasonable person will not count on the strength of those odors remaining within the range that, while detectible by a dog, cannot be smelled by a human.

For these reasons, I would hold that no search within the meaning of the Fourth Amendment took place in this case, and I would reverse the decision below.

I

The opinion of the Court may leave a reader with the mistaken impression that Detective Bartelt and Franky remained on respondent's property for a prolonged period of time and conducted a far-flung exploration of the front yard. But that is not what happened.

Detective Bartelt and Franky approached the front door via the driveway and a paved path—the route that any visitor would customarily use[4]—and Franky was on the kind of leash that any dog owner might employ.[5] As Franky approached the door, he started to track an airborne odor. He held his head high and began "bracketing" the area (pacing back and forth) in order to determine the strongest source of the smell. Detective Bartelt knew "the minute [he] observed" this behavior that Franky had detected drugs. Upon locating the odor's strongest source, Franky sat at the base of the front door, and at this point, Detective Bartelt and Franky immediately returned to their patrol car.

A critical fact that the Court omits is that, as respondent's counsel explained at oral argument, this entire process—walking down the driveway and front path to the front door, waiting for Franky to find the strongest source of the odor, and walking back to the car—took approximately a minute or two. Thus, the amount of time that Franky and the detective remained at the front porch was even less. The Court also fails to mention that, while Detective Bartelt apparently did not personally smell the odor of marijuana coming from the house, another officer who subsequently stood on the front porch, Detective Pedraja, did notice that smell and was able to identify it.

From Supreme Court of the United States, March 26, 2013.

II

The Court concludes that the conduct in this case was a search because Detective Bartelt exceeded the boundaries of the license to approach the house that is recognized by the law of trespass, but the Court's interpretation of the scope of that license is unfounded.

A

It is said that members of the public may lawfully proceed along a walkway leading to the front door of a house because custom grants them a license to do so. *Breard v. Alexandria,* 341 U. S. 622, 626 (1951); *Lakin v. Ames,* 64 Mass. 198, 220 (1852); J. Bishop, Commentaries on the Non-Contract Law §823, p. 378 (1889). This rule encompasses categories of visitors whom most homeowners almost certainly wish to allow to approach their front doors—friends, relatives, mail carriers, persons making deliveries. But it also reaches categories of visitors who are less universally welcome—"solicitors," "hawkers," "peddlers," and the like. The law might attempt to draw fine lines between categories of welcome and unwelcome visitors, distinguishing, for example, between tolerable and intolerable door-to-door peddlers (Girl Scouts selling cookies versus adults selling aluminum siding) or between police officers on agreeable and disagreeable missions (gathering information about a bothersome neighbor versus asking potentially incriminating questions). But the law of trespass has not attempted such a difficult taxonomy. See *Desnick v. American Broadcasting Cos.,* 44 F. 3d 1345, 1351 (CA7 1995) ("[C]onsent to an entry is often given legal effect even though the entrant has intentions that if known to the owner of the property would cause him for perfectly understandable and generally ethical or at least lawful reasons to revoke his consent"); cf. *Skinner v. Ogallala Public School Dist.,* 262 Neb. 387, 402, 631 N. W. 2d 510, 525 (2001) ("[I n order to determine if a business invitation is implied, the inquiry is not a subjective assessment of why the visitor chose to visit the premises in a particular instance"); *Crown Cork & Seal Co. v. Kane,* 213 Md. 152, 159, 131 A. 2d 470, 473–474 (1957) (noting that "there are many cases in which an invitation has been implied from circumstances, such as custom," and that this test is "objective in that it stresses custom and the appearance of things" as opposed to "the undisclosed intention of the visitor").

Of course, this license has certain spatial and temporal limits. A visitor must stick to the path that is typically used to approach a front door, such as a paved walkway. A visitor cannot traipse through the garden, meander into the backyard, or take other circuitous detours that veer from the pathway that a visitor would customarily use. See, *e.g., Robinson v. Virginia,* 47 Va. App. 533, 549–550, 625 S. E. 2d 651, 659 (2006) (en banc); *United States v. Wells,* 648 F. 3d 671, 679–680 (CA8 2011) (police exceeded scope of their implied invitation when they bypassed the front door and proceeded directly to the back yard); *State v. Harris,* 919 S. W. 2d 619, 624 (Tenn. Crim. App. 1995) ("Any substantial and unreasonable departure from an area where the public is impliedly invited exceeds the scope of the implied invitation . . . " (internal quotation marks and brackets omitted)); 1 W. LaFave, Search and Seizure §2.3(c), p. 578 (2004) (hereinafter LaFave); *id.,* §2.3(f), at 600–603 ("[W]hen the police come on to private property to conduct an investigation or for some other legitimate purpose and restrict their movements to places visitors could be expected to go (e.g., walkways, driveways, porches), observations made from such vantage points are not covered by the Fourth Amendment" (footnotes omitted)).

Nor, as a general matter, may a visitor come to the front door in the middle of the night without an express invitation. See *State v. Cada,* 129 Idaho 224, 233, 923 P. 2d 469, 478 (App. 1996) ("Furtive intrusion late at night or in the predawn hours is not conduct that is expected from ordinary visitors. Indeed, if observed by a resident of the premises, it could be a cause for great alarm.")

Similarly, a visitor may not linger at the front door for an extended period. See 9 So. 3d 1, 11 (Fla. App. 2008) (case below) (Cope, J., concurring in part and dissenting in part) ("[T]here is no such thing as squatter's rights on a front porch. A stranger may not plop down uninvited to spend the afternoon in the front porch rocking chair, or throw down a sleeping bag to spend the night, or lurk on the front porch, looking in the windows"). The license is limited to the amount of time it would customarily take to approach the door, pause long enough to see if someone is home, and (if not expressly invited to stay longer), leave.

As I understand the law of trespass and the scope of the implied license, a visitor who adheres to these limitations is not necessarily required to ring the doorbell, knock on the door, or attempt to speak with an occupant. For example, mail carriers, persons making deliveries, and individuals distributing flyers may leave the items they are carrying and depart without making any attempt to converse. A pedestrian or motorist looking for a particular address may walk up to a front door in order to check a house number that is hard to see from the sidewalk or road. A neighbor who knows that the residents are away may approach the door to retrieve an accumulation of newspapers that might signal to a potential burglar that the house is unoccupied.

As the majority acknowledges, this implied license to approach the front door extends to the police. As we recognized in *Kentucky v. King,* 563 U. S. ___ (2011), police officers do not engage in a search when they approach the front door of a residence and seek to engage in what is termed a "knock and talk," *i.e.,* knocking on the door and seeking to speak to an occupant for the purpose of gathering evidence. See *id.,* at ___ (slip op., at 16) ("When law enforcement officers who are not armed with a warrant knock on a door, they do no more than any private citizen might do"). See also 1 LaFave §2.3(e), at 592 ("It is not objectionable for an officer to come upon that part of the property which has been opened to public common use" (internal quotation marks omitted)). Even when the objective of a "knock and talk" is to obtain evidence that will lead to the homeowner's arrest and prosecution, the license to approach still applies. In other words, gathering evidence—even damning evidence—is a lawful activity that falls within the scope of the license to approach. And when officers walk up to the front door of a house, they are permitted to see, hear, and smell whatever can be detected from a lawful vantage point. *California v. Ciraolo,* 476 U. S. 207, 213 (1986) ("The Fourth Amendment protection of the home has never been extended to require law enforcement officer to shield their eyes when passing by a home on public thoroughfares"); *Cada, supra,* at 232, 923 P. 2d, at 477 ("[P]olice officers restricting their activity to [areas to which the public is impliedly invited] are permitted the same intrusion and the same level of observation as would be expected from a reasonably respectful citizen" (internal quotation marks omitted)); 1 LaFave §§2.2(a), 2.3(c), at 450–452, 572–577.

B

Detective Bartelt did not exceed the scope of the license to approach respondent's front door. He adhered to the customary path; he did not approach in the middle of the night; and he remained at the front door for only a very short period (less than a minute or two).

The Court concludes that Detective Bartelt went too far because he had the "*objectiv[e] . . . purpose* to conduct a search." *Ante,* at 8 (emphasis added). What this means, I take it, is that anyone aware of what Detective Bartelt did would infer that his subjective purpose was to gather evidence. But if this is the Court's point, then a standard "knock and talk" and most other police visits would likewise constitute searches. With the exception of visits to serve warrants or civil process, police almost always approach homes with a purpose of discovering information. That is certainly the objective of a "knock and talk."

The Court offers no meaningful way of distinguishing the "objective purpose" of a "knock and talk" from the "objective purpose" of Detective Bartelt's conduct here.

The Court contends that a "knock and talk" is different because it involves talking, and "all are invited" to do that. *Ante,* at 7–8, n. 4 (emphasis deleted). But a police officer who approaches the front door of a house in accordance with the limitations already discussed may gather evidence by means other than talking. The officer may observe items in plain view and smell odors coming from the house. So the Court's "objective purpose" argument cannot stand.

What the Court must fall back on, then, is the particular instrument that Detective Bartelt used to detect the odor of marijuana, namely, his dog. But in the entire body of common-law decisions, the Court has not found a single case holding that a visitor to the front door of a home commits a trespass if the visitor is accompanied by a dog on a leash. On the contrary, the common law allowed even unleashed dogs to wander on private property without committing a trespass. G. Williams, Liability for Animals 136–146 (1939); J. Ingham, A Treatise on Property in Animals Wild and Domestic and the Rights and Respon-sibilities Arising Therefrom 277–278 (1900). Cf. B. Markesinis & S. Deakin, Tort Law 511 (4th ed. 1999).

The Court responds that "[i]t is not the dog that is the problem, but the behavior that here involved use of the dog." *Ante,* at 7, n. 3. But where is the support in the law of trespass for *this* proposition? Dogs' keen sense of smell has been used in law enforcement for centuries. The antiquity of this practice is evidenced by a Scottish law from 1318 that made it a crime to "disturb a tracking dog or the men coming with it for pursuing thieves or seizing malefactors." K. Brown et al., The Records of the Parliaments of Scotland to 1707, (St Andrews, 2007–2013), online at http://www.rps.ac.uk/mss/1318/9. If bringing a tracking dog to the front door of a home constituted a trespass, one would expect at least one case to have arisen during the past 800 years. But the Court has found none.

For these reasons, the real law of trespass provides no support for the Court's holding today. While the Court claims that its reasoning has "ancient and durable roots," *ante,* at 4, its trespass rule is really a newly struck counterfeit.

III

The concurring opinion attempts to provide an alternative ground for today's decision, namely, that Detective Bartelt's conduct violated respondent's reasonable expectations of privacy. But we have already rejected a very similar, if not identical argument, see *Illinois v. Caballes,* 543 U. S. 405, 409–410 (2005), and in any event I see no basis for concluding that the occupants of a dwelling have a reasonable expectation of privacy in odors that emanate from the dwelling and reach spots where members of the public may lawfully stand.

It is clear that the occupant of a house has no reasonable expectation of privacy with respect to odors that can be smelled by human beings who are standing in such places. See *United States v. Johns,* 469 U. S. 478, 482 (1985) ("After the officers came closer and detected the distinct odor of marihuana, they had probable cause to believe that the vehicles contained contraband"); *United States v. Ventresca,* 380 U. S. 102, 111 (1965) (scent of fermenting mash supported probable cause for warrant); *United States v. Johnston,* 497 F. 2d 397, 398 (CA9 1974) (there is no "reasonable expectation of privacy from drug agents with inquisitive nostrils"). And I would not draw a line between odors that can be smelled by humans and those that are detectible only by dogs.

Consider the situation from the point of view of the occupant of a building in which marijuana is grown or methamphetamine is manufactured. Would such an occupant reason as follows? "I know that odors may emanate from my building and that atmospheric conditions, such as the force and direction of the wind, may affect the strength of those odors when they reach a spot where members of the public may lawfully stand. I also know that some people have a much more acute sense of smell than others,[6] and I have no idea who might be standing in one of the spots in question when the odors from my house reach that location. In addition, I know that odors coming from my building, when they reach these locations, may be strong enough to be detected by a dog. But I am confident that they will be so faint that they cannot be smelled by any human being." Such a finely tuned expectation would be entirely unrealistic, and I see no evidence that society is prepared to recognize it as reasonable.

In an attempt to show that respondent had a reasonable expectation of privacy in the odor of marijuana wafting from his house, the concurrence argues that this case is just like *Kyllo v. United States,* 533 U. S. 27 (2001), which held that police officers conducted a search when they used a thermal imaging device to detect heat emanating from a house. *Ante,* at 3–4 (opinion of KAGAN, J.). This Court, however, has already rejected the argument that the use of a drug-sniffing dog is the same as the use of a thermal imaging device. See *Caballes,* 543 U. S., at 409–410. The very argument now advanced by the concurrence appears in Justice Souter's *Caballes* dissent. See *id.,* at 413, and n. 3. But the Court was not persuaded.

Contrary to the interpretation propounded by the concurrence, *Kyllo* is best understood as a decision about the use of new technology. The *Kyllo* Court focused on the fact that the thermal imaging device was a form of "sense-enhancing technology" that was "not in general public use," and it expressed concern that citizens would be "at the mercy of advancing technology" if its use was not restricted. 533 U. S., at 34–35. A dog, however, is not a new form of "technology or a device." And, as noted, the use of dogs' acute sense of smell in law enforcement dates back many centuries.

The concurrence suggests that a *Kyllo*-based decision would be "much like" the actual decision of the Court, but that is simply not so. The holding of the Court is based on what the Court sees as a "'physical intrusion of a constitutionally protected area.'" *Ante,* at 3 (quoting *United States v. Knotts,* 460 U. S. 276, 286 (1983) (Brennan, J., concurring in judgment)). As a result, it does not apply when a dog alerts while on a public sidewalk or street or in the corridor of a building to which the dog and handler have been lawfully admitted.

The concurrence's *Kyllo*-based approach would have a much wider reach. When the police used the thermal imaging device in *Kyllo,* they were on a public street, 533 U. S., at 29, and "committed no trespass." *Ante,* at 3. Therefore, if a dog's nose is just like a thermal imaging device for Fourth Amendment purposes, a search would occur if a dog alerted while on a public sidewalk or in the corridor of an apartment building. And the same would be true if the dog was trained to sniff, not for marijuana, but for more dangerous quarry, such as explosives or for a violent fugitive or kidnaped child. I see no ground for hampering legitimate law enforcement in this way.

IV

The conduct of the police officer in this case did not constitute a trespass and did not violate respondent's reasonable expectations of privacy. I would hold that this conduct was not a search, and I therefore respectfully dissent.

Notes

1. See, *e.g.,* Sloane, Dogs in War, Police Work and on Patrol, 46 *J. Crim. L., C. & P. S.* 385 (1955–1956) (hereinafter Sloane).

2. M. Derr, A Dog's History of America 68–92 (2004); K. Olsen Daily Life in 18th-Century England 32–33 (1999).
3. Sloane 388–389.
4. See App. 94; App. to Brief for Respondent 1A (depiction of respondent's home).
5. The Court notes that Franky was on a 6-foot leash, but such a leash is standard equipment for ordinary dog owners. See, *e.g.*, J. Stregowski, Four Dog Leash Varieties, http://dogs.about.com /od/toyssupplies/tp/Dog-Leashes.htm (all Internet materials as visited Mar. 21, 2013, and available in Clerk of Court's case file).
6. Some humans naturally have a much more acute sense of smell than others, and humans can be trained to detect and distinguish odors that could not be detected without such training. See E. Hancock, A Primer on Smell, http://www.jhu .edu/jhumag/996web/smell.html. Some individuals employed in the perfume and wine industries, for example, have an amazingly acute sense of smell. *Ibid.*

SAMUEL ANTHONY ALITO, JR. is an associate justice of the Supreme Court of the United States. He is a graduate of Princeton University and Yale Law School, and he served as U.S. Attorney for the District of New Jersey and as a judge on the United States Court of Appeals for the Third Circuit. He was nominated by President George W. Bush and has served on the court since January 31, 2006.

EXPLORING THE ISSUE

Is a Dog Sniffing for Drugs Outside a Home a Search Prohibited by the Fourth Amendment?

Critical Thinking and Reflection

1. What are the guarantees under the Fourth Amendment?
2. Is a governmental agency ever allowed to enter someone's property? If yes, under what conditions?
3. Why does the State argue that this dog search is allowed?
4. What was the view of the Court in the case of *Kentucky v. King* about police knocking at a citizen's door to get information? How did Justice Alito think this was relevant in this case? How did Justice Scalia limit this activity?

Is There Common Ground?

This appears to have been a challenging case for the justices. Not only was it decided by a 5 to 4 vote but the grouping of justices in the majority and minority was unusual. Joining Justice Scalia were Justices Kagan, Ginsburg and Sotomayor, three of the more liberal justices, and Justice Thomas. In the minority were Justice Alito, joined by Justices Roberts, Kennedy, and Breyer, the last being one of the more liberal justices. Breyer does not write a separate opinion, but his vote is interesting in that he sided with Justices Scalia in the *Kyllo* case, which found the use of thermal imaging equipment unconstitutional. It is not clear what, in particular, Justice Breyer thought was different about this case.

One instructive recent case that was decided in 2012 was *United States v. Jones*, 132 S.Ct. 945 (2012). *Jones* involved a GPS device that the government attached to a car and then monitored for a month. All nine justices agreed that this was impermissible. The majority opinion found this a violation of the Fourth Amendment largely because physically attaching a device constituted trespass. The four in the minority, in which Justice Breyer was again included, agreed that this was not permitted. The basis for their believing this, however, was not that there was a physical intrusion but that the owner of the car had an "expectation of privacy" that was being interfered with.

In the case at issue here, Justice Scalia finds a physical intrusion into part of a home and thus an illegal search. The minority feels that a dog sniffing around the outside of a home does not interfere with any "expectation of privacy." While Justice Scalia's opinion is viewed as pro-privacy, its rational may be difficult to apply in future cases where more and more occurs at a distance and without any physical intrusion.

Additional Resources

Tobias W. Mock, "The TSA's New X-Ray Vision: The Fourth Amendment Implications of 'Body-Scan' Searches at Domestic Airport Security Checkpoints," 49 *Santa Clara L. Rev.* 213 (2009).

Helen Nissenbaum, *Privacy in Context: Technology, Policy, and the Integrity of Social Life* (Stanford University Press, 2009).

Ian James Samuel, "Warrantless Location Tracking," 83 *N.Y.U.L. Rev.* 1324 (2008).

Daniel Solove, *Understanding Privacy* (Harvard University Press, 2010).

Internet References . . .

Scotus Blog Case File on *Florida v. Jardines*

www.scotusblog.com/case-files/cases/florida
-v-jardines/

Fourth Amendment Search and Seizure Materials

http://constitution.findlaw.com/amendment4
/amendment.html

Wall Street Journal

This article, "Justices Rein in Police on GPS Tracker," reports on the decision in *United States v. Jones* of the Supreme Court restricting law enforcements use of GPS to track suspects without a warrant.

http://online.wsj.com/article
/SB10001424052970203806504577178811800873358
.html

Selected, Edited, and with Issue Framing Material by:
M. Ethan Katsh, *University of Massachusetts, Amherst*

ISSUE

Does the "Cruel and Unusual Punishment" Clause of the Eighth Amendment Bar the Imposition of the Death Penalty on Juveniles?

YES: Anthony Kennedy, from "Majority Opinion, *Donald P. Roper, Superintendent, Potosi Correctional Center, Petitioner v. Christopher Simmons,*" *United States Supreme Court* (2005)

NO: Antonin Scalia, from "Minority Opinion, *Donald P. Roper, Superintendent, Potosi Correctional Center, Petitioner v. Christopher Simmons,*" *United States Supreme Court* (2005)

Learning Outcomes

After reading this issue, you will be able to:

- Identify the similarities between the death penalty's application to the mentally retarded and to juveniles.
- Discuss how changing standards within our society can affect the interpretation of the Constitution.
- Discuss differing opinions of justices on the application of international law and norms to our own jurisprudence.

ISSUE SUMMARY

YES: Supreme Court Justice Anthony Kennedy holds that the Constitution prohibits the execution of a person who was under the age of 18 at the time of the offense.

NO: Supreme Court Justice Antonin Scalia believes that the Constitution does not preclude the execution of a juvenile.

The questions of how a society punishes its wrongdoers, and to what extent it does so, are central to the very structure of social organization. These questions are particularly complex in democratic societies. Modern states, democratic or not, claim a monopoly over the use of violence. When democratic states punish, they do so in the name of its citizens. Such questions are particularly urgent when they deal with capital punishment. Death, it is often said, is different. If someone takes a life, should the state take his or hers in return? These questions are informed by centuries of debate. For example, in 428 B.C.E., Thucydides recorded the following arguments by Cleon in support of the death penalty:

Punish them as they deserve, and teach your other allies by a striking example that the penalty of rebellion is death. Let them once understand this and you will not so often have to neglect your enemies while you are fighting with your confederates.

In response, Diodotus wrote:

All states and individuals are alike prone to err, and there is no law that will prevent them, or why should men have exhausted the list of punishments in search of enactments to protect them from evildoers? It is probable that in early times the penalties for the greatest offenses were less severe, and that as these were disregarded, the penalty of death has been by degrees in most cases arrived at, which is itself disregarded in like manner. Either some means of terror more terrible than this must be discovered, or it must be owned that this restraint is useless. . . . We must make up our minds to look for our protection not to legal terrors but to careful administration.

During the last four decades, the U.S. Supreme Court has frequently been confronted with death penalty cases. The most significant was that of *Furman v. Georgia,* 408 U.S. 238 (1972). Furman, a 26-year-old African American, had killed a homeowner during a break-in and was sentenced to death. In a 5 to 4 decision, the Court overturned the sentence. It held that the procedure used by Georgia (and most other states at the time) was "cruel and unusual" and, therefore, a violation of the Eighth Amendment of the Constitution. Two justices, Thurgood Marshall and William Brennan, believed that at that point in the development of American society, infliction of the death penalty under any circumstances violated the Cruel and Unusual Punishments Clause of the Eighth Amendment. The three other justices in the *Furman* majority, however, held that the death penalty was not inherently unconstitutional, but that the procedures through which it was applied in that specific case were. In particular, Georgia law left it to the discretion of the jury to decide whether or not capital punishment was appropriate in each case, leading the death penalty to be administered in an arbitrary and potentially discriminatory fashion.

Furman resulted in a nationwide moratorium on capital punishment that lasted until the Supreme Court revisited the issue in 1976 in *Gregg v. Georgia,* 428 U.S. 153. In *Gregg,* the Court upheld a revised Georgia death penalty statute that, in keeping with the *Furman* guidelines, was intended to limit the capital jury's discretion. The process effected a bifurcated trial—divided into a "guilt phase" and a "penalty phase"—that aimed at greater equalization of punishment, while, at the same time, remaining sensitive to the unique characteristics of the individual defendant and the circumstances of the crime.

Actual executions resumed in 1977 and 35 states currently have a death penalty. From the 1970s to the present, the U.S. Supreme Court has continued to examine various aspects of the administration of capital punishment, but a majority of the Court has continued to find that the death penalty in itself is consistent with the requirements of the Eighth Amendment. A majority of the Court has also held, however, that the meaning of the Eighth Amendment is not fixed but continues to evolve. Accordingly, in 2002, the Court found in *Atkins v. Virginia,* 536 U.S. 304, that a "national consensus" had evolved against the execution of the mentally retarded and held that such punishment now violates the Eighth Amendment's prohibition of cruel and unusual punishment.

The United States is not alone in the world in employing capital punishment, but it does have some curious bedfellows. In 2012, the United States executed the fifth most people, behind China, Iran, Iraq, and Saudi Arabia, and was followed by Yemen and Sudan. Within the U.S. penal system, there is not a preference for the death penalty as a form of punishment, but rather these numbers are the product of the extraordinary number of incarcerated individuals in this country. With more than 2.2 million people under lock and key, the United States has the highest rate of incarceration of any country in the world, with more than 730 people per 100,000 behind bars.

Just as the U.S. Supreme Court appears to be evolving in its opinion, so too does the rest of the world. The number of countries that employ the death penalty has slowly been falling with only 25 countries in 2012 carrying out death sentences, and in December 2012, the United Nations passed a resolution calling for a moratorium on the use of the death penalty with a view to its abolishment. More than half the world's countries—111—voted in favor of the resolution, and approximately 150 countries have either abolished or no longer practice capital punishment.

Roper v. Simmons presented the U.S. Supreme Court with the question of whether or not the execution of someone who was 16 or 17 at the time of their capital offense is "cruel and unusual." Clearly, the Eighth Amendment does not explicitly prohibit capital punishment. What is far less clear is what the language of that amendment *means* when we attempt to apply it under ever-changing historical and cultural conditions. Does the language of the Eighth Amendment mean today what it meant at the end of the eighteenth century when it was written? If not, what is the proper mechanism for determining its changed meaning? And, who should be the authoritative agent for interpreting this change, Congress, the Courts, or the people themselves?

The interpretive problems that attend the meaning of the Eighth Amendment are one manifestation of more general disagreements about constitutional interpretation. Justice Kennedy assumes a central role for the courts—the Supreme Court in particular—in determining the meaning of the Eighth Amendment. Kennedy's interpretive approach requires the courts to "read" public opinion to comprehend dominant trends in state legislative enactments, and to be aware of comparative legal developments in the international arena. Justice Scalia, however, believes that each of these moves is but a part of a more general problem of misunderstanding the proper nature of the judicial role, a misunderstanding that risks the legitimacy of the court itself.

Does the Cruel and Unusual Punishment Clause of the 8th Amendment Bar the Imposition of the Death Penalty on Juveniles? by Katsh

199

YES

Anthony Kennedy

Majority Opinion, *Donald P. Roper, Superintendent, Potosi Correctional Center, Petitioner v. Christopher Simmons*

JUSTICE KENNEDY delivered the opinion of the Court.

This case requires us to address, for the second time in a decade and a half, whether it is permissible under the Eighth and Fourteenth Amendments to the Constitution of the United States to execute a juvenile offender who was older than 15 but younger than 18 when he committed a capital crime. In *Stanford v. Kentucky,* 492 U.S. 361 (1989), a divided Court rejected the proposition that the Constitution bars capital punishment for juvenile offenders in this age group. We reconsider the question. . . .

After these proceedings in Simmons' case had run their course, this Court held that the Eighth and Fourteenth Amendments prohibit the execution of a mentally retarded person. *Atkins v. Virginia,* 536 U.S. 304 (2002). Simmons filed a new petition for state postconviction relief, arguing that the reasoning of *Atkins* established that the Constitution prohibits the execution of a juvenile who was under 18 when the crime was committed.

The Missouri Supreme Court agreed. *State ex rel. Simmons v. Roper,* 112 S. W. 3d 397 (2003) (en banc). It held that since *Stanford,*

> "a national consensus has developed against the execution of juvenile offenders, as demonstrated by the fact that eighteen states now bar such executions for juveniles, that twelve other states bar executions altogether, that no state has lowered its age of execution below 18 since *Stanford,* that five states have legislatively or by case law raised or established the minimum age at 18, and that the imposition of the juvenile death penalty has become truly unusual over the last decade." 112 S. W. 3d, at 399.

On this reasoning it set aside Simmons' death sentence and resentenced him to "life imprisonment without eligibility for probation, parole, or release except by act of the Governor." *Id.,* at 413.

We granted certiorari, 540 U.S. 1160 (2004), and now affirm.

The Eighth Amendment provides: "Excessive bail shall not be required, nor excessive fines imposed, nor cruel and unusual punishments inflicted." The provision is applicable to the States through the Fourteenth Amendment. As the Court explained in *Atkins,* the Eighth Amendment guarantees individuals the right not to be subjected to excessive sanctions. The right flows from the basic "'precept of justice that punishment for crime should be graduated and proportioned to [the] offense.'" By protecting even those convicted of heinous crimes, the Eighth Amendment reaffirms the duty of the government to respect the dignity of all persons.

The prohibition against "cruel and unusual punishments," like other expansive language in the Constitution, must be interpreted according to its text, by considering history, tradition, and precedent, and with due regard for its purpose and function in the constitutional design. To implement this framework we have established the propriety and affirmed the necessity of referring to "the evolving standards of decency that mark the progress of a maturing society" to determine which punishments are so disproportionate as to be cruel and unusual.

In *Thompson v. Oklahoma,* 487 U.S. 815 (1988), a plurality of the Court determined that our standards of decency do not permit the execution of any offender under the age of 16 at the time of the crime. *Id.,* at 818–838. The plurality opinion explained that no death penalty State that had given express consideration to a minimum age for the death penalty had set the age lower than 16. *Id.,* at

826–829. The plurality also observed that "[t]he conclusion that it would offend civilized standards of decency to execute a person who was less than 16 years old at the time of his or her offense is consistent with the views that have been expressed by respected professional organizations, by other nations that share our Anglo-American heritage, and by the leading members of the Western European community." *Id.*, at 830. . . .

The next year, in *Stanford v. Kentucky*, the Court, . . . referred to contemporary standards of decency in this country and concluded the Eighth and Fourteenth Amendments did not proscribe the execution of juvenile offenders over 15 but under 18. . . . A plurality of the Court also "emphatically reject[ed]" the suggestion that the Court should bring its own judgment to bear on the acceptability of the juvenile death penalty.

The same day the Court decided *Stanford*, it held that the Eighth Amendment did not mandate a categorical exemption from the death penalty for the mentally retarded. *Penry v. Lynaugh*, 492 U.S. 302 (1989). In reaching this conclusion it stressed that only two States had enacted laws banning the imposition of the death penalty on a mentally retarded person convicted of a capital offense. *Id.*, at 334. According to the Court, "the two state statutes prohibiting execution of the mentally retarded, even when added to the 14 States that have rejected capital punishment completely, [did] not provide sufficient evidence at present of a national consensus." *Ibid.*

Three Terms ago the subject was reconsidered in *Atkins*. We held that standards of decency have evolved since *Penry* and now demonstrate that the execution of the mentally retarded is cruel and unusual punishment. The Court noted objective indicia of society's standards, as expressed in legislative enactments and state practice with respect to executions of the mentally retarded. When *Atkins* was decided only a minority of States permitted the practice, and even in those States it was rare. 536 U.S., at 314–315. On the basis of these indicia the Court determined that executing mentally retarded offenders "has become truly unusual, and it is fair to say that a national consensus has developed against it." *Id.*, at 316. . . .

The *Atkins* Court neither repeated nor relied upon the statement in *Stanford* that the Court's independent judgment has no bearing on the acceptability of a particular punishment under the Eighth Amendment. Instead we returned to the rule, established in decisions predating *Stanford*, that "'the Constitution contemplates that in the end our own judgment will be brought to bear on the question of the acceptability of the death penalty under the Eighth Amendment.'" . . . Based on these considerations and on the finding of national consensus against executing the mentally retarded, the Court ruled that the death penalty constitutes an excessive sanction for the entire category of mentally retarded offenders, and that the Eighth Amendment "'places a substantive restriction on the State's power to take the life' of a mentally retarded offender."

Just as the *Atkins* Court reconsidered the issue decided in *Penry*, we now reconsider the issue decided in *Stanford*. The beginning point is a review of objective indicia of consensus, as expressed in particular by the enactments of legislatures that have addressed the question. This data gives us essential instruction. We then must determine, in the exercise of our own independent judgment, whether the death penalty is a disproportionate punishment for juveniles.

❧

The evidence of national consensus against the death penalty for juveniles is similar, and in some respects parallel, to the evidence *Atkins* held sufficient to demonstrate a national consensus against the death penalty for the mentally retarded. . . .

Though less dramatic than the change from *Penry* to *Atkins* . . . we still consider the change from *Stanford* to this case to be significant. . . . The number of States that have abandoned capital punishment for juvenile offenders since *Stanford* is smaller than the number of States that abandoned capital punishment for the mentally retarded after *Penry*; yet we think the same consistency of direction of change has been demonstrated. Since *Stanford*, no State that previously prohibited capital punishment for juveniles has reinstated it. This fact, coupled with the trend toward abolition of the juvenile death penalty, carries special force in light of the general popularity of anti-crime legislation, and in light of the particular trend in recent years toward cracking down on juvenile crime in other respects. . . .

As in *Atkins*, the objective indicia of consensus in this case—the rejection of the juvenile death penalty in the majority of States; the infrequency of its use even where it remains on the books; and the consistency in the trend toward abolition of the practice—provide sufficient evidence that today our society views juveniles, in the words *Atkins* used respecting the mentally retarded, as "categorically less culpable than the average criminal." 536 U.S., at 316.

❧

A majority of States have rejected the imposition of the death penalty on juvenile offenders under 18, and we now hold this is required by the Eighth Amendment.

Because the death penalty is the most severe punishment, the Eighth Amendment applies to it with special force. Capital punishment must be limited to those offenders who commit "a narrow category of the most serious crimes" and whose extreme culpability makes them "the most deserving of execution." . . .

Three general differences between juveniles under 18 and adults demonstrate that juvenile offenders cannot with reliability be classified among the worst offenders. First, . . .

The second area of difference . . .

The third broad difference . . .

These differences render suspect any conclusion that a juvenile falls among the worst offenders. The susceptibility of juveniles to immature and irresponsible behavior means "their irresponsible conduct is not as morally reprehensible as that of an adult." *Thompson, supra,* at 835 (plurality opinion). Their own vulnerability and comparative lack of control over their immediate surroundings mean juveniles have a greater claim than adults to be forgiven for failing to escape negative influences in their whole environment. See *Stanford,* 492 U.S., at 395 (Brennan, J., dissenting). The reality that juveniles still struggle to define their identity means it is less supportable to conclude that even a heinous crime committed by a juvenile is evidence of irretrievably depraved character. From a moral standpoint it would be misguided to equate the failings of a minor with those of an adult, for a greater possibility exists that a minor's character deficiencies will be reformed. Indeed, "[t]he relevance of youth as a mitigating factor derives from the fact that the signature qualities of youth are transient; as individuals mature, the impetuousness and recklessness that may dominate in younger years can subside." *Johnson, supra,* at 368; see also Steinberg & Scott 1014 ("For most teens, [risky or antisocial] behaviors are fleeting; they cease with maturity as individual identity becomes settled. Only a relatively small proportion of adolescents who experiment in risky or illegal activities develop entrenched patterns of problem behavior that persist into adulthood"). . . .

Once the diminished culpability of juveniles is recognized, it is evident that the penological justifications for the death penalty apply to them with lesser force than to adults. We have held there are two distinct social purposes served by the death penalty: "'retribution and deterrence of capital crimes by prospective offenders.'" As for retribution, we remarked in *Atkins* that "[i]f the culpability of the average murderer is insufficient to justify the most extreme sanction available to the State, the lesser culpability of the mentally retarded offender surely does not merit that form of retribution." The same conclusions follow from the lesser culpability of the juvenile offender. Whether viewed as an attempt to express the community's moral outrage or as an attempt to right the balance for the wrong to the victim, the case for retribution is not as strong with a minor as with an adult. Retribution is not proportional if the law's most severe penalty is imposed on one whose culpability or blameworthiness is diminished, to a substantial degree, by reason of youth and immaturity.

As for deterrence, it is unclear whether the death penalty has a significant or even measurable deterrent effect on juveniles, as counsel for the petitioner acknowledged at oral argument. . . .

In concluding that neither retribution nor deterrence provides adequate justification for imposing the death penalty on juvenile offenders, we cannot deny or overlook the brutal crimes too many juvenile offenders have committed. . . .

Drawing the line at 18 years of age is subject, of course, to the objections always raised against categorical rules. The qualities that distinguish juveniles from adults do not disappear when an individual turns 18. By the same token, some under 18 have already attained a level of maturity some adults will never reach. For the reasons we have discussed, however, a line must be drawn. The plurality opinion in *Thompson* drew the line at 16. In the intervening years the *Thompson* plurality's conclusion that offenders under 16 may not be executed has not been challenged. The logic of *Thompson* extends to those who are under 18. The age of 18 is the point where society draws the line for many purposes between childhood and adulthood. It is, we conclude, the age at which the line for death eligibility ought to rest. . . .

❧

Our determination that the death penalty is disproportionate punishment for offenders under 18 finds confirmation in the stark reality that the United States is the only country in the world that continues to give official sanction to the juvenile death penalty. This reality does not become controlling, for the task of interpreting the Eighth Amendment remains our responsibility. Yet at least from the time of the Court's decision in *Trop,* the Court has referred to the laws of other countries and to international authorities as instructive for its interpretation of the

Eighth Amendment's prohibition of "cruel and unusual punishments." . . .

As respondent and a number of *amici* emphasize, Article 37 of the United Nations Convention on the Rights of the Child, which every country in the world has ratified save for the United States and Somalia, contains an express prohibition on capital punishment for crimes committed by juveniles under 18. . . .

Respondent and his *amici* have submitted, and petitioner does not contest, that only seven countries other than the United States have executed juvenile offenders since 1990: Iran, Pakistan, Saudi Arabia, Yemen, Nigeria, the Democratic Republic of Congo, and China. Since then each of these countries has either abolished capital punishment for juveniles or made public disavowal of the practice. Brief for Respondent 49–50. In sum, it is fair to say that the United States now stands alone in a world that has turned its face against the juvenile death penalty. . . .

It is proper that we acknowledge the overwhelming weight of international opinion against the juvenile death penalty, resting in large part on the understanding that the instability and emotional imbalance of young people may often be a factor in the crime. See Brief for Human Rights Committee of the Bar of England and Wales et al. as *Amici Curiae* 10–11. The opinion of the world community, while not controlling our outcome, does provide respected and significant confirmation for our own conclusions.

Over time, from one generation to the next, the Constitution has come to earn the high respect and even, as Madison dared to hope, the veneration of the American people. See The Federalist No. 49, p. 314 (C. Rossiter ed. 1961). The document sets forth, and rests upon, innovative principles original to the American experience, such as federalism; a proven balance in political mechanisms through separation of powers; specific guarantees for the accused in criminal cases; and broad provisions to secure individual freedom and preserve human dignity. These doctrines and guarantees are central to the American experience and remain essential to our present-day self-definition and national identity. Not the least of the reasons we honor the Constitution, then, is because we know it to be our own. It does not lessen our fidelity to the Constitution or our pride in its origins to acknowledge that the express affirmation of certain fundamental rights by other nations and peoples simply underscores the centrality of those same rights within our own heritage of freedom.

⇛

The Eighth and Fourteenth Amendments forbid imposition of the death penalty on offenders who were under the age of 18 when their crimes were committed. The judgment of the Missouri Supreme Court setting aside the sentence of death imposed upon Christopher Simmons is affirmed.

It is so ordered.

ANTHONY KENNEDY is an associate justice of the U.S. Supreme Court. He received his LLB from Harvard Law School in 1961 and worked for law firms in San Francisco and Sacramento, California, until he was nominated by President Gerald Ford to the U.S. Court of Appeals for the Ninth Circuit in 1975. He was nominated by President Ronald Reagan to the Supreme Court in 1988.

Antonin Scalia

 **NO**

Minority Opinion, *Donald P. Roper, Superintendent, Potosi Correctional Center, Petitioner v. Christopher Simmons*

JUSTICE SCALIA, with whom THE CHIEF JUSTICE and JUSTICE THOMAS join, dissenting.

In urging approval of a constitution that gave life-tenured judges the power to nullify laws enacted by the people's representatives, Alexander Hamilton assured the citizens of New York that there was little risk in this, since "[t]he judiciary . . . ha[s] neither FORCE nor WILL but merely judgment." The Federalist No. 78, p. 465 (C. Rossiter ed. 1961). But Hamilton had in mind a traditional judiciary, "bound down by strict rules and precedents which serve to define and point out their duty in every particular case that comes before them." *Id.,* at 471. Bound down, indeed. What a mockery today's opinion makes of Hamilton's expectation, announcing the Court's conclusion that the meaning of our Constitution has changed over the past 15 years—not, mind you, that this Court's decision 15 years ago was *wrong,* but that the Constitution *has changed.* The Court reaches this implausible result by purporting to advert, not to the original meaning of the Eighth Amendment, but to "the evolving standards of decency," *ante,* at 6 (internal quotation marks omitted), of our national society. It then finds, on the flimsiest of grounds, that a national consensus which could not be perceived in our people's laws barely 15 years ago now solidly exists. Worse still, the Court says in so many words that what our people's laws say about the issue does not, in the last analysis, matter: "[I]n the end our own judgment will be brought to bear on the question of the acceptability of the death penalty under the Eighth Amendment." *Ante,* at 9 (internal quotation marks omitted). The Court thus proclaims itself sole arbiter of our Nation's moral standards—and in the course of discharging that awesome responsibility purports to take guidance from the views of foreign courts and legislatures. Because I do not believe that the meaning of our Eighth Amendment, any more than the meaning of other provisions of our Constitution, should be determined by the subjective views of five Members of this Court and like-minded foreigners, I dissent. . . .

❧

We have held that this determination should be based on "objective indicia that reflect the public attitude toward a given sanction"—namely, "statutes passed by society's elected representatives." As in *Atkins v. Virginia,* 536 U.S. 304, 312 (2002), the Court dutifully recites this test and claims half-heartedly that a national consensus has emerged since our decision in *Stanford,* because 18 States—or 47% of States that permit capital punishment—now have legislation prohibiting the execution of offenders under 18, and because all of four States have adopted such legislation since *Stanford.*

Words have no meaning if the views of less than 50% of death penalty States can constitute a national consensus. Our previous cases have required overwhelming opposition to a challenged practice, generally over a long period of time. . . .

In an attempt to keep afloat its implausible assertion of national consensus, the Court throws overboard a proposition well established in our Eighth Amendment jurisprudence. "It should be observed," the Court says, "that the *Stanford* Court should have considered those States that had abandoned the death penalty altogether as part of the consensus against the juvenile death penalty . . . ; a State's decision to bar the death penalty altogether of necessity demonstrates a judgment that the death penalty is inappropriate for all offenders, including juveniles." The insinuation that the Court's new method of counting contradicts only "the *Stanford* Court" is misleading. *None* of our cases dealing with an alleged constitutional limitation upon the death penalty has counted, as States supporting a consensus in favor

From Supreme Court of the United States, March 1, 2005.

of that limitation, States that have eliminated the death penalty entirely. And with good reason. Consulting States that bar the death penalty concerning the necessity of making an exception to the penalty for offenders under 18 is rather like including old-order Amishmen in a consumer-preference poll on the electric car. Of *course* they don't like it, but that sheds no light whatever on the point at issue. That 12 States favor no executions says something about consensus against the death penalty, but nothing—absolutely nothing—about consensus that offenders under 18 deserve special immunity from such a penalty. In repealing the death penalty, those 12 States considered *none* of the factors that the Court puts forth as determinative of the issue before us today—lower culpability of the young, inherent recklessness, lack of capacity for considered judgment, etc. What might be relevant, perhaps, is how many of those States permit 16- and 17-year-old offenders to be treated as adults with respect to non-capital offenses. (They all do;[1] indeed, some even *require* that juveniles as young as 14 be tried as adults if they are charged with murder.[2]) The attempt by the Court to turn its remarkable minority consensus into a faux majority by counting Amishmen is an act of nomological desperation. . . .

The Court's reliance on the infrequency of executions, for under-18 murderers, *ante,* at 10–11, 13, credits an argument that this Court considered and explicitly rejected in *Stanford.* That infrequency is explained, we accurately said, both by "the undisputed fact that a far smaller percentage of capital crimes are committed by persons under 18 than over 18," 492 U.S., at 374, and by the fact that juries are required at sentencing to consider the offender's youth as a mitigating factor. Thus, "it is not only possible, but overwhelmingly probable, that the very considerations which induce [respondent] and [his] supporters to believe that death should *never* be imposed on offenders under 18 cause prosecutors and juries to believe that it should *rarely* be imposed." *Stanford, supra,* at 374. . . .

❧❦❧

Of course, the real force driving today's decision is not the actions of four state legislatures, but the Court's "' "own judgment" ' " that murderers younger than 18 can never be as morally culpable as older counterparts. The Court claims that this usurpation of the role of moral arbiter is simply a "retur[n] to the rul[e] established in decisions predating *Stanford.*" That supposed rule—which is reflected solely in dicta and never once in a *holding* that purports to

supplant the consensus of the American people with the Justices' views[3]—was repudiated in *Stanford* for the very good reason that it has no foundation in law or logic. If the Eighth Amendment set forth an ordinary rule of law, it would indeed be the role of this Court to say what the law is. But the Court having pronounced that the Eighth Amendment is an ever-changing reflection of "the evolving standards of decency" of our society, it makes no sense for the Justices then to *prescribe* those standards rather than discern them from the practices of our people. On the evolving-standards hypothesis, the only legitimate function of this Court is to identify a moral consensus of the American people. By what conceivable warrant can nine lawyers presume to be the authoritative conscience of the Nation?[4]

The reason for insistence on legislative primacy is obvious and fundamental: "'[I]n a democratic society legislatures, not courts, are constituted to respond to the will and consequently the moral values of the people.'" *Gregg v. Georgia,* 428 U.S. 153, 175–176 (1976) (joint opinion of Stewart, Powell, and STEVENS, JJ.) (quoting *Furman v. Georgia,* 408 U.S. 238, 383 (1972) (Burger, C. J., dissenting)). For a similar reason we have, in our determination of society's moral standards, consulted the practices of sentencing juries: Juries "'maintain a link between contemporary community values and the penal system'" that this Court cannot claim for itself. *Gregg, supra,* at 181 (quoting *Witherspoon v. Illinois,* 391 U.S. 510, 519, n. 15 (1968)).

Today's opinion provides a perfect example of why judges are ill equipped to make the type of legislative judgments the Court insists on making here. To support its opinion that States should be prohibited from imposing the death penalty on anyone who committed murder before age 18, the Court looks to scientific and sociological studies, picking and choosing those that support its position. It never explains why those particular studies are methodologically sound; none was ever entered into evidence or tested in an adversarial proceeding. . . .

In other words, all the Court has done today, to borrow from another context, is to look over the heads of the crowd and pick out its friends. . . .

That "almost every State prohibits those under 18 years of age from voting, serving on juries, or marrying without parental consent," *ante,* at 15, is patently irrelevant—and is yet another resurrection of an argument that this Court gave a decent burial in *Stanford.* . . . As we explained in *Stanford,* it is "absurd to think that one must be mature enough to drive carefully, to drink responsibly, or to vote intelligently, in order to be mature enough to understand that murdering another human being is profoundly wrong, and to conform one's conduct to that

Does the Cruel and Unusual Punishment Clause of the 8th Amendment Bar the Imposition of the Death Penalty on Juveniles? by Katsh

205

most minimal of all civilized standards." Serving on a jury or entering into marriage also involve decisions far more sophisticated than the simple decision not to take another's life. . . .

The Court's contention that the goals of retribution and deterrence are not served by executing murderers under 18 is also transparently false. The argument that "[r]etribution is not proportional if the law's most severe penalty is imposed on one whose culpability or blameworthiness is diminished," is simply an extension of the earlier, false generalization that youth *always* defeats culpability. The Court claims that "juveniles will be less susceptible to deterrence," *ante,* at 18, because "'[t]he likelihood that the teenage offender has made the kind of cost-benefit analysis that attaches any weight to the possibility of execution is so remote as to be virtually nonexistent.'" The Court unsurprisingly finds no support for this astounding proposition, save its own case law. The facts of this very case show the proposition to be false. Before committing the crime, Simmons encouraged his friends to join him by assuring them that they could "get away with it" because they were minors. This fact may have influenced the jury's decision to impose capital punishment despite Simmons' age. Because the Court refuses to entertain the possibility that its own unsubstantiated generalization about juveniles could be wrong, it ignores this evidence entirely.

❧

Though the views of our own citizens are essentially irrelevant to the Court's decision today, the views of other countries and the so-called international community take center stage.

The Court begins by noting that "Article 37 of the United Nations Convention on the Rights of the Child, entered into force Sept. 2, 1990, which every country in the world has ratified save *for the United States* and Somalia, contains an express prohibition on capital punishment for crimes committed by juveniles under 18.". . .

Unless the Court has added to its arsenal the power to join and ratify treaties on behalf of the United States, I cannot see how this evidence favors, rather than refutes, its position. That the Senate and the President—those actors our Constitution empowers to enter into treaties, see Art. II, §2—have declined to join and ratify treaties prohibiting execution of under-18 offenders can only suggest that *our country* has either not reached a national consensus on the question, or has reached a consensus contrary to what the Court announces. . . .

More fundamentally, however, the basic premise of the Court's argument—that American law should conform to the laws of the rest of the world—ought to be rejected out of hand. In fact the Court itself does not believe it. In many significant respects the laws of most other countries differ from our law—including not only such explicit provisions of our Constitution as the right to jury trial and grand jury indictment, but even many interpretations of the Constitution prescribed by this Court itself. The Court-pronounced exclusionary rule, for example, is distinctively American. . . .

The Court has been oblivious to the views of other countries when deciding how to interpret our Constitution's requirement that "Congress shall make no law respecting an establishment of religion. . . ."

And let us not forget the Court's abortion jurisprudence, which makes us one of only six countries that allow abortion on demand until the point of viability. . . .

The Court should either profess its willingness to reconsider all these matters in light of the views of foreigners, or else it should cease putting forth foreigners' views as part of the *reasoned basis* of its decisions. To invoke alien law when it agrees with one's own thinking, and ignore it otherwise, is not reasoned decisionmaking, but sophistry.[5]

❧

To add insult to injury, the Court affirms the Missouri Supreme Court without even admonishing that court for its flagrant disregard of our precedent in *Stanford*. Until today, we have always held that "it is this Court's prerogative alone to overrule one of its precedents." . . . Today, however, the Court silently approves a state-court decision that blatantly rejected controlling precedent.

One must admit that the Missouri Supreme Court's action, and this Court's indulgent reaction, are, in a way, understandable. In a system based upon constitutional and statutory text democratically adopted, the concept of "law" ordinarily signifies that particular words have a fixed meaning. Such law does not change, and this Court's pronouncement of it therefore remains authoritative until (confessing our prior error) we overrule. The Court has purported to make of the Eighth Amendment, however, a mirror of the passing and changing sentiment of American society regarding penology. The lower courts can look into that mirror as well as we can; and what we saw 15 years ago bears no necessary relationship to what they see today. Since they are not looking at the same text, but at a different scene, why should our earlier decision control their judgment?

However sound philosophically, this is no way to run a legal system. We must disregard the new reality that, to the extent our Eighth Amendment decisions constitute something more than a show of hands on the current Justices' current personal views about penology, they purport to be nothing more than a snapshot of American public opinion at a particular point in time (with the timeframes now shortened to a mere 15 years). We must treat these decisions just as though they represented *real* law, *real* prescriptions democratically adopted by the American people, as conclusively (rather than sequentially) construed by this Court. Allowing lower courts to reinterpret the Eighth Amendment whenever they decide enough time has passed for a new snapshot leaves this Court's decisions without any force—especially since the "evolution" of our Eighth Amendment is no longer determined by objective criteria. To allow lower courts to behave as we do, "updating" the Eighth Amendment as needed, destroys stability and makes our case law an unreliable basis for the designing of laws by citizens and their representatives, and for action by public officials. The result will be to crown arbitrariness with chaos.

Notes

1. See Alaska Stat. §47.12.030 (Lexis 2002); Haw. Rev. Stat. §571-22 (1999); Iowa Code §232.45 (2003); Me. Rev. Stat. Ann., Tit. 15, §3101(4) (West 2003); Mass. Gen. Laws Ann., ch. 119, §74 (West 2003); Mich. Comp. Laws Ann. §764.27 (West 2000); Minn. Stat. §260B.125 (2002); N. D. Cent. Code §27-20-34 (Lexis Supp. 2003); R. I. Gen. Laws §14-1-7 (Lexis 2002); Vt. Stat. Ann., Tit. 33, §5516 (Lexis 2001); W. Va. Code §49-5-10 (Lexis 2004); Wis. Stat. §938.18 (2003–2004); see also National Center for Juvenile Justice, Trying and Sentencing Juveniles as Adults: An Analysis of State Transfer and Blended Sentencing Laws 1 (Oct. 2003). The District of Columbia is the only jurisdiction without a death penalty that specifically exempts under-18 offenders from its harshest sanction—life imprisonment without parole. See D. C. Code §22-2104 (West 2001).

2. See Mass. Gen. Laws Ann., ch. 119, §74 (West 2003); N. D. Cent. Code §27-20-34 (Lexis Supp. 2003); W. Va. Code §49-5-10 (Lexis 2004).

3. See, e.g., *Enmund v. Florida,* 458 U.S. 782, 801 (1982) ("[W]e have no reason to disagree with th[e] judgment [of the state legislatures] for purposes of construing and applying the Eighth Amendment"); *Coker v. Georgia,* 433 U.S. 584, 597 (1977) (plurality opinion) ("[T]he legislative rejection of capital punishment for rape strongly confirms our own judgment").

4. JUSTICE O'CONNOR agrees with our analysis that no national consensus exists here, *ante,* at 8–12 (dissenting opinion). She is nonetheless prepared (like the majority) to override the judgment of America's legislatures if it contradicts her own assessment of "moral proportionality," *ante,* at 12. She dissents here only because it does not. The votes in today's case demonstrate that the offending of selected lawyers' moral sentiments is not a predictable basis for law—much less a democratic one.

5. JUSTICE O'CONNOR asserts that the Eighth Amendment has a "special character," in that it "draws its meaning directly from the maturing values of civilized society." *Ante,* at 19. Nothing in the text reflects such a distinctive character—and we have certainly applied the "maturing values" rationale to give brave new meaning to other provisions of the Constitution, such as the Due Process Clause and the Equal Protection Clause. See, *e.g., Lawrence v. Texas,* 539 U.S. 558, 571–573 (2003); *United States v. Virginia,* 518 U.S. 515, 532–534 (1996); *Planned Parenthood of Southeastern Pa. v. Casey,* 505 U.S. 833, 847–850 (1992). Justice O'Connor asserts that an international consensus can at least "serve to confirm the reasonableness of a consonant and genuine American consensus." Ante, at 19. Surely not unless it can also demonstrate the unreasonableness of such a consensus. Either America's principles are its own, or they follow the world; one cannot have it both ways. Finally, Justice O'Connor finds it unnecessary to consult foreign law in the present case because there is "no . . . domestic consensus" to be confirmed. *Ibid.* But since she believes that the Justices can announce their own requirements of "moral proportionality" despite the absence of consensus, why would foreign law not be relevant to *that* judgment? If foreign law is powerful enough to supplant the judgment of the American people, surely it is powerful enough to change a personal assessment of moral proportionality.

ANTONIN SCALIA is an associate justice of the U.S. Supreme Court. He taught law at the University of Virginia, the American Enterprise Institute, Georgetown University, and the University of Chicago before being nominated to the U.S. Court of Appeals by President Ronald Reagan in 1982. He served in that capacity until he was nominated by Reagan to the Supreme Court in 1986.

Does the Cruel and Unusual Punishment Clause of the 8th Amendment Bar the Imposition of the Death Penalty on Juveniles? by Katsh

207

EXPLORING THE ISSUE

Does the "Cruel and Unusual Punishment" Clause of the Eighth Amendment Bar the Imposition of the Death Penalty on Juveniles?

Critical Thinking and Reflection

1. Is the Constitution best applied based on the intended meaning of the original drafters or based on our present-day conceptions of its meaning?
2. Do you agree with Justice Scalia that the Court's legitimacy is at risk if it is willing to evolve its opinions based on outside factors?
3. Should U.S. courts look to the laws of other nations for guidance in its rulings?
4. Do you believe that the standards of an entire society, such as that of the United States, can change within 15 years?
5. If our legislatures fail to reflect our changing standards as a society, should judges be allowed to?

Is There Common Ground?

Finding common ground in the majority and dissenting opinions of *Simmons* is a particularly difficult task given the fundamental philosophical differences in constitutional interpretation that form the bases for each opinion. Whether the Constitution is a living document to be interpreted as the United States evolves or whether we should look directly to the wisdom of the Founding Fathers to rule on our most pressing issues is a debate that will continue to fill the halls of Congress, law school classrooms, and the Supreme Court chamber. The choice may seem a simple one to some, and in viewing the easiest of cases, it can appear to be so. However, a living document proponent cannot dismiss the intellect and forethought of the Founding Fathers any more than an originalist can deem them sufficiently clairvoyant to have anticipated the constitutional implications of Facebook.

At the end of the day, it is the decision of the majority of nine individuals that determines the law of the land in cases dealing with fundamental rights. Justice Scalia chastises the majority's opinion for substituting its "own judgment" for the application of precedent and the law. However, is it possible that any person is so acutely capable as to be able to completely separate his or her personal beliefs from the facts before them so as to be only judge?

Additional Resources

Stuart Banner, *The Death Penalty: An American History* (Harvard, 2003).

Hugo Adam Bedau, *Debating the Death Penalty* (Oxford, 2003) and *The Death Penalty in America* (Oxford, 1998).

Timothy Kaufman-Osborn, *From Noose to Needle: Capital Punishment and the Late Liberal State* (Michigan, 2002).

Austin Sarat, *When the State Kills: Capital Punishment and the American Condition* (Princeton, 2002).

James Q. Whitman, *Harsh Justice: Capital Punishment and the Widening Divide Between America and Europe* (Oxford, 2003).

Internet References . . .

Abstract and Recording of Oral Arguments of *Roper v. Simmons*

www.oyez.org/cases/2000-2009/2004/2004_03_633/

Abstract and Recording of Oral Arguments of *Stanford v. Kentucky*

www.oyez.org/cases/1980-1989/1988/1988_87_5765

Abstract and Recording of Oral Arguments of *Atkins v. Virginia*

www.oyez.org/cases/2000-2009/2001/2001_00_8452/

The Guardian

This article provides recent statistics and infographics on the death penalty around the world.

www.guardian.co.uk/news/datablog/2011/mar/29/death-penalty-countries-world

The United Nations Resolution

This link provides a description of the U.N. resolution calling for a moratorium on countries' use of the death penalty.

www.un.org/sg/statements/index.asp?nid=6448

Death Penalty Information Center

The Death Penalty Information Center provides useful background information on capital punishment in the United States.

www.deathpenaltyinfo.org

Bureau of Justice Statistics

This website details prison population data.

www.bjs.gov/index.cfm?ty=tp&tid=131

Bloomberg

This article, "U.S. Jails More People Than Any Other Country: Chart of the Day," details U.S. incarceration statistics.

www.bloomberg.com/news/2012-10-15/u-s-jails-more-people-than-any-other-country-chart-of-the-day.html

Does Sex in Title IX Allow Transgender Students to Use Restrooms Aligned with Their Gender Identity, Not Their Biological Sex? by Katsh

209

Selected, Edited, and with Issue Framing Material by:
M. Ethan Katsh, *University of Massachusetts, Amherst*

ISSUE

Does the Definition of "Sex" in Title IX Include Gender Identity and Allow Transgender Students to Use the Restrooms That Align with Their Gender Identities and Not Their Biological Sex?

YES: Henry Franklin Floyd, from "Majority Opinion, *G.G. v. Gloucester County School Board*," *U.S. Court of Appeals for the Fourth Circuit* (2016)

NO: Counsel for Amici Curiae, from "Amicus Brief of Christian Educators Association International, *Gloucester County School Board v. G.G.*," *U.S. Supreme Court* (2017)

Learning Outcomes
After reading this issue, you will be able to: <ul><li>Consider the constitutional protections currently afforded to transgender individuals.</li><li>Understand the difference between biological sex and gender identity and the constitutional protections afforded to each group.</li><li>Analyze when and how the U.S. government may interpret statutes and regulations, and if such interpretations are legally binding or merely suggestions.</li></ul>

ISSUE SUMMARY

YES: Circuit Judge Henry Franklin Floyd held that the term "sex" was ambiguous and that it must include gender identity and not just biological sex.

NO: The Christian Educators Association International argues that the term "sex" is unambiguous, and subject to one interpretation, that of biological sex.

The past half-century has been subject to extreme social and public change. The widespread use of the Internet has expanded communications capabilities and allowed people to gather and rally, both physically and virtually, in historic numbers in efforts to fight for specific interests that will lead to specific social results. On January 21, 2017, for example, an estimated 2.6 million people united worldwide to raise awareness at the 2017 Women's March. Seven hundred fifty thousand people attended in Los Angeles alone.

Social media, and the speed of communicating and organizing online, have also influenced constitutional disputes, rulings, and the interpretation of fundamental human rights and liberties. A recent example is the Supreme Court's 2015 decision in *Obergefell v. Hodges*, where it was held that the definition of "marriage" was no longer a legally binding union between men and women but was interpreted as a legally binding union between two people, regardless of "sex."

Within the United States, issues regarding civil rights and fundamental liberties have been at the center of much legislative and judicial attention. Roughly one year after the Supreme Court decided that the definition of "marriage" was not based on "sex," the Court accepted a case about whether the definition of "sex" includes one's gender identity; a phrase used to describe the difference between one's biological gender and the gender they identify with. In other words, a transmale (born as a biological female) is deemed to have a male gender identity. The question that has raised much social and legal controversy is which bathroom should a transmale be allowed to use in public?

Many states have enacted legislation that permit individuals to use public restrooms aligning with their gender identity. A few of the states banning discrimination in public accommodations based on gender identity are California, Connecticut, Delaware, Massachusetts, Washington, and also Washington, DC. In Virginia, however, that is not the case.

The case that the Supreme Court decided to hear was *G.G. v. Gloucester County School Board*. G.G. was a transmale at Gloucester High School in Gloucester County, Virginia. Gloucester High School initially allowed G.G. to use the boys' room in the high school per G.G.'s request. According to numerous complaints, such action invaded the privacy of teenage male students using the boys' room and resulted in an outpouring of complaints and concerns from students and parents alike. The Gloucester County School Board considered the matter at public board meetings, where the administrators determined, citing firsthand knowledge and information concerning the dynamics, behaviors, and safety of all students and facility at the high school, that it should continue the practice of separate bathroom facilities based on biological sex.

After review by the federal government, specifically the Department of Justice and the Department of Education, the Board received a letter on January 7, 2015, from the Department of Education, stating: "Title IX regulations permit schools to provide sex-segregated restrooms, locker rooms, shower facilities, housing, athletic teams, and single-sex classes under certain circumstances. When a school elects to separate or treat students differently on the basis of sex in those situations, a school generally must treat transgender students consistent with their gender identity." In other words, the Department of Education said that a school receiving federal funding must allow a transmale to use the boy's restroom and other facilities. On May 13, 2016, the Department of Education sent a letter to every Title IX recipient in Gloucester County, repeating the Department's January 7, 2015, letter, including the following requirement that the schools must comply with: a school may no longer require a student to use the bathroom, locker room, or shower of the opposite sex if the student or his/her parent or guardian asserts a "gender identity" different from his/her sex.

In March 2017, shortly before the Court was scheduled to hold oral arguments in the case, it decided to return the case to the Court of Appeals. The Trump Administration had decided that it would not follow the Department of Education regulation that the YES opinion below relies on. We have decided to include both the issue and the readings here because the issue will not go away. Other courts are considering the issue and a court can decide to rule in favor of the plaintiff even without the Department of Education regulation. Undoubtedly, a case involving transgender rights will reach the Supreme Court in the next few years.

Does Sex in Title IX Allow Transgender Students to Use Restrooms Aligned with Their Gender Identity, Not Their Biological Sex?   by Katsh

211

YES ↰

Henry Franklin Floyd

Majority Opinion, *G.G. v. Gloucester County School Board*

G.G., a transgender boy, seeks to use the boys' restrooms at his high school. After G.G. began to use the boys' restrooms with the approval of the school administration, the local school board passed a policy banning G.G. from the boys' restroom.

G.G. alleges that the school board impermissibly discriminated against him in violation of Title IX and the Equal Protection Clause of the Constitution. The district court dismissed G.G.'s Title IX claim and denied his request for a preliminary injunction. This appeal followed. Because we conclude the district court did not accord appropriate deference to the relevant Department of Education regulations, we reverse its dismissal of G.G.'s Title IX claim.

. . .

I.

At the heart of this appeal is whether Title IX requires schools to provide transgender students access to restrooms congruent with their gender identity. Title IX provides: "[n]o person . . . shall, on the basis of sex, be excluded from participation in, be denied the benefits of, or be subjected to discrimination under any education program or activity receiving federal financial assistance" (20 U.S.C. § 1681(a)). The Department of Education's regulations implementing Title IX permit the provision of "separate toilet, locker room, and shower facilities on the basis of sex, but such facilities provided for students of one sex shall be comparable to such facilities for students of the other sex." In an opinion letter dated January 7, 2015, the Department's Office for Civil Rights (OCR) interpreted how this regulation should apply to transgender individuals: "When a school elects to separate or treat students differently on the basis of sex . . . a school generally must treat transgender students consistent with their gender identity."

. . .

A.

G.G. is a transgender boy now in his junior year at Gloucester High School. G.G.'s birth-assigned sex, or the so-called "biological sex," is female, but G.G.'s gender identity is male. G.G. has been diagnosed with gender dysphoria, a medical condition characterized by clinically significant distress caused by an incongruence between a person's gender identity and the person's birth-assigned sex. Since the end of his freshman year, G.G. has undergone hormone therapy and has legally changed his name to G., a traditionally male name. G.G. lives all aspects of his life as a boy. G.G. has not, however, had sex reassignment surgery.[1]

Before beginning his sophomore year, G.G. and his mother told school officials that G.G. was a transgender boy. The officials were supportive and took steps to ensure that he would be treated as a boy by teachers and staff. Later, at G.G.'s request, school officials allowed G.G. to use the boys' restroom.[2] G.G. used this restroom without incident for about seven weeks. G.G.'s use of the boys' restroom, however, excited the interest of others in the community, some of whom contacted the Gloucester County School Board (the Board) seeking to bar G.G. from continuing to use the boys' restroom.

Board Member Carla B. Hook added an item to the agenda for the November 11, 2014, board meeting titled "Discussion of Use of Restrooms/Locker Room Facilities." J.A.15. Hook proposed the following resolution (hereinafter the "transgender restroom policy" or "the policy"):

> Whereas the GCPS (i.e., Gloucester County Public Schools) recognizes that some students question their gender identities, and
>
> Whereas the GCPS encourages such students to seek support, advice, and guidance from parents, professionals, and other trusted adults, and

Majority Opinion, G.G. v. Gloucester County School Board, U.S. Court of Appeals, 4th Cir., April 19, 2016.

Whereas the GCPS seeks to provide a safe learning environment for all students and to protect the privacy of all students, therefore

It shall be the practice of the GCPS to provide male and female restroom and locker room facilities in its schools, and the use of said facilities shall be limited to the corresponding biological genders, and students with gender identity issues shall be provided an alternative appropriate private facility.

At the November 11, 2014, meeting, 27 people spoke during the Citizens' Comment Period, a majority of whom supported Hook's proposed resolution. Many of the speakers displayed hostility to G.G., including by referring pointedly to him as a "young lady." Others claimed that permitting G.G. to use the boys' restroom would violate the privacy of other students and would lead to sexual assault in restrooms. One commenter suggested that if the proposed policy was not adopted, nontransgender boys would come to school wearing dresses in order to gain access to the girls' restrooms. G.G. and his parents spoke against the proposed policy. Ultimately, the Board postponed a vote on the policy until its next meeting on December 9, 2014.

At the December 9 meeting, approximately 37 people spoke during the Citizens' Comment Period. Again, most of those who spoke were in favor of the proposed resolution. Some speakers threatened to vote the Board members out of office if the Board members voted against the proposed policy. Speakers again referred to G.G. as a "girl" or "young lady." One speaker called G.G. a "freak" and compared him to a person who thinks he is a "dog" and wants to urinate on fire hydrants. Following this second comment period, the Board voted 6-1 to adopt the proposed policy, thereby barring G.G. from using the boys' restroom at school.

G.G. alleges that he cannot use the girls' restroom because women and girls in those facilities "react[] negatively because they perceive[] G.G. to be a boy." Further, using the girls' restroom would "cause severe psychological distress" to G.G. and would be incompatible with his treatment for gender dysphoria. As a corollary to the policy, the Board announced a series of updates to the school's restrooms to improve general privacy for all students, including adding or expanding partitions between urinals in male restrooms, adding privacy strips to the doors of stalls in all restrooms, and constructing single-stall unisex restrooms available to all students. G.G. alleges that he cannot use these new unisex restro because they "make him feel even more stigmatized . . . . Being required to use the separate restrooms sets him apart from his peers,

and serves as a daily reminder that the school views him as 'different.'" G.G. further alleges that, because of this stigma and exclusion, his social transition is undermined and he experiences "severe and persistent emotional and social harms." G.G. avoids using the restroom while at school and has, as a result of this avoidance, developed multiple urinary tract infections.

B.

G.G. sued the Board on June 11, 2015. G.G. seeks an injunction allowing him to use the boys' restroom and brings underlying claims that the Board impermissibly discriminated against him in violation of Title IX of the Education Amendments Act of 1972 and the Equal Protection Clause of the Constitution.

On July 27, 2015, the district court held a hearing on G.G.'s motion for a preliminary injunction and on the Board's motion to dismiss G.G.'s lawsuit. . . .

In its September 17, 2015, order, the district court reasoned that Title IX prohibits discrimination on the basis of sex and not on the basis of other concepts such as gender, gender identity, or sexual orientation. The district court observed that the regulations implementing Title IX specifically allow schools to provide separate restrooms on the basis of sex. The district court concluded that G.G.'s sex was female and that requiring him to use the female restroom facilities did not impermissibly discriminate against him on the basis of sex in violation of Title IX. With respect to G.G.'s request for an injunction, the district court found that G.G. had not made the required showing that the balance of equities was in his favor. The district court found that requiring G.G. to use the unisex restrooms during the pendency of this lawsuit was not unduly burdensome and would result in less hardship than requiring other students made uncomfortable by G.G.'s presence in the boys' restroom to themselves use the unisex restrooms.

This appeal followed. . . .

II.

We turn first to the district court's dismissal of G.G.'s Title IX claim. We review de novo the district court's grant of a motion to dismiss. "To survive a motion to dismiss, a complaint must contain sufficient factual matter, accepted as true, to state a claim to relief that is plausible on its face."

As noted earlier, Title IX provides: "[n]o person . . . shall, on the basis of sex, be excluded from participation in, be denied the benefits of, or be subjected to discrimination under any education program or activity receiving federal financial assistance" (20 U.S.C. § 1681(a)). To allege a violation of Title IX, G.G. must allege (1) that he was excluded from participation in an education program because of his sex, (2) that the educational institution was receiving federal financial assistance at the time of his exclusion, and (3) that the improper discrimination caused G.G. harm.[3] . . . We look to case law interpreting Title VII of the Civil Rights Act of 1964 for guidance in evaluating a claim brought under Title IX.

Not all distinctions on the basis of sex are impermissible under Title IX. For example, Title IX permits the provision of separate living facilities on the basis of sex: "nothing contained [in Title IX] shall be construed to prohibit any educational institution receiving funds under this Act, from maintaining separate living facilities for the different sexes." The Department's regulations implementing Title IX permit the provision of "separate toilet, locker room, and shower facilities on the basis of sex, but such facilities provided for students of one sex shall be comparable to such facilities provided for students of the other sex." The Department recently delineated how this regulation should be applied to transgender individuals. In an opinion letter dated January 7, 2015, the Department's OCR wrote: "When a school elects to separate or treat students differently on the basis of sex . . . a school generally must treat transgender students consistent with their gender identity."

A.

G.G., and the United States as amicus curiae, ask us to give the Department's interpretation of its own regulation controlling weight pursuant to Auer v. Robbins (519 U.S. 452, 1997). Auer requires that an agency's interpretation of its own ambiguous regulation be given controlling weight unless the interpretation is plainly erroneous or inconsistent with the regulation or statute. Agency interpretations need not be well-settled or long-standing to be entitled to deference. They must, however, "reflect the agency's fair and considered judgment on the matter in question."

. . .

The district court declined to afford deference to the Department's interpretation of 34 C.F.R. § 106.33. The district court found the regulation to be unambiguous because "[i]t clearly allows the School Board to limit bathroom access 'on the basis of sex,' including birth or biological sex." The district court also found, alternatively, that the interpretation advanced by the

Department was clearly erroneous and inconsistent with the regulation. The district court reasoned that, because "on the basis of sex" means, at most, on the basis of sex and gender together, it cannot mean on the basis of gender alone.

The United States contends that the regulation clarifies statutory ambiguity by making clear that schools may provide separate restrooms for boys and girls "without running afoul of Title IX." However, the Department also considers § 106.33 itself to be ambiguous as to transgender students because "the regulation is silent on what the phrases 'students of one sex' and 'students of the other sex' mean in the context of transgender students."

. . .

Our analysis begins with a determination of whether 34 C.F.R. § 106.33 contains an ambiguity.

. . .

Although the regulation may refer unambiguously to males and females, it is silent as to how a school should determine whether a transgender individual is a male or female for the purpose of access to sex-segregated restrooms. We conclude that the regulation is susceptible to more than one plausible reading because it permits both the Board's reading—determining maleness or femaleness with reference exclusively to genitalia—and the Department's interpretation—determining maleness or femaleness with reference to gender identity. . . . It is not clear to us how the regulation would apply in a number of situations—even under the Board's own "biological gender" formulation. For example, which restroom would a transgender individual who had undergone sex-reassignment surgery use? What about an intersex individual? What about an individual born with X–X–Y sex chromosomes? What about an individual who lost external genitalia in an accident? The Department's interpretation resolves ambiguity by providing that in the case of a transgender individual using a sex-segregated facility, the individual's sex as male or female is to be generally determined by reference to the student's gender identity.

C.

Because we conclude that the regulation is ambiguous as applied to transgender individuals, the Department's interpretation is entitled to Auer deference unless the Board demonstrates that the interpretation is plainly erroneous or inconsistent with the regulation or statute. . . .

Title IX regulations were promulgated by the Department of Health, Education, and Welfare in 1975 and were adopted unchanged by the Department in 1980 (45 Fed. Reg. 30802, 30955, May 9, 1980). Two dictionaries from the drafting era inform our analysis of how the term "sex" was understood at that time. The first defines "sex" as "the character of being either male or female" or "the sum of those anatomical and physiological differences with reference to which the male and female are distinguished . . . ." American College Dictionary 1109 (1970). The second defines "sex" as:

> the sum of the morphological, physiological, and behavioral peculiarities of living beings that subserves biparental reproduction with its concomitant genetic segregation and recombination which underlie most evolutionary change, that in its typical dichotomous occurrence is usu[ally] genetically controlled and associated with special sex chromosomes, and that is typically manifested as maleness and femaleness . . . . (Webster's Third New International Dictionary 2081, 1971)

Although these definitions suggest that the word "sex" was understood at the time, the regulation was adopted to connote male and female and that maleness and femaleness were determined primarily by reference to the factors the district court termed "biological sex," namely, reproductive organs, the definitions also suggest that a hard-and-fast binary division on the basis of reproductive organs—although useful in most cases—was not universally descriptive. The dictionaries, therefore, used qualifiers such as reference to the "sum of" various factors, "typical dichotomous occurrence," and "typically manifested as maleness and femaleness." Section 106.33 assumes a student population composed of individuals of what has traditionally been understood as the usual "dichotomous occurrence" of male and female where the various indicators of sex all point in the same direction. It sheds little light on how exactly to determine the "character of being either male or female" where those indicators diverge. . . . The regulation is silent as to which restroom transgender individuals are to use when a school elects to provide sex-segregated restrooms, and the Department's interpretation, although perhaps not the intuitive one, is permitted by the varying physical, psychological, and social aspects—or, in the words of an older dictionary, "the morphological, physiological, and behavioral peculiarities"—included in the term "sex."

D.

Finally, we consider whether the Department's interpretation of § 106.33 is the result of the agency's fair and considered judgment. . . .

Finally, this interpretation cannot properly be considered a post hoc rationalization because it is in line with the existing guidances and regulations of a number of federal agencies—all of which provide that transgender individuals should be permitted access to the restroom that corresponds with their gender identities (U.S. Br. 17 n.5 & n.6; citing publications by the Occupational Safety and Health Administration, the Equal Employment Opportunity Commission, the Department of Housing and Urban Development, and the Office of Personnel Management).

. . .

E.

We conclude that the Department's interpretation of its own regulation, § 106.33, as it relates to restroom access by transgender individuals, is to be accorded controlling weight in this case. We reverse the district court's contrary conclusion and its resultant dismissal of G.G.'s Title IX claim.

. . .

V.

For the foregoing reasons, the judgment of the district court is reversed in part, vacated in part, and remanded.

Notes

1. The World Professional Association for Transgender Health (WPATH) has established Standards of Care for individuals with gender dysphoria. These Standards of Care are accepted as authoritative by organizations such as the American Medical Association and the American Psychological Association. The WPATH Standards of Care do not permit sex reassignment surgery for persons who are under the legal age of majority.
2. G.G. does not participate in the school's physical education programs. He does not seek here,

Does Sex in Title IX Allow Transgender Students to Use Restrooms Aligned with Their Gender Identity, Not Their Biological Sex? by Katsh

215

and never has sought, use of the boys' locker room. Only restroom use is at issue in this case.

3. The Board suggests that a restroom may not be educational in nature and thus is not an educational program covered by Title IX. Appellee's Br. 35 (quoting Johnston v. Univ. of Pittsburgh, 97 F. Supp. 3d 657, 682 (W.D. Pa. 2015)). The Department's regulation pertaining to "Education programs or activities" provides:

Except as provided in this subpart, in providing any aid, benefit, or service to a student, a recipient shall not, on the basis of sex:

(1) Treat one person differently from another in determining whether such person satisfies any requirement or condition for the provision of such aid, benefit, or service;

(2) Provide different aid, benefits, or services or provide aid, benefits, or services in a different manner;

(3) Deny any person any such aid, benefit, or service;

. . .

(7) Otherwise limit any person in the enjoyment of any right, privilege, advantage, or opportunity.

34 C.F.R. § 106.31(b). We have little difficulty concluding that access to a restroom at a school, under this regulation, can be considered either an "aid, benefit, or service" or a "right, privilege, advantage, or opportunity," which, when offered by a recipient institution, falls within the meaning of "educational program" as used in Title IX and defined by the Department's implementing regulations.

HENRY FRANKLIN FLOYD is a judge of the United States Fourth Circuit Court of Appeals. He had been nominated by President George W. Bush to a seat on the United States District Court in 2003. On January 26, 2011, President Barack Obama nominated Floyd to serve on the United States Court of Appeals for the Fourth Circuit. He was confirmed by a 96-0 vote. In 2005, Judge Floyd had presided over the case of José Padilla, a U.S. citizen detained as an enemy combatant. Judge Floyd ruled that President Bush did not have the authority to hold Padilla as an enemy combatant.

Counsel for Amici Curiae

 **NO**

Amicus Brief of Christian Educators Association International, *Gloucester County School Board v. G.G.*

Brief of Christian Educators Association International and Dr. Douglas R. Jackson, the President of Both the Great Lakes Educators' Convention and the Michigan Association of Christian Schools as *Amici Curiae* in Support of Petitioner

Statement of Identity and Interests of *Amici Curiae*

Pursuant to Supreme Court Rule 37, *Amici Curiae*, the Christian Educators Association International and Dr. Douglas R. Jackson, the President of both the Great Lakes Educators' Convention and the Michigan Association of Christian Schools, respectfully submit this brief. *Amici Curiae* urge the court to protect the rights and privacy of students, school faculty, parents, and Christians nationwide and to uphold the concept of subsidiarity, as required by the U.S. Constitution, Federal law, and State law.

The Christian Educators Association International has a significant interest in the protection of the constitutional rights, privacy rights, and religious freedom of students, teachers, school faculty, and parents nationwide. The Christian Educators Association International is an international organization that encourages, equips, and empowers educators to be faithful to their Christian beliefs in all aspects of their lives, including their professions. The Christian Educators Association International promotes educational excellence committed to Biblical principles and the values of the Judeo-Christian heritage. It also promotes the protection of all Christians' legal rights in the public schools. The Christian Educators Association International is the only professional association that specifically serves Christians within the public schools. The organization has 18 formal chapters throughout the United States.

. . .

Background

In 1979, the U.S. Congress enacted and President Carter signed the Department of Education Organization Act, establishing the Department of Education (20 U.S.C. § 3401, *et seq*). Seven years earlier in 1972, the Congress passed and President Nixon signed Title IX of the 1972 Education Amendments into law (20 U.S.C. § 1681, *et seq*). Title IX sought to rectify the inequity women faced in the workforce and to address the earnings gap between the sexes by enabling the progress of women and girls in education. See, for example, U.S. Department of Justice, Civil Rights Division, "Title IX Legal Manual," *available at* https://www.justice.gov/sites/default/files/crt/legacy/2010/12/14/ixlegal.pdf, last visited January 4, 2017. As legislative history reveals, the law focused on combating the economic disadvantages women faced in the workplace by addressing differential treatment on the basis of sex in education. See, for example, 118 Cong. Rec. 5803-07 (1972).

Title IX provides:

> No person in the United States shall, on the basis of sex, be excluded from participation in, be denied the benefits of, or be subjected to discrimination under any education program or activity receiving federal financial assistance

. . .

20 U.S.C. § 1681(a).

Notably, Title IX recognizes the biological and physiological differences between men and women. Title IX also importantly provides that,

Notwithstanding anything to the contrary contained in this chapter, nothing contained herein shall be construed to prohibit any educational institution receiving funds under this Act, from maintaining separate living facilities for the different sexes.

20 U.S.C. § 1686.

Likewise, Title IX's implementing regulation, 34 C.F.R. § 106.33, expressly allows for schools to designate separate facilities based upon sex:

A recipient may provide separate toilet, locker room, and shower facilities on the basis of sex, but such facilities provided for students of one sex shall be comparable to such facilities provided for students of the other sex.

Id. The terms or concept of "gender identity," "transgenderism," and "transsexuality" appear nowhere in Title IX, its enacting regulations, or its legislative history.[1] In sum, Title IX: (1) requires that schools not discriminate on the basis of sex in order to receive federal funding; (2) clearly states that separate "toilet, locker room, and shower facilities" on the basis sex are permissible; and (3) includes *no* provisions, legal or otherwise, pertaining to the special treatment of "gender identity," "transgenderism," or "transsexuality."

For over 40 years, Title IX permitted schools to provide separate bathrooms, changing rooms, and showering facilities on the basis of sex, with discretion resting at the state and local school levels. The clear meaning of the legislation was never questioned.

The Petitioner in the present case initially allowed the Respondent, a biological female, to use the boys' room in the high school per Respondent's request (App. 144a, 149a). Such action invaded the privacy of teenaged male students using the boys' room and resulted in an outpouring of complaints and concerns from students and parents alike (App. 144a). Petitioner carefully considered the matter at public board meetings on November 11 and December 9, 2014. See Gloucester County School Board Meeting November 11, 2014, *available at* http://www.gloucesterva.info/channels47and48, last visited January 4, 2017; Gloucester County School Board Meeting 12/9/2014, *available at* http://bit.ly/2bsVO6h, last visited January 4, 2017. Additionally, the administrators at Respondent's high school determined, based on firsthand knowledge and information concerning the dynamics, behaviors, and safety of all students and facility at the high school, that it should continue the practice of separate bathroom facilities based on sex (App. 144a-151a).

These decisions generated national publicity from "transgender" activists, including an attorney who requested that the federal government review Petitioner's informed and considered determination (App. 118a-120a). In response to the attorney's inquiry, Petitioner received a letter on January 7, 2015. In the letter, the Department of Education opined: "Title IX regulations permit schools to provide sex-segregated restrooms, locker rooms, shower facilities, housing, athletic teams, and single-sex classes under certain circumstances. When a school elects to separate, or treat students differently on the basis of sex in those situations, a school generally must treat transgender students consistent with their gender identity" (App. 121a, 123a). In other words, the Department said that a school must allow a biological girl to use the boy's restroom and shower if the girl says she's a boy.

School officials rightly discerned that the Department's new "transgender" exception swallowed the express rule that permits a school to provide separate restrooms based on sex.

On May 13, 2016, during the pendency of the appeal in this case, the Department of Education sent a letter to every Title IX recipient in the county (App. 126a-142a). The letter essentially replicates the Department's first letter to Petitioner and adds a detailed mandate of compliance:

1. A school may no longer require a student to use the bathroom, locker room, or shower of the opposite sex if the student or his/her parent or guardian asserts a "gender identity" different from his/her sex (App. 130a).
2. The assertion by the student or his/her parent or guardian does not need to be supported by a psychological diagnosis, a medical diagnosis, or any evidence of treatment (App. 130a).
3. Students who, as a consequence of this new policy, no longer feels comfortable using the bathroom, locker room, or shower of their own sex for reasons of privacy, modesty, sincerely held religious beliefs, or safety concerns, may be relegated to a separate facility (App. 134a).
4. Yet, no school can require that a student whose "gender identity" does not match his/her biological sex use a separate facility (App. 134a).

Only nontransgendered students will be required to use a separate facility.

Respondents argue that Petitioner's action violates Title IX, in part, because the Department of Education letters provide the "controlling interpretation" of Title IX. It is undisputed that the agency's letters fail to address Title IX's implementing regulations, including 34 C.F.R. § 106.33, which allows for the separation of toilets, locker rooms, and showers based on sex (App. 121a, 123a, 126a-142a). It is also undisputed that the Department of Education never published the letters and has never issued notice of rulemaking regarding its radical new "interpretation" of Title IX.

. . .

Adopting the Department of Education's Unlawful Interpretation of Title IX Would Create a Hostile and Discriminatory Environment for Religious Administrators, Teachers, Parents, and Students Throughout Our Nation

. . .

The Department of Education's interpretation violates: (1) the fundamental right of parents to control and direct the upbringing of their children; (2) the procedural due process requirements of the 14th Amendment; (3) the First Amendment constitutional freedoms of students, faculty, and staff (whose valid religious, moral, political, and cultural views necessarily conflict with a political agenda that denies biology, ignores Biblical teaching, and diminishes student privacy); (4) the fundamental constitutional liberty and equal protection interests judicially recognized by this court in the recent decision in *Obergefell v. Hodges*, 135 S. Ct. 2584 (2015) (i.e., the personal identity rights of students, faculty, and staff who find their personal identity not in their sexuality but in Jesus Christ or other faith orientation); and (5) the principle of subsidiarity and the proper constitutional role of state and local governments.

A. The Agency's Proposed Interpretation of Title IX Unconstitutionally Infringes on the Fundamental Right of Parents to Direct and Control the Upbringing of Their Children

The Department of Education's "interpretation" of Title IX substantially infringes upon the parents' right to participate in the education and upbringing of their children. The interpretation imposes immorality into schools by promoting conduct (selecting a "gender identity")

contrary to biological and Biblical teachings. The interpretation fails to even allow parents to be notified if their child requests to enter, or if their child will be forced to use a bathroom, shower, or changing room with a child or adult of the opposite sex.

This Court recognizes parental rights to be fundamental rights. See, for example, *Meyer v. Nebraska*, 262 U.S. 390 (1923); *Pierce v. Society of Sisters*, 268 U.S. 510 (1925). Such liberty serves as a powerful limitation on exercises of government authority, including those exercises of authority that impact the parental role in educational matters.

Courts strictly scrutinize government actions that substantially interfere with a citizen's fundamental rights:

> The essence of all that has been said and written on the subject is that only those interests of the highest order and those not otherwise served can overbalance legitimate claims to the free exercise of [a fundamental right].

Wisconsin v. Yoder, 406 U.S. 205, 215 (1972); *see also Adarand Constructors, Inc. v. Pena*, 515 U.S. 200 (1995); *Widmar v. Vincent*, 454 U.S. 263 (1981); *Church of the Lukumi Babalu Aye, Inc., v. Hialeah*, 508 U.S. 520 (1993).

The fundamental rights standard preserves fit parents' fundamental liberty to control and direct the upbringing of their children. The historical underpinnings of the fundamental right of parents to direct and control the upbringing of their children, and the case law in support of it, compels the conclusion that the agency's imposition here violates constitutionally protected fundamental liberty, especially when it infringes upon parental choices grounded in religious conscience. Certainly, no compelling governmental interest exists which would allow a governmental regime to impose immorality into schools by promoting conduct (selecting a "gender identity") contrary to Biblical, biological, and other scientific teachings. None. And even if a compelling interest did exist, the least restrictive means of accomplishing this interest surely must not be the promulgation of a sexual facility policy that threatens both the privacy and safety of other students using the facilities.

The Department of Education's expansion of Title IX also conflicts with controlling state laws protecting parents' fundamental right to control the upbringing of their children in contexts outside of exercising their freedom of religious conscience. For example, in Michigan, MCL § 380.10 (rights of parents and legal guardians; duties of public schools) expressly provides that parents *do have a fundamental right* to direct and control the upbringing of their children. MCL § 380.10 provides:

Does Sex in Title IX Allow Transgender Students to Use Restrooms Aligned with Their Gender Identity, Not Their Biological Sex?   by Katsh

219

It is the natural, fundamental right of parents and legal guardians to determine and direct the care, teaching, and education of their children. The public schools of this state serve the needs of the pupils by cooperating with the pupil's parents and legal guardians to develop the pupil's intellectual capabilities and vocational skills in a safe and positive environment.

MCL § 380.10; see also *In re A.P.*, 770 N.W.2d 403, 412 (Mich. Ct. App. 2009) ("[D]ue process precludes a government from interfering with parents' fundamental liberty interest in making decisions regarding the care, custody, and control of their children"). The Department of Education's letter ignores such protections that states have enacted to safeguard parents' rights and unlawfully pushes parents to the sidelines.

Both the Constitution and state law protect the fundamental right of parents to control and direct the upbringing of their children, including in the sensitive and private matters relevant here. Because the agency's interpretation of Title IX infringes on the rights of parents, it would be inappropriate to defer to the agency's interpretation of the statute.

. . .

C. The Agency's Interpretation Unconstitutionally Infringes Fundamental First Amendment Rights of Conscience and Expression

The agency's interpretation of Title IX will lead to censorship and punishment for students, faculty, and administrators whose valid religious, moral, political, and cultural views necessarily conflict with the radical new "gender identity" political agenda. For these students, faculty, and administrators, the Department of Education's interpretation of Title IX unconstitutionally interferes with and discriminates against their sincerely held religious beliefs and identity, as well as their freedom of speech (by disallowing any dissent to the federally mandated promotion and acceptance of allowing students, faculty, and administrators into the showers, bathrooms, and locker rooms of the opposite sex and by promoting gender-confused behavior).

Under the Constitution, no federal agency can dictate what is acceptable and not acceptable on matters of religion and politics. The government cannot silence and punish all objecting discourse to promote one political or religious viewpoint. Yet, this is exactly what the Department of Education seeks to do.

For over the last half-century, the U.S. Supreme Court has repeatedly upheld the First Amendment rights of students. Indeed, it is axiomatic that students do not "shed their constitutional rights to freedom of speech or expression at the school house gate" (*Tinker v. Des Moines Indep. Cmty. Sch. Dist.*, 393 U.S. 503, 1969).

> Any word spoken, in class, in the lunchroom, or on the campus, that deviates from the views of another person may start an argument or cause a disturbance. But our Constitution says we must take this risk, and our history says that it is this sort of hazardous freedom—this kind of openness—that is the basis of our national strength and of the independence and vigor of Americans who grow up and live in this relatively permissive and often disputatious society.

> In order for the [government] to justify prohibition of a particular expression of opinion, it must be able to show that its action was caused by something more than a mere desire to avoid the discomfort and unpleasantness that always accompany an unpopular viewpoint. Certainly, where there is no finding and no showing that engaging in the forbidden conduct would "materially and substantially interfere with the requirements of appropriate discipline in the operation of the school," the prohibition cannot be sustained.

Id. at 508–09.

Here, the effect of the agency's expansion of Title IX will inhibit, if not ban, the expression of a particular viewpoint and religious belief without any evidence that the belief materially and substantially interferes with the operation of all schools within the United States. The agency's interpretation creates "the ironic, and unfortunate, paradox of . . . celebrating 'diversity' by refusing to permit the presentation to students of an 'unwelcomed' viewpoint on the topic of homosexuality and religion, while actively promoting the competing view" (*Hansen v. Ann Arbor Pub. Schools*, 293 F. Supp. 2d 780, 782; E.D. Mich. 2003). This rewriting of Title IX requires that everyone get on board with the politically correct "gender identity" or "transsexual" agenda or lose all federal funding.

This unlawful policy limits the viewpoint of allowable student speech and compels school faculty to politically normalize LGBTQ behavior.

. . .

Students, faculty, and administrators have a right to articulate their disapproval or concerns with "gender identity" or "transgenderism" on religious grounds. See, for example, *Zamecnik v. Indian Prairie School Dist. # 204*, 636 F.3d 874, 875 (7th Cir. 2011). Students have a constitutional right to advocate their religious, political, and moral beliefs about homosexuality "provided the statements are not inflammatory—that is, are not 'fighting words,' which means speech likely to provoke a violent response amounting to a breach of the peace" (Id.).

Indeed, "a school that permits advocacy of the rights of homosexual students cannot be allowed to stifle criticism of homosexuality . . . people in our society do not have a legal right to prevent criticism of their beliefs or even their way of life" (Id. at 876). A statutory interpretation that punishes a dissenting opinion by promoting another is unconstitutional.. . . .

Further, the policy fails to adequately respect the First Amendment freedoms of school faculty. It requires school administrators, teachers, and support staff to adopt, implement, and enforce policies that promote the LGBTQ lifestyle. The federally mandated support, encouragement, and affirmation of LGBTQ behaviors necessarily coerces school faculty members who believe this lifestyle to be sinful to either violate their religious conscience and endorse a pro-LGBTQ message under the compulsion of governmental power or face punishment. Nowhere in the agency's revision of Title IX does the Department of Education protect dissenting opinions or sincerely held religious conscience. It must be remembered that "[t]olerance is a two-way street. Otherwise, the rule mandates orthodoxy, not antidiscrimination" (*Ward v. Polite*, 667 F.3d 727, 735, 6th Cir. 2012).

As this court has emphasized, government officials are not thought police: "If there is any fixed star in our constitutional constellation, it is that no official, high or petty, can prescribe what shall be orthodox in politics, nationalism, religion, or other matters of opinion or force citizens to confess by word or act their faith therein" (*W. Virginia State Bd. of Ed. v. Barnette*, 319 U.S. 624, 642, 1943). The Department's new directive patently violates this critical principle.

The Department of Education claims to promote nondiscrimination, by discriminating against, silencing, and punishing those who cannot and do not support the LGBTQ lifestyle. This is still a free country, however, and such censorship is still unconstitutional. The federal government cannot and should not create an environment that will undoubtedly chill the First Amendment freedoms of those students and faculty who disagree with the LGBTQ political agenda for valid religious, moral, political, and cultural reasons.

D. The Agency's Interpretation Unconstitutionally Infringes on the Constitutional Liberty and Equal Protection Interests Recognized by the Supreme Court in *Obergefell*

This Court's recent ruling in *Obergefell v. Hodges*, 135 S. Ct. 2584 (2015) created a new constitutional right of personal identity for all citizens. This Court held that one's right of personal identity precluded any state from proscribing same-sex marriage. In *Obergefell*, the justices in the majority held that "The Constitution promises liberty to all within its reach, a liberty that includes certain specific rights that allow persons, within a lawful realm, to define and express their identity" (*Id.* at 2593).

Because this Court defined a fundamental liberty right as including "most of the rights enumerated in the Bill of Rights," and "liberties [that] extend to certain personal choices central to individual dignity and autonomy, including intimate choices that define personal identity and beliefs," this new right of personal identity must also comprehend factual contexts well beyond same-sex marriage. Clearly, this newly created right of personal identity applies not just to those who find their identity in their sexuality and sexual preferences—but also to citizens who define their identity by their religious beliefs.

Many Christian people, for example, find their identity in Jesus Christ and the ageless, sacred tenets of his word in the Holy Bible. For followers of Jesus, adhering to his commands is *the* most personal choice central to their individual dignity and autonomy. A Christian, whose identity inheres in their religious faith orientation, is entitled to at least as much constitutional protection as those who find their identity in their sexual preference orientation. There can be no doubt that this newly created right of personal identity protects against government authorities who use public policy to persecute, oppress, and discriminate against Christian people.

The agency's revision of Title IX unconstitutionally infringes on the personal identity, liberty, and equal protection this Court established in *Obergefell*. *Id.* at 2607

Does Sex in Title IX Allow Transgender Students to Use Restrooms Aligned with Their Gender Identity, Not Their Biological Sex? by Katsh

221

("The First Amendment ensures that religious organizations and persons are given proper protection as they seek to teach the principles that are so fulfilling and so central to their lives and faiths, and to their own deep aspirations to continue the family structure they have long revered.").

According to *Obergefell*, then, beyond the First Amendment religious liberty protections expressly enshrined in the Bill of Rights, the new judicially created substantive due process right to personal identity now provides Christian and other religious people additional constitutional protection. Henceforth, government action not only must avoid compelling a religious citizen to facilitate or participate in policies that are contrary to their freedoms of expression and religious conscience protected by the First Amendment, but it must also refrain from violating their personal identity rights secured by substantive due process.

The Department of Education's statutory interpretation imposed against Christian or other religious people will violate their First Amendment rights and also the new constitutional "identity" rights that this Court created in *Obergefell*.

. . .

Conclusion

This Honorable Court should vacate and reverse the decisions of the appellate court to prevent the unauthorized governmental overreach of an executive agency and to protect the privacy and constitutional rights of all Americans.

Respectfully submitted,
Erin Elizabeth Mersino
Counsel of Record William Wagner John Kane

Great Lakes Justice Center,
5600 W. Mount Hope Hwy
Lansing, MI 48917, USA.
(517) 322-3207.
Contact@GreatLakesJC.org

Counsel for Amici Curiae

Note

1. *Amici* reject the legitimacy of these recently coined terms as unfounded in science or reason. Instead, the terminology is the self-serving political rhetoric of a small group of activists. See, for example, Reilly, *Making Gay Okay—How Rationalizing Homosexual Behavior Is Changing Everything*, pp. 11, 47–48, 64, 117–29 (Ignatius Press, 2014) (acceptance and promotion of homosexual behavior is based on politics rather than science). *Amici* believe—along with practically all of humanity throughout all of human history—that if a boy says he is a girl, he is not "transgender"; he is denying biology and pretending to be a sex other than his own. We will not participate in adding to such confusion. See id. at 131 (scientific research suggests that at least to some extent "differences in sexual behavior cause (rather than are caused by) differences in the brain").

THE CHRISTIAN EDUCATORS ASSOCIATION INTERNATIONAL is a professional association for Christian educators in both public and private school.

EXPLORING THE ISSUE

Does the Definition of "Sex" in Title IX Include Gender Identity and Allow Transgender Students to Use the Restrooms That Align with Their Gender Identities and Not Their Biological Sex?

Critical Thinking and Reflection

1. After reviewing the readings in this chapter, do you think the definition of "sex" is ambiguous, thus subject to more than one meaning?
2. Who should be the proper authority to determine the definition of "sex"?
3. What constitutional protections, if any, are afforded to transgender individuals?

Is There Common Ground?

In 2017, there does not appear to be a more clashing view on legal issues than the sides taken regarding transgender rights. While the Court of Appeals for the Fourth Circuit and the Christian Educators Association International (CEAI) have fundamental differences on the rights afforded to transgender individuals under Title IX, both find common ground on the importance of students being comfortable in their academic surroundings. It is mutually agreed that transgender students should not be forced to use bathrooms and facilities that strictly align with their biological sex; with the understanding that such would be cruel and unfair to those individuals. But with the withdrawal of the Department of Justice (DOJ) and Department of Education's (DOE's) guides on the issue, the Fourth Circuit, on remand, will have to find a new ground to support their interpretation that "sex" is ambiguous and encompasses gender identity. Neither the Fourth Circuit nor the CEAI may argue that the DOJ and DOE's input on the matter is legally binding, as it no longer exists. With the new Trump Administration issuing executive orders on a frequent basis, additional legal arguments on both sides will be needed.

Additional Resources

Harvey Molotoch and Laura Noren, *Toilet: Public Restrooms and the Politics of Sharing* (NYU Press, 2010).

Proceedings and Orders of *Gloucester County School Board v. G.G.*, http://www.scotusblog.com/case-files/cases/gloucester-county-school-board-v-g-g/.

Title IX Legal Manual, U.S. Department of Justice, Civil Rights Division, https://www.justice.gov/sites/default/files/crt/legacy/2010/12/14/ixlegal.pdf.

U.S. Department of Justice, Civil Rights Division and U.S. Department of Education, Office for Civil Rights, *Dear Colleague Letter on Transgender Students*, May 13, 2016, https://www2.ed.gov/about/offices/list/ocr/letters/colleague-201605-title-ix-transgender.pdf.

U.S. Department of Justice, Civil Rights Division and U.S. Department of Education, Office for Civil Rights, *Dear Colleague Letter Withdrawing Prior Statements of Policy and Guidance*, February 22, 2017, http://www.scotusblog.com/wp-content/uploads/2017/02/16-273-2.22.17-DOJ-Cover-Letter-Guidance.pdf.

Does Sex in Title IX Allow Transgender Students to Use Restrooms Aligned with Their Gender Identity, Not Their Biological Sex?   by Katsh

223

Internet References . . .

American Civil Liberties Union (ACLU)

This webpage created by the ACLU is devoted to *G.G. v. Gloucester County School Board*. The page houses docket filings starting with the District Court proceeding, as well as news sources, press releases, and updates on the issue.

https://www.aclu.org/cases/gg-v-gloucester-county-school-board

National Conference of State Legislatures

Pew Research Center

This Pew Research poll from 2016 reflects Americans' views over which bathrooms transgender individuals should use.

http://www.pewresearch.org/fact-tank/2016/10/03/americans-are-divided-over-which-public-bathrooms-transgender-people-should-use/

The New Yorker

This article in *The New Yorker* discusses the current U.S. debate regarding the rights afforded to transgender individuals to use public restrooms that align with their gender identity.

http://www.newyorker.com/news/news-desk/public-bathroom-regulations-could-create-a-title-ix-crisis

Thomson Reuters

This article and video-bit in *Thomson Reuters* details the Trump Administration's revocation of the Obama Administration's guidelines regarding transgender bathroom use, and "sex" meaning gender identity.

http://www.reuters.com/article/us-usa-trump-lgbt-idUSKBN161243

Selected, Edited, and with Issue Framing Material by:
M. Ethan Katsh, *University of Massachusetts, Amherst*

ISSUE

Does a Facebook Poster Need More Than "General Intent" for a Post to Be Considered a "True Threat" Under Criminal Law?

YES: **John G. Roberts, Jr.**, from "Majority Opinion, *Elonis v. United States*," U.S. Supreme Court (2015)

NO: **Samuel Anthony Alito, Jr.**, from "Dissenting Opinion, *Elonis v. United States*," U.S. Supreme Court (2015)

Learning Outcomes

After reading this issue, you will be able to:

- Discuss the contested role of mental intent and general intent in establishing the criminal culpability of a threat.Understand how Facebook posts could count as threats in the context of criminal law.
- Understand why the Supreme Court refused to decide the role of recklessness in determining a true threat, leaving it to the lower courts to determine.

ISSUE SUMMARY

YES: Supreme Court Chief Justice John Roberts holds that more than a "general intent," standard is required to hold a Facebook poster criminally liable for the contents of the post.

NO: Supreme Court Justice Samuel Alito argues that the majority is unclear as to the state of mind necessary for someone posting a threat on Facebook to be criminally liable for a "true threat."

Although the First Amendment prescribes that "Congress shall make no law . . . abridging the freedom of speech," in practice judges have declared that certain categories of expression are legally unprotected. These categories are often anchored in metaphors, such as "shouting fire in a crowded theater" or "fighting words," which have transcended the language of legal opinions.

One such category of traditionally unprotected speech is "true threats," established inferentially by the Supreme Court in *Watts v. United States*. In 1966, an antidraft activist named Watts told a group of protestors, "If they ever make me carry a rifle the first man I want to get in my sights is L.B.J." Watts was arrested and charged under a federal law that makes it illegal to threaten the life of the president. The Supreme Court quickly concluded,

however, that this statement was "political hyperbole" and that, "taken in context," was not a "true threat," and reversed Watts' conviction.

The Supreme Court was so convinced of its correctness of its ruling in *Watts* that it didn't bother to hear arguments or issue a full decision. Instead, its short *per curiam* opinion skips over the question of what *would* constitute a true threat, including whether intent to carry out the threat—or what the Court in *Watts* calls "willfulness"—is required for a threat to be a true threat. This unanswered question of the role of intent in establishing the trust of a threat has now come again before the Court with a little help from an amusement park employee with a troubling Facebook account.

In May 2010, Anthony Elonis, a 27-year-old employee of the Wildwater Kingdom amusement park in Allentown,

PA, began posting public, violent updates to his Facebook page. In one post, he wrote: "If I only knew then what I know now . . . I would have smothered your ass with a pillow. Dumped your body in the back seat. Dropped you off in Toad Creek and made it look like a rape and murder." Elonis, who had recently been left by his wife of seven years, contacted his sister-in-law to make sure that his wife had read the post, and she soon filed a restraining order against him. A week later, he posted another public status update that began "Fold up your [restraining order] and put it in your pocket/Is it thick enough to stop a bullet?. . . ."

Elonis soon was fired from his job at the amusement park after he posted a picture of himself holding a knife to the throat of a female employee who had filed five sexual harassment complaints against him. A few days later, he posted about shooting up a kindergarten classroom, which earned him a visit from an FBI special agent. After the agent left his house, Elonis posted publicly that it "Took all the strength I had not to turn the bitch ghost/ Pull my knife flick my wrist and slit her throat/Leave her bleedin' from the jugular in the arms of her partner. . . ." He was soon indicted, tried, and found guilty of multiple counts of the interstate communication of threats.

Elonis appealed his conviction on First Amendment grounds, arguing that he did not actually intend to threaten anyone or to carry out the acts described in his posts, which he compared to rap lyrics and other forms of violent but protected expression. Indeed, he had specifically characterized some of his posts as lyrics when he posted them, and in several had linked to the Wikipedia entry on the First Amendment. His case was heard by the Supreme Court on December 1, 2014, and was decided on June 1, 2015, with Chief Justice John Roberts authoring the majority opinion.

At issue in the case was how to interpret 18 U.S. Code § 875(c), a 1939 law that states: "Whoever transmits in interstate or foreign commerce any communication containing any threat to kidnap any person or *any threat to injure the person of another*, shall be fined under this title or imprisoned not more than five years, or both." While prior legislation had only criminalized extortion through interstate commerce, Congress authored 875(c) specifically with examples such as "a mentally irresponsible fellow who might send a threatening letter to a judge" in mind.

The question at the heart of *Elonis* is this: Who decides what counts as a true threat? At trial, a federal judge instructed the jury that it could find Elonis guilty if an average person would believe his posts were intended as a threat, but Elonis argued that such a standard could find him guilty of a state of mind he had never actually held. Upon agreeing to hear the case, the Supreme Court asked this specific question, whether 875(c) "requires proof of the defendant's subjective intent to threaten." Put another way, does the law require the state to prove that Elonis actually intended to threaten his wife, his employer, or the FBI agent, or merely that they (or any reasonable person) would find his posts threatening?

Chief Justice Roberts, in his majority opinion, found that a Facebook user could not be punished solely on the fact that a "friend" found their post threatening. The Court has historically been reluctant to infer a "reasonable person" standard in criminal statutes. The Court further found that mere negligence was an insufficient standard for an individual to be held criminally liable under 875(c). Circumventing that determination, the prosecution argued that Elonis's recklessness should suffice under 875(c). Following usual practice, Chief Justice Roberts decided to leave it to the to the lower courts to collect more facts and legal arguments. So, the takeaways from the majority are that a "true threat" under 875(c) requires more than negligence and a reasonable person standard, the question of recklessness is still uncertain, and temporarily, your Facebook friends do not have the power to unilaterally incriminate you from unintended "threats." But, as shown, Justice Samuel Alito was not persuaded.

Disagreeing with the majority, Justice Alito argued that a general intent/reasonable person standard was in fact proper, and the Court's avoidance of the recklessness issue creates uncertainty for courts and citizens since there is no standard to follow, leaving just guesswork and inferences. Justice Alito relied on the Court's ordinary presumption that absent an explicit mental state, the Court requires only proof of general intent, meaning no criminal intent is necessary. Accordingly, Elonis's conviction should have only be upheld if he had knowledge of the conduct that made his actions illegal, but he did not need to know that the conduct was in fact illegal/criminal. The concern is that if 875(c) requires mental intent, any person could just claim he or she was unaware of the law; and unless the jury is equipped with psychic powers, proving otherwise is nearly impossible. This legal tension is evident in the opinions of both the Chief Justice and Justice Alito.

YES ↵

John G. Roberts, Jr.

Majority Opinion, *Elonis v. United States*

CHIEF JUSTICE ROBERTS delivered the opinion of the Court. Federal law makes it a crime to transmit in interstate commerce "any communication containing any threat . . . to injure the person of another" (18 U. S. C. §875(c)). Petitioner was convicted of violating this provision under instructions that required the jury to find that he communicated what a reasonable person would regard as a threat. The question is whether the statute also requires that the defendant be aware of the threatening nature of the communication, and—if not—whether the First Amendment requires such a showing.

I

A

Anthony Douglas Elonis was an active user of the social networking website Facebook. Users of that website may post items on their Facebook page that are accessible to other users, including Facebook "friends" who are notified when new content is posted. In May 2010, Elonis's wife of nearly seven years left him, taking with her their two young children. Elonis began "listening to more violent music" and posting self-styled "rap" lyrics inspired by the music. Eventually, Elonis changed the user name on his Facebook page from his actual name to a rap-style nom de plume, "Tone Dougie," to distinguish himself from his "online persona." The lyrics Elonis posted as "Tone Dougie" included graphically violent language and imagery. This material was often interspersed with disclaimers that the lyrics were "fictitious," with no intentional "resemblance to real persons." Elonis posted an explanation to another Facebook user that "I'm doing this for me. My writing is therapeutic." . . .

Elonis's coworkers and friends viewed the posts in a different light. Around Halloween of 2010, Elonis posted a photograph of himself and a coworker at a "Halloween Haunt" event at the amusement park where they worked. In the photograph, Elonis was holding a toy knife against his coworker's neck, and in the caption Elonis wrote, "I wish." Elonis was not Facebook friends with the coworker and did not "tag" her, a Facebook feature that would have alerted her to the posting. But the chief of park security was a Facebook "friend" of Elonis, saw the photograph, and fired him.

In response, Elonis posted a new entry on his Facebook page:

> Moles! Didn't I tell y'all I had several? Y'all sayin' I had access to keys for all the f . . . in' gates. That I have sinister plans for all my friends and must have taken home a couple. Y'all think it's too dark and foggy to secure your facility from a man as mad as me? You see, even without a paycheck, I'm still the main attraction. Whoever thought the Halloween Haunt could be so f . . . in' scary?

This post became the basis for Count One of Elonis's subsequent indictment, threatening park patrons and employees.

Elonis's posts frequently included crude, degrading, and violent material about his soon-to-be ex-wife. Shortly after he was fired, Elonis posted an adaptation of a satirical sketch that he and his wife had watched together. In the actual sketch, called "It's Illegal to Say . . . ," a comedian explains that it is illegal for a person to say he wishes to kill the President, but not illegal to explain that it is illegal for him to say that. When Elonis posted the script of the sketch, however, he substituted his wife for the president. The posting was part of the basis for Count Two of the indictment, threatening his wife:

> Hi, I'm Tone Elonis.
> Did you know that it's illegal for me to say I want to kill my wife? . . .
> It's one of the only sentences that I'm not allowed to say. . . .
> Now it was okay for me to say it right then because I was just telling you that it's illegal for me to say I want to kill my wife. . . .

Majority Opinion, Elonis v. U.S., U.S. Supreme Court, 135 S. Ct. 2001, June 1, 2015.

Um, but what's interesting is that it's very illegal to say I really, really think someone out there should kill my wife. . . .
But not illegal to say with a mortar launcher.
Because that's its own sentence. . . .
I also found out that it's incredibly illegal, extremely illegal to go on Facebook and say something like the best place to fire a mortar launcher at her house would be from the cornfield behind it because of easy access to a getaway road and you'd have a clear line of sight through the sun room. . . .
Yet even more illegal to show an illustrated diagram.
[diagram of the house]. . . .

The details about the home were accurate. At the bottom of the post, Elonis included a link to the video of the original skit, and wrote, "Art is about pushing limits. I'm willing to go to jail for my Constitutional rights. Are you?"

After viewing some of Elonis's posts, his wife felt "extremely afraid for [her] life." A state court granted her a three-year protection-from-abuse order against Elonis (essentially, a restraining order). Elonis referred to the order in another post on his "Tone Dougie" page, also included in Count Two of the indictment:

Fold up your [protection-from-abuse order] and put it in your pocket
Is it thick enough to stop a bullet?
Try to enforce an Order
that was improperly granted in the first place
Me thinks the Judge needs an education
on true threat jurisprudence
And prison time'll add zeros to my settlement . . .
And if worse comes to worse
I've got enough explosives
to take care of the State Police and the Sheriff's Department.

At the bottom of this post was a link to the Wikipedia article on "Freedom of speech." Elonis's reference to the police was the basis for Count Three of his indictment, threatening law enforcement officers.

That same month, interspersed with posts about a movie Elonis liked and observations on a comedian's social commentary, Elonis posted an entry that gave rise to Count Four of his indictment:

That's it, I've had about enough
I'm checking out and making a name for myself
Enough elementary schools in a ten mile radius

to initiate the most heinous school shooting ever imagined
And hell hath no fury like a crazy man in a Kindergarten class
The only question is . . . which one?

Meanwhile, park security had informed both local police and the Federal Bureau of Investigation about Elonis's posts, and FBI Agent Denise Stevens had created a Facebook account to monitor his online activity. After the post about a school shooting, Agent Stevens and her partner visited Elonis at his house. Following their visit, during which Elonis was polite but uncooperative, Elonis posted another entry on his Facebook page, called "Little Agent Lady," which led to Count Five:

You know your s***'s ridiculous
when you have the FBI knockin' at yo' door
Little Agent lady stood so close
Took all the strength I had not to turn the b**** ghost
Pull my knife, flick my wrist, and slit her throat
Leave her bleedin' from her jugular in the arms of her partner
[laughter]
So the next time you knock, you best be serving a warrant
And bring yo' SWAT and an explosives expert while you're at it
Cause little did y'all know, I was strapped wit' a bomb
Why do you think it took me so long to get dressed with no shoes on?
I was jus' waitin' for y'all to handcuff me and pat me down
Touch the detonator in my pocket and we're all goin'
[BOOM!]
Are all the pieces comin' together?
S***, I'm just a crazy sociopath
that gets off playin' you stupid f***s like a fiddle
And if y'all didn't hear, I'm gonna be famous
Cause I'm just an aspiring rapper who likes the attention
who happens to be under investigation for terrorism
cause y'all think I'm ready to turn the Valley into Fallujah
But I ain't gonna tell you which bridge is gonna fall
into which river or road
And if you really believe this s***
I'll have some bridge rubble to sell you tomorrow
[BOOM!][BOOM!][BOOM!]

B

A grand jury indicted Elonis for making threats to injure patrons and employees of the park, his estranged wife, police officers, a kindergarten class, and an FBI agent, all in violation of 18 U. S. C. §875(c). In the District Court, Elonis moved to dismiss the indictment for failing to allege that he had intended to threaten anyone. The District Court denied the motion, holding that Third Circuit precedent required only that Elonis "intentionally made the communication, not that he intended to make a threat." At trial, Elonis testified that his posts emulated the rap lyrics of the well-known performer Eminem, some of which involve fantasies about killing his ex-wife. In Elonis's view, he had posted "nothing . . . that hasn't been said already." The Government presented as witnesses Elonis's wife and co-workers, all of whom said they felt afraid and viewed Elonis's posts as serious threats.

Elonis requested a jury instruction that "the government must prove that he intended to communicate a true threat." The District Court denied that request. The jury instructions instead informed the jury that

> A statement is a true threat when a defendant intentionally makes a statement in a context or under such circumstances wherein a reasonable person would foresee that the statement would be interpreted by those to whom the maker communicates the statement as a serious expression of an intention to inflict bodily injury or take the life of an individual.

The Government's closing argument emphasized that it was irrelevant whether Elonis intended the postings to be threats—"it doesn't matter what he thinks." A jury convicted Elonis on four of the five counts against him, acquitting only on the charge of threatening park patrons and employees. Elonis was sentenced to three years, eight months' imprisonment, and three years' supervised release.

Elonis renewed his challenge to the jury instructions in the Court of Appeals, contending that the jury should have been required to find that he intended his posts to be threats. The Court of Appeals disagreed, holding that the intent required by Section 875(c) is only the intent to communicate words that the defendant understands and that a reasonable person would view as a threat.

We granted certiorari.

II

A

An individual who "transmits in interstate or foreign commerce any communication containing any threat to kidnap any person or any threat to injure the person of another" is guilty of a felony and faces up to five years' imprisonment (18 U. S. C. §875(c)). This statute requires that a communication be transmitted and that the communication contain a threat. It does not specify that the defendant must have any mental state with respect to these elements. In particular, it does not indicate whether the defendant must intend that his communication contain a threat.

Elonis argues that the word "threat" itself in Section 875(c) imposes such a requirement. According to Elonis, every definition of "threat" or "threaten" conveys the notion of an intent to inflict harm. ("to declare (usually conditionally) one's intention of inflicting injury upon"); Webster's New International Dictionary 2633 (2d ed. 1954). . . .

These definitions, however, speak to what the statement conveys—not to the mental state of the author. For example, an anonymous letter that says "I'm going to kill you" is "an expression of an intention to inflict loss or harm" regardless of the author's intent. A victim who receives that letter in the mail has received a threat, even if the author believes (wrongly) that his message will be taken as a joke.

For its part, the Government argues that Section 875(c) should be read in light of its neighboring provisions, Sections 875(b) and 875(d). Those provisions also prohibit certain types of threats but expressly include a mental state requirement of an "intent to extort." See 18 U. S. C. §875(b) (proscribing threats to injure or kidnap made "with intent to extort"); §875(d) (proscribing threats to property or reputation made "with intent to extort"). According to the Government, the express "intent to extort" requirements in Sections 875(b) and (d) should preclude courts from implying an unexpressed "intent to threaten" requirement in Section 875(c). . . .

The Government takes this *expressio unius est exclusio alterius* canon too far. The fact that Congress excluded the requirement of an "intent to extort" from Section 875(c) is strong evidence that Congress did not mean to confine Section 875(c) to crimes of extortion. But that does not suggest that Congress, at the same time, also meant to exclude a requirement that a defendant act with a certain mental state in communicating a threat. The most we can conclude from the language of Section 875(c) and its neighboring provisions is that Congress meant to proscribe a broad class of threats in Section 875(c) but did not identify what mental state, if any, a defendant must have to be convicted.

In sum, neither Elonis nor the Government has identified any indication of a particular mental state requirement in the text of Section 875(c).

B

The fact that the statute does not specify any required mental state, however, does not mean that none exists. We have repeatedly held that "mere omission from a criminal enactment of any mention of criminal intent" should not be read "as dispensing with it" (*Morissette v. United States*, 342 U.S. 246, 250, 1952). This rule of construction reflects the basic principle that "wrongdoing must be conscious to be criminal." As Justice Jackson explained, this principle is "as universal and persistent in mature systems of law as belief in freedom of the human will and a consequent ability and duty of the normal individual to choose between good and evil." The "central thought" is that a defendant must be "blameworthy in mind" before he can be found guilty. . . . We therefore generally "interpret[ ] criminal statutes to include broadly applicable scienter requirements, even where the statute by its terms does not contain them." . . .

This is not to say that a defendant must know that his conduct is illegal before he may be found guilty. The familiar maxim "ignorance of the law is no excuse" typically holds true. Instead, our cases have explained that a defendant generally must "know the facts that make his conduct fit the definition of the offense," . . . even if he does not know that those facts give rise to a crime.

Morissette, for example, involved an individual who had taken spent shell casings from a Government bombing range, believing them to have been abandoned. During his trial for "knowingly convert[ing]" property of the United States, the judge instructed the jury that the only question was whether the defendant had knowingly taken the property without authorization. This Court reversed the defendant's conviction, ruling that he had to know not only that he was taking the casings but also that someone else still had property rights in them. He could not be found liable "if he truly believed [the casings] to be abandoned." . . .

To take another example, in *Posters 'N' Things, Ltd. v. United States*, this Court interpreted a federal statute prohibiting the sale of drug paraphernalia (511 U. S. 513, 1994). Whether the items in question qualified as drug paraphernalia was an objective question that did not depend on the defendant's state of mind. But, we held, an individual could not be convicted of selling such paraphernalia unless he "knew that the items at issue [were] likely to be used with illegal drugs." Such a showing was necessary to establish the defendant's culpable state of mind.

And again, in *X-Citement Video*, we considered a statute criminalizing the distribution of visual depictions of minors engaged in sexually explicit conduct. We rejected a reading of the statute which would have required only that a defendant knowingly send the prohibited materials, regardless of whether he knew the age of the performers. We held instead that a defendant must also know that those depicted were minors, because that was "the crucial element separating legal innocence from wrongful conduct."

. . .

C

Section 875(c), as noted, requires proof that a communication was transmitted and that it contained a threat. The "presumption in favor of a scienter requirement should apply to *each* of the statutory elements that criminalize otherwise innocent conduct." . . . The parties agree that a defendant under Section 875(c) must know that he is transmitting a communication. But communicating *something* is not what makes the conduct "wrongful." Here "the crucial element separating legal innocence from wrongful conduct" is the threatening nature of the communication. The mental state requirement must therefore apply to the fact that the communication contains a threat.

Elonis's conviction, however, was premised solely on how his posts would be understood by a reasonable person. Such a "reasonable person" standard is a familiar feature of civil liability in tort law but is inconsistent with "the conventional requirement for criminal conduct— *awareness* of some wrongdoing." . . . Under these principles, "what [Elonis] thinks" does matter.

The Government is at pains to characterize its position as something other than a negligence standard, emphasizing that its approach would require proof that a defendant "comprehended [the] contents and context" of the communication. The Government gives two examples of individuals who, in its view, would lack this necessary mental state—a "foreigner, ignorant of the English language," who would not know the meaning of the words at issue, or an individual mailing a sealed envelope without knowing its contents. But the fact that the Government would require a defendant to actually know the words of and circumstances surrounding a communication does not amount to a rejection of negligence. Criminal negligence standards often incorporate "the circumstances known" to a defendant. . . . Courts then ask, however, whether a reasonable person equipped with that knowledge, not the actual defendant, would have recognized the harmfulness of his conduct. That is precisely the Government's position here: Elonis can be convicted, the Government contends, if he himself knew the contents and context of his posts, and a reasonable person would have recognized that the posts would be read as genuine threats. That is a negligence standard.

In support of its position, the Government relies most heavily on *Hamling v. United States*, 418 U.S. 87 (1974). In that case, the Court rejected the argument that individuals could be convicted of mailing obscene material only if they knew the "legal status of the materials" distributed. Absolving a defendant of liability because he lacked the knowledge that the materials were legally obscene "would permit the defendant to avoid prosecution by simply claiming that he had not brushed up on the law." It was instead enough for liability that "a defendant had knowledge of the contents of the materials he distributed, and that he knew the character and nature of the materials."

This holding does not help the Government. In fact, the Court in *Hamling* approved a state court's conclusion that requiring a defendant to know the character of the material incorporated a "vital element of scienter" so that "not innocent but *calculated purveyance* of filth . . . is exorcised." . . . In this case, "calculated purveyance" of a threat would require that Elonis know the threatening nature of his communication. Put simply, the mental state requirement the Court approved in *Hamling* turns on whether a defendant knew the *character* of what was sent, not simply its contents and context.

Contrary to the dissent's suggestion, see *post*, at 4–5, 9–10 (opinion of Thomas, J.), nothing in *Rosen v. United States*, 161 U.S. 29 (1896), undermines this reading. The defendant's contention in *Rosen* was that his indictment for mailing obscene material was invalid because it did not allege that he was aware of the contents of the mailing. That is not at issue here; there is no dispute that Elonis knew the words he communicated. The defendant also argued that he could not be convicted of mailing obscene material if he did not know that the material "could be properly or justly characterized as obscene." The Court correctly rejected this "ignorance of the law" defense; no such contention is at issue here.

. . .

In light of the foregoing, Elonis's conviction cannot stand. The jury was instructed that the Government need prove only that a reasonable person would regard Elonis's communications as threats, and that was an error. Federal criminal liability generally does not turn solely on the results of an act without considering the defendant's mental state. That understanding "took deep and early root in American soil" and Congress left it intact here: Under Section 875(c), "wrongdoing must be conscious to be criminal."

There is no dispute that the mental state requirement in Section 875(c) is satisfied if the defendant transmits a communication for the purpose of issuing a threat, or with knowledge that the communication will be viewed as a threat. In response to a question at oral argument, Elonis stated that a finding of recklessness would not be sufficient. . . .

The judgment of the U.S. Court of Appeals for the Third Circuit is reversed, and the case is remanded for further proceedings consistent with this opinion.

It is so ordered.

John G. Roberts, Jr., is the current chief justice of the U.S. Supreme Court. He received an AB from Harvard College in 1976 and a JD from Harvard Law School in 1979. He served as a law clerk for former U.S. Supreme Court Chief Justice William Rehnquist during the 1980 term, and in various other legal capacities until his appointment to the U.S. Court of Appeals for the District of Columbia Circuit in 2003. President George W. Bush nominated him as a chief justice in 2005.

Samuel Anthony Alito, Jr.

 **NO**

Dissenting Opinion, *Elonis v. United States*

JUSTICE ALITO concurring in part and dissenting in part.

In *Marbury v. Madison*, 1 Cranch 137, 177 (1803), the Court famously proclaimed: "It is emphatically the province and duty of the judicial department to say what the law is." Today, the Court announces: It is emphatically the prerogative of this Court to say only what the law is not.

The Court's disposition of this case is certain to cause confusion and serious problems. Attorneys and judges need to know which mental state is required for conviction under 18 U. S. C. §875(c), an important criminal statute. This case squarely presents that issue, but the Court provides only a partial answer. The Court holds that the jury instructions in this case were defective because they required only negligence in conveying a threat. But the Court refuses to explain what type of intent was necessary. Did the jury need to find that Elonis had the *purpose* of conveying a true threat? Was it enough if he *knew* that his words conveyed such a threat? Would *recklessness* suffice? The Court declines to say. Attorneys and judges are left to guess.

This will have regrettable consequences. While this Court has the luxury of choosing its docket, lower courts and juries are not so fortunate. They must actually decide cases, and this means applying a standard. If purpose or knowledge is needed and a district court instructs the jury that recklessness suffices, a defendant may be wrongly convicted. On the other hand, if recklessness is enough, and the jury is told that conviction requires proof of more, a guilty defendant may go free. . . .

I

Section 875(c) provides in relevant part:

> Whoever transmits in interstate or foreign commerce any communication containing . . . any threat to injure the person of another, shall be fined under this title or imprisoned not more than five years, or both.

Thus, conviction under this provision requires proof that: (1) the defendant transmitted something, (2) the thing transmitted was a threat to injure the person of another, and (3) the transmission was in interstate or foreign commerce.

At issue in this case is the *mens rea* required with respect to the second element—that the thing transmitted was a threat to injure the person of another. This Court has not defined the meaning of the term "threat" in §875(c), but in construing the same term in a related statute, the Court distinguished a "true 'threat'" from facetious or hyperbolic remarks (*Watts v. United States*, 394 U.S. 705, 708, 1969; *per curiam*). In my view, the term "threat" in §875(c) can fairly be defined as a statement that is reasonably interpreted as "an expression of an intention to inflict evil, injury, or damage on another" (Webster's Third New International Dictionary 2382, 1976). Conviction under §875(c) demands proof that the defendant's transmission was in fact a threat, that is, that it is reasonable to interpret the transmission as an expression of an intent to harm another. In addition, it must be shown that the defendant was at least reckless as to whether the transmission met that requirement.

Why is recklessness enough? My analysis of the *mens rea* issue follows the same track as the Court's, as far as it goes. I agree with the Court that we should presume that criminal statutes require some sort of *mens rea* for conviction. To be sure, this presumption marks a departure from the way in which we generally interpret statutes. We "ordinarily resist reading words or elements into a statute that do not appear on its face" (*Bates v. United States*, 522 U.S. 23, 29, 1997). But this step is justified by a well-established pattern in our criminal laws. "For several centuries (at least since 1600), the different common law crimes have been so defined as to require, for guilt, that the defendant's acts or omissions be accompanied by one or more of the various types of fault (intention, knowledge, recklessness or—more rarely—negligence)" (1 W. LaFave, Substantive Criminal Law §5.5, p. 381, 2003). Based on these "background rules of the common law, in which the requirement of some *mens rea* for a crime is firmly embedded," we require "some indication of congressional

Dissenting Opinion, Elonis v. U.S., U.S. Supreme Court, 135 S. Ct. 2001, June 1, 2015.

intent, express or implied, . . . to dispense with *mens rea* as an element of a crime" (*Staples v. United States*, 511 U.S. 600–606, 1994).

For a similar reason, I agree with the Court that we should presume that an offense like that created by §875(c) requires more than negligence with respect to a critical element like the one at issue here. As the Court states, "[w] hen interpreting federal criminal statutes that are silent on the required mental state, we read into the statute 'only that *mens rea* which is necessary to separate wrongful conduct from "otherwise innocent conduct.'" . . . Whether negligence is morally culpable is an interesting philosophical question, but the answer is at least sufficiently debatable to justify the presumption that a serious offense against the person that lacks any clear common-law counterpart should be presumed to require more.

Once we have passed negligence, however, no further presumptions are defensible. In the hierarchy of mental states that may be required as a condition for criminal liability, the *mens rea* just above negligence is recklessness. Negligence requires only that the defendant "should [have] be[en] aware of a substantial and unjustifiable risk," . . . While recklessness exists "when a person disregards a risk of harm of which he is aware" (*Farmer v. Brennan*, 511 U.S. 825, 837, 1994). And when Congress does not specify a *mens rea* in a criminal statute, we have no justification for inferring that anything more than recklessness is needed. It is quite unusual for us to interpret a statute to contain a requirement that is nowhere set out in the text. Once we have reached recklessness, we have gone as far as we can without stepping over the line that separates interpretation from amendment.

There can be no real dispute that recklessness regarding a risk of serious harm is wrongful conduct. In a wide variety of contexts, we have described reckless conduct as morally culpable. . . . Indeed, this Court has held that "reckless disregard for human life" may justify the death penalty (*Tison v. Arizona*, 481 U.S. 137, 157, 1987). Someone who acts recklessly with respect to conveying a threat necessarily grasps that he is not engaged in innocent conduct. He is not merely careless. He is aware that others could regard his statements as a threat, but he delivers them anyway.

Accordingly, I would hold that a defendant may be convicted under §875(c) if he or she consciously disregards the risk that the communication transmitted will be interpreted as a true threat. Nothing in the Court's noncommittal opinion prevents lower courts from adopting that standard.

II

There remains the question whether interpreting §875(c) to require no more than recklessness with respect to the element at issue here would violate the First Amendment. Elonis contends that it would. I would reject that argument.

It is settled that the Constitution does not protect true threats. . . . And there are good reasons for that rule: true threats inflict great harm and have little if any social value. A threat may cause serious emotional stress for the person threatened and those who care about that person, and a threat may lead to a violent confrontation. It is true that a communication containing a threat may include other statements that have value and are entitled to protection. But that does not justify constitutional protection for the threat itself.

Elonis argues that the First Amendment protects a threat if the person making the statement does not actually intend to cause harm. In his view, if a threat is made for a "'therapeutic'" purpose, "to 'deal with the pain' . . . of a wrenching event," or for "cathartic" reasons, the threat is protected. Brief for Petitioner 52–53. But whether or not the person making a threat intends to cause harm, the damage is the same. And the fact that making a threat may have a therapeutic or cathartic effect for the speaker is not sufficient to justify constitutional protection. Some people may experience a therapeutic or cathartic benefit only if they know that their words will cause harm or only if they actually plan to carry out the threat, but surely the First Amendment does not protect them.

Elonis also claims his threats were constitutionally protected works of art. Words like his, he contends, are shielded by the First Amendment because they are similar to words uttered by rappers and singers in public performances and recordings. To make this point, his brief includes a lengthy excerpt from the lyrics of a rap song in which a very well-compensated rapper imagines killing his ex-wife and dumping her body in a lake. If this celebrity can utter such words, Elonis pleads, amateurs like him should be able to post similar things on social media. But context matters. "Taken in context," lyrics in songs that are performed for an audience or sold in recorded form are unlikely to be interpreted as a real threat to a real person. Statements on social media that are pointedly directed at their victims, by contrast, are much more likely to be taken seriously. To hold otherwise would grant a license to anyone who is clever enough to dress up a real threat in the guise of rap lyrics, a parody, or something similar.

Does a Facebook Poster Need More Than "General Intent" for a Post to Be Considered a "True Threat" Under Criminal Law? by Katsh

233

The facts of this case illustrate the point. Imagine the effect on Elonis's estranged wife when she read this: "'If I only knew then what I know now . . . I would have smothered your ass with a pillow, dumped your body in the back seat, dropped you off in Toad Creek and made it look like a rape and murder'" (730 F. 3d 321, 324, CA3, 2013). Or this: "There's one way to love you but a thousand ways to kill you. I'm not going to rest until your body is a mess, soaked in blood and dying from all the little cuts" (Ibid). Or this: "Fold up your [protection from abuse order] and put it in your pocket[.] Is it thick enough to stop a bullet?" (Id., at 325).

There was evidence that Elonis made sure his wife saw his posts. And she testified that they made her feel "'extremely afraid'" and "'like [she] was being stalked'" (Ibid). Considering the context, who could blame her? Threats of violence and intimidation are among the most favored weapons of domestic abusers, and the rise of social media has only made those tactics more commonplace. . . . A fig leaf of artistic expression cannot convert such hurtful, valueless threats into protected speech.

It can be argued that §875(c), if not limited to threats made with the intent to harm, will chill statements that do not qualify as true threats, for example, statements that may be literally threatening but are plainly not meant to be taken seriously. We have sometimes cautioned that it is necessary to "exten[d] a measure of strategic protection" to otherwise unprotected false statements of fact in order to ensure enough "'breathing space'" for protected speech (*Gertz v. Robert Welch, Inc.*, 418 U.S. 323, 342, 1974; quoting *NAACP v. Button*, 371 U.S. 415, 433, 1963). A similar argument might be made with respect to threats. But we have also held that the law provides adequate breathing space when it requires proof that false statements were made with reckless disregard of their falsity.

. . .

Samuel Anthony Alito, Jr., is an associate justice of the Supreme Court of the United States. He is a graduate of Princeton University and Yale Law School, and he served as U.S. Attorney for the District of New Jersey and as a judge on the U.S. Court of Appeals for the Third Circuit. He was nominated by President George W. Bush and has served on the court since January 31, 2006.

EXPLORING THE ISSUE

Does a Facebook Poster Need More Than "General Intent" for a Post to Be Considered a "True Threat" Under Criminal Law?

Critical Thinking and Reflection

1. Considering the Supreme Court's decision that a true threat requires more than a general intent and negligence standard to be held criminally liable, what impact might that have on victims of domestic violence or other forms of assault?
2. Have you ever posted anything (perhaps a joke) on Facebook that could be considered threatening by a jury in light of the holding in *Elonis*? After reading the majority and Justice Alito's dissent, what would qualify as a true threat, and why?
3. What guidelines, if any, did the Supreme Court provide in determining whether a Facebook post is a true threat?
4. Do you think different laws should apply to Facebook and other social media sites?

Is There Common Ground?

Chief Justice Roberts and Justice Alito agree on many issues brought before the Court. Legislating from the bench or aggressive judicial policy-making is a common concern of both Roberts and Alito. Both justices view a limited judicial role for the Court, preferring to have elected representatives, not unelected lawyers making policy. *Elonis's* sole dispute involved the question of how to determine the state of mind requirement of a statute when none was provided.

Justice Alito acknowledges the differing legal grounds set forth in the dissent and majority. "As the majority correctly explains," wrote Justice Alito, "nothing in the text of § 875(c) itself requires proof of an intent to threaten." When there is a statute requiring the Court to read in a requisite mental state, the Court's decision is limited to no more than a recklessness standard. Neither Justice Roberts and the majority nor Justice Alito would adopt an intent-to-threaten requirement, for if this was Congress's intent, it is mutually agreed that the statute would have included that standard.

In *Elonis*, the core difference between the majority and Justice Alito's dissent was the requisite mental state that categorizes a communication as a "true threat." Does a true threat require the intent to threaten, or the intent to communicate what a reasonable person would interpret as threatening? Justice Alito believes that requiring the intent to communicate a true threat would allow individuals to escape prosecution by "simply claiming that [they] . . . had not brushed up on the law," resulting in the guilty going free. Chief Justice Roberts argues that a general intent standard relying on a reasonable person's interpretation, regardless of what the defendant thinks or intended, "reduces the culpability on the all-important element of the crime to negligence," which the Court has been reluctant to infer in criminal statutes. The dissent is under the perspective that we cannot allow the guilty to get off easy, while the majority argues that we must protect the innocent from unfair prosecution.

If you were looking for the Court to resolve the ambiguity of a "true threat," *Elonis* may not satisfy your urge for confirmation or for a clear-cut legal doctrine. This is because the Court has not yet decided the full extent of what mental state is required for a "true threat." The door is still open to determine whether a true threat requires a recklessness standard, with the case on remand to "help ensure that [the Court] decide[s] it correctly." Solace may be found in the majority's explanation of what a true threat is not, which is a communication relying solely on a general intent/reasonable person standard. But maybe *Elonis* will be in front of the Court again, hopefully to identify more clearly what a true threat is.

Does a Facebook Poster Need More Than "General Intent" for a Post to Be Considered a "True Threat" Under Criminal Law? by Katsh

235

Additional Resources

Argument Analysis: Taking Ownership of an Internet Rant, www.scotusblog.com/2014/12/argument-analysis-taking-ownership-of-an-internet-rant.

Oral Arguments in *Elonis v. US*, www.oyez.org/cases/2010-2019/2014/2014_13_983.

Proceedings and Orders of *Elonis v. US*, www.scotusblog.com/case-files/cases/elonis-v-united-states/.

Proceedings and Orders of *Elonis v. US*, www.scotusblog.com/case-files/cases/elonis-v-united-states/.

Internet References . . .

Drawing the Line between Therapy and Threats: In Plain English

www.scotusblog.com/2014/11/drawing-a-line-between-therapy-and-threats-in-plain-english/

First Amendment: Speech: *Elonis v. United States*

harvardlawreview.org/2015/11/elonis-v-united-states/

Oral Arguments in *Elonis v. US*

www.oyez.org/cases/2010-2019/2014/2014_13_983

Proceedings and Orders of *Elonis v. US*

www.scotusblog.com/case-files/cases/elonis-v-united-states/

The Nuances of Threats on Facebook

www.newyorker.com/news/news-desk/nuances-threat-facebook/

What Is a True Threat on Facebook?

www.nytimes.com/2014/12/02/opinion/what-is-a-true-threat-on-facebook.html

Unit 4

UNIT

Law and the Community

*W*hile *we are all citizens of a state, we are also participants in various communities whose members generally hold shared values and hope to satisfy shared goals. The challenge of finding appropriate relationships among the individual, the state, and the community is examined in this section.*

Selected, Edited, and with Issue Framing Material by:
M. Ethan Katsh, *University of Massachusetts, Amherst*

ISSUE

Is There a Constitutional Right to Possess a Firearm for Private Use?

YES: Antonin Scalia, from "Majority Opinion, *District of Columbia, et al., v. Heller,*" *United States Supreme Court* (2008)

NO: John Paul Stevens, from "Dissenting Opinion, *District of Columbia, et al., v. Heller,*" *United States Supreme Court* (2008)

Learning Outcomes

After reading this issue, you will be able to:

- Explain what the main issue was in the *Miller* case of 1939 and why Justice Stevens thought that the decision was relevant to this case but Justice Scalia thought it was not relevant.
- Explain what Justice Scalia meant when he said that the rights guaranteed by the Second Amendment were not unlimited.
- Describe what was Justice Breyer's "interest balancing inquiry" vis-à-vis the District of Columbia gun law and explain Justice Scalia's criticism of this view.
- Explain what Justice Stevens meant when he wrote that for most of our history, it has been understood that legislatures could regulate the use and misuse of firearms. Which legislatures does this cover? What are the limitations of this regulation?
- Explain what is meant by Second Amendment-based objections to firearms regulation.

ISSUE SUMMARY

YES: Supreme Court Justice Antonin Scalia argues that the Second Amendment protects the right of a private citizen to own a handgun for self-defense.

NO: Supreme Court Justice John Paul Stevens argues that a previous case, *United States v. Miller,* held that the Second Amendment did not protect the right of a private citizen to own a handgun for self-defense.

The Supreme Court routinely hears cases requiring it to interpret the vague language of the Bill of Rights and determine how to apply the often-abstract principles to concrete situations in modern American society. The Court frequently addresses the meaning of the First Amendment guarantee of freedom of speech, the Fifth Amendment right to due process, the Eighth Amendment prohibition on cruel and unusual punishment, and numerous other constitutional guarantees of individual rights and civil liberties. The Second Amendment, however, has historically been conspicuously absent from the Court's docket. The Court has addressed the Second Amendment so rarely that until 2008, more than two centuries after ratification of the Bill of Rights, the Court had never even made a definitive statement about what the right to "bear arms"

*Levinson, "The Embarrassing Second Amendment," 99 *Yale L. J.* 637 (1989).

encompassed—and what government action would violate that right.

As law professor Sanford Levinson once wryly noted, "No one has ever described the Constitution as a marvel of clarity, and the Second Amendment is perhaps one of the worst drafted of all its provisions."* The Second Amendment states, "A well-regulated militia, being necessary to the security of a free state, the right of the people to keep and bear arms, shall not be infringed." One of the central questions in interpreting the amendment is how to understand the connection between its two clauses. Is the first clause intended to limit the right to bear arms to military situations or military-type weapons, or is it simply announcing a purpose and not otherwise circumscribing the right? (Those who endorse the latter view claim that the first clause is merely "prefatory.") Is the "right to keep and bear arms" one that even applies to individual persons, or does the language about the militia in the first clause turn it into a "collective" right that is relevant only to a group?

The amendment's confusing language has led to other interpretive debates. Are all "arms" protected under the amendment, or only certain types of weapons? Who is prohibited from infringing on the right to bear arms: Congress or the individual states? Does the right belong to everyone—including, say, dangerous criminals? Do gun-control laws that regulate but do not outlaw gun ownership, such as licensing requirements, constitute infringement?

The Supreme Court was forced to grapple with these issues in the 2008 case of *District of Columbia v. Heller*. Washington, DC, had one of the strictest gun-control laws in the country, and Robert Levy, a Washington lawyer affiliated with the libertarian Cato Institute, decided to organize and bankroll a legal challenge to the constitutionality of the District of Columbia gun law. Levy found six District of Columbia residents who were willing to serve as plaintiffs in a lawsuit against the District; one of them was Dick Heller, a District of Columbia police officer who wanted to purchase a handgun to keep in his home for self-defense. Although an appeals court dismissed the other five plaintiffs from the lawsuit, it allowed Heller's case to go forward and sided with his argument that the District of Columbia law violated the Second Amendment. Faced with losing what its leaders saw as an important tool for fighting crime, the District appealed the decision to the Supreme Court, which agreed to hear the case.

In the readings that follow, Justices Scalia and Stevens provide two strikingly different interpretations of the Second Amendment. Both agree on the importance,

in interpreting the text of the amendment, of looking at how it would have been understood at the time it was drafted and ratified. However, by relying on different historical sources and putting emphasis on different pieces of evidence, the two justices reach very divergent conclusions about the "original" meaning of the amendment. Furthermore, the justices disagree about how to interpret the Court's decision in a prior Second Amendment case, *United States v. Miller* (307 U.S. 174, 1939), and how much weight to assign that decision. While Justice Scalia, writing for the five-person majority, asserts that *Miller* supports his argument that the Second Amendment protects the right of a private citizen like Heller to own a handgun for self-defense, Justice Stevens claims that the majority is ignoring *Miller*'s clear holding to the contrary, simply because it does not agree with the prior Court's decision.

Justice Scalia has long been an advocate of "originalism," the idea that the Constitution is properly interpreted by looking at how its provisions were "originally" understood when it was drafted and ratified. He relies on this methodology in his *Heller* opinion to determine the meaning of the Second Amendment. While Justice Stevens has never been a committed originalist, he attempts to rebut much of Justice Scalia's argument using originalist arguments. For Justice Stevens, the primary problem with Justice Scalia's opinion is not that the interpretive method is wrong, but that Justice Scalia relies on the wrong historical evidence in trying to use that method to understand the Second Amendment.

One could, however, also object to Justice Scalia's argument on methodological grounds. Instead of arguing about who is correct with historical details, one could claim that the historical details are not the most important determinant of how the Constitution should be interpreted. In a separate dissent, Justice Stephen Breyer made just such a claim. As he sees it:

> The majority's conclusion is wrong for two independent reasons. The first reason is that set forth by Justice Stevens—namely, that the Second Amendment protects militia-related, not self-defense-related, interests. . . . The second independent reason is that the protection the Amendment provides is not absolute. The Amendment permits government to regulate the interests that it serves. Thus, irrespective of what those interests are—whether they do or do not include an independent interest in self-defense—the majority's view cannot be correct unless it can show that the District's regulation is unreasonable or inappropriate in Second Amendment terms. This the majority cannot do.

In Justice Breyer's view, the Court should not be relying solely on originalism to determine the scope of the Second Amendment. Instead, the Court should be considering the governmental interests at stake, taking into account that violent crime in urban areas like Washington, DC, is a significant problem today but was not when the Second Amendment was drafted. For Breyer, history may be illuminating, but the meaning of the Constitution was not fixed at the time it was written, rather the text sets out broad principles that can be interpreted in various ways, and it is the job of the courts to determine how those principles can be best applied to the specific circumstances of modern-day America. As you read the following selections, ask yourself how much weight you think should be given to what the drafters of the amendment were thinking.

YES ←

Antonin Scalia

Majority Opinion, *District of Columbia, et al., v. Heller*

JUSTICE SCALIA delivered the opinion of the Court.

We consider whether a District of Columbia prohibition on the possession of usable handguns in the home violates the Second Amendment to the Constitution.

I

. . .

II

We turn first to the meaning of the Second Amendment. . . .

The two sides in this case have set out very different interpretations of the Amendment. Petitioners and today's dissenting Justices believe that it protects only the right to possess and carry a firearm in connection with militia service. . . . Respondent argues that it protects an individual right to possess a firearm unconnected with service in a militia, and to use that arm for traditionally lawful purposes, such as self-defense within the home. . . .

Presser said nothing about the Second Amendment's meaning or scope, beyond the fact that it does not prevent the prohibition of private paramilitary organizations.

JUSTICE STEVENS places overwhelming reliance upon this Court's decision in *United States v. Miller,* 307 U.S. 174 (1939). "[H]undreds of judges," we are told, "have relied on the view of the amendment we endorsed there," *post,* at 2, and "[e]ven if the textual and historical arguments on both sides of the issue were evenly balanced, respect for the well-settled views of all of our predecessors on this Court, and for the rule of law itself . . . would prevent most jurists from endorsing such a dramatic upheaval in the law," *post,* at 4. And what is, according to JUSTICE STEVENS, the holding of *Miller* that demands such obeisance? That the Second Amendment "protects the right to keep and bear arms for certain military purposes, but that it does not curtail the legislature's power to regulate the nonmilitary use and ownership of weapons." *Post,* at 2.

Nothing so clearly demonstrates the weakness of JUSTICE STEVENS' case. *Miller* did not hold that and cannot possibly be read to have held that. The judgment in the case upheld against a Second Amendment challenge two men's federal convictions for transporting an unregistered short-barreled shotgun in interstate commerce, in violation of the National Firearms Act, 48 Stat. 1236. It is entirely clear that the Court's basis for saying that the Second Amendment did not apply was *not* that the defendants were "bear[ing] arms" not "for . . . military purposes" but for "nonmilitary use," *post,* at 2. Rather, it was that the *type of weapon at issue* was not eligible for Second Amendment protection: "In the absence of any evidence tending to show that the possession or use of a [short-barreled shotgun] at this time has some reasonable relationship to the preservation or efficiency of a well regulated militia, we cannot say that the Second Amendment guarantees the right to keep and bear *such an instrument.*" 307 U.S., at 178 (emphasis added). "Certainly," the Court continued, "it is not within judicial notice that this weapon is any part of the ordinary military equipment or that its use could contribute to the common defense." *Ibid.* Beyond that, the opinion provided no explanation of the content of the right.

This holding is not only consistent with, but positively suggests, that the Second Amendment confers an individual right to keep and bear arms (though only arms that "have some reasonable relationship to the preservation or efficiency of a well regulated militia"). Had the Court believed that the Second Amendment protects only those serving in the militia, it would have been odd to examine the character of the weapon rather than simply note that the two crooks were not militiamen. JUSTICE STEVENS can say again and again that *Miller* did "not turn on the difference between muskets and sawed-off shotguns, it turned, rather, on the basic difference between the military and nonmilitary use and possession of guns," *post,* at 42–43, but the words of the opinion prove otherwise. The most JUSTICE STEVENS can plausibly claim for *Miller* is that it declined to decide the nature of the Second Amendment

From Supreme Court of the United States, June 26, 2008.

right, despite the Solicitor General's argument (made in the alternative) that the right was collective, see Brief for United States, O. T. 1938, No. 696, pp. 4–5. *Miller* stands only for the proposition that the Second Amendment right, whatever its nature, extends only to certain types of weapons.

It is particularly wrongheaded to read *Miller* for more than what it said, because the case did not even purport to be a thorough examination of the Second Amendment. JUSTICE STEVENS claims, *post,* at 42, that the opinion reached its conclusion "[a]fter reviewing many of the same sources that are discussed at greater length by the Court today." Not many, which was not entirely the Court's fault. The respondent made no appearance in the case, neither filing a brief nor appearing at oral argument; the Court heard from no one but the Government (reason enough, one would think, not to make that case the beginning and the end of this Court's consideration of the Second Amendment). See Frye, The Peculiar Story of *United States v. Miller,* 3 N. Y. U. J. L. & Liberty 48, 65–68 (2008). The Government's brief spent two pages discussing English legal sources, concluding "that at least the carrying of weapons without lawful occasion or excuse was always a crime" and that (because of the class-based restrictions and the prohibition on terrorizing people with dangerous or unusual weapons) "the early English law did not guarantee an unrestricted right to bear arms." Brief for United States, O. T. 1938, No. 696, at 9–11. It then went on to rely primarily on the discussion of the English right to bear arms in *Aymette v. State,* 21 Tenn. 154, for the proposition that the only uses of arms protected by the Second Amendment are those that relate to the militia, not self-defense. See Brief for United States, O. T. 1938, No. 696, at 12–18. The final section of the brief recognized that "some courts have said that the right to bear arms includes the right of the individual to have them for the protection of his person and property," and launched an alternative argument that "weapons which are commonly used by criminals," such as sawed-off shotguns, are not protected. See *id.,* at 18–21. The Government's *Miller* brief thus provided scant discussion of the history of the Second Amendment—and the Court was presented with no counterdiscussion. As for the text of the Court's opinion itself, that discusses *none* of the history of the Second Amendment. It assumes from the prologue that the Amendment was designed to preserve the militia, 307 U.S., at 178 (which we do not dispute), and then reviews some historical materials dealing with the nature of the militia, and in particular with the nature of the arms their members were expected to possess, *id.,* at 178–182. Not a word *(not a word)* about the

history of the Second Amendment. This is the mighty rock upon which the dissent rests its case.[1]

We may as well consider at this point (for we will have to consider eventually) *what* types of weapons *Miller* permits. Read in isolation, *Miller's* phrase "part of ordinary military equipment" could mean that only those weapons useful in warfare are protected. That would be a startling reading of the opinion, since it would mean that the National Firearms Act's restrictions on machineguns (not challenged in *Miller)* might be unconstitutional, machineguns being useful in warfare in 1939. We think that *Miller's* "ordinary military equipment" language must be read in tandem with what comes after: "[O]rdinarily when called for [militia] service [able-bodied] men were expected to appear bearing arms supplied by themselves and of the kind in common use at the time." 307 U.S., at 179. The traditional militia was formed from a pool of men bringing arms "in common use at the time" for lawful purposes like self-defense. "In the colonial and revolutionary war era, [small-arms] weapons used by militiamen and weapons used in defense of person and home were one and the same." *State v. Kessler,* 289 Ore. 359, 368, 614 P. 2d 94, 98 (1980) (citing G. Neumann, Swords and Blades of the American Revolution 6–15, 252–254 (1973)). Indeed, that is precisely the way in which the Second Amendment's operative clause furthers the purpose announced in its preface. We therefore read *Miller* to say only that the Second Amendment does not protect those weapons not typically possessed by law-abiding citizens for lawful purposes, such as short-barreled shotguns. That accords with the historical understanding of the scope of the right, see Part III, *infra.*[2]

We conclude that nothing in our precedents forecloses our adoption of the original understanding of the Second Amendment. It should be unsurprising that such a significant matter has been for so long judicially unresolved. For most of our history, the Bill of Rights was not thought applicable to the States, and the Federal Government did not significantly regulate the possession of firearms by law-abiding citizens. Other provisions of the Bill of Rights have similarly remained unilluminated for lengthy periods. This Court first held a law to violate the First Amendment's guarantee of freedom of speech in 1931, almost 150 years after the Amendment was ratified, see *Near v. Minnesota ex rel. Olson,* 283 U.S. 697 (1931), and it was not until after World War II that we held a law invalid under the Establishment Clause, see *Illinois ex rel. McCollum v. Board of Ed. of School Dist. No. 71, Champaign Cty.,* 333 U.S. 203 (1948). Even a question as basic as the scope of proscribable libel was not addressed by this Court until 1964, nearly two centuries after the founding. See *New York Times Co. v. Sullivan*, 376 U.S. 254 (1964). It is demonstrably not true that, as JUSTICE STEVENS claims, *post*, at 41–42, "for most of our history, the invalidity of Second-Amendment-based objections to firearms regulations has been well settled and uncontroversial." For most of our history the question did not present itself.

III

Like most rights, the right secured by the Second Amendment is not unlimited. From Blackstone through the 19th-century cases, commentators and courts routinely explained that the right was not a right to keep and carry any weapon whatsoever in any manner whatsoever and for whatever purpose. See, *e.g.*, *Sheldon*, in 5 Blume 346; Rawle 123; Pomeroy 152–153; Abbott 333. For example, the majority of the 19th-century courts to consider the question held that prohibitions on carrying concealed weapons were lawful under the Second Amendment or state analogues. See, *e.g.*, *State v. Chandler*, 5 La. Ann., at 489-490; *Nunn v. State*, 1 Ga., at 251; see generally 2 Kent *340, n. 2; The American Students' Blackstone 84, n. 11 (G. Chase ed. 1884). Although we do not undertake an exhaustive historical analysis today of the full scope of the Second Amendment, nothing in our opinion should be taken to cast doubt on longstanding prohibitions on the possession of firearms by felons and the mentally ill, or laws forbidding the carrying of firearms in sensitive places such as schools and government buildings, or laws imposing conditions and qualifications on the commercial sale of arms.[3]

We also recognize another important limitation on the right to keep and carry arms. *Miller* said, as we have explained, that the sorts of weapons protected were those "in common use at the time." 307 U.S., at 179. We think that limitation is fairly supported by the historical tradition of prohibiting the carrying of "dangerous and unusual weapons." See 4 Blackstone 148–149 (1769); 3 B. Wilson, Works of the Honourable James Wilson 79 (1804); J. Dunlap, The New-York Justice 8 (1815); C. Humphreys, A Compendium of the Common Law in Force in Kentucky 482 (1822); 1 W. Russell, A Treatise on Crimes and Indictable Misdemeanors 271–272 (1831); H. Stephen, Summary of the Criminal Law 48 (1840); E. Lewis, An Abridgment of the Criminal Law of the United States 64 (1847); F. Wharton, A Treatise on the Criminal Law of the United States 726 (1852). See also *State v. Langford*, 10 N. C. 381, 383–384 (1824); *O'Neill v. State*, 16 Ala. 65, 67 (1849);

English v. State, 35 Tex. 473, 476 (1871); *State v. Lanier*, 71 N. C. 288, 289 (1874).

It may be objected that if weapons that are most useful in military service—M-16 rifles and the like—may be banned, then the Second Amendment right is completely detached from the prefatory clause. But as we have said, the conception of the militia at the time of the Second Amendment's ratification was the body of all citizens capable of military service, who would bring the sorts of lawful weapons that they possessed at home to militia duty. It may well be true today that a militia, to be as effective as militias in the 18th century, would require sophisticated arms that are highly unusual in society at large. Indeed, it may be true that no amount of small arms could be useful against modern-day bombers and tanks. But the fact that modern developments have limited the degree of fit between the prefatory clause and the protected right cannot change our interpretation of the right.

IV

We turn finally to the law at issue here. As we have said, the law totally bans handgun possession in the home. It also requires that any lawful firearm in the home be disassembled or bound by a trigger lock at all times, rendering it inoperable.

As the quotations earlier in this opinion demonstrate, the inherent right of self-defense has been central to the Second Amendment right. The handgun ban amounts to a prohibition of an entire class of "arms" that is overwhelmingly chosen by American society for that lawful purpose. The prohibition extends, moreover, to the home, where the need for defense of self, family, and property is most acute. Under any of the standards of scrutiny that we have applied to enumerated constitutional rights,[4] banning from the home "the most preferred firearm in the nation to 'keep' and use for protection of one's home and family," 478 F. 3d, at 400, would fail constitutional muster.

Few laws in the history of our Nation have come close to the severe restriction of the District's handgun ban. And some of those few have been struck down. In *Nunn v. State*, the Georgia Supreme Court struck down a prohibition on carrying pistols openly (even though it upheld a prohibition on carrying concealed weapons). See 1 Ga., at 251. In *Andrews v. State*, the Tennessee Supreme Court likewise held that a statute that forbade openly carrying a pistol "publicly or privately, without regard to time or place, or circumstances," 50 Tenn., at 187, violated the state constitutional provision (which the court equated with the Second Amendment). That was so even though the statute did not restrict the carrying of long guns. *Ibid.* See also *State v. Reid,* 1 Ala. 612, 616–617 (1840) ("A statute which, under the pretence of regulating, amounts to a destruction of the right, or which requires arms to be so borne as to render them wholly useless for the purpose of defence, would be clearly unconstitutional").

It is no answer to say, as petitioners do, that it is permissible to ban the possession of handguns so long as the possession of other firearms (*i.e.,* long guns) is allowed. It is enough to note, as we have observed, that the American people have considered the handgun to be the quintessential self-defense weapon. There are many reasons that a citizen may prefer a handgun for home defense: It is easier to store in a location that is readily accessible in an emergency; it cannot easily be redirected or wrestled away by an attacker; it is easier to use for those without the upper-body strength to lift and aim a long gun; it can be pointed at a burglar with one hand while the other hand dials the police. Whatever the reason, handguns are the most popular weapon chosen by Americans for self-defense in the home, and a complete prohibition of their use is invalid.

We must also address the District's requirement (as applied to respondent's handgun) that firearms in the home be rendered and kept inoperable at all times. This makes it impossible for citizens to use them for the core lawful purpose of self-defense and is hence unconstitutional. The District argues that we should interpret this element of the statute to contain an exception for self-defense. See Brief for Petitioners 56–57. But we think that is precluded by the unequivocal text, and by the presence of certain other enumerated exceptions: "Except for law enforcement personnel . . . , each registrant shall keep any firearm in his possession unloaded and disassembled or bound by a trigger lock or similar device unless such firearm is kept at his place of business, or while being used for lawful recreational purposes within the District of Columbia." D. C. Code §7–2507.02. The nonexistence of a self-defense exception is also suggested by the D. C. Court of Appeals' statement that the statute forbids residents to use firearms to stop intruders, see *McIntosh v. Washington,* 395 A. 2d 744, 755–756 (1978).[5]

Apart from his challenge to the handgun ban and the trigger-lock requirement respondent asked the District Court to enjoin petitioners from enforcing the separate licensing requirement "in such a manner as to forbid the carrying of a firearm within one's home or possessed land without a license." App. 59a. The Court of Appeals did not invalidate the licensing requirement, but held only that the District "may not prevent [a handgun] from being moved throughout one's house." 478 F. 3d, at 400. It then ordered the District Court to enter summary judgment "consistent with [respondent's] prayer for relief." *Id.,* at 401. Before this Court petitioners have stated that "if the handgun ban is struck down and respondent registers a handgun, he could obtain a license, assuming he is not otherwise disqualified," by which they apparently mean if he is not a felon and is not insane. Brief for Petitioners 58. Respondent conceded at oral argument that he does not "have a problem with . . . licensing" and that the District's law is permissible so long as it is "not enforced in an arbitrary and capricious manner." Tr. of Oral Arg. 74–75. We therefore assume that petitioners' issuance of a license will satisfy respondent's prayer for relief and do not address the licensing requirement.

Justice Breyer has devoted most of his separate dissent to the handgun ban. He says that, even assuming the Second Amendment is a personal guarantee of the right to bear arms, the District's prohibition is valid. He first tries to establish this by founding-era historical precedent, pointing to various restrictive laws in the colonial period. These demonstrate, in his view, that the District's law "imposes a burden upon gun owners that seems proportionately no greater than restrictions in existence at the time the Second Amendment was adopted." *Post,* at 2. Of the laws he cites, only one offers even marginal support for his assertion. A 1783 Massachusetts law forbade the residents of Boston to "take into" or "receive into" "any Dwelling House, Stable, Barn, Out-house, Ware-house, Store, Shop or other Building" loaded firearms, and permitted the seizure of any loaded firearms that "shall be found" there. Act of Mar. 1, 1783, ch. 13, 1783 Mass. Acts p. 218. That statute's text and its prologue, which makes clear that the purpose of the prohibition was to eliminate the danger to firefighters posed by the "depositing of loaded Arms" in buildings, give reason to doubt that colonial Boston authorities would have enforced that general prohibition against someone who temporarily loaded a firearm to confront an intruder (despite the law's application in that case). In any case, we would not stake our interpretation of the Second Amendment upon a single law, in effect in a single city, that contradicts the overwhelming weight of other evidence regarding the right to keep and bear arms for defense of the home. The other laws Justice Breyer cites are gunpowder-storage laws that he concedes did not clearly prohibit loaded weapons, but required only that excess gunpowder be kept in a special container or on the top floor of the home. *Post,* at 6–7. Nothing about those fire-safety laws undermines our analysis; they do not remotely burden the right of self-defense as much as an absolute ban on handguns. Nor, correspondingly, does our analysis suggest the invalidity of laws regulating the storage of firearms to prevent accidents.

JUSTICE BREYER points to other founding-era laws that he says "restricted the firing of guns within the city limits to at least some degree" in Boston, Philadelphia and New York. *Post*, at 4 (citing Churchill, Gun Regulation, the Police Power, and the Right to Keep Arms in Early America, 25 Law & Hist. Rev. 139, 162 (2007)). Those laws provide no support for the severe restriction in the present case. The New York law levied a fine of 20 shillings on anyone who fired a gun in certain places (including houses) on New Year's Eve and the first two days of January, and was aimed at preventing the "great Damages . . . frequently done on [those days] by persons going House to House, with Guns and other Firearms and being often intoxicated with Liquor." 5 Colonial Laws of New York 244–246 (1894). It is inconceivable that this law would have been enforced against a person exercising his right to self-defense on New Year's Day against such drunken hooligans. The Pennsylvania law to which JUSTICE BREYER refers levied a fine of 5 shillings on one who fired a gun or set off fireworks in Philadelphia without first obtaining a license from the governor. See Act of Aug. 26, 1721, §4, in 3 Stat. at Large 253–254. Given Justice Wilson's explanation that the right to self-defense with arms was protected by the Pennsylvania Constitution, it is unlikely that this law (which in any event amounted to at most a licensing regime) would have been enforced against a person who used firearms for self-defense. JUSTICE BREYER cites a Rhode Island law that simply levied a 5-shilling fine on those who fired guns in *streets* and *taverns,* a law obviously inapplicable to this case. See An Act for preventing Mischief being done in the town of Newport, or in any other town in this Government, 1731, Rhode Island Session Laws. Finally, JUSTICE BREYER points to a Massachusetts law similar to the Pennsylvania law, prohibiting "discharg[ing] any Gun or Pistol charged with Shot or Ball in the Town of *Boston.*" Act of May 28, 1746, ch. X, Acts and Laws of Mass. Bay 208. It is again implausible that this would have been enforced against a citizen acting in self-defense, particularly given its preambulatory reference to "the *indiscreet* firing of Guns." *Ibid,* (preamble) (emphasis added).

A broader point about the laws that JUSTICE BREYER cites: All of them punished the discharge (or loading) of guns with a small fine and forfeiture of the weapon (or in a few cases a very brief stay in the local jail), not with significant criminal penalties.[6] They are akin to modern penalties for minor public-safety infractions like speeding or jaywalking. And although such public-safety laws may

not contain exceptions for self-defense, it is inconceivable that the threat of a jaywalking ticket would deter someone from disregarding a "Do Not Walk" sign in order to flee an attacker, or that the Government would enforce those laws under such circumstances. Likewise, we do not think that a law imposing a 5-shilling fine and forfeiture of the gun would have prevented a person in the founding era from using a gun to protect himself or his family from violence, or that if he did so the law would be enforced against him. The District law, by contrast, far from imposing a minor fine, threatens citizens with a year in prison (five years for a second violation) for even obtaining a gun in the first place. See D. C. Code §7-2507.06.

JUSTICE BREYER moves on to make a broad jurisprudential point: He criticizes us for declining to establish a level of scrutiny for evaluating Second Amendment restrictions. He proposes, explicitly at least, none of the traditionally expressed levels (strict scrutiny, intermediate scrutiny, rational basis), but rather a judge-empowering "interest-balancing inquiry" that "asks whether the statute burdens a protected interest in a way or to an extent that is out of proportion to the statute's salutary effects upon other important governmental interests." *Post*, at 10. After an exhaustive discussion of the arguments for and against gun control, JUSTICE BREYER arrives at his interest-balanced answer: because handgun violence is a problem, because the law is limited to an urban area, and because there were somewhat similar restrictions in the founding period (a false proposition that we have already discussed), the interest-balancing inquiry results in the constitutionality of the handgun ban. QED.

We know of no other enumerated constitutional right whose core protection has been subjected to a freestanding "interest-balancing" approach. The very enumeration of the right takes out of the hands of government—even the Third Branch of Government—the power to decide on a case-by-case basis whether the right is *really worth* insisting upon. A constitutional guarantee subject to future judges' assessments of its usefulness is no constitutional guarantee at all. Constitutional rights are enshrined with the scope they were understood to have when the people adopted them, whether or not future legislatures or (yes) even future judges think that scope too broad. We would not apply an "interest-balancing" approach to the prohibition of a peaceful neo-Nazi march through Skokie. See *National Socialist Party of America v. Skokie*, 432 U.S. 43 (1977) *(per curiam)*. The First Amendment contains the freedom-of-speech guarantee that the people ratified, which included exceptions for obscenity, libel, and disclosure of state secrets, but not for the expression of extremely unpopular and wrong-headed views. The Second Amendment is no different. Like the First, it is the very *product* of an interest-balancing by the people—which JUSTICE BREYER would now conduct for them anew. And whatever else it leaves to future evaluation, it surely elevates above all other interests the right of law-abiding, responsible citizens to use arms in defense of hearth and home.

JUSTICE BREYER chides us for leaving so many applications of the right to keep and bear arms in doubt, and for not providing extensive historical justification for those regulations of the right that we describe as permissible. See *post,* at 42–43. But since this case represents this Court's first in-depth examination of the Second Amendment, one should not expect it to clarify the entire field, any more than *Reynolds v. United States,* 98 U.S. 145 (1879), our first in-depth Free Exercise Clause case, left that area in a state of utter certainty. And there will be time enough to expound upon the historical justifications for the exceptions we have mentioned if and when those exceptions come before us.

In sum, we hold that the District's ban on handgun possession in the home violates the Second Amendment, as does its prohibition against rendering any lawful firearm in the home operable for the purpose of immediate self-defense. Assuming that Heller is not disqualified from the exercise of Second Amendment rights, the District must permit him to register his handgun and must issue him a license to carry it in the home.

✦

We are aware of the problem of handgun violence in this country, and we take seriously the concerns raised by the many *amici* who believe that prohibition of handgun ownership is a solution. The Constitution leaves the District of Columbia a variety of tools for combating that problem, including some measures regulating handguns, see *supra,* at 54–55, and n. 26. But the enshrinement of constitutional rights necessarily takes certain policy choices off the table. These include the absolute prohibition of handguns held and used for self-defense in the home. Undoubtedly some think that the Second Amendment is outmoded in a society where our standing army is the pride of our Nation, where well-trained police forces provide personal security, and where gun violence is a serious problem. That is perhaps debatable, but what is not debatable is that it is not the role of this Court to pronounce the Second Amendment extinct.

We affirm the judgment of the Court of Appeals.

It is so ordered.

Notes

[1.] As for the "hundreds of judges," *post,* at 2, who have relied on the view of the Second Amendment JUSTICE STEVENS claims we endorsed in *Miller:* If so, they overread *Miller.* And their erroneous reliance upon an uncontested and virtually unreasoned case cannot nullify the reliance of millions of Americans (as our historical analysis has shown) upon the true meaning of the right to keep and bear arms. In any event, it should not be thought that the cases decided by these judges would necessarily have come out differently under a proper interpretation of the right.

[2.] *Miller* was briefly mentioned in our decision in *Lewis v. United States,* 445 U.S. 55 (1980), an appeal from a conviction for being a felon in possession of a firearm. The challenge was based on the contention that the prior felony conviction had been unconstitutional. No Second Amendment claim was raised or briefed by any party. In the course of rejecting the asserted challenge, the Court commented gratuitously, in a footnote, that "[t]hese legislative restrictions on the use of firearms are neither based upon constitutionally suspect criteria, nor do they trench upon any constitutionally protected liberties. See *United States v. Miller* . . . (the Second Amendment guarantees no right to keep and bear a firearm that does not have 'some reasonable relationship to the preservation or efficiency of a well regulated militia')." *Id.,* at 65–66, n. 8. The footnote then cites several Court of Appeals cases to the same effect. It is inconceivable that we would rest our interpretation of the basic meaning of any guarantee of the Bill of Rights upon such a footnoted dictum in a case where the point was not at issue and was not argued.

[3.] We identify these presumptively lawful regulatory measures only as examples; our list does not purport to be exhaustive.

[4.] JUSTICE BREYEE correctly notes that this law, like almost all laws, would pass rational-basis scrutiny. *Post,* at 8. But rational-basis scrutiny is a mode of analysis we have used when evaluating laws under constitutional commands that are themselves prohibitions on irrational laws. See, *e.g., Engquist v. Oregon Dept. of Agriculture,* 553 U.S. ___, ___ (2008) (slip op., at 9–10). In those cases, "rational basis" is not just the standard of scrutiny, but the very substance of the constitutional guarantee. Obviously, the same test could not be used to evaluate the extent to which a legislature may regulate a specific, enumerated right, be it the freedom of speech, the guarantee against double jeopardy, the right to counsel, or the right to keep and bear arms. See *United States v. Carolene Products Co.,* 304 U.S. 144, 152, n. 4 (1938) ("There may be narrower scope for operation of the presumption of constitutionality [*i.e.,* narrower than that provided by rational-basis review] when legislation appears on its face to be within a specific prohibition of the Constitution, such as those of the first ten amendments. . ."). If all that was required to overcome the right to keep and bear arms was a rational basis, the Second Amendment would be redundant with the separate constitutional prohibitions on irrational laws, and would have no effect.

[5.] *McIntosh* upheld the law against a claim that it violated the Equal Protection Clause by arbitrarily distinguishing between residences and businesses. See 395 A. 2d, at 755. One of the rational bases listed for that distinction was the legislative finding "that for each intruder stopped by a firearm there are four gun-related accidents within the home." *Ibid.* That tradeoff would not bear mention if the statute did not prevent stopping intruders by firearms.

[6.] The Supreme Court of Pennsylvania described the amount of five shillings in a contract matter in 1792 as "nominal consideration." *Morris's Lessee v. Smith,* 4 Dall. 119, 120 (Pa. 1792). Many of the laws cited punished violation with fines in a similar amount; the 1783 Massachusetts gunpowder-storage law carried a somewhat larger fine of £10 (200 shillings) and forfeiture of the weapon.

ANTONIN SCALIA is an associate justice of the U.S. Supreme Court. He taught law at the University of Virginia, the American Enterprise Institute, Georgetown University, and the University of Chicago before being nominated to the U.S. Court of Appeals by President Ronald Reagan in 1982. He served in that capacity until he was nominated by Reagan to the Supreme Court in 1986.

John Paul Stevens

 **NO**

Dissenting Opinion, *District of Columbia, et al., v. Heller*

JUSTICE STEVENS, with whom JUSTICE SOUTER, JUSTICE GINSBURG, and JUSTICE BREYER join, dissenting.

The question presented by this case is not whether the Second Amendment protects a "collective right" or an "individual right." Surely it protects a right that can be enforced by individuals. But a conclusion that the Second Amendment protects an individual right does not tell us anything about the scope of that right.

Guns are used to hunt, for self-defense, to commit crimes, for sporting activities, and to perform military duties. The Second Amendment plainly does not protect the right to use a gun to rob a bank; it is equally clear that it *does* encompass the right to use weapons for certain military purposes. Whether it also protects the right to possess and use guns for nonmilitary purposes like hunting and personal self-defense is the question presented by this case. The text of the Amendment, its history, and our decision in *United States v. Miller,* 307 U.S. 174 (1939), provide a clear answer to that question.

The Second Amendment was adopted to protect the right of the people of each of the several States to maintain a well-regulated militia. It was a response to concerns raised during the ratification of the Constitution that the power of Congress to disarm the state militias and create a national standing army posed an intolerable threat to the sovereignty of the several States. Neither the text of the Amendment nor the arguments advanced by its proponents evidenced the slightest interest in limiting any legislature's authority to regulate private civilian uses of firearms. Specifically, there is no indication that the Framers of the Amendment intended to enshrine the common-law right of self-defense in the Constitution.

In 1934, Congress enacted the National Firearms Act, the first major federal firearms law. Upholding a conviction under that Act, this Court held that, "[i]n the absence of any evidence tending to show that possession or use of a 'shotgun having a barrel of less than eighteen inches in length' at this time has some reasonable relationship to

the preservation or efficiency of a well regulated militia, we cannot say that the Second Amendment guarantees the right to keep and bear such an instrument." *Miller,* 307 U.S., at 178. The view of the Amendment we took in *Miller*—that it protects the right to keep and bear arms for certain military purposes, but that it does not curtail the Legislature's power to regulate the nonmilitary use and ownership of weapons—is both the most natural reading of the Amendment's text and the interpretation most faithful to the history of its adoption.

Since our decision in *Miller,* hundreds of judges have relied on the view of the Amendment we endorsed there;[1] we ourselves affirmed it in 1980. See *Lewis v. United States,* 445 U.S. 55, 65–66, n. 8 (1980).[2] No new evidence has surfaced since 1980 supporting the view that the Amendment was intended to curtail the power of Congress to regulate civilian use or misuse of weapons. Indeed, a review of the drafting history of the Amendment demonstrates that its Framers *rejected* proposals that would have broadened its coverage to include such uses.

The opinion the Court announces today fails to identify any new evidence supporting the view that the Amendment was intended to limit the power of Congress to regulate civilian uses of weapons. Unable to point to any such evidence, the Court stakes its holding on a strained and unpersuasive reading of the Amendment's text; significantly different provisions in the 1689 English Bill of Rights, and in various 19th-century State Constitutions; postenactment commentary that was available to the Court when it decided *Miller;* and, ultimately, a feeble attempt to distinguish *Miller* that places more emphasis on the Court's decisional process than on the reasoning in the opinion itself.

Even if the textual and historical arguments on both sides of the issue were evenly balanced, respect for the well-settled views of all of our predecessors on this Court, and for the rule of law itself, see *Mitchell v. W. T. Grant Co.,* 416 U.S. 600, 636 (1974) (Stewart, J., dissenting), would prevent most jurists from endorsing such a dramatic upheaval in the law.[3] As Justice Cardozo observed years ago, the "labor of judges would be increased almost to the breaking point if every past decision could be reopened in every case, and one could not lay one's own course of bricks on the secure foundation of the courses laid by others who had gone before him." The Nature of the Judicial Process 149 (1921).

In this dissent I shall first explain why our decision in *Miller* was faithful to the text of the Second Amendment and the purposes revealed in its drafting history. I shall then comment on the postratification history of the Amendment, which makes abundantly clear that the Amendment should not be interpreted as limiting the authority of Congress to regulate the use or possession of firearms for purely civilian purposes. . . .

II

The proper allocation of military power in the new Nation was an issue of central concern for the Framers. The compromises they ultimately reached, reflected in Article I's Militia Clauses and the Second Amendment, represent quintessential examples of the Framers' "splitting the atom of sovereignty."[4]

Two themes relevant to our current interpretive task ran through the debates on the original Constitution. "On the one hand, there was a widespread fear that a national standing Army posed an intolerable threat to individual liberty and to the sovereignty of the separate States." *Perpich v. Department of Defense,* 496 U.S. 334, 340 (1990).[5] Governor Edmund Randolph, reporting on the Constitutional Convention to the Virginia Ratification Convention, explained: "With respect to a standing army, I believe there was not a member in the federal Convention, who did not feel indignation at such an institution." 3 J. Elliot, Debates in the Several State Conventions on the Adoption of the Federal Constitution 401 (2d ed. 1863) (hereinafter Elliot). On the other hand, the Framers recognized the dangers inherent in relying on inadequately trained militia members "as the primary means of providing for the common defense," *Perpich,* 496 U.S., at 340; during the Revolutionary War, "[t]his force, though armed, was largely untrained, and its deficiencies were the subject of bitter complaint." Wiener, The Militia Clause of the Constitution, 54 Harv. L. Rev. 181, 182 (1940).[6] In order to respond to those twin concerns, a compromise was reached: Congress would be authorized to raise and support a national Army and Navy, and also to organize, arm, discipline, and provide for the calling forth of "the Militia." U.S. Const., Art. I, §8, cls. 12–16. The President,

at the same time, was empowered as the "Commander in Chief of the Army and Navy of the United States, and of the Militia of the several States, when called into the actual Service of the United States." Art. II, §2. But, with respect to the militia, a significant reservation was made to the States: Although Congress would have the power to call forth, organize, arm, and discipline the militia, as well as to govern "such Part of them as may be employed in the Service of the United States," the States respectively would retain the right to appoint the officers and to train the militia in accordance with the discipline prescribed by Congress. Art. I, §8, cl. 16.

But the original Constitution's retention of the militia and its creation of divided authority over that body did not prove sufficient to allay fears about the dangers posed by a standing army. For it was perceived by some that Article I contained a significant gap: While it empowered Congress to organize, arm, and discipline the militia, it did not prevent Congress from providing for the militia's disarmament. As George Mason argued during the debates in Virginia on the ratification of the original Constitution:

> "The militia may be here destroyed by that method which has been practiced in other parts of the world before; that is, by rendering them useless—by disarming them. Under various pretences, Congress may neglect to provide for arming and disciplining the militia; and the state governments cannot do it, for Congress has the exclusive right to arm them." . . .

This sentiment was echoed at a number of state ratification conventions; indeed, it was one of the primary objections to the original Constitution voiced by its opponents. The Anti-Federalists were ultimately unsuccessful in persuading state ratification conventions to condition their approval of the Constitution upon the eventual inclusion of any particular amendment. But a number of States did propose to the first Federal Congress amendments reflecting a desire to ensure that the institution of the militia would remain protected under the new Government. The proposed amendments sent by the States of Virginia, North Carolina, and New York focused on the importance of preserving the state militias and reiterated the dangers posed by standing armies. New Hampshire sent a proposal that differed significantly from the others; while also invoking the dangers of a standing army, it suggested that the Constitution should more broadly protect the use and possession of weapons, without tying such a guarantee expressly to the maintenance of the militia. The States of Maryland, Pennsylvania, and Massachusetts sent no relevant proposed amendments to Congress, but in each of those States a minority of the delegates advocated related amendments. While the Maryland minority proposals were exclusively concerned with standing armies and conscientious objectors, the unsuccessful proposals in both Massachusetts and Pennsylvania would have protected a more broadly worded right, less clearly tied to service in a state militia. Faced with all of these options, it is telling that James Madison chose to craft the Second Amendment as he did.

The relevant proposals sent by the Virginia Ratifying Convention read as follows:

> "17th, That the people have a right to keep and bear arms; that a well regulated Militia composed of the body of the people trained to arms is the proper, natural and safe defence of a free State. That standing armies are dangerous to liberty, and therefore ought to be avoided, as far as the circumstances and protection of the Community will admit; and that in all cases the military should be under strict subordination to and be governed by the civil power." Elliot 659.
>
> "19th. That any person religiously scrupulous of bearing arms ought to be exempted, upon payment of an equivalent to employ another to bear arms in his stead." *Ibid.*

North Carolina adopted Virginia's proposals and sent them to Congress as its own, although it did not actually ratify the original Constitution until Congress had sent the proposed Bill of Rights to the States for ratification. . . .

New York produced a proposal with nearly identical language. It read:

> "That the people have a right to keep and bear Arms; that a well regulated Militia, including the body of the People capable of bearing Arms, is the proper, natural, and safe defence of a free State. . . . That standing Armies, in time of Peace, are dangerous to Liberty, and ought not to be kept up, except in Cases of necessity; and that at all times, the Military should be kept under strict Subordination to the civil Power." 2 Schwartz 912.

Notably, each of these proposals used the phrase "keep and bear arms," which was eventually adopted by Madison. And each proposal embedded the phrase within a group of principles that are distinctly military in meaning. . . .

Madison, charged with the task of assembling the proposals for amendments sent by the ratifying States, was the principal draftsman of the Second Amendment.

He had before him, or at the very least would have been aware of, all of these proposed formulations. In addition, Madison had been a member, some years earlier, of the committee tasked with drafting the Virginia Declaration of Rights. That committee considered a proposal by Thomas Jefferson that would have included within the Virginia Declaration the following language: "No freeman shall ever be debarred the use of arms [within his own lands or tenements]." 1 Papers of Thomas Jefferson 363 (J. Boyd ed. 1950). But the committee rejected that language, adopting instead the provision drafted by George Mason.[7]

With all of these sources upon which to draw, it is strikingly significant that Madison's first draft omitted any mention of nonmilitary use or possession of weapons. Rather, his original draft repeated the essence of the two proposed amendments sent by Virginia, combining the substance of the two provisions succinctly into one, which read: "The right of the people to keep and bear arms shall not be infringed; a well armed, and well regulated militia being the best security of a free country; but no person religiously scrupulous of bearing arms, shall be compelled to render military service in person." . . .

Madison's decision to model the Second Amendment on the distinctly military Virginia proposal is therefore revealing, since it is clear that he considered and rejected formulations that would have unambiguously protected civilian uses of firearms. When Madison prepared his first draft, and when that draft was debated and modified, it is reasonable to assume that all participants in the drafting process were fully aware of the other formulations that would have protected civilian use and possession of weapons and that their choice to craft the Amendment as they did represented a rejection of those alternative formulations. . . .

The history of the adoption of the Amendment thus describes an overriding concern about the potential threat to state sovereignty that a federal standing army would pose, and a desire to protect the States' militias as the means by which to guard against that danger. But state militias could not effectively check the prospect of a federal standing army so long as Congress retained the power to disarm them, and so a guarantee against such disarmament was needed. As we explained in *Miller*: "With obvious purpose to assure the continuation and render possible the effectiveness of such forces the declaration and guarantee of the Second Amendment were made. It must be interpreted and applied with that end in view." 307 U.S., at 178. The evidence plainly refutes the claim that the Amendment was motivated by the Framers' fears that Congress might act to regulate any civilian uses of weapons. And even if the historical record were genuinely ambiguous, the burden would remain on the parties advocating a change in the law to introduce facts or arguments "'newly ascertained,'" *Vasquez,* 474 U.S., at 266; the Court is unable to identify any such facts or arguments. . . .

[F]or most of our history, the invalidity of Second-Amendment-based objections to firearms regulations has been well settled and uncontroversial. Indeed, the Second Amendment was not even mentioned in either full House of Congress during the legislative proceedings that led to the passage of the 1934 Act. Yet enforcement of that law produced the judicial decision that confirmed the status of the Amendment as limited in reach to military usage. After reviewing many of the same sources that are discussed at greater length by the Court today, the *Miller* Court unanimously concluded that the Second Amendment did not apply to the possession of a firearm that did not have "some reasonable relationship to the preservation or efficiency of a well regulated militia." 307 U.S., at 178.

The key to that decision did not, as the Court belatedly suggests, . . . turn on the difference between muskets and sawed-off shotguns; it turned, rather, on the basic difference between the military and nonmilitary use and possession of guns. Indeed, if the Second Amendment were not limited in its coverage to military uses of weapons, why should the Court in *Miller* have suggested that some weapons but not others were eligible for Second Amendment protection? If use for self-defense were the relevant standard, why did the Court not inquire into the suitability of a particular weapon for self-defense purposes? . . .

The Court is simply wrong when it intones that *Miller* contained *"not a word"* about the Amendment's history. . . . The Court plainly looked to history to construe the term "Militia," and, on the best reading of *Miller,* the entire guarantee of the Second Amendment. After noting the original Constitution's grant of power to Congress and to the States over the militia, the Court explained:

> "With obvious purpose to assure the continuation and render possible the effectiveness of such forces the declaration and guarantee of the Second Amendment were made. It must be interpreted and applied with that end in view.
>
> "The Militia which the States were expected to maintain and train is set in contrast with Troops which they were forbidden to keep without the consent of Congress. The sentiment of the time strongly disfavored standing armies; the common view was that adequate defense of country

and laws could be secured through the Militia—civilians primarily, soldiers on occasion.

> "The signification attributed to the term Militia appears from the debates in the Convention, the history and legislation of Colonies and States, and the writings of approved commentators." *Miller,* 307 U.S., at 178–179.

The majority cannot seriously believe that the *Miller* Court did not consider any relevant evidence; the majority simply does not approve of the conclusion the *Miller* Court reached on that evidence. Standing alone, that is insufficient reason to disregard a unanimous opinion of this Court, upon which substantial reliance has been placed by legislators and citizens for nearly 70 years.

V

The Court concludes its opinion by declaring that it is not the proper role of this Court to change the meaning of rights "enshrine[d]" in the Constitution. *Ante,* at 64. But the right the Court announces was not "enshrined" in the Second Amendment by the Framers; it is the product of today's law-changing decision. The majority's exegesis has utterly failed to establish that as a matter of text or history, "the right of law-abiding, responsible citizens to use arms in defense of hearth and home" is "elevate[d] above all other interests" by the Second Amendment. . . .

Until today, it has been understood that legislatures may regulate the civilian use and misuse of firearms so long as they do not interfere with the preservation of a well-regulated militia. The Court's announcement of a new constitutional right to own and use firearms for private purposes upsets that settled understanding, but leaves for future cases the formidable task of defining the scope of permissible regulations. Today judicial craftsmen have confidently asserted that a policy choice that denies a "law-abiding, responsible citize[n]" the right to keep and use weapons in the home for self-defense is "off the table." . . . Given the presumption that most citizens are law abiding, and the reality that the need to defend oneself may suddenly arise in a host of locations outside the home, I fear that the District's policy choice may well be just the first of an unknown number of dominoes to be knocked off the table.

I do not know whether today's decision will increase the labor of federal judges to the "breaking point" envisioned by Justice Cardozo, but it will surely give rise to a far more active judicial role in making vitally important national policy decisions than was envisioned at any time in the 18th, 19th, or 20th centuries.

The Court properly disclaims any interest in evaluating the wisdom of the specific policy choice challenged in this case, but it fails to pay heed to a far more important policy choice—the choice made by the Framers themselves. The Court would have us believe that over 200 years ago, the Framers made a choice to limit the tools available to elected officials wishing to regulate civilian uses of weapons, and to authorize this Court to use the common-law process of case-by-case judicial lawmaking to define the contours of acceptable gun control policy. Absent compelling evidence that is nowhere to be found in the Court's opinion, I could not possibly conclude that the Framers made such a choice.

For these reasons, I respectfully dissent.

Notes

[1.] Until the Fifth Circuit's decision in *United States v. Emerson*, 270 F. 3d 203 (2001), every Court of Appeals to consider the question had understood *Miller* to hold that the Second Amendment does not protect the right to possess and use guns for purely private, civilian purposes. See, *e.g., United States v. Haney*, 264 F. 3d 1161, 1164–1166 (CA10 2001); *United States v. Napier*, 233 F. 3d 394, 402–404 (CA6 2000); *Gillespie v. Indianapolis*, 185 F. 3d 693, 710–711 (CA7 1999); *United States v. Scanio*, No. 97-1584, 1998 WL 802060, *2 (CA2, Nov. 12, 1998) (unpublished opinion); *United States v. Wright*, 117 F. 3d 1265, 1271–1274 (CA11 1997); *United States v. Rybar*, 103 F. 3d 273, 285–286 (CA3 1996); *Hickman v. Block*, 81 F. 3d 98, 100–103 (CA9 1996); *United States v. Hale*, 978 F. 2d 1016, 1018–1020 (CA8 1992); *Thomas v. City Council of Portland*, 730 F. 3d 41, 42 (CA1 1984) *(per curiam); United States v. Johnson*, 497 F. 2d 548, 550 (CA4 1974) *(per curiam); United States v. Johnson*, 441 F. 2d 1134, 1136 (CA5 1971); see also *Sandidge v. United States*, 520 A. 2d 1057, 1058–1059 (DC App. 1987). And a number of courts have remained firm in their prior positions, even after considering *Emerson*. See, *e.g., United States v. Lippman*, 369 F. 3d 1039, 1043–1045 (CA8 2004); *United States v. Parker*, 362 F. 3d 1279, 1282–1284 (CA10 2004); *United States v. Jackubowski*, 63 Fed. Appx. 959, 961 (CA7 2003) (unpublished opinion); *Silveira v. Lockyer*, 312 F. 3d 1052, 1060–1066 (CA9 2002);. *United States v. Milheron*, 231 F. Supp. 2d 376, 378 (Me.

2002); *Bach v. Pataki*, 289 F. Supp. 2d 217, 224–226 (NDNY 2003); *United States v. Smith*, 56 M. J. 711, 716 (C. A. Armed Forces 2001).

[2.] Our discussion in *Lewis* was brief but significant. Upholding a conviction for receipt of a firearm by a felon, we wrote: "These legislative restrictions on the use of firearms are neither based upon constitutionally suspect criteria, nor do they entrench upon any constitutionally protected liberties. See *United States v. Miller*, 307 U.S. 174, 178 (1939) (the Second Amendment guarantees no right to keep and bear a firearm that does not have 'some reasonable relationship to the preservation or efficiency of a well regulated militia')." 445 U.S., at 65, n. 8.

[3.] See *Vasquez v. Hillery*, 474 U.S. 254, 265, 266 (1986) ("*[Stare decisis]* permits society to presume that bedrock principles are founded in the law rather than in the proclivities of individuals, and thereby contributes to the integrity of our constitutional system of government, both in appearance and in fact. While *stare decisis* is not an inexorable command, the careful observer will discern that any detours from the straight path of *stare decisis* in our past have occurred for articulable reasons, and only when the Court has felt obliged 'to bring its opinions into agreement with experience and with facts newly ascertained.' *Burnet v. Coronado Oil & Gas Co.*, 285 U.S. 393, 412 (1932) (Brandeis, J., dissenting)"); *Pollock v. Farmers' Loan & Trust Co.*, 157 U.S. 429, 652 (1895) (White, J., dissenting) ("The fundamental conception of a judicial body is that of one hedged about by precedents which are binding on the court without regard to the personality of its members. Break down this belief in judicial continuity and let it be felt that on great constitutional questions this Court is to depart from the settled conclusions of its predecessors, and to determine them all according to the mere opinion of those who temporarily fill its bench, and our Constitution will, in my judgment, be bereft of value and become a most dangerous instrument to the rights and liberties of the people").

[4.] By "'splitt[ing] the atom of sovereignty,'" the Framers created "'two political capacities, one state and one federal, each protected from incursion by the other. The resulting Constitution created a legal system unprecedented in form and design, establishing two orders of government, each with its own direct relationship, its own privity, its own set of mutual rights and obligations to the people who sustain it and are governed by it.'" *Saenz v. Roe*, 526 U.S. 489, 504, n. 17 (1999) (quoting *U.S. Term Limits, Inc. v. Thornton*, 514 U.S. 779, 838 (1995) (KENNEDY, J., concurring)).

[5.] Indeed, this was one of the grievances voiced by the colonists: Paragraph 13 of the Declaration of Independence charged of King George, "He has kept among us, in times of peace, Standing Armies without the Consent of our legislatures."

[6.] George Washington, writing to Congress on September 24, 1776, warned that for Congress "[t]o place any dependance upon Militia, is, assuredly, resting upon a broken staff." 6 Writings of George Washington 106, 110 (J. Fitzpatrick ed. 1932). Several years later he reiterated this view in another letter to Congress: "Regular Troops alone are equal to the exigencies of modern war, as well for defence as offence. . . . *No Militia* will ever acquire the habits necessary to resist a regular force. . . . The firmness requisite for the real business of fighting is only to be attained by a constant course of discipline and service." 20 *id.*, at 49, 49–50 (Sept. 15, 1780). And Alexander Hamilton argued this view in many debates. In 1787, he wrote:

"Here I expect we shall be told that the militia of the country is its natural bulwark, and would be at all times equal to the national defense. This doctrine, in substance, had like to have lost us our independence. . . . War, like most other things, is a science to be acquired and perfected by diligence, by perseverance, by time, and by practice." The Federalist No. 25, p. 166 (C. Rossiter ed. 1961).

[7.] The adopted language, Virginia Declaration of Rights ¶13 (1776), read as follows: "That a well-regulated Militia, composed of the body of the people, trained to arms, is the proper, natural, and safe defence of a free State; that Standing Armies, in time of peace, should be avoided as dangerous to liberty; and that, in all cases, the military should be under strict subordination to, and governed by, the civil power." 1 Schwartz 234.

JOHN PAUL STEVENS retired as an associate justice of the U.S. Supreme Court in June 2010. He worked in law firms in Chicago, Illinois, for 20 years before being nominated by President Richard Nixon to the U.S. Court of Appeals in 1970. He served in that capacity until he was nominated to the Supreme Court by President Gerald Ford in 1975.

EXPLORING THE ISSUE

Is There a Constitutional Right to Possess a Firearm for Private Use?

Critical Thinking and Reflection

1. Explain the Second Amendment and what Justice Scalia meant when he wrote that these rights were limited.
2. What was the majority view about the right to own guns when one is not a military person? How was this view different from that of the minority?
3. Why was Justice Scalia's rationale for not banning handguns based on their popularity?
4. How was the ratification of the Second Amendment related to the historical events of the time? What were states worried about?
5. Compare Justice Stevens' view that Second Amendment-based objections to firearms control are invalid with that of Justice Scalia.

Is There Common Ground?

The United States has a population of over 300 million persons, and there are approximately 300 million guns owned by civilians. About 100 million of these guns are handguns. It is estimated that 40–45 percent (47–53 million) of households have a gun. Currently, gun ownership is a particularly controversial and polarizing topic for several reasons. There have been highly publicized shootings in Newtown, Connecticut, and Aurora, Colorado, with killings of school children and persons attending a movie. Estimates are that over 90 percent of the public is in favor of greater use of background checks for persons attempting to purchase a gun. In April 2013, the Senate voted on three bills, one for background checks, one involving mental health, and one concerning gun-trafficking. Each received more than 50 votes but none received the 60 votes necessary for passage.

According to a recent Institute of Medicine report, "the U.S. rate of firearm-related homicide is higher than that of any other industrialized country: 19.5 times higher than the rates in other high-income countries." In the absence of congressional action, President Obama has issued several executive orders to promote sharing of information among states and promote a greater focus on prevention, such as locks and some technological approaches that would allow a gun to be used only by a particular owner. Most significantly, he has ordered the Centers for Disease Control and Prevention (CDC) to begin funding gun-violence research. In 1996, at the urging of the National Rifle Association, Congress banned CDC funding for any research to "advocate or promote gun control." This led to a reduction in funding for gun-violence research from $2.5 million per year in the early 1990s to $100,000 per year today.

Additional Resources

Saul Cornell, *A Well-Regulated Militia: The Founding Fathers and the Origins of Gun Control in America* (Oxford University Press, 2008).

Institute of Medicine, *Priorities for Research to Reduce the Threat of Firearm-Related Violence*, June 5, 2013.

Joyce Lee Malcolm, *To Keep and Bear Arms: The Origins of an Anglo-American Right* (Harvard University Press, 1996).

Internet References . . .

Audio of the Oral Argument in *District of Columbia v. Heller*

www.intellectualtakeout.org/library/video-podcast
-media/audio-district-columbia-v-heller-oral
-arguments

Transcript of the Oral Argument in *District of Columbia v. Heller*

www.supremecourt.gov/oral_arguments/argument
_transcripts/07-290.pdf

Pew Research Center, "Gun Control: Key Data Points from Pew Research" (June 10, 2013)

www.pewresearch.org/key-data-points/gun-control
-key-data-points-from-pew-research/

Becky Bowers, Angie Drobnic Holan, Louis Jacobson, "Special Report: Examining the State of Gun Research"

www.politifact.com/truth-o-meter/article/2013/apr/26
/special-report-examining-state-gun-research/

Selected, Edited, and with Issue Framing Material by:
M. Ethan Katsh, *University of Massachusetts, Amherst*

ISSUE

Are Blanket Prohibitions on Cross Burnings Unconstitutional?

YES: Sandra Day O'Connor, from "Plurality Opinion, *Virginia v. Black*," *United States Supreme Court* (2003)

NO: Clarence Thomas, from "Dissenting Opinion, *Virginia v. Black*," *United States Supreme Court* (2003)

Learning Outcomes

After reading this issue, you will be able to:

- Discuss the origins and history of the Ku Klux Klan's use of cross burning.
- Identify under what circumstances cross burning can be prohibited.
- Distinguish the different results involving cross burning statutes in *R.A.V. v. City of St. Paul* and *Virginia v. Black*.
- Discuss the application and regulation of symbolic conduct under the First Amendment.

ISSUE SUMMARY

YES: Supreme Court Justice Sandra Day O'Connor argues that part of a Virginia statute proscribing cross burning with the intent to intimidate is constitutional because it is content discrimination based on the very reasons that make it constitutional; however, part of the statute is unconstitutional insofar as it requires an inference of intent to intimidate solely based on the action of cross burning itself, which is symbolic speech.

NO: Supreme Court Justice Clarence Thomas disagrees with part of the statute being held unconstitutional, arguing that the history and nature of cross burning in the United States inextricably links the act to threatening and menacing violence and that the intent to intimidate can therefore be inferred solely from the act of cross burning itself.

We do not live in tranquil, quiet, and harmonious times. Terrorism, as a domestic threat, is a fairly new challenge for the United States. Hate crimes, however, have occurred throughout the nation's history. The Community Relations Service of the U.S. Department of Justice has defined hate crime as "the violence of intolerance and bigotry, intended to hurt and intimidate someone because of their race, ethnicity, national origin, religion, sexual orientation, or disability."

Since 1991 the Hate Crimes Statistics Act has required the FBI to keep statistics on hate crimes. In general, these crimes are not separate, distinct crimes but traditional offenses, such as assault, that are motivated by the offender's bias. The following readings, which are from a case involving cross burning, focus on a criminal statute that explicitly targets bias activities.

In the United States, among the few categories of speech that can be constitutionally prohibited are "fighting words," defined by the Supreme Court as statements "which by their very utterance inflict injury or tend to incite an immediate breach of the peace" (see *Chaplinsky v. New Hampshire,* 315 U.S. 568, 1942). The "fighting words" exception applies not only to actual speech but also to "symbolic" speech, actions that are not speech per se but convey certain messages and thus, the Supreme Court has held, deserve the same First Amendment protection as audible words. Because of the importance of free speech to political discourse and debate, the "fighting words" prohibition has been narrowly construed throughout its history. The government can only prohibit speech that constitutes an immediate threat, and even calls for violence may be permissible if they are rhetorical in nature and will probably not incite any actual violence.

In *R. A. V. v. City of St. Paul,* 505 U.S. 377 (1992), the Supreme Court applied the "fighting words" doctrine to one particularly controversial form of symbolic speech: cross burning. St. Paul, Minnesota, had passed a city ordinance that outlawed "plac[ing] on public or private property a symbol . . . including, but not limited to, a burning cross or Nazi swastika, which one knows or has reasonable grounds to know arouses anger, alarm or resentment in others on the basis of race, color, creed, religion or gender." The Supreme Court struck down the ordinance, ruling that to be constitutionally permissible, speech codes regulating "fighting words" must address only the *outcome* of the speech: whether it is foreseeable that the speech will make others feel threatened or encourage physical violence. Writing for the majority, Justice Antonin Scalia noted that "[t]he First Amendment generally prevents government from proscribing speech . . . or even expressive conduct [i.e., symbolic speech] . . . because of disapproval of the ideas expressed. Content-based regulations are presumptively invalid." According to the majority, the problem with the St. Paul ordinance was that it focused only on speech that "insult[s] or provoke[s] violence, 'on the basis of race, color, creed, religion, or gender.'" To fulfill the demands of content neutrality, however, the ordinance would have to outlaw *all* speech that provoked violence; the ordinance could not specify that some subject matter, such as race or gender, was prohibited, while ignoring, in the words of the Court, "those who wish to use 'fighting words' in connection with other ideas—to express hostility, for example, on the basis of political affiliation, union membership, or homosexuality."

In the case that follows, the Supreme Court once again addresses the constitutionality of laws intended to outlaw cross burnings. Under the *R. A. V.* precedent, legislatures are allowed to outlaw symbolic speech, such as cross burnings, as long as such prohibitions are content-neutral and apply only to speech that constitutes "fighting words" (or one of the other limited categories of speech that fall outside constitutional protection). In *Virginia v. Black,* the Court addresses the question of whether the intent to

intimidate—a prerequisite for establishing "fighting words" status—can be inferred from the nature of the act itself. In so doing, the Court tackles the social history of such acts as cross burning that help define what they stand for in the specific context of twenty-first-century America.

The Court also tackles the philosophical nature of symbolic actions. Among the various forms of "symbolic speech," cross burning straddles the poorly defined line that distinguishes speech from conduct. In the history of the Supreme Court, this distinction has been a central cause of controversy surrounding what does and does not deserve First Amendment protection. According to Justice Thomas, it is one of the key issues in *Virginia v. Black:* He asserts that the majority reaches the wrong conclusion because it refuses to recognize cross burning as "conduct" that the state may constitutionally outlaw. "A conclusion," he writes, "that the statute prohibiting cross burning with intent to intimidate sweeps beyond a prohibition on certain conduct into the zone of expression overlooks not only the words of the statute but also reality."

Justice Thomas's argument suggests one solution: Limit First Amendment protection only to actual speech. Such an approach to the First Amendment might be consistent with its actual words—that "Congress shall make no law . . . abridging the freedom of speech"—but could undermine some of the greater ends that the First Amendment attempts to accomplish, such as allowing citizens to express their objections to government policies with which they disagree.

In some instances, symbolic speech may better express political ideas than actual words ever could. Take, for example, the 1969 case of *Tinker v. Des Moines,* in which the Supreme Court had to consider whether students who wore black armbands to school to protest the Vietnam War were engaging in a form of protected symbolic speech. An important aspect of the Court's decision in favor of the students was that wearing armbands in class was a "silent, passive expression of opinion, unaccompanied by any disorder or disturbance." Actual speech, yelled in the middle of a school class, would probably have been viewed as disruptive; perhaps even creating the type of "breach of the peace" that would make it fall under the "fighting words" exception to the First Amendment. Symbolic speech, by contrast, allowed the students to effectively convey their political views in a calm, peaceful fashion, one that the Supreme Court recognized as precisely the type of dissent that the First Amendment was designed to protect.

YES ↵

Sandra Day O'Connor

Plurality Opinion, *Virginia v. Black*

In this case we consider whether the Commonwealth of Virginia's statute banning cross burning with "an intent to intimidate a person or group of persons" violates the First Amendment. We conclude that while a State, consistent with the First Amendment, may ban cross burning carried out with the intent to intimidate, the provision in the Virginia statute treating any cross burning as prima facie evidence of intent to intimidate renders the statute unconstitutional in its current form.

I

Respondents Barry Black, Richard Elliott, and Jonathan O'Mara were convicted separately of violating Virginia's cross-burning statute, §18.2–423. That statute provides:

> "It shall be unlawful for any person or persons, with the intent of intimidating any person or group of persons, to burn, or cause to be burned, a cross on the property of another, a highway or other public place. Any person who shall violate any provision of this section shall be guilty of a Class 6 felony.
>
> "Any such burning of a cross shall be prima facie evidence of an intent to intimidate a person or group of persons."

On August 22, 1998, Barry Black led a Ku Klux Klan rally in Carroll County, Virginia. Twenty-five to thirty people attended this gathering, which occurred on private property with the permission of the owner, who was in attendance. The property was located on an open field just off Brushy Fork Road (State Highway 690) in Cana, Virginia.

When the sheriff of Carroll County learned that a Klan rally was occurring in his county, he went to observe it from the side of the road. During the approximately one hour that the sheriff was present, about 40 to 50 cars passed the site, a "few" of which stopped to ask the sheriff what was happening on the property. Eight to ten houses were located in the vicinity of the rally. Rebecca Sechrist, who was related to the owner of the property where the rally took place, "sat and watched to see wha[t] [was] going on" from the lawn of her in-laws' house. She looked on as the Klan prepared for the gathering and subsequently conducted the rally itself.

During the rally, Sechrist heard Klan members speak about "what they were" and "what they believed in." The speakers "talked real bad about the blacks and the Mexicans." One speaker told the assembled gathering that "he would love to take a .30/.30 and just random[ly] shoot the blacks." The speakers also talked about "President Clinton and Hillary Clinton," and about how their tax money "goes to . . . the black people." Sechrist testified that this language made her "very . . . scared."

At the conclusion of the rally, the crowd circled around a 25- to 30-foot cross. The cross was between 300 and 350 yards away from the road. According to the sheriff, the cross "then all of a sudden . . . went up in a flame." As the cross burned, the Klan played Amazing Grace over the loudspeakers. Sechrist stated that the cross burning made her feel "awful" and "terrible."

When the sheriff observed the cross burning, he informed his deputy that they needed to "find out who's responsible and explain to them that they cannot do this in the State of Virginia." The sheriff then went down the driveway, entered the rally, and asked "who was responsible for burning the cross." Black responded, "I guess I am because I'm the head of the rally." The sheriff then told Black, "[T]here's a law in the State of Virginia that you cannot burn a cross and I'll have to place you under arrest for this."

Black was charged with burning a cross with the intent of intimidating a person or group of persons, in violation of §18.2-423. At his trial, the jury was instructed that "intent to intimidate means the motivation to intentionally put a person or a group of persons in fear of bodily harm. Such fear must arise from the willful conduct of the accused rather than from some mere temperamental timidity of the victim." The trial court also instructed the jury that "the burning of a cross by itself is sufficient

From Supreme Court of the United States, April 7, 2003.

evidence from which you may infer the required intent." When Black objected to this last instruction on First Amendment grounds, the prosecutor responded that the instruction was "taken straight out of the [Virginia] Model Instructions." The jury found Black guilty, and fined him $2,500. The Court of Appeals of Virginia affirmed Black's conviction.

On May 2, 1998, respondents Richard Elliott and Jonathan O'Mara, as well as a third individual, attempted to burn a cross on the yard of James Jubilee. Jubilee, an African-American, was Elliott's next-door neighbor in Virginia Beach, Virginia. Four months prior to the incident, Jubilee and his family had moved from California to Virginia Beach. Before the cross burning, Jubilee spoke to Elliott's mother to inquire about shots being fired from behind the Elliott home. Elliott's mother explained to Jubilee that her son shot firearms as a hobby, and that he used the backyard as a firing range.

On the night of May 2, respondents drove a truck onto Jubilee's property, planted a cross, and set it on fire. Their apparent motive was to "get back" at Jubilee for complaining about the shooting in the backyard. Respondents were not affiliated with the Klan. The next morning, as Jubilee was pulling his car out of the driveway, he noticed the partially burned cross approximately 20 feet from his house. After seeing the cross, Jubilee was "very nervous" because he "didn't know what would be the next phase," and because "a cross burned in your yard . . . tells you that it's just the first round."

Elliott and O'Mara were charged with attempted cross burning and conspiracy to commit cross burning. O'Mara pleaded guilty to both counts, reserving the right to challenge the constitutionality of the cross-burning statute. The judge sentenced O'Mara to 90 days in jail and fined him $2,500. The judge also suspended 45 days of the sentence and $1,000 of the fine.

At Elliott's trial, the judge originally ruled that the jury would be instructed "that the burning of a cross by itself is sufficient evidence from which you may infer the required intent." At trial, however, the court instructed the jury that the Commonwealth must prove that "the defendant intended to commit cross burning," that "the defendant did a direct act toward the commission of the cross burning," and that "the defendant had the intent of intimidating any person or group of persons." The court did not instruct the jury on the meaning of the word "intimidate," nor on the prima facie evidence provision of §18.2-423. The jury found Elliott guilty of attempted cross burning and acquitted him of conspiracy to commit cross burning. It sentenced Elliott to 90 days

in jail and a $2,500 fine. The Court of Appeals of Virginia affirmed the convictions of both Elliott and O'Mara.

Each respondent appealed to the Supreme Court of Virginia, arguing that §18.2-423 is facially unconstitutional. The Supreme Court of Virginia consolidated all three cases, and held that the statute is unconstitutional on its face. It held that the Virginia cross-burning statute "is analytically indistinguishable from the ordinance found unconstitutional in *R. A. V. [v. St. Paul]*. The Virginia statute, the court held, discriminates on the basis of content since it "selectively chooses only cross burning because of its distinctive message." The court also held that the prima facie evidence provision renders the statute overbroad because "[t]he enhanced probability of prosecution under the statute chills the expression of protected speech."

Three justices dissented, concluding that the Virginia cross-burning statute passes constitutional muster because it proscribes only conduct that constitutes a true threat. The justices noted that unlike the ordinance found unconstitutional in *R. A. V. v. St. Paul,* the Virginia statute does not just target cross burning "on the basis of race, color, creed, religion or gender." Rather, "the Virginia statute applies to any individual who burns a cross for any reason provided the cross is burned with the intent to intimidate." The dissenters also disagreed with the majority's analysis of the prima facie provision because the inference alone "is clearly insufficient to establish beyond a reasonable doubt that a defendant burned a cross with the intent to intimidate." The dissent noted that the burden of proof still remains on the Commonwealth to prove intent to intimidate. We granted certiorari.

II

Cross burning originated in the 14th century as a means for Scottish tribes to signal each other. . . . Cross burning in this country, however, long ago became unmoored from its Scottish ancestry. Burning a cross in the United States is inextricably intertwined with the history of the Ku Klux Klan.

The first Ku Klux Klan began in Pulaski, Tennessee, in the spring of 1866. Although the Ku Klux Klan started as a social club, it soon changed into something far different. The Klan fought Reconstruction and the corresponding drive to allow freed blacks to participate in the political process. Soon the Klan imposed "a veritable reign of terror" throughout the South. The Klan employed tactics such as whipping, threatening to burn people at the stake, and murder. The Klan's victims included blacks, southern whites who disagreed with the Klan, and "carpetbagger" northern whites.

The activities of the Ku Klux Klan prompted legislative action at the national level. In 1871, "President Grant sent a message to Congress indicating that the Klan's reign of terror in the Southern States had rendered life and property insecure." In response, Congress passed what is now known as the Ku Klux Klan Act. President Grant used these new powers to suppress the Klan in South Carolina, the effect of which severely curtailed the Klan in other States as well. By the end of Reconstruction in 1877, the first Klan no longer existed.

The genesis of the second Klan began in 1905, with the publication of Thomas Dixon's The Clansmen: An Historical Romance of the Ku Klux Klan. Dixon's book was a sympathetic portrait of the first Klan, depicting the Klan as a group of heroes "saving" the South from blacks and the "horrors" of Reconstruction. Although the first Klan never actually practiced cross burning, Dixon's book depicted the Klan burning crosses to celebrate the execution of former slaves. Cross burning thereby became associated with the first Ku Klux Klan. When D. W. Griffith turned Dixon's book into the movie The Birth of a Nation in 1915, the association between cross burning and the Klan became indelible. In addition to the cross burnings in the movie, a poster advertising the film displayed a hooded Klansman riding a hooded horse, with his left hand holding the reins of the horse and his right hand holding a burning cross above his head. Soon thereafter, in November 1915, the second Klan began.

From the inception of the second Klan, cross burnings have been used to communicate both threats of violence and messages of shared ideology. The first initiation ceremony occurred on Stone Mountain near Atlanta, Georgia. While a 40-foot cross burned on the mountain, the Klan members took their oaths of loyalty. This cross burning was the second recorded instance in the United States. The first known cross burning in the country had occurred a little over one month before the Klan initiation, when a Georgia mob celebrated the lynching of Leo Frank by burning a "gigantic cross" on Stone Mountain that was "visible throughout" Atlanta.

The new Klan's ideology did not differ much from that of the first Klan. As one Klan publication emphasized, "We avow the distinction between [the] races, . . . and we shall ever be true to the faithful maintenance of White Supremacy and will strenuously oppose any compromise thereof in any and all things." Violence was also an elemental part of this new Klan. By September 1921, the New York World newspaper documented 152 acts of Klan violence, including 4 murders, 41 floggings, and 27 tar-and-featherings.

Often, the Klan used cross burnings as a tool of intimidation and a threat of impending violence. For example, in 1939 and 1940, the Klan burned crosses in front of synagogues and churches. After one cross burning at a synagogue, a Klan member noted that if the cross burning did not "shut the Jews up, we'll cut a few throats and see what happens." In Miami in 1941, the Klan burned four crosses in front of a proposed housing project, declaring, "We are here to keep niggers out of your town. . . . When the law fails you, call on us." And in Alabama in 1942, in "a whirlwind climax to weeks of flogging and terror," the Klan burned crosses in front of a union hall and in front of a union leader's home on the eve of a labor election. These cross burnings embodied threats to people whom the Klan deemed antithetical to its goals. And these threats had special force given the long history of Klan violence.

The Klan continued to use cross burnings to intimidate after World War II. In one incident, an African-American "school teacher who recently moved his family into a block formerly occupied only by whites asked the protection of city police . . . after the burning of a cross in his front yard." And after a cross burning in Suffolk, Virginia, during the late 1940's, the Virginia Governor stated that he would "not allow any of our people of any race to be subjected to terrorism or intimidation in any form by the Klan or any other organization." These incidents of cross burning, among others, helped prompt Virginia to enact its first version of the cross-burning statute in 1950.

The decision of this Court in Brown v. Board of Education, 347 U.S. 483 (1954), along with the civil rights movement of the 1950's and 1960's, sparked another outbreak of Klan violence. These acts of violence included bombings, beatings, shootings, stabbings, and mutilations. Members of the Klan burned crosses on the lawns of those associated with the civil rights movement, assaulted the Freedom Riders, bombed churches, and murdered blacks as well as whites whom the Klan viewed as sympathetic toward the civil rights movement.

Throughout the history of the Klan, cross burnings have also remained potent symbols of shared group identity and ideology. The burning cross became a symbol of the Klan itself and a central feature of Klan gatherings. According to the Klan constitution (called the kloran), the "fiery cross" was the "emblem of that sincere, unselfish devotedness of all klansmen to the sacred purpose and principles we have espoused." And the Klan has often published its newsletters and magazines under the name The Fiery Cross.

At Klan gatherings across the country, cross burning became the climax of the rally or the initiation. Posters advertising an upcoming Klan rally often featured a Klan member holding a cross. Typically, a cross burning would start with a prayer by the "Klavern" minister, followed by the singing of Onward Christian Soldiers. The Klan would then light the cross on fire, as the members raised their left arm toward the burning cross and sang The Old Rugged Cross. Throughout the Klan's history, the Klan continued to use the burning cross in their ritual ceremonies.

For its own members, the cross was a sign of celebration and ceremony. During a joint Nazi-Klan rally in 1940, the proceeding concluded with the wedding of two Klan members who "were married in full Klan regalia beneath a blazing cross." In response to antimasking bills introduced in state legislatures after World War II, the Klan burned crosses in protest. On March 26, 1960, the Klan engaged in rallies and cross burnings throughout the South in an attempt to recruit 10 million members. Later in 1960, the Klan became an issue in the third debate between Richard Nixon and John Kennedy, with both candidates renouncing the Klan. After this debate, the Klan reiterated its support for Nixon by burning crosses. And cross burnings featured prominently in Klan rallies when the Klan attempted to move toward more nonviolent tactics to stop integration. In short, a burning cross has remained a symbol of Klan ideology and of Klan unity.

To this day, regardless of whether the message is a political one or whether the message is also meant to intimidate, the burning of a cross is a "symbol of hate." And while cross burning sometimes carries no intimidating message, at other times the intimidating message is the *only* message conveyed. For example, when a cross burning is directed at a particular person not affiliated with the Klan, the burning cross often serves as a message of intimidation, designed to inspire in the victim a fear of bodily harm. Moreover, the history of violence associated with the Klan shows that the possibility of injury or death is not just hypothetical. The person who burns a cross directed at a particular person often is making a serious threat, meant to coerce the victim to comply with the Klan's wishes unless the victim is willing to risk the wrath of the Klan. Indeed, as the cases of respondents Elliott and O'Mara indicate, individuals without Klan affiliation who wish to threaten or menace another person sometimes use cross burning because of this association between a burning cross and violence.

In sum, while a burning cross does not inevitably convey a message of intimidation, often the cross burner intends that the recipients of the message fear for their lives. And when a cross burning is used to intimidate, few if any messages are more powerful.

III

A

The First Amendment, applicable to the States through the Fourteenth Amendment, provides that "Congress shall make no law . . . abridging the freedom of speech." The hallmark of the protection of free speech is to allow "free trade in ideas"—even ideas that the overwhelming majority of people might find distasteful or discomforting. Thus, the First Amendment "ordinarily" denies a State "the power to prohibit dissemination of social, economic and political doctrine which a vast majority of its citizens believes to be false and fraught with evil consequence." The First Amendment affords protection to symbolic or expressive conduct as well as to actual speech.

The protections afforded by the First Amendment, however, are not absolute, and we have long recognized that the government may regulate certain categories of expression consistent with the Constitution. The First Amendment permits "restrictions upon the content of speech in a few limited areas, which are 'of such slight social value as a step to truth that any benefit that may be derived from them is clearly outweighed by the social interest in order and morality.'"

Thus, for example, a State may punish those words "which by their very utterance inflict injury or tend to incite an immediate breach of the peace." We have consequently held that fighting words—"those personally abusive epithets which, when addressed to the ordinary citizen, are, as a matter of common knowledge, inherently likely to provoke violent reaction"—are generally proscribable under the First Amendment. Furthermore, "the constitutional guarantees of free speech and free press do not permit a State to forbid or proscribe advocacy of the use of force or of law violation except where such advocacy is directed to inciting or producing imminent lawless action and is likely to incite or produce such action." And the First Amendment also permits a State to ban a "true threat."

"True threats" encompass those statements where the speaker means to communicate a serious expression of an intent to commit an act of unlawful violence to a particular individual or group of individuals. The speaker need not actually intend to carry out the threat. Rather, a prohibition on true threats "protect[s] individuals from the fear of violence" and "from the disruption that fear engenders," in addition to protecting people "from the possibility that the threatened violence will occur." Intimidation in the constitutionally proscribable sense of the word is a type of true threat, where a speaker directs a threat to a person or group of persons with the intent of placing the victim in fear of bodily harm or death. Respondents do not contest that some cross burnings fit within this meaning of intimidating speech, and rightly so. As noted in Part II, *supra,* the history of cross burning in this country shows that cross burning is often intimidating, intended to create a pervasive fear in victims that they are a target of violence.

B

The Supreme Court of Virginia ruled that in light of *R. A. V. v. City of St. Paul,* even if it is constitutional to ban cross burning in a content-neutral manner, the Virginia cross-burning statute is unconstitutional because it discriminates on the basis of content and viewpoint. It is true, as the Supreme Court of Virginia held, that the burning of a cross is symbolic expression. The reason why the Klan burns a cross at its rallies, or individuals place a burning cross on someone else's lawn, is that the burning cross represents the message that the speaker wishes to communicate. Individuals burn crosses as opposed to other means of communication because cross burning carries a message in an effective and dramatic manner.[1]

The fact that cross burning is symbolic expression, however, does not resolve the constitutional question. The Supreme Court of Virginia relied upon *R. A. V. v. City of St. Paul* to conclude that once a statute discriminates on the basis of this type of content, the law is unconstitutional. We disagree.

In *R. A. V.,* we held that a local ordinance that banned certain symbolic conduct, including cross burning, when done with the knowledge that such conduct would "'arouse anger, alarm or resentment in others on the basis of race, color, creed, religion or gender'" was unconstitutional. We held that the ordinance did not pass constitutional muster because it discriminated on the basis of content by targeting only those individuals who "provoke violence" on a basis specified in the law. The ordinance did not cover "[t]hose who wish to use 'fighting words' in connection with other ideas—to express hostility, for example, on the basis of political affiliation, union membership, or homosexuality." This content-based discrimination was unconstitutional because it allowed the city "to impose special prohibitions on those speakers who express views on disfavored subjects."

We did not hold in *R. A. V.* that the First Amendment prohibits *all* forms of content-based discrimination within a proscribable area of speech. Rather, we specifically stated

that some types of content discrimination did not violate the First Amendment:

> "When the basis for the content discrimination consists entirely of the very reason the entire class of speech at issue is proscribable, no significant danger of idea or viewpoint discrimination exists. Such a reason, having been adjudged neutral enough to support exclusion of the entire class of speech from First Amendment protection, is also neutral enough to form the basis of distinction within the class."

Indeed, we noted that it would be constitutional to ban only a particular type of threat: "[T]he Federal Government can criminalize only those threats of violence that are directed against the President . . . since the reasons why threats of violence are outside the First Amendment . . . have special force when applied to the person of the President." And a State may "choose to prohibit only that obscenity which is the most patently offensive *in its prurience—i.e.,* that which involves the most lascivious displays of sexual activity." Consequently, while the holding of *R. A. V.* does not permit a State to ban only obscenity based on "offensive *political* messages" or "only those threats against the President that mention his policy on aid to inner cities," the First Amendment permits content discrimination "based on the very reasons why the particular class of speech at issue . . . is proscribable."

Similarly, Virginia's statute does not run afoul of the First Amendment insofar as it bans cross burning with intent to intimidate. Unlike the statute at issue in *R. A. V.,* the Virginia statute does not single out for opprobrium only that speech directed toward "one of the specified disfavored topics." It does not matter whether an individual burns a cross with intent to intimidate because of the victim's race, gender, or religion, or because of the victim's "political affiliation, union membership, or homosexuality." Moreover, as a factual matter it is not true that cross burners direct their intimidating conduct solely to racial or religious minorities. Indeed, in the case of Elliott and O'Mara, it is at least unclear whether the respondents burned a cross due to racial animus.

The First Amendment permits Virginia to outlaw cross burnings done with the intent to intimidate because burning a cross is a particularly virulent form of intimidation. Instead of prohibiting all intimidating messages, Virginia may choose to regulate this subset of intimidating messages in light of cross burning's long and pernicious history as a signal of impending violence. Thus, just as a

State may regulate only that obscenity which is the most obscene due to its prurient content, so too may a State choose to prohibit only those forms of intimidation that are most likely to inspire fear of bodily harm. A ban on cross burning carried out with the intent to intimidate is fully consistent with our holding in *R. A. V.* and is proscribable under the First Amendment.

IV

The Supreme Court of Virginia ruled in the alternative that Virginia's cross-burning statute was unconstitutionally overbroad due to its provision stating that "[a]ny such burning of a cross shall be prima facie evidence of an intent to intimidate a person or group of persons." The Commonwealth added the prima facie provision to the statute in 1968. The court below did not reach whether this provision is severable from the rest of the cross-burning statute under Virginia law. In this Court, as in the Supreme Court of Virginia, respondents do not argue that the prima facie evidence provision is unconstitutional as applied to any one of them. Rather, they contend that the provision is unconstitutional on its face.

The Supreme Court of Virginia has not ruled on the meaning of the prima facie evidence provision. It has, however, stated that "the act of burning a cross alone, with no evidence of intent to intimidate, will nonetheless suffice for arrest and prosecution and will insulate the Commonwealth from a motion to strike the evidence at the end of its case-in-chief." The jury in the case of Richard Elliott did not receive any instruction on the prima facie evidence provision, and the provision was not an issue in the case of Jonathan O'Mara because he pleaded guilty. The court in Barry Black's case, however, instructed the jury that the provision means: "The burning of a cross, by itself, is sufficient evidence from which you may infer the required intent."

The prima facie evidence provision, as interpreted by the jury instruction, renders the statute unconstitutional. Because this jury instruction is the Model Jury Instruction, and because the Supreme Court of Virginia had the opportunity to expressly disavow the jury instruction, the jury instruction's construction of the prima facie provision "is a ruling on a question of state law that is as binding on us as though the precise words had been written into" the statute. As construed by the jury instruction, the prima facie provision strips away the very reason why a State may ban cross burning with the intent to intimidate. The prima facie evidence provision permits a jury to convict in every cross-burning case in which defendants

exercise their constitutional right not to put on a defense. And even where a defendant like Black presents a defense, the prima facie evidence provision makes it more likely that the jury will find an intent to intimidate regardless of the particular facts of the case. The provision permits the Commonwealth to arrest, prosecute, and convict a person based solely on the fact of cross burning itself.

It is apparent that the provision as so interpreted "'would create an unacceptable risk of the suppression of ideas.'" The act of burning a cross may mean that a person is engaging in constitutionally proscribable intimidation. But that same act may mean only that the person is engaged in core political speech. The prima facie evidence provision in this statute blurs the line between these two meanings of a burning cross. As interpreted by the jury instruction, the provision chills constitutionally protected political speech because of the possibility that a State will prosecute—and potentially convict—somebody engaging only in lawful political speech at the core of what the First Amendment is designed to protect.

As the history of cross burning indicates, a burning cross is not always intended to intimidate. Rather, sometimes the cross burning is a statement of ideology, a symbol of group solidarity. It is a ritual used at Klan gatherings, and it is used to represent the Klan itself. Thus, "[b]urning a cross at a political rally would almost certainly be protected expression." Indeed, occasionally a person who burns a cross does not intend to express either a statement of ideology or intimidation. Cross burnings have appeared in movies such as Mississippi Burning, and in plays such as the stage adaptation of Sir Walter Scott's The Lady of the Lake.

The prima facie provision makes no effort to distinguish among these different types of cross burnings. It does not distinguish between a cross burning done with the purpose of creating anger or resentment and a cross burning done with the purpose of threatening or intimidating a victim. It does not distinguish between a cross burning at a public rally or a cross burning on a neighbor's lawn. It does not treat the cross burning directed at an individual differently from the cross burning directed at a group of like-minded believers. It allows a jury to treat a cross burning on the property of another with the owner's acquiescence in the same manner as a cross burning on the property of another without the owner's permission. To this extent I agree with Justice Souter that the prima facie evidence provision can "skew jury deliberations toward conviction in cases where the evidence of intent to intimidate is relatively weak and arguably consistent with a solely ideological reason for burning."

It may be true that a cross burning, even at a political rally, arouses a sense of anger or hatred among the vast majority of citizens who see a burning cross. But this sense of anger or hatred is not sufficient to ban all cross burnings. As Gerald Gunther has stated, "The lesson I have drawn from my childhood in Nazi Germany and my happier adult life in this country is the need to walk the sometimes difficult path of denouncing the bigot's hateful ideas with all my power, yet at the same time challenging any community's attempt to suppress hateful ideas by force of law." The prima facie evidence provision in this case ignores all of the contextual factors that are necessary to decide whether a particular cross burning is intended to intimidate. The First Amendment does not permit such a shortcut.

For these reasons, the prima facie evidence provision, as interpreted through the jury instruction and as applied in Barry Black's case, is unconstitutional on its face. We recognize that the Supreme Court of Virginia has not authoritatively interpreted the meaning of the prima facie evidence provision. Unlike Justice Scalia, we refuse to speculate on whether any interpretation of the prima facie evidence provision would satisfy the First Amendment. Rather, all we hold is that because of the interpretation of the prima facie evidence provision given by the jury instruction, the provision makes the statute facially invalid at this point. We also recognize the theoretical possibility that the court, on remand, could interpret the provision in a manner different from that so far set forth in order to avoid the constitutional objections we have described. We leave open that possibility. We also leave open the possibility that the provision is severable, and

if so, whether Elliott and O'Mara could be retried under §18.2–423.

V

With respect to Barry Black, we agree with the Supreme Court of Virginia that his conviction cannot stand, and we affirm the judgment of the Supreme Court of Virginia. With respect to Elliott and O'Mara, we vacate the judgment of the Supreme Court of Virginia, and remand the case for further proceedings.

It is so ordered.

Note

1. Justice Thomas argues in dissent that cross burning is "conduct, not expression." While it is of course true that burning a cross is conduct, it is equally true that the First Amendment protects symbolic conduct as well as pure speech. As Justice Thomas has previously recognized, a burning cross is a "symbol of hate," and a "a symbol of white supremacy."

SANDRA DAY O'CONNOR was an associate justice of the U.S. Supreme Court. She worked in various legal capacities both in the United States and in Germany until she was appointed to the Arizona State Senate in 1969. She served as a state senator for 4 years and served in the Arizona judiciary for 6 years before she was nominated to the Supreme Court by President Ronald Reagan in 1981.

Clarence Thomas

Dissenting Opinion, *Virginia v. Black*

Justice Thomas, dissenting.

In every culture, certain things acquire meaning well beyond what outsiders can comprehend. That goes for both the sacred and the profane. I believe that cross burning is the paradigmatic example of the latter.

I

Although I agree with the majority's conclusion that it is constitutionally permissible to "ban . . . cross burning carried out with intent to intimidate," I believe that the majority errs in imputing an expressive component to the activity in question (relying on one of the exceptions to the First Amendment's prohibition on content-based discrimination outlined in *R. A. V. v. St. Paul*). In my view, whatever expressive value cross burning has, the legislature simply wrote it out by banning only intimidating conduct undertaken by a particular means. A conclusion that the statute prohibiting cross burning with intent to intimidate sweeps beyond a prohibition on certain conduct into the zone of expression overlooks not only the words of the statute but also reality.

A

"In holding [the ban on cross burning with intent to intimidate] unconstitutional, the Court ignores Justice Holmes' familiar aphorism that 'a page of history is worth a volume of logic.'"

To me, the majority's brief history of the Ku Klux Klan only reinforces [the] common understanding of the Klan as a terrorist organization, which, in its endeavor to intimidate, or even eliminate those it dislikes, uses the most brutal of methods.

Such methods typically include cross burning—"a tool for the intimidation and harassment of racial minorities, Catholics, Jews, Communists, and any other groups hated by the Klan." For those not easily frightened, cross burning has been followed by more extreme measures, such as beatings and murder. As the Solicitor General

points out, the association between acts of intimidating cross burning and violence is well documented in recent American history. Indeed, the connection between cross burning and violence is well ingrained, and lower courts have so recognized. . . .

But the perception that a burning cross is a threat and a precursor of worse things to come is not limited to blacks. Because the modern Klan expanded the list of its enemies beyond blacks and "radical[s]," to include Catholics, Jews, most immigrants, and labor unions, a burning cross is now widely viewed as a signal of impending terror and lawlessness. I wholeheartedly agree with the observation made by the Commonwealth of Virginia that

> "A white, conservative, middle-class Protestant, waking up at night to find a burning cross outside his home, will reasonably understand that someone is threatening him. His reaction is likely to be very different than if he were to find, say, a burning circle or square. In the latter case, he may call the fire department. In the former, he will probably call the police." Brief of Petitioner, at 26.

In our culture, cross burning has almost invariably meant lawlessness and understandably instills in its victims well-grounded fear of physical violence.

B

Virginia's experience has been no exception. In Virginia, though facing widespread opposition in 1920s, the KKK developed localized strength in the southeastern part of the State, where there were reports of scattered raids and floggings. Although the KKK was disbanded at the national level in 1944, a series of cross burnings in Virginia took place between 1949 and 1952.

Most of the crosses were burned on the lawns of black families, who either were business owners or lived in predominantly white neighborhoods. At least one of the cross burnings was accompanied by a shooting. The crosses burned near residences were about five to six feet tall; while a "huge cross reminiscent of the Ku Klux Klan days" burned "atop a hill" as part of the initiation ceremony of the secret organization of the Knights of Kavaliers, was twelve feet tall. These incidents were, in the words of the time, "*terroristic* [sic] . . . un-American act[s], designed to *intimidate* Negroes from seeking their rights as citizens."

In February 1952, in light of this series of cross burnings and attendant reports that the Klan, "long considered dead in Virginia, is being revitalized in Richmond," Governor Battle announced that "Virginia 'might well consider passing legislation' to restrict the activities of the Ku Klux Klan." As newspapers reported at the time, the bill was "to ban the burning of crosses and other similar evidences of *terrorism.*" The bill was presented to the House of Delegates by a former FBI agent and future two-term Governor, Delegate Mills E. Godwin, Jr. "Godwin said law and order in the State were impossible if organized groups could *create fear by intimidation.*"

That in the early 1950s the people of Virginia viewed cross burning as creating an intolerable atmosphere of terror is not surprising: Although the cross took on some religious significance in the 1920's when the Klan became connected with certain southern white clergy, by the postwar period it had reverted to its original function "as an instrument of intimidation."

Strengthening Delegate Godwin's explanation, as well as my conclusion, that the legislature sought to criminalize terrorizing *conduct* is the fact that at the time the statute was enacted, racial segregation was not only the prevailing practice, but also the law in Virginia. And, just two years after the enactment of this statute, Virginia's General Assembly embarked on a campaign of "massive resistance" in response to *Brown v. Board of Education.*

It strains credulity to suggest that a state legislature that adopted a litany of segregationist laws self-contradictorily intended to squelch the segregationist message. Even for segregationists, violent and terroristic conduct, the Siamese twin of cross burning, was intolerable. The ban on cross burning with intent to intimidate demonstrates that even segregationists understood the difference between intimidating and terroristic conduct and racist expression. It is simply beyond belief that, in passing the statute now under review, the Virginia legislature was concerned with anything but penalizing conduct it must have viewed as particularly vicious.

Accordingly, this statute prohibits only conduct, not expression. And, just as one cannot burn down someone's house to make a political point and then seek refuge in the First Amendment, those who hate cannot terrorize and intimidate to make their point. In light of my conclusion

that the statute here addresses only conduct, there is no need to analyze it under any of our First Amendment tests.

II

Even assuming that the statute implicates the First Amendment, in my view, the fact that the statute permits a jury to draw an inference of intent to intimidate from the cross burning itself presents no constitutional problems. Therein lies my primary disagreement with the plurality.

A

"The threshold inquiry is ascertaining the constitutional analysis applicable to [a jury instruction involving a presumption] is to determine the nature of the presumption it describes." We have categorized the presumptions as either permissive inferences or mandatory presumptions.

To the extent we do have a construction of this statute by the Virginia Supreme Court, we know that both the majority and the dissent agreed that the presumption was "a statutorily supplied *inference.*" Under Virginia law, the term "inference" has a well-defined meaning and is distinct from the term "presumption."

> A presumption is a rule of law that compels the fact finder to draw a certain conclusion or a certain inference from a given set of facts. [FN1: In contrast, *an inference,* sometimes loosely referred to as a presumption of fact, *does not compel a specific conclusion. An inference merely applies to the rational potency or probative value of an evidentiary fact to which the fact finder may attach whatever force or weight it deems best.*] The primary significance of a presumption is that it operates to shift to the opposing party the burden of producing evidence tending to rebut the presumption. [FN2: *An inference, on the other hand, does not invoke this procedural consequence of shifting the burden of production.*] No presumption, however, can operate to shift the ultimate burden of persuasion from the party upon whom it was originally cast.

Both the majority and the dissent below classified the clause in question as an "inference," and I see no reason to disagree, particularly in light of the instructions given to the jury in Black's case, requiring it to find guilt beyond a reasonable doubt both as to the fact that "the defendant burned or caused to burn a cross in a public place," and that "he did so with the intent to intimidate any person or persons."

Even though under Virginia law the statutory provision at issue here is characterized as an "inference," the Court must still inquire whether the label Virginia attaches corresponds to the categorization our cases have given such clauses. In this respect, it is crucial to observe that what Virginia law calls an "inference" is what our cases have termed "a permissive inference or presumption."[1] Given that this Court's definitions of a "permissive inference" and a "mandatory presumption" track Virginia's definitions of "inference" and "presumption," the Court should judge the Virginia statute based on the constitutional analysis applicable to "inferences:" they raise no constitutional flags unless "no rational trier could make a connection permitted by the inference." As explained in Part I, *not* making a connection between cross burning and intimidation would be irrational.

But even with respect to statutes containing a mandatory irrebuttable presumption as to intent, the Court has not shown much concern. For instance, there is no scienter requirement for statutory rape. That is, a person can be arrested, prosecuted, and convicted for having sex with a minor, without the government ever producing any evidence, let alone proving beyond a reasonable doubt, that a minor did not consent. In fact, "[f]or purposes of the child molesting statute . . . consent is irrelevant. The legislature has determined in such cases that children under the age of sixteen (16) cannot, as a matter of law, consent to have sexual acts performed upon them, or consent to engage in a sexual act with someone over the age of sixteen (16)." The legislature finds the behavior so reprehensible that the intent is satisfied by the mere act committed by a perpetrator. Considering the horrific effect cross burning has on its victims, it is also reasonable to presume intent to intimidate from the act itself.

Statutes prohibiting possession of drugs with intent to distribute operate much the same way as statutory rape laws. Under these statutes, the intent to distribute is effectively satisfied by possession of some threshold amount of drugs. As with statutory rape, the presumption of intent in such statutes is irrebuttable—not only can a person be arrested for the crime of possession with intent to distribute (or "trafficking") without any evidence of intent beyond quantity of drugs, but such person cannot even mount a defense to the element of intent. However, as with statutory rape statutes, our cases do not reveal any controversy with respect to the presumption of intent in these drug statutes.

Because the prima facie clause here is an inference, not an irrebuttable presumption, there is all the more basis under our Due Process precedents to sustain this statute.

B

The plurality, however, is troubled by the presumption because this is a First Amendment case. The plurality laments the fate of an innocent cross-burner who burns a cross, but does so without an intent to intimidate. The plurality fears the chill on expression because, according to the plurality, the inference permits "the Commonwealth to arrest, prosecute and convict a person based solely on the fact of cross burning itself." First, it is, at the very least, unclear that the inference comes into play during arrest and initiation of a prosecution, that is, prior to the instructions stage of an actual trial. Second, as I explained above, the inference is rebuttable and, as the jury instructions given in this case demonstrate, Virginia law still requires the jury to find the existence of each element, including intent to intimidate, beyond a reasonable doubt.

Moreover, even in the First Amendment context, the Court has upheld such regulations where conduct that initially appears culpable, ultimately results in dismissed charges. A regulation of pornography is one such example. While possession of child pornography is illegal, possession of adult pornography, as long as it is not obscene, is allowed. As a result, those pornographers trafficking in images of adults who look like minors, may be not only deterred but also arrested and prosecuted for possessing what a jury might find to be legal materials. This "chilling" effect has not, however, been a cause for grave concern with respect to overbreadth of such statutes among the members of this Court.

That the First Amendment gives way to other interests is not a remarkable proposition. What is remarkable is that, under the plurality's analysis, the determination of whether an interest is sufficiently compelling depends not on the harm a regulation in question seeks to prevent, but on the area of society at which it aims. For instance, in *Hill v. Colorado*, the Court upheld a restriction on protests near abortion clinics, explaining that the State had a legitimate interest, which was sufficiently narrowly tailored, in protecting those seeking services of such establishments "from unwanted advice" and "unwanted communication." In so concluding, the Court placed heavy reliance on the "vulnerable physical and emotional conditions" of patients. Thus, when it came to the rights of those seeking abortions, the Court deemed restrictions on "unwanted advice," which, notably, can be given only from a distance of at least 8 feet from a prospective patient, justified by the countervailing interest in obtaining abortion. Yet, here, the plurality strikes down the statute because one day an individual might wish to burn a cross, but might do so without an intent to intimidate anyone. That cross burning subjects its targets, and, sometimes, an unintended audience, to extreme emotional distress, and is virtually never viewed merely as "unwanted communication," but rather, as a physical threat, is of no concern to the plurality. Henceforth, under the plurality's view, physical safety will be valued less than the right to be free from unwanted communications.

III

Because I would uphold the validity of this statute, I respectfully dissent.

Note

1. As the Court explained in [*County Court of Ulster City v.*] *Allen,* a permissive inference or presumption "allows—but does not require—the trier of fact to infer the elemental fact from proof by the prosecutor of the basic one and which places no burden of any kind on the defendant. In that situation the basic fact may constitute prima facie evidence of the elemental fact. . . . Because

this permissive presumption leaves the trier of fact free to credit or reject the inference and does not shift the burden of proof, it affects the application of the 'beyond a reasonable doubt' standard only if, under the facts of the case, there is no rational way the trier could make the connection permitted by the inference." *Id.* at 157 (internal citations omitted). By contrast, "a mandatory presumption . . . may affect not only the strength of the 'no reasonable doubt' burden but also the placement of that burden; it tells the trier that he or they *must* find the elemental fact upon proof of the basic fact, at least unless the defendant has come forward with some evidence to rebut the presumed connection between the two facts." *Id.*

CLARENCE THOMAS is an associate justice of the U.S. Supreme Court. A former judge on the U.S. Court of Appeals for the District of Columbia, he was nominated by President George H. W. Bush to the Supreme Court in 1991. He received his JD from the Yale University School of Law in 1974.

EXPLORING THE ISSUE

Are Blanket Prohibitions on Cross Burnings Unconstitutional?

Critical Thinking and Reflection

1. How might this issue be different if it were not a cross being burned, but a symbol from another religion?
2. Do you think it is possible to fairly and predictably determine what conduct is speech and what conduct is simply conduct?
3. Would there be any changes to the meaning or application of Virginia's cross-burning statute if the words "with the intent of intimidating any person" were replaced with "to the extent possible under the law?"
4. Is there a valid danger that the First Amendment can now be used as a shield by those who wish to threaten violence upon others?

Is There Common Ground?

In *Virginia v. Black*, history takes center stage. Both the majority and dissent devote a substantial portion of their opinions to the origin and practices of the Ku Klux Klan and their use of cross burning as an intimidation technique, and both opinions do not shy away from expressing their repugnance for the group's activities and beliefs. Although the justices differ on the constitutional scope and means of restricting certain symbolic conduct, it is abundantly clear that they strongly believe that a State has the right to enact laws to protect the safety of its citizens.

With the exception of the prima facie evidence provision, both the majority and dissent also agree that the Virginia legislature carefully crafted a law that banned cross burning. Both opinions agree that by invoking within the law itself the constitutional standard by which First Amendment speech may be restricted, Virginia successfully prohibited cross burning and distinguished itself from other state cross-burning statutes, namely that in *R.A.V.* Justice Thomas, however, went even further, opining that a state has the power to regulate any conduct based on the text of the Constitution. While many of the justices are hesitant to side with Justice Thomas's textualism, there is little doubt that all would agree that one of the principal functions of government is to provide security to its citizens. Furthermore, this security extends beyond freedom from actual violence, and includes direct threats of violence as well. *Virginia v. Black* solidifies this proposition. In fact, it could be argued that the social contract between the state and individual requires it.

Additional Resources

Randall P. Bezanson, *Speech Stories: How Free Can Speech Be?* (New York University Press, 1998).

Edward J. Cleary, *Beyond the Burning Cross: The First Amendment and the Landmark R. A. V. Case* (Random House, 1994).

Steven Gey, "The Nuremberg Files and the First Amendment Value of Threats," 78 *Tex. L. Rev.* 541 (2000).

Frederick Schauer, *Free Speech: A Philosophical Enquiry* (Cambridge University Press, 1982).

Geoffrey R. Stone, *Perilous Times: Free Speech in Wartime from the Sedition Act of 1789 to the War on Terrorism* (W. W. Norton & Co., 2004).

Wyn Craig Wade, *The Fiery Cross: The Ku Klux Klan in America* (Simon & Schuster, 1987).

Internet References . . .

Abstract and Recording of Oral Arguments of *Virginia v. Black*

www.oyez.org/cases/2000-2009/2002/2002_01_1107

Abstract and Recording of Oral Arguments of *R. A. V. v. City of St. Paul*

www.oyez.org/cases/1990-1999/1991/1991_90_7675

Abstract and Recording of Oral Arguments of *Tinker v. Des Moines*

www.oyez.org/cases/1960-1969/1968/1968_21

Department of Justice, Federal Bureau of Investigation Hate Crimes Statistics

The Hate Crimes Statistics Act requires the FBI to keep statistics on hate crimes across the country. A copy of the 2012 Hate Crimes Report is available at the link below.

www.fbi.gov/news/stories/2012/december/annual -hate-crimes-report-released/annual-hate-crimes -report-released

Selected, Edited, and with Issue Framing Material by:
M. Ethan Katsh, *University of Massachusetts, Amherst*

ISSUE

Does the Fourth Amendment Prohibit the Police from Collecting a DNA Sample from a Person Arrested, but Not Yet Convicted on Felony Charges?

YES: Anthony Kennedy, from "Majority Opinion, *Maryland v. King*," *United States Supreme Court* (2013)

NO: Antonin Scalia, from "Dissenting Opinion, *Maryland v. King*," *United States Supreme Court* (2013)

Learning Outcomes

After reading this issue, you will be able to:

- Describe generally the manner by which law enforcement collects and analyzes DNA samples from people after they are arrested.
- Identify the various ways in which a DNA profile may be used after it is created.
- Compare and contrast DNA identification to other historical methods of identifying arrested individuals.
- Identify the arguments for and against the reasonableness of government collection of DNA samples at the time of arrest.

ISSUE SUMMARY

YES: Justice Anthony Kennedy rules that using a cheek swab to collect a person's DNA during post-arrest processing is a reasonable search under the Fourth Amendment because it is predominantly used to confirm the identity of the arrestee.

NO: Justice Antonin Scalia argues that DNA collection at the time of arrest is an unreasonable search because the arrestee's DNA profile is predominantly used to investigate unrelated crimes.

Most human cells contain 46 chromosomes, each of which is composed of highly compacted and extraordinarily long strands of deoxyribonucleic acid, or DNA. DNA is a complex molecule composed of sugar and phosphate backbones to which chemical nucleotides attach. The order of nucleotides dictates the production of various proteins in the body, which in turn determine all aspects of the body's function, including physical development. The order of nucleotides is different for each person, and therefore acts as a unique genetic code.

Because of DNA's powerful ability to serve as a personal identifier, it has become an important tool in criminal investigations. In 1986, British police were able to identify a rapist by matching DNA found at the crime scene to that of a suspect. American law enforcement took notice, and within a few years state governments in the United States began collecting DNA samples from individuals convicted of certain crimes. At first, many states limited DNA collection to those convicted of sex offenses. Today, however, nearly all states and the U.S. federal government require people convicted of *any* felony to provide a DNA sample.

More recently, states and the U.S. federal government have sought to extend DNA collection to individuals who have been arrested, but not yet convicted, of qualifying offenses. The DNA Fingerprint Act of 2005 mandated that any adult arrested for a federal crime provide a DNA sample as part of the booking process. Twenty-eight states similarly require that individuals provide a DNA sample upon arrest. The range of qualifying offenses varies from state to state: in some states, DNA is collected only at an incident of an arrest for a sex crime or violent offense; in others, DNA is collected for any felony arrest; in a third group of states, DNA is collected even for misdemeanor arrests.

Unlike blood samples, DNA collection is quick and painless. During the booking process, the inside of the arrestee's cheek is lightly swabbed to collect his or her DNA. The DNA sample is then sent to a crime laboratory for processing. Laboratory technicians translate the DNA sample into a profile consisting of a numerical sequence. That profile is then entered into the U.S. federal Combined DNA Index System (CODIS) database, a central repository of federal, state, and local DNA databases. CODIS was established by federal law in 1994 and is operated by the FBI. The CODIS database currently contains more than 10 million convicted offender profiles and another 1.5 million arrestee profiles.

DNA profiles in CODIS do not contain any personal information attached to convicted offenders or arrestees. Rather, the profile information is limited to genetic information gleaned from 13 predetermined loci, or regions, of an individual's DNA. These loci contain sequences of repeating nucleotides known as short tandem repeats (STRs). The number and size of STRs at each of the 13 loci vary extensively from person to person and collectively form the person's unique DNA profile.

Once a profile is in the database, it may be compared against DNA profiles of suspected perpetrators in unsolved crimes. For example, perpetrator DNA collected from a victim of a sexual assault, or from other forensic evidence left at a crime scene, is processed and converted into an unknown perpetrator profile. If an arrestee or convict's profile matches that of an unknown perpetrator, the laboratory must undertake procedures to confirm the match, at which point the identity of the suspected can be obtained. Law enforcement may then use this match to further investigate the matched individual's involvement in the unsolved crime.

Some arrestees who ultimately are not convicted of a crime may request that their DNA profile be expunged from CODIS. The complexity and availability of the expungement procedure vary from state to state. A few states remove the profile automatically. Most states and the federal government, however, require the arrestee to formally request that the profile be removed. Critics have argued that this requirement unfairly places the burden of expungement entirely on the innocent individual.

Advocates for DNA collection at the time of arrest stress that the swabbing procedure is minimally invasive, especially in comparison to the benefits of using DNA to convict or exonerate people of major crimes. Critics of pre-conviction DNA collection counter that the practice violates the Fourth Amendment's prohibition on unreasonable searches and seizures by the government. As the Supreme Court has interpreted the Fourth Amendment, police may not search a person without a warrant unless there is reasonable suspicion that the person has been or will be involved in a crime, based on specific facts and circumstances. As DNA can be used to link a person to a crime that is unrelated to the crime for which the person was arrested, critics argue that DNA collection constitutes an unreasonable search.

The Fourth Amendment question was raised and addressed by several state and federal courts in the mid-to-late 2000s. These courts reached different conclusions on the issue, with some courts holding that collecting DNA from an arrestee was constitutionally sound, and others holding that such collection amounted to an unreasonable search. A legal challenge to Maryland's DNA collection statute finally reached the Supreme Court in 2013. Justice Anthony Kennedy, writing for a majority of five justices, held that collecting DNA at the time of arrest was not an unreasonable search, because the primary purpose of the DNA collection was administrative: to confirm the identity of the arrestee. Justice Antonin Scalia, writing in dissent for a four-justice minority, argued that the primary purpose of collecting an arrestee's DNA was to compare it to the DNA of unknown perpetrators in the CODIS database, rendering it a search undertaken without reasonable suspicion of the arrestee's involvement.

YES ⤶

Anthony Kennedy

Majority Opinion, *Maryland v. King*

JUSTICE KENNEDY delivered the opinion of the Court.

In 2003 a man concealing his face and armed with a gun broke into a woman's home in Salisbury, Maryland. He raped her. The police were unable to identify or apprehend the assailant based on any detailed description or other evidence they then had, but they did obtain from the victim a sample of the perpetrator's DNA.

In 2009 Alonzo King was arrested in Wicomico County, Maryland, and charged with first- and second-degree assault for menacing a group of people with a shotgun. As part of a routine booking procedure for serious offenses, his DNA sample was taken by applying a cotton swab or filter paper—known as a buccal swab—to the inside of his cheeks. The DNA was found to match the DNA taken from the Salisbury rape victim. King was tried and convicted for the rape. Additional DNA samples were taken from him and used in the rape trial, but there seems to be no doubt that it was the DNA from the cheek sample taken at the time he was booked in 2009 that led to his first having been linked to the rape and charged with its commission.

The Court of Appeals of Maryland, on review of King's rape conviction, ruled that the DNA taken when King was booked for the 2009 charge was an unlawful seizure because obtaining and using the cheek swab was an unreasonable search of the person. It set the rape conviction aside. This Court granted certiorari and now reverses the judgment of the Maryland court.

I

When King was arrested on April 10, 2009, for menacing a group of people with a shotgun and charged in state court with both first- and second-degree assault, he was processed for detention in custody at the Wicomico County Central Booking facility. Booking personnel used a cheek swab to take the DNA sample from him pursuant to provisions of the Maryland DNA Collection Act (or Act).

On July 13, 2009, King's DNA record was uploaded to the Maryland DNA database, and three weeks later, on August 4, 2009, his DNA profile was matched to the DNA sample collected in the unsolved 2003 rape case. Once the DNA was matched to King, detectives presented the forensic evidence to a grand jury, which indicted him for the rape. Detectives obtained a search warrant and took a second sample of DNA from King, which again matched the evidence from the rape. He moved to suppress the DNA match on the grounds that Maryland's DNA collection law violated the Fourth Amendment. The Circuit Court Judge upheld the statute as constitutional. King pleaded not guilty to the rape charges but was convicted and sentenced to life in prison without the possibility of parole.

In a divided opinion, the Maryland Court of Appeals struck down the portions of the Act authorizing collection of DNA from felony arrestees as unconstitutional. The majority concluded that a DNA swab was an unreasonable search in violation of the Fourth Amendment because King's "expectation of privacy is greater than the State's purported interest in using King's DNA to identify him." . . .

Both federal and state courts have reached differing conclusions as to whether the Fourth Amendment prohibits the collection and analysis of a DNA sample from persons arrested, but not yet convicted, on felony charges. This Court granted certiorari, 568 U. S. ___ (2012), to address the question. . . .

II

The advent of DNA technology is one of the most significant scientific advancements of our era. The full potential for use of genetic markers in medicine and science is still being explored, but the utility of DNA identification in the criminal justice system is already undisputed. Since the first use of forensic DNA analysis to catch a rapist and murderer in England in 1986, law enforcement, the defense bar, and the courts have acknowledged DNA testing's "unparalleled ability both to exonerate the wrongly convicted and to identify the guilty. It has the potential to significantly improve both the criminal justice system and police investigative practices."

From Supreme Court of the United States, June 3, 2013.

A

The current standard for forensic DNA testing relies on an analysis of the chromosomes located within the nucleus of all human cells. "The DNA material in chromosomes is composed of 'coding' and 'noncoding' regions. The coding regions are known as *genes* and contain the information necessary for a cell to make proteins. . . . Non-protein-coding regions . . . are not related directly to making proteins, [and] have been referred to as 'junk' DNA." The adjective "junk" may mislead the layperson, for in fact this is the DNA region used with near certainty to identify a person. . . .

Many of the patterns found in DNA are shared among all people, so forensic analysis focuses on "repeated DNA sequences scattered throughout the human genome," known as "short tandem repeats" (STRs). The alternative possibilities for the size and frequency of these STRs at any given point along a strand of DNA are known as "alleles," and multiple alleles are analyzed in order to ensure that a DNA profile matches only one individual. Future refinements may improve present technology, but even now STR analysis makes it "possible to determine whether a biological tissue matches a suspect with near certainty."

The Act authorizes Maryland law enforcement authorities to collect DNA samples from "an individual who is charged with . . . a crime of violence or an attempt to commit a crime of violence; or . . . burglary or an attempt to commit burglary." . . . Once taken, a DNA sample may not be processed or placed in a database before the individual is arraigned (unless the individual consents). It is at this point that a judicial officer ensures that there is probable cause to detain the arrestee on a qualifying serious offense. If "all qualifying criminal charges are determined to be unsupported by probable cause . . . the DNA sample shall be immediately destroyed." DNA samples are also destroyed if "a criminal action begun against the individual . . . does not result in a conviction," "the conviction is finally reversed or vacated and no new trial is permitted," or "the individual is granted an unconditional pardon."

The Act also limits the information added to a DNA database and how it may be used. Specifically, "[o]nly DNA records that directly relate to the identification of individuals shall be collected and stored." No purpose other than identification is permissible: "A person may not willfully test a DNA sample for information that does not relate to the identification of individuals as specified in this subtitle." . . . The officers involved in taking and analyzing respondent's DNA sample complied with the Act in all respects.

Respondent's DNA was collected in this case using a common procedure known as a "buccal swab." "Buccal cell collection involves wiping a small piece of filter paper or a cotton swab similar to a Q-tip against the inside cheek of an individual's mouth to collect some skin cells." The procedure is quick and painless. The swab touches inside an arrestee's mouth, but it requires no "surgical intrusio[n] beneath the skin," and it poses no "threa[t] to the health or safety" of arrestees.

B

Respondent's identification as the rapist resulted in part through the operation of a national project to standardize collection and storage of DNA profiles. Authorized by Congress and supervised by the Federal Bureau of Investigation, the Combined DNA Index System (CODIS) connects DNA laboratories at the local, state, and national level. Since its authorization in 1994, the CODIS system has grown to include all 50 [s]tates and a number of federal agencies. CODIS collects DNA profiles provided by local laboratories taken from arrestees, convicted offenders, and forensic evidence found at crime scenes. To participate in CODIS, a local laboratory must sign a memorandum of understanding agreeing to adhere to quality standards and submit to audits to evaluate compliance with the federal standards for scientifically rigorous DNA testing.

One of the most significant aspects of CODIS is the standardization of the points of comparison in DNA analysis. The CODIS database is based on 13 loci at which the STR alleles are noted and compared. These loci make possible extreme accuracy in matching individual samples, with a "random match probability of approximately 1 in 100 trillion (assuming unrelated individuals)." . . . In short, CODIS sets uniform national standards for DNA matching and then facilitates connections between local law enforcement agencies who can share more specific information about matched STR profiles. . . .

Twenty-eight states and the Federal Government have adopted laws similar to the Maryland Act authorizing the collection of DNA from some or all arrestees. Although those statutes vary in their particulars, such as what charges require a DNA sample, their similarity means that this case implicates more than the specific Maryland law. At issue is a standard, expanding technology already in widespread use throughout the Nation.

III

A

. . . The Fourth Amendment, binding on the States by the Fourteenth Amendment, provides that "[t]he right of the people to be secure in their persons, houses, papers, and effects, against unreasonable searches and seizures, shall not be violated." It can be agreed that using a buccal swab on the inner tissues of a person's cheek in order to obtain DNA samples is a search. Virtually any "intrusio[n] into the human body," will work an invasion of "'cherished personal security' that is subject to constitutional scrutiny," The Court has applied the Fourth Amendment to police efforts to draw blood, scraping an arrestee's fingernails to obtain trace evidence, and even to "a breathalyzer test, which generally requires the production of alveolar or 'deep lung' breath for chemical analysis."

A buccal swab is a far more gentle process than a venipuncture to draw blood. It involves but a light touch on the inside of the cheek; and although it can be deemed a search within the body of the arrestee, it requires no "surgical intrusions beneath the skin." The fact than an intrusion is negligible is of central relevance to determining reasonableness, although it is still a search as the law defines that term.

B

To say that the Fourth Amendment applies here is the beginning point, not the end of the analysis. . . . "As the text of the Fourth Amendment indicates, the ultimate measure of the constitutionality of a governmental search is 'reasonableness.'" In giving content to the inquiry whether an intrusion is reasonable, the Court has preferred "some quantum of individualized suspicion . . . [as] a prerequisite to a constitutional search or seizure. But the Fourth Amendment imposes no irreducible requirement of such suspicion."

In some circumstances, such as "[w]hen faced with special law enforcement needs, diminished expectations of privacy, minimal intrusions, or the like, the Court has found that certain general, or individual, circumstances may render a warrantless search or seizure reasonable." Those circumstances diminish the need for a warrant, either because "the public interest is such that neither a warrant nor probable cause is required," or because an individual is already on notice, for instance because of his employment, or the conditions of his release from government custody, that some reasonable police intrusion on his privacy is to be expected. The need for a warrant is perhaps least when the search involves no discretion that could properly be limited by the "interpo[lation of] a neutral magistrate between the citizen and the law enforcement officer."

The instant case can be addressed with this background. The Maryland DNA Collection Act provides that, in order to obtain a DNA sample, all arrestees charged with serious crimes must furnish the sample on a buccal swab applied, as noted, to the inside of the cheeks. The arrestee is already in valid police custody for a serious offense supported by probable cause. The DNA collection is not subject to the judgment of officers whose perspective might be "colored by their primary involvement in 'the often competitive enterprise of ferreting out crime.'" . . .

Even if a warrant is not required, a search is not beyond Fourth Amendment scrutiny; for it must be reasonable in its scope and manner of execution. . . . This application of "traditional standards of reasonableness" requires a court to weigh "the promotion of legitimate governmental interests" against "the degree to which [the search] intrudes upon an individual's privacy." . . .

IV

A

The legitimate government interest served by the Maryland DNA Collection Act is one that is well established: the need for law enforcement officers in a safe and accurate way to process and identify the persons and possessions they must take into custody. It is beyond dispute that "probable cause provides legal justification for arresting a person suspected of crime, and for a brief period of detention to take the administrative steps incident to arrest." Also uncontested is the "right on the part of the Government, always recognized under English and American law, to search the person of the accused when legally arrested." . . . [I]ndividual suspicion is not necessary, because "[t]he constitutionality of a search incident to an arrest does not depend on whether there is any indication that the person arrested possesses weapons or evidence. The fact of a lawful arrest, standing alone, authorizes a search."

The "routine administrative procedure[s] at a police station house incident to booking and jailing the suspect" derive from different origins and have different constitutional justifications than, say, the search of a place, for the search of a place not incident to an arrest depends on the "fair probability that contraband or evidence of a crime will be found in a particular place." The interests are further different when an individual is formally processed into police custody. . . . When probable cause exists to remove an individual from the normal channels of society and hold him in legal custody, DNA identification plays a critical role in serving those interests.

First, "[i]n every criminal case, it is known and must be known who has been arrested and who is being tried." An individual's identity is more than just his name or

Social Security number, and the government's interest in identification goes beyond ensuring that the proper name is typed on the indictment. Identity has never been considered limited to the name on the arrestee's birth certificate. In fact, a name is of little value compared to the real interest in identification at stake when an individual is brought into custody. "It is a well recognized aspect of criminal conduct that the perpetrator will take unusual steps to conceal not only his conduct, but also his identity. Disguises used while committing a crime may be supplemented or replaced by changed names, and even changed physical features." . . .

A suspect's criminal history is a critical part of his identity that officers should know when processing him for detention. . . . Police already seek this crucial identifying information. They use routine and accepted means as varied as comparing the suspect's booking photograph to sketch artists' depictions of persons of interest, showing his mugshot to potential witnesses, and of course making a computerized comparison of the arrestee's fingerprints against electronic databases of known criminals and unsolved crimes. In this respect the only difference between DNA analysis and the accepted use of fingerprint databases is the unparalleled accuracy DNA provides. . . .

A DNA profile is useful to the police because it gives them a form of identification to search the records already in their valid possession. In this respect the use of DNA for identification is no different than matching an arrestee's face to a wanted poster of a previously unidentified suspect; or matching tattoos to known gang symbols to reveal a criminal affiliation; or matching the arrestee's fingerprints to those recovered from a crime scene. . . . Finding occurrences of the arrestee's CODIS profile in outstanding cases is consistent with this common practice. It uses a different form of identification than a name or fingerprint, but its function is the same.

Second, law enforcement officers bear a responsibility for ensuring that the custody of an arrestee does not create inordinate "risks for facility staff, for the existing detainee population, and for a new detainee." DNA identification can provide untainted information to those charged with detaining suspects and detaining the property of any felon. For these purposes officers must know the type of person whom they are detaining, and DNA allows them to make critical choices about how to proceed. . . .

Third, looking forward to future stages of criminal prosecution, "the Government has a substantial interest in ensuring that persons accused of crimes are available for trials." A person who is arrested for one offense but knows that he has yet to answer for some past crime may be more inclined to flee the instant charges, lest continued contact with the criminal justice system expose one or more other serious offenses. . . .

Fourth, an arrestee's past conduct is essential to an assessment of the danger he poses to the public, and this will inform a court's determination whether the individual should be released on bail. . . . DNA identification of a suspect in a violent crime provides critical information to the police and judicial officials in making a determination of the arrestee's future dangerousness. . . . Knowing that the defendant is wanted for a previous violent crime based on DNA identification is especially probative of the court's consideration of "the danger of the defendant to the alleged victim, another person, or the community." . . .

Finally, in the interests of justice, the identification of an arrestee as the perpetrator of some heinous crime may have the salutary effect of freeing a person wrongfully imprisoned for the same offense. "[P]rompt [DNA] testing . . . would speed up apprehension of criminals before they commit additional crimes, and prevent the grotesque detention of . . . innocent people." . . .

B

DNA identification represents an important advance in the techniques used by law enforcement to serve legitimate police concerns . . . Law enforcement agencies routinely have used scientific advancements in their standard procedures for the identification of arrestees. "Police had been using photography to capture the faces of criminals almost since its invention." . . .

Beginning in 1887, some police adopted more exacting means to identify arrestees, using the system of precise physical measurements pioneered by the French anthropologist Alphonse Bertillon. Bertillon identification consisted of 10 measurements of the arrestee's body, along with a "scientific analysis of the features of the face and an exact anatomical localization of the various scars, marks, etc., of the body." "[W]hen a prisoner was brought in, his photograph was taken according to the Bertillon system, and his body measurements were then made. The measurements were made . . . and noted down on the back of a card or a blotter, and the photograph of the prisoner was expected to be placed on the card. This card, therefore, furnished both the likeness and description of the prisoner, and was placed in the rogues' gallery, and copies were sent to various cities where similar records were kept." As in the present case, the point of taking this information about each arrestee was not limited to verifying that the proper name was on the indictment. These procedures were used to "facilitate the recapture of escaped prisoners," to aid "the investigation of their past records and personal history," and "to preserve the means of identification for . . . future supervision after discharge." . . .

Perhaps the most direct historical analogue to the DNA technology used to identify respondent is the familiar practice of fingerprinting arrestees. From the advent of this technique, courts had no trouble determining that fingerprinting was a natural part of "the administrative steps incident to arrest." . . .

By the middle of the 20th century, it was considered "elementary that a person in lawful custody may be required to submit to photographing and fingerprinting as part of routine identification processes."

DNA identification is an advanced technique superior to fingerprinting in many ways, so much so that to insist on fingerprints as the norm would make little sense to either the forensic expert or a layperson. The additional intrusion upon the arrestee's privacy beyond that associated with fingerprinting is not significant, and DNA is a markedly more accurate form of identifying arrestees. A suspect who has changed his facial features to evade photographic identification or even one who has undertaken the more arduous task of altering his fingerprints cannot escape the revealing power of his DNA.

The respondent's primary objection to this analogy is that DNA identification is not as fast as fingerprinting, and so it should not be considered to be the 21st-century equivalent. But rapid analysis of fingerprints is itself of recent vintage. The FBI's vaunted Integrated Automated Fingerprint Identification System (IAFIS) was only "launched on July 28, 1999. Prior to this time, the processing of . . . fingerprint submissions was largely a manual, labor-intensive process, taking weeks or months to process a single submission." . . . It was not the advent of this technology that rendered fingerprint analysis constitutional in a single moment. The question of how long it takes to process identifying information obtained from a valid search goes only to the efficacy of the search for its purpose of prompt identification, not the constitutionality of the search. Given the importance of DNA in the identification of police records pertaining to arrestees and the need to refine and confirm that identity for its important bearing on the decision to continue release on bail or to impose of new conditions, DNA serves an essential purpose despite the existence of delays such as the one that occurred in this case. Even so, the delay in processing DNA from arrestees is being reduced to a substantial degree by rapid technical advances. . . . New technology will only further improve its speed and therefore its effectiveness. . . . By identifying not only who the arrestee is but also what other available records disclose about his past to show who he is, the police can ensure that they have the proper person under arrest and that they have made the necessary arrangements for his custody; and, just as important, they can also prevent suspicion against or prosecution of the innocent.

In sum, there can be little reason to question "the legitimate interest of the government in knowing for an absolute certainty the identity of the person arrested, in knowing whether he is wanted elsewhere, and in ensuring his identification in the event he flees prosecution." . . . DNA identification of arrestees, of the type approved by the Maryland statute here at issue, is "no more than an extension of methods of identification long used in dealing with persons under arrest." In the balance of reasonableness required by the Fourth Amendment, therefore, the Court must give great weight both to the significant government interest at stake in the identification of arrestees and to the unmatched potential of DNA identification to serve that interest.

V

A

By comparison to this substantial government interest and the unique effectiveness of DNA identification, the intrusion of a cheek swab to obtain a DNA sample is a minimal one. True, a significant government interest does not alone suffice to justify a search. The government interest must outweigh the degree to which the search invades an individual's legitimate expectations of privacy. In considering those expectations in this case, however, the necessary predicate of a valid arrest for a serious offense is fundamental. "Although the underlying command of the Fourth Amendment is always that searches and seizures be reasonable, what is reasonable depends on the context within which a search takes place." . . .

The reasonableness of any search must be considered in the context of the person's legitimate expectations of privacy. . . .

The expectations of privacy of an individual taken into police custody "necessarily [are] of a diminished scope." . . .

In this critical respect, the search here at issue differs from the sort of programmatic searches of either the public at large or a particular class of regulated but otherwise law-abiding citizens that the Court has previously labeled as "special needs" searches. When the police stop a motorist at a checkpoint, or test a political candidate for illegal narcotics, they intrude upon substantial expectations of privacy. So the Court has insisted on some purpose other than "to detect evidence of ordinary criminal wrongdoing" to justify these searches in the absence of individualized suspicion. Once an individual has been arrested on probable cause for a dangerous offense that may require detention before trial, however, his or her expectations of privacy and freedom from police scrutiny are reduced. DNA identification like that at issue here thus does not require consideration of any unique needs that would be required to justify searching the average citizen. The special needs cases, though in full accord with the result reached here, do not have a direct bearing on the issues presented in this case, because unlike the search of a citizen who has not been suspected of a wrong, a detainee has a reduced expectation of privacy.

The reasonableness inquiry here considers two other circumstances in which the Court has held that particularized suspicion is not categorically required: "diminished expectations of privacy [and] minimal intrusions." This is not to suggest that any search is acceptable solely because a person is in custody. Some searches, such as invasive surgery, or a search of the arrestee's home, involve either greater intrusions or higher expectations of privacy than are present in this case. In those situations, when the Court must "balance the privacy-related and law enforcement-related concerns to determine if the intrusion was reasonable," the privacy-related concerns are weighty enough that the search may require a warrant, notwithstanding the diminished expectations of privacy of the arrestee.

Here, by contrast to the approved standard procedures incident to any arrest detailed above, a buccal swab involves an even more brief and still minimal intrusion. A gentle rub along the inside of the cheek does not break the skin, and it "involves virtually no risk, trauma, or pain." "A crucial factor in analyzing the magnitude of the intrusion . . . is the extent to which the procedure may threaten the safety or health of the individual," and nothing suggests that a buccal swab poses any physical danger whatsoever. A brief intrusion of an arrestee's person is subject to the Fourth Amendment, but a swab of this nature does not increase the indignity already attendant to normal incidents of arrest.

B

In addition the processing of respondent's DNA sample's 13 CODIS loci did not intrude on respondent's privacy in a way that would make his DNA identification unconstitutional.

First, . . . the CODIS loci come from noncoding parts of the DNA that do not reveal the genetic traits of the arrestee. . . .

And even if non-coding alleles could provide some information, they are not in fact tested for that end. It is undisputed that law enforcement officers analyze DNA for the sole purpose of generating a unique identifying number against which future samples may be matched. . . . If in the future police analyze samples to determine, for instance, an arrestee's predisposition for a particular disease or other hereditary factors not relevant to identity, that case would present additional privacy concerns not present here.

Finally, the Act provides statutory protections that guard against further invasion of privacy. As noted above, the Act requires that "[o]nly DNA records that directly relate to the identification of individuals shall be collected and stored." No purpose other than identification is permissible. . . . In light of the scientific and statutory safeguards, once respondent's DNA was lawfully collected the STR analysis of respondent's DNA pursuant to CODIS procedures did not amount to a significant invasion of privacy that would render the DNA identification impermissible under the Fourth Amendment.

* * *

In light of the context of a valid arrest supported by probable cause respondent's expectations of privacy were not offended by the minor intrusion of a brief swab of his cheeks. By contrast, that same context of arrest gives rise to significant state interests in identifying respondent not only so that the proper name can be attached to his charges but also so that the criminal justice system can make informed decisions concerning pretrial custody. Upon these considerations the Court concludes that DNA identification of arrestees is a reasonable search that can be considered part of a routine booking procedure. When officers make an arrest supported by probable cause to hold for a serious offense and they bring the suspect to the station to be detained in custody, taking and analyzing a cheek swab of the arrestee's DNA is, like fingerprinting and photographing, a legitimate police booking procedure that is reasonable under the Fourth Amendment.

The judgment of the Court of Appeals of Maryland is reversed.

It is so ordered.

ANTHONY KENNEDY is an associate justice of the U.S. Supreme Court. He received his LLB from Harvard Law School in 1961 and worked for law firms in San Francisco and Sacramento, California, until he was nominated by President Gerald Ford to the U.S. Court of Appeals for the Ninth Circuit in 1975. He was nominated by President Ronald Reagan to the Supreme Court in 1988.

Antonin Scalia

Dissenting Opinion, *Maryland v. King*

JUSTICE SCALIA, with whom JUSTICE GINSBURG, JUSTICE SOTOMAYOR, and JUSTICE KAGAN join, dissenting.

The Fourth Amendment forbids searching a person for evidence of a crime when there is no basis for believing the person is guilty of the crime or is in possession of incriminating evidence. That prohibition is categorical and without exception; it lies at the very heart of the Fourth Amendment. Whenever this Court has allowed a suspicionless search, it has insisted upon a justifying motive apart from the investigation of crime.

It is obvious that no such noninvestigative motive exists in this case. The Court's assertion that DNA is being taken, not to solve crimes, but to *identify* those in the State's custody, taxes the credulity of the credulous. And the Court's comparison of Maryland's DNA searches to other techniques, such as fingerprinting, can seem apt only to those who know no more than today's opinion has chosen to tell them about how those DNA searches actually work.

I

A

At the time of the Founding, Americans despised the British use of so-called "general warrants"—warrants not grounded upon a sworn oath of a specific infraction by a particular individual, and thus not limited in scope and application. The first Virginia Constitution declared that "general warrants, whereby any officer or messenger may be commanded to search suspected places without evidence of a fact committed," or to search a person "whose offence is not particularly described and supported by evidence," "are grievous and oppressive, and ought not be granted." The Maryland Declaration of Rights similarly provided that general warrants were "illegal."

In the ratification debates, Antifederalists sarcastically predicted that the general, suspicionless warrant would be among the Constitution's "blessings." "Brutus" of New York asked why the Federal Constitution contained no provision like Maryland's, and Patrick Henry warned that the new Federal Constitution would expose the citizenry to searches and seizures "in the most arbitrary manner, without any evidence or reason."

Madison's draft of what became the Fourth Amendment answered these charges by providing that the "rights of the people to be secured in their persons . . . from all unreasonable searches and seizures, shall not be violated by warrants issued without probable cause . . . or not particularly describing the places to be searched." As ratified, the Fourth Amendment's Warrant Clause forbids a warrant to "issue" except "upon probable cause," and requires that it be "particula[r]" (which is to say, *individualized*) to "the place to be searched, and the persons or things to be seized." And we have held that, even when a warrant is not constitutionally necessary, the Fourth Amendment's general prohibition of "unreasonable" searches imports the same requirement of individualized suspicion.

Although there is a "closely guarded category of constitutionally permissible suspicionless searches" that has never included searches designed to serve "the normal need for law enforcement." Even the common name for suspicionless searches—"special needs" searches—itself reflects that they must be justified, *always*, by concerns "other than crime detection." We have approved random drug tests of railroad employees, yes—but only because the Government's need to "regulat[e] the conduct of railroad employees to ensure safety" is distinct from "normal law enforcement." So too we have approved suspicionless searches in public schools—but only because there the government acts in furtherance of its "responsibilities . . . as guardian and tutor of children entrusted to its care."

So while the Court is correct to note that there are instances in which we have permitted searches without individualized suspicion, "[i]n none of these cases. . . did we indicate approval of a [search] whose primary purpose was to detect evidence of ordinary criminal wrongdoing." That limitation is crucial. It is only when a governmental purpose aside from crime-solving is at stake that we engage in the free-form "reasonableness" inquiry that the Court indulges at length today. To put it another way, both the legitimacy of the Court's method and the correctness of its outcome hinge entirely on the truth of a single proposition: that the primary purpose of these DNA searches is something other than simply discovering evidence of criminal wrongdoing. As I detail below, that proposition is wrong.

B

The Court alludes at several points to the fact that King was an arrestee, and arrestees maybe validly searched incident to their arrest. But the Court does not really *rest* on this principle, and for good reason: The objects of a search incident to arrest must be either (1) weapons or evidence that might easily be destroyed, or (2) evidence relevant to the crime of arrest. Neither is the object of the search at issue here.

The Court hastens to clarify that it does not mean to approve invasive surgery on arrestees or warrantless searches of their homes. That the Court feels the need to disclaim these consequences is as damning a criticism of its suspicionless-search regime as any I can muster. And the Court's attempt to distinguish those hypothetical searches from this real one is unconvincing. We are told that the "privacy-related concerns" in the search of a home "are weighty enough that the search may require a warrant, notwithstanding the diminished expectations of privacy of the arrestee." But why are the "privacy-related concerns" not also "weighty" when an intrusion into the *body* is at stake? (The Fourth Amendment lists "persons" *first* among the entities protected against unreasonable searches and seizures.) And could the police engage, without any suspicion of wrongdoing, in a "brief and . . . minimal" intrusion into the home of an arrestee—perhaps just peeking around the curtilage a bit? Obviously not.

At any rate, all this discussion is beside the point. No matter the degree of invasiveness, suspicionless searches are *never* allowed if their principal end is ordinary crime solving. A search incident to arrest either serves other ends (such as officer safety, in a search for weapons) or is not suspicionless (as when there is reason to believe the arrestee possesses evidence relevant to the crime of arrest).

Sensing (correctly) that it needs more, the Court elaborates at length the ways that the search here served the special purpose of "identifying" King. But that seems to me quite wrong—unless what one means by "identifying" someone is "searching for evidence that he has committed crimes unrelated to the crime of his arrest." At points the Court does appear to use "identifying" in that peculiar sense—claiming, for example, that knowing "an arrestee's past conduct is essential to an assessment of the danger he poses." If identifying someone means finding out what unsolved crimes he has committed, then identification is indistinguishable from the ordinary law-enforcement aims that have never been thought to justify a suspicionless search. Searching every lawfully stopped car, for example, might turn up information about unsolved crimes the driver had committed, but no one would say that such a search was aimed at "identifying" him, and no court would hold such a search lawful. I will therefore assume that the Court means that the DNA search at issue here was useful to "identify" King in the normal sense of that word—in the sense that would identify the author of Introduction to the Principles of Morals and Legislation as Jeremy Bentham.

1

The portion of the Court's opinion that explains the identification rationale is strangely silent on the actual workings of the DNA search at issue here. To know those facts is to be instantly disabused of the notion that what happened had anything to do with identifying King.

King was arrested on April 10, 2009, on charges unrelated to the case before us. That same day, April 10, the police searched him and seized the DNA evidence at issue here. What happened next? Reading the Court's opinion, particularly its insistence that the search was necessary to know "who [had] been arrested," one might guess that King's DNA was swiftly processed and his identity thereby confirmed—perhaps against some master database of known DNA profiles, as is done for fingerprints. After all, was not the suspicionless search here crucial to avoid "inordinate risks for facility staff" or to "existing detainee population"? Surely, then— *surely*—the State of Maryland got cracking on those grave risks immediately, by rushing to identify King with his DNA as soon as possible.

Nothing could be further from the truth. Maryland officials did not even begin the process of testing King's DNA that day. Or, actually, the next day. Or the day after that. And that was for a simple reason: Maryland law forbids them to do so. A "DNA sample collected from an individual charged with a crime . . . *may not* be tested or placed in the statewide DNA data base system prior to the first scheduled arraignment date." And King's first appearance in court was not until three days after his arrest. (I suspect, though, that they did not wait three days to ask his name or take his fingerprints.)

This places in a rather different light the Court's solemn declaration that the search here was necessary so that King could be identified at "every stage of the criminal process." I hope that the Maryland officials who read the Court's opinion do not take it seriously. Acting on the Court's misperception of Maryland law could lead to jail time. Does the Court really believe that Maryland did not know whom it was arraigning? The Court's response is to imagine that release on bail could take so long that the DNA results are returned in time, or perhaps that bail could be revoked if the DNA test turned up incriminating information. That is no answer at all. If the purpose of this Act is to assess "whether [King] should be released on bail," why would it *possibly* forbid the DNA testing process to *begin* until King was arraigned? Why would Maryland resign itself to simply hoping that the bail decision will drag out long enough that the "identification" can succeed before the arrestee is released? The truth, known to Maryland and increasingly to the reader: this search had nothing to do with establishing King's identity.

It gets worse. King's DNA sample was not received by the Maryland State Police's Forensic Sciences Division until April 23, 2009—two weeks after his arrest. It sat in that office, ripening in a storage area, until the custodians got around to mailing it to a lab for testing on June 25, 2009—two months after it was received, and nearly *three* since King's arrest. After it was mailed, the data from the lab tests were not available for several more weeks, until July 13, 2009, which is when the test results were entered into Maryland's DNA database, *together with information identifying the person from whom the sample was taken.* Meanwhile, bail had been set, King had engaged in discovery, and he had requested a speedy trial—presumably not a trial of John Doe. It was not until August 4, 2009—four months after King's arrest—that the forwarded sample transmitted (*without* identifying information) from the Maryland DNA database to the Federal Bureau of Investigation's national database was matched with a sample taken from the scene of an unrelated crime years earlier.

A more specific description of exactly what happened at this point illustrates why, by definition, King could not have been *identified* by this match. The FBI's DNA database (known as CODIS) consists of two distinct collections. One of them, the one to which King's DNA was submitted, consists of DNA samples taken from known convicts or arrestees. I will refer to this as the "Convict and Arrestee Collection." The other collection consists of samples taken from crime scenes; I will refer to this as the "Unsolved Crimes Collection." The Convict and Arrestee Collection stores "no names or other personal identifiers of the offenders, arrestees, or detainees." Rather, it contains only the DNA profile itself, the name of the agency that submitted it, the laboratory personnel who analyzed it, and an identification number for the specimen. This

is because the submitting state laboratories are expected *already* to know the identities of the convicts and arrestees from whom samples are taken. (And, of course, they do.)

Moreover, the CODIS system works by checking to see whether any of the samples in the Unsolved Crimes Collection match any of the samples in the Convict and Arrestee Collection. That is sensible, if what one wants to do is solve those cold cases, but note what it requires: that the identity of the people whose DNA has been entered in the Convict and Arrestee Collection *already be known.*[1] If one wanted to identify someone in custody using his DNA, the logical thing to do would be to compare that DNA against the Convict and Arrestee Collection: to search, in other words, the collection that could be used (by checking back with the submitting state agency) to identify people, rather than the collection of evidence from unsolved crimes, whose perpetrators are by definition unknown. But that is not what was done. And that is because this search had nothing to do with identification.

In fact, if anything was "identified" at the moment that the DNA database returned a match, it was not King—his identity was already known. (The docket for the original criminal charges lists his full name, his race, his sex, his height, his weight, his date of birth, and his address.) Rather, what the August 4 match "identified" was *the previously-taken sample from the earlier crime.* That sample was genuinely mysterious to Maryland; the State knew that it had probably been left by the victim's attacker, but nothing else. King was not identified by his association with the sample; rather, the sample was identified by its association with King. The Court effectively destroys its own "identification" theory when it acknowledges that the object of this search was "to see what [was] already known about [King]." King was who he was, and volumes of his biography could not make him any more or any less King. No minimally competent speaker of English would say, upon noticing a known arrestee's similarity "to a wanted poster of a previously unidentified suspect," that the *arrestee* had thereby been identified. It was the previously unidentified suspect who had been identified—just as, here, it was the previously unidentified rapist.

2

That taking DNA samples from arrestees has nothing to do with identifying them is confirmed not just by actual practice (which the Court ignores) but by the enabling statute itself (which the Court also ignores). The Maryland Act at issue has a section helpfully entitled "Purpose of collecting and testing DNA samples." (One would expect such a section to play a somewhat larger role in the Court's analysis of the Act's purpose—which is to say, at least *some* role.) That provision lists five purposes for which DNA samples may be tested. By this point, it will not surprise the reader to learn that the Court's imagined purpose is not among them.

Instead, the law provides that DNA samples are collected and tested, as a matter of Maryland law, "as part of a official investigation into a crime." (Or, as our suspicionless-search cases would put it: for ordinary law-enforcement purposes.) That is certainly how everyone has always understood the Maryland Act until today. The Governor of Maryland, in commenting on our decision to hear this case, said that he was glad, because "[a]llowing law enforcement to collect DNA samples . . . is absolutely critical to our efforts to continue driving down crime," and "bolsters our efforts to resolve open investigations and bring them to a resolution." The attorney general of Maryland remarked that he "look[ed] forward to the opportunity to defend this important crime-fighting tool," and praised the DNA database for helping to "bring to justice violent perpetrators." Even this Court's order staying the decision below states that the statute "provides a valuable tool for investigating unsolved crimes and thereby helping to remove violent offenders from the general population"—with, unsurprisingly, no mention of identity.

More devastating still for the Court's "identification" theory, the statute *does* enumerate two instances in which a DNA sample may be tested for the purpose of identification: "to help identify *human remains*," and "to help identify *missing individuals*." No mention of identifying arrestees. And note again that Maryland forbids using DNA records "for any purposes other than those specified"—it is actually a crime to do so.

The Maryland regulations implementing the Act confirm what is now monotonously obvious: These DNA searches have nothing to do with identification. For example, if someone is arrested and law enforcement determines that "a convicted offender Statewide DNA Data Base sample already exists" for that arrestee, "the agency is not required to obtain a new sample." But how could the State know if an arrestee has already had his DNA sample collected, if the point of the sample is to identify who he is? Of course, if the DNA sample is instead taken in order to investigate crimes, this restriction makes perfect sense: Having previously placed an identified someone's DNA on file to check against available crime-scene evidence, there is no sense in going to the expense of taking a new sample. . . .

So, to review: DNA testing does not even begin until after arraignment and bail decisions are already made.

The samples sit in storage for months, and take weeks to test. When they are tested, they are checked against the Unsolved Crimes Collection—rather than the Convict and Arrestee Collection, which could be used to identify them. The Act forbids the Court's purpose (identification), but prescribes as its purpose what our suspicionless-search cases forbid ("official investigation into a crime"). Against all of that, it is safe to say that if the Court's identification theory is not wrong, there is no such thing as error.

II

The Court also attempts to bolster its identification theory with a series of inapposite analogies.

Is not taking DNA samples the same, asks the Court, as taking a person's photograph? No—because that is not a Fourth Amendment search at all. It does not involve a physical intrusion onto the person, and we have never held that merely taking a person's photograph invades any recognized "expectation of privacy." Thus, it is unsurprising that the cases the Court cites as authorizing photo-taking do not even mention the Fourth Amendment.

But is not the practice of DNA searches, the Court asks, the same as taking "Bertillon" measurements—noting an arrestee's height, shoe size, and so on, on the back of a photograph? No, because that system was not, in the ordinary case, used to solve unsolved crimes. It is possible, I suppose, to imagine situations in which such measurements might be useful to generate leads. (If witnesses described a very tall burglar, all the "tall man" cards could then be pulled.) But the obvious primary purpose of such measurements, as the Court's description of them makes clear, was to verify that, for example, the person arrested today is the same person that was arrested a year ago. Which is to say, Bertillon measurements were *actually* used as a system of identification, and drew their primary usefulness from that task.

It is on the fingerprinting of arrestees, however, that the Court relies most heavily. The Court does not actually say whether it believes that taking a person's fingerprints is a Fourth Amendment search, and our cases provide no ready answer to that question. Even assuming so, however, law enforcement's post-arrest use of fingerprints could not be more different from its post-arrest use of DNA. Fingerprints of arrestees are taken primarily to identify them (though that process sometimes solves crimes); the DNA of arrestees is taken to solve crimes (and nothing else). Contrast CODIS, the FBI's nationwide DNA database, with IAFIS, the FBI's Integrated Automated Fingerprint Identification System.

Fingerprints	DNA Samples
The "average response time for an electronic criminal fingerprint submission is about 27 minutes."	DNA analysis can take months—far too long to be useful for identifying someone.
IAFIS includes detailed identification information, including "criminal histories; mug shots; scars and tattoo photos; physical characteristics like height, weight, and hair and eye color."	CODIS contains "[n]o names or other personal identifiers of the offenders, arrestees, or detainees."
"Latent prints" recovered from crime scenes are not systematically compared against the database of known fingerprints, since that requires further forensic work.[2]	The entire *point* of the DNA database is to check crime scene evidence against the profiles of arrestees and convicts as they come in.

The Court asserts that the taking of fingerprints was "constitutional for generations prior to the introduction" of the FBI's rapid computer-matching system. This bold statement is bereft of citation to authority because there is none for it. The "great expansion in fingerprinting came before the modern era of Fourth Amendment jurisprudence," and so we were never asked to decide the legitimacy of the practice. As fingerprint databases expanded from convicted criminals, to arrestees, to civil servants, to immigrants, to everyone with a driver's license, Americans simply "became accustomed to having our fingerprints on file in some government database." But it is wrong to suggest that this was uncontroversial at the time, or that this Court blessed universal fingerprinting for "generations" before it was possible to use it effectively for identification.

The Court also assures us that "the delay in processing DNA from arrestees is being reduced to a substantial degree by rapid technical advances." The idea, presumably, is that the snail's pace in this case is atypical, so that DNA is now readily usable for identification. The Court's proof, however, is nothing but a pair of press releases—each of which turns out to undercut this argument. We learn in them that reductions in backlog have enabled Ohio and Louisiana crime labs to analyze a submitted DNA sample in twenty days. But that is *still longer* than the *eighteen* days that Maryland needed to analyze King's sample, once it worked its way through the State's labyrinthine bureaucracy. What this illustrates is that these times do not take into account the many other sources of delay. So if the Court means to suggest that Maryland is unusual, that may be right—it may qualify in this context as a paragon of efficiency. . . .

Meanwhile, the Court's holding will result in the dumping of a large number of arrestee samples—many from minor offenders—onto an already overburdened system: Nearly one-third of Americans will be arrested for some offense by age 23. See Brame, Turner, Paternoster, & Bushway, Cumulative Prevalence of Arrest From Ages 8 to 23 in a National Sample, 129 Pediatrics 21 (2011).

The Court also accepts uncritically the Government's representation at oral argument that it is developing devices that will be able to test DNA in mere minutes. At most, this demonstrates that it may one day be possible to design a program that uses DNA for a purpose other than crime-solving—not that Maryland has in fact designed such a program today. And that is the main point, which the Court's discussion of the brave new world of instant DNA analysis should not obscure. The issue before us is not whether DNA can *some day* be used for identification; nor even whether it can *today* be used for identification; but whether it *was used for identification here.*

Today, it can fairly be said that fingerprints really are used to identify people—so well, in fact, that there would be no need for the expense of a separate, wholly redundant DNA confirmation of the same information. What DNA adds—what makes it a valuable weapon in the law-enforcement arsenal—is the ability to solve unsolved crimes, by matching old crime-scene evidence against the profiles of people whose identities are already known. That is what was going on when King's DNA was taken, and we should not disguise the fact. Solving unsolved crimes is a noble objective, but it occupies a lower place in the American pantheon of noble objectives than the protection of our people from suspicionless law-enforcement searches. The Fourth Amendment must prevail.

* * *

The Court disguises the vast (and scary) scope of its holding by promising a limitation it cannot deliver. The Court repeatedly says that DNA testing, and entry into a national DNA registry, will not befall thee and me, dear reader, but only those arrested for "serious offense[s]." I cannot imagine what principle could possibly justify this limitation, and the Court does not attempt to suggest any. If one believes that DNA will "identify" someone arrested for assault, he must believe that it will "identify" someone arrested for a traffic offense. This Court does not base its judgments on senseless distinctions. At the end of the day, *logic will out.* When there comes before us the taking of DNA from an arrestee for a traffic violation, the Court will predictably (and quite rightly) say, "We can find no significant difference between this case and *King.*" Make no mistake about it: As an entirely predictable consequence of today's decision, your DNA can be taken and entered into a national DNA database if you are ever arrested, rightly or wrongly, and for whatever reason.

The most regrettable aspect of the suspicionless search that occurred here is that it proved to be quite unnecessary. All parties concede that it would have been entirely permissible, as far as the Fourth Amendment is concerned, for Maryland to take a sample of King's DNA as a consequence of his conviction for second-degree assault. So the ironic result of the Court's error is this: The only arrestees to whom the outcome here will ever make a difference are those who *have been acquitted* of the crime of arrest (so that their DNA could not have been taken upon conviction). In other words, this Act manages to burden uniquely the sole group for whom the Fourth Amendment's protections ought to be most jealously guarded: people who are innocent of the State's accusations.

Today's judgment will, to be sure, have the beneficial effect of solving more crimes; then again, so would the taking of DNA samples from anyone who flies on an airplane (surely the Transportation Security Administration needs to know the "identity" of the flying public), applies for a driver's license, or attends a public school. Perhaps the construction of such a genetic panopticon is wise. But I doubt that the proud men who wrote the charter of our liberties would have been so eager to open their mouths for royal inspection.

I therefore dissent, and hope that today's incursion upon the Fourth Amendment, like an earlier one,[3] will some day be repudiated.

Notes

1. By the way, this procedure has nothing to do with exonerating the wrongfully convicted, as the Court soothingly promises. The FBI CODIS database includes DNA from *unsolved* crimes. I know of no indication (and the Court cites none) that it also includes DNA from all—or even any—crimes whose perpetrators have already been convicted.

2. See, *e.g.*, FBI, Privacy Impact Assessment: Integrated Automated Fingerprint Identification System (IAFIS)/Next Generation Identification (NGI) Repository for Individuals of Special Concern (RISC), http://www.fbi.gov/foia/privacy-impact-assessments/iafis-ngi-risc (searches of the "Unsolved Latent File" may "take considerably more time").

3. Compare, *New York* v. *Belton*, 453 U. S. 454 (1981) (suspic ionless search of a car permitted upon arrest of the driver), with *Arizona* v. *Gant*, 556 U. S. 332 (2009) (on second thought, no).

Antonin Scalia is an associate justice of the U.S. Supreme Court. He taught law at the University of Virginia, the America n Enterprise Institute, Georgetown University, and the University of Chicago before being nominated to the U.S. Court of Appeals by President Ronald Reagan in 1982. He served in that capacity until he was nominated by Reagan to the Supreme Court in 1986.

Does the 4th Amendment Prohibit Police in Collecting DNA Samples of Persons Arrested but Not Convicted on Felony Charges? by Katsh

287

EXPLORING THE ISSUE

Does the Fourth Amendment Prohibit the Police from Collecting a DNA Sample from a Person Arrested, but Not Yet Convicted on Felony Charges?

Critical Thinking and Reflection

1. Is fingerprinting an apt analogy to the use of DNA profiles in law enforcement? Why or why not?
2. How do the timing of DNA collection and the creation of DNA profiles influence each side's argument?
3. What are the government's interests in collecting DNA samples from arrestees? How do they compare to the interests of the individual to not be subjected to a cheek swab?

Is There Common Ground?

There is a well-established legal framework for determining whether a government search or seizure satisfies the Fourth Amendment, and both Justice Kennedy and Justice Scalia accept this framework. First, searches may be executed pursuant to a properly issued warrant. If (as here) no warrant has been issued, the reasonableness of the search is determined by balancing the legitimate interests of the government against the degree of intrusion upon the individual's privacy. Both sides recognize the important government interests in collecting DNA evidence, such as helping to crack unsolved crimes, identifying dangerous suspects, and preventing the incarceration of the innocent. Both sides also recognize that individual privacy is violated by any physical invasion, even a painless one like a cheek swab. The debate centers on how to weigh the value of the government's legitimate interests against the value of freedom from unreasonable government intrusion into one's body. This is probably a closer call than either opinion lets on, for a free society and a safe society are both strongly desirable. Justice Kennedy strikes the balance on the side of emerging technology, whereas Justice Scalia places the criminal justice benefits of DNA analysis "in a lower place on the American pantheon of noble objectives than the protection of our people from suspicionless law-enforcement searches."

Justices Kennedy and Scalia also agree that the collection of DNA from someone convicted of a crime would not violate the Fourth Amendment's prohibition on unreasonable searches and seizures. This practice has been ongoing for many years and is relatively uncontroversial. Although the Supreme Court did not address this issue specifically in *Maryland v. King*, it is useful to ask why the collection of DNA from convicted individuals has been deemed unproblematic from a legal standpoint.

Additional Resources

Berson, Sarah B., "Debating DNA Collection." *NIJ J*, 26, (November 2009).

Biancamano, John D., "Arresting DNA: The Evolving Nature of DNA Collection Statutes and their Fourth Amendment Justifications." 70 *Ohio State Law J.* 613 (2009).

Monteleoni, Paul M., "DNA Databases, Universality, and the Fourth Amendment." 82 *New York Univ. Law Rev.* 247 (2007).

Internet References . . .

Federal Bureau of Investigation, CODIS and NDIS Fact Sheet

This site presents official details on the CODIS program and the operation of the National DNA Index System.

**www.fbi.gov/about-us/lab/biometric-analysis/codis
/codis-and-ndis-fact-sheet**

The Brookings Institution

This article by Brookings Visiting Fellow Richard Lempert lays out a variety of detailed arguments against the collection of DNA after an arrest, including arguments that were not raised in Justice Scalia's dissent.

**www.brookings.edu/blogs/up-front/posts/2013/06/06
-maryland-king-supreme-court-dna-samples-lempert**

SCOTUSBlog

This page provides summaries of the *Maryland v. King* oral arguments before the Supreme Court, and links to the briefs filed by the parties and other interested organizations.

www.scotusblog.com/?p=164386

Stanford Law School Center for Law and Biosciences

This blog contains several illuminating posts on *Maryland v. King* and its aftermath, including an exploration of how the decision will affect similar cases in California.

**http://blogs.law.stanford.edu/lawandbiosciences
/2013/06/08/maryland-v-king-%E2%80%93-the
-coming-california-sequels/**

Selected, Edited, and with Issue Framing Material by:
M. Ethan Katsh, *University of Massachusetts, Amherst*

ISSUE

Is Same-sex Marriage Protected by the Fourteenth Amendment to the U.S. Constitution?

YES: **Anthony Kennedy**, from "Majority Opinion, *Obergefell v. Hodges*," *U.S. Supreme Court* (2015)

NO: **John G. Roberts, Jr.**, from "Dissenting Opinion, *Obergefell v. Hodges*," *U.S. Supreme Court* (2015)

Learning Outcomes
After reading this issue, you will be able to:
• Consider different ways to interpret guarantees of equal protection in the U.S. Constitution.
• Discuss the arguments surrounding how to apply constitutional protections of minority rights to the issue of same-sex marriage.
• Assess different views about the role of the courts in setting public policy.

ISSUE SUMMARY

YES: Supreme Court Justice Anthony Kennedy holds that marriage is a fundamental right, and bans on same-sex marriage are unconstitutional under the Due Process and Equal Protection Clauses of the Fourteenth Amendment.

NO: Supreme Court Chief Justice John Roberts argues that it is no place for the Court, as unelected lawyers, to make the determination of what defines "marriage," as that is the job of the legislature and not the judiciary.

Few major issues have traveled the journey from taboo to national movement faster than the issue of same-sex marriage in America. Same-sex marriage has become both an issue in its own right and a symbol of a large culture war between traditionalists and progressives, as it crosses the bounds of several subjects of great import to many Americans. What is the definition of "marriage?" What does it mean to be married? Is it a religious or civil union, a legal relationship, a moral bond, or a fundamental right? Is it the government's role to make decisions regarding family? If so, upon which part of the government does the Constitution bestow this power?

Given its history, the institution of marriage has become a commonly used unit of measurement and consequence for many facets of our lives. Over 1,000 federal statutes and countless regulations refer to the institution of marriage in some form. Checking the box labeled single or married has serious implications that affect how we interact with government and private businesses. Income taxes, health insurance, estate planning, housing, and child-rearing all of these life decisions may have quite different ramifications for single and married people.

Prior to 2004, no state in the United States permitted same-sex couples to marry. The status quo changed after the Massachusetts Supreme Judicial Court issued its opinion in *Goodridge v. Department of Public Health* (798 N.E.2d 941, Mass. 2003), holding that "[l]imiting the protections, benefits, and obligations of civil marriage to opposite-sex couples violates the basic premises of individual liberty and equality under law protected by the Massachusetts Constitution." The decision provoked a backlash that was evident in the 2004 general elections. Both major candidates in the presidential race, George W. Bush and John Kerry, voiced their opposition to same-sex marriage, and 11 states (Arkansas, Georgia, Kentucky, Michigan, Ohio, and Utah) overwhelmingly passed ballot initiatives that contained same-sex marriage bans.

Despite popular opposition to same-sex marriage, many states continued passing laws recognizing same-sex civil unions and domestic partnerships. In 1999, Beth Robinson, currently a Justice of the Vermont Supreme Court, was cocounsel in the groundbreaking case *Baker v. State* (744 A.2d 864, Vt. 1999), resulting in Vermont becoming the first state in the country to recognize civil unions. Same-sex marriage proponents were also successful in persuading state courts in Iowa, California, and Connecticut that a right to same-sex marriage was protected by their respective state constitutions. Equally important, a dramatic shift in public opinion began, likely due to the public attention that these lawsuits and political campaigns brought to the real practical difficulties that marriage bans inflicted on same-sex couples. In stark contrast to only a decade ago, polls now show that a majority of Americans support equal marriage rights for same-sex couples.

In 2013, the U.S. Supreme Court issued a landmark ruling on same-sex marriage in *United States v. Windsor*, striking down as unconstitutional a portion of the federal Defense of Marriage Act ("DOMA"), which had been passed in 1996 to ensure that only opposite-sex couples would be recognized as legally married under federal law. The *Windsor* decision harshly denounced DOMA as being motivated by antigay prejudice, finding that its "principal purpose [was] to impose inequality" and "demean" same-sex couples. Although directly applicable only to federal law, the *Windsor* decision had clear implications for state same-sex marriage bans. Indeed, almost immediately, lawsuits were filed in the lower federal courts arguing that, after *Windsor*, there was no way to view state same-sex marriage bans as constitutionally permissible: just like DOMA, such bans were the product of unconstitutional "animus" rather than any legitimate political ends. For over a year, same-sex marriage advocates won every single one of these cases, as each federal circuit court to consider the issue agreed that *Windsor's* reasoning required it to strike down the state bans.

In November 2014, a panel for the Sixth Circuit Court of Appeals surprised many by upholding a series of same-sex marriage laws in the states under its geographic purview. The panel decided, 2–1, that the constitutional issue was not as clear-cut as other federal courts had held. Writing for the two-judge majority, Judge Jeffrey Sutton said that there were arguably some legitimate reasons why states might want to limit marriage to opposite-sex couples, and it was not the place of the courts to second-guess such determinations made through the democratic process. The Supreme Court accepted this case for review.

In one of, if not the most anticipated opinions of the 2014–2015 term, Justice Anthony Kennedy authored the majority opinion in *Obergefell v. Hodges*, which was decided on June 26, 2015. The Court, in a 5–3 split, held that marriage is a fundamental right, thus same-sex marriage is protected under the Due Process and Equal Protection Clauses of the Fourteenth Amendment. As same-sex marriage bans are now deemed unconstitutional, the ruling in *Obergefell* further requires states to recognize lawful same-sex marriages executed in other states. The judgment was based on the overwhelming "insights and societal understandings," that were used to identify the inequalities in the institution of marriage based on sex-based classifications, which "vindicate[ed] precepts of liberty . . . under the Constitution."

Chief Justice John Roberts authored one of the two dissents, with the other by the late Justice Antonin Scalia. The Chief Justice argued that the majority essentially legislated from the bench and made judicial decisions based on their "desire to remake society according to [their] 'new insight' into the 'nature of injustice [and fundamental liberties].'" Attempting to keep personal views aside, Chief Justice Roberts made clear that his disagreement was not with the outcome, but with allowing five unelected lawyers to make the determination of what constitutes "marriage," instead of by "the people acting through their elected representatives [as intended through our democratic republic]."

With the recent appointment of a new Supreme Court justice, and the likely appointment of more during the next four years of Republican congressional and presidential tenure, the legal community as well as the country should keep an eye on the status of *Obergefell*. If the decision is one day reversed, it will likely cause confusion and procedural chaos for those once affected by the Court's holding.

YES ↵

Anthony Kennedy

Majority Opinion, *Obergefell v. Hodges*

JUSTICE KENNEDY delivered the opinion of the Court.

The Constitution promises liberty to all within its reach, a liberty that includes certain specific rights that allow persons, within a lawful realm, to define and express their identity. The petitioners in these cases seek to find that liberty by marrying someone of the same sex and having their marriages deemed lawful on the same terms and conditions as marriages between persons of the opposite sex.

I

These cases come from Michigan, Kentucky, Ohio, and Tennessee, states that define marriage as a union between one man and one woman. The petitioners are 14 same-sex couples and two men whose same-sex partners are deceased. The respondents are state officials responsible for enforcing the laws in question. The petitioners claim the respondents violate the Fourteenth Amendment by denying them the right to marry or to have their marriages, lawfully performed in another state, given full recognition.

Petitioners filed these suits in U.S. District Courts in their home states. Each District Court ruled in their favor. The respondents appealed the decisions against them to the U.S. Court of Appeals for the Sixth Circuit. It consolidated the cases and reversed the judgments of the District Courts (*DeBoer v. Snyder*, 772 F. 3d 388, 2014). The Court of Appeals held that a state has no constitutional obligation to license same-sex marriages or to recognize same-sex marriages performed out of state.

The petitioners sought certiorari. This Court granted review, limited to two questions. The first, presented by the cases from Michigan and Kentucky, is whether the Fourteenth Amendment requires a state to license a marriage between two people of the same sex. The second, presented by the cases from Ohio, Tennessee, and, again, Kentucky, is whether the Fourteenth Amendment requires a state to recognize a same-sex marriage licensed and performed in a state which does grant that right.

II

A

From their beginning to their most recent page, the annals of human history reveal the transcendent importance of marriage. The lifelong union of a man and a woman always has promised nobility and dignity to all persons, without regard to their station in life. Marriage is sacred to those who live by their religions and offers unique fulfillment to those who find meaning in the secular realm. Its dynamic allows two people to find a life that could not be found alone, for a marriage becomes greater than just the two persons. Rising from the most basic human needs, marriage is essential to our most profound hopes and aspirations.

The centrality of marriage to the human condition makes it unsurprising that the institution has existed for millennia and across civilizations.

· · ·

That history is the beginning of these cases. The respondents say it should be the end as well. To them, it would demean a timeless institution if the concept and lawful status of marriage were extended to two persons of the same sex. Marriage, in their view, is by its nature a gender-differentiated union of man and woman. This view long has been held—and continues to be held—in good faith by reasonable and sincere people here and throughout the world.

The petitioners acknowledge this history but contend that these cases cannot end there. Were their intent to demean the revered idea and reality of marriage, the petitioners' claims would be of a different order. But that is neither their purpose nor their submission. To the contrary, it is the enduring importance of marriage that underlies the petitioners' contentions. This, they say, is their whole point. Far from seeking to devalue marriage, the petitioners seek it for themselves because of their respect—and need—for its privileges and responsibilities.

Majority Opinion, Obergefell v. Hodges, U.S. Supreme Court, 135 S. Ct. 2071, 2015.

And their immutable nature dictates that same-sex marriage is their only real path to this profound commitment.

Recounting the circumstances of three of these cases illustrates the urgency of the petitioners' cause from their perspective. Petitioner James Obergefell, a plaintiff in the Ohio case, met John Arthur over two decades ago. They fell in love and started a life together, establishing a lasting, committed relation. In 2011, however, Arthur was diagnosed with amyotrophic lateral sclerosis, or ALS. This debilitating disease is progressive, with no known cure. Two years ago, Obergefell and Arthur decided to commit to one another, resolving to marry before Arthur died. To fulfill their mutual promise, they traveled from Ohio to Maryland, where same-sex marriage was legal. It was difficult for Arthur to move, and so the couple were wed inside a medical transport plane as it remained on the tarmac in Baltimore. Three months later, Arthur died. Ohio law does not permit Obergefell to be listed as the surviving spouse on Arthur's death certificate. By statute, they must remain strangers even in death, a state-imposed separation Obergefell deems "hurtful for the rest of time." He brought suit to be shown as the surviving spouse on Arthur's death certificate.

April DeBoer and Jayne Rowse are co-plaintiffs in the case from Michigan. They celebrated a commitment ceremony to honor their permanent relation in 2007. They both work as nurses, DeBoer in a neonatal unit and Rowse in an emergency unit. In 2009, DeBoer and Rowse fostered and then adopted a baby boy. Later that same year, they welcomed another son into their family. The new baby, born prematurely and abandoned by his biological mother, required around-the-clock care. The next year, a baby girl with special needs joined their family. Michigan, however, permits only opposite-sex married couples or single individuals to adopt, so each child can have only one woman as his or her legal parent. If an emergency were to arise, schools and hospitals may treat the three children as if they had only one parent. And, were tragedy to befall either DeBoer or Rowse, the other would have no legal rights over the children she had not been permitted to adopt. This couple seeks relief from the continuing uncertainty their unmarried status creates in their lives.

Army Reserve Sergeant First Class Ijpe DeKoe and his partner Thomas Kostura, co-plaintiffs in the Tennessee case, fell in love. In 2011, DeKoe received orders to deploy to Afghanistan. Before leaving, he and Kostura married in New York. A week later, DeKoe began his deployment, which lasted for almost a year. When he returned, the two settled in Tennessee, where DeKoe works full-time for the Army Reserve. Their lawful marriage is stripped from them whenever they reside in Tennessee, returning and disappearing as they travel across state lines. DeKoe, who served this Nation to preserve the freedom the Constitution protects, must endure a substantial burden.

The cases now before the Court involve other petitioners as well, each with their own experiences. Their stories reveal that they seek not to denigrate marriage but rather to live their lives, or honor their spouses' memory, joined by its bond.

B

The ancient origins of marriage confirm its centrality, but it has not stood in isolation from developments in law and society. The history of marriage is one of both continuity and change. That institution—even as confined to opposite-sex relations—has evolved over time.

For example, marriage was once viewed as an arrangement by the couple's parents based on political, religious, and financial concerns; but by the time of the Nation's founding, it was understood to be a voluntary contract between a man and a woman. As the role and status of women changed, the institution further evolved. Under the centuries-old doctrine of coverture, a married man and woman were treated by the state as a single, male-dominated legal entity. As women gained legal, political, and property rights and as society began to understand that women have their own equal dignity, the law of coverture was abandoned. These and other developments in the institution of marriage over the past centuries were not mere superficial changes. Rather, they worked deep transformations in its structure, affecting aspects of marriage long viewed by many as essential.

These new insights have strengthened, not weakened, the institution of marriage. Indeed, changed understandings of marriage are characteristic of a Nation where new dimensions of freedom become apparent to new generations, often through perspectives that begin in pleas or protests and then are considered in the political sphere and the judicial process.

This dynamic can be seen in the Nation's experiences with the rights of gays and lesbians. Until the mid-20th century, same-sex intimacy long had been condemned as immoral by the state itself in most Western nations, a belief often embodied in the criminal law. For this reason, among others, many persons did not deem homosexuals to have dignity in their own distinct identity.

A truthful declaration by same-sex couples of what was in their hearts had to remain unspoken. Even when a greater awareness of the humanity and integrity of homosexual persons came in the period after World War II, the argument that gays and lesbians had a just claim to dignity was in conflict with both law and widespread social conventions. Same-sex intimacy remained a crime in many states. Gays and lesbians were prohibited from most government employment, barred from military service, excluded under immigration laws, targeted by police, and burdened in their rights to associate.

For much of the 20th century, moreover, homosexuality was treated as an illness. When the American Psychiatric Association published the first Diagnostic and Statistical Manual of Mental Disorders in 1952, homosexuality was classified as a mental disorder, a position adhered to until 1973. Only in more recent years have psychiatrists and others recognized that sexual orientation is both a normal expression of human sexuality and immutable.

In the late 20th century, following substantial cultural and political developments, same-sex couples began to lead more open and public lives and to establish families. This development was followed by a quite extensive discussion of the issue in both governmental and private sectors and by a shift in public attitudes toward greater tolerance. As a result, questions about the rights of gays and lesbians soon reached the courts, where the issue could be discussed in the formal discourse of the law.

This Court first gave detailed consideration to the legal status of homosexuals in *Bowers v. Hardwick*, 478 U.S. 186 (1986). There it upheld the constitutionality of a Georgia law deemed to criminalize certain homosexual acts. Ten years later, in *Romer v. Evans*, 517 U.S. 620 (1996), the Court invalidated an amendment to Colorado's Constitution that sought to foreclose any branch or political subdivision of the state from protecting persons against discrimination based on sexual orientation. Then, in 2003, the Court overruled *Bowers*, holding that laws making same-sex intimacy a crime "demea[n] the lives of homosexual persons" (*Lawrence v. Texas*, 539 U.S. 558, 575).

Against this background, the legal question of same-sex marriage arose. In 1993, the Hawaii Supreme Court held Hawaii's law restricting marriage to opposite-sex couples constituted a classification on the basis of sex and was therefore subject to strict scrutiny under the Hawaii Constitution (*Baehr v. Lewin*, 74 Haw. 530, 852 P. 2d 44). Although this decision did not mandate that same-sex marriage be allowed, some states were concerned by its implications and reaffirmed in their laws that marriage is defined as a union between opposite-sex partners. So too in 1996, Congress passed the Defense of Marriage Act (DOMA), 110 Stat. 2419, defining marriage for all

federal-law purposes as "only a legal union between one man and one woman as husband and wife" (1 U.S. C. §7).

The new and widespread discussion of the subject led other states to a different conclusion. In 2003, the Supreme Judicial Court of Massachusetts held the State's Constitution guaranteed same-sex couples the right to marry (see *Goodridge v. Department of Public Health*, 440 Mass. 309, 798 N. E. 2d 941, 2003). After that ruling, some additional states granted marriage rights to same-sex couples, either through judicial or legislative processes. Two terms ago, in *United States v. Windsor*, 570 U.S. (2013), this Court invalidated DOMA to the extent it barred the federal government from treating same-sex marriages as valid even when they were lawful in the state where they were licensed. DOMA, the Court held, impermissibly disparaged those same-sex couples "who wanted to affirm their commitment to one another before their children, their family, their friends, and their community."

. . .

III

Under the Due Process Clause of the Fourteenth Amendment, no state shall "deprive any person of life, liberty, or property, without due process of law." The fundamental liberties protected by this Clause include most of the rights enumerated in the Bill of Rights. In addition, these liberties extend to certain personal choices central to individual dignity and autonomy, including intimate choices that define personal identity and beliefs.

The identification and protection of fundamental rights is an enduring part of the judicial duty to interpret the Constitution. That responsibility, however, "has not been reduced to any formula." Rather, it requires courts to exercise reasoned judgment in identifying interests of the person so fundamental that the state must accord them its respect. That process is guided by many of the same considerations relevant to the analysis of other constitutional provisions that set forth broad principles rather than specific requirements. History and tradition guide and discipline this inquiry but do not set its outer boundaries. That method respects our history and learns from it without allowing the past alone to rule the present.

The nature of injustice is that we may not always see it in our own times. The generations that wrote and ratified the Bill of Rights and the Fourteenth Amendment did not presume to know the extent of freedom in all of its dimensions, and so they entrusted to future generations a charter protecting the right of all persons to enjoy liberty as we learn its meaning. When new insight reveals discord between the Constitution's central protections and a received legal stricture, a claim to liberty must be addressed.

Applying these established tenets, the Court has long held the right to marry is protected by the Constitution. In *Loving v. Virginia*, 388 U.S. 1, 12 (1967), which invalidated bans on interracial unions, a unanimous Court held marriage is "one of the vital personal rights essential to the orderly pursuit of happiness by free men." The Court reaffirmed that holding in *Zablocki v. Redhail*, 434 U.S. 374, 384 (1978), which held the right to marry was burdened by a law prohibiting fathers who were behind on child support from marrying. The Court again applied this principle in *Turner v. Safley*, 482 U.S. 78, 95 (1987), which held the right to marry was abridged by regulations limiting the privilege of prison inmates to marry. Over time and in other contexts, the Court has reiterated that the right to marry is fundamental under the Due Process Clause.

It cannot be denied that this Court's cases describing the right to marry presumed a relationship involving opposite-sex partners. The Court, like many institutions, has made assumptions defined by the world and time of which it is a part. This was evident in *Baker v. Nelson*, 409 U.S. 810, a one-line summary decision issued in 1972, holding the exclusion of same-sex couples from marriage did not present a substantial federal question.

Still, there are other, more instructive precedents. This Court's cases have expressed constitutional principles of broader reach. In defining the right to marry, these cases have identified essential attributes of that right based in history, tradition, and other constitutional liberties inherent in this intimate bond. And in assessing whether the force and rationale of its cases apply to same-sex couples, the Court must respect the basic reasons why the right to marry has been long protected.

This analysis compels the conclusion that same-sex couples may exercise the right to marry. The four principles and traditions to be discussed demonstrate that the reasons marriage is fundamental under the Constitution apply with equal force to same-sex couples.

A first premise of the Court's relevant precedents is that the right to personal choice regarding marriage is inherent in the concept of individual autonomy. This abiding connection between marriage and liberty is why *Loving* invalidated interracial marriage bans under the Due Process Clause. Like choices concerning contraception, family relationships, procreation, and child-rearing, all of which are protected by the Constitution, decisions concerning marriage are among the most intimate that an individual can make. Indeed, the Court has noted it would be contradictory "to recognize a right of privacy with respect to other matters of family life and not with respect to the decision to enter the relationship that is the foundation of the family in our society."

Choices about marriage shape an individual's destiny. As the Supreme Judicial Court of Massachusetts has explained, because "it fulfils yearnings for security, safe haven, and connection that express our common humanity, civil marriage is an esteemed institution, and the decision whether and whom to marry is among life's momentous acts of self-definition" (*Goodridge*, 440 Mass., at 322, 798 N. E. 2d, at 955).

The nature of marriage is that, through its enduring bond, two persons together can find other freedoms, such as expression, intimacy, and spirituality. This is true for all persons, whatever their sexual orientation. There is dignity in the bond between two men or two women who seek to marry and in their autonomy to make such profound choices.

A second principle in this Court's jurisprudence is that the right to marry is fundamental because it supports a two-person union unlike any other in its importance to the committed individuals. This point was central to *Griswold v. Connecticut*, which held the Constitution protects the right of married couples to use contraception (381 U.S., at 485). Suggesting that marriage is a right "older than the Bill of Rights," *Griswold* described marriage this way:

> Marriage is a coming together for better or for worse, hopefully enduring, and intimate to the degree of being sacred. It is an association that promotes a way of life, not causes; a harmony in living, not political faiths; a bilateral loyalty, not commercial or social projects. Yet it is an association for as noble a purpose as any involved in our prior decisions. (Id., at 486)

. . .

As this Court held in *Lawrence*, same-sex couples have the same right as opposite-sex couples to enjoy intimate association. *Lawrence* invalidated laws that made same-sex intimacy a criminal act. And it acknowledged that "[w]hen sexuality finds overt expression in intimate conduct with another person, the conduct can be but one element in a personal bond that is more enduring." But while *Lawrence* confirmed a dimension of freedom that allows individuals to engage in intimate association without criminal liability, it does not follow that freedom stops there. Outlaw to outcast may be a step forward, but it does not achieve the full promise of liberty.

A third basis for protecting the right to marry is that it safeguards children and families and thus draws meaning from related rights of child-rearing, procreation, and education. The Court has recognized these connections by describing the varied rights as a unified whole: "[T]he right to 'marry, establish a home and bring up children' is a central part of the liberty protected by the Due Process Clause" (*Zablocki*, 434 U.S., at 384). Under the laws of the several states, some of marriage's protections for children and families are material. But marriage also confers more profound benefits. By giving recognition and legal structure to their parents' relationship, marriage allows children "to understand the integrity and closeness of their own family and its concord with other families in their community and in their daily lives." Marriage also affords the permanency and stability important to children's best interests.

As all parties agree, many same-sex couples provide loving and nurturing homes to their children, whether biological or adopted. And hundreds of thousands of children are presently being raised by such couples. Most states have allowed gays and lesbians to adopt, either as individuals or as couples, and many adopted and foster children have same-sex parents. This provides powerful confirmation from the law itself that gays and lesbians can create loving, supportive families.

Excluding same-sex couples from marriage thus conflicts with a central premise of the right to marry. Without the recognition, stability, and predictability marriage offers, their children suffer the stigma of knowing their families are somehow lesser. They also suffer the significant material costs of being raised by unmarried parents, relegated through no fault of their own to a more difficult and uncertain family life. The marriage laws at issue here thus harm and humiliate the children of same-sex couples.

That is not to say the right to marry is less meaningful for those who do not or cannot have children. An ability, desire, or promise to procreate is not and has not been a prerequisite for a valid marriage in any state. In light of precedent protecting the right of a married couple not to procreate, it cannot be said the Court or the states have conditioned the right to marry on the capacity or commitment to procreate. The constitutional marriage right has many aspects, of which childbearing is only one.

Fourth and finally, this Court's cases and the Nation's traditions make clear that marriage is a keystone of our social order. In *Maynard v. Hill*, 125 U.S. 190, 211 (1888), the Court echoed de Tocqueville, explaining that marriage is "the foundation of the family and of society, without which there would be neither civilization nor progress." Marriage, the Maynard Court said, has long been "'a great public institution, giving character to our whole civil polity.'" This idea has been reiterated even as the institution has evolved in substantial ways over time, superseding rules related to parental consent, gender, and race once thought by many to be essential. Marriage remains a building block of our national community.

For that reason, just as a couple vows to support each other, so does society pledge to support the couple, offering symbolic recognition and material benefits to protect and nourish the union. Indeed, while the states are in general free to vary the benefits they confer on all married couples, they have throughout our history made marriage the basis for an expanding list of governmental rights, benefits, and responsibilities.

These aspects of marital status include taxation; inheritance and property rights; rules of intestate succession; spousal privilege in the law of evidence; hospital access; medical decision-making authority; adoption rights; the rights and benefits of survivors; birth and death certificates; professional ethics rules; campaign finance restrictions; workers' compensation benefits; health insurance; and child custody, support, and visitation rules. Valid marriage under state law is also a significant status for over a thousand provisions of federal law. The states have contributed to the fundamental character of the marriage right by placing that institution at the center of so many facets of the legal and social order.

There is no difference between same- and opposite-sex couples with respect to this principle. Yet by virtue of their exclusion from that institution, same-sex couples are denied the constellation of benefits that the states have linked to marriage. This harm results in more than just material burdens. Same-sex couples are consigned to an instability many opposite-sex couples would deem intolerable in their own lives. As the state itself makes marriage all the more precious by the significance it attaches to it, exclusion from that status has the effect of teaching that gays and lesbians are unequal in important respects. It demeans gays and lesbians for the state to lock them out of a central institution of the Nation's society. Same-sex couples, too, may aspire to the transcendent purposes of marriage and seek fulfillment in its highest meaning.

The limitation of marriage to opposite-sex couples may long have seemed natural and just, but its inconsistency with the central meaning of the fundamental right to marry is now manifest. With that knowledge must come the recognition that laws excluding same-sex couples from the marriage right impose stigma and injury of the kind prohibited by our basic charter . . .

The right to marry is fundamental as a matter of history and tradition, but rights come not from ancient sources alone. They rise, too, from a better informed understanding of how constitutional imperatives define a liberty that remains urgent in our own era. Many who deem same-sex marriage to be wrong reach that conclusion based on decent and honorable religious or philosophical premises, and neither they nor their beliefs are disparaged here. But when that sincere, personal opposition becomes enacted law and public policy, the necessary consequence is to put the imprimatur of the state itself on an exclusion that soon demeans or stigmatizes those whose own liberty is then denied. Under the Constitution, same-sex couples seek in marriage the same legal treatment as opposite-sex couples, and it would disparage their choices and diminish their personhood to deny them this right . . .

These considerations lead to the conclusion that the right to marry is a fundamental right inherent in the liberty of the person, and under the Due Process and Equal Protection Clauses of the Fourteenth Amendment couples of the same-sex may not be deprived of that right and that liberty. The Court now holds that same-sex couples may exercise the fundamental right to marry. No longer may this liberty be denied to them. Baker *v.* Nelson must be and now is overruled, and the state laws challenged by Petitioners in these cases are now held invalid to the extent they exclude same-sex couples from civil marriage on the same terms and conditions as opposite-sex couples.

IV

There may be an initial inclination in these cases to proceed with caution—to await further legislation, litigation, and debate. The respondents warn there has been insufficient democratic discourse before deciding an issue so basic as the definition of marriage. In its ruling on the cases now before this Court, the majority opinion for the Court of Appeals made a cogent argument that it would be appropriate for the respondents' states to await further public discussion and political measures before licensing same-sex marriages.

Yet there has been far more deliberation than this argument acknowledges. There have been referenda, legislative debates, and grassroots campaigns, as well as countless studies, papers, books, and other popular and scholarly writings. There has been extensive litigation in state and federal courts. Judicial opinions addressing the issue have been informed by the contentions of parties and counsel, which, in turn, reflect the more general, societal discussion of same-sex marriage and its meaning that has occurred over the past decades. As more than 100 *amici* make clear in their filings, many of the central institutions in American life—state and local governments, the military, large and small businesses, labor unions, religious organizations, law enforcement, civic groups, professional organizations, and universities—have devoted substantial attention to the question. This has led to an enhanced understanding of the issue—an understanding reflected in the arguments now presented for resolution as a matter of constitutional law.

. . .

The dynamic of our constitutional system is that individuals need not await legislative action before asserting a fundamental right. The Nation's courts are open to injured individuals who come to them to vindicate their own direct, personal stake in our basic charter. An individual can invoke a right to constitutional protection when he or she is harmed, even if the broader public disagrees and even if the legislature refuses to act. The idea of the Constitution "was to withdraw certain subjects from the vicissitudes of political controversy, to place them beyond the reach of majorities and officials and to establish them as legal principles to be applied by the courts" (*West Virginia Bd. of Ed. v. Barnette*, 319 U.S. 624, 638, 1943). This is why "fundamental rights may not be submitted to a vote; they depend on the outcome of no elections" (Ibid). It is of no moment whether advocates of same-sex marriage now enjoy or lack momentum in the democratic process. The issue before the Court here is the legal question whether the Constitution protects the right of same-sex couples to marry.

. . .

The respondents also argue allowing same-sex couples to wed will harm marriage as an institution by leading to fewer opposite-sex marriages. This may occur, the respondents contend, because licensing same-sex marriage severs the connection between natural procreation and marriage. That argument, however, rests on a counterintuitive view of opposite-sex couple's decision-making processes regarding marriage and parenthood. Decisions about whether to marry and raise children are based on many personal, romantic, and practical considerations; and it is unrealistic to conclude that an opposite-sex couple would choose not to marry simply because same-sex couples may do so. The respondents have not shown a foundation for the conclusion that allowing same-sex marriage will cause the harmful outcomes they describe. Indeed, with respect to this asserted basis for excluding same-sex couples from the right to marry, it is appropriate to observe these cases involve only the rights of two consenting adults whose marriages would pose no risk of harm to themselves or third parties.

Finally, it must be emphasized that religions, and those who adhere to religious doctrines, may continue to advocate with utmost, sincere conviction that, by divine precepts, same-sex marriage should not be condoned. The First Amendment ensures that religious organizations and persons are given proper protection as they seek to teach the principles that are so fulfilling and so central to their lives and faiths, and to their own deep aspirations to continue the family structure they have long revered. The same is true of those who oppose same-sex marriage for other reasons. In turn, those who believe allowing same-sex marriage is proper or indeed essential, whether as a matter of religious conviction or secular belief, may engage those who disagree with their view in an open and searching debate. The Constitution, however, does not permit the state to bar same-sex couples from marriage on the same terms as accorded to couples of the opposite sex.

V

These cases also present the question whether the Constitution requires states to recognize same-sex marriages validly performed out of state. As made clear by the case of Obergefell and Arthur, and by that of DeKoe and Kostura, the recognition bans inflict substantial and continuing harm on same-sex couples.

Being married in one state but having that valid marriage denied in another is one of "the most perplexing and distressing complication[s]" in the law of domestic relations (*Williams v. North Carolina*, 317 U.S. 287, 299, 1942). Leaving the current state of affairs in place would maintain and promote instability and uncertainty. For some couples, even an ordinary drive into a neighboring state to visit family or friends risks causing severe hardship in the event of a spouse's hospitalization while across state lines.

In light of the fact that many states already allow same-sex marriage—and hundreds of thousands of these marriages already have occurred—the disruption caused by the recognition bans is significant and ever-growing.

As counsel for the respondents acknowledged at argument, if states are required by the Constitution to issue marriage licenses to same-sex couples, the justifications for refusing to recognize those marriages performed elsewhere are undermined. The Court, in this decision, holds same-sex couples may exercise the fundamental right to marry in all states. It follows that the Court must also hold—and it now does hold—that there is no lawful basis for a state to refuse to recognize a lawful same-sex marriage performed in another state on the ground of its same-sex character.

. . .

No union is more profound than marriage, for it embodies the highest ideals of love, fidelity, devotion, sacrifice, and family. In forming a marital union, two people become something greater than once they were. As some of the petitioners in these cases demonstrate, marriage embodies a love that may endure even past death. It would misunderstand these men and women to say they disrespect the idea of marriage. Their plea is that they do respect it, respect it so deeply that they seek to find its fulfillment for themselves. Their hope is not to be condemned to live in loneliness, excluded from one of civilization's oldest institutions. They ask for equal dignity in the eyes of the law. The Constitution grants them that right.

The judgment of the Court of Appeals for the Sixth Circuit is reversed.

It is so ordered.

Anthony Kennedy is an associate justice of the U.S. Supreme Court. He received his LLB from Harvard Law School in 1961 and worked for law firms in San Francisco and Sacramento, CA, until he was nominated by President Gerald Ford to the U.S. Court of Appeals for the Ninth Circuit in 1975. He was nominated by President Ronald Reagan to the Supreme Court in 1988.

John G. Roberts, Jr.  **NO**

Dissenting Opinion, *Obergefell v. Hodges*

Cᴴɪᴇꜰ Jᴜꜱᴛɪᴄᴇ Rᴏʙᴇʀᴛꜱ, with whom Jᴜꜱᴛɪᴄᴇ Sᴄᴀʟɪᴀ ᴀɴᴅ Jᴜꜱᴛɪᴄᴇ Tʜᴏᴍᴀꜱ join, dissenting.

Petitioners make strong arguments rooted in social policy and considerations of fairness. They contend that same-sex couples should be allowed to affirm their love and commitment through marriage, just like opposite-sex couples. That position has undeniable appeal; over the past six years, voters and legislators in 11 states and the District of Columbia have revised their laws to allow marriage between two people of the same sex.

But this Court is not a legislature. Whether same-sex marriage is a good idea should be of no concern to us. Under the Constitution, judges have power to say what the law is, not what it should be. The people who ratified the Constitution authorized courts to exercise "neither force nor will but merely judgment" (The Federalist No. 78, p. 465; C. Rossiter ed. 1961; A. Hamilton; capitalization altered).

Although the policy arguments for extending marriage to same-sex couples may be compelling, the legal arguments for requiring such an extension are not. The fundamental right to marry does not include a right to make a state change its definition of marriage. And a state's decision to maintain the meaning of marriage that has persisted in every culture throughout human history can hardly be called irrational. In short, our Constitution does not enact any one theory of marriage. The people of a state are free to expand marriage to include same-sex couples or to retain the historic definition.

Today, however, the Court takes the extraordinary step of ordering every state to license and recognize same-sex marriage. Many people will rejoice at this decision, and I begrudge none their celebration. But for those who believe in a government of laws, not of men, the majority's approach is deeply disheartening. Supporters of same-sex marriage have achieved considerable success persuading their fellow citizens—through the democratic process—to adopt their view. That ends today. Five lawyers have closed the debate and enacted their own vision of marriage as a matter of constitutional law. Stealing this issue from the people will for many cast a cloud over same-sex marriage, making a dramatic social change that much more difficult to accept.

The majority's decision is an act of will, not legal judgment. The right it announces has no basis in the Constitution or this Court's precedent. The majority expressly disclaims judicial "caution" and omits even a pretense of humility, openly relying on its desire to remake society according to its own "new insight" into the "nature of injustice." As a result, the Court invalidates the marriage laws of more than half the states and orders the transformation of a social institution that has formed the basis of human society for millennia, for the Kalahari Bushmen and the Han Chinese, the Carthaginians and the Aztecs. Just who do we think we are?

It can be tempting for judges to confuse our own preferences with the requirements of the law. But as this Court has been reminded throughout our history, the Constitution "is made for people of fundamentally differing views." Accordingly, "courts are not concerned with the wisdom or policy of legislation." The majority today neglects that restrained conception of the judicial role. It seizes for itself a question the Constitution leaves to the people, at a time when the people are engaged in a vibrant debate on that question. And it answers that question based not on neutral principles of constitutional law, but on its own "understanding of what freedom is and must become."

I have no choice but to dissent.

Understand well what this dissent is about: it is not about whether, in my judgment, the institution of marriage should be changed to include same-sex couples. It is instead about whether, in our democratic republic, that decision should rest with the people acting through their elected representatives or with five lawyers who happen to hold commissions authorizing them to resolve legal disputes according to law. The Constitution leaves no doubt about the answer.

Dissenting Opinion, Obergefell v. Hodges, U.S. Supreme Court, 135 S. Ct. 2071, 2016.

I

Petitioners and their *amici* base their arguments on the "right to marry" and the imperative of "marriage equality." There is no serious dispute that, under our precedents, the Constitution protects a right to marry and requires states to apply their marriage laws equally. The real question in these cases is what constitutes "marriage," or—more precisely—*who decides* what constitutes "marriage"?

The majority largely ignores these questions, relegating ages of human experience with marriage to a paragraph or two. Even if history and precedent are not "the end" of these cases, I would not "sweep away what has so long been settled" without showing greater respect for all that preceded us.

A

As the majority acknowledges, marriage "has existed for millennia and across civilizations." For all those millennia, across all those civilizations, "marriage" referred to only one relationship: the union of a man and a woman. As the Court explained two terms ago, "until recent years, . . . marriage between a man and a woman no doubt had been thought of by most people as essential to the very definition of that term and to its role and function throughout the history of civilization."

This universal definition of marriage as the union of a man and a woman is no historical coincidence. Marriage did not come about as a result of a political movement, discovery, disease, war, religious doctrine, or any other moving force of world history—and certainly not as a result of a prehistoric decision to exclude gays and lesbians. It arose in the nature of things to meet a vital need: ensuring that children are conceived by a mother and father committed to raising them in the stable conditions of a lifelong relationship.

The premises supporting this concept of marriage are so fundamental that they rarely require articulation. The human race must procreate to survive. Procreation occurs through sexual relations between a man and a woman. When sexual relations result in the conception of a child, that child's prospects are generally better if the mother and father stay together rather than going their separate ways. Therefore, for the good of children and society, sexual relations that can lead to procreation should occur only between a man and a woman committed to a lasting bond.

Society has recognized that bond as marriage. And by bestowing a respected status and material benefits on married couples, society encourages men and women to conduct sexual relations within marriage rather than without. As one prominent scholar put it, "Marriage is a socially arranged solution for the problem of getting people to stay together and care for children that the mere desire for children, and the sex that makes children possible, does not solve" (J. Q. Wilson, The Marriage Problem 41, 2002).

This singular understanding of marriage has prevailed in the United States throughout our history. The majority accepts that at "the time of the Nation's founding [marriage] was understood to be a voluntary contract between a man and a woman."

. . .

The Constitution itself says nothing about marriage, and the Framers thereby entrusted the states with "[t]he whole subject of the domestic relations of husband and wife" (*Windsor*, 570 U.S., at slip op., at 17). There is no dispute that every state at the founding—and every state throughout our history until a dozen years ago—defined marriage in the traditional, biologically rooted way. The four states in these cases are typical. Their laws, before and after statehood, have treated marriage as the union of a man and a woman. Even when state laws did not specify this definition expressly, no one doubted what they meant (see *Jones v. Hallahan*, 501 S.W. 2d 588, 589, Ky. App. 1973). The meaning of "marriage" went without saying.

. . .

This Court's precedents have repeatedly described marriage in ways that are consistent only with its traditional meaning. Early cases on the subject referred to marriage as "the union for life of one man and one woman" (*Murphy v. Ramsey*, 114 U.S. 15, 45, 1885), which forms "the foundation of the family and of society, without which there would be neither civilization nor progress" (*Maynard v. Hill*, 125 U.S. 190, 211, 1888). We later described marriage as "fundamental to our very existence and survival," an understanding that necessarily implies a procreative component. More recent cases have directly connected the right to marry with the "right to procreate."

As the majority notes, some aspects of marriage have changed over time. Arranged marriages have largely given way to pairings based on romantic love. States have replaced coverture, the doctrine by which a married man and woman became a single legal entity, with laws that respect each participant's separate status. Racial restrictions on marriage, which "arose as an incident to slavery" to promote "White Supremacy," were repealed by many states and ultimately struck down by this Court.

The majority observes that these developments "were not mere superficial changes" in marriage, but rather "worked deep transformations in its structure." . . . The majority may be right that the "history of marriage is one of both continuity and change," but the core meaning of marriage has endured.

B

Shortly after this Court struck down racial restrictions on marriage in *Loving*, a gay couple in Minnesota sought a marriage license. They argued that the Constitution required states to allow marriage between people of the same sex for the same reasons that it requires states to allow marriage between people of different races. The Minnesota Supreme Court rejected their analogy to *Loving*, and this Court summarily dismissed an appeal (*Baker v. Nelson*, 409 U.S. 810, 1972).

In the decades after *Baker*, greater numbers of gays and lesbians began living openly, and many expressed a desire to have their relationships recognized as marriages. Over time, more people came to see marriage in a way that could be extended to such couples. Until recently, this new view of marriage remained a minority position. After the Massachusetts Supreme Judicial Court in 2003 interpreted its State Constitution to require recognition of same-sex marriage, many states—including the four at issue here—enacted constitutional amendments formally adopting the long-standing definition of marriage.

Over the last few years, public opinion on marriage has shifted rapidly.

. . .

In all, voters and legislators in 11 states and the District of Columbia have changed their definitions of marriage to include same-sex couples. The highest courts of five states have decreed that same result under their own Constitutions. The remainder of the states retain the traditional definition of marriage.

Petitioners brought lawsuits contending that the Due Process and Equal Protection Clauses of the Fourteenth Amendment compel their states to license and recognize marriages between same-sex couples. In a carefully reasoned decision, the Court of Appeals acknowledged the democratic "momentum" in favor of "expand[ing] the definition of marriage to include gay couples," but concluded that petitioners had not made "the case for constitutionalizing the definition of marriage and for removing the issue from the place it has been since the founding: in the hands of state voters" (772 F. 3d, at 396, 403). That decision interpreted the Constitution correctly, and I would affirm.

II

Petitioners first contend that the marriage laws of their states violate the Due Process Clause. The Solicitor General of the United States, appearing in support of petitioners, expressly disowned that position before this Court. The majority nevertheless resolves these cases for petitioners based almost entirely on the Due Process Clause.

The majority purports to identify four "principles and traditions" in this Court's due process precedents that support a fundamental right for same-sex couples to marry. In reality, however, the majority's approach has no basis in principle or tradition, except for the unprincipled tradition of judicial policy-making that characterized discredited decisions such as *Lochner v. New York*, 198 U.S. 45. Stripped of its shiny rhetorical gloss, the majority's argument is that the Due Process Clause gives same-sex couples a fundamental right to marry because it will be good for them and for society. If I were a legislator, I would certainly consider that view as a matter of social policy. But as a judge, I find the majority's position indefensible as a matter of constitutional law.

A

Petitioners' "fundamental right" claim falls into the most sensitive category of constitutional adjudication. Petitioners do not contend that their states' marriage laws violate an *enumerated* constitutional right, such as the freedom of speech protected by the First Amendment. There is, after all, no "Companionship and Understanding" or "Nobility and Dignity" Clause in the Constitution. They argue instead that the laws violate a right *implied* by the Fourteenth Amendment's requirement that "liberty" may not be deprived without "due process of law."

This Court has interpreted the Due Process Clause to include a "substantive" component that protects certain liberty interests against state deprivation "no matter what process is provided" (*Reno v. Flores*, 507 U.S. 292, 302, 1993). The theory is that some liberties are "so rooted in the traditions and conscience of our people as to be ranked as fundamental," and therefore cannot be deprived without compelling justification (*Snyder v. Massachusetts*, 291 U.S. 97, 105, 1934).

Allowing unelected federal judges to select which unenumerated rights rank as "fundamental"—and to strike down state laws on the basis of that determination—raises obvious concerns about the judicial role. Our precedents have accordingly insisted that judges "exercise the utmost care" in identifying implied fundamental rights, "lest the liberty protected by the Due Process Clause be subtly transformed into the policy preferences of the Members of this Court" (*Washington v. Glucksberg*, 521 U.S. 702, 720, 1997).

. . .

The need for restraint in administering the strong medicine of substantive due process is a lesson this Court has learned the hard way. The Court first applied substantive due process to strike down a statute in *Dred Scott v. Sandford*, 19 How. 393 (1857). There the Court invalidated the Missouri Compromise on the ground that legislation restricting the institution of slavery violated the implied rights of slaveholders. The Court relied on its own conception of liberty and property in doing so. It asserted that "an act of Congress which deprives a citizen of the United States of his liberty or property, merely because he came himself or brought his property into a particular Territory of the United States . . . could hardly be dignified with the name of due process of law" (Id., at 450). In a dissent that has outlasted the majority opinion, Justice Curtis explained that when the "fixed rules which govern the interpretation of laws [are] abandoned, and the theoretical opinions of individuals are allowed to control" the Constitution's meaning, "we have no longer a Constitution; we are under the government of individual men, who for the time being have power to declare what the Constitution is, according to their own views of what it ought to mean" (Id., at 621).

Dred Scott's holding was overruled on the battlefields of the Civil War and by constitutional amendment after Appomattox, but its approach to the Due Process Clause reappeared. In a series of early 20th-century cases, most prominently *Lochner v. New York*, this Court invalidated state statutes that presented "meddlesome interferences with the rights of the individual," and "undue interference with liberty of person and freedom of contract" (198 U.S., at 60, 61). In *Lochner* itself, the Court struck down a New York law setting maximum hours for bakery employees, because there was "in our judgment, no reasonable foundation for holding this to be necessary or appropriate as a health law" (Id., at 58).

The dissenting Justices in *Lochner* explained that the New York law could be viewed as a reasonable response to legislative concern about the health of bakery employees, an issue on which there was at least "room for debate and for an honest difference of opinion" (Id., at 72; opinion of Harlan, J.).

In the decades after *Lochner*, the Court struck down nearly 200 laws as violations of individual liberty, often over strong dissents contending that "[t]he criterion of constitutionality is not whether we believe the law to be for the public good" (*Adkins v. Children's Hospital of D. C.*, 261 U.S. 525, 570, 1923; opinion of Holmes, J.). By empowering judges to elevate their own policy judgments to the status of constitutionally protected "liberty," the *Lochner* line of cases left "no alternative to regarding the court as a . . . legislative chamber" (L. Hand, The Bill of Rights 42, 1958).

Eventually, the Court recognized its error and vowed not to repeat it. "The doctrine that . . . due process authorizes courts to hold laws unconstitutional when they believe the legislature has acted unwisely," we later explained, "has long since been discarded. We have returned to the original constitutional proposition that courts do not substitute their social and economic beliefs for the judgment of legislative bodies, who are elected to pass laws" (*Ferguson v. Skrupa*, 372 U.S. 726, 730, 1963).

Rejecting *Lochner* does not require disavowing the doctrine of implied fundamental rights, and this Court has not done so. But to avoid repeating *Lochner*'s error of converting personal preferences into constitutional mandates, our modern substantive due process cases have stressed the need for "judicial self-restraint" (*Collins v. Harker Heights*, 503 U.S. 115, 125, 1992). Our precedents have required that implied fundamental rights be "objectively, deeply rooted in this Nation's history and tradition," and "implicit in the concept of ordered liberty, such that neither liberty nor justice would exist if they were sacrificed" (*Glucksberg*, 521 U.S., at 720–721).

B

The majority acknowledges none of this doctrinal background, and it is easy to see why: its aggressive application of substantive due process breaks sharply with decades of precedent and returns the Court to the unprincipled approach of *Lochner*.

1

The majority's driving themes are that marriage is desirable and petitioners desire it. The opinion describes the "transcendent importance" of marriage and repeatedly insists that petitioners do not seek to "demean," "devalue," "denigrate," or "disrespect" the institution. Nobody disputes those points. Indeed, the compelling personal accounts of petitioners and others like them are likely a primary reason why many Americans have changed their minds about whether same-sex couples should be allowed to marry. As a matter of constitutional law, however, the sincerity of petitioners' wishes is not relevant.

When the majority turns to the law, it relies primarily on precedents discussing the fundamental "right to marry." These cases do not hold, of course, that anyone who wants to get married has a constitutional right to do so. They instead require a state to justify barriers to marriage as that institution has always been understood. In *Loving*, the Court held that racial restrictions on the right to marry lacked a compelling justification. In *Zablocki*, restrictions based on child support debts did not suffice. In *Turner*, restrictions based on status as a prisoner were deemed impermissible.

None of the laws at issue in those cases purported to change the core definition of marriage as the union of a man and a woman.

. . .

In short, the "right to marry" cases stand for the important but limited proposition that particular restrictions on access to marriage *as traditionally defined* violate due process. These precedents say nothing at all about a right to make a state change its definition of marriage, which is the right petitioners actually seek here. Neither petitioners nor the majority cites a single case or other legal source providing any basis for such a constitutional right. None exists, and that is enough to foreclose their claim.

2

The majority suggests that "there are other, more instructive precedents" informing the right to marry. Although not entirely clear, this reference seems to correspond to a line of cases discussing an implied fundamental "right of privacy" (*Griswold*, 381 U.S., at 486). In the first of those cases, the Court invalidated a criminal law that banned the use of contraceptives. The Court stressed the invasive nature of the ban, which threatened the intrusion of "the police to search the sacred precincts of marital bedrooms." In the Court's view, such laws infringed the right to privacy in its most basic sense: the "right to be let alone" (*Eisenstadt v. Baird*, 405 U.S. 438, 453–454, n. 10, 1972; see *Olmstead v. United States*, 277 U.S. 438, 478, 1928; Brandeis, J., dissenting).

The Court also invoked the right to privacy in *Lawrence v. Texas*, 539 U.S. 558 (2003), which struck down a Texas statute criminalizing homosexual sodomy. *Lawrence* relied on the position that criminal sodomy laws, like bans on contraceptives, invaded privacy by inviting "unwarranted government intrusions" that "touc[h] upon the most private human conduct, sexual behavior . . . in the most private of places, the home."

Neither *Lawrence* nor any other precedent in the privacy line of cases supports the right that petitioners assert here. Unlike criminal laws banning contraceptives and sodomy, the marriage laws at issue here involve no government intrusion. They create no crime and impose no punishment. Same-sex couples remain free to live together, to engage in intimate conduct, and to raise their families as they see fit. No one is "condemned to live in loneliness" by the laws challenged in these cases—no one. At the same time, the laws in no way interfere with the "right to be let alone."

. . .

In sum, the privacy cases provide no support for the majority's position, because petitioners do not seek privacy. Quite the opposite, they seek public recognition of their relationships, along with corresponding government benefits.

. . .

3

It is strking how much of the majority's reasoning would apply with equal force to the claim of a fundamental right to plural marriage. If "[t]here is dignity in the bond between two men or two women who seek to marry and in their autonomy to make such profound choices," why would there be any less dignity in the bond between three people, who, in exercising their autonomy, seek to make the profound choice to marry? If a same-sex couple has the constitutional right to marry because children would otherwise "suffer the stigma of knowing their families are somehow lesser," why wouldn't the same reasoning apply to a family of three or more persons raising children? If not having the opportunity to marry "serves to disrespect and subordinate" gay and lesbian couples, why wouldn't the same "imposition of this disability" serve to disrespect and subordinate people who find fulfillment in polyamorous relationships? See Bennet, Polyamory: The Next Sexual Revolution? Newsweek, July 28, 2009 (estimating

500,000 polyamorous families in the United States); Li, Married Lesbian "Throuple" Expecting First Child, N.Y. Post, April 23, 2014; Otter, Three May Not be a Crowd: The Case for a Constitutional Right to Plural Marriage, 64 Emory L. J. 1977 (2015).

I do not mean to equate marriage between same-sex couples with plural marriages in all respects. There may well be relevant differences that compel different legal analysis. But if there are, petitioners have not pointed to any. When asked about a plural marital union at oral argument, petitioners asserted that a state "doesn't have such an institution." But that is exactly the point: the states at issue here do not have an institution of same-sex marriage, either.

. . .

IV

The legitimacy of this Court ultimately rests "upon the respect accorded to its judgments" (*Republican Party of Minn. v. White*, 536 U.S. 765, 793, 2002; KENNEDY, J., concurring). That respect flows from the perception—and reality—that we exercise humility and restraint in deciding cases according to the Constitution and law. The role of the Court envisioned by the majority today, however, is anything but humble or restrained. Over and over, the majority exalts the role of the judiciary in delivering social change. In the majority's telling, it is the courts, not the people, who are responsible for making "new dimensions of freedom . . . apparent to new generations," for providing "formal discourse" on social issues, and for ensuring "neutral discussions, without scornful or disparaging commentary."

Nowhere is the majority's extravagant conception of judicial supremacy more evident than in its description—and dismissal—of the public debate regarding same-sex marriage. Yes, the majority concedes, on one side are thousands of years of human history in every society known to have populated the planet. But on the other side, there has been "extensive litigation," "many thoughtful District Court decisions," "countless studies, papers, books, and other popular and scholarly writings," and "more than 100" *amicus* briefs in these cases alone. What would be the point of allowing the democratic process to go on? It is high time for the Court to decide the meaning of marriage, based on five lawyers' "better informed understanding" of "a liberty that remains urgent in our own era." The answer is surely there in one of those *amicus* briefs or studies.

Those who founded our country would not recognize the majority's conception of the judicial role. They after all risked their lives and fortunes for the precious right to govern themselves. They would never have imagined yielding that right on a question of social policy to unaccountable and unelected judges. And they certainly would not have been satisfied by a system empowering judges to override policy judgments so long as they do so after "a quite extensive discussion." In our democracy, debate about the content of the law is not an exhaustion requirement to be checked off before courts can impose their will. "Surely the Constitution does not put either the legislative branch or the executive branch in the position of a television quiz show contestant so that when a given period of time has elapsed and a problem remains unresolved by them, the federal judiciary may press a buzzer and take its turn at fashioning a solution" (Rehnquist, The Notion of a Living Constitution, 54 Texas L. Rev. 693, 700, 1976). As a plurality of this Court explained just last year, "It is demeaning to the democratic process to presume that voters are not capable of deciding an issue of this sensitivity on decent and rational grounds" (*Schuette v. BAMN*, 572 U.S., 2014; slip op., at 16–17).

The Court's accumulation of power does not occur in a vacuum. It comes at the expense of the people. And they know it. Here and abroad, people are in the midst of a serious and thoughtful public debate on the issue of same-sex marriage. They see voters carefully considering same-sex marriage, casting ballots in favor or opposed, and sometimes changing their minds. They see political leaders similarly reexamining their positions, and either reversing course or explaining adherence to old convictions confirmed anew. They see governments and businesses modifying policies and practices with respect to same-sex couples, and participating actively in the civic discourse. They see countries overseas democratically accepting profound social change, or declining to do so. This deliberative process is making people take seriously questions that they may not have even regarded as questions before.

When decisions are reached through democratic means, some people will inevitably be disappointed with the results. But those whose views do not prevail at least know that they have had their say, and accordingly are—in the tradition of our political culture—reconciled to the result of a fair and honest debate. In addition, they can gear up to raise the issue later, hoping to persuade enough on the winning side to think again. "That is exactly how our system of government is supposed to work."

But today the Court puts a stop to all that. By deciding this question under the Constitution, the Court removes it from the realm of democratic decision.

. . .

Federal courts are blunt instruments when it comes to creating rights. They have constitutional power only to resolve concrete cases or controversies; they do not have the flexibility of legislatures to address concerns of parties not before the court or to anticipate problems that may arise from the exercise of a new right. Today's decision, for example, creates serious questions about religious liberty. Many good and decent people oppose same-sex marriage as a tenet of faith, and their freedom to exercise religion is—unlike the right imagined by the majority—actually spelled out in the Constitution.

Respect for sincere religious conviction has led voters and legislators in every state that has adopted same-sex marriage democratically to include accommodations for religious practice. The majority's decision imposing same-sex marriage cannot, of course, create any such accommodations. The majority graciously suggests that religious believers may continue to "advocate" and "teach" their views of marriage. The First Amendment guarantees, however, the freedom to "*exercise*" religion. Ominously, that is not a word the majority uses.

Hard questions arise when people of faith exercise religion in ways that may be seen to conflict with the new right to same-sex marriage—when, for example, a religious college provides married student housing only to opposite-sex married couples, or a religious adoption agency declines to place children with same-sex married couples. Indeed, the Solicitor General candidly acknowledged that the tax exemptions of some religious institutions would be in question if they opposed same-sex marriage. There is little doubt that these and similar questions will soon be before this Court. Unfortunately, people of faith can take no comfort in the treatment they receive from the majority today.

. . .

If you are among the many Americans—of whatever sexual orientation—who favor expanding same-sex marriage, by all means celebrate today's decision. Celebrate the achievement of a desired goal. Celebrate the opportunity for a new expression of commitment to a partner. Celebrate the availability of new benefits. But do not celebrate the Constitution. It had nothing to do with it.

I respectfully dissent.

John G. Roberts, Jr., is the current Chief Justice of the U.S. Supreme Court. He received an AB from Harvard College in 1976 and a JD from Harvard Law School in 1979. He served as a law clerk for former U.S. Supreme Court Chief Justice William Rehnquist during the 1980 term, and in various other legal capacities until his appointment to the U.S. Court of Appeals for the District of Columbia Circuit in 2003. President George W. Bush nominated him as a Chief Justice in 2005.

EXPLORING THE ISSUE

Is Same-sex Marriage Protected by the Fourteenth Amendment to the U.S. Constitution?

Critical Thinking and Reflection

1. Should the laws governing marital unions be created and enforced by state governments or the federal government? If federal, should these decisions be left up to elected representatives or should courts intervene to protect the rights of a traditionally marginalized minority group?
2. According to the Supreme Court, what is the definition of "marriage" and who is responsible for determining the meaning? Is the Supreme Court's view proper? Pro-social?
3. Can you think of any common words with a definition that have changed over time? Does a word/phrase commonly used in the 21st century have an utterly different meaning from its origin?
4. Both sides consider what social policies prompted states to pass or prohibit same-sex marriage bans. Does the motivation of legislators matter or should courts focus on the ramifications of the laws in deciding whether they are constitutional?

Is There Common Ground?

The greatest commonality between the majority and dissent is their shared view on the importance of social discourse to shape the laws regarding same-sex marriage. Although the federal government may regulate marriage in certain circumstances, these instances are limited. Both opinions stress the history and tradition of marriage in this nation's culture, although Justice Kennedy and the majority cannot come to a common ground with Chief Justice Roberts on what is the definition of marriage. Throughout the numerous cases before the Supreme Court reviewing laws relating to, and the constitutionality of same-sex marriage, the United States as a whole had been awaiting this final resolution to be determined.

Chief Justice Roberts in his quite critical dissent similarly relied on the prevalence of today's strong social discourse in arguing that the Court is not properly suited to resolve such a prominent and widespread social issue. Falling in line with his predecessor, Chief Justice Rehnquist, Roberts asserted that judges are interpreters, not architects of law. In other words, "the decision should rest with the people acting through their elected representatives," just as the Founding Fathers intended and expressly provided in the Constitution. Although the definition of marriage is apparently ambiguous to the Court—with the majority finding it is between two people, and the dissent interpreting it as between a man and a woman—the view of the people at large clearly influenced the thinking of both the majority and dissent.

Additional Resources

Debbie Cenziper and Jim Obergefell, *Love Wins: The Lovers and Lawyers Who Fought the Landmark Case for Marriage Equality* (Headline Publishing Group, 2016).

Evan Gerstmann, *Same-sex Marriage and the Constitution*, 2nd ed. (Cambridge University Press, 2008).

Maggie Gallagher, "What Marriage Is For," *Weekly Standard* (August 4–11, 2003).

Oral Arguments in *Obergefell v. Hodges*, https://www.oyez.org/cases/2014/14–556

Proceedings and Orders of *Obergefell v. Hodges*, http://www.scotusblog.com/case-files/cases/obergefell-v-hodges/

Stephanie Coontz, *Marriage, A History: How Love Conquered Marriage* (Penguin, 2006).

Internet References . . .

Gallup Survey

This May 2016 *Gallup* survey illustrates Americans' positions on the same-sex marriage issue.

http://www.gallup.com/poll/191645/americans-support-gay-marriage-remains-high.aspx

National Public Radio (NPR)

This NPR article and sound-bit reviews how opponents of same-sex marriage are responding to the Supreme Court's decision in *Obergefell v. Hodges*.

http://www.npr.org/2015/06/27/418038177/for-same-sex-marriage-opponents-the-fight-is-far-from-over

National Review

This *National Review* article reviews the Supreme Court's decision in *Obergefell v. Hodges*, and how this will affect the legal and political landscape of the United States.

http://www.nationalreview.com/article/420420/supreme-court-has-legalized-same-sex-marriage-now-what-nro-symposium

The Opinion of the U.S. Supreme Court in *United States v. Windsor*

https://www.supremecourt.gov/opinions/12pdf/12-307_6j37.pdf

The Weekly Standard

A conservative perspective on same-sex marriage by Stanley Kurtz in his article, *The End of Marriage in Scandinavia* (February 2, 2004).

http://www.weeklystandard.com/the-end-of-marriage-in-scandinavia/article/4891

Selected, Edited, and with Issue Framing Material by:
M. Ethan Katsh, *University of Massachusetts, Amherst*

ISSUE

Are Race-conscious Public University Admissions Policies Permitted Under the Fourteenth Amendment?

YES: Anthony Kennedy, from "Majority Opinion, *Fisher v. University of Texas at Austin II*," *U.S. Supreme Court* (2016)

NO: Samuel Anthony Alito, **Jr.**, from "Dissenting Opinion, *Fisher v. University of Texas at Austin II*," *U.S. Supreme Court* (2016)

Learning Outcomes

After reading this issue, you will be able to:

- Articulate the political process doctrine and describe what it is intended to do.
- Describe how Texas's voter-initiated amendment changed the procedure for setting admissions policies, and whether race may be taken into consideration when reviewing applicants for admission to public universities.
- Distinguish between the policy arguments for and against affirmative action programs and the broader procedural arguments over who should be allowed to decide whether affirmative action programs are implemented.

ISSUE SUMMARY

YES: Justice Anthony Kennedy holds that the race-conscious admissions program in use at the University of Texas does not violate the Equal Protection Clause of the Fourteenth Amendment.

NO: Justice Samuel Alito argues that the university failed to effectively demonstrate that its admission policy needs a racial element and that the one it employs does, in fact, foster diversity.

Affirmative action continues to be one of the most hotly debated issues in the United States. Proponents justify the use of affirmative action policies by arguing that government should use race-conscious programs both to redress the continuing effects of past racial discrimination and to achieve more racially diverse educational and work environments. Opponents of affirmative action view it as unnecessary and unfair, arguing that it is, in essence, nothing more than "reverse discrimination" and, as such, a violation of the Fourteenth Amendment's guarantee of equal protection under the law. Opponents also assert that affirmative action policies stigmatize the beneficiaries of such programs, marking them as unable to succeed on their own merits.

The constitutionality of affirmative action in college and university admissions has occupied the Supreme Court for nearly four decades. In *Regents of the University of California v. Bakke*, 438 U.S. 265 (1978), the Court held that race could be taken into account in a public university's admission decisions. But the Court was deeply divided in reaching that conclusion: the Justices produced six separate opinions, none of which was able to garner a majority. Justice Lewis F. Powell was joined by four other members of the Court in invalidating the admissions policy of the University of California at Davis Medical School—a race-based "set aside"—on the grounds that it constituted an impermissible race-based classification. However, Powell was joined by four different members of the Court in holding that public universities may nonetheless use race as one factor in the admissions decision. Because of the splintered nature of the Court's statement on affirmative action and because of the inherently contested nature of the problem of race in American law and politics, further litigation was almost inevitable.

During the last two decades, the Supreme Court has continued to grapple with the constitutional implications of affirmative action policies. The University of Texas (UT) at Austin relies upon a complex system of admissions that has undergone significant evolution over the past two decades. In 1996, the Court of Appeals for the Fifth Circuit held that any consideration of race in college admissions violates the Equal Protection Clause. One year later, the University adopted a new admissions policy based on an applicant's "Academic Index" (AI) and Personal Achievement Index" (PAI). The PAI was a numerical score based on a holistic review of an application. Included in the number were the applicant's essays, leadership and work experience, extracurricular activities, community service, and other "special characteristics" that might give the admissions committee insight into a student's background. Race was not a consideration in calculating an applicant's AI or PAI.

In 2003, the University changed their admissions policy one again after the U.S. Supreme Court decided the companion cases of *Grutter v. Bollinger*, and *Gratz v. Bollinger*. In *Gratz*, the Court struck down the University of Michigan's undergraduate system of admissions, which at the time allocated predetermined points to racial minority candidates. In *Grutter*, however, the Court upheld the University of Michigan Law School's system of holistic review—a system that did not assign predetermined points but rather treated race as a relevant feature within a candidate's application.

In light of the Court's two decisions regarding race-conscious admissions policy, the UT at Austin submitted a proposal to the Board of Regents that requested permission to begin taking race into consideration as one of "the many ways in which [an] academically qualified individual might contribute to, and benefit from, the rich, diverse, and challenging educational environment of the University." After the board approved the proposal, the University adopted a new admissions policy to implement it.

Abigail Fisher applied for admission to the University's 2008 freshman class. She was not in the top 10 percent of her high school class, so she was evaluated for admission through holistic, full-file review. When her application was rejected, she filed suit alleging that the University's consideration of race as part of its holistic-review process disadvantaged her and other Caucasian applicants, in violation of the Equal Protection Clause.

The District Court found in favor of the University, and the Court of Appeals affirmed. The Supreme Court granted certiorari, and in *Fisher v. University of Texas at Austin I*, vacated the judgment of the Court of Appeals because it had applied an overly deferential "good faith" standard in assessing the constitutionality of the University's program. The Court remanded the case for the Court of Appeals to assess the parties' claims under the correct legal standard. On remand, the Court of Appeals again affirmed the judgment in the University's favor. The Supreme Court granted certiorari for a second time, and on June 23, 2016, affirmed the Court of Appeals judgment in favor of University, finding that the race-conscious admissions policy was constitutional and within the guidelines of the Equal Protection Clause. Excerpted below are the majority opinion of Justice Kennedy and a dissenting opinion by Justice Samuel Alito.

YES ⬅

Anthony Kennedy

Majority Opinion, *Fisher v. University of Texas at Austin II*

JUSTICE KENNEDY delivered the opinion of the Court.

The Court is asked once again to consider whether the race-conscious admissions program at the University of Texas (UT) is lawful under the Equal Protection Clause.

I

The UT at Austin (or University) relies upon a complex system of admissions that has undergone significant evolution over the past two decades. Until 1996, the University made its admissions decisions primarily based on a measure called "Academic Index" (or AI), which is calculated by combining an applicant's SAT score and academic performance in high school. In assessing applicants, preference was given to racial minorities.

In 1996, the Court of Appeals for the Fifth Circuit invalidated this admissions system, holding that any consideration of race in college admissions violates the Equal Protection Clause (see *Hopwood* v. *Texas*, 78 F. 3d 932, 934–935, 948).

One year later, the University adopted a new admissions policy. Instead of considering race, the University began making admissions' decisions based on an applicant's AI and his or her "Personal Achievement Index" (PAI). The PAI was a numerical score based on a holistic review of an application. Included in the number were the applicant's essays, leadership and work experience, extracurricular activities, community service, and other "special characteristics" that might give the admissions committee insight into a student's background. Consistent with *Hopwood*, race was not a consideration in calculating an applicant's AI or PAI.

The Texas Legislature responded to *Hopwood* as well. It enacted H. B. 588, commonly known as the Top Ten Percent Law. Tex. Educ. Code Ann. §51.803 (West Cum. Supp. 2015). As its name suggests, the Top Ten Percent Law guarantees college admission to students who graduate from a Texas high school in the top 10 percent of their class.

Those students may choose to attend any of the public universities in the state.

The University implemented the Top Ten Percent Law in 1998. After first admitting any student who qualified for admission under that law, the University filled the remainder of its incoming freshman class using a combination of an applicant's AI and PAI scores—again, without considering race.

The University used this admissions system until 2003, when this Court decided the companion cases of *Grutter* v. *Bollinger*, 539 U.S. 306, and *Gratz* v. *Bollinger*, 539 U.S. 244.

In *Gratz*, this Court struck down the University of Michigan's undergraduate system of admissions, which at the time allocated predetermined points to racial minority candidates. In *Grutter*, however, the Court upheld the University of Michigan Law School's system of holistic review—a system that did not mechanically assign points but rather treated race as a relevant feature within the broader context of a candidate's application. In upholding this nuanced use of race, *Grutter* implicitly overruled *Hopwood*'s categorical prohibition.

In the wake of *Grutter*, the University embarked upon a yearlong study seeking to ascertain whether its admissions policy was allowing it to provide "the educational benefits of a diverse student body . . . to all of the University's undergraduate students." The University concluded that its admissions policy was not providing these benefits.

To change its system, the University submitted a proposal to the Board of Regents that requested permission to begin taking race into consideration as one of "the many ways in which [an] academically qualified individual might contribute to, and benefit from, the rich, diverse, and challenging educational environment of the University." After the board approved the proposal, the University adopted a new admissions policy to implement it. The University has continued to use that admissions policy to this day.

Majority Opinion, Fisher v. University of Texas at Austin II, U.S. Supreme Court, 136 S. Ct. 2198, June 23, 2016.

Although the University's new admissions policy was a direct result of *Grutter*, it is not identical to the policy this Court approved in that case. Instead, consistent with the state's legislative directive, the University continues to fill a significant majority of its class through the Top Ten Percent Plan (or Plan). Today, up to 75 percent of the places in the freshman class are filled through the Plan. As a practical matter, this 75 percent cap, which has now been fixed by statute, means that, while the Plan continues to be referenced as a "Top Ten Percent Plan," a student actually needs to finish in the top seven or eight percent of his or her class in order to be admitted under this category.

The University did adopt an approach similar to the one in *Grutter* for the remaining 25 percent or so of the incoming class. This portion of the class continues to be admitted based on a combination of their AI and PAI scores. Now, however, race is given weight as a subfactor within the PAI. The PAI is a number from 1 to 6 (6 is the best) that is based on two primary components. The first component is the average score a reader gives the applicant on two required essays. The second component is a full-file review that results in another 1-to-6 score, the "Personal Achievement Score" or PAS. The PAS is determined by a separate reader, who (1) rereads the applicant's required essays, (2) reviews any supplemental information the applicant submits (letters of recommendation, resumes, an additional optional essay, writing samples, artwork, etc.), and (3) evaluates the applicant's potential contributions to the University's student body based on the applicant's leadership experience, extracurricular activities, awards/honors, community service, and other "special circumstances."

"Special circumstances" include the socioeconomic status of the applicant's family, the socioeconomic status of the applicant's school, the applicant's family responsibilities, whether the applicant lives in a single-parent home, the applicant's SAT score in relation to the average SAT score at the applicant's school, the language spoken at the applicant's home, and, finally, the applicant's race.

Both the essay readers and the full-file readers who assign applicants their PAI undergo extensive training to ensure that they are scoring applicants consistently. The Admissions Office also undertakes regular "reliability analyses" to "measure the frequency of readers scoring within one point of each other." Both the intensive training and the reliability analyses aim to ensure that similarly situated applicants are being treated identically regardless of which admissions officer reads the file.

Once the essay and full-file readers have calculated each applicant's AI and PAI scores, admissions officers from each school within the University set a cutoff PAI/AI score combination for admission and then admit all of the applicants who are above that cutoff point. In setting the cutoff, those admissions officers only know how many applicants received a given PAI/AI score combination. They do not know what factors went into calculating those applicants' scores. The admissions officers who make the final decision as to whether a particular applicant will be admitted make that decision without knowing the applicant's race. Race enters the admissions process, then, at one stage and one stage only—the calculation of the PAS.

Therefore, although admissions officers can consider race as a positive feature of a minority student's application, there is no dispute that race is but a "factor of a factor of a factor" in the holistic-review calculus (645 F. Supp. 2d 587, 608, WD Tex. 2009). Furthermore, consideration of race is contextual and does not operate as a mechanical plus factor for underrepresented minorities. Id., at 606 ("Plaintiffs cite no evidence to show racial groups other than African Americans and Hispanics are *excluded* from benefitting from UT's consideration of race in admissions. As the Defendants point out, the consideration of race, within the full context of the entire application, may be beneficial to any UT Austin applicant—including whites and Asian Americans"); see also Brief for Asian American Legal Defense and Education Fund et al. as *Amici Curiae* 12 (the contention that the University discriminates against Asian Americans is "entirely unsupported by evidence in the record or empirical data"). There is also no dispute, however, that race, when considered in conjunction with other aspects of an applicant's background, can alter an applicant's PAS score. Thus, race, in this indirect fashion, considered with all of the other factors that make up an applicant's AI and PAI scores, can make a difference to whether an application is accepted or rejected.

Petitioner Abigail Fisher applied for admission to the University's 2008 freshman class. She was not in the top 10 percent of her high school class, so she was evaluated for admission through holistic, full-file review. Petitioner's application was rejected.

Petitioner then filed suit alleging that the University's consideration of race as part of its holistic-review process disadvantaged her and other Caucasian applicants, in violation of the Equal Protection Clause (see U.S. Const., Amdt. 14, §1; no State shall "deny to any person within its jurisdiction the equal protection of the laws"). The District Court entered summary judgment in the University's favor, and the Court of Appeals affirmed.

This Court granted certiorari and vacated the judgment of the Court of Appeals, *Fisher* v. *University of Tex.*

At Austin, 570 U. S. ___ (2013) (*Fisher I*), because it had applied an overly deferential "good faith" standard in assessing the constitutionality of the University's program. The Court remanded the case for the Court of Appeals to assess the parties' claims under the correct legal standard.

Without further remanding to the District Court, the Court of Appeals again affirmed the entry of summary judgment in the University's favor (758 F. 3d 633, CA5 2014). This Court granted certiorari for a second time, 576 U. S. ___ (2015), and now affirms.

II

Fisher I set forth three controlling principles relevant to assessing the constitutionality of a public university's affirmative action program. First, "because racial characteristics so seldom provide a relevant basis for disparate treatment," *Richmond* v. *J. A. Croson Co.,* 488 U.S. 469, 505 (1989), "[r]ace may not be considered [by a university] unless the admissions process can withstand strict scrutiny," Strict scrutiny requires the university to demonstrate with clarity that its "'purpose or interest is both constitutionally permissible and substantial, and that its use of the classification is necessary . . . to the accomplishment of its purpose'" (Ibid).

Second, *Fisher I* confirmed that "the decision to pursue 'the educational benefits that flow from student body diversity' . . . is, in substantial measure, an academic judgment to which some, but not complete, judicial deference is proper." A university cannot impose a fixed quota or otherwise "define diversity as 'some specified percentage of a particular group merely because of its race or ethnic origin.'" Once, however, a university gives "a reasoned, principled explanation" for its decision, deference must be given "to the University's conclusion, based on its experience and expertise, that a diverse student body would serve its educational goals."

Third, *Fisher I* clarified that no deference is owed when determining whether the use of race is narrowly tailored to achieve the university's permissible goals. A university, *Fisher I* explained, bears the burden of proving a "nonracial approach" would not promote its interest in the educational benefits of diversity "about as well and at tolerable administrative expense." Though "[n]arrow tailoring does not require exhaustion of every conceivable race-neutral alternative" or "require a university to choose between maintaining a reputation for excellence [and] fulfilling a commitment to provide educational opportunities to members of all racial groups," *Grutter,* 539 U.S., at 339, it does impose "on the university the ultimate burden

of demonstrating" that "race-neutral alternatives" that are both "available" and "workable" "do not suffice."

. . .

III

The University's program is *sui generis.* Unlike other approaches to college admissions considered by this Court, it combines holistic review with a percentage plan. This approach gave rise to an unusual consequence in this case: the component of the University's admissions policy that had the largest impact on petitioner's chances of admission was not the school's consideration of race under its holistic-review process but rather the Top Ten Percent Plan. Because petitioner did not graduate in the top 10 percent of her high school class, she was categorically ineligible for more than ¾ of the slots in the incoming freshman class. It seems quite plausible, then, to think that petitioner would have had a better chance of being admitted to the University if the school used race-conscious holistic review to select its entire incoming class, as was the case in *Grutter.*

Despite the Top Ten Percent Plan's outsized effect on petitioner's chances of admission, she has not challenged it. For that reason, throughout this litigation, the Top Ten Percent Plan has been taken, somewhat artificially, as a given premise.

Petitioner's acceptance of the Top Ten Percent Plan complicates this Court's review. In particular, it has led to a record that is almost devoid of information about the students who secured admission to the University through the Plan. The Court thus cannot know how students admitted solely based on their class rank differ in their contribution to diversity from students admitted through holistic review.

. . .

In seeking to reverse the judgment of the Court of Appeals, petitioner makes four arguments. First, she argues that the University has not articulated its compelling interest with sufficient clarity. According to petitioner, the University must set forth more precisely the level of minority enrollment that would constitute a "critical mass." Without a clearer sense of what the University's ultimate goal is, petitioner argues, a reviewing court cannot assess whether the University's admissions program is narrowly tailored to that goal.

As this Court's cases have made clear, however, the compelling interest that justifies consideration of race in college admissions is not an interest in enrolling a certain number of minority students. Rather, a university may institute a race-conscious admissions program as a means of obtaining "the educational benefits that flow from student body diversity."

As this Court has said, enrolling a diverse student body "promotes cross-racial understanding, helps to break down racial stereotypes, and enables students to better understand persons of different races." Equally important, "student body diversity promotes learning outcomes, and better prepares students for an increasingly diverse workforce and society."

Increasing minority enrollment may be instrumental to these educational benefits, but it is not, as petitioner seems to suggest, a goal that can or should be reduced to pure numbers. Indeed, since the University is prohibited from seeking a particular number or quota of minority students, it cannot be faulted for failing to specify the particular level of minority enrollment at which it believes the educational benefits of diversity will be obtained.

On the other hand, asserting an interest in the educational benefits of diversity writ large is insufficient. A university's goals cannot be elusory or amorphous—they must be sufficiently measurable to permit judicial scrutiny of the policies adopted to reach them.

The record reveals that in first setting forth its current admissions policy, the University articulated concrete and precise goals. On the first page of its 2004 "Proposal to Consider Race and Ethnicity in Admissions," the University identifies the educational values it seeks to realize through its admissions process: the destruction of stereotypes, the "'promot[ion of] cross-racial understanding,'" the preparation of a student body "'for an increasingly diverse workforce and society,'" and the "'cultivat[ion of] a set of leaders with legitimacy in the eyes of the citizenry.'" . . . Later in, . . . The University has provided in addition a "reasoned, principled explanation" for its decision to pursue these goals. The University's 39-page proposal was written following a yearlong study, which concluded that "[t]he use of race-neutral policies and programs ha[d] not been successful" in "provid[ing] an educational setting that fosters cross-racial understanding, provid[ing] enlightened discussion and learning, [or] prepar[ing] students to function in an increasingly diverse workforce and society." . . . Further support for the University's conclusion can be found in the depositions and affidavits from various admissions officers, all of whom articulate the same, consistent "reasoned, principled explanation."

. . . Petitioner's contention that the University's goal was insufficiently concrete is rebutted by the record.

Second, petitioner argues that the University has no need to consider race because it had already "achieved critical mass" by 2003 using the Top Ten Percent Plan and race-neutral holistic review. Petitioner is correct that a university bears a heavy burden in showing that it had not obtained the educational benefits of diversity before it turned to a race-conscious plan. The record reveals, however, that, at the time of petitioner's application, the University could not be faulted on this score. Before changing its policy, the University conducted "months of study and deliberation, including retreats, interviews, [and] review of data" and concluded that "[t]he use of race-neutral policies and programs ha[d] not been successful in achieving" sufficient racial diversity at the University. At no stage in this litigation has petitioner challenged the University's good faith in conducting its studies, and the Court properly declines to consider the extra record materials the dissent relies upon, many of which are tangential to this case at best and none of which the University has had a full opportunity to respond to. See, for example, *post* at 45–46 (opinion of ALITO, J.)

The record itself contains significant evidence, both statistical and anecdotal, in support of the University's position. To start, the demographic data the University has submitted show consistent stagnation in terms of the percentage of minority students enrolling at the University from 1996 to 2002. In 1996, for example, 266 African American freshmen enrolled, a total that constituted 4.1 percent of the incoming class. In 2003, the year *Grutter* was decided, 267 African American students enrolled—again, 4.1 percent of the incoming class. The numbers for Hispanic and Asian American students tell a similar story. Although demographics alone are by no means dispositive, they do have some value as a gauge of the University's ability to enroll students who can offer underrepresented perspectives.

In addition to this broad demographic data, the University put forward evidence that minority students admitted under the *Hopwood* regime experienced feelings of loneliness and isolation.

This anecdotal evidence is, in turn, bolstered by further, more nuanced quantitative data. In 2002, 52 percent of undergraduate classes with at least five students had no African American students enrolled in them, and 27 percent had only one African American student. In other words, only 21 percent of undergraduate classes with five or more students in them had more than one African American student enrolled. Twelve percent of these classes had no Hispanic students, as compared to 10 percent in 1996. Though a college must continually reassess its need for race-conscious review, here that assessment appears to have been done with care, and a reasonable determination was made that the University had not yet attained its goals.

Third, petitioner argues that considering race was not necessary because such consideration has had only a "'minimal impact' in advancing the (University's) compelling interest." Again, the record does not support this assertion. In 2003, 11 percent of the Texas residents enrolled through holistic review were Hispanic and 3.5 percent were African American. In 2007, by contrast, 16.9 percent of the Texas holistic-review freshmen were Hispanic and 6.8 percent were African American. Those increases—of 54 percent and 94 percent, respectively—show that consideration of race has had a meaningful, if still limited, effect on the diversity of the University's freshman class.

. . .

Petitioner's final argument is that "there are numerous other available race-neutral means of achieving" the University's compelling interest. A review of the record reveals, however, that, at the time of petitioner's application, none of her proposed alternatives was a workable means for the University to attain the benefits of diversity it sought. For example, petitioner suggests that the University could intensify its outreach efforts to African American and Hispanic applicants. But the University submitted extensive evidence of the many ways in which it already had intensified its outreach efforts to those students. The University has created three new scholarship programs, opened new regional admissions centers, increased its recruitment budget by half-a-million dollars, and organized over 1,000 recruitment events. Perhaps more significantly, in the wake of *Hopwood*, the University spent seven years attempting to achieve its compelling interest using race-neutral holistic review. None of these efforts succeeded, and petitioner fails to offer any meaningful way in which the University could have improved upon them at the time of her application.

Petitioner also suggests altering the weight given to academic and socioeconomic factors in the University's admissions calculus. This proposal ignores the fact that the University tried, and failed, to increase diversity through enhanced consideration of socioeconomic and other factors. And it further ignores this Court's precedent making clear that the Equal Protection Clause does not force universities to choose between a diverse student body and a reputation for academic excellence.

Petitioner's final suggestion is to uncap the Top Ten Percent Plan, and admit more—if not all—the University's students through a percentage plan. As an initial matter, petitioner overlooks the fact that the Top Ten Percent Plan, though facially neutral, cannot be understood apart from its basic purpose, which is to boost minority enrollment. Percentage plans are "adopted with racially segregated neighborhoods and schools front and center stage" (*Fisher I*, 570 U.S., at; Ginsburg, J., dissenting) "It is race consciousness, not blindness to race, that drives such plans." Consequently, petitioner cannot assert simply that increasing the University's reliance on a percentage plan would make its admissions policy more race neutral.

Even if, as a matter of raw numbers, minority enrollment would increase under such a regime, petitioner would be hard-pressed to find convincing support for the proposition that college admissions would be improved if they were a function of class rank alone. That approach would sacrifice all other aspects of diversity in pursuit of enrolling a higher number of minority students. A system that selected every student through class rank alone would exclude the star athlete or musician whose grades suffered because of daily practices and training. It would exclude a talented young biologist who struggled to maintain above-average grades in humanities classes. And it would exclude a student whose freshman-year grades were poor because of a family crisis but who got herself back on track in her last three years of school, only to find herself just outside of the top decile of her class.

These are but examples of the general problem. Class rank is a single metric, and like any single metric, it will capture certain types of people and miss others. This does not imply that students admitted through holistic review are necessarily more capable or more desirable than those admitted through the Top Ten Percent Plan. It merely reflects the fact that privileging one characteristic above all others does not lead to a diverse student body. Indeed, to compel universities to admit students based on class rank alone is in deep tension with the goal of educational diversity as this Court's cases have defined it.

. . .

In addition to these fundamental problems, an admissions policy that relies exclusively on class rank creates perverse incentives for applicants. Percentage plans "encourage parents to keep their children in low-performing segregated schools and discourage students from taking challenging classes that might lower their grade point averages" (*Gratz*, 539 U.S., at 304, n. 10; Ginsburg, J., dissenting).

For all these reasons, although it may be true that the Top Ten Percent Plan in some instances may provide a path out of poverty for those who excel at schools lacking in resources, the Plan cannot serve as the admissions solution that petitioner suggests. Wherever the balance between percentage plans and holistic review should rest, an effective admissions policy cannot prescribe, realistically, the exclusive use of a percentage plan.

In short, none of petitioner's suggested alternatives—nor other proposals considered or discussed in the course of this litigation—have been shown to be "available" and "workable" means through which the University could have met its educational goals, as it understood and defined them in 2008. The University has thus met its burden of showing that the admissions policy it used at the time it rejected petitioner's application was narrowly tailored.

. . .

A university is in large part defined by those intangible "qualities which are incapable of objective measurement but which make for greatness" (*Sweatt* v. *Painter*, 339 U.S. 629, 634, 1950). Considerable deference is owed to a university in defining those intangible characteristics, like student body diversity, that are central to its identity and educational mission. But still, it remains an enduring challenge to our Nation's education system to reconcile the pursuit of diversity with the constitutional promise of equal treatment and dignity.

In striking this sensitive balance, public universities, like the states themselves, can serve as "laboratories for experimentation" (*United States v. Lopez*, 514 U.S. 549, 581, 1995; Kennedy, J., concurring; see also *New State Ice Co. v. Liebmann*, 285 U.S. 262, 311, 1932; Brandeis, J., dissenting). The UT at Austin has a special opportunity to learn and to teach. The University now has at its disposal valuable data about the manner in which different approaches to admissions may foster diversity or instead dilute it. The University must continue to use this data to scrutinize the fairness of its admissions program; to assess whether changing demographics have undermined the need for a race-conscious policy; and to identify the effects, both positive and negative, of the affirmative action measures it deems necessary.

The Court's affirmance of the University's admissions policy today does not necessarily mean the University may rely on that same policy without refinement. It is the University's ongoing obligation to engage in constant deliberation and continued reflection regarding its admissions policies.

The judgment of the Court of Appeals is affirmed.

It is so ordered.

Anthony Kennedy is an associate justice of the U.S. Supreme Court. He received his LLB from Harvard Law School in 1961 and worked for law firms in San Francisco and Sacramento, CA, until he was nominated by President Gerald Ford to the U.S. Court of Appeals for the Ninth Circuit in 1975. He was nominated by President Ronald Reagan to the Supreme Court in 1988.

Samuel Anthony Alito, Jr.

 **NO**

Dissenting Opinion, *Fisher v. University of Texas at Austin II*

JUSTICE ALITO, with whom The Chief Justice and Justice Thomas join, dissenting.

Something strange has happened since our prior decision in this case (see *Fisher v. University of Texas at Austin*, 570 U.S. ___, 2013; *Fisher I*). In that decision, we held that strict scrutiny requires the University of Texas at Austin (UT or University) to show that its use of race and ethnicity in making admissions decisions serves compelling interests and that its plan is narrowly tailored to achieve those ends. Rejecting the argument that we should defer to UT's judgment on those matters, we made it clear that UT was obligated (1) to identify the interests justifying its plan with enough specificity to permit a reviewing court to determine whether the requirements of strict scrutiny were met and (2) to show that those requirements were in fact satisfied. On remand, UT failed to do what our prior decision demanded. The University has still not identified with any degree of specificity the interests that its use of race and ethnicity is supposed to serve. Its primary argument is that merely invoking "the educational benefits of diversity" is sufficient and that it need not identify any metric that would allow a court to determine whether its plan is needed to serve, or is actually serving, those interests. This is nothing less than the plea for deference that we emphatically rejected in our prior decision. Today, however, the Court inexplicably grants that request.

To the extent that UT has ever moved beyond a plea for deference and identified the relevant interests in more specific terms, its efforts have been shifting, unpersuasive, and, at times, less than candid. When it adopted its race-based plan, UT said that the plan was needed to promote classroom diversity. It pointed to a study showing that African American, Hispanic, and Asian American students were underrepresented in many classes. But UT has never shown that its race-conscious plan actually ameliorates this situation. The University presents no evidence that its admissions officers, in administering the "holistic" component of its plan, make any effort to determine whether an African American, Hispanic, or Asian American student is likely to enroll in classes in which minority students are underrepresented. And although UT's records should permit it to determine without much difficulty whether holistic admittees are any more likely than students admitted through the Top Ten Percent Law, Tex. Educ. Code Ann. §51.803 (West Cum. Supp. 2015), to enroll in the classes lacking racial or ethnic diversity, UT either has not crunched those numbers or has not revealed what they show. Nor has UT explained why the underrepresentation of Asian American students in many classes justifies its plan, which discriminates *against* those students.

At times, UT has claimed that its plan is needed to achieve a "critical mass" of African American and Hispanic students, but it has never explained what this term means. According to UT, a critical mass is neither some absolute number of African American or Hispanic students nor the percentage of African Americans or Hispanics in the general population of the State. The term remains undefined, but UT tells us that it will let the courts know when the desired end has been achieved. This is a plea for deference—indeed, for blind deference—the very thing that the Court rejected in *Fisher I*.

UT has also claimed at times that the race-based component of its plan is needed because the Top Ten Percent Plan admits *the wrong kind* of African American and Hispanic students, namely, students from poor families who attend schools in which the student body is predominantly African American or Hispanic. As UT put it in its brief in *Fisher I*, the race-based component of its admissions plan is needed to admit "[t]he African-American or Hispanic child of successful professionals in Dallas."

. . .

Although UT now disowns the argument that the Top Ten Percent Plan results in the admission of the wrong kind of African American and Hispanic students, the Fifth Circuit majority bought a version of that claim.

As the panel majority put it, the Top Ten African American and Hispanic admittees cannot match the holistic African American and Hispanic admittees when it comes to "records of personal achievement," a "variety of perspectives" and "life experiences," and "unique skills" (758 F. 3d 633, 653, 2014). All in all, according to the panel majority, the Top Ten Percent students cannot "enrich the diversity of the student body" in the same way as the holistic admittees. As Judge Garza put it in dissent, the panel majority concluded that the Top Ten Percent admittees are "somehow more homogenous, less dynamic, and more undesirably stereotypical than those admitted under holistic review" (Id., at 669–670; Garza, J., dissenting).

The Fifth Circuit reached this conclusion with little direct evidence regarding the characteristics of the Top Ten Percent and holistic admittees. Instead, the assumption behind the Fifth Circuit's reasoning is that most of the African American and Hispanic students admitted under the race-neutral component of UT's plan were able to rank in the top decile of their high school classes only because they did not have to compete against white and Asian American students. This insulting stereotype is not supported by the record. African American and Hispanic students admitted under the Top Ten Percent Plan receive higher college grades than the African-American and Hispanic students admitted under the race-conscious program.

It should not have been necessary for us to grant review a second time in this case, and I have no greater desire than the majority to see the case drag on. But that need not happen. When UT decided to adopt its race-conscious plan, it had every reason to know that its plan would have to satisfy strict scrutiny and that this meant that it would be *its burden* to show that the plan was narrowly tailored to serve compelling interests. UT has failed to make that showing. By all rights, judgment should be entered in favor of petitioner.

But if the majority is determined to give UT yet another chance, we should reverse and send this case back to the District Court. What the majority has now done—awarding a victory to UT in an opinion that fails to address the important issues in the case—is simply wrong.

. . .

II

UT's race-conscious admissions program cannot satisfy strict scrutiny. UT says that the program furthers its interest in the educational benefits of diversity, but it has failed to define that interest with any clarity or to demonstrate that its program is narrowly tailored to achieve that or any other particular interest. By accepting UT's rationales as sufficient to meet its burden, the majority licenses UT's perverse assumptions about different groups of minority students—the precise assumptions strict scrutiny is supposed to stamp out.

A

"The moral imperative of racial neutrality is the driving force of the Equal Protection Clause" (*Richmond v. J. A. Croson Co.*, 488 U.S. 469, 518, 1989; Kennedy, J., concurring in part and concurring in judgment). "At the heart of the Constitution's guarantee of equal protection lies the simple command that the Government must treat citizens as individuals, not as simply components of a racial, religious, sexual or national class" (*Miller v. Johnson*, 515 U.S. 900, 911, 1995; internal quotation marks omitted). "Race-based assignments embody stereotypes that treat individuals as the product of their race, evaluating their thoughts and efforts—their very worth as citizens—according to a criterion barred to the Government by history and the Constitution" (Id., at 912; internal quotation marks omitted). Given our constitutional commitment to "the doctrine of equality," "'[d]istinctions between citizens solely because of their ancestry are by their very nature odious to a free people'" (*Rice v. Cayetano*, 528 U.S. 495, 517, 2000; quoting *Hirabayashi v. United States*, 320 U.S. 81, 100, 1943).

"[B]ecause racial characteristics so seldom provide a relevant basis for disparate treatment, the Equal Protection Clause demands that racial classifications . . . be subjected to the most rigid scrutiny" (*Fisher I*, 570 U.S., at ___; slip op., at 8; internal quotation marks and citations omitted). "[J]udicial review must begin from the position that 'any official action that treats a person differently on account of his race or ethnic origin is inherently suspect'" (Ibid.; see also *Grutter*, 539 U.S., at 388; Kennedy, J., dissenting; "'Racial and ethnic distinctions of any sort are inherently suspect and thus call for the most exacting judicial examination'"). Under strict scrutiny, the use of race must be "necessary to further a compelling governmental interest," and the means employed must be "'specifically and narrowly'" tailored to accomplish the compelling interest (Id., at 327, 333; O'Connor, J., for the Court).

The "higher education dynamic does not change" this standard (*Fisher I*, *supra*, at ____; slip op., at 12). "Racial discrimination [is] invidious in all contexts" (*Edmonson v. Leesville Concrete Co.*, 500 U.S. 614, 619, 1991), and "'[t]he analysis and level of scrutiny applied to determine the validity of [a racial] classification do not vary simply because the objective appears acceptable'" (*Fisher I, supra,* at ____, slip op., at 12).

Nor does the standard of review "'depen[d] on the race of those burdened or benefited by a particular classification.'" *Gratz v. Bollinger*, 539 U. S. 244, 270 (2003) (quoting *Adarand Constructors, Inc.* v. *Peña*, 515 U. S. 200, 224 (1995)); see also *Miller, supra,* at 904 ("This rule obtains with equal force regardless of 'the race of those burdened or benefited by a particular classification'" (quoting *Croson, supra,* at 494 (plurality opinion of O'Connor, J.)). "Thus, 'any person, of whatever race, has the right to demand that any governmental actor subject to the Constitution justify any racial classification subjecting that person to unequal treatment under the strictest of judicial scrutiny'" (*Gratz, supra,* at 270; quoting *Adarand, supra,* at 224).

In short, in "all contexts," *Edmonson, supra,* at 619, racial classifications are permitted only "as a last resort," when all else has failed, *Croson, supra,* at 519 (opinion of Kennedy, J.). "Strict scrutiny is a searching examination, and it is the government that bears the burden" of proof. *Fisher I,* 570 U.S., at ____ (slip op., at 8). To meet this burden, the government must "demonstrate *with clarity* that its 'purpose or interest is both constitutionally permissible and substantial, and that its use of the classification is necessary . . . to the accomplishment of its purpose'" (Id., at ____; slip op., at 7; emphasis added).

B

Here, UT has failed to define its interest in using racial preferences with clarity. As a result, the narrow tailoring inquiry is impossible, and UT cannot satisfy strict scrutiny.

When UT adopted its challenged policy, it characterized its compelling interest as obtaining a "'critical mass'" of underrepresented minorities (Id., at ____; slip op., at 1). The 2004 Proposal claimed that "[t]he use of race-neutral policies and programs has not been successful in achieving a critical mass of racial diversity." Supp. App. 25a; see *Fisher v. University of Tex. at Austin*, 631 F. 3d 213, 226 (CA5 2011) ("[T]he *2004 Proposal* explained that UT had not yet achieved the critical mass of underrepresented minority students needed to obtain the full educational benefits of diversity"). But to this day, UT has not explained in anything other than the vaguest terms what it means by "critical mass." In fact, UT argues that it need not identify *any* interest more specific than "securing the educational benefits of diversity." Brief for Respondents 15.

UT has insisted that critical mass is not an absolute number. See Tr. of Oral Arg. 39 (October 10, 2012) (declaring that UT is not working toward any particular number of African-American or Hispanic students); App.

315a (confirming that UT has not defined critical mass as a number and has not projected when it will attain critical mass). Instead, UT prefers a deliberately malleable "we'll know it when we see it" notion of critical mass. It defines "critical mass" as "an adequate representation of minority students so that the . . . educational benefits that can be derived from diversity can actually happen," and it declares that it "will . . . know [that] it has reached critical mass" when it "see[s] the educational benefits happening" (Id., at 314a–315a). In other words: Trust us.

This intentionally imprecise interest is designed to insulate UT's program from meaningful judicial review. As Judge Garza explained:

> [T]o meet its narrow tailoring burden, the University must explain its goal to us in some meaningful way. We cannot undertake a rigorous ends-to-means narrow tailoring analysis when the University will not define the ends. We cannot tell whether the admissions program closely "fits" the University's goal when it fails to objectively articulate its goal. Nor can we determine whether considering race is necessary for the University to achieve "critical mass," or whether there are effective race-neutral alternatives, when it has not described what 'critical mass' requires. 758 F. 3d, at 667 (dissenting opinion).

Indeed, without knowing in reasonably specific terms what critical mass is or how it can be measured, a reviewing court cannot conduct the requisite "careful judicial inquiry" into whether the use of race was "'necessary'" (*Fisher I, supra,* at ____; slip op., at 10).

To be sure, I agree with the majority that our precedents do not require UT to pinpoint "an interest in enrolling a certain number of minority students." *Ante,* at 11. But in order for us to assess whether UT's program is narrowly tailored, the University must identify *some sort of concrete interest.* "Classifying and assigning" students according to race "requires more than . . . an amorphous end to justify it." *Parents Involved in Community Schools* v. *Seattle School Dist. No. 1,* 551 U. S. 701, 735 (2007). Because UT has failed to explain "with clarity," *Fisher I, supra,* at ____ (slip op., at 7), why it needs a race-conscious policy and how it will know when its goals have been met, the narrow tailoring analysis cannot be meaningfully conducted. UT therefore cannot satisfy strict scrutiny.

The majority acknowledges that "asserting an interest in the educational benefits of diversity writ large is insufficient," and that "[a] university's goals cannot be elusory or amorphous—they must be sufficiently measurable to permit judicial scrutiny of the policies adopted to reach them" (*Ante*, at 12). According to the majority, however, UT has articulated the following "concrete and precise goals": "the destruction of stereotypes, the promot[ion of] cross-racial understanding, the preparation of a student body for an increasingly diverse workforce and society, and the cultivat[ion of] a set of leaders with legitimacy in the eyes of the citizenry" (Ibid.; internal quotation marks omitted).

These are laudable goals, but they are not concrete or precise, and they offer no limiting principle for the use of racial preferences. For instance, how will a court ever be able to determine whether stereotypes have been adequately destroyed? Or whether cross-racial understanding has been adequately achieved? If a university can justify racial discrimination simply by having a few employees opine that racial preferences are necessary to accomplish these nebulous goals, see *ante*, at 12–13 (citing *only* self-serving statements from UT officials), then the narrow tailoring inquiry is meaningless. Courts will be required to defer to the judgment of university administrators, and affirmative action policies will be completely insulated from judicial review.

By accepting these amorphous goals as sufficient for UT to carry its burden, the majority violates decades of precedent rejecting blind deference to government officials defending "'inherently suspect'" classifications. *Miller*, 515 U.S., at 904 (citing *Regents of Univ. of Cal. v. Bakke*, 438 U.S. 265, 291 (1978) (opinion of Powell, J.)); see also, for example, *Miller, supra*, at 922 ("Our presumptive skepticism of all racial classifications . . . prohibits us . . . from accepting on its face the Justice Department's conclusion" (citation omitted)); *Croson*, 488 U.S., at 500 ("[T]he mere recitation of a 'benign' or legitimate purpose for a racial classification is entitled to little or no weight"); id., at 501 ("The history of racial classifications in this country suggests that blind judicial deference to legislative or executive pronouncements of necessity has no place in equal protection analysis"). Most troublingly, the majority's uncritical deference to UT's self-serving claims blatantly contradicts our decision in the prior iteration of this very case, in which we faulted the Fifth Circuit for improperly "deferring to the University's good faith in its use of racial classifications" (*Fisher I*, 570 U.S., at ____; slip op., at 12). As we emphasized just three years ago, our precedent "ma[kes] clear that it is for the courts, not for university

administrators, to ensure that" an admissions process is narrowly tailored (Id., at ____; slip op., at 10).

A court cannot ensure that an admissions process is narrowly tailored if it cannot pin down the goals that the process is designed to achieve. UT's vague policy goals are "so broad and imprecise that they cannot withstand strict scrutiny" (*Parents Involved, supra*, at 785; Kennedy, J., concurring in part and concurring in judgment).

. . .

IV

It is important to understand what is and what is not at stake in this case. *What is not at stake* is whether UT or any other university may adopt an admissions plan that results in a student body with a broad representation of students from all racial and ethnic groups. UT previously had a race-neutral plan that it claimed had "effectively compensated for the loss of affirmative action," App. 396a, and UT could have taken other steps that would have increased the diversity of its admitted students without taking race or ethnic background into account.

What is at stake is whether university administrators may justify systematic racial discrimination simply by asserting that such discrimination is necessary to achieve "the educational benefits of diversity," without explaining—much less proving—why the discrimination is needed or how the discriminatory plan is well crafted to serve its objectives. Even though UT has never provided any coherent explanation for its asserted need to discriminate on the basis of race, and even though UT's position relies on a series of unsupported and noxious racial assumptions, the majority concludes that UT has met its heavy burden. This conclusion is remarkable—and remarkably wrong.

Because UT has failed to satisfy strict scrutiny, I respectfully dissent.

Samuel Anthony Alito, Jr., is an associate justice of the Supreme Court of the United States. He is a graduate of Princeton University and Yale Law School, and he served as U.S. Attorney for the District of New Jersey and as a judge on the U.S. Court of Appeals for the Third Circuit. He was nominated by President George W. Bush and has served on the court since January 31, 2006.

EXPLORING THE ISSUE

Are Race-conscious Public University Admissions Policies Permitted Under the Fourteenth Amendment?

Critical Thinking and Reflection

1. Does the desire for "diversity" on campus mean that every university should reflect the demographics of the United States as a whole?
2. To what degree, if at all, should the courts take into account the progress that has been made regarding diversity on campuses?
3. Are the admissions policies of the UT at Austin synonymous with affirmative action?
4. Should race be taken into consideration when reviewing applicants for admission to public universities? And who should be allowed to decide whether affirmative action programs are implemented?

Is There Common Ground?

The world is not a homogenous playground. We come from many different backgrounds and are born with various privileges and challenges. The sad history of this country is that being born black in the south in the first half of nineteenth century meant almost certainly being born into slavery. No justice would deny today that this was wrong, nor can they deny that this was a fact.

For some, race-conscious remedies designed to cure the ills of past discrimination have done nothing to ease racial tensions and have resulted only in creating new problems, putting some people at a disadvantage for the sins of others. For others, race-conscious programs have threatened the very integrity of the Constitution, risking one of its most sacred principles: that all stand equal before the law, regardless of race, class, or other personal characteristics. Yet the fact remains that nearly half a century after *Brown v. Board of Education*, far too many of America's colleges and universities remain predominantly white but for race-conscious admissions programs of the sort at issue in *Fisher v. University of Texas at Austin II*. None

of the Supreme Court justices seem to disagree on that single point; the question is what to do about it.

Interestingly, both the majority and dissenting opinions appear to be in agreement regarding the need to right the wrongs of the past, although they disagree with how state institutions may attempt this onerous and challenging feat. *Fisher II* is only a step in the direction of promoting equal access to education for all, regardless of one's demographic or race.

Additional Resources

Derek Bok and William Bowen, *The Shape of the River: Long-Term Consequences of Considering Race in College and University Admissions* (Princeton University Press, 1998).

Michael Rosenfeld, *Affirmative Action and Justice: A Philosophical and Constitutional Inquiry* (Yale University Press, 1991).

Lisa M. Stulberg and Sharon Lawner Weinberg, *Diversity in American Higher Education: Toward a More Comprehensive Approach* (Routledge, 2011).

Internet References . . .

New England Law Review

This faculty blog, "Analyzing Race-Based Classifications After Fisher," discusses the latest Supreme Court decision to address race in college and university admissions, *Fisher v. University of Texas at Austin II*.

https://newenglrev.com/2016/07/05/faculty-blog-how-scotus-analyzes-race-based-classifications-after-fisher/

Oral Arguments in *Fisher v. University of Texas at Austin II*

https://www.oyez.org/cases/2015/14-981

Proceedings and Orders of *Fisher v. University of Texas at Austin II*

http://www.scotusblog.com/case-files/cases/fisher-v-university-of-texas-at-austin-2/

Students for Fair Admissions (SFFA)

SFFA is a nonprofit, anti-affirmative action membership organization suing colleges and universities for allegedly enforcing discriminatory admissions policies that deny admission based on race.

https://studentsforfairadmissions.org/

The University of Texas: Not Fair

Students for Fair Admissions' website soliciting students who were denied admission to the University of Texas at Austin in hopes of finding cases to bring a new legal challenge to the policies constitutionality.

https://utnotfair.com/

Selected, Edited, and with Issue Framing Material by:
M. Ethan Katsh, *University of Massachusetts, Amherst*

ISSUE

Is It Unconstitutional for States to Imprison Undocumented Immigrants?

YES: Anthony Kennedy, from "Opinion of the Court, *Arizona v. United States*," *United States Supreme Court* (2012)

NO: Antonin Scalia, from "Dissenting Opinion, *Arizona v. United States*," *United States Supreme Court* (2012)

Learning Outcomes

After reading this issue, you will be able to:

- Describe under what situations the requirements of a state law can be more stringent than the federal statute and still be constitutional.
- Explain what Justice Kennedy meant in this case when he wrote: "When congress occupies an entire field . . . even complementary state regulation is impermissible."
- Contrast the views of Justices Kennedy and Scalia about whether the Arizona law is constitutional and why each holds his position.
- Explain the Privileges and Immunity Clause of the Constitution and its relevance to this case.

ISSUE SUMMARY

YES: Justice Anthony Kennedy argues that a recent state law making it a crime to be an undocumented immigrant in Arizona impinges on the U.S. federal government's authority to regulate immigration.

NO: Justice Antonin Scalia argues that it is not unconstitutional for a state to supplement U.S. federal immigration law with its own, harsher penalties for illegal immigration.

Two major cases about federalism and the relationship between the states and the U.S. federal government reached the Supreme Court in 2011–2012. The first concerned health care, an issue that traditionally had been left to the states. The second dealt with the reverse situation: a state's involvement in immigration policy, an area that had traditionally been the responsibility of the U.S. federal government.

The Constitution specifically gives Congress the power to address national issues for which the Framers believed there needed to be a uniform policy across the entire country, rather than many different state-based policies. The Constitution does not mention immigration, but the Supreme Court has long held that federal control over immigration policy follows from the U.S. federal government's exclusive power to regulate foreign affairs. Because "[o]ne of the most important and delicate of all international relationships . . . has to do with the protection of the just rights of a country's own nationals when those nationals are in another country,"[1] the Court has held that the U.S. federal government could not effectively engage in international diplomacy and carry out its explicit responsibilities in foreign affairs—including nationalization, war-making, and international commerce—if it did not have control over immigration. The Court has also held, for over two centuries, that where federal law and state law both are valid but conflict, federal law is supreme. Coupled together, these precedents mean that any state laws that interfere with U.S. federal immigration policy must be viewed as invalid.

In 2010, Arizona passed a sweeping immigration-related law, the Support Our Law Enforcement and Safe Neighborhoods Act, usually referred to by the number of the bill in the state senate, Senate Bill (S.B.) 1070. The law was designed to make it harder for undocumented immigrants to continue living in Arizona. Arizona claimed that the presence of so many undocumented immigrants in the state was having a seriously detrimental effect on the safety and well-being of its legal residents, and that its pleas to the U.S. federal government to enforce federal immigration law more aggressively were falling on deaf ears.

S.B. 1070 made it a crime for any noncitizen to be present in the state without properly registering with the U.S. federal government, which would essentially criminalize being an undocumented immigrant. As Kennedy notes in the YES selection, being undocumented may violate U.S. federal civil statutes and possibly lead to deportation, but it is not criminal in the sense that the undocumented immigrant status alone could lead to imprisonment. Another provision of S.B. 1070 made it a crime for undocumented immigrants to work in Arizona, and a third provision gave state law enforcement the authority to arrest anyone suspected of being an undocumented immigrant.

None of S.B. 1070's provisions explicitly conflicted with federal immigration laws, and thus Arizona argued that it was not trying to interfere with federal policy but merely to supplement it. Indeed, in the NO selection, Scalia accepts that as a valid argument to uphold the constitutionality of S.B. 1070. However, as Kennedy argues, a state law need not explicitly conflict with U.S. federal policy for the Court to declare it unconstitutional. Under the legal doctrine of *field preemption*, a state law is invalid if it tries to legislate on a topic where the U.S. federal government has already established a comprehensive policy, and where the U.S. federal government's aims might be undermined by a separate state policy. In this case, Kennedy notes, part of U.S. federal immigration policy is to give U.S. federal officials discretion about whom to deport in order to ensure that enforcing immigration law does not undermine other policy interests. If S.B. 1070's provisions criminalizing being an undocumented immigrant were upheld, the state would start arresting undocumented immigrants rather than letting U.S. federal officials decide how to handle their presence.

The case discussed in this issue is a *facial challenge* to the constitutionality of S.B. 1070. Facial challenges are made before a law is ever enforced, as opposed to *as-applied* challenges, which occur when someone is aggrieved by a law in operation. They are often unsuccessful because federal courts like to base their decisions on facts about a law's impact, rather than speculation about what that effect may be in the future. A facial challenge is, therefore, successful only if it is abundantly clear ahead of time that a law cannot possibly be enforced in accordance with the Constitution. Here, Kennedy argued that, no matter how enacted, the three provisions struck down by the Court would unconstitutionally infringe upon the U.S. federal government's authority in immigration matters.

A fourth controversial provision in the law was not declared unconstitutional in this particular case. That provision encourages and sometimes mandates that state police stopping or arresting someone for a non-immigration-related offense check the suspect's immigration status. Opponents of S.B. 1070 have argued that that provision will lead to racial profiling and may encourage state police to stop people under false pretenses to check their immigration status. However, the Supreme Court held that it was possible for that provision to be constitutional, depending on how it is enforced. The Court said that it would allow the law to stand under this facial challenge, but that it was open in the future to as-applied challenges if evidence arose that the law was indeed resulting in racial profiling or pretextual arrests. In other words, despite the Supreme Court's decision in this case, litigation about the constitutionality of S.B. 1070 may continue for several years.

One attempt to deal with part of the immigration issue is the DREAM Act, which stands for the Development, Relief, and Education for Alien Minor. The DREAM Act has been introduced in Congress several times since 2001 and is intended to provide permanent residency, but not citizenship, to minors who have lived in the United States for a number of years, graduated from high school, and met a number of other conditions. On June 15, 2012, President Obama issued an executive order stopping the deportation of at least 800,000 illegal immigrants who were brought to the United States as children and who meet many of the same conditions as contained in the DREAM Act. It differs from the DREAM Act in that the Act would provide permanent residency status, whereas the executive order bars deportation but does not change anyone's legal status.

YES ↵

Anthony Kennedy

Opinion of the Court, *Arizona v. United States*

JUSTICE KENNEDY delivered the opinion of the Court.

To address pressing issues related to the large number of aliens within its borders who do not have a lawful right to be in this country, the State of Arizona in 2010 enacted a statute called the Support Our Law Enforcement and Safe Neighborhoods Act. The law is often referred to as S. B. 1070, the version introduced in the state senate. Its stated purpose is to "discourage and deter the unlawful entry and presence of aliens and economic activity by persons unlawfully present in the United States." The law's provisions establish an official state policy of "attrition through enforcement." The question before the Court is whether federal law preempts and renders invalid four separate provisions of the state law.

I

The United States filed this suit against Arizona, seeking to enjoin S. B. 1070 as preempted. Four provisions of the law are at issue here. Two create new state offenses. Section 3 makes failure to comply with federal alien-registration requirements a state misdemeanor. Section 5, in relevant part, makes it a misdemeanor for an unauthorized alien to seek or engage in work in the State; this provision is referred to as §5(C). . . . Section 6 authorizes officers to arrest without a warrant a person "the officer has probable cause to believe . . . has committed any public offense that makes the person removable from the United States." . . .

The United States District Court for the District of Arizona issued a preliminary injunction preventing the provisions at issue from taking effect. The Court of Appeals for the Ninth Circuit affirmed. . . . This Court granted certiorari to resolve important questions concerning the interaction of state and federal power with respect to the law of immigration and alien status.

II

A

The Government of the United States has broad, undoubted power over the subject of immigration and the status of aliens. This authority rests, in part, on the National Government's constitutional power to "establish an uniform Rule of Naturalization," and its inherent power as sovereign to control and conduct relations with foreign nations.

The federal power to determine immigration policy is well settled. Immigration policy can affect trade, investment, tourism, and diplomatic relations for the entire Nation, as well as the perceptions and expectations of aliens in this country who seek the full protection of its laws. Perceived mistreatment of aliens in the United States may lead to harmful reciprocal treatment of American citizens abroad.

It is fundamental that foreign countries concerned about the status, safety, and security of their nationals in the United States must be able to confer and communicate on this subject with one national sovereign, not the 50 separate States. This Court has reaffirmed that "[o]ne of the most important and delicate of all international relationships . . . has to do with the protection of the just rights of a country's own nationals when those nationals are in another country."

Federal governance of immigration and alien status is extensive and complex. Congress has specified categories of aliens who may not be admitted to the United States. Unlawful entry and unlawful reentry into the country are federal offenses. Once here, aliens are required to register with the Federal Government and to carry proof of status on their person. Failure to do so is a federal misdemeanor. Federal law also authorizes States to deny noncitizens a range of public benefits, and it imposes sanctions on employers who hire unauthorized workers.

Congress has specified which aliens may be removed from the United States and the procedures for doing so. Aliens may be removed if they were inadmissible at the time of entry, have been convicted of certain crimes, or meet other criteria set by federal law. Removal is a civil, not criminal, matter. A principal feature of the removal system is the broad discretion exercised by immigration officials. Federal officials, as an initial matter, must decide whether it makes sense to pursue removal at all. If removal proceedings commence, aliens may seek asylum and other discretionary relief allowing them to remain in the country or at least to leave without formal removal.

Discretion in the enforcement of immigration law embraces immediate human concerns. Unauthorized workers trying to support their families, for example, likely pose less danger than alien smugglers or aliens who commit a serious crime. The equities of an individual case may turn on many factors, including whether the alien has children born in the United States, long ties to the community, or a record of distinguished military service. Some discretionary decisions involve policy choices that bear on this Nation's international relations. Returning an alien to his own country may be deemed inappropriate even where he has committed a removable offense or fails to meet the criteria for admission. The foreign state may be mired in civil war, complicit in political persecution, or enduring conditions that create a real risk that the alien or his family will be harmed upon return. The dynamic nature of relations with other countries requires the Executive Branch to ensure that enforcement policies are consistent with this Nation's foreign policy with respect to these and other realities.

Agencies in the Department of Homeland Security play a major role in enforcing the country's immigration laws. United States Customs and Border Protection (CBP) is responsible for determining the admissibility of aliens and securing the country's borders. In 2010, CBP's Border Patrol apprehended almost half a million people. Immigration and Customs Enforcement (ICE), a second agency, "conducts criminal investigations involving the enforcement of immigration-related statutes." ICE also operates the Law Enforcement Support Center. LESC, as the Center is known, provides immigration status information to federal, state, and local officials around the clock. ICE officers are responsible "for the identification, apprehension, and removal of illegal aliens from the United States." Hundreds of thousands of aliens are removed by the Federal Government every year.

B

The pervasiveness of federal regulation does not diminish the importance of immigration policy to the States. Arizona bears many of the consequences of unlawful immigration. Hundreds of thousands of deportable aliens are apprehended in Arizona each year. Unauthorized aliens who remain in the State comprise, by one estimate, almost six percent of the population. And in the State's most populous county, these aliens are reported to be responsible for a disproportionate share of serious crime.

Statistics alone do not capture the full extent of Arizona's concerns. Accounts in the record suggest there is an "epidemic of crime, safety risks, serious property damage, and environmental problems" associated with the influx of illegal migration across private land near the Mexican border. Phoenix is a major city of the United States, yet signs along an interstate highway 30 miles to the south warn the public to stay away. One reads, "DANGER—PUBLIC WARNING—TRAVEL NOT RECOMMENDED / Active Drug and Human Smuggling Area / Visitors May Encounter Armed Criminals and Smuggling Vehicles Traveling at High Rates of Speed." The problems posed to the State by illegal immigration must not be underestimated.

These concerns are the background for the formal legal analysis that follows. The issue is whether, under preemption principles, federal law permits Arizona to implement the state-law provisions in dispute.

III

Federalism, central to the constitutional design, adopts the principle that both the National and State Governments have elements of sovereignty the other is bound to respect. From the existence of two sovereigns follows the possibility that laws can be in conflict or at cross-purposes. The Supremacy Clause provides a clear rule that federal law "shall be the supreme Law of the Land; and the Judges in every State shall be bound thereby, any Thing in the Constitution or Laws of any State to the Contrary notwithstanding." Under this principle, Congress has the power to preempt state law. There is no doubt that Congress may withdraw specified powers from the States by enacting a statute containing an express preemption provision.

State law must also give way to federal law in at least two other circumstances. First, the States are precluded from regulating conduct in a field that Congress, acting within its proper authority, has determined must be regulated by its exclusive governance. The intent to displace state law altogether can be inferred from a framework of regulation "so pervasive . . . that Congress left no room for the States to supplement it" or where there is a "federal interest . . . so dominant that the federal system will be assumed to preclude enforcement of state laws on the same subject."

Second, state laws are preempted when they conflict with federal law. This includes cases where "compliance with both federal and state regulations is a physical impossibility," and those instances where the challenged state law "stands as an obstacle to the accomplishment and execution of the full purposes and objectives of Congress." In preemption analysis, courts should assume that "the historic police powers of the States" are not superseded "unless that was the clear and manifest purpose of Congress."

The challenged provisions of the state law each must be examined under these preemption principles.

IV

A

Section 3

Section 3 of S. B. 1070 creates a new state misdemeanor. It forbids the "willful failure to complete or carry an alien registration document . . . in violation of 8 United States Code section 1304(e) or 1306(a)." In effect, §3 adds a state-law penalty for conduct proscribed by federal law. The United States contends that this state enforcement mechanism intrudes on the field of alien registration, a field in which Congress has left no room for States to regulate.

The Court discussed federal alien-registration requirements in *Hines* v. *Davidowitz,* 312 U. S. 52. In 1940, as international conflict spread, Congress added to federal immigration law a "complete system for alien registration." The new federal law struck a careful balance. It punished an alien's willful failure to register but did not require aliens to carry identification cards. There were also limits on the sharing of registration records and fingerprints. The Court found that Congress intended the federal plan for registration to be a "single integrated and all-embracing system." Because this "complete scheme . . . for the registration of aliens" touched on foreign relations, it did not allow the States to "curtail or complement" federal law or to "enforce additional or auxiliary regulations." As a consequence, the Court ruled that Pennsylvania could not enforce its own alien-registration program.

The present regime of federal regulation is not identical to the statutory framework considered in *Hines,* but it remains comprehensive. Federal law now includes a requirement that aliens carry proof of registration. Other aspects, however, have stayed the same. Aliens who remain in the country for more than 30 days must apply for registration and be fingerprinted. Detailed information is required, and any change of address has to be reported to the Federal Government. The statute continues to provide penalties for the willful failure to register.

The framework enacted by Congress leads to the conclusion here, as it did in *Hines,* that the Federal Government has occupied the field of alien registration. The federal statutory directives provide a full set of standards governing alien registration, including the punishment for noncompliance. It was designed as a "'harmonious whole.'" Where Congress occupies an entire field, as it has in the field of alien registration, even complementary state regulation is impermissible. Field preemption reflects a congressional decision to foreclose any state regulation in the area, even if it is parallel to federal standards.

Federal law makes a single sovereign responsible for maintaining a comprehensive and unified system to keep track of aliens within the Nation's borders. If §3 of the Arizona statute were valid, every State could give itself independent authority to prosecute federal registration violations, "diminish[ing] the [Federal Government]'s control over enforcement" and "detract[ing] from the 'integrated scheme of regulation' created by Congress." Even if a State may make violation of federal law a crime in some instances, it cannot do so in a field (like the field of alien registration) that has been occupied by federal law.

Arizona contends that §3 can survive preemption because the provision has the same aim as federal law and adopts its substantive standards. This argument not only ignores the basic premise of field preemption—that States may not enter, in any respect, an area the Federal Government has reserved for itself—but also is unpersuasive on its own terms. Permitting the State to impose its own penalties for the federal offenses here would conflict with the careful framework Congress adopted. Were §3 to come into force, the State would have the power to bring criminal charges against individuals for violating a federal law even in circumstances where federal officials in charge of the comprehensive scheme determine that prosecution would frustrate federal policies.

There is a further intrusion upon the federal scheme. Even where federal authorities believe prosecution is appropriate, there is an inconsistency between §3 and federal law with respect to penalties. Under federal law, the failure to carry registration papers is a misdemeanor that may be punished by a fine, imprisonment, or a term of probation. State law, by contrast, rules out probation as a possible sentence (and also eliminates the possibility of a pardon). This state framework of sanctions creates a conflict with the plan Congress put in place.

These specific conflicts between state and federal law simply underscore the reason for field preemption. As it did in *Hines,* the Court now concludes that, with respect to the subject of alien registration, Congress intended to preclude States from "complement[ing] the federal law, or enforc[ing] additional or auxiliary regulations." Section 3 is preempted by federal law.

B

Section 5(C)

Unlike §3, which replicates federal statutory requirements, §5(C) enacts a state criminal prohibition where no federal counterpart exists. The provision makes it a state misdemeanor for "an unauthorized alien to knowingly apply for work, solicit work in a public place or perform work as an employee or independent contractor" in Arizona. Violations can be punished by a $2,500 fine and incarceration for up to six months. The United States contends that the provision upsets the balance struck by the Immigration Reform and Control Act of 1986 (IRCA) and must be preempted as an obstacle to the federal plan of regulation and control. . . .

Congress enacted IRCA as a comprehensive framework for "combating the employment of illegal aliens." The law makes it illegal for employers to knowingly hire, recruit, refer, or continue to employ unauthorized workers. It also requires every employer to verify the employment authorization status of prospective employees. These requirements are enforced through criminal penalties and an escalating series of civil penalties tied to the number of times an employer has violated the provisions.

This comprehensive framework does not impose federal criminal sanctions on the employee side (*i.e.*, penalties on aliens who seek or engage in unauthorized work). Under federal law some civil penalties are imposed instead. With certain exceptions, aliens who accept unlawful employment are not eligible to have their status adjusted to that of a lawful permanent resident. Aliens also may be removed from the country for having engaged in unauthorized work. In addition to specifying these civil consequences, federal law makes it a crime for unauthorized workers to obtain employment through fraudulent means. Congress has made clear, however, that any information employees submit to indicate their work status "may not be used" for purposes other than prosecution under specified federal criminal statutes for fraud, perjury, and related conduct.

The legislative background of IRCA underscores the fact that Congress made a deliberate choice not to impose criminal penalties on aliens who seek, or engage in, unauthorized employment. A commission established by Congress to study immigration policy and to make recommendations concluded these penalties would be "unnecessary and unworkable." To make unauthorized work a criminal offense were debated and discussed during the long process of drafting IRCA. But Congress rejected them. In the end, IRCA's framework reflects a considered judgment that making criminals out of aliens engaged in unauthorized work—aliens who already face the possibility of employer exploitation because of their removable status—would be inconsistent with federal policy and objectives.

IRCA's express preemption provision, which in most instances bars States from imposing penalties on employers of unauthorized aliens, is silent about whether additional penalties may be imposed against the employees themselves. But the existence of an "express pre-emption provisio[n] does *not* bar the ordinary working of conflict pre-emption principles" or impose a "special burden" that would make it more difficult to establish the preemption of laws falling outside the clause.

The ordinary principles of preemption include the well-settled proposition that a state law is preempted where it "stands as an obstacle to the accomplishment and execution of the full purposes and objectives of Congress." Arizona law would interfere with the careful balance struck by Congress with respect to unauthorized employment of aliens. Although §5(C) attempts to achieve one of the same goals as federal law—the deterrence of unlawful employment—it involves a conflict in the method of enforcement. The Court has recognized that a "[c]onflict in technique can be fully as disruptive to the system Congress enacted as conflict in overt policy." The correct instruction to draw from the text, structure, and history of IRCA is that Congress decided it would be inappropriate to impose criminal penalties on aliens who seek or engage in unauthorized employment. It follows that a state law to the contrary is an obstacle to the regulatory system Congress chose. Section 5(C) is preempted by federal law.

C

Section 6

Section 6 of S. B. 1070 provides that a state officer, "without a warrant, may arrest a person if the officer has probable cause to believe . . . [the person] has committed any public offense that makes [him] removable from the United States." The United States argues that arrests authorized by this statute would be an obstacle to the removal system Congress created.

As a general rule, it is not a crime for a removable alien to remain present in the United States. If the police stop someone based on nothing more than possible removability, the usual predicate for an arrest is absent. When an alien is suspected of being removable, a federal official issues an administrative document called a Notice to Appear. The form does not authorize an arrest. Instead, it gives the alien information about the proceedings, including the time and date of the removal hearing. If an alien fails to appear, an *in absentia* order may direct removal.

The federal statutory structure instructs when it is appropriate to arrest an alien during the removal process. For example, the Attorney General can exercise discretion to issue a warrant for an alien's arrest and detention "pending a decision on whether the alien is to be removed from the United States." And if an alien is ordered removed after a hearing, the Attorney General will issue a warrant. In both instances, the warrants are executed by federal officers who have received training in the enforcement of immigration law. If no federal warrant has been issued, those officers have more limited authority. They may arrest an alien for being "in the United States in violation of any [immigration] law or regulation," for example, but only where the alien "is likely to escape before a warrant can be obtained."

Section 6 attempts to provide state officers even greater authority to arrest aliens on the basis of possible removability than Congress has given to trained federal immigration officers. Under state law, officers who believe an alien is removable by reason of some "public offense" would have the power to conduct an arrest on that basis regardless of whether a federal warrant has issued or the alien is likely to escape. This state authority could be exercised without any input from the Federal Government about whether an arrest is warranted in a particular case. This would allow the State to achieve its own immigration policy. The result could be unnecessary harassment of some aliens (for instance, a veteran, college student, or someone assisting with a criminal investigation) whom federal officials determine should not be removed.

This is not the system Congress created. Federal law specifies limited circumstances in which state officers may perform the functions of an immigration officer. A principal example is when the Attorney General has granted that authority to specific officers in a formal agreement with a state or local government. Officers covered by these agreements are subject to the Attorney General's direction and supervision. There are significant complexities involved in enforcing federal immigration law, including the determination whether a person is removable. As a result, the agreements reached with the Attorney General must contain written certification that officers have received adequate training to carry out the duties of an immigration officer.

By authorizing state officers to decide whether an alien should be detained for being removable, §6 violates the principle that the removal process is entrusted to the discretion of the Federal Government. A decision on removability requires a determination whether it is appropriate to allow a foreign national to continue living in the United States. Decisions of this nature touch on foreign relations and must be made with one voice. . . .

Congress has put in place a system in which state officers may not make warrantless arrests of aliens based on possible removability except in specific, limited circumstances. By nonetheless authorizing state and local officers to engage in these enforcement activities as a general matter, §6 creates an obstacle to the full purposes and objectives of Congress. Section 6 is preempted by federal law. . . .

V

Immigration policy shapes the destiny of the Nation. On May 24, 2012, at one of this Nation's most distinguished museums of history, a dozen immigrants stood before the tattered flag that inspired Francis Scott Key to write the National Anthem. There they took the oath to become American citizens. These naturalization ceremonies bring together men and women of different origins who now share a common destiny. They swear a common oath to renounce fidelity to foreign princes, to defend the Constitution, and to bear arms on behalf of the country when required by law. The history of the United States is in part made of the stories, talents, and lasting contributions of those who crossed oceans and deserts to come here.

The National Government has significant power to regulate immigration. With power comes responsibility, and the sound exercise of national power over immigration depends on the Nation's meeting its responsibility to base its laws on a political will informed by searching, thoughtful, rational civic discourse. Arizona may have understandable frustrations with the problems caused by illegal immigration while that process continues, but the State may not pursue policies that undermine federal law. . . .

ANTHONY KENNEDY is an associate justice of the U.S. Supreme Court. He received his LLB from Harvard Law School in 1961 and worked for law firms in San Francisco and Sacramento, California, until he was nominated by President Gerald Ford to the U.S. Court of Appeals for the Ninth Circuit in 1975. He was nominated by President Ronald Reagan to the Supreme Court in 1988.

Antonin Scalia

 **NO**

Dissenting Opinion, *Arizona v. United States*

JUSTICE SCALIA, concurring in part and dissenting in part.

The United States is an indivisible "Union of sovereign States." Today's opinion . . . deprives States of what most would consider the defining characteristic of sovereignty: the power to exclude from the sovereign's territory people who have no right to be there. Neither the Constitution itself nor even any law passed by Congress supports this result. I dissent.

I

As a sovereign, Arizona has the inherent power to exclude persons from its territory, subject only to those limitations expressed in the Constitution or constitutionally imposed by Congress. That power to exclude has long been recognized as inherent in sovereignty. . . .

There is no doubt that "before the adoption of the constitution of the United States" each State had the authority to "prevent [itself] from being burdened by an influx of persons." And the Constitution did not strip the States of that authority. To the contrary, two of the Constitution's provisions were designed to enable the States to prevent "the intrusion of obnoxious aliens through other States." The Articles of Confederation had provided that "the free inhabitants of each of these States, paupers, vagabonds and fugitives from justice excepted, shall be entitled to all privileges and immunities of free citizens in the several States." This meant that an unwelcome alien could obtain all the rights of a citizen of one State simply by first becoming an *inhabitant* of another. To remedy this, the Constitution's Privileges and Immunities Clause provided that "[t]he *Citizens* of each State shall be entitled to all Privileges and Immunities of Citizens in the several States." But if one State had particularly lax citizenship standards, it might still serve as a gateway for the entry of "obnoxious aliens" into other States. This problem was solved "by authorizing the general government to establish a uniform rule of naturalization throughout the United States." In other words, the naturalization power was given to Congress not to abrogate States' power to exclude those they did not want, but to vindicate it.

Two other provisions of the Constitution are an acknowledgment of the States' sovereign interest in protecting their borders. Article I provides that "[n]o State shall, without the Consent of the Congress, lay any Imposts or Duties on Imports or Exports, *except what may be absolutely necessary for executing it's inspection Laws.*" This assumed what everyone assumed: that the States could exclude from their territory dangerous or unwholesome goods. A later portion of the same section provides that "[n]o State shall, without the Consent of Congress, . . . engage in War, *unless actually invaded, or in such imminent Danger as will not admit of delay.*" This limits the States' sovereignty (in a way not relevant here) but leaves intact their inherent power to protect their territory.

Notwithstanding "[t]he myth of an era of unrestricted immigration" in the first 100 years of the Republic, the States enacted numerous laws restricting the immigration of certain classes of aliens, including convicted criminals, indigents, persons with contagious diseases, and (in Southern States) freed blacks. State laws not only provided for the removal of unwanted immigrants but also imposed penalties on unlawfully present aliens and those who aided their immigration. . . .

In *Mayor of New York* v. *Miln*, this Court considered a New York statute that required the commander of any ship arriving in New York from abroad to disclose "the name, place of birth, and last legal settlement, age and occupation . . . of all passengers . . . with the intention of proceeding to the said city." After discussing the sovereign authority to regulate the entrance of foreigners the Court said:

> "The power . . . of New York to pass this law having undeniably existed at the formation of the constitution, the simply inquiry is, whether by that instrument it was taken from the states, and granted to congress; for if it were not, it yet remains with them."

And the Court held that it remains.

From Supreme Court of the United States, 2012.

II

One would conclude from the foregoing that after the adoption of the Constitution there was some doubt about the power of the Federal Government to control immigration, but no doubt about the power of the States to do so. Since the founding era (though not immediately), doubt about the Federal Government's power has disappeared. Indeed, primary responsibility for immigration policy has shifted from the States to the Federal Government. Congress exercised its power "[t]o establish an uniform Rule of Naturalization," very early on. But with the fleeting exception of the Alien Act, Congress did not enact any legislation regulating *immigration* for the better part of a century. . . . Of course, it hardly bears mention that Federal immigration law is now extensive.

I accept that as a valid exercise of federal power—not because of the Naturalization Clause (it has no necessary connection to citizenship) but because it is an inherent attribute of sovereignty no less for the United States than for the States. As this Court has said, it is an "'accepted maxim of international law, that every sovereign nation has the power, as inherent in sovereignty, and essential to self-preservation, to forbid the entrance of foreigners within its dominions.'" That is why there was no need to set forth control of immigration as one of the enumerated powers of Congress. . . .

In light of the predominance of federal immigration restrictions in modern times, it is easy to lose sight of the States' traditional role in regulating immigration—and to overlook their sovereign prerogative to do so. I accept as a given that State regulation is excluded by the Constitution when (1) it has been prohibited by a valid federal law, or (2) it conflicts with federal regulation—when, for example, it admits those whom federal regulation would exclude, or excludes those whom federal regulation would admit.

Possibility (1) need not be considered here: there is no federal law prohibiting the States' sovereign power to exclude (assuming federal authority to enact such a law). The mere existence of federal action in the immigration area—and the so-called field preemption arising from that action, upon which the Court's opinion so heavily relies—cannot be regarded as such a prohibition. We are not talking here about a federal law prohibiting the States from regulating bubble-gum advertising, or even the construction of nuclear plants. We are talking about a federal law going to the *core* of state sovereignty: the power to exclude. Like elimination of the States' other inherent sovereign power, immunity from suit, elimination of the States' sovereign power to exclude requires that "Congress . . .

unequivocally expres[s] its intent to abrogate." Implicit "field preemption" will not do.

Nor can federal power over illegal immigration be deemed exclusive because of what the Court's opinion solicitously calls "foreign countries['] concern[s] about the status, safety, and security of their nationals in the United States." The Constitution gives all those on our shores the protections of the Bill of Rights—but just as those rights are not expanded for foreign nationals because of their countries' views (some countries, for example, have recently discovered the death penalty to be barbaric), neither are the fundamental sovereign powers of the States abridged to accommodate foreign countries' views. Even in its international relations, the Federal Government must live with the inconvenient fact that it is a Union of independent States, who have their own sovereign powers. . . . Though it may upset foreign powers—and even when the Federal Government desperately wants to avoid upsetting foreign powers—the States have the right to protect their borders against foreign nationals, just as they have the right to execute foreign nationals for murder.

What this case comes down to, then, is whether the Arizona law conflicts with federal immigration law— whether it excludes those whom federal law would admit, or admits those whom federal law would exclude. It does not purport to do so. It applies only to aliens who neither possess a privilege to be present under federal law nor have been removed pursuant to the Federal Government's inherent authority. I proceed to consider the challenged provisions in detail. . . .

§6

"A peace officer, without a warrant, may arrest a person if the officer has probable cause to believe . . . [t]he person to be arrested has committed any public offense that makes the person removable from the United States."

This provision of S. B. 1070 expands the statutory list of offenses for which an Arizona police officer may make an arrest without a warrant. If an officer has probable cause to believe that an individual is "removable" by reason of a public offense, then a warrant is not required to make an arrest. The Government's primary contention is that §6 is pre-empted by federal immigration law because it allows state officials to make arrests "without regard to federal priorities." The Court's opinion focuses on limits that Congress has placed on *federal* officials' authority to arrest removable aliens and the possibility that state officials will make arrests "to achieve [Arizona's] own immigration policy" and "without any input from the Federal Government."

Of course on this pre-enforcement record there is no reason to assume that Arizona officials will ignore federal immigration policy (unless it be the questionable policy of not wanting to identify illegal aliens who have committed offenses that make them removable). As Arizona points out, federal law expressly provides that state officers may "cooperate with the Attorney General in the identification, apprehension, detention, or removal of aliens not lawfully present in the United States;" and "cooperation" requires neither identical efforts nor prior federal approval. It is consistent with the Arizona statute, and with the "cooperat[ive]" system that Congress has created, for state officials to arrest a removable alien, contact federal immigration authorities, and follow their lead on what to do next. And it is an assault on logic to say that identifying a removable alien and holding him for federal determination of whether he should be removed "violates the principle that the removal process is entrusted to the discretion of the Federal Government. The State's detention does not represent commencement of the removal process unless the Federal Government makes it so.

But that is not the most important point. The most important point is that, as we have discussed, Arizona is *entitled* to have "its own immigration policy"—including a more rigorous enforcement policy—so long as that does not conflict with federal law. The Court says, as though the point is utterly dispositive, that "it is not a crime for a removable alien to remain present in the United States." It is not a federal crime, to be sure. But there is no reason Arizona cannot make it a state crime for a removable alien (or any illegal alien, for that matter) to remain present in Arizona. . . .

The Court raises concerns about "unnecessary harassment of some aliens . . . whom federal officials determine should not be removed." But we have no license to assume, without any support in the record, that Arizona officials would use their arrest authority under §6 to harass anyone. And it makes no difference that federal officials might "determine [that some unlawfully present aliens] should not be removed." They may well determine not to remove from the United States aliens who have no right to be here; but unless and until these aliens have been given the right to remain, Arizona is entitled to arrest them and *at least* bring them to federal officials' attention, which is all that §6 necessarily entails. (In my view, the State can go further than this, and punish them for their unlawful entry and presence in Arizona.)

The Government complains that state officials might not heed "federal priorities." Indeed they might not,

particularly if those priorities include willful blindness or deliberate inattention to the presence of removable aliens in Arizona. The State's whole complaint—the reason this law was passed and this case has arisen—is that the citizens of Arizona believe federal priorities are too lax. The State has the sovereign power to protect its borders more rigorously if it wishes, absent any valid federal prohibition. The Executive's policy choice of lax federal enforcement does not constitute such a prohibition.

§3

> "In addition to any violation of federal law, a person is guilty of willful failure to complete or carry an alien registration document if the person is in violation of 8 [U. S. C] §1304(e) or §1306(a)."

It is beyond question that a State may make violation of federal law a violation of state law as well. We have held that to be so even when the interest protected is a distinctively federal interest, such as protection of the dignity of the national flag, or protection of the Federal Government's ability to recruit soldiers . . . . Much more is that so when, as here, the State is protecting its *own* interest, the integrity of its borders. And we have said that explicitly with regard to illegal immigration: "Despite the exclusive federal control of this Nation's borders, we cannot conclude that the States are without any power to deter the influx of persons entering the United States against federal law, and whose numbers might have a discernible impact on traditional state concerns."

The Court's opinion relies upon *Hines v. Davidowitzr.* But that case did not, as the Court believes, establish a "field preemption" that implicitly eliminates the States' sovereign power to exclude those whom federal law excludes. It held that the States are not permitted to establish "additional or auxiliary" registration requirements for aliens. But §3 does not establish additional or auxiliary registration requirements. It merely makes a violation of state law the *very same* failure to register and failure to carry evidence of registration that are violations of federal law. *Hines* does not prevent the State from relying on the federal registration system as "an available aid in the enforcement of a number of statutes of the state applicable to aliens whose constitutional validity has not been questioned." . . .

In some areas of uniquely federal concern—*e.g.,* fraud in a federal administrative process or perjury in violation of a federally required oath—this Court has held that a State has no legitimate interest in enforcing a federal scheme. But the federal alien registration system is

→ Confusion of punishment

certainly not of uniquely federal interest. States, private entities, and individuals rely on the federal registration system (including the E-Verify program) on a regular basis. Arizona's legitimate interest in protecting (among other things) its unemployment-benefits system is an entirely adequate basis for making the violation of federal registration and carry requirements a violation of state law as well.

The Court points out, however, that in some respects the state law exceeds the punishments prescribed by federal law: It rules out probation and pardon, which are available under federal law. The answer is that it makes no difference. Illegal immigrants who violate §3 violate *Arizona* law. It is one thing to say that the Supremacy Clause prevents Arizona law from excluding those whom federal law admits. It is quite something else to say that a violation of Arizona law cannot be punished more severely than a violation of federal law. Especially where (as here) the State is defending its own sovereign interests, there is no precedent for such a limitation. The sale of illegal drugs, for example, ordinarily violates state law as well as federal law, and no one thinks that the state penalties cannot exceed the federal. As I have discussed, moreover, "field preemption" cannot establish a prohibition of additional state penalties in the area of immigration.

Finally, the Government also suggests that §3 poses an obstacle to the administration of federal immigration law, but "there is no conflict in terms, and no possibility of such conflict, [if] the state statute makes federal law its own."

It holds no fear for me, as it does for the Court, that "[w]ere §3 to come into force, the State would have the power to bring criminal charges against individuals for violating a federal law even in circumstances where federal officials in charge of the comprehensive scheme determine that prosecution would frustrate federal policies." That seems to me entirely appropriate when the State uses the federal law (as it must) as the criterion for the exercise of *its own power,* and the implementation of *its own policies* of excluding those who do not belong there. What I do fear—and what Arizona and the States that support it fear—is that "federal policies" of nonenforcement will leave the States helpless before those evil effects of illegal immigration that the Court's opinion dutifully recites in its prologue but leaves unremedied in its disposition.

§5(C)

"It is unlawful for a person who is unlawfully present in the United States and who is an unauthorized alien to knowingly apply for work, solicit work in a public place or

perform work as an employee or independent contractor in this state."

. . . The Court concludes "that Congress made a deliberate choice not to impose criminal penalties on aliens who seek, or engage in, unauthorized employment." But that is not the same as a deliberate choice to prohibit the States from imposing criminal penalties. Congress's intent with regard to exclusion of state law need not be guessed at, but is found in the law's express pre-emption provision, which excludes "any State or local law imposing civil or criminal sanctions (other than through licensing and similar laws) upon *those who employ, or recruit or refer for a fee for employment,* unauthorized aliens." Common sense . . . suggests that the specification of pre-emption for laws punishing "those who employ" implies the lack of pre-emption for other laws, including laws punishing "those who seek or accept employment."

The Court has no credible response to this. It quotes our jurisprudence to the effect that an "express preemption provisio[n] does *not* bar the ordinary working of conflict pre-emption principles." True enough—*conflict* preemption principles. It then goes on [to] say that since "Congress decided it would be inappropriate to impose criminal penalties on aliens who seek or engage in unauthorized employment," "[i]t follows that a state law to the contrary is an obstacle to the regulatory system Congress chose." For "'[w]here a comprehensive federal scheme intentionally leaves a portion of the regulated field without controls, *then* the pre-emptive inference can be drawn.'" All that is a classic description not of *conflict* pre-emption but of *field* pre-emption, which (concededly) does not occur beyond the terms of an express pre-emption provision.

The Court concludes that §5(C) "would interfere with the careful balance struck by Congress" (another field pre-emption notion, by the way), but that is easy to say and impossible to demonstrate. The Court relies primarily on the fact that "[p]roposals to make unauthorized work a criminal offense were debated and discussed during the long process of drafting [the Immigration Reform and Control Act of 1980 (IRCA)]," "[b]ut Congress rejected them." There is no more reason to believe that this rejection was expressive of a desire that there be no sanctions on employees, than expressive of a desire that such sanctions be left to the States. To tell the truth, it was most likely expressive of what inaction ordinarily expresses: nothing at all. It is a "naive assumption that the failure of a bill to make it out of committee, or to be adopted when reported to the floor, is the same as a congressional rejection of what the bill contained."

* * *

The brief for the Government in this case asserted that "the Executive Branch's ability to exercise discretion and set priorities is particularly important because of the need to allocate scarce enforcement resources wisely." Of course there is no reason why the Federal Executive's need to allocate *its* scarce enforcement resources should disable Arizona from devoting *its* resources to illegal immigration in Arizona that in its view the Federal Executive has given short shrift. Despite Congress's prescription that "the immigration laws of the United States should be enforced vigorously and uniformly," Arizona asserts without contradiction and with supporting citations:

> "[I]n the last decade federal enforcement efforts have focused primarily on areas in California and Texas, leaving Arizona's border to suffer from comparative neglect. The result has been the funneling of an increasing tide of illegal border crossings into Arizona. Indeed, over the past decade, over a third of the Nation's illegal border crossings occurred in Arizona."

Must Arizona's ability to protect its borders yield to the reality that Congress has provided inadequate funding for federal enforcement—or, even worse, to the Executive's unwise targeting of that funding?

. . . The Court opinion's looming specter of inutterable horror—"[i]f §3 of the Arizona statute were valid, every State could give itself independent authority to prosecute federal registration violations,"—seems to me not so horrible and even less looming. But there has come to pass, and is with us today, the specter that Arizona and the States that support it predicted: A Federal Government that does not want to enforce the immigration laws as written, and leaves the States' borders unprotected against immigrants whom those laws would exclude. So the issue is a stark one. Are the sovereign States at the mercy of the Federal Executive's refusal to enforce the Nation's immigration laws?

A good way of answering that question is to ask: Would the States conceivably have entered into the Union if the Constitution itself contained the Court's holding? Today's judgment surely fails that test. At the Constitutional Convention of 1787, the delegates contended with

"the jealousy of the states with regard to their sovereignty." Through ratification of the fundamental charter that the Convention produced, the States ceded much of their sovereignty to the Federal Government. But much of it remained jealously guarded—as reflected in the innumerable proposals that never left Independence Hall. Now, imagine a provision—perhaps inserted right after Art. I, §8, cl. 4, the Naturalization Clause—which included among the enumerated powers of Congress "To establish Limitations upon Immigration that will be exclusive and that will be enforced only to the extent the President deems appropriate." The delegates to the Grand Convention would have rushed to the exits.

As is often the case, discussion of the dry legalities that are the proper object of our attention suppresses the very human realities that gave rise to the suit. Arizona bears the brunt of the country's illegal immigration problem. Its citizens feel themselves under siege by large numbers of illegal immigrants who invade their property, strain their social services, and even place their lives in jeopardy. Federal officials have been unable to remedy the problem, and indeed have recently shown that they are unwilling to do so. Thousands of Arizona's estimated 400,000 illegal immigrants—including not just children but men and women under 30—are now assured immunity from enforcement, and will be able to compete openly with Arizona citizens for employment.

Arizona has moved to protect its sovereignty—not in contradiction of federal law, but in complete compliance with it. The laws under challenge here do not extend or revise federal immigration restrictions, but merely enforce those restrictions more effectively. If securing its territory in this fashion is not within the power of Arizona, we should cease referring to it as a sovereign State. I dissent.

Antonin Scalia is an associate justice of the U.S. Supreme Court. He taught law at the University of Virginia, the American Enterprise Institute, Georgetown University, and the University of Chicago before being nominated to the U.S. Court of Appeals by President Ronald Reagan in 1982. He served in that capacity until he was nominated by President Reagan to the Supreme Court in 1986.

EXPLORING THE ISSUE

Is It Unconstitutional for States to Imprison Undocumented Immigrants?

Critical Thinking and Reflection

1. Why did Justice Scalia think that having a more stringent immigration law was constitutional? Give examples of other laws he cited that were more stringent in some states.
2. Why did Congress assign all matters involving immigration to the federal level? Why couldn't Arizona have a law with more requirements, according to Justice Kennedy?
3. What is the "Privilege and Immunity Clause," and how does each justice interpret the law in relation to this case?
4. Justice Scalia cited the 1837 case of *New York v. Miln* to support the argument of Arizona. What were the facts and decisions of that case that Justice Scalia thinks are important in this case? What did the decision in that case prove to Justice Scalia?

Is There Common Ground?

In late June 2013, the U.S. Senate passed an immigration bill that would provide a path to citizenship for some of the 11 million undocumented immigrants residing in the country. The bill also prevented further deportations, which have often separated family members. Included in the bipartisan agreement were tough new border regulations intended to thwart almost all illegal entrance to the United States. The bill passed in a 68 to 32 vote, with all the Democratic senators joined by 14 Republicans.

As this is being written, Republicans in the House of Representatives are considering whether and how to respond to this new bill. The Senate bill was drafted by a group of Republicans and Democrats but it is unclear what will happen in the House. Whether common ground with the Senate can be reached is hard to predict, but a recent speech by former President George W. Bush suggests that there may be room for compromise. Bush urged an overhaul of the immigration laws, saying that "the laws governing the immigration system aren't working. The system is broken." He also added that he hoped that during the debate over reform, "there is a benevolent spirit in mind and we understand the contributions that immigrants make to our country."

This is an issue in which the challenge of finding common ground has come and gone before. The DREAM Act (Development, Relief, and Education for Alien Minors), for example, was first introduced in the Senate on August 1, 2001. As noted earlier, the bill would provide conditional permanent residency to certain immigrants who had arrived as children. They needed to have arrived in the United States as minors, graduated from U.S. high schools, and lived in the country continuously for at least five years before the bill's enactment. They also needed to meet other criteria. This bill would have included illegal aliens as old as 35 years of age.

The DREAM Act has never been approved as a federal law but it has been reintroduced over the years. The Senate immigration bill discussed above had the best DREAM Act provisions, shortening the waiting period to a five-year path to legal permanent residency. To qualify, Dreamers would have had to meet certain requirements, including having been present in the United States since December 31, 2011, entered the United States before the age of 16, and either graduated from a U.S. high school or obtained a GED.

A few states have their own versions of the DREAM Act, which deal mostly with tuition prices and financial aid for state universities. These states include Texas, California, Illinois, Utah, Nebraska, Kansas, New Mexico, New York, Washington, Wisconsin, Massachusetts, Maryland, and Minnesota.

Additional Resources

Roger Daniels, *Coming to America: A History of Immigration and Ethnicity in American Life* (2002).

Peter H. Schuck, "Taking Immigration Federalism Seriously," *University of Chicago Legal Forum*, vol. 57 (2007).

Carol M. Swain (ed.), *Debating Immigration* (2007).

Internet References . . .

Summary of President Obama's Executive Order on Immigration

www.dhs.gov/files/enforcement/deferred-action
-process-for-young-people-who-arelaw-enforcement
-priorities.shtm

History of Immigration

www.immigrationpolicy.org/issues/history

Immigration Statistics

www.dhs.gov/immigration-statistics

Frequently Requested Statistics on Immigrants and Immigration in the United States

www.migrationinformation.org/USfocus
/display.cfm?id=886